Appealing Because He Is Appalling

Appealing Because He Is Appalling

Black Masculinities, Colonialism, and Erotic Racism

TAMARI KITOSSA, *Editor*

UNIVERSITY *of* **ALBERTA** PRESS

Published by

University of Alberta Press
1–16 Rutherford Library South
11204 89 Avenue NW
Edmonton, Alberta, Canada T6G 2J4
Amiskwaciwâskahican | Treaty 6 | Métis Territory
uap.ualberta.ca

LIBRARY AND ARCHIVES CANADA
CATALOGUING IN PUBLICATION

Title: Appealing because he is appalling : Black masculinities, colonialism, and erotic racism / Tamari Kitossa, editor.
Names: Kitossa, Tamari, editor.
Description: Includes bibliographical references and index.
Identifiers: Canadiana (print) 20210119500 | Canadiana (ebook) 20210120789 | ISBN 9781772125436 (softcover) | ISBN 9781772125535 (EPUB) | ISBN 9781772125559 (PDF)
Subjects: LCSH: Men, Black. | LCSH: Sexual attraction. | LCSH: Racism. | LCSH: Sex. | LCSH: Desire. | LCSH: Lust. | LCSH: Sexual excitement. | LCSH: Sexual ethics.
Classification: LCC HQ18.6 .A67 2021 | DDC 306.70811—dc23

First edition, first printing, 2021.
First printed and bound in Canada by Houghton Boston Printers, Saskatoon, Saskatchewan.
Copyediting and proofreading by Kay Rollans.
Indexing by Stephen Ullstrom.

University of Alberta Press gratefully acknowledges the support received for its publishing program from the Government of Canada, the Canada Council for the Arts, and the Government of Alberta through the Alberta Media Fund.

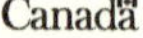

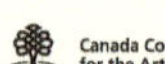

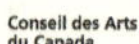

For my son, Jelani.

"This is my Son, whom I love; with him I am well pleased."

Contents

Foreword

Black Maleness as a Deleterious Category

BLACK MALE STUDIES has demanded a reappraisal of the previous scholarship concerning the role that maleness, manhood, and masculinity have played in white patriarchal societies for Black men in the United States, Canada, the United Kingdom, and elsewhere (Curry, 2017a). This collection of essays is a welcomed advancement of the conversation. With authors writing from all over the world, *Appealing Because He Is Appalling* builds on various interdisciplinary tools alongside the psychosexual perspectives of Fanon and Baldwin to reframe dominant narratives of Black male experience. Current analyses of Black males found in history, feminist thought, and popular culture literature are dominated by narratives emphasizing the lack, hypermasculinity, or sexism of Black males. This collection of essays is critical to challenging and changing these narratives. In order to understand the significance of this book's contribution to the field of Black male studies, however, it is first necessary to understand both the field itself and the broader landscapes of which it is a part.

Unpacking Black Male Studies

The dominant view of Black masculinity presented by intersectional and Black feminist theories in American universities asserts that Black men are less powerful white men and that they desire power and embrace social hierarchy in order to dominate Black women and other marginalized Black groups in the Black community (cf. Cooper, 2006; White, 2008).

These theories, which have reduced the study of Black males to a mimetic endeavour, are promulgated as the cumulative advance of gender studies over the last several decades.

This scholarship begins with the assertion that Black males' desire for completeness and manhood is achieved through their imitation of white masculinity (Curry, 2021). These works assert that Black men are lesser men because of racism and that Black men use violence to compensate for centuries of racial discrimination and injury. Because these theories are primarily applied to Black men and boys, very little effort has been made to empirically verify or ethnographically demonstrate and validate these theories. The idea that Black men were violent sexual predators who take pleasure in the murder and rape of others was a cornerstone of the subculture-of-violence theories coming out of criminology in the 1960s as well as the feminist theories of the 1970s. Despite there being relatively few attempts to verify whether Black males are driven to imitate the character of white men, mimeticism has come to be the premise from which all work on Black males begins. Theoretical research on Black men throughout various fields attempts to either affirm or refute the idea that Black men are deviant. In both cases, the attempts to affirm or refute the idea of Black male deviance (e.g., criminality, hypermasculinity, misogyny, violence) centre pathology as the origin of thinking about the Black male. The time has come for Black men and boys to be thought of and theorized differently.

Understanding Black Males' Disproportionate Death and Dying as Gendercide

The intensification of anti-Black racism, xenophobia, and right-wing ideology in the United States and Europe make the intellectual reconsideration of Black men and boys a timely and much-needed project. Heightened levels of fear, hatred, and xenophobia directed at negatively racialized groups throughout the world have especially made Black men a target for white and right-wing vigilantism, police brutality, and state violence. Black male death not only deserves scholarly attention, but also warrants an invigorated demand for understanding how Black male life is critical to the preservation of right-wing and white supremacist structures and order throughout the world. Understanding the life, death, and dying of Black men and boys in the United States (the chief right-wing and white supremacist global hegemon) and elsewhere requires a systemic analysis of how the necropolitical destruction of Black male death plays into, supports, and enables racism—or, more specifically, racial domination. This requires an area of study dedicated to analyzing the global program of targeting and demonizing Black males not only throughout the Western world but also in other regions where anti-Black misandry may be less expected.

According to historian Amy E. Randall (2015):

> As scholars, human rights activists, and policymakers grapple with the challenges of how to stop genocidal violence before its starts...a focus on gender-specific actions and patterns might yield insights. Scholars have pointed out there is a high correlation between certain types of gender violence and genocide...In present-day conflicts, if gender-selective slaughter of a specific ethnic/racial/national group of male civilians occurs, it could be a warning that the more generalized destruction and mass murder of that population might soon follow. (p. 4)

The dehumanizing caricatures whites created and other non-white people have since inherited of Black males are the bases of the racist stereotypes imposed on the whole group (Ghavami & Peplau, 2013; McConnaughy, 2017; McConnaughy & White, 2011; Thiem et al., 2019).

The proximity that caricatures of Black males have to the stereotypes of their larger racial group suggest that analyses of the distancing negativity associated with Black males are central to understanding the intent of racial violence throughout contemporary patriarchal societies. The killing of negatively racialized men and boys is connected to historical patterns of mass violence used to dominate and manage subjugated or conquered populations (Miller, 1994, 2004). These killings are enduring features of social organization within Western and other racialized patriarchal societies. Negatively racialized males are the canaries in the coal mine, so to speak, for genocidal processes. Their condemnation, degradation, and, ultimately, elimination indicate rising levels of dehumanization for the groups to which they belong.

Black male studies scholars have suggested that racism is a form of misandric aggression (Curry, 2018). This statement adds nuance to formulations of racism that often articulate racism as a claim concerning the status or hierarchy between different racial groups, where one dominant racial group is thought superior to an inferior racial group. Conceptualizing racism as a complex system is often difficult. Ramon Grosfoguel (2016) defines racism as "a global hierarchy of superiority and inferiority along the line of the human that have been politically, culturally and economically produced and reproduced for centuries by the institutions of the 'capitalist/patriarchal western-centric/Christian-centric modern/colonial world system' (Grosfoguel, 2011)" (p. 10). As thorough as this definition may be, it says little about how racism is enforced or about the role violence against men plays in racist oppression. It is nonetheless clear that the disproportionality of lethal violence directed against Black males compared to whites or women in racist societies warrants serious study.

This difference in the magnitude of violence imposed on Black men through homicide, incarceration, police killings, and economic isolation offers evidence that the targeting of Black males (and other non-white racial male groups) plays a significant role in enforcing hierarchies and accentuating systems of racial domination. Despite this fact, it is not often analyzed. In my book *The Man-Not*, I argue that racism aims for the death and dying of the subjugated group such that the dominant racial group can aspire for a more prosperous and less perilous future for its progeny (Curry, 2017a). One of the primary strategies of racism is misandric aggression, or sex-specific targeting, of Black males in white supremacist societies. The benefits of the present volume include its expansion of this frame of analysis to the world and over time, and its incorporation of subtler methods of necropolitics.

The sex-specific killing of Black males by state agents and vigilantes, or what has been called (male) gendercide by some scholars, is empirically substantiated (Jones, 2000; Curry, 2017a). Yet it remains a theoretically neglected area of concern for scholars working in Black studies and on race and gender more broadly. The extermination of Black men and boys operates to maintain social order and racial hierarchy. This is a sex-specific strategy of scholarly discourse that attempts to exclude the Black male from civil society through punitive programs and dehumanizing rhetoric (Wynter, 1994). As Augusta Del Zotto (2004) explains,

> In the United States, the systematic objectification and control of poor, particularly black males, likewise play an important role in maintaining the desired social order. In this case, it is informed by the long historical tradition of objectifying black males. While the black female as threat can be controlled through policies of manipulation, the black male as threat requires the implementation of policies of direct force to keep him at the margins, and policies of containment to ensure that he does not encroach upon the serenity of growing industrial parks and gated communities. (pp. 163–64)

This removal of Black males from American society through lethal violence, the prison industrial complex, and the poverty draft into the military has previously been described as a program of institutional decimation (Stewart & Scott, 1978).

Unlike previous research into the precarity of being Black and male in the United States and elsewhere, Black male studies seeks to illuminate *how* the oppression of Black men and boys is part of a historic aspect of racist patriarchal societies around the world. Such societies seek to exclude and eliminate negatively racialized males who are outside the racial kinship of the dominant group. Perceiving them as cultural and biological threats to the continuity of racial domination, whites and non-white groups in their own national contexts severely sanction Black men and boys. As shown in the United States by Shervin Assari and myself, Black men and boys are more severely restricted in their freedoms and their ability to elevate themselves than any other group (Assari & Curry, 2020). Because societies frame Black men and boys primarily as deviants and criminals, their deaths are deemed to be necessary for the survival of the dominant groups of these same societies.

The emphasis of this latter observation is not meant to be specifically placed on the identity of being Black and male; rather, it is meant to reveal a repetitive pattern throughout history in Western patriarchal societies: that of subjugating and eliminating negatively racialized males. Even excluded from any particular kinship or racial bonds, the societal male "outgroup" has been found in most patriarchal societies throughout history to be the target of many of the most dehumanizing stereotypes and the most lethal violence. As Errol Miller (1991) explained several decades ago:

> Patriarchy has historically marginalized men not covered by the covenant of kinship...Throughout history such men have been perceived as threats and treated as such. Patriarchy's treatment of such men has always been more brutal and harsh than its treatment of women. This contradictory and inconsistent feature of patriarchy has been mostly ignored. (p. 342)

By focusing on the motivation patriarchal societies have to exclude rather than incorporate negatively racialized males, it becomes easier to see how lethal violence against Black males is not simply the product of fear or aversion, as many psychoanalytic theorists proclaim. It is instead a program aimed at securing a numerical majority, resources, and cultural influence within a particular geography. The effects of Black male death—and the ways in which dominant groups in society benefit from it—are cumulative.

The removal of Black males and their subsequent absence in a society produces an underclass of Black males that, economically, politically, and socially, fall below many of the women in that very same society (Chetty et al., 2020; Sidanius & Pratto, 1999). In other words, maleness, when claimed under the duress of racialization and white supremacy, is a deleterious category that inverts the gender relation found among whites in the metropole. The targeting of Black men is merely one example of how gender is an apparatus of racial propagation for whites but of racial diminishment and disposability for Blacks.

Obstacles to the Theorizing of Black Male Vulnerability to Sexual Violence

Over the last decade, there has been mounting evidence that Black men were routinely raped and subject to sexual violence during slavery and Jim Crow. The homoerotic violence of white men that manifested in sodomizing Black males has slowly come to the fore in our attempts to rethink the institution of slavery (Aidoo, 2018). While there is substantial evidence that white women systematically raped and sexually coerced Black men and boys during slavery and segregation, these historical facts have been resisted and deemphasized as an area of theorization (Foster, 2011; Sweet, 2003; Wells, 2010). The history of sexual violence against Black males requires a paradigmatic shift in how scholars understand what gender-based violence means.

That Black men are and have been vulnerable to rape and sexual violence has not only been an understudied aspect of anti-Black racism, but an aspect shrouded by denial. A more accurate history of colonization and slavery shows that anti-Black sexual violence was not restricted only to heterosexually oriented white males who violated Black women. The erotic dimension of anti-Black racism, colonialism, and slavery not only erases this fact but flips it on its head. The representation of Black men as hypersexual brutes and insatiable rapists precludes the possibility that Black men *could* be raped. In 1942, J.A. Rogers explained that

> [m]ost Southerners still believe, or will proclaim very loudly, that it is and has been unthinkable that any white woman in her sane mind will have any relations with a Negro...However, the records show something entirely different. They show that the white woman ran a not too far distant second from the white man in miscegenation in spite of the severe restrictions against her, and which by the way, shows what she might have done if she had been as free as the white man. (p. 232; see also Wells, 2010)

Despite the evidence of Black male sexual victimization, there has been a hesitancy in reformulating theories of gender and sexual violence to reflect this fact. As I have shown in *The Man-Not*, the history of Black men being victims of rape and sexual violence is related to how Black males experience sexual assault in our present day (Curry, 2017a). The suffering of Black males has been solely attributed to the effects of racism; the effects of gender have largely been ignored. This account of Black male existence has made experiences of sexual violence appear to be exceptional and rare rather than systemic and repetitive.

This is, however, far from the case. In the United States and Africa, Black men who have been victims of slavery and apartheid remain disproportionately at risk for rape, sexual violence, and abuse. This research would help explain the current sexual victimization findings in the United States and South Africa concerning Black males. In the United States, Black males report higher levels of contact sexual violence (which includes rape, being made to penetrate, sexual coercion, and unwanted sexual contact) than Black women and white women over a 12-month period (Smith et al., 2017). Unlike some European countries, the Optimus Study in South Africa similarly found that the sexual assault of South African boys (who were often victimized by older African women) was higher than that of their female counterparts (Artz et al., 2016). Likewise, in the United States today, decades after the repressive regimes of slavery and Jim Crow were formally abolished, Black men and boys remain disproportionately vulnerable to interracial and intraracial sexual assault and violence (Curry & Utley, 2018).

The neglect of male sexual victimization, specifically Black male sexual victimization at the hands of women, is actually quite staggering. Until recently, the US Department of Justice defined rape specifically as "the carnal knowledge of a female forcibly and against her will" (Carbon, 2012, para. 1). This definition was updated in 2013 to read, "penetration, no matter how slight, of the vagina or anus with any body part or object, or oral penetration by a sex organ of another person, without the consent of the victim" (Carbon, 2012, para. 2). This new definition changes how rape victimization and perpetration is understood: male rape victims are now more accounted for in US data. Recent scholarship that takes this change of definition into account showed that men were raped and/or made to penetrate at similar rates to women in a 12-month period in the United States (Stemple & Meyer, 2014). The most surprising finding, however, has been the high rates of female perpetration of sexual coercion, unwanted sexual contact, and made-to-penetrate violence against men (Stemple et al., 2017; Smith et al., 2017, p. 32).

Smith et al. (2017) found that, in the United States over a 12-month period, Black males reported higher rates (6.5%) of contact sexual violence than both Black women (5.8%) and white women (3.6%) (pp. 18, 21, 28). They also found that, over a 12-month period, Black women in the United States reported roughly 262,000 cases of rape while Black men reported roughly 272,000 cases of made-to-penetrate violence (Smith et al., 2017, pp. 21, 28). In the same period, Black men reported 865,000 cases of contact sexual violence while Black women reported 849,000 cases. These numbers show that Black men experience sexual violence at rates comparable to, if not more than, most women in the United States. And yet the racist mythology of Black men as sexual brutes—a myth that pervades the US imagination—has neutralized the study of Black males as sexual victims (Curry, 2019).

But this myth does not belong to the United States alone. In general, feminist theory has also had considerable difficulty imagining women as perpetrators of sexual violence and rape. As Claire Cohen (2014) explains, "rape is still the most gender-specific of all crimes [where] only a man...can be the actual perpetrator, only a woman the victim" (p. 3). This is an ontological problem that implicates the normative assumptions surrounding how maleness excludes particular outgroup males from the identity of the rape victim. Some scholars might suggest that intersectionality, specifically intersectional invisibility, might be more open to discussing the rape of Black males and other subordinate male groups given its origin in Black feminism in the United States. This, however, is not the case: Black feminist authors have insisted since the 1980s that Black men were not systematically raped during slavery or even now as part of police violence in the United States (Davis, 1983; James 1999). This view of Black males being invulnerable to sexual violence and rape, despite the overwhelming evidence that Black men and boys have been and still are victims of sexual violence and rape, suggests the intersectional frame of analysis as mobilized by Black feminists has no way of analyzing the sexual victimization of subordinate males (see Jacobs, 2017). In other words, the apparent *need* of feminist theorists to proximally locate Black males within regimes of privilege and power *because* of their *maleness* is an obstacle to acknowledging the historic role that sexual violence has played in the oppression and subjugation of Black men by white men and women across the globe.

Many of the early feminist theorizations suggesting that Black men have power over Black women were based on the writings of subculture-of-violence theorists in the sixties and seventies. Theorists such as Marvin E. Wolfgang and Franco Ferracutti (1967), authors of *The Subculture of Violence: Towards an Integrated Theory in Criminology*, and Menachem Amir (1971), author of *Patterns in Forcible Rape*, were authoritatively cited as evidence that Black men rape more often and more brutally than white men. Despite their indebtedness to white male–inspired pathological accounts of Black male sexuality, feminist authors such as Susan Brownmiller (1975), and Karen A. Holmes and Joyce E. Williams (1981) feature prominently in Kimberlé Crenshaw's (1991) original formulation of intersectionality. Said differently, our present theories of intersectionality, race, and male gender identity tend towards viewing Black males as perpetrators of sexual violence and away from viewing Black males as victims of such violence. Black feminist discourse on sexual violence merely reproduces the more general problem of previous criminological and feminist anti-Black misandry. Masculinity framed as a rapist category does not allow for masculinity that is endemically vulnerable to rape. History reveals the latter is a part of the condition of Black maleness, contrary to the insistence of our present categories and disciplinary preoccupations with gender, masculinity, or patriarchy.

A Sterling Contribution to Black Male Studies

Black male studies offers a corrective to this skewing of Black male reality. It offers a way to empirically test and theorize visions that affirm Black males—that help them and, by extension, their communities thrive. Tamari Kitossa's edited collection *Appealing Because He Is Appalling* makes a distinct and vital contribution to this endeavour by deeroticizing Black masculinity and reclaiming the facticity of Black male life from the anti-Black misandric gender analytic.

Appealing Because He Is Appalling reconfigures the boundaries of gender theory and of thought itself, which today remain deeply ingrained in various feminist-inspired accounts of a racist anti-Black male imaginary. Expanding the male category to include erotic subjugation under colonial and slaveocratic orders contributes to the establishment of a new register by which to think Black men and boys in relation to patriarchy, sexuality, and violence. Grounded in James Baldwin's and Frantz Fanon's affirmations of Black maleness, Kitossa's edited collection takes as its central focus the expansion of the erotic landscape that Black maleness makes possible: a landscape that is one of desire, horror, and terror (as in the case of the rapist) as well as one of sexual caricature and misrepresentation. In Chapter 1, Kitossa uses the works of James Baldwin and Frantz Fanon to reflect upon how and why "the presumption that Black men are hypersexual, priapic, and prone to rape White women has been a central animating theme in Western cultural psychology." This tripartite assemblage of Black men expresses what Kitossa calls the Black Phallic Fantastic. My own reflections on phallicism have striven to clarify the transubstantiation of Black male flesh through phallic representations surrounding savagery and feminization (Curry, 2017b, 2018). This simultaneity of the hypersexual rapist and the effeminate male (that is, the male who is capable of being raped) occupies a significant dynamic in the racial negativing of maleness. Kitossa similarly provokes our thinking towards the psychosexual construction of the Black male as a pathological entity without neglecting the vulnerability and coercive trauma Black male flesh endures during this process.

Whereas Black male studies insists upon the end of the presumptive teleologism of gender imposed upon our considerations of the Black male, this collection reintroduces the Black male as a sociohistorical entity capable of inquiry without the pathological sexual apriorism entailed by current gender theories after this teleological suspension. The deeroticization of the Black male enables *genuine study and analysis* of the Black male "as is"—that is, study and analysis of Black manhood that is not preoccupied, as current disciplinary dialectics are, with where to locate Black males on the line between "rapist" and "nonrapist." The starting point for scholarly inquiry into the Black male must be reconfigured. The seemingly intuitive and obvious ends of gender analyses that suggest Black men are sexually aggressive and invulnerable to sexual assault, made-to-penetrate violence, and rape are not the results of inquiry. Rather, they are analytic assertions attached to the general category of maleness. The historical and sociological evidence simply does not confirm or conform to the prevalent ideologies used to analyze Black male sexual victimization. Feminists, gender theorists, and criminologists continue to assert that Black males are predominately the perpetrators of sexual violence. This is despite the fact that Black males experience higher rates of sexual victimization than whites, Black females, and other female groups in the United States. This suggests that the sexual vulnerability Black males have had to sodomization and sexual coercion at the hands of white men and women historically, and Black women currently, challenge the analytic assumptions undergirding the intervention of gender into our contemporary analyses, showing that these analyses fail to accurately represent the full extent of the violence *gender* intends to clarify.

Appealing Because He Is Appalling leads the reader through an impressive conceptual terrain making visible new topographical constructs through the exegetical approach deployed by Kitossa and the collection contributors. By emphasizing the vulnerability of Black males, the chapters in this volume unveil a positive phenomenology of Black male life that exceeds the limitations and descriptions of the corpse. From this excess, we gain an understanding of Black male disability, queerness, transnational context, and *being*—an understanding that is currently veiled by the dominant disciplinary episteme.

Ultimately, this collection shows that there is far more to Black masculinity throughout the world than the tropes that dominate in anti-Black racist societies today. Our present mode of intellectually engaging the Black male is found wanting. The historical, sociological, criminological, and philosophical assertions of masculinity draw legitimacy not from meeting the standards of evidence in history, sociology, criminology, or philosophy, but from the analytic presumptions of the gender category itself. These presumptions project a Fanonist phobogenetic framing of Black masculinity and sexuality (Oyěwùmí, 1997). These paradigmatic constraints on how we think about Black men and boys render much of our present scholarship not only empirically incorrect but inefficacious in the task of study. The essays in this collection are an essential contribution to Black male studies; their commendable interventions reject the mimeticism of the dominant intersectional mode of race and gender theory and show the urgent need for a genre study of Black male death and dying within this context.

TOMMY J. CURRY
University of Edinburgh
2020

Bibliography

Aidoo, L. (2018). *Slavery unseen: Sex, power, and violence in Brazilian history.* Duke University Press.

Amir, M. (1971). *Patterns in forcible rape.* University of Chicago Press.

Artz, L., Burton, P., Ward, C.L., Leoschut, L., Phyfer, J., Lloyd, S., Kassanjee, R., & Le Mottee, C. (2016). *Sexual victimisation of children in South Africa: Final report of the Optimus Foundation study.* UBS Optimus Foundation. http://www.ci.uct.ac.za/overview-violence/reports/sexual-victimisation-of-children-in-SA

Assari, S., & Curry, T.J. (2020, July 21). Black men face high discrimination and depression, even as their education and incomes rise. *The Conversation.* https://theconversation.com/black-men-face-high-discrimination-and-depression-even-as-their-education-and-incomes-rise-141027

Brownmiller, S. (1975). *Against our will: Men, women and rape.* Simon and Schuster.

Carbon, S.B. (2012, January 6). *An updated definition of rape.* U.S. Department of Justice. https://www.justice.gov/archives/opa/blog/updated-definition-rape

Chetty, R., Hendren, N., Jones, M.R., & Porter, S.R. (2020). Race and economic opportunity in the United States: An intergenerational perspective. *The Quarterly Journal of Economics, 135*(2), 711–83. https://doi.org/10.1093/qje/qjz042

Cohen, C. (2014). *Male rape is a feminist issue: Feminism, governmentality and male rape.* Palgrave Macmillan.

Cooper, F.R. (2006). Against bipolar Black masculinity: Intersectionality, assimilation, identity performance, and hierarchy. *UC Davis Law Review, 39*, 853–906.

Crenshaw, K.W. (1991). Mapping the margins: Intersectionality, identity politics, and violence against women of color. *Stanford Law Review, 43*(6), 1241–99. https://doi.org/10.2307/1229039

Curry, T.J. (2017a). *The man-not: Race, class, genre, and the dilemmas of Black manhood*. Temple University Press.

Curry, T.J. (2017b). This nigger's broken: Hyper-masculinity, the buck, and the role of physical disability in white anxiety toward the Black male body. *Journal of Social Philosophy, 48*(3), 321–43. https://doi.org/10.1111/josp.12193

Curry, T.J. (2018). Killing boogeymen: Phallicism and the misandric mischaracterizations of Black males in theory. *Res Philosophica, 95*(2), 235–72. https://doi.org/10.11612/resphil.1612

Curry, T.J. (2019). Expendables for whom: Terry Crews and the erasure of Black male victims of sexual assault and rape. *Women's Studies in Communication, 42*(3), 287–307. https://doi.org/10.1080/07491409.2019.1641874

Curry, T.J. (2021). Decolonizing the intersection: Black male studies as a critique of intersectionality's indebtedness to subculture of violence theory. In R.K. Beshara (Ed.), *Critical psychology praxis: Psychosocial non-alignment to modernity/coloniality* (pp. 132–54). Routledge.

Curry, T.J., & Utley, E.A. (2018). She touched me: Five snapshots of adult sexual violations of Black boys. *Kennedy Institute of Ethics Journal, 28*(2), 205–41. https://doi.org/10.1353/ken.2018.0014

Davis, A.Y. (1983). *Women, race, and class*. Vintage Books.

Del Zotto, A.C. (2004). Gendercide in a historical-structural context: The case of Black male gendercide in the United States. In A. Jones (Ed.), *Gendercide and genocide* (pp. 157–71). Vanderbilt University Press.

Foster, T.A. (2011). The sexual abuse of Black men under American slavery. *Journal of the History of Sexuality, 20*(3), 445–64. https://doi.org/10.1353/sex.2011.0059

Ghavami, N., & Peplau, L.A. (2013). An intersectional analysis of gender and ethnic stereotypes. *Psychology of Women Quarterly, 37*(1), 113–27. https://doi.org/10.1177/0361684312464203

Grosfoguel, R. (2016). What is racism? *Journal of World-Systems Research, 22*(1), 9–15. https://doi.org/10.5195/jwsr.2016.609

Jacobs, M.S. (2017). The violent state: Black women's invisible struggle against police violence. *William & Mary Journal of Race, Gender, and Social Justice, 24*(1), 39–100.

James, J. (1999). Black revolutionary icons and "neoslave" narratives. *Social Identities, 5*(2), 135–59. https://doi.org/10.1080/13504639951536

Jones, A. (2000). Gendercide and genocide. *Journal of Genocide Research, 2*(2), 185–211. https://doi.org/10.1080/713677599

McConnaughy, C. (2017, June 29–July 2). *Black men, white women, and demands from the state: How race and gender jointly shape protest expectations and legitimate state response* [Conference presentation]. International Society of Political Psychology Conference, ISPP at 40: Revisiting Core Themes of Tyranny, Intergroup Relations and Leadership, Edinburgh, Scotland.

http://www.dannyhayes.org/uploads/6/9/8/5/69858539/mcconnaughy_race_gender_protest_workshop_june2017.pdf

McConnaughy, C., & White, I.K. (2011, March 4–5). *Racial politics complicated: The work of gendered race cues in American politics* [Conference presentation]. New Research on Gender in Political Psychology Conference, Rutgers University. https://polisci.osu.edu/sites/polisci.osu.edu/files/mcconnaughy_white.pdf

Miller, E. (1991). *Men at risk*. Jamaica Publishing House Ltd.

Miller, E. (1994). *Marginalization of the Black male: Insights from the development of the teaching profession*. Canoe Publishing.

Miller, E. (2004). Male marginalization revisited. In E. Leo-Rhynie & B. Bailey (Eds.), *Gender in the 21st Century: Caribbean perspectives, visions, and possibilities* (pp. 99–133). Ian Randle Publishers.

Oyěwùmí, O. (1997). *The invention of women: Making an African sense of Western gender discourses*. University of Minnesota Press.

Randall, A.E. (2015). Gendering genocide studies. In A.E. Randall (Ed.), *Genocide and gender in the 20th Century: A comparative study* (pp. 1–34). Bloomsbury.

Rogers, J.A. (1942). *Sex and race* (Vol. 2). Helga M. Rogers.

Sidanius, J., & Pratto, F. (1999). *Social dominance: An intergroup theory of social hierarchy and oppression*. Cambridge University Press.

Smith, S.G., Basile, K., Gilbert, L.K., Merrick, M.T., Patel, N., Walling, M., & Jain, A. (2017). *National intimate partner and sexual violence survey (NISVS): 2010–2012 state report*. Atlanta, GA: National Center for Injury Prevention and Control, Division of Violence Prevention, Centers for Disease Control and Prevention. https://stacks.cdc.gov/view/cdc/46305

Stemple, L., Flores, A., & Meyer, I.H. (2017). Sexual victimization perpetrated by women: Federal data reveal surprising prevalence. *Aggression and Violent Behavior, 34*, 302–11. https://doi.org/10.1016/j.avb.2016.09.007

Stemple, L., & Meyer, I.H. (2014). The sexual victimization of men in America: New data challenge old assumptions. *American Journal of Public Health, 104*(6), e19–e26. https://doi.org/10.2105/AJPH.2014.301946

Stewart, J.B., & Scott, J.W. (1978). The institutional decimation of Black American males. *The Western Journal of Black Studies, 2*(2), 82–92. https://www.proquest.com/docview/1311832674?accountid=14474

Sweet, J.H. (2003). *Recreating Africa: Culture, kinship and religion in the African-Portuguese world, 1441–1770*. University of North Carolina Press.

Thiem, K.C., Neel, R., Simpson, A.J., & Todd, A.R. (2019). Are Black women and girls associated with danger? Implicit racial bias at the intersection of target age and gender. *Personality and Social Psychology Bulletin, 45*(10), 1427–39. https://doi.org/10.1177/0146167219829182

Wells, I.B. (2010). *Ida B. Wells versus Judge Lynch: The anti-lynching trilogy* (J. H. Mitchell, Ed.). CreateSpace Independent Publishing Platform.

White, A.M. (2008). *Ain't I a feminist? African American men speak out on fatherhood, friendship, forgiveness, and freedom*. State University of New York Press.

Williams, J.E., & Holmes, K.A. (1981). *The second assault: Rape and public attitudes*. Greenwood Press.

Wolfgang, M.E., & Ferracuti, F. (1967). *The subculture of violence: Towards an integrated theory in criminology* (M.E. Wolfgang, Ed.). Tavistock Publications.

Wynter, S. (1994). "No humans involved": An open letter to my colleagues. *Forum N.H.I.: Knowledge for the 21st Century, 1*(1), 42–73.

Preface

FROM ACROSS TIME, and different places and spaces, this book narrates the construction and the sociopolitical and psychological implications of the representation of the hegemonic Black[1] man as hypersexual, priapic, and prone to commit rape. However imperfect, I have taken to calling this unified and overdetermining fantasy the *Black Phallic Fantastic*. Asking who invented this fantastic spectacle, this recursive and persistent trope, and how, in spite of its irrationality, it continues to be invested with meaning, is as important as examining how it is renewed and recycled. It is equally important to demontrate the concrete and psychosocial uses to which it is put, how it is accommodated and appropriated, and—not least—how and at what cost it is resisted. For Black men, all too often, the cost is their lives.

There is something sticky, yet slippery, about how Blackness and maleness have come to be imagined, and which makes the Black Phallic Fantastic commonsensical. With few exceptions, masculinity studies, and much of feminist and gender writing, have done little to coherently deconstruct and explicate this trope. In fact, there seems to be a dependence on it, principally, I think, because these fields are largely Eurocentric, middle-class preoccupied, and deeply informed by sexual mythologies about Black men. Manifesting as a form of "bad faith," there is a tacit dependence on representing Black men as sexualized beings and refusing their humanity. I think that academia's epistemic dependence on sexualized tropes of Black men is a protective shield that prohibits deconstruction. What is at stake is not only the stability of the aforementioned academic disciplines, but also the uses to which they are put for the state and capital in the maintenance of social order and the oppression of Black communities. Also implicated are the identities and the personalities of theorists, being themselves the product of anti-Black misandry. As with the Black Phallic Fantastic, its historical foundations, and the social bases for its reproduction through discursive formations and regimes of representation, we must ask questions about how it has come to stick to the very insides of academic disciplines and theory. These questions are tied up together; this book is a series of meditations on them. Here, I offer four central points from which to begin.

First, the White supremacist invention of the Black-man-as-sexual-demon is an epistemic object for the normative claims of scholastic feminism, gender studies, and White-male-determined masculinities studies. As a productive commodity for knowledge workers, abstractified Black men are transformed from complex, whole, and varied human beings into theoretical objects for (unaccountable) scopophilic, dependent ontology. In other words, since no one innocently theorizes about the social, ontologies, which consist of preexisting conceptions and sentiments rigorously denied as such, are in many respects biographical sketches inductively applied to the world. Black men are, in effect, brought into being as spectacularized objects of sexual desire and revulsion. They are constituted as bestial, framed as archetypes of "toxic masculinity"; imagined as overcompensating "patriarchs"; framed as supremely misogynistic; understood to be quintessentially homophobic; regarded as sexually unrestrained, crotch grabbing "thugs"; assumed to be violent rapists; and so on. Conceptualized as genital and as being concerned only with their genitals as a compensatory negritude for "possessing" so little else, there is at the heart of academia and White supremacist popular culture an eroticized desire for *the* Black man as a problem upon whom, and through whom, others work out their sense of themselves and their place in the world. The tacit overdetermined sexualization of the Black man simultaneously visibilizes and invisibilizes him as a negated personhood for the ontological productivity of theorists for whom the social is gendered, masculine, and patriarchal. In short, the sexualized, tropical Black man, always able-bodied and heterosexual, is a scapegoat object for the working-out of the agency and moral innocence of various theorists.

Second, as a sexualized discursive formation, the Black man is a compendium of negative traits, assuring that correcting and disciplining him is a constant procedure achieved even at the price of killing him— for how else can he be saved. "Crisis," "problem," "crotch-fixated," "misogynist," "homophobe," "transphobe," and "toxic" are the watchwords for Black men. This is evident in middle-class projective fantasies—irrespective of the theorist's race and sex—and none of it seems aware of itself, nor of the real Black men who are desired, feared, and loathed. Even as agents doing things—adapting, accommodating, challenging, resisting—they are crushed by the weight of sexualization that overdetermines how they are imagined: as always in need of correction, tutelage, and direction. It seems that the genitalized Black man whom James Baldwin and Frantz Fanon made known to us exists, especially among the academic class, as a universal type—a problem to be changed, criticized, and fixed. To be "cool," for example, is imagined as the socially constructed poor, urban, and young Black man appealing to an embedded sexual repertoire rather than other possibilities. How else can others make themselves socially useful except by self-righteously correcting and pontificating about "him"?

Third, as nonbeings constructed to serve others, what is missed in all this is that the quality of Black men's lives, irrespective of social station and whether the most marginal among them live or are killed by those who imagine them to be monsters, is in no small measure informed by the unified trope of the Black Phallic Fantastic. However Black men cope, handle it or are handled by it, no Black man goes untouched. I know from personal experience how deforming and devastating is the notion that Black boys and men are neither (sexually) fragile nor vulnerable. I have spoken to Black men from Africa, the Caribbean, Europe, Latin America, and North America about the implication of this tripartite trope on their lives. Various men told me of being sexually abused as children by males and females, of being sexually exploited in their adolescence by women two and three times their age, and of being sexually manipulated as adults.

Being sexually abused by males was coded in speech, discerned only by inference; being sexually abused by females was equally mystified through the use of the term "sexual experience." These sorts of encounters shape the identities, self-esteem, sexual and social lives of Black men, indeed their sovereignty; yet the implications are hardly considered a topic worthy of inquiry in the scholarly literature. Blackness and maleness, it would seem, make it unimaginable that boys and men can be sexually endangered and hurt. In addition to witnessing and listening to Black men about their vulnerabilities, we should scrutinize Kimberlé Crenshaw's (1989) point of departure—borrowed from the groundbreaking collection edited by Gloria Hull, Patricia Bell-Scott and Barbara Smith (1982)—that "all the women are white; all the blacks are men, but some of us are brave." Equally dubious is bell hooks's (1984, 1990, 1992a, 1992b, 2004) claim that from the plantation to the present, Black men have been both fixated on their genitals and have colluded with White men to oppress Black women. The *au courant* idea among some that "straight Black men are the White people of the Black community," also demands an account for the demonizing, invisibilizing, and "woke" profiteering from the dehumanization and murder of (straight) Black boys and men. It ought not to be accepted as an article of faith that Black men are both beneficiaries and responsible for the invisibilization of Black women.

How can it be that Ralph Ellison's complaint that Black men are invisible rings as true today as in 1952? What is not being seen when so many Black men and boys languish in prisons; are murdered by police, vigilantes, and their peers; commit suicide; are detained in schools when not pushed out of them; are locked out of employment; are unhoused; are deprived of the vote; and are forced to "scavenge," as Tommy Curry (2017) puts it, a living on the margins and underworld of society? This is the privilege of being a Black boy and man? The idea that the lives of Black men and women should be examined as separate realities, rather than the *we-ness* of their relational differences under White supremacy, leaves little room to imagine, in fact and theory, the reality of their mutual dependence and that what affects one affects the other. I hasten to add, this is not a Polyanna view which obviates the tangle of conflict, contradiction, difference and paradox within Blackness.

Finally, despite sound criticism of the thesis that patriarchy is the "gender domination" of women by men, there seems, both intellectually and politically, little appreciation that this is an innovation of nineteenth-century White male intellectuals who were heavily invested in colonialism, Eurocentricsm, and White supremacy. Black men in the West were enslaved, were just recently emancipated, or had lived through the reality of the partition of Africa and settler colonialism at precisely the time that Freidrich Engels, Henry Maine, Lewis Henry Morgan, and other White men were elaborating the matriarchal and patriarchal theses from which theories of gender and feminism were born. We would do well to return to the origin of this theorizing to apprehend, as did James Baldwin and Frantz Fanon, that "patriarchy" should be understood not as the domination of universal man over universal woman, but instead as an articulation of the antagonism and contest between groups. This does not, however, displace the dialogic between gender and sexual contradiction *within* groups, necessarily stratified to engage in intergroup conflict. That the discourse of "patriarchy" has been displaced in the West in favour of "masculinities" and, at the same time, has been outsourced, through the "war on terror," to the Global South as a means of explaining suicide bombing and the refusal to permit women to drive or go to school, makes little difference to my mind. As will be shown throughout this book, "patriarchy," as an epistemic construct, not only suppresses cognitive awareness that it is an intergroup, competitive, racial dynamic in and through which males are the first targets of other males attacking minoritized communities, but also that women from the dominant group are directly complicit in maintaining and sustaining patriarchy as a form of "in-group" dominance of "outgroups."

In my opinion, sexualized tropes about *the* Black man deny Black men personhood in the eyes of others, make of him an object toward the ontological and theoretical affirmation of others, obfuscate his experience of trauma and coping with sexualized objectification, and stabilize and mystify the imperialist and white supremacist theory of "patriarchy." If there is merit to these opinions—opinions which inspired the composition of this book—there is an urgent need to reimagine how Black men are sexually imagined. I think doing so needs to begin with an honest appraisal of *the* Black man, especially the eroticized and sexualized trope of the Black man, as a fiction made real by a vast range of constituencies who continue to recreate him as a disembodied and unruly penis. The eroticized objectification of Black men that forms the backdrop to this book is both personal to me and informs the perspective of the book's contributors who are concerned with generating alternative accounts of Black men and the implications of their sexualization through the component parts of the Black Phallic Fantastic.

It is my hope that this book reveals the (re)production of the actual and symbolic nakedness of Black men. As a result, I hope that readers will understand that Black men are routinely violated, and that bad faith toward their Blackness and their maleness not only obfuscates this violation but legitimates it. With the eroticized snuff film of George Floyd[2] being sadistically murdered by Derek Chauvin in mind, I want this book to help make it impossible to avoid the fact that the Black man is sexually gazed at, fixed in the scopophilic gaze as always genital, and imagined as a defective being by virtue of the debased meanings of sex—meanings attached to his body. My wish is that this book contributes to other works that aim to refract the scopophilic gaze on the Black man back to its source, compelling those who derive innocence from the Black Phallic Fantastic to come to terms with the cultural and ontological magnitude of their dependence on this fiction. The prospect of an empathetic and humanizing orientation toward Black men, without apology, without qualification, is what is at stake.

This is a book of big thoughts and daring ideas, and it comes with risk-taking. As its curator, I present it to everyone who will read it—with the humility of a student. If there are errors that I and the contributors are responsible for, my hope is that we are clear about them so that we may be just as clearly corrected.

TAMARI KITOSSA
Brock University
2020

Notes

1. Capitalization of race/colour adjectives is not consistent throughout this volume. Each contributor to this book uses these adjectives in ways that suit their sensibilities and politics.
2. Elsewhere (Kitossa, 2020), I present an integrative analysis of how the sexual demonization of Black men and women leads to their actual and ritual destruction.

Bibliography

Crenshaw, K. (1989). Demarginalizing the intersection of race and sex: A Black feminist critique of antidiscrimination doctrine, feminist theory, and antiracist politics. *University of Chicago Legal Forum*, *1*(8), 139–67.

Hull, G.T., Scott, P.B., & Smith, B. (Eds.). (1982). *All the women are White, all the Blacks are men, but some of us are brave: Black women's studies*. Feminist Press.

Kitossa, T. (2020, December 4). *Anti-Black sexual racism: Linking white police violence, COVID-19, and popular culture* [Symposium paper]. Intervention Symposium—Black Humanity: Bearing Witness to COVID-19, online. https://antipodeonline.org/2020/12/04/black-humanity-bearing-witness-to-covid-19/

Acknowledgements

SOCIAL THEORISTS WORK ALONE, but never in isolation of historical developments, patterns, trends, the immediacy of their relations, and the mediated world around them. From these dynamics, which interact with their consciousness and experience, theorists select, include and exclude in their work ideas they test, and which are tested on them. There are many to whom I owe a great deal for debating, discussing, clarifying, and sharing their wisdom. Not all, of course, can be mentioned, but I will try. My first thank-you is to the dearly departed Gwen and Lenny Johnson, once proud owners of Third World Bookstore in Toronto. When I went there to buy books and attend discussion groups in the late 1980s and into the early 1990s, it was an oasis in a desert of panic about Jamaicans and "crime." I owe the early sharpening of my critical faculties not only to the Johnsons, but also to the brothers and sisters with whom I turned pages and broke bread at both Third World Books and the Bear Pit at York University. I am grateful for my breddrins Andre Clarke, Gregory Balgobind, Patrick Knight, Whitney Sanford, Paul Scotland, and Charles Simon-Aaron. These men helped me become a man.

I am indebted, too, to my colleagues at Brock University. They, knowing of my research interests, never failed to make inquiries; issue encouraging words; and, ever thoughtfully, provide newspaper clippings, weblinks, and books they thought relevant to my research. Among them are Jonah Butovsky, Maureen Connolly, Ann Duffy, June Corman, Jane Helleiner, Chris Lytle, Mary-Beth Raddon, and Felipe Ruan. I am grateful for former grad students Tierney Kobryn-Dietrich and Anson Nater who, on top of believing in what I was doing, provided much-needed technical support out of the kindness of their hearts. Appreciation to Aline Carmo, Glorie Tapo Chimbganda, Richard Christie, Alejandra Aguilar Dornelles, Charu Gupta, Scott Kouri, Kwamena Kwansah-Aidoo, Seulghee Lee, Virginia Mapedzahama, Roxana Escobar Ñañez, Cathy Skott-Myhre, Hans Skott-Myrhe, Charles Quiste-Adade, Elaine Rocha, Rosario del Pilar Rodríguez Romaní, and Brad Elliott Stone.

I recognize my non-Black chosen brothers and sisters whose Black consciousness and support of my ideas is unwavering: Laura Banfield, Antje Deckert, Nicole Gruel, Patty Krawec, Scott Milne, Gordon Pon, and Caroline Schöepf.

I am grateful to the Black women who are my sisters from other mothers and fathers: Jennifer Adkins, Akua Benjamin, Mutsa Charamba, Lindis Bacchus, Lana Burchell, Lydia Forge, Aisha Francis, Amoaba Gooden, Annette Henry, Erica Lawson, Kerry Goring, Nyarai Kapisavanhu, Delores Mullings, Evelyn Myrie, Kimberly Nesbeth, Adele Norris, Doret Phillips, Zamani Ra, L.A. Wade and Lana Burchell.

I am thankful to the Black men who, over the years, befriended me and shared their lives and stories with me: Eugene Bacchus, Victor Beausoleil, Ryan Burke, Warren Clarke, Dave Francis, Davaun Francis, Dr. Vibe, Menelik Girma, Brandon Hay, Tony Hayes, Ajamu Ikwe-Tyehimba, Sheldon Holder, Winston Husbands, Francis Jeffers, Olivier Kaitaba, Shaka Licorish, Louis March, Kenrick McKinnon, Tibab McNeish, Desmond Miller, Anthony Morgan, Jason Murray, Dionisio Nyaga, Paul Scotland, Michael St. George, Emmanuel Tabi, Martin Tshibabwa, Khalil West, Tristan Williams, and Kumsa Yuya. I am grateful for the friendship and the intellectual inspiration of David Austin and Barrington Walker. My dear colleagues, friends, and brothers in the struggle at Brock University—John Kaethler, Richard Ndyazigamiye, and Jean Ntakirutimana—thank you.

Big up to mi' likkle cousin dem who struggle and rise like roses in concrete: Carlington Luke, Kadeem Ellis, Menelik Luke, Negus Luke, Prince Luke, and Rodney Malcolm. Fi mi bigga cousin dem who shared conversation and references with me: Ustinov Luke and Sekou Luke. Thanks to my uncle Junior Luke who kept me alive and taught me the ways of the world. Thanks to my sisters Dorothy Luke and Nadine Luke-Moraghan and her husband Mike Moraghan who gave me the run of their home on my sabbatical in 2014 to think through the issues that are the fruit of this book. Big up, too, to the rest of my family and especially my grandparents aunt May and mas' Alti.

I am grateful to my chosen brothers and sisters in the intellectual community: Biko Agozino, Boulou Ebanda de B'béri, Horace Campbell, Tommy J. Curry, Henry Daniel, George Dei, Cecil Foster, Lorne Foster, Awad Ibrahim, Carl E. James, Anthony Stewart, Handel Kashope Wright. I am especially grateful to Wesley Crichlow, Dennis Yeo, and Christopher J. Williams—their emotional and intellectual nurturing is unconditional.

I deeply appreciate of the confidential examiners of this book. Their commitment is evident in their thoughtful and helpful commentary. I must also thank my PHD supervisor, Kari Dehli, for encouraging my interest in the eroticization of Black men.

This book is indebted to the outstanding contributors. They were patient and walked hand-in-hand with me since the journey officially began in 2014. It has been a wonderful experience working with you. I am grateful to the press committee and the staff of the University of Alberta Press, namely Cathie Crooks and Duncan Turner, for their abiding commitment. Mat Buntin, the editor with the patience of a saint, was gracious to a fault. I especially want to thank Doug Hildebrand, Director of the University of Alberta press, who found my pitch "eye-raisingly interesting" and did not waver in his support. I am eternally grateful to the copy editor assigned to this book—Kay Rollans. She pored over every word and line of this text, raising both the clarity and quality of scholarship. This book is possible because of the financial support of SSHRC Exchange Grant from Brock University and the University of Alberta Press.

This book honours two dearly departed friends. More than friends, they were sounding boards, teachers, mentors. First, Courtney "Cedric" Licorish (1945–2018) who entertained me in conversation, read everything I wrote, even when it was horrible, and bequeathed me his extensive library. Cedric's friendship would have meant nothing without the kindness and support of his widow, Lynette Profitt. Second, I am thankful to Sidney McLarty Willhelm (1834–2018), author of *Who Needs the Negro,* who always made the time for me. He was my window into a different era and the tradition of the life of the mind to which I aspire. He helped me to understand what *was*, so that I could see what *might* be. "The struggle is the victory," he would say.

This book would not be possible without my family who were my sounding board, analysts of my arguments, and providers of references. My children Jelani and Adisa, you have watched me with concern as I pulled one too many late nights. Thanks for the love and the times you compelled me to go to bed: it made all the difference. Finally, this book would not have been possible without my life-partner and research collaborator, Katerina Deliovsky. We share a life and all this entails: time, pillow, ideas, research, writing, and children these past 32 years—She is my rock. This book is a testament to our shared vision of a life together, proving Baldwin and Fanon right that living and loving authentically, as we see it, is possible.

Introduction

TAMARI KITOSSA

If one wants to understand the racial situation psychoanalytically, not from a universal viewpoint but as it is experienced by individual consciousness, considerable importance must be given to the sexual phenomenon. In the case of the Jew, one thinks of money and its cognates. In that of the Negro, one thinks of sex.

—FRANTZ FANON, *Black Skin, White Masks*

[I]t is absolutely certain that white men, who invented the nigger's big black prick, are still at the mercy of this nightmare, and are still, for the most part doomed, in one way or another, to attempt to make this prick their own.

—JAMES BALDWIN, *No Name in the Street*

THIS BOOK IS PERSONAL. I have spent the better part of my intellectual career and near all of my life in Canada pondering what makes Black[1] men's bodies, my body, so available to non-Black people, to hate, to love, to desire, to touch, to grab, to possess. I have struggled to understand why my body, at least in the minds of others, belongs to them and not to me. Let me wrest "the personal is political" and the auto-ethnographic concept of "standpoint" from feminism to explain.

When I was in grade six, I was infatuated with a female classmate of Mediterranean heritage. I thought she was the most beautiful girl in the world and I told her so. Her reaction was startling: it was one of horror, as if she had been infected by the plague, and she basically told *me* so. The child in me still remembers the feeling that something was wrong with me because of who and what I am; that a part of me, in the eyes of non-Black, but especially White others, is unworthy. As it turns out, a few years ago when I met up with some high school friends, I was told that this girl, now a woman, married a Jamaican and has lived, I suppose and hope, having resolved the paradox the White world presented her, happily ever after.

But I was to discover inasmuch as hatred lays claim to a part of me in the eyes of others, they desired me, and that they could and did take a part of me at their whim. The first time this happened was when I was 16 and riding the subway in Toronto. I was standing in the car holding onto the above-head railings. I felt my ass fulsomely clutched. Shocked and perplexed I look around, only to see the smirking faces of older White men and women. I shrugged it off, until again my ass was clutched, this time even more firmly. I had no words. Embarrassed, ashamed, and hyperventilating, I rushed to another part of the car and exited to wait for another train. When I was 22, I was frisked by a cop for smoking a joint in front of an apartment building. He spent more time clutch-and-grasping at my crotch than patting my pockets. I wanted to fucking kill him. Seeing the water in my eyes, he smiled and remarked, "Oh, your ticklish eh?"[2]

The nightclub scene also proved to be unpredictable and terrible. At one downtown Toronto club, not 10 paces into the place, an attractive White woman about my age walked directly in my way. As I stopped, so did she. Next, as she looked me dead in the eyes, she moved closer to me, clutched my crotch, gave a light squeeze, squinted her eyes, smiled and walked off. At another club, my friend and I danced the night away with two women we had met. Then, being gentlemen, we walked them to their car. Next thing we knew, we were being driven to their place. We had to tell them to turn around as we hadn't planned on this, didn't know where we were going, and our friends wouldn't know where we were. Looking back now, I can only conclude it was their habit to kidnap Black men for their sexual gratification. Given the many conversations I have had and continue to have with Black men, saying "no," can, in some instances, be fraught with risk. That night, my friend and I could have been accused of attempted rape, and who would believe we had not.

I had a White female student attend my office hours to discuss her term paper. Within five minutes, she began to shake and sob. TAs and students have routinely remarked that they find me "intimidating," and so thinking I was being too intellectually demanding, for what else could it be, and concerned for her well-being, I paused to ask what I had done to make her so upset. She replied, "Professor, I have never been this close to a Black man before."

Finally, after yet another blackface incident at Brock University in 2014 (Kitossa, 2014), I gave a lecture to my third year class about neoliberalism, White privilege, and blackface. A cabal of at least four White female students was so incensed by the lecture that in the weeks following they plotted to either try to damage my car by pouring sugar into the gas tank, or, much more frighteningly, attempt to kill me by cutting the car's brake lines. These are the sorts of experiences that have shaped my interest in understanding how the Black man has come to be imagined as an object that is appealing because he is appalling. And it is James Baldwin and Frantz Fanon who have most helped me to make sense of how a part of me and parts of other Black men have come to be desired and "owned" by those who imagine us this way.

Lay of the Land

Focused on discourse, history, and representation in race-based group conflict articulated through psychosexual dynamics, the fact of racial patriarchy considered in this book centres on the ways that ideologies about sex constitute a method by which fear, loathing, and desire occupy the same place at the same time in the domination of Black men.[3] I introduce a tripartite concept that condenses how Black men's bodies are reduced to the status of objects and are seen as simultaneously appealing and appalling. This concept, which I call the *Black Phallic Fantastic*, encapsulates three core traits according to which Black men's (and boy's) bodies are imagined and defined: priapic, hypersexual, and prone to commit rape. Ultimately, the Black Phallic Fantastic summarizes a contradiction that both reaffirms and intensifies the domination and positional inferiority of Black men. Moreover, because men are the first targets of other men[4] (a statement that, I concede, may at this point be controversial for some), and because the totality of dominant groups is oriented toward the actual and symbolic subordination of "outgroup" males (a position that will be argued below), we are at this moment, to borrow the words of James Baldwin (1972), deep into "history's ass-pocket" (p. 61). And we know it! The continued plantation-like eroticized breaking, bludgeoning, butchering, caging, and mutilating of Black men's bodies and minds are proof of it.[5] There are too many examples, but one need look no farther than Eric Garner, Freddy Gray, Ahmaud Arbery, and George Floyd in the USA; Jermaine Carby and Junior Manon in Canada; Raymond Lawrence and Mark Dugganin the UK; Solomon Teka and Abraham Damati in Israel; Willy Monteiro Duarte in Italy; the countless young Black men murdered by police in Brazil's favelas; and in India African students are berated, beaten and killed (see chapter 10 this volume). Whether you are a Black man in the geographic regions covered in this book—Canada, the Caribbean, China, the United Kingdom and Europe, India, Japan, North Africa, the Philippines, and the United States—it is not seriously disputed, as Baldwin (1961) avers, that to be a Black man "is to be a walking phallic symbol: which means that one pays in one's own personality, for the sexual insecurity of others" (para. 3). But what sort of insecurity is it that arises in those that desire and revile the Black man who is their own creation?

This book puts forward the thesis that the problem of the colour-line has always been one of sexualized racial patriarchy. To be sure, this is not an original idea; it runs through the works of, for example, James Baldwin and Frantz Fanon, who are the touchstones of this collection, but also Eldridge Cleaver (1968/1992, pp. 176–90).[6] What *is* new is the intensive *application* of these ideas to the depth psychology of representations and experiences of men defined as Black across time, place, and space. As such, the focus is on confronting, elucidating, and naming the erotic and sexual racist ideologies about Black men in the minds of other men, women, and non-Black peoples. Facing up to these ideologies will not be comfortable and will not be easy; the normative and conceptual inertia about gender, masculinity, race, rape, sexualities, and patriarchy as given to us by the West will and must be unsettled (Thomas, 2007). Indeed, it will be shown throughout this book that inasmuch as Western colonialism and imperialism is the major engine for circulating eroticized tropes of Black men around the world, other cultures, too, either had prior conceptions of Black men derived from ancient Greece and Rome or have made these tropes all their own to understand Africa, Blackness, Black men, and themselves.

Certainly, the credibility of the foregoing thesis may be denied, evaded, obfuscated and disputed. But consider Greg Thomas's (2007) observation that, whether in the past or present of plantation America, "[t]here is no universal man socialized in opposition to a universal woman, or vice versa; there is a white man and a white woman specified over and against [Black people]" (p. 42). To theorize otherwise is to be complicit with the trope that woman is the archetypical victim of patriarchy and to deny that patriarchy is a colonialist, dominative, imperialist group and White supremacist racial phenomenon. We must face up to the fact that, within this context, a fundamental tension underlies the attacks on Black men and boys: that which makes them objects of sexualized gender violence is also that which makes them desirable. We can no longer avoid directly confronting the sexual dynamic in anti-Black misandry[7] that is also central to the subordination of Black women (Kitossa, 2020; Roberts, 1993), nor we can sustain discrete nineteenth-century mechanistic conceptual verbiage such as *intersection*,[8] which is taken to imply the particular gendered object of patriarchy is biological *woman* (see Curry, 2017; Thomas, 2007; Trexler, 1995).

Black men exist in the ontologically determined psychosexual imaginary of Others as appealing because they are appalling. What might explain this? Elsewhere, I have suggested that a strictly materialist analysis that positions class as the essential determinant for racism will not do (Kitossa, 2020). Precisely for this reason, Fanon (1963/1968) asserts that

> [w]hen you examine at close quarters the colonial [and racist] context, it is evident that what parcels out the world is to begin with the fact of belonging to or not belonging to a given race, a given species...This is why Marxist analysis should always be slightly stretched every time we have to do with the colonial problem. (p. 40).[9]

Earlier, Fanon cites Karl Jaspers emphasizing that "[i]t is not so much the number of cases seen that matters in phenomenology but the extent of the inner exploration of the individual case, which needs to be carried to the furthest possible limit" (cited in Fanon, 1952/2008, p. 146).[10]

The phenomenological approach to psychosexual pathology is important for Fanon because what is said by a culture, especially a colonialist, imperialist, and White supremacist one that speaks with a forked tongue, is not what its members practice. To this end, Fanon (1967) asserts that "[i]f in England, in Belgium, or in France, despite the democratic principles affirmed by these respective nations, there are still racists, it is these racists who, in their opposition to the country as a whole, are logically consistent" (p. 40). As a consequence, Fanon adds:

> The racist in a culture with racism is therefore normal. He has achieved a perfect harmony of economic relations and ideology. The idea that one forms of man, to be sure, is never totally dependent on economic relations, in other words—and this must not be forgotten—on relations existing historically and geographically among men and groups. (p. 40)

One must therefore go behind the manifest expressions of a culture to expose what constitutes the taken-for-granted ideals and practices that are the cohering resonance that reproduce White supremacist culture.

At a conceptual level then, the depth of psychosexual pathology of collective White supremacist patriarchy escapes us because, in cognitive terms, sex is *obviously* linked to darker and dirtier people (Hoch, 1979). Baldwin drew attention to this taken-for-grantedness when he asserted that, in the United States,

> [i]f you're a Negro, you're in the center of the peculiar affliction because anybody [read: White people] can touch you—when the sun goes down. You know, you're the target for everybody's fantasies. If you're a Negro female whore, he comes to you and asks you to do for him what he wouldn't ask his wife to do—nor any other white woman. But you're a black woman! So you can do it—because you know how to do dirty things! And if you're a black boy you wouldn't believe the holocaust that opens over your head—with all these despicable—males—looking for somebody to act out their fantasies on. And it happens in this case—if you're sixteen years old—to be you! (Baldwin cited in Eckman, 1968, pp. 32–33)

We will see later that Baldwin's indictment was not only of White men, but also of White women who themselves established their conceptions of beauty, femininity, and racial authority through their communion with White men and children at lynching picnics.

But this was more than a phenomenon at the heart of the global hegemon. It was a phenomenon of White world supremacy. As noted by Ronald Hyam (1991):

> Sex is at the very heart of racism. Racism is not caused simply by sexual apprehensions, and there are many other factors involved, such as fear of the unfamiliar, fear bred by memory of historic conflicts, fear of demographic swamping by the superior numbers of a culture perceived as alien and inferior, fear of disease, fear of economic competition for limited resources—but the peculiarly emotional hostility towards black men[11] which it has so often engendered[12] requires a sexual explanation. (p. 203; see also Hernton, 1965; Hoch, 1979; Kovel, 1971; Mason, 1971)

From anxieties about immigration and citizenship, Black liberation, rape, social order, and beyond (Austin, 2013; Curry, 2017; Ferber, 2007; C. James, in press; Preibisch & Binford, 2007; Thomas, 2007; Walker, 2010), now more than ever we must attend to the sexual implications of what Du Bois (1914/1986) in his essay "The Prize Fighter" called "this unforgivable blackness" (pp. 1161–62).

Indeed, conceptions of race, sex, and civilization are tightly enmeshed in regimes of fantasy and projection, both for individuals and societal complexes. Erotic and sexual racism as group patriarchy is at the heart of colonialism and imperialism (Baldwin, 1955/1984, 1972, 1976; Fanon, 1968, 1952/1977; Farmanfarmaian, 1992; Hall, 1996; Stannard, 1992). As noted by the likes of Freud (1930), Jung (1966), and Mead (1918), cooperation and peace are the manifest imperatives for "in-group" cultural sublimation of the sexual instinct and impulse. But in the uneasy truce between individual and "society," where each (re)produces the other, where does the dammed energy of aggressive sexuality go? What are its psychosexual articulations manifested in expressive modes of representation and projection onto a scapegoated, "animalized," and sexualized Other that bring ontological coherence and stability? If the production of sexual demons are foundational to the establishment and maintenance of both ontology and social order, then enemies who are marked by the psychological and social distance of the "difference" they represent must always be manufactured and constructed. This book examines *the* Black man as such a construction—one that occupies the space of the sexual demon for a variety of cultures, groups, and individuals.

The canalization outward, released in orgies of symbolic and physical violence, expropriates all that the Other is and possesses, and in the practice and psychology of domination a culture is born, reinforcing its members' sense of we-ness against them. As noted by George Herbert Mead (1918), war, both internal and external, symbolic and practical, proceeds by way of channelling and substituting the sexual drive that underlies cooperation with the desire to destroy the enemy as a means of experiencing and benefiting from in-group communion. Before the enemy is destroyed or enslaved—or at least before the attempt is made—they are ritually and symbolically imagined as subhuman, if not "animal." Importantly, they are specifically imagined as sexual beasts. Freud, like Jung, imagined that at the heart of civilization there is a lingering ambivalence that, despite all efforts to separate ourselves from the world, we have not transcended; sex and the guilt associated with it are central to hierarchical social orders and articulations of the mark between "civilization" and "barbarism." At least in the contemporary West, nonhuman animal totems, mythic beast-humans, and archetypes are constant reminders of a struggle within to transcend the primordial ooze.[13] Human civilization, used here in the broadest and most relativistic anthropological sense of the term, differs only with regards to the quality of quantitative distinction between "complex" and "simple" social organization—for within and between tribes, clans, and nations, the Other is judged by taboos, including those around sex (Elias, 2008; Raybeck, 1991).[14] As noted by Mary Douglas (1970), "dirtiness" and "pollution" are moral counterpoints to "cleanliness" and "purity," which, in the psychoanalytics of depth psychology, reveal themselves to be discourses and representations of sexual propriety and civility versus sexual impropriety and barbarism.

With these vital anthropological and psychosocial observations in the background, the purpose of this book is to explain and to explore the historical, transhistorical, and transnational creation, reproduction, and implications of the tripartite myth that Black men are hypersexual, priapic, and prone to commit rape: the Black Phallic Fantastic (see also Kitossa, Chapter 1 in this volume). In A.A. Roback's (1944) *Dictionary of International Slurs*, he coined the term *ethnophaulism* to account for ethnic and racial stereotypes that appear unalterably tied to specific disparaged groups. Persisting in the dominant culture through diffusion in art and other media is what Hortense Spillers (1987) calls "pornotroping."[15] In the case of this book, the concern is a historical and transnational pornotroping of Black men.[16] What James Baldwin and Frantz Fanon show, however, is that this tripartite trope has deep psychosexual implications: erotic and sexual racism merge with scopophilia,[17] that fixes the Black man's body as both mental and actual prosthetic, and which produces a presumably unique sexual experience (see Chapter 3). More than any other theorists of erotic and sexual racism, Baldwin and Fanon are sensitive to culture, history, and psychology in order to provide an account of the distinct social mythology of the Black man as the unsurpassed master of sexual delight and debauchery.

With Baldwin and Fanon as our guides, contributors to this collection explore a range of questions: What accounts for the persistent myth from antiquity to the present of the Black man as hypersexual, priapic, and prone to commit rape? What are its effects on men of African descent? What "work" is done in constructing hegemonic masculinity for other men? How does the Black Phallic Fantastic inform how non-Black women construct and experience their sexual autonomy, especially in the tourist and transnational context? What are the means and varied communicative modes by which one or more aspects of the tripartite trope mentioned above is transmitted globally? How does this trope enable a desiring, exoticization, fetishization, and objectification of Black men—by non-Black men, gay and straight alike, and by White and other non-Black women—as a *thing*, there to serve their psychoexistential "liberation" through sexual play? How and in what ways is this trope relevant to a critical understanding of the constructs of gender, White hegemonic femininity and masculinity, and patriarchy?

Baldwin and Fanon: Rethinking Masculinities, Unthinking Patriarchy for the Deeroticization of Black Men

The purpose of this section is to demonstrate why Baldwin and Fanon are unique in enabling the theoretical space to confront the paradox of Black men's location in the psychosexual imaginary of the Other. I suggest that in their concern for liberating the constructed Black man, Baldwin and Fanon provide a way toward the deeroticization of real Black men. Their methods neither imply that the highly charged anti-Black misandrist sexual tropes cannot be transcended, nor pretend that they can. Rather, they suggest the only way out of this paradox is to go deeper into the psychosocial pathology of it all; for if there is to be any liberation at all from it, there can be no innocents. It is of critical importance, here, to remember that, in providing analysis and conceptual tools to confront the psychosexual pathology of erotic and sexual racism in the colonialist and White supremacist context, certain creed-like assumptions must be challenged. For example, the expectation that Black men are sexual aggressors and that they cannot be sexually abused or exploited *because* they are men must be abandoned.

What Fanon and Baldwin show is that in critically analyzing psychosexual pathologies in colonialist and racist contexts, it is necessary to reconceptualize patriarchy. Again, patriarchy is not a regime of an essential and universal *man* dominating an equally essential and universal *woman*. It must, rather, be understood in the colonial, imperial, and White supremacist context as a group racial dynamic that ontologically grants both females and males of the dominant group a shared investment in the sexual domination of Black men.

Baldwin and Fanon both consistently emphasize how the Black man is constructed in the ontological psychology of White men. To this effect, Baldwin (1963/1985) asserts that "the white man's unadmitted—and apparently, to him, unspeakable—private fears and longings are projected onto the Negro" (p. 129) while Fanon (1952/1977) contends that "[t]he civilized white man...project[s] his own desires onto the Negro...[and] behaves 'as if' the Negro really had them" (p. 165).

The study of Baldwin's and Fanon's criticism of White supremacy through their exposure of White men is a well-worn track throughout the scholarly literature. My track, and that of this collection, offers an alternative—one that is less travelled and is certain to unsettle. My track demonstrates that biological sex essentialism must be delinked from bodies if we are to liberate Black men from the deficient and pathological understandings of them as sexual demons—understandings culturally imposed on them and recycled through feminist theory and White masculinity studies. I propose, in this introduction, to show Fanon and Baldwin converge in their thesis of White racial patriarchy and its sexual demonization of Black men. To do so, I will focus on their *divergent* readings of Boris Vian's 1946 novel *J'irai cracher sur vos tombes* [*I Shall Spit on Your Graves*].

What I want to show is that if one accepts Baldwin's (1976) critique of Vian's novel in *The Devil Finds Work*, one sees contradiction of and divergence from Fanon's (1957/1977) clinical psychoanalytic mobilization of Vian's text in *Black Skin, White Masks*. Vian's novel is a flashpoint in *Black Skin, White Masks* because it brings together key themes in

Fanonn's account of the psychosexual pathology of White men though the psychosexual pathology of White women vis-à-vis the trope of the Black Phallic Fantastic. But where *The Devil Finds Work* reveals a James Baldwin who lapses into the Protestant puritanism of the culture of the United States, a country that he elsewhere excoriates for its anti-Black psychosexual pathology, it is in the short story "Going to Meet the Man" (Baldwin, 1965/1998) and the novel *Just Above My Head* (Baldwin, 1964/1977) where Baldwin the artist-cum-psychoanalyst meets and meshes with Fanon the psychologist-cum-cultural-critic. I suggest that between them the singular instance of Vian's text reveals a deep disjuncture between them that, when it bottoms out, in fact reveals a deep interpenetration of their ideas and opens what I believe is a radical vista for divesting ourselves of the pornotropic Black man. Baldwin and Fanon suggest that, in cultures of sexual racism, the commodification and fetishization of sexualized ideas of the Black man in fact make him a fantasy and a fillip to sexual dénouement, precisely because he is constituted as a mental prosthetic and a means of sustaining innocence in the performance of the primal—sex—and the innocence of all who rely on the pathologized Black man for their very ontological sense of innocence! In the cultural imaginary where the pornotropic Black man is the existential opposite of decent people, there is no good Black man: only a putative philanderer or rapist. And every Black man knows it. The tripartite trope of the Black Phallic Fantastic allows White men and women, and other non-Black people to imagine real Black men as both compendia of pornotropic-inspired deficits and unparalleled playthings of desires rooted in their own racial, sexual, and social domination. To be sure, this project of divestiture entails a high-risk strategy of rethinking the terms of engagement themselves: *gender*, *masculinity*, *patriarchy*, *rape*, and the contradictory construction of the agency of women championed by feminism.

Diverging to Converge: Baldwin, Fanon, Women, and "Patriarchy"

In *The Devil Finds Work*, James Baldwin (1976) excoriates Boris Vian's 1946 novel *I Shall Spit on Your Graves* as an amateur attempt by a Frenchman to transubstantiate into the bodily experience of an African American. Baldwin seemed to simultaneously appreciate and be bothered by the fact that a White Frenchman both cared and presumed to know something about the fine texture of the African American experience from what he absorbed through reading Richard Wright and Chester Himes and listening to jazz musicians at seedy Parisian dives. The novel is supposed to be an attack on White racism. In it, Vian, according to Baldwin, gets some things right and others terribly wrong. The novel's protagonist, a White-passing African American man who, in seeking to avenge his murdered darker-skinned brother, a GI, is shown by Baldwin to be not dissimilar to Richard Wright's character Bigger Thomas, the protagonist of *Native Son*,. Baldwin (1976) is scathing on two counts. First, as he says, "the novel takes place in America, and the black man looks like a white man—this double remove liberating both fantasy and hope, which is, perhaps, at bottom, what pornography is all about" (p. 38). Second, Baldwin claims Vian's protagonist was ruled by vindictive sexual passion with the White woman as target. He asserts that Vian made the mistake of trapping the Black protagonist by what the White imagination made of the Black man. To some extent, Baldwin is recapitulating his 1949 excoriation of Richard Wright's Bigger Thomas, who also commits rape and murder.[18] With a character like Bigger Thomas, Baldwin claimed that Wright, failed to present a whole person in the fullness of Black humanity, offering only a pathological exemplar of an African American man who could not transcend self-hatred and blind rage.

For Baldwin, things are as bad with Vian as they were with Wright. Vian's protagonist is "caught, and hanged—hung like a horse, his sex, according to Vian, mocking his murderers to the last" (Baldwin, 1976, p. 38). For Baldwin, Vian is ignorant of the real-life combustibility of the material with which he works. "Vian," continues Baldwin, "did not know that this particular nigger would almost certainly have been castrated: which is but another and deadlier way for White men to be mocked by the terror and fury by which they are engulfed upon the discovery the black man is a man" (p. 39). In short, for Baldwin, Vian is performing Blackbody through literary transubstantiation and the "weary, misogynistic humor" (p. 41) which runs through the novel to fulfill what White people and others think of Black men anyway—cock-centred misogynists.

While it is very likely that Baldwin, who read French fluently, at some point probably read *Black Skin, White Masks* (Fanon, 1952/1977), and while Vian's novel enables Fanon to make a number of critical discoveries, it is nonetheless interesting that in the final analysis both Baldwin and Fanon were to conclude that a key participant in the reproduction of sexual tropes about the Black man were White women. But it was in "Going to Meet the Man" and *Just Above My Head* that Baldwin would draw the same conclusions in literature that Fanon drew from his psychoanalytic treatment of White women.

Unlike Baldwin, Fanon (1952/1977) expressed no misgiving of Vian's novel in *Black Skin, White Masks*. In fact, Vian's widely read novel played an important role in Fanon's therapeutic practice. For example, a White female patient who read the book claimed to have subsequently developed a phobia of Black men. She claimed to fear being raped by any and all of them. What Fanon concluded from his patient's neurosis is that she was exhibiting a classic instance of reaction formation: her antipathy toward Black men concealed her sexual repression, which concealed her sexual desire—not, that is, her desire for Black men, but for liberation from her guilt at desiring sex at all. In this sense, the Black man was a "scapegoat" (Fanon, 1952/1977, p. 194) on whom could be projected the guilt for lascivious desire. Fanon failed to persuade his patient that in Vian's novel the "victimized white women were as sick as the Negro" (p. 159). And besides, Fanon tried to persuade his patient, Vian's text was not autobiographical and the author was a White Frenchman. Fanon could not dissuade his patient from the racial conceit that the fictional Black man in Vian's novel personified the desire of actually existing Black men to sexually ravage her. Her steadfast refusal led Fanon to conclude that, in psychoanalytic terms, her obsessive fear and protest signified a hidden desire. He notes, based on his experience as a soldier and clinician, "All the Negrophobic women I have known have had abnormal sex lives" (p. 158). The "Negrophobic" White woman, he continues, "endowed the Negro with [sexual powers] other men (husbands, transient lovers) did not have" (p. 158). The woman's obsession with the Black rapist, her imagining of him as a penis, is a sort of cultural psychosis that, for Fanon, was at the heart of psychosexual pathology. That culture, which persistently recycles myths and tropes, and which also represses women's sexuality, enables the "Negrophobic woman" (Fanon, 1952/1977, p. 156) as much as the Negrophic man to imagine the Black man as "the keeper of the impalpable gate that opens into the realm of orgies, of bacchanals, of delirious sexual sensations" (Fanon, 1952/1977, p. 177).[19]

Like the "Negrophobic" white man who finds the Black man sexually appalling because he is a putative sexual partner or, alternatively, a transubstantive object, Fanon (1952/1977) says the "Negrophobic woman is in fact nothing but a putative sexual partner" (p. 156). As a consequence, the "Negrophobic" White woman's cultural Whiteness takes on the power of patriarchy to be a sexual aggressor towards, to possess, or even kill her putative Black male partner.[20] Implicitly in Fanon's work, the biological essentialist thesis that penetration *is* domination (ergo only males can rape, ergo only females are truly victims of it) is neutralized by inversion in the context of White supremacy. Here is the high-risk deessentializing of feminist conceptions I noted earlier if we are to rethink masculinity and patriarchy. What does Fanon (1952/1977) mean when he writes "whoever says *rape* says Negro" (p. 166) and vice versa? And what, further, is he asking when citing Octave Mannoni, who asserts "there are sensitive spots in the human soul at a level where thought becomes confused and where sexual excitement is strangely linked with violence and aggression" (p. 166)?

Fanon is getting at the fact that the Black-man-as-rapist occupies a distinctive space in the psychosexual and symbolic life of White individuals at an intuitive level and in the totality of the Western cultural complex. A space and place in which sexual ascetism both gives rise to and clashes with fantasy projection. Case in point: The instance of Clarence Moses-El, falsely charged, convicted, and imprisoned for 27 years because the White woman who was raped dreamt that his face was that of her attacker (Hesse, 2015) is by no means an anomaly.[21] But in the presence of exculpatory evidence in the

Moses-El case, not least of which her attacker appeared to her in a dream, the Black rapist takes on a quality that exceeds all evidence to the contrary. Chester Himes (1984) describes just this fact in *A Case of Rape*, observing that no amount of exculpatory evidence can rescue any Black man accused of the rape of a (White) woman, since *all* Black men and boys are imagined as putative rapists. Indeed, in *Yearning: Race, Gender, and Cultural Politics* (1992b), bell hooks waxes with eloquent certainty on the warped vengeful misogyny of the boys now known as the Central Park Five:

> The Central Park crime involves aspects of the sexism, male domination, misogyny, and the use of rape as an instrument of terror...No one can truly believe that the young black males involved in the Central Park incident were not engaged in a suicidal ritual enactment of a dangerous masculinity that will ultimately threaten their lives, their well-being.
> (pp. 62–63)

To this day, she has not retracted her indictment of them, which might suggest some Black feminists, too, despite knowing full well what Ida B. Wells did—that women do not always tell the truth, that women, too, project, and that White supremacy has Black men as its primary target for destruction—see through the lens of the Black Phallic Fantastic. This is only to state the ubiquity of the belief, made good by "second wave" feminists like Susan Brownmiller (1993), Shulamith Firestone (1971), and Michele Wallace (1979), that not only the abstract Black man, but also real Black men are uniquely disposed to being rapists.[22]

Given the persistence of the myth of the Black-man-as-(putative)-rapist, Fanon's patient is neither an extreme nor an isolated instance of this particular neurosis. It is a fact that US courts have recognized White women's phobia of Black men as justification for employment compensation (Armour, 1994). This, in effect, gives legal sanction to the psychosexual pathology of White supremacy. As suggested by Ida B. Wells (2010), the myth of the Black rapist—the proclamation that White women should *rightly* fear being raped by Black men—is meant as an economic attack on Black people by attacking

Black men. Given that the many instances Wells documented of this myth in action centred on White women's absolution of responsibility for consummating their desire for Black flesh, this is a phenomenon to be explained psychoanalytically.[23] Fanon (1952/1977) repeatedly notes that, in a White world, the Devil is Black and always associated with hypersexuality. He further notes that, in a sexually repressed culture, liberation requires a scapegoat. This means, in Fanon's view, that whether it is White men imagining or simulating *being* transubstantiatively Black in the act of coitus or White women holding onto the "fantasy...that a Negro is raping me" (p. 178), a dangerous and troubling labyrinthine psychology is at play.[24]

Fanon here makes a number of claims. First, he claims that what is missed is not that men do not rape women—for they do—but that in the cultural complex of the West, the myth of the Black-man-as-rapist conceals the realities of White women's sexual aggression toward Black men and the sexual victimization of Black men. From this first claim, two others follow: that women can also rape men (and other women);[25] and that, if we accept patriarchy as a racial dynamic of a given dominant group, women can and do internalize phallocentric misogyny.[26] Fanon (1952/1977) also suggests that because of sexual dimorphism and gendered regimes of domination coded as female and male, sexual reception and penetration can give way to a psychoanalytic paradox. In this instance, the supercharged erotic racial fantasy of a racist White woman fearing/desiring being raped by a Black man unsettles feminist certainties about consent/nonconsent and that some (neurotic) women accept the gendered terms of dominance by semiconsciously turning the tables on themselves:

> If we go further into the labyrinth, we discover that when a woman lives the fantasy of rape by a Negro, it is in some way the fulfillment of a private dream, an inner wish. Accomplishing the phenomenon of turning against itself, it is the woman who rapes herself.[27] We can find clear proof of this in the fact that it is commonplace for women, during the sexual act, to cry to their partners: "Hurt me!" They are merely expressing this idea: Hurt me as I would hurt me if I were in your place. The fantasy of rape by a Negro

is a variation of this emotion: "I wish the Negro would rip me open as I would have ripped a woman open." (Fanon, 1952/1977, p. 179)[28]

There is no question that Fanon could be wrong, since both the male sexual organ, which provisionally signifies the phallus, and the ego are more than vulnerable to an alternative discourse of ingestion. But these are not the "ordinary" terms of reference in the case of Fanon's patient. Indeed, Baldwin's (1976) personal objection to rape narratives lead him to the false conclusion that "the straight-laced French...considered the novel pornographic" (p. 38). Fanon on the other hand, was both writing and treating patients at the time Vian's novel was being widely read in spite of the censors. Baldwin missed what Fanon did not: despite being censored, Vian's novel was so widely read because the trope of "Negro rape" figured prominently. That is *why* it was read so widely, and by Fanon's patient at that.

Despite Baldwin's assertion that Vian's text was pornographic, Baldwin's own works revealed the intense pornographic desire around Black men as sexually desirable and threatening all at once. Baldwin himself comes, though more implicitly than Fanon, close to a similar antiessentialist perspective on the role of racist White women in erotic and sexual racism.

Baldwin's (1965/1998) short story "Going to Meet the Man" is interpreted most obviously as a story about a White Southern police officer, Jesse. Jesse has a visceral and obsessive hate of African Americans. As a child, he experienced the eroticism that shot through the White crowd at lynching picnics. His early learning that racial hate is connected to sexual power warped his ability to experience nonpsychopathological sex—a fact that plays out in his relationship with his White wife, Grace. He tells himself that she can neither compare to nor do the "spicey" things that he "could ask a nigger girl to do" (Baldwin, 1965/1998, p. 191). Prior to the civil rights protests that crimped Jesse's style, "he would drive over yonder pick up a [black] piece or arrest her, it came to the same thing" (p. 191).[29] But with Black men, the nature of Jesse's sexual pathology differed. He got a sexual thrill from savagely beating African American men and boys, experiencing an erection afterward. Such violent erotic pathologies in *fiction* are in fact drawn from *reality*. Judith Butler (1993a), for instance, reminds us that the four Los Angeles police officers—Powell, Koon, Wind, and Briseno—who savagely bludgeoned Rodney King did so while making sexual utterances that signified the event was in fact a rape. Fanon (1952/1977) reminds us that racism produces sexual jealousy and, by consequence, there is "much of sexuality...in all cruelties, tortures, beatings" (p. 159). In fact, for Jesse, sex with his wife Grace demands transubstantiation; the highest charge of sexual experience manifests, for him, only when he "becomes" a Black man. He says to her, "Come on, sugar, I'm going to do you like a nigger, just like a nigger, come on, sugar, and love me just like you'd love a nigger" (Baldwin, 1965/1998, p. 207).[30] Baldwin paints a picture of Jesse as a sadistic man, doubly demoralized because his racism grants him violent licence.

Jesse's psychosexual pathology is obvious. But is Grace *only* a passive object in his real-life pornography film? Commentators like David McCracken (2018), in their rush to imagine Jesse as an ogre and Grace as her namesake, have missed the forest for the trees: in a colonialist and racist context, women from the dominant group are not victims *just* because they are women—for sometimes they are. White womanhood, which confers racial patriarchal authority to White women, ensures that they are complicit with the reproduction of White patriarchal supremacy. As such, White women through White womanhood are active agents in the sexual psychopathology of White supremacy. I suggest that what Baldwin seeks to expose is *not* Grace's victimization by her husband's racist psychosexual pathology, but rather her complicity (and the complicity of other White women in the story), through White womanhood, in that very same pathology. What carries the story, then, are the White women who relished lynching picnics as an opportunity to primp, preen, and encourage their men in the ecstatic, orgiastic lynchings and castrations of Black men.

Baldwin offers us nothing of Fanon's (1952/1977) deep interpretive psychoanalytic disquisitions that riff on Helen Deutsch's and Marie Bonaparte's accounts of the psychology of (White) women and (White) female sexuality (p. 178). Nor does he offer us anything like the Frenchwoman in Fanon's (1959/1965) "Algeria Unveiled" in *A Dying Colonialism*, who shrieked with exhortation when French soldiers captured Algerian liberation fighters, "They've been caught! They're going to get their what-you-call'ems cut off!" (p. 56). Here, it is admitted that the phallus is as important to women colonizers as it is to men. Algerian men are imagined as and reduced to their penises, signified in the French imaginary as the actional symbol of resistance to colonization as rape, an act in which colonialism is metaphorized by Fanon as unconsensual sexual penetration. Obviously, from Fanon's viewpoint, women colonizers, as much as institutionalized, state-sanctioned feminism, were key parts of the whole. Baldwin is subtler than Fanon, but his point is just as strong.

Like Fanon, however, Baldwin suggests that in colonialist and racist contexts, it cannot be taken for granted that White women are innocents—passive objects at the mercy of White men's sexual ends. Indeed, as affirmation of the point that White women and Black men have nothing at all in common in the context of "patriarchy" as racial group domination, Baldwin's (and Fanon's) point is unambiguously stated by Zeus Leonardo and Erica Boas (2013):

> Just as every army is composed of different tactical positions in order to secure or conquer a territory, so does whiteness consist of its own foot soldiers, officers, and generals who perform different functions but whose allegiance to whiteness is not the question. With respect to White women, although they may not call the shots, they often pull the trigger... Understanding their role in the upkeep of whiteness is critical if educators wish to explain the specific battleground called schooling. Often, White women are drafted to carry out the reproductive work of whiteness as education becomes a para-caring profession, not unlike nursing. For centuries, as the "caring gender," White women have occupied a space different from White men within the enactment of racism. From enslavement to colonialism, White women have done the work of White supremacy specific to their own place in the hierarchy, producing their own contradictions in the process. (p. 315)

But, in hegemonic terms, inasmuch as White women occupy different "institutional" gender–sex locations (e.g., in "caring professions" such as nursing, teaching, and social work) and social status (e.g., income) than White men, their commitment to Whiteness as group patriarchy is *not* coerced. Eschewing White supremacy as a function of extremist males (and females), Dawn McIntosh (2018) validates the conclusions of social dominance psychologists that gender–sex and patriarchy in White women's racial performance is saturated and mutually intelligible in reifying White supremacy:

> White supremacy is not often associated with White women and that, in and of itself, is a strategic working of whiteness for and through White women. In a post-racial, colorblind era, White women have regained their privilege to be clandestinely racist.[31] In turn, White women play an imperative role in recentering whiteness. If White women are culturally organized as nurturing, innocent, and pure, then they are never racist. White supremacy is secured through White feminine enactments of whiteness while simultaneously running covertly under the radar as never marked in these [six] hostile ways. (p. 109)[32]

Implicating the social protective function granted to women conceals the dangerous complicity of White women and White men in the pursuit of White group dominance. McIntosh adds, as a practical matter, that

> [t]he reason White women's bodies continue to be carefully cloaked from connections with White supremacy is because our White feminine bodies serve, as Chow (1990) frames, [as] "sutures" to White men and whiteness (p. 89). White women's bodies conjoin White masculinity to patriarchy and ensure that White power be maintained through our relationship to it. Ware (1992) claims White women help create a racially divided and patriarchal world (p. 68–69). [White women's] bodies do this both in obligated service to whiteness and patriarchy and in doing so reap the empowering benefits for our services. Each of these six performative

> frameworks reveal the codependency White femininity has to White patriarchy. The embodiment of the White Female Employee performing victimization relies on the performance of a White masculine savior. The White Supermom's performance of domesticity perpetuates White patriarchal norms. (p. 110)

The idea that women in general, and White women in particular, are complicit with patriarchy rather than oppressed by it is, of course, contrary to feminist doctrine. Indeed, Black feminists such as bell hooks (1984), however much she may assert fundamental distinctions between Black and White women, effectively unify with White feminist constructions of patriarchy as the domination of women.[33]

Baldwin and Fanon expose White women as complicit in the reproduction of White supremacy.[34] They also, as is shown by Katerina Deliovsky (Chapter 3 in this volume), play a part in mobilizing, desiring, and sustaining the Black Phallic Fantastic as a property in the "collective unconscious" as much as White men. They can and do participate in sexual "race play" that reduces Black men to a mental and physical prosthetic and, by this means, achieves the poetics of sexual racism. In the novel *Just Above My Head,* James Baldwin (1964/1977) has the protagonist, Hall Montana, speak *the* unutterable, inevitable, and irrefutable truth: that in his experience of sleeping with both White men and their girlfriends (at the same time), when it came to his penis, "[i]t was more a matter of its color than its size...[I]ts color *was* its size" (p. 102). We are confronted here with the irrational view that Black men are imagined not only to have big penises, but to be their penises (Fanon, 1952/1977).

Grace, therefore, like the many other women in "Going to Meet the Man" and in *Just Above My Head,* is a person whose sexual agency, whose desire for sexual fulfillment, is a "property right of whiteness" (see C. Harris, 1993) that enables White men and women to experience erotic pleasure through the *power* of anti-Black misandry. The theme of White women's complicity in the reproduction of sexual racism is at the very core of the story. As depicted by Baldwin, the quiet horror in "Going to Meet the Man" is that

White mothers are raising children to learn the sexual ritual of violence—a dynamic that Katerina Deliovsky (Chapter 3 in this volume) refers to as "racialized gender power."

Baldwin retheorizes "gender" in a way that acknowledges the power of White women in the racial–sexual oppression of Black men. He explicitly connects this power to White women's oppression of Black mothers and women. In doing so, Baldwin reveals the sorrow that hangs over Black motherhood—a sorrow that White mothers can never experience because they are one of its sources. To this end, Baldwin (1972) notes poetically that sexual racism from slavery onward not only imposed terror and tyranny on the "fearfully mistreated [Black woman]" (p. 69) and "despised Black mother," but also denied that her "children are also the issue of the Holy Ghost" (p. 197). Terkel (1961/1989) punctuates the point further, deepening the mutual struggle of Black men, women, and children in the resistance of capitalist White group racial patriarchy:

> It is a terrible thing: the Negro women for generations raised white children, who sometimes lynched their children, and they have tried to raise their own child, like a man; and yet in the full knowledge that if he really walks around like a man he is going to be cut down...A terrible price to ask anybody to pay. In this country, Negro women have been paying it for 300 years; 100 of those when they were legally and technically free. (pp. 9–10)

Baldwin presents us with an open terrain to reconsider the sorts of biocultural essentialism that feminist scholars have attempted—but failed—to eschew (see, for example, Hartmann, 1979; Mouffe, 1993). The incapacity to locate "woman" outside essentialist categories of analysis such as "gender" (J. Butler, 1993b) is built into the very flawed proposition that the objective of "patriarchy" is the oppression of women.[35] Doubt is cast on this idea, however unintended, by Gerda Lerner's (1986) admission that "[t]he system of patriarchy can function *only* [emphasis added] with the cooperation of women" (p. 217). With this, the entire complex of the feminist project resting on the props of women's "oppression"[36] and male "domination" falls away, not least because men as much as women, following the classic Marxist line of reasoning, are bound by definite constraints to change, at will, the social conditions they have inherited (Grande, 2003; Rowbotham, 1981).[37]

Baldwin and Fanon lead us to understand that in the colonialist and racist context, "patriarchy" is a White group racial phenomenon of domination that brings death and destruction. That racially subordinated Black men and boys are personified as enemies is evident in Baldwin's statement: "I know what a no-knock, stop-and-frisk law means. It means search and destroy" (cited in Frost, 1970/1989, p. 95). J. Edgar Hoover's COINTELPRO and other state strategies that saw the assassination and incarceration of African American male leaders is testimony, at the highest level, to what occurs in more quotidian ways (Curry, 2017; Flowe, 2020; Mutua, 2013; Thomas, 2007).[38] In service to their group (and again with the collusion of their women), Baldwin (1972) asserts "men have an enormous need to debase other men—and only because they are *men*—is a truth which history forbids us to labor" (p. 63). It might be said that in a world where there are no innocents save children, the severely disabled, and the elderly, "men know something of other men" as do women know something of the men from the opposing group: that in the capitalist, colonialist, and racist context, the powerful and the powerless know they occupy two different and antagonist worlds, and that they are locked in a death struggle. Under such conditions, the proposition that Black men are privileged rather than oppressed by "gender" is self-refuting. As Katerina Deliovsky (Chapter 3 in this volume) demonstrates, thinking otherwise leads to absurd conclusions in which, for example, feminist researchers and White sex tourist women alike assume that indigent young Black men plying the beaches of the Caribbean have the status of lords of the polis.

Baldwin (1972) describes the terrible paradox that Black men find themselves in: they are at once hypervisible as sexual demons and, like Ralph Ellison's invisible man, nonhuman beings. Thus,he observes,

> Every Black man walking[39]...pays a tremendous price for walking: for men are not women, and a man's balance depends on the weight he carries between his legs. All men, however they may handle, or be handled by it, know something about each other, which is simply that a man without balls is not a man; that the world genesis describes the male, involves the phallus, and refers to the seed which gives life. When one man can no longer honor this in another man—and this remains true even if that man is his lover—he has abdicated from a man's estate, and, hard upon the heels of that abdication chaos arrives. (p. 64)

That chaos is the labyrinthine zone of the "Black superhumanizing bias" (Waytz et al., 2014) where sexual racism enables the conditions for the sexual exploitation of Black boys and men.

Precisely because they are imagined as sexual demons, Black men and boys[40] are not seen as human. In demonstrating that "patriarchy" is a group dynamic of racial domination, Baldwin and Fanon were ahead of their time, anticipating theories and perspectives that today empirically verify the endangerment that Black men and boys routinely face. Now, social dominance theorists are not only revealing that the racially subordinated males are disproportionately targeted for intensive discrimination, but that women from the dominant group are directly implicated (Navarette et al., 2010; Pearson et al., 2007; Sidanius & Pratto, 1999). Male "expendability/disposability" (theorists are now affirming Baldwin's and Fanon's thesis that "patriarchy" is preeminently about men attacking other men) show that this manifests in male-on-male genocide, castrations, and rape. Augusta Del Zotto and Adam Jones (2002) further show that global policy makers and feminist organizations suppress the extent and impact of rape on boys and men (see also Goldstein, 2004; A. Jones, 2002, 2004; Trexler, 1995). Indeed, they demonstrate that private and state funders dictate that women's groups addressing rape do not provide services to males, thus incentivizing women's groups to treat rape as a province of women and girls. As a result, the age-old practice and threat of male-on-male "penetrative penality" (Trexler, 1995, p. 7) is erased, silenced, and normalized.[41]

Journalists and legal scholars are also demonstrating that, despite the tight discursive connection between human trafficking and women and girls, the scale and scope of boys and men being trafficked is grossly underestimated (Dennis, 2008, "Hundreds of boys," 2019; S. Jones, 2010). Social psychologists of harm and obedience (FeldmanHall et al., 2016; Doliński et al., 2017) and legal theorists and philosophers of anti-Black-misandry (Curry, 2017; D. Hutchinson, 2001; Mutua, 2013) all emphasize that "patriarchy" is a group racial dynamic that both emphasizes the racialized competition between men and boys and is protective of women from the dominant group.[42] What these scholars effectively affirm is Baldwin's (1963/1985) thesis that "[w]hen a white man faces a black man, especially a black man that is helpless, terrible things are revealed" (p. 75). The Other that (re)creates the Black man as a sexual monstrosity and psychosexual prop is revealed as stunted and undeveloped. And for the Black man, it reveals that the erotic and sexual racism saturating their social definition is not a property they need to own.

Baldwin's (1964/1977) recognition that "its colour was is its size" (p. 102)—a recognition that can also be attributed to Fanon—demands direct confrontation with exactly how much the Black Phallic Fantastic— the tripartite trope of the Black man as hypersexual, priapic, and prone to commit rape—saturates the whole culture's view of him. When it is recognized that erotic and sexual racism lubricate the practices of capitalism and supremacy, then it becomes possible to come to terms with the fact that the *only* way out of the paradox that Black men are appealing because they are appalling is to go deeper into it.

What to Expect From This Book?

This introduction has aimed to clear the ground for a way to unthink the ways that representations of Black men are constituted, both in academia and popular culture. This book, as a whole, is designed to bring within one cover as much of a transnational viewpoint on the erotic construction of Black men as possible. Because Baldwin and Fanon speak to this internationalization and offer cultural theory and psychoanalytic treatment, they are vital touchstones. But I must make three points so that readers are not mislead in expecting what they will not find, and thus condemn this book on that score.

First, this collection is not a hagiography of two supposedly infallible and worldly savants of anti-Black, antiracist, and anticolonial psychosexual philosophy. Both Baldwin and Fanon abhorred saint-making. (This is true of Baldwin in particular, who to his detriment symbolically slew one too many giants—Richard Wright, for example—without just cause). Neither would have appreciated being beatified; both would have preferred that their lives and works be colours that added to the palette of the radical humanism they believed in and struggled for. In this vein, we are not reducing them to their interests in the ways that the sexual impulses shape identity, experience, and social organization in relation to the sex act. Indeed, focused on compassion and love, both saw sexual pleasure as a complicated space in which the universe of one's *being* either opened to freedom and human mutuality or closed in on itself to stunt a human personality obedient to authority and which projected internal fears outward onto scapegoats.

Second, this book is not a complete review of the huge and accelerating body of scholarship on both Baldwin and Fanon. If one includes here either offhand mentions or references to them in biographies of figures such as Sartre and de Beauvoir, or in social histories of the 1950s to 1970s, the scholarly landscape grows even larger. The task of this volume is not to survey that landscape's peaks, valleys, and substrate to articulate what else might be said of both or to correct errors of analysis about them. Indeed, whole libraries can be filled with dedicated journals and special issues, biographies, and the voluminous body of books and journal articles that bring both men into sharper focus by discussing their ideas, their relation to their time, and their contrast with other thinkers. When confronted with Baldwin's and Fanon's bodies of work and the enormous volumes of exegetical and secondary literature built up about and around them—almost like a fortress that dissuades all but the already-expert, the daring, the innocent, or the foolish—a curious alchemy of humility and risk-taking is required of us in this book. Confronted with the enormity of the literature on Baldwin and Fanon, one might turn away to seek other pastures not already well-mowed. I can only hope some of what is said in this book will be found refreshing.

Third, inasmuch as engagement with secondary literature on these two thinkers would take us too far afield from the practical application of their ideas, this book does not pretend that this substantive body of literature does not exist. Though some experts might take umbrage that they are not cited here and there throughout the text, the literature is simply too vast for perfunctory mentions. To be sure, some of this literature (and some issues of debate ranging across it) are visible throughout this book. More importantly, however, the ongoing and vital domains of specifying in detail the meaning of what Baldwin or Fanon said in this sentence or that or this or that work is left to the more expert.

If this book is neither hagiography nor an explicit engagement with the secondary literature on Baldwin and Fanon, what then is it? It is a collection of interdisciplinary thought on erotic racism and Black masculinities with four related aims: First, it aims to elucidate across time, place, and space a humane account of the impact of the Black Phallic Fantastic on Black men's lives; their communities; and the ways they accommodate, deploy, and resist. Second, it aims to contribute to ongoing critical and empathetic empirical and theoretical research that values the humanity of Black men. Third, through an account of the ways Black men are commodified, desired, loathed, objectified, and mortified, this book analyzes the psychosexual imperatives and ontology of anti-Black cultures, nations, and peoples. Finally, gender and masculinities studies have got away for far too long with drawing on the insights of Baldwin and Fanon without giving them due recognition. It is my hope this book generates not only debate, discussion and research, but enables Black men, in all their diversity, to be valued as human beings.

Organization of This Book

Erotic Racism, Tropes, and Interracial Sex: Art, Nations, and Transnationalism

Writing from Canada, I have written Chapter 1, "Can the Black Man Be Nude in a Culture That Imagines Him as Naked? A Baldwinian and Fanonian Psychosexual Reading of Black Masculinity in 'Western' Art and Cinema." I outline a tranhistorical, psychosexual analysis of the Black man as hypersexual, priapic, and prone to commit rape from the visual arts and science in Greece and Rome to contemporary art and cinema.

John G. Russell (Japan) gives us Chapter 2: "Anaconda East: Fetishes, Phallacies, *Chimbo* Chauvinism, and the Displaced Discourse of Black Male Sexuality in Japan ." Russell explores the fetishistic tropes of the Black man's body and the construction of Black men as hypersexual, bestial Others in the context of contemporary Japanese popular culture. It specifically examines how these tropes connect to and replicate transnational, but primarily American-derived, constructions of fetishized Blackness. It goes on to explore domestic sites of and for the articulation of Japanese masculinity and patriarchy though a discussion of the Japanese discourse on "yellow cabs."

In Chapter 3, "White Femininity, Black Masculinity, Sex/Romance Tourism, and the Politics of Feminist Theory: Theorizing Desire and Erotic Racism," Katerina Deliovsky (Canada) uses a Fanonist epistemology alongside antiracist and critical race feminist approaches to examine the research on White women's sex/romance tourism with local Black men in the Caribbean. She explores how White womanhood, oftentimes aided and abetted by researchers and scholars, is implicated in and empowered by "white imperial tourism" (Alexander, 1997) to mobilize desire, power, and colonialist tropes of the Black male Other in transnational contexts.

What Does a Black Man Want? Situating the Lives of Black Men

In Chapter 4, "Beyond the Exotic and the Grotesque: Toward a Theology of Black Men and Radical Self-Love in the United Kingdom," Delroy Hall (United Kingdom)—a Christian pastoral theologian, minister, and registered counselling psychotherapist—undertakes a Black pastoral theology for Black men's self-love in an anti-Black world that imagines them as both exotic and grotesque. Hall's interest is to contribute a conversation about the possibility of authentic love within an anti-Black social context. For Hall, this possibility is rooted in self-care.

Chapter 5, written by Leroy F. Moore Jr. (United States) and myself, is titled "A Krip-Hop Theory of Disabled Black Men: Challenging the Disabling of Black America, Resisting Killing and Erasure Through the Arts and Self-Empowerment." This chapter collaboration explores sex, sexuality, and masculinity for disabled Black men, building on Moore's concept of Krip-Hop and its application for a cultural and political theory of Black masculinities and disabilities. We assert that, from slavery to the present, Black disability is a productive space and source for a radical Black resistance to the necropolitics of capitalism, slavery, and White supremacy, and argue that disability is foundational to the artistic and political culture of Black America. We bridge the divide that exists between theorists asserting the ontology of disability and the ways in which anti-Black racism produces disabilities through physical, mental, economic, and political disablement.

National Culture, Transqueering Black Masculinities, Challenging Hegemonic Masculinity

In Chapter 6, "Carrying Corporeal Narratives: Weighing the Burden of Antiqueer Representations in Jamaica," Kemar McIntosh (Jamaica; United States) employs intersectional theory to explore the psychosocial effects of antiqueer visual representations of what he calls lower-class-black-queer males in the drawings of Clovis Brown, a long-time cartoonist at the *Jamaica Observer*. McIntosh shows that coming to terms with queerness is vital to the radical humanism of Baldwin and Fanon.

Watufani M. Poe, a US researcher who lives and studies in Brazil, meditates on James Baldwin's resistance to "terror of the flesh" in Chapter 7, "A Quare Eye to Slavery: Black Homoerotic Encounters in Brazil and Cuba." Poe articulates the connections between heteronormativity, masculinity, race, and sexuality. Taking a case study approach, his attention centres on Black queer individuals in Brazil and Cuba during slavery.

Focusing on archival ethnographies and nineteenth- and twentieth-century Brazilian fiction, he deconstructs the fear-mongering stereotypes of the Black homosexual and the conceptual emergence hegemonic masculinity, nationalism, and anxieties over male-to-male interracial love.

In Chapter 8, Dennis O. Howard (Jamaica) writes about masculinities and heterosexual gender relations in "'7 Eleven': Dialectics of Jamaican Popular Music Culture and Hegemonic Masculinity." He examines how Jamaican popular music culture challenges and resists taboos around hypermasculinity and female sexuality. He explores how the controversial lyrics of the popular Jamaican musical artist Dexta Daps is part of a historical trajectory of male artists that push the margins of middle-class propriety, challenge hegemonic masculinity, and engage with the sexual autonomy of Jamaican women.

The *Other* Other and the Black Man

In Chapter 9, "*Sila ay Malaki*: Anti-African Racism, the 'Filipino Gaze,' and the Paradox of Black Masculinity in Collegiate Basketball in the Philippines," Satwinder Singh Rehal (Philippines; Australia) draws upon Frantz Fanon's *Black Skin, White Masks* to theorize the double entendre of *sila ay malaki* [they are big]. The chapter examines the growing scapegoating and moral panic about African male athletes. It draws attention to the homoerotic (re)production of sexual tropes about on African varsity basketball players as a foil against which nativist Filipino hegemonic masculinity produces a narrative of heroic nationalistic resistance against Spanish and US colonization.

Finally, in Chapter 10, "Siddis, African Students, Anti-Blackness, and Psychosexual Politics in the Indian Ocean World and Its Diaspora: A Fanonist Reading of Anti-Black Sexual Racism in the Indian Imaginary," Elishma Noel Khokhar (Canada), Mohan Siddi (India), and myself undertake a panoramic social history of the African Siddi presence in India and how Gandhian–Nerhuvian and post-Bandung imaginings of African sexuality influence continued sexual anxieties about Africans in India.

Author's Note

I am grateful to Erica Lawson for commenting on an earlier iteration of this chapter and to Katerina Deliovsky for providing feedback and editorial assistance on this version.

Notes

1. Cultural and group appellations are sociopolitical constructions, precisely because they reflect the fact that human existence, identities, and materiality are, through symbols and representation, constantly in conflict, motion, and negotiation. Especially in abstract, alienating, bureaucratic, and nation-state social formations, group appellations are contested, signifying conflict over material and social goods. To this end, I use *black* in lower case and *Black* in upper case throughout this chapter to connote definite meanings, which are at once contingent and historically specific. I use the lowercase forms of this duality to signify abstractions with anthropomorphic implications. Within double-heliacal, Manichean, integrative yin and yang and simple dualisms, *black/blackness* versus *white/whiteness* are near universal expressions. As forms of abstract representation, they are "condensation symbols" that connote negative/positive and subordinate/supraordinate aesthetic, affective, moral, and normative meanings (see Douglas, 1970; Maybury-Lewis, 1992). In all binaries the opposing principles follow asymmetrical articulations of social power. Thus, following, Derrida, Stuart Hall (1997) asserts: "One pole of the binary...is usually the dominant one, the one which includes the other within its field of operations" (p. 235). In this context, "blackness," existing in a dialectic with "whiteness," is anthropomorphized to take on axiological meanings and lexical referents of a negative character, even when framed positively (Ani, 1994; C.L. Brown, 1967; Deliovsky & Kitossa, 2013; Fanon, 1952/2008; Gergen, 1967; Gossett, 1997; Isaacs, 1967; A. James, 1981; Jordan, 1968/1977; Kovel, 1971; Wagatsumo, 1967; Williams & Carter, 1967). I do not, therefore, use the lowercase *b* as an inclusive descriptor for all non-White groups, as is still common in the United Kingdom and its commonwealth (see J. James, 1996, pp. 234–35). Capitalized as a proper noun, I intend the word *Black* to have the connotation given it by the global Black Power Movement in the United States, Canada, the Caribbean, and the United Kingdom. This Pan-African worldview resisted the appellation "Negro" and inverted the anthropomorphic attributes of blackness in the White imaginary. It regarded African-descended people of the diaspora as having definite shared experiences and characteristics, irrespective of national and colonial differences among them. I use the word *White* with a capital *W* in a similar way.
2. Black men are 4% of the city of Toronto's population, but represent 25% of all sexual assault complaints against the Metro Toronto police force (Ontario Human Rights Commission, 2020). The majority of the over 22,000 strip searches conducted annually by police in Ontario occur in the Greater Toronto Area, and of these 75% to 80% are conducted on males (Office of the Independent Review of Police Directorate, 2019). While these data are not disaggregated by age or race, there is no reason to suspect that Black men in Toronto are not disproportionately impacted (see R. v. Darteh, 2013; Special Investigations Unit, 2013). In the United States,

stop-and-frisk, which disproportionately affects African American and Latinx males, is criticized as state-sanctioned sexual assault (Ross, 2018).

3. Focused as the contributors in this collection are on the politics of construction and meanings of tropic significations and symbols in the sexual representation of Black masculinities, this collection falls within the domain of cultural materialism (Hall et al., 1978; M. Harris, 1980).
4. Richard Trexler (1995) provides copious contemporary and historical evidence to this effect. Without eschewing women's experience with gendered domination, all of course with appreciation of differential stratification based on age, ability, class, race, sexuality, and so on, Trexler (1995) observes that sexual practices such as castration, dismemberment, homicide, rape, and anal rupture "were used in the first place to represent the power of one group of men over another" (p. 5). This argument, elaborated through an engagement with Baldwin and Fanon, takes a dialectical view of patriarchy. This means that in order to dominate women, men must first be dominated by other men, thereby rendering them "feminine" through the act of domination, even when dominated males are imagined as hypermasculine. This may seem like a simplistic argument, but in order for the first man to have dominated a woman, he would have had to go through her father and all male relations. But what of women? Trexler assumes too much of what is presumed to be the case in the sense that women are written out of the picture as victims, always, of the "patriarchy." But surely women were and remain agentic. Could, therefore, "patriarchy," if it is a group dynamic, not have begun with females conspiring, cajoling, goading, manipulating, and scheming with males of their group to overpower and dominate "outgroup" females and males? This possibility is suggested, even if unintentionally, by feminists themselves (Lerner, 1986), but also by social dominance inquiry that exposes the implicit methods that women use in pursuit of personal and group power (Sidanius & Pratto, 1999; Sidanius & Veniegas, 2000); by behavioural studies and evolutionary and critical psychology examinations of gendered aggression and authority in interpersonal relationships and group dynamics (Bagner et al., 2007; Crick & Grotpeter, 1995; Denson et al., 2018; Doliński et al., 2017; Dube & Harish, 2019; Stroebe et al., 2017); critical cultural histories of women, state and interpersonal power (Chinweizu, 1990; Goldstein, 2004; Vilar, 1972); and anthropologists (Mauss, 1925/1990). What must be rejected here is the assumption of the timeless and universal innocence of women as much as their timeless and universal oppression. Indeed, James Baldwin (1961, 1963/1985) repeatedly warns against the dangerous epistemic and political effects when groups and individuals assert self-innocence and the blame-worthiness of others. Equally rejected is the concept of "gender," taken as an asymmetrical social relation of power corresponding to sex, but assumed to reference biological woman as the only gendered subject. With gender tangentially linked to biology, social hierarchy, and imbalances of power between men and groups, the universal category of woman and its relation to "gender" oppression is inherently unstable over time, place, and space and within as well as between societies. Moreover, because women from the dominant group *are* from the dominant group, with all perquisites pertaining to their stratified station as members of a dominant racial caste, they are only provisionally opposed to in-group expressions of masculinity to the extent they are excluded from

the rewards and overt exercise of racial domination (see Daniels, 1997; Hodes, 1997; Newman, 1999; Ware, 1992). Greg Thomas (2007) draws on Toni Cade Bambara to deconstruct the colonial and imperial madness of the epistemic construction of "gender" (pp. 25–55; see also Combahee River Collective, 1983/2000; Grande, 2003; Lugones, 2007, 2010). Pursuant to Thomas's rejection of the Western imperialist constructions of gender and patriarchy, it is vital to confront the ethnocentric erasure of the possibility, reality, and practicality that there are cultures in which biology is delinked from gender–sex roles and performance as conceived in the West. "Patriarchy," though an inappropriate nomenclature, is constitutive of social androgyny in which there are female sons, female fathers, male daughters, and male mothers (see Amadiume, 1987; Clarke, 1976).

5. While throughout *Black Skin, White Masks* Fanon (1952/1977) establishes a clear relationship between sex, sexuality, sadomasochistic degradation, humiliation, and violence, both Richard Trexler (1995) and David Brion Davis (2006, 2014) provide supporting historical evidence on the psychosexual lexicology of militarized metaphors, animalization, and rituals of slaughter relevant to the sex act, penetrative penality, sexual domination, and the conquest of groups. The deep psychology of purity and taboo signified by this connection that "slaughterhouse vocabulary and practice is part of a broad human tendency first to emasculate or desexualize, consequently to dehumanize, and thus finally to treat our enemies as dirt" (Trexler, 1995, p. 17; see Kitossa, Chapter 1 in this volume for an application of this concept to depth psychology of the Western representations of the Black man as *naked* as opposed to *nude*; see also n. 27).

6. To be sure, feminists such as Dorothy E. Roberts (1993) have connected racism and patriarchy: "Racism is patriarchal. Patriarchy is racist" (p. 3). Problematically, the assumption that women are the objects of patriarchy is not destabilized. Thus, the universal woman that Roberts seeks to critique is in the final analysis sustained because she refuses to question the gender = woman essentialism.

7. The term *misandrynoir*, however accurate and appropriate, is not used for two reasons. First, I want to avoid any competition with what Black feminist academic Moya Bailey (2010) has called *misogynoir*. Second, following Toni Cade Bambara (1970) and Greg Thomas (2007), I question the implied exceptionality that (a) women are the only gendered subjects and (b) that Black women, because of "intersectionality," are granted distinct, separate, and privileged subjectivity from Black men, children, and communities (see Kitossa, 2020). Relevant to "citational politics," both concepts are fiercely defended as the property and intellectual labour of Black women. Interestingly, Kathy Davis (2008) finds that for feminist theory the weakness of "intersectionality"—its ambiguity and open-endedness—is its strength. Others are less indifferent to that which feminism takes for granted as the central and essentialist node around which female subjectivity is supposed to hinge: the gender–woman dialectic to the exclusion of males as also gendered subjects, especially Black men (Cooper, 2006; Curry, 2017; D. Hutchinson, 2001; Mutua, 2013; Thomas, 2007). Needless to say, none of this criticism rejects misogyny or misogynoir as realities, be they practices of females or males in the maintenance of the racial order.

8. See note 7, above, for a discussion of intersectionality.

9. Marxist psychoanalysis does exist with the likes of Walter Abell (1957/1966), whose concept of depth psychology I mobilize in Chapter 1 of this volume. Significantly, despite alienation and consciousness being key psychological concepts in Marxist theory, much of Marxist theory continues to treat race and as an "epiphenomenon" of class. Still to this day, aside from Baldwin and Fanon, the materialist psychoanalysis of sexual racism elaborated by Joel Kovel (1971), Paul Hoch (1979), and Noel Manganyi (1977) remain rare.

10. I cite here Richard Philcox's translation rather than Charles Lam Markmann.

11. Hyam is here using the word *black* in the adjectival form historically understood in Britain as an inclusive term now apprehended by "people of colour" or "world majority."

12. If the reader of Hyam's (1991) book keeps in mind his acerbic and brief commentary on the analytical disutility of hegemonic feminism toward understanding the psychological and practical dimensions in the doing of sex in the lives of imperial administrators and soldiers alike (see pp. 16–19), his use of the intransitive verb may suggest irony and playfulness.

13. With Emile Durkheim (1995) and Sigmund Freud (1913/1989) as exemplars of Western cognitive imperialism, totem and taboo are imagined as signs of "primitive" and "backward" cultures, steeped in superstition, stuck at elemental stages of consciousness—meaning, since they have not transcended being *of* nature to being *in* nature, non-Western cultures/societies are not "civilized." Indeed, by these lights, even if they have managed the accomplishment of "civilization," they are in a state of arrested development. Yet, the fetishes of nation, science, state, and the totemic qualities associated with them in the forms of doctrine, ritual, and political despotism are taken as problems of "modernity" rather than of the universalization of Europe's cultural particularism.

14. "Mortification of the flesh," both as concept and practice derived from Roman Catholicism, remains a powerful psychological force in its offshoots—notably Protestantism—and plays a major role in colonialism and conquest. The Puritans, for example, who imagined themselves as the "New Israelites taming the wilds of New Canaan," spurred their murderous campaign of dispossessing the indigenous peoples of what became the United States of America through what Philip Greven (1977) calls "the furtive gratifications of an ascetic sadism" (cited in Stannard, 1992, p. 231). This ideology, as noted by Greven (1977), was deeply inculcated into the cultural norms of child-rearing. As this pertains to continental and hemispheric supremacy, global imperialism, and White supremacy in the United States, sexual anxieties became manifest, as James Baldwin (cited in Terkel, 1961/1989) remarks:

> And the sexual paranoia. It is very important what it means to be born in a Protestant Puritan country, with all the taboos placed on the flesh, and have at the same time in this country to have such a vivid example of a decent pagan imagination and the sexual liberty with which white people invest Negroes—and then penalize them for. (p. 8; see also Baldwin, 1963/1985, 1968; Goldstein, 1984/2014).

This was a psychosexual pathology of Whiteness in the United States of America; it was also evident in European nationalism and its global imperialism at their inception (Farmanfarmaian, 1992; Gordon, 1998; Hall, 1996, p. 210; Hoch, 1979, pp. 43–64; Hyam, 1991; Mason, 1971, pp. 87–103; Segal, 1994, pp. 168–81; Spongberg, 1997; Stannard, 1992, pp. 149–246).

15. Conceptually, theoretically, and even lexically, Spillers's (1987) essay owes a tremendous debt to both Baldwin and Fanon, particularly the distinction she makes between "body" (which Fanon [1952/1977] makes in *Black Skin, White Masks*) and "flesh" (which courses through virtually all of Baldwin's work; see also Terkel, 1961/1989, pp. 8–11). Significantly, unlike bell hooks (1992a) who reluctantly cites Fanon, all the while pilfering his ideas, Spillers acknowledges neither Baldwin or Fanon. Despite erasing Baldwin and Fanon, Spillers offers an outstanding theoretical exposition of the limits of the discourse of gender and provides an excellent example of the we-ness of African descended men and women under White supremacy.

16. As noted by Baldwin (1955/1984, 1972) and Fanon (1952/1977) the Black man is imagined as a penis, and in the race-group patriarchal supremacist context, the penis can hardly be imagined without also taking on the embodiment of the Black man. There is a very close association in the public imagination between Black men and pornography in the United States, where 70% of pornography consumers are White men, the remaining 30% being classified as "Other" (Poulson-Bryant, 2005). According to Bill Marigold, pioneer of "interracial porn"—a category that refers, more specifically, to Black men with White women—"That more blacks are viewing this material is purely accidental. When I put blacks in my videos, I project my fantasies, not theirs" (cited in Poulson-Bryant, 2005, p. 140). Pornhub Insights found that in 15 US states, *Big Black Dick* is the most searched term on Gay PornHub (Matters, 2016). In Japan, as John Russell (Chapter 2 in this volume) shows, words used to refer to Black people such as *kokojin* return significant numbers of pornographic "hits." Russell also documents the massive Japanese penis enhancement industry, which uses Black men as the archetype.

17. See Kitossa (Chapter 1 in this volume) for discussions on the tripartite trope of the Black Phallic Fantastic, non-Black ontology, and pornotropic representations of the Black man.

18. Baldwin's essay "Everybody's Protest Novel" was printed in *Zero* magazine in 1949, and subsequently reprinted in 1955 in *Notes of a Native Son*, the title of which is a sideways compliment to Wright.

19. Chester Himes is among many African American novelists to attempt to exorcise the sexual demons of his country's culture. Himes's (1945/2002) classic *If He Hollers Let Him Go*, like Wright's *Native Son* and Vian's *I Shall Spit on Your Graves*, revolves around a Black man raping and murdering a White woman. This novel deeply impacted Fanon's thesis of the psychosexual pathology of White supremacy. Mixed-race like Fanon, Himes is a man with a complex biography and was acutely sensitive to Black and White anxiety, fascination, and preoccupation with disciplining and surveilling intimacy between Black men and White women. A character from his novel *Plan B* (1993) asserts with anger and resignation: "It is said that black men inspire the baser emotions in women because they don't consider us as human. Therefore, they can indulge in any depravity at all with us because it doesn't count" (cited in Thomas, 2007, n.15, p. 189). Like Vian

and Wright, the warping of love and sexual desire by ascetism and the human degradation of racism on its perpetrators and victims alike are themes that Himes (1956/1984) brilliantly distilled in his short story *A Case of Rape*.

20. Fanon's thesis has considerable explanatory power in the cases of Botham Jean, who was killed by Amber Guyger, his White female neighbour and an off-duty police officer (McLaughlin & Almasy, 2019); and that of a White female postal worker who won a claim of permanent disability because she feared African American (men) (Armour, 1994).
21. The Scotsboro Nine, the Central Park Five, the Iowa State Four, Lennon Lacey, and countless others lynched or thrown in prison to waste away because they were either falsely accused, wrongly convicted, or simply envied by White males for dating, marrying, or sleeping with White women are eloquent testimony of the reality that every Black man is imagined as a putative rapist.
22. Feminists (i.e., Brownmiller, 1993; Firestone, 1971) and others treat Eldrige Cleaver's (1968/1992) *Soul on Ice* as empirical verification of their claims that Black men, generalis, are rapists by nature. It hardly enters consideration that a polemical and antagonistic Cleaver gave White America the fear they desired. If Black men in the United States were hung from trees for less, it is unclear how Cleaver remained at large for so long. Black feminists, too, such as Nell Irvin Painter (1992), excoriate Cleaver as a degenerate serial rapist of Black women, and for good measure, disparage Black radical men such as David Walker and Frantz Fanon as inveterate misogynists. It is of consequence that feminist readings of *Soul on Ice* deliberately exclude Cleaver's own statement of contrition, self-repudiation for harming his victims, and love of Black women (pp. 15–17, 176–190, and 205–210). Along the way to excommunicating Cleaver from the human community, though she should know better, Painter insists on repeating the myth that *only* Black women were sexually abused during slavery, thereby reifying the myths of womanhood between enslaved and slave-owning women and patriarchal solidarity between enslaved men and slave-owning men. I encourage reading chapter 2 of Greg Thomas's (2007) *The Sexual Demon of Colonial Power*, where he critiques (bourgeois) Black feminist plantation historiography that mystifies gender and mythologizes sexual domination on the plantation alongside chapter 6 of Joy James's (1996) *Resisting State Violence*, where she presents sobering commentary on right-wing Black feminist excesses brought to bear in defending an equally right-wing Anita Hill. Yet Joy James (1996), like Angela Davis (1983, 1971), Saidiya Hartman (1997), bell hooks (1981/1990, 1990/1992b), and Lorde (1994), repeats Painter's contradictions and errors, which universalize gender, manhood, and womanhood, exceptionalize Black women, and understand them to be the only ones subjected to sexual violence on the plantation and into the contemporary period. Such perspectives are clearly contrary to the collective communal knowledge about "buck breaking" on plantations and rape in US prisons (see Chapter 10). One may also find more specific and probing examination of Cleaver in Biko Agozino's (2003) brief treatment (pp. 78–80) and Tommy Curry's (2017) more extensive disquisition (pp. 73–103). Thus, when particular feminists hold up Cleaver as the *cause célèbre* to affirm the Black-man-as-rapist myth, as well as the myths that rape is solely a violation experienced by women and that women themselves are incapable of it, rape becomes no more than an ideology to sustain the essentialist universalism of women as victims of male

patriarchy. But as shown by Tommy Curry (2017, Foreword to this volume), Leroy Moore and myself (Chapter 5 in this volume), Biko Agozino (2003), Thomas Foster (2011, 2019), Anthony Lemelle (2010), Stemple et al., (2016), James H. Sweet (2003), Richard Trexler (1995), and Greg Thomas (2007), there is no reason that theorizing rape as an act of gender violence should either exclude men or women as homosexual or heterosexual perpetrators. Indeed, without disavowing sexual violence toward women and girls, gender-based sexual violence is more likely to be reduced when it is recognized how brutal, pervasive, and routine is the sexual trafficking and violation of boys and men (Allegra, 2019; Del Zotto & Jones, 2002; Dennis, 2008; A. Jones, 2004, 2002; S. Jones, 2010; Teixeira, 2017).

23. Having documented many instances of White women lying about their dalliances with Black men for which the men were lynched or run out of town, Ida B. Wells, were she alive today, would certainly not endorse #Metoo or "believe women" simply because they are women (i.e., good) and not men (i.e., bad). In Chapter 3 of this volume, Katerina Deliovsky details the procedures of exoneration mobilized by White women sex tourists and White feminist researchers of "romance tourism."

24. As I (Chapter 1 of this volume) show, the Black-man-as-rapist trope is a staple in cinema in the Western World; John Russell (Chapter 2 of this volume) shows the same in the context of Japanese pornography. In Chapter 5, Moore and I discuss the state and public tolerance for the crisis of rape of men in the United States prisons. We suggest the rape of Black men and boys contributes to the production of mental and physical disabilities inasmuch as males with preexisting disabilities are the most susceptible to sexual abuse.

25. The logical conclusion of Fanon's deessentialization of rape opens us to thinking about female same-sex rape under colonialism and slavery. The slave narrative of Harriet Jacobs (1861/2001) is eloquent testimony of this fact. Interestingly, the small body of work demonstrating that White women routinely sexually assaulted Black men during slavery (Foster 2011, 2019) has not crossed over to reveal how prevalent cases like Jacobs's were. In part, the problem is that there would be few criminal cases, since the authority of White men were not perturbed, and because public discourse of female-to-female sex was even more coded and repressed that male-to-male sex.

26. The question of Fanon as "misogynist," "sexist," and "phallocentric" as raised by Anne McClintock (1995) and Atu Sekyi-Out (1996) cannot be taken up in detail here. There are, however, excellent opposing responses to this criticism (see Haddour, 2010; Sharpley-Whiting, 1996; Thomas, 2007). Given the (Black and White) feminist attack on Fanon, Denean Sharpley-Whiting (1996) asserts that there is "a recurring antiblack male bias [in feminist theories, which] appropriate indiscriminately the equally masculinist, oftentimes virulently racist–sexist thought of Freud, Lacan, Foucault, and Nietzsche...even as they aggressively critique Fanon for his 'misogeny'" (cited in Thomas, 2007, p. 96; see also Chinweizu, 1990; Wynter, 1994). Interestingly, in "Algeria Unveiled," Fanon exposed the collusion of French feminists and feminist organizations with the French government's effort to induct Algerian women as a fifth column among the colonized Algerians. Algeria, however, was not alone. Other Western governments and *their* feminists

worked to spread feminism as a benign force of disruption into the heart of what was then called the "Third World." In *The Mighty Wurlitzer: How the CIA Played America*, Hugh Wilford (2008) details that from 1952 onward, feminists in the United States actively colluded with the CIA to "spread feminism" into the "Third World." With "gender" and "woman" as key weapons against "Orientalist patriarchal despotism" and "oversexed patriarchs" of the "Third World," these weaponized discursive formations (Ozyegin, 2018; Shome, 2014; Thomas, 2007) spread the faith of Western patriarchal feminism at the barrel of a gun (e.g., the US/NATO invasion of Afghanistan so that women and girls can go to school) and through aid (e.g., family planning advocated by the Kissinger Report, 1974). The essential problem of colonialism and imperialism, however, resolves itself as that posed by males from opposing, conquered, and/or dominated groups who might likely resist White supremacist patriarchal imperial domination. They are thus demonized as archetypes of hetero-hypermasculinity, patriarchy, toxic masculinity, and as oversexed rapists. This is why non-White males are specified as a problem to be controlled outright or prevented from being born so that they do not staff anti-imperial insurgencies and governments that could challenge the colonial and imperial dominance of the US/West at home and abroad (e.g., "Harvard fellow," 2010; Faler, 2005; Kissinger, 1974, pp. 58, 75; Wynter, 1994); or are made use of by induction into the military (e.g., Moynihan, 1965, pp. 16, 40–43). In the context of the Cold War (and now in the "age of terror"), assuring "women's rights" has been tied to ensuring the control of countries that challenge the West or are farthest away from the orbit of the United States and the West. Indeed, Gloria Steinem's inglorious and unapologetic shilling for the CIA stands as eloquent condemnation of institutionalized feminism ("C.I.A. subsidize," 1967; Lofton, 1975). It is difficult to find current information on weaponized Western feminism telescoped into the Global South. Little wonder that radical Black men in the 1960s and 1970s not only raised the alarm about feminism, but were specifically targeted for destruction by the nationalizing of the KKK into the FBI's COINTELPRO (Thomas, 2007). It is for these reasons that Fanon and other revolutionary males who oppose feminism are dubbed as "misogynists" by female and male sympathizers of Western racial patriarchal imperial feminism.

27. Fanon challenges us to rethink the idea that women are paragons of virtue in terms of sexual pathology and violence. Recent attention is turning to sexual violence perpetrated by women against women and men. Lara Stemple et al. (2017) assert that researchers have been hindered from inquiry into this area because "feminist theory posits that sexual victimization is a result of socially constructed male power and privilege, employed as a tool to subordinate women" (p. 32). They note that women sexual abusers not only force men to penetrate them, but also that "[l]esbian and bisexual women abused by women report feeling that their victimization is delegitimized due to heterosexist assumptions" (p. 32; see also Agozino, 2003). The case of Ghislaine Maxwell, Jeffrey Epstein's accused sex recruiter and co-sexual exploiter of young women, raised eyebrows (J. Harris, 2019; Whitehead, 2019), but largely because of the refusal to admit that women are not passive victims. This mythology also leads to lack of interest in intimate partner and sexual violence among lesbian and same sex unions that are higher than heterosexual unions (Brown & Herman, 2015; Edwards & Sylaska, 2014; Langenderfer-Magruder et al., 2016).

28. The idea that no woman, or man for that matter, can ever find pain sexually ecstatic is largely the result of the merging of the puritanical Judeo-Christianity with the minority, but hegemonic, feminist opinion that heterosexual sex (i.e., male insertion) amounts to "sexual violence" and domination (Hyam, 1991). The great irony is that the literatures of the early desert Christian sects and the pre-Renaissance Roman Catholic accounts of the lives of saints brim with pornographic sadomasochism and descriptions of mortification of the flesh pronounced and narrated in sexually graphic detail (Schäfer-Althaus, 2014). Though it might belabour the point, it seems important to add that the sensualism of biological and medical discourses—which assert that the human organism, as any other, avoids pain and pursues pleasure—too sharply divides desire of and for violence with the experience of sex to justify conceptions of deviance and pathology (Baldwin 1955/1984; Fanon, 1952/1977; Foucault, 1978/1990). Human cultures—no more than individuals—across time, place, and space have found ingenious ways to bridge the divide for transiting pain into ecstasy. Initiation rituals are but one example. The thriving subculture of sadomasochism and race play are evidence of this fact. And, excluding sexually charged hetero- and homoerotic encounters between captor/captive and torturer/tortured, consensual sex is of a piece with vocabularies of violence (i.e., *bang, frig, fuck, hit it, pound, punch, stab, strike, screw,* etc.; these metaphors cross gender and sexual orientation), mortification (e.g., orgasm named a *petite mort* [little death] and communicated through terms such as *harder, your killing me*, and *I'm dying*), and modified torture (i.e., asphyxiation, binding, slapping, etc.) See also note 5 above.
29. The case of Daniel Holtzclaw is emblematic of a significant problem in Canada and the United states of male police officers sexually assaulting women (McLaughlin et al., 2016; Sedensky & Merchant, 2015). Tommy Curry (2017) also notes, however, that the nature of police sexual assault against Black men is particularly violent and even more suppressed.
30. I take up the issue of White men transubstantiating into Black men in Chapter 1 of this volume. This is a recursive theme in North American literature (Baldwin, 1961; Cleaver, 1968/1992; Hoch, 1979). In the context of "cuckolding" in the swinging lifestyle, Caribbean sex tourism, and so-called interracial pornography, White men and women, with the complicity of Black men, engage in what is called "race play," which includes feigned rape, role play, BDSM, and general fetishizing of Black men as "bulls," "horses," and "studs" (see Lambert, 2012; Trott, 2017). In other instances, Black women participate in "race play" (Mistress A, 2011, 2012).
31. Courttia Newland (2019), a British author who is a Black man, revealed that for many years White women in the publishing industry sexually harassed him and threatened his career if he did not submit to their sexual advances. In quotidian ways, too, using rumour, innuendo, and cries for help, the memes "Becky" and "Karen" capture the ways White women have consciously and deliberately contributed to the assaults, murders, and suspicion of Black men by calling the police and vigilantes (Curry, 2017; Lord, 2020; Wong, 2020). Both in the past and the present, and within White supremacist groups and outside of them, they have also participated in physical violence and acted as human shields to enable White men to do the physical assaults (Daniels, 1997; Curry, 2017). These past and current events support findings by social dominance

theorists that women from the dominant racial group mobilize the discriminatory power of their group through covert, implicit, and subtle ways (Navarrete et al., 2010; Sidanius & Pratto, 1999).

32. McIntosh identifies six performative typologies that both regulate and privilege White women's reproduction of White patriarchal supremacy: White virgin, good White female employee, White pinup, White supermom, White trash mama, and White lady. Lynn Stuart Parramore's (2017) analysis is an elegant, thoughtful, and compelling critical examination of the Faustian bargain White women make with White men to dominate other racial groups.

33. Seeking to establish a position of moral sanctity for Black women, bell hooks (1984), in a remarkable stretch of illogic, asserts:

> As a group, black women are in an unusual position in this society, for not only are we collectively at the bottom of the occupational ladder, but our social status is lower than any other group. Occupying such a position, we bear the brunt of sexist, racist, and classist oppression. At the same time, we are the group that has not been socialized to assume the role of exploiter/oppressor in that we are allowed no institutional "other" that we can exploit or oppress. (Children do not represent an institutionalized other even though they may be oppressed by parents.) White women and black men have it both ways. They can be oppressor or be oppressed. Black men may be victimized by racism, but sexism allows them to act as exploiters and oppressors of women. White women may be victimized by sexism, but racism enables them to act as exploiters and oppressors of black people. *Both* groups have led liberation movements for *their* interests [emphasis added] and support the continued oppression of other groups. (pp. 14–15)

However much hooks (2004, 1992a, 1990/1992b) claims to profess a complex viewpoint of Black men (cf. E. Hutchinson, 1996), her prevarications about Black men's diversity personifies academia's and the Black bourgeois feminist intelligentsia's mocking tone. This perspective is voiced by Gloria Naylor: "All the good [Black] men are dead or waiting to be born" (cited in Segal, 1995, p. 196) or more recently by the "woke" gay, lesbian, #Blackgirlmagic, and Black feminist/womynist memes "Straight black men are the white people of black people" and "Straight black men are trash" (Anyabwele, 2017; H.K., 2017; Watkins, 2019; Young, 2017). Whether as a commodity for the careers of academics and novelists or the "property" of "woke" Black "necro-activists" (Williams, 2018; see also Curry, 2021; Kitossa, 2019, pp. 90–98), the wishing of death and destruction to straight and presumably "bad" (Cooper, 2006), disreputable, undisciplined, and unintegrateable Black men is indisputable. In the parlance of bell hooks, *he* is: (a) cock-centred and "root[ed] in patriarchal phallocentrism" (hooks, 1992a, p. 111); (b) "the erect phallus" that helps to forge "a bond between oppressed black men and their white male oppressors" to oppress all women, but especially Black women (hooks, 1990/1992b, p. 58); and (c) one who "[d]espite all popular arguments that claim black men were figuratively castrated [during slavery]" was "allowed to maintain some semblance of their societally defined masculine role" (hooks, 1981/1990, p. 21). In these statements, it strikes me that hooks's grasp of history and the sociology of the oppressed in slavery and contemporary Black men's reality is grotesquely impoverished, if not surreal.

hooks (1992a) lists non-patriarchal Black men she was fascinate with growing up: "Felix, a hobo who jumped trains, never worked a regular job, and had a missing thumb" and "Kid, who lived out in the country and hunted rabbits and coons that came to our table" and "Daddy Gus, who spoke in hushed tones, sharing his sense of spiritual mysticism" (p. 88). And "[t]he list could go on" (p. 88). So, the down and out moved her. There are plenty more where they came from. But how and why could hooks have crafted a theory of Black men that constructs them as demons? Did these outcast Black men in her community collude with White men and women to oppress Black women? If hooks fails to translate these positive experiences into a coherent theory of Black men, what of her account of slavery? Her mobilization of "plantation patriarchy" and the way she narrates transatlantic slavery does not hold up to scrutiny (Dusinberre, 2000; V. Brown, 2008, 2020; Craton, 1982; Foster, 2019, 2011; Patterson, 1969, 1982, Sweet, 2003; Thomas, 2007; Woodard, 2014). hooks's work, and others of its ilk, erase the vital roles Black men undertook as leaders of slave revolts (e.g., in the United States, Denmark Vessay and Nat Turner). It would do for hooks and others certain of Black men's universal collusion with the oppressors of Black women to consider the role that Black women in Africa played in aiding and abetting the Danes and other Europeans to sell other African children, men, and women into the horrors of transatlantic slavery (see Ipsen, 2015). It would be impolitic for hooks and her ilk to consider the contribution of Black men to civil rights and Black Power, and who were jailed and assassinated for it. Finally, how does hooks square the economic exclusion, mass incarceration, and contemporary lynchings of gay, straight, and transgendered Black men (Assari & Caldwell, 2018; Blackwell, 2014; Flowe, 2020; Gilbert & Ray, 2015; Hudson et al., 2012; "Hundreds of boys," 2019; Khan, 2020; Martinez & Law, 2020; Mooney, 2014; Ogungbure, 2019; Slotkin, 2020; Smith, et al., 2011). All of these empirical facts indict any claim that Black men are in cahoots with White men (and women) to oppress Black women as mendacious and misandrist. Interestingly, the sanctification, advocated by hooks and the "woke," of Black women as the ultimate victims of men and White supremacy plays dangerously with an inverted cult of true womanhood in the form of the strong Black woman who is everybody's mule. But can Black women harm Black boys and men, be it "institutionally" or interpersonally, with little to no accountability? In spite of Black mothers' concern, fears, and protectiveness of their sons (Golden,1995; Lawson, 2019), the answer is yes, and in many ways: bidirectional intimate partner violence (see Curry, 2017); collusion with institutional domination of Black men and boys (see Curry, 2017; Lemelle, 2010); and child abandonment and neglect (Balkissoon, 2018; Curry, 2017), however much the problem is blamed on overzealous White female (and sometimes Black and other women "of colour") social workers (Maynard, 2017). The vulnerability of Black boys to sexual abuse and the resulting trauma that shapes their lives is an experience without a name. An extreme but not unusual instance appears in the opening paragraph of Iceberg Slim's autobiography. He describes, as a three-year old, being forced to perform cunnilingus, repeatedly, on his Holy Roller babysitter, a young widow who was the same age as his mother (1969/2011, p. 1).

Other examples include James Baldwin (1963/1985, p. 39), Tommy Davidson (2020, p. 26), and D.L. Hughley (djvlad, 2018, 55:56–58:30). The sexual abuse of boys transcends race, time, place, and space. Ronald Hyam remarks that "[e]ven [Sigmund] Freud was seduced by his nurse" (1991, p. 59). Could Freud's psycho-genital theory (and his love of big cigars) be an effort to reclaim his sexual sovereignty? This is question for Freudians to answer. The sexual abuse of boys and men still remains largely underdeveloped in spite of calls for more research (Biehler, 2019; C. Butler, 2015; Curry, 2017, 2018; Del Zotto & Jones, 2002; Dennis, 2008; Foster, 2011; Holmes & Slap, 1998; Trexler, 1995; Sivagurunathana et al., 2019; Stemple & Meyer, 2014; Winbush, 2002).

34. Scholars are now turning the critical gaze onto White women as slave holders who, no differently from White men, imposed all manner of mental and physical tortures and sexual abuses on enslaved African men and women (Curry, 2017; Foster, 2011, 2019; Jones-Rogers, 2019; Sweet, 2003; Woodard, 2014). Significantly, this turn is happening almost 40 years after Gilbert Osofsky (1969) encouraged scholars to rethink

> [t]he image of the blessed, genteel, white Southern femininity [to] find some place for the [mistress] who tried to kill Moses Roper because he looked too like her husband, or for the ladies the Clarke brothers referred to as she-wolves, screech owls, and she-bears. (p. 43)

35. The flaws in this proposition are many. For instance, it should be noted that Marcel Mauss's (1925/1990) publication *The Gift* provides a critical basis for asserting that a key failing in the feminist assertion of "patriarchy" is that it refuses to acknowledge the powerful role that women occupy as "gift givers." Crucially for Mauss, social protection is a part of that exchange. Gerda Lerner's (1986) thesis conceptually linking the emergence of "patriarchy" with the slavery of women falls apart under the weight of numerous examples showing that women could only *be* enslaved *because* the males of their group were, as one authority she cites puts it, "brained on the spot" (p. 79). David Brion Davis (2006), citing Lerner, observes that from "Homeric and biblical literature...the males defeated in wars were usually slaughtered while foreign women were used for household service as well as for sex and heavy labor" (p. 38). It is, therefore, surprising that Davis should uncritically accept Lerner's thesis that women were "the archetypical slave" (D. Davis, 2006, p. 38). Even perceptive theorists such as Richard Trexler (1995, p. 13), whose work on sex and conquest was in part inspired by Lerner, accepts some of Lerner's claims such as conquerors learning to subordinate women from outgroups because they had already subordinated their own. Of course, as I point out in note 6 above, this is conjecture that falls apart once the category of "woman" is deessentialized and women are recognized as having agency that is as diabolic and parasitic as that of which men are capable. Rosalind Coward (1983) provides a thoughtful and detailed social history of "patriarchy" as a concept, while Marvin Harris (1974) gives an interesting anthropological critique of feminist essentialism. Only subsequently, once captive women were incorporated and populations increased through their forced breeding, were slaveholding protostates able to raise large armies and local police forces composed of males

mothered by captured women. With such male children adopted and raised into allegiance to their father's dominant group was there the *man-power* to hold enslaved men in check. Even then, captured males were routinely disabled and "domesticated" through blinding, castration, and hamstringing (Scott, 2008; Trexler, 1995). No such precautionary debilitations were routinely meted out to female captives, who were regarded as a resource and not as a threat to the conquering group. Hilary Clinton's (1998) statement that "[w]omen have always been the *primary* [emphasis added] victims of war...because...[w]omen lose their husbands, their fathers, their sons in combat" (para. 9) is disingenuous. It is an erasure of male victims of war, an affirmation of the social privileging of females, and a denial of her own role as a perpetrator of the war on Libya (Comissiong, 2017) and the coup in Honduras (Naiman, 2017) which cost the lives of tens of thousands of women and girls their male relations. The facts, then—we could even look to the Bible—do not bear Clinton out that women are the sole or even primary victims of war; males are *always* the first targets for genocide and the destruction of groups (Del Zotto & Jones, 2002; "Hundreds of boys," 2019; A. Jones, 2004; Sidanius & Pratto, 1999; Quilty, 2020; Trexler, 1995). It is out of place also for Chandra Mohanty (2003) to criticize Vandana Shiva for rejecting the feminist patriarchal creed that hives off women from the men in their communities. Like Clinton, therefore, Mohanty espouses the illogic that "[p]oor women and girls are the hardest hit by the degradation of environmental conditions, wars, famines, privatization of services and deregulation of governments, the dismantling of welfare states, the restructuring of paid and unpaid work, increasing surveillance and incarceration in prisons, and so on" (p. 514). And bell hooks (1981/1990, 1990/1992b, 1992a) asserts in many of her works that "patriarchy" is a relationship of collusion in which Black men make common cause with men to oppress Black women (see also note 32 above). All evidence, from slave rebellions and quotidian acts of resistance to the civil rights and Black Power movements and beyond, nonetheless stands in stark rebuke of the verity of her claims.

36. The totalizing argument that women as a universal category are "oppressed" and men cannot be because they are men, and that women qua women are as a consequence "weak" has not held up, nor is it saved by constructions of heroism such as the use of the term *survivor*. No one really and seriously believes that enslaved African peoples were weak, judging by the frequency of outright revolts and low-intensity resistance (i.e., playing stupid, going slow, malingering, sabotaging machinery, etc.). James C. Scott (1985) notes that weapons of the weak are not to be found in grand movements organized by the disaffected bourgeoisie, but in the thousand pin-pricks of everyday (and every night) acts of resistance. Why, then, should it be thought that women are disempowered and oppressed by "patriarchy" and that not until feminism was there resistance? Arguing that "gender" and "patriarchy" are culturally variable and that "patriarchy" cannot be understood as the single cause of women's subordination, Sheila Rowbotham (1981) insists on the rejection of static models of "man" and "woman" in place of an account of contradictory, dynamic, and mutual dependencies (see alsoStemple et al., 2017; Thomas, 2007). "Patriarchy," Rowbotham notes, gives us no sense of men's dependence on women. Nor does it reveal how "women have resolutely manoeuvred for a better position within the general context of

subordination—by shifting for themselves, turning the tables, ruling the roost, wearing the trousers, hen-pecking, gossiping, hustling, or (in the words of a woman I overheard) just 'going drip, drip at him'" (p. 364). In much the same way, Ronald Hyam (1991) cites Vern and Bonnie Bullough as stating that (female) sex work "is an outstanding example of the perverse resilience of human beings, since women, including prostitutes, have turned their sexual subordination into a weapon that allows them in turn to victimize men" (p. 24, n. 58; see also Ringdal, 2004).

37. Based on a "structural" analysis of "gender relations" that is in part rooted in biological sexual dimorphism, Sally Alexander and Barbara Taylor (1981) offer a counterperspective to that of Rowbotham (1981). To the extent that Alexander and Taylor's defence of patriarchy both excludes other axes of difference (e.g., class, colour, language) and regimes of power (e.g., colonialism and imperialism) and leaves women outside of "gender relations" as victims only, rather than agents with a stake in the reproduction of "patriarchy," their "defence of patriarchy" is less than persuasive. See note 4 above.
38. David Austin (2013) recounts the parallel dynamic with the Royal Canadian Mounted Police in the 1960s, while Paul Gilroy (1991) describes police tactics to undermine the Black Power Movement in the United Kingdom.
39. Leroy Moore Jr. and myself show (Chapter 5 of this volume) that however much this language is ableist, Baldwin (and Fanon) laid the groundwork for Black disabilities studies over 50 years ago.
40. Blackness and maleness uniquely exposes Black boys to the presumption of noninnocence (Goff et al., 2014), thus exposing them to mental, physical, and sexual abuse. Recent reports of women (notably, mostly White) teachers are beginning to cause alarm among African American educators. Raymond Winbush (2002) notes anecdotally, "I have spoken to other black educators about this subject, and many of them tell how they have overheard white female teachers talk in sexual terms about their black male students" (p. 120–21). He points out also that "the sexual anxiety felt by many of these teachers could easily translate into rejection and avoidance of their pubescent male students" (p. 121).
41. Omar Khadr, the 16-year-old child soldier apprehended by the US invading forces in Afghanistan and subsequently transferred to Guantamo, was threatened by his interrogator in Afghanistan, Sergeant Joshua Claus, that he would be sent to prison in the United States where "big black guys" would be let to rape him ("Interrogator warned," 2010).
42. Experimental research studies indicate there is a greater tendency for women and men alike to hurt and sacrifice men more than women (Doliński et al., 2017; FeldmanHall et al., 2016).

Bibliography

Abell, W. (1966). *The collective dream in art*. New York: Schocken Books. (Original work published 1957)

Agozino, B. (2003). *Counter-colonial criminology: A critique of imperialist reason*. Pluto Press.

Alexander, S., & Taylor, B. (1981). In defence of "patriarchy." In R. Samuel (Ed.), *People's history and socialist theory* (pp. 364–69). Routledge.

Allegra, C. (2019, September 7). Unspeakable crime: Rape as a weapon of war in Libya. *Al Jazeera*. https://www.aljazeera.com/programmes/specialseries/2019/09/unspeakable-crime-rape-weapon-war-libya-190903102146596.html

Amadiume, I. (1987). *Male daughters, female husbands: Gender and sex in an African society*. Zed Books.

Ani, M. (1994). *Yurugu: An African-centered critique of European cultural thought and behavior*. African World Press, Inc.

Anyabwele, T.V. (2017, September 23). My response to "straight Black men are the White people of Black people." *Huffpost*. https://www.huffpost.com/entry/black-girl-responds-to-straight-black-men-are-the_b_59c630ede4b0f2df5e83ae88

Armour, J.D. (1994). Race ipsa loquitur: Of reasonable racists, intelligent Bayesians, and involuntary Negrophobes. *Stanford Law Review, 46*(4), 781–816.

Assari, S., & Caldwell, C.H. (2018). High risk of depression in high-income African American boys. *Journal of Racial and Ethnic Health Disparities, 5*, pp. 808–19. https://doi.org/10.1007/s40615-017-0426-1

Austin, D. (2013). *Fear of a Black nation: Race, sex, and security in sixties Montreal*. Between the Lines.

Bagner, D.M., Storch, E.A., & Preston, A.S. (2007). Romantic relational aggression: What about gender? *Journal of family violence, 22*, 19–24. https://doi.org/10.1007/s10896-006-9055-x

Bailey, M. (2010, March 14). They aren't talking about me... *Crunk Feminist Collective*. http://www.crunkfeministcollective.com/2010/03/14/they-arent-talking-about-me/

Baldwin, J. (1961, May 1). The Black boy looks at the White boy Norman Mailer. *Esquire*. https://classic.esquire.com/article/1961/5/1/the-black-boy-looks-at-the-white-boy-norman-mailer

Baldwin, J. (1972). *No name in the street*. The Dial Press.

Baldwin, J. (1976). *The devil finds work: An essay*. The Dial Press.

Baldwin, J. (1977). *Just above my head*. Random House. (Original work published 1964)

Baldwin, J. (1984). *Notes of a native son*. Beacon Press. (Original work published 1955)

Baldwin, J. (1985). *The fire next time*. Laurel. (Original work published 1963)

Baldwin, J. (1998). Going to meet the man. In T. Morrison (Ed.), *Baldwin: Early novels & stories* (pp. 933–50). The Library of America. (Original interview published 1965)

Balkissoon, D. (2018, July 17). What good data mean for Black youth in foster care. *The Globe and Mail*. https://www.theglobeandmail.com/canada/toronto/article-what-good-data-mean-for-black-youth-in-foster-care/

Bambara, T.C. (1970). On the issue of roles. In T.C. Bambara (Ed.), *The Black woman: An anthology* (pp. 101–10). Mentor.

Bieler, D. (2019, May 3). AAU basketball coach who sexually exploited more than 400 boys gets 180 years in prison. *Washington Post*. https://www.washingtonpost.com/sports/2019/05/03/aau-basketball-coach-who-sexually-exploited-more-than-boys-gets-years-prison/?noredirect=on&utm_term=.d59688bc9e56

Blackwell, V. (2014). N.C. teen's hanging death ruled a suicide; mother says it was a lynching. *CNN*. https://www.cnn.com/2014/12/15/justice/north-carolina-lennon-lacy

Brown, C.L. (1967). Color in northern Africa. *Daedalus*, 96(2), 464–82.

Brown, T.N.T., & Herman, J.L. (2015). *Intimate partner violence and sexual abuse among LGBT people: A review of existing research*. The Williams Institute. https://williamsinstitute.law.ucla.edu/wp-content/uploads/IPV-Sexual-Abuse-Among-LGBT-Nov-2015.pdf

Brown, V. (2008). *The reaper's garden: Death and power in the world of Atlantic slavery*. Harvard University Press.

Brown, V. (2020). *Tacky's revolt: The story of an Atlantic slave war*. The Belknap Press of Harvard University Press.

Brownmiller, S. (1993). *Against our will: Men, women and rape*. Fawcett Columbine.

Bullough, V., & Bullough, B. (1987). *Women and prostitution: A social history*. Prometheus Books

Butler, C.N. (2015). The racial roots of human trafficking. *UCLA law review*, *62*, 1464–514.

Butler, J. (1993a). Endangered/endangering: Schematic racism and white paranoia. In R. Gooding-Williams (Ed.), *Reading Rodney King / Reading urban uprising* (pp. 15–22). Routledge.

Butler, J. (1993b). *Gender trouble: Feminism and the subversion of identity*. Routledge.

C.I.A. subsidized festival trips: Hundreds of students were sent to world gathering. (1967, February 21). *The New York Times*. https://timesmachine.nytimes.com/timesmachine/1967/02/21/90263931.html?pageNumber=33

Chinweizu, I. (1990). *Anatomy of female power: A masculinist dissection of matriarchy*. Pero Press.

Chow, R. (1990). Violence in the other country. In C. Mohanty, A. Russo, & L. Torres (Eds.), *Third world women and the politics of feminism* (pp. 81–100). Indiana University Press.

Clarification: Ferguson activists-deaths story. (2019, March 21). *Associated Press*. https://apnews.com/article/436251b8a58c470eb4f69099f43f2231

Clarke, E. (1976). *My mother who fathered me: A study of the families in three selected communities of Jamaica*. G. Allen & Unwin.

Cleaver, E. (1992). *Soul on Ice*. Ramparts. (Original work published 1968)

Clinton, H. (1998, November 17). *First Lady Hillary Rodham Clinton: First Ladies' conference on domestic violence, San Salvador, El Salvador* [Speech transcript]. National Archives. https://clintonwhitehouse3.archives.gov/WH/EOP/First_Lady/html/generalspeeches/1998/19981117.html

Combahee River Collective. (2000). The Combahee River Collective statement. In B. Smith (Ed.), *Home girls: A Black feminist anthology* (pp. 264–74). Rutgers University Press. (Original work published 1983)

Comissiong, S. (2017, December 6). How Barack Obama and Hillary Clinton contributed to Libya's slavery crisis. *Black Agenda Report*. https://blackagendareport.com/how-barack-obama-and-hillary-clinton-contributed-libyas-slavery-crisis

Conrad, P., & Schneider, J.W. (1992). *Deviance and medicalization: From badness to sickness*. Temple University Press.

Cooper, F.R. (2006). Against bipolar Black masculinity: Intersectionality, assimilation, identity performance, and hierarchy. *UC Davis Law Review*, *39*(3), 853–904.

Coward, R. (1983). *Patriarchal precedents: Sexuality and social relations*. Routledge / Kegan Paul.

Craton, M. (1982). *Testing the chains: Resistance to slavery in the British West Indies*. Cornell University Press.

Crenshaw, K. (1991). Mapping the margins: Intersectionality, identity politics, and violence against women of color. *Stanford Law Review, 43*(6), pp. 1241–300.

Crick, N.R., & Grotpeter, J.K. (1995). Relational aggression, gender, and social-psychological adjustment. *Child development, 66*(3). 710–22. https://doi.org/10.1111/j.1467-8624.1995.tb00900.x

Curry, T.J. (2017). *The man-not: Race, class, genre, and the dilemmas of Black manhood*. Temple University Press.

Curry, T.J. (2018). Expendables for whom: Terry Crews and the erasure of Black male victims of sexual assault and rape. *Women's studies in communication, 42*(3), 287–307. https://doi.org/10.1080/07491409.2019.1641874

Curry, T.J. (in press). He never mattered: Poor Black males and the dark logic of intersectional invisibility. In M. Cholbi, B. Hogan, A. Mavda, & B. Yost (Eds.), *The movement for Black lives: Philosophical perspectives*. Oxford University Press.

Daniels, J. (1997). *White lies: Race, class, gender and sexuality in White supremacist discourse*. Routledge

Davidson, T. (2020). *Living in color: What's funny about me*. Kensington Books.

Davis, A.Y. (1971). The Black woman's role in the community of slaves. *The Black Scholar, 3*(4), 1–14.

Davis, A.Y. (1983). *Women, race, and class*. Random House.

Davis, D.B. (2006). *Inhuman bondage: The rise and fall of slavery in the New World*. Oxford University Press.

Davis, D.B. (2014). *The problem of slavery in the age of emancipation*. Alfred A. Knopf.

Davis, K. (2008). Intersectionality as buzzword: A sociology of science perspective on what makes a feminist theory successful. *Feminist Theory, 9*(1), 67–85. https://doi.org/10.1177/1464700108086364

Del Zotto, A., & Jones, A. (2002, March 23–27). *Male-on-male sexual violence in wartime: Human rights' last taboo?* [Conference presentation]. Annual Convention of the International Studies Association (ISA), New Orleans, LA. http://adamjones.freeservers.com/malerape.htm

Deliovsky, K., & Kitossa, T. (2013). Beyond Black and White: When going beyond may take us out of bounds. *Journal of Black Studies, 44*(2), 158–81. https://doi.org/10.3138/ijcs.56.2017-0005

Dennis, J.P. (2008). Women are victims, men make choices: The invisibility of men and boys in the global sex trade. *Gender Issues, 25*(1), 11–25. https://doi.org/10.1007/s12147-008-9051-y

Denson, T.F., O'Dean, S.M., Blake, K.R., & Beames, J.R. (2018). Aggression in women: Behavior, brain and hormones. *Frontiers in Behavioural Neuroscience, 12*, 1–20. https://doi.org/10.3389/fnbeh.2018.00081

djvlad. (2018, August 28). *DL Hughley on Kim K, Kanye, Kevin Hart, Bill Cosby, Steve Harvey (full interview)* [Video]. YouTube. https://www.youtube.com/watch?v=IWBn_aFxaBM

Doliński, D., Grzyb, T., Folwarczny, M., Grzybała, P., Krzyszycha, K., Martynowska, K., & Trojanowski, J. (2017). Would you deliver an electric shock in 2015? Obedience in the experimental paradigm developed by Stanley Milgram in the 50 years following the original studies. *Social Psychological and Personality Science*, *8*(8), 927–33. https://doi.org/10.1177/1948550617693060

Douglas, M. (1970). *Natural symbols: Explorations in cosmology*. Pantheon Books

Du Bois, W.E.B. (1986). The prize fighter. In N.I. Huggins (Ed.), *W.E.B. Du Bois: Writings* (pp. 1161–62). The Library of America/Viking Press. (Original work published 1914)

Du Bois, W.E.B. (2004). *Darkwater: Voices from within the veil*. Washington Square Press. (Original work publishd 1920)

Dube, O., & Harish, S.P. (2019). *Queens* (National Bureau of Economic Research working paper #23337). https://www.nber.org/papers/w23337

Durkheim, E. (1995). *The elementary forms of religious life*. The Free Press.

Dusinberre, W. (2000). *Them dark days: Slavery in the American rice swamps*. University of Georgia Press

Eckman, F.M. (1968). *The furious passage of James Baldwin*. Michael Joseph.

Edwards, K., & Sylaska, K. (2014, Spring). Intimate partner violence among LGBTQ+ college students. Carsey Institute (Carsey Institute Issue Brief #69). https://scholars.unh.edu/cgi/viewcontent.cgi?referer=&httpsredir=1&article=1209&context=carsey

Elias, N. (2008). *The civilizing process: Sociogenic and psychogenetic investigations*. Wiley-Blackwell.

Faler, B. (2005, September 30). Bennett under fire for remark on crime and Black abortions. *The Washington Post*. http://www.csun.edu/~bashforth/155_PDF/BennettBlackBabiesandAbortion.pdf

Fanon, F. (1965). *A dying colonialism* (H. Chevalier, Trans.). Grove Press. (Original work published 1959)

Fanon, F. (1967). *Toward the African revolution* (H. Chevalier, Trans.). Grove Press.

Fanon, F. (1968). *The wretched of the earth* (C. Farrington, Trans.). Grove Press. (Original work published 1963)

Fanon, F. (1977). *Black skin, White masks* (C.L. Markmann, Trans.). Grove Press. (Original work published 1952)

Fanon, F. (2008). *Black skin, White masks* (R. Philcox, Trans). Grove Press. (Original work published 1952)

Farmanfarmaian, A. (1992). Did you measure up? The role of race and sexuality in the Gulf War. In C. Peters (Ed.), *Collateral damage: The new world order at home and abroad* (pp. 111–37). South End Press.

FeldmanHall, O., Dalgleish, T., Evans, D., Navrady, L., Tedeschi, E., & Mobbs, D. (2016). Moral chivalry: Gender and harm sensitivity predict costly altruism. *Social Psychological and Personality Science*, *7*(6), 542–51. https://doi.org/10.1177/1948550616647448

Ferber, A.L. (2007). The construction of Black masculinity: White supremacy now and then. *Journal of Sport and Social Issues*, *31*(1), 11–24. https://doi.org/10.1177/0193723506296829

Firestone, S. (1971). *The dialectic of sex: The case for feminist revolution*. Bantam Books.

Flowe, D.J. (2020). *Uncontrollable Blackness: African American men and criminality in Jim Crow New York*. University of North Carolina Press.

Foster, T.A. (2011). The sexual abuse of Black men under American slavery. *Journal of the History of Sexuality*, *20*(3), 445–64. https://doi.org/10.1353/sex.2011.0059

Foster, T.A. (2019). *Rethinking Rufus: Sexual violations of enslaved men*. University of Georgia Press.

Foucault, M. (1990). *The history of sexuality: An introduction* (Vol. 1; R. Hurley, Trans.). Vintage Books. (Original work published 1978)

Freud, S. (1930). *Civilization and its discontents* (J. Riviere, Trans.). Hogarth Press and Institute of Psychoanalysis.

Freud, S. (1989). *Totem and taboo: Some points of agreement between mental lives of savages and neurotics*. W.W. Norton. (Original work published 1913)

Frost, D. (1989). Are we on the edge of civil war? [Interview]. In F.L. Standley & L.H. Pratt (Eds.), *Conversations with James Baldwin* (pp. 93–97). (Original interview published 1970)

Gergen, K.T. (1967). The significance of skin color in human relations. *Daedalus, 96*(2), 390–406. https://www.jstor.org/stable/20027044

Gilbert, K.L., & Ray, R. (2015). Why police kill Black males with impunity: Applying public health critical race praxis (PHCRP) to address the determinants of policing behaviors and "justifiable" homicides in the USA. *Journal of Urban Health: Bulletin of the New York Academy of Medicine*, 93(1), 122–40. https://doi.org/10.1007/s11524-015-0005-x

Gilroy, P. (1991). *"There ain't no black in the Union Jack": The cultural politics of race and nation*. University of Chicago Press.

Goff, P.A., Jackson, M.C., Di Leone, B.A.L., Culotta, C.M., & DiTomasso, N.A. (2014). The essence of innocence: Consequences of dehumanizing Black children. *Journal of Personality and Social Psychology, 106*(4), 526–45. https://doi.org/10.1037/a0035663

Golden, M. (1995). *Saving our sons: Raising Black children in a turbulent world*. Anchor Books.

Goldstein, J.S. (2004). War and gender. In M. Ember & C.R. Ember (Eds.), *Encyclopedia of sex and gender: Men and women in the world's cultures* (pp. 107–16). Kluwer Academic / Plenum Publishers.

Goldstein, R. (2014). "Go the way your blood beats": An interview with James Baldwin. In *James Baldwin: The last interview and other conversations* (pp. 55–74). Melville House. (Original work published 1984)

Gordon, R. (1998). The rise of the bushman penis: Germans, genitalia and genocide. *African Studies*, 57(1), pp. 27–54.

Gossett, T. (1997). *Race: The history of an idea*. Oxford University Press.

Grande, S. (2003). Whitestream feminism and the colonialist project: A review of contemporary feminist pedagogy and praxis. *Educational Theory, 53*(3), 329–46.

Greven, P.J. (1977). *The Protestant temperament: Patterns of child-rearing, religious experience, and the self in early America*. Alfred A. Knopf.

H.K. (2017, September 21). A woman's response to "straight Black men are the White people of Black people." *Huffpost*. https://www.huffpost.com/entry/a-womans-response-to-straight-black-men-are-the-white_b_59c3cf05e4b0c87def8835c8

Haddour, A. (2010). Torture unveiled: Rereading Fanon and Bourdieu in the context of May 1958. *Theory, Culture & Society, 27*(7–8), 66–90. https://doi.org/10.1177/0263276410383710

Hall, S. (1996). The West and the rest: Discourse and power. In S. Hall, D. Held, D. Hubert, & K. Thompson (Eds.), *Modernity: An introduction to modern societies* (pp. 184–227). Wiley-Blackwell.

Hall, S. (1997). The work of representation. In S. Hall (Ed.), *Representation: Cultural representations and signifying practices* (pp. 223–79). SAGE / The Open University.

Hall, S., Critcher, C., Jefferson, T., Clarke, J., & Roberts, B. (1978). *Policing the crisis: Mugging, the state, and law and order.* Palgrave Macmillan.

Harris, C. (1993). Whiteness as property. *Harvard Law Review, 106*(8), 1707–91.

Harris, J.A. (2019, August 29). How a ring of women allegedly recruited girls for Jeffrey Epstein. *New York Times*. https://www.nytimes.com/2019/08/29/nyregion/jeffrey-epstein-ghislaine-maxwell.html

Harris, M. (1974). *Cows, pigs, wars & witches: The riddles of culture*. Vintage.

Harris, M. (1980). *Cultural materialism: The struggle for a science of culture*. Vintage Books.

Hartman, S.V. (1997). *Scenes of subjection: Terror, slavery, and self-making in nineteenth-century America*. Oxford University Press.

Hartmann, H.I. (1979). The unhappy marriage of Marxism and feminism: Towards a more progressive union. *Capital & Class, 3*(2), 1–33. https://doi.org/10.1177/030981687900800102

Harvard fellow calls for genocidal measure to curb Palestinian births. (2010, February 22). The *Electronic Intifada*. http://electronicintifada.net/v2/article11091.shtml

Hayes, M. (2018, May 1). "One woman or girl every other day": 57 women killed in Canada this year. *Globe and Mail*. https://www.theglobeandmail.com/canada/article-femicide-occurs-on-regular-basis-in-canada-data/

Hernton, C.C. (1965). *Sex and racism in America*. Doubleday.

Hesse, J. (2015, December 24). Convicted of rape based on a dream, man relishes freedom after 28 years. *The Guardian*. https://www.theguardian.com/us-news/2015/dec/24/clarence-moses-el-free-denver-rape-case

Himes, C. (1984). *A case of rape*. Howard University Press. (Original work published 1956)

Himes, C. (1993). *Plan B*. University of Press of Mississippi.

Himes, C. (2002). *If he hollers let him go*. Thunder's Mouth Press. (Original work published 1945)

Hoch, P. (1979). *White hero, Black beast: Racism, sexism, and the mask of masculinity*. Pluto Press.

Hodes, M. (1997). *White women, Black men: Illicit sex in the nineteenth-century South*. Yale University Press.

Holloway, L. (2014, December 20). Lennon Lacy's White girlfriend speaks out; Says he was murdered. *Nation*. https://newsone.com/3078313/lennon-lacy-girlfriend-claims-he-was-murdered/

Holmes, W., & Slap, G. (1998). Sexual abuse of boys: Definition, prevalence, correlates, sequelae, and management. *JAMA, 280*(21), 1855–62.

hooks, b. (1984). *Feminist theory: From margin to center*. South End Press.

hooks, b. (1990). *Ain't I a woman? Black women and feminism*. South End Press. (Original work published 1981)

hooks, b. (1992a). *Black looks: Race and representation*. Between The Lines.

hooks, b. (1992b). *Yearning: Race, gender, and cultural politics*. Between The Lines. (Original work published 1990)

hooks, b. (2004). *We real cool: Black men and masculinity*. Routledge

Hudson, D.L., Bullard, K.M., Neighbors, H.W., Geronimus, A.T., Yang, J., & Jackson, S.J. (2012). Are benefits conferred with greater socioeconomic position undermined by racial discrimination among African American men? *Journal of mens health*, 9(2), 127–36. https://doi.org/10.1016/j.jomh.2012.03.006

Hundreds of boys, men freed from torture building in Nigeria. (2019, September 27). *NBC News*. https://www.nbcnews.com/news/world/hundreds-boys-men-freed-torture-building-nigeria-n1059716

Hutchinson, D.L. (2001). Identity crisis: "Intersectionality," "multidimensionality," and the development of an adequate theory of subordination. *Michigan Journal of Race & Law*, 6, 1–33.

Hutchinson, E.O. (1996). *The assassination of the Black male image*. Simon and Schuster.

Hyam, R. (1991). *Empire and sexuality: The British experience*. Manchester University Press.

Interrogator warned teenaged Omar Khadr about threat of gang rape in U.S. prison. (2010, October 29). *Hamilton Spectator.* https://www.thespec.com/news/world/2010/10/29/interrogator-warned-teenaged-omar-khadr-about-threat-of-gang-rape-in-u-s-prison.html

Ipsen, P. (2015). *Daughters of the trade: Atlantic slavers and interracial marriage on the Gold Coast*. University of Pennsylvania Press.

Isaacs, H.R. (1967). Group identity and political change: The role of color and physical characteristics. *Daedalus*, 96(2), 353–75. https://www.jstor.org/stable/20027042

Jacobs, H. (2001). *Incidents in the life of a slave girl*. Dover Publications Inc. (Original work published 1861)

James, A. (1981). "Black": An inquiry into the pejorative associations of an English word. *New Community*, 9(1), 19–30. https://doi.org/10.1080/1369183X.1981.9975656

James, C.E. (in press). "The Jamaicans are here and working": Race and community responses. In D. Keyes & L.L.M. Aguiar (Eds.), *White space: Race, privilege, and cultural economies of the Okanagan Valley.* University of British Columbia Press.

James, J. (1996). *Resisting state violence: Radicalism, gender & race in U.S. culture*. University of Minnesota Press.

Jones-Rogers, S.E. (2019). *They were her property: White women as slave owners in the American South*. Yale University Press.

Jones, A. (2002). Gender and genocide in Rwanda. *Journal of Genocide Research*, *4*(1), 65–94. https://doi.org/10.1080/14623520120113900

Jones, A. (2004). *The murdered men of Ciudad Juárez*. http://adamjones.freeservers.com/juarez.htm

Jones, S.V. (2010). The invisible man: The conscious neglect of men and boys in the war on human trafficking. *Utah Law Review*, *2010*(4), 1143–88.

Jordan, W.D. (1977). *White over Black: American attitudes toward the Negro, 1550–1812*. W.W. Norton. (Original work published 1968)

Jung, C. (1966). *The collected works*. Princeton University Press.

Kelly, L. (2003). Disabusing the definition of domestic violence: How women batter men and the role of the feminist state. *Florida State University Law Review, 30*(4), 791–855.

Khan, S. (2020, June 15). Another lynching? Black man found hanging from a tree in Victorville, California. *HNGN*. https://www.hngn.com/articles/230019/20200615/another-lynching-black-man-found-hanging-tree-victorville-california.htm

King, J. (2020). James Byrd Jr. and the modern-day lynching. *D Magazine*. https://www.dmagazine.com/frontburner/2020/06/james-byrd-jr-and-the-modern-day-lynching/

Kissinger, H. (1974). Implications of worldwide population growth (National security study memorandum #200). https://pdf.usaid.gov/pdf_docs/PCAAB500.pdf

Kitossa, T. (2014, November 19). Black face at Brock: "Is it racist if they didn't mean it?". *Brock Press*. http://www.brockpress.com/2014/11/black-face-at-brock-is-it-racist-if-they-didnt-mean-it/

Kitossa, T. (2019). Metaphoricality of "crisis" in African Canadian leadership: Theorizing African Canadian leadership. In T. Kitossa, E. Lawson, & P.S.S. Howard (Eds.), *African Canadian Leadership: Continuity, transition and transformation* (pp. 71–110). University of Toronto Press.

Kitossa, T. (2020, December 4). *Anti-Black sexual racism: Linking White police violence, COVID-19, and popular culture* [Symposium paper]. Intervention Symposium—Black Humanity: Bearing Witness to COVID-19, online. https://antipodeonline.org/2020/12/04/black-humanity-bearing-witness-to-covid-19/

Kovel, J. (1971). *White racism: A psychohistory*. Pantheon Books.

Lambert, S. (2012, July 18). Man at centre of Manitoba judge scandal accused of sex for money. *The Globe and Mail*. https://www.theglobeandmail.com/news/national/man-at-centre-of-manitoba-judge-scandal-accused-of-sex-for-money/article4425491/

Langenderfer-Magruder, L., Walls, N.E., Whitfield, D.L., Brown, S. M., & Barrett, C.M. (2016). Partner violence victimization among lesbian, gay, bisexual, transgender, and queer youth: Associations among risk factors. *Child and Adolescent Social Work Journal, 33*, 55–68. https://doi.org/10.1007/s10560-015-0402-8

Lawson, E. (2019). Mercy for their children: A feminist reading of Black women's maternal activism and leadership practices. In T. Kitossa, E. Lawson, & P.S.S. Howard (Eds.), *African Canadian leadership: Continuity, transition, and transformation* (pp. 190–210). University of Toronto Press.

Lemelle, A. (2010). *Black masculinity and sexual politics*. Routledge.

Leonardo, Z., & Boas, E. (2013). Other kid's teachers: What children of color learn from White women and what this says about race, Whiteness, and gender. In M. Lynn & A. Dixson (Eds.), *Handbook of critical race theory in education* (pp. 313–24). Routledge.

Lerner, G. (1986). *The creation of patriarchy*. Oxford University Press.

Lofton, J. (1975, May 10). Ms. Steinem's CIA connection. *Human Events*. CIA: Freedom of Information Act Electronic Reading Room. https://www.cia.gov/library/readingroom/docs/CIA-RDP88-01315R000300380009-2.pdf

Lord, C. (2020, July 10). Ottawa police apologize after 911 call where White woman reports Black man on trail. *Global News*. https://globalnews.ca/news/7161684/ottawa-police-white-woman-911-call/

Lorde, A. (1994). *Age, race, class and sex: Women redefining difference.* In M. Evans (Ed.), *The woman question* (pp. 36–41). Sage Publications.

Lugones, M. (2007). Heterosexualism and the Colonial/Modern Gender System. *Hypatia, 22*(1), 186–209.

Lugones, M. (2010). Toward a decolonial feminism. *Hypatia, 25*(4), 742–59.

Manganyi, N. (1977). *Alienation and the body in a racist society: A study of the society that invented Soweto.* NOK Publishers.

Martinez, G. & Law, T. (2020). Two recent murders of Black trans women in Texas reveal a nationwide crisis, advocates say. *Time.* https://time.com/5601227/two-black-trans-women-murders-in-dallas-anti-trans-violence/

Mason, P. (1971). *Patterns of dominance.* Oxford University Press.

Matters, R. (2016, May 23). "Big Black dick" on gay PornHub is most searched for in these 15 states. *RonaldMatters.* http://www.ronaldmatters.com/big-black-dick-gay-pornhub-searched-15-states

Mauss, M. (1990). *The gift: The form and reason for exchange in archaic societies.* W.W. Norton. (Original work published 1925)

Maybury-Lewis, D. (1992). Introduction: The quest for harmony. In D. Maybury-Lewis & U. Almagor (Eds.), *The attraction of opposites: Thought and society in the dualistic mode* (pp. 1–18). University of Michigan Press.

Maynard, R. (2017). *Policing Black lives: State violence in Canada from slavery to the present.* Fernwood Publishing.

McClintock, A. (1995). *Imperial leather: Race, gender and sexuality in the colonial contest.* Routledge.

McCracken, D. (2018). Missing the "moment of grace" in James Baldwin's Going to Meet the Man. *The Explicator, 76*(4), 212–16. https://doi.org/10.1080/00144940.2018.1539698

McIntosh, D.M.D. (2018). From White ladies to White trash mamas: (Re)Locating the performances of White femininity. In D.G. Moon, D.M.D. McIntosh, & T.K. Nakayama (Eds.), *Interrogating the communicative power of Whiteness* (pp. 94–116). Routledge.

McLaughlin, E.C., & Almasy, S. (2019, October 3). Amber Guyger gets 10-year murder sentence for fatally shooting Botham Jean. *CNN.* https://www.cnn.com/2019/10/02/us/amber-guyger-trial-sentencing/index.html

McLaughlin, E.C., Sidner, S., & Martinez, M. (2016, January 22). Oklahoma City cop Daniel Holtzclaw sentenced to 263 years. *CNN.* http://www.cnn.com/2016/01/21/us/oklahoma-city-officer-daniel-holtzclaw-rape-sentencing/

Mead, G.H. (1918). The psychology of punitive justice. *American Journal of Sociology, 23*(5), 577–602. https://doi.org/10.1086/212795

Mistress A. (2011, December 9). Confessions of a Black dominatrix. *Afropunk.* https://afropunk.com/2011/12/confessions-of-a-black-dominatrix/

Mistress A. (2012, January 13). Confessions of a Black dominatrix — Part 2: Race play? *Afropunk.* https://afropunk.com/2012/01/confessions-of-a-black-dominatrix-part-2-race-play/

Mohanty, C.T. (2003). "Under Western Eyes" revisited: Feminist solidarity through anticapitalist struggles. *Signs: Journal of Women in Culture and Society, 28*(2), 499–535. https://doi.org/10.1086/342914

Mooney, C. (2014, December 1). The science of why cops shoot young Black men: And how to reform our bigoted brains. *Mother Jones*. http://www.motherjones.com/politics/2014/11/science-of-racism-prejudice

Mouffe, C. (1993). *Return of the political*. Verso Books.

Moynihan, P. (1965, March). *The Negro family: The case for national action office of policy* [The Moynihan Report]. Planning and Research; United States Department of Labor.

Mutua, A.D. (2013). Multidimensionality is to masculinities what intersectionality is to feminism. *Nevada Law Journal, 13*(2), 341–67. https://ssrn.com/abstract=2498732

Naiman, R. (2017, February 19). Did Secretary of State Hillary Clinton enable the coup in Honduras? *Huffpost*. https://www.huffpost.com/entry/secretary-of-state-hillar_b_9273712

Navarrete, C.D., McDonald, M.M., Molina, L.E., & Sidanius, J. (2010). Prejudice at the nexus of race and gender: An outgroup male target hypothesis. *Journal of Personality and Social Psychology*, 98(6), 933–45. https://doi.org/10.1037/a0017931

Newland, C. (2019, February 27). I had to submit to being exoticised by White women. If I didn't, I was punished. *The Guardian*. https://www.theguardian.com/world/2019/feb/27/white-privilege-is-used-by-women-against-black-men-as-a-tool-of-oppression

Newman, L.M. (1999). *White women's rights: The racial origins of feminism in the United States*. Oxford University Press.

Office of the Independent Review of Police Directorate. (2019). *Breaking the golden rule: A review of police strip searches in Ontario.* https://www.oiprd.on.ca/wp-content/uploads/OIPRD_Breaking-the-Golden-Rule_Report.pdf

Ogungbure, A. (2019). The political economy of Niggerdom: W.E.B. Du Bois and Martin Luther King Jr. on the racial and economic discrimination of Black males in America. *Journal of Black Studies*, 50(3), 273–97. https://doi.org/10.1177/0021934719834828

Ontario Human Rights Commission. (2020). *A disparate impact: Second interim report on the inquiry into racial profiling and racial discrimination of Black persons by the Toronto Police Service*. http://www.ohrc.on.ca/en/disparate-impact-second-interim-report-inquiry-racial-profiling-and-racial-discrimination-black

Osofsky, G. (1969). *Puttin' one ole massa: The slave narratives of Henry Bibb, William Wells Brown, and Solomon Northup*. Harper Torchbooks.

Ozyegin, G. (2018). Rethinking patriarchy through unpatriarchal male desires. In J.W. Messerschmidt, P.Y. Martin, M. A. Messner., & Connell, R. (Eds.), *Gender reckonings: New social theory and research* (pp. 233–53). New York University Press.

Painter, N.I. (1992). Hill, Thomas, and the use of racial stereotype. In T. Morrison (Ed.), *Race-ing justice, en-gendering power: Essays on Anita Hill, Clarence Thomas, and the construction of social reality* (pp. 200–14). Pantheon.

Parramore, L.S. (2017, August 2). White females from hell: Meet the new monster in the house. *Lapham's Quarterly*. https://www.laphamsquarterly.org/roundtable/white-females-hell

Patterson, O. (1969). *The sociology of slavery: an analysis of the origins, development and structure of Negro slave society in Jamaica*. Fairleigh Dickinson University Press

Patterson, O. (1982). *Slavery and social death: A comparative study*. Harvard University Press.

Pearson, A.R., Dovidio, J.F., & Pratto, F. (2007). Racial prejudice, intergroup hate, and blatant and subtle bias of Whites toward Blacks in legal decision making in the United States. *International Journal of Psychology and Psychological Therapy*, *7*(2), 145–58. https://www.redalyc.org/pdf/560/56070203.pdf

Poulson-Bryant, S. (2005). *Hung: A meditation on the measure of Black men in America*. Harlem Moon / Broadway Books.

Preibisch, K., & Binford, L. (2007). Interrogating racialized global labour supply: An exploration of the racial/national replacement of foreign agricultural workers in Canada. *Canadian Review of Sociology/Revue Canadienne de Sociologie*, *44*(1), 5–36. https://doi.org/10.1111/j.1755-618X.2007.tb01146.x

Quilty, A. (2020, December 18). The CIA's Afghan death squads: A U.S.-backed militia that kills children may be America's exit strategy from its longest war. *The Intercept*. https://theintercept.com/2020/12/18/afghanistan-cia-militia-01-strike-force/

R. v. Darteh, 233 Ontario Supreme Court of Justice. (2013).

Raybeck, D. (1991). Hard versus soft deviance: Anthropology and labeling theory. In M. Freilich, D. Raybeck, & J. Savishinsky (Eds.), *Deviance: Anthropological perspectives* (pp. 51–72). Bergin and Harvey.

Ringdal, N.J. (2004). *Love for sale: A world history of prostitution* (R. Daly, Trans.). Grove Press.

Roback, A.A. (1944). *A dictionary of international slurs: Ethnophaulisms, with a supplementary essay on aspects of ethnic prejudice*. Sci-Art Publishers.

Roberts, D.E. (1993). Racism and patriarchy in the meaning of motherhood. *Faculty Scholarship at Penn Law*, article 595. https://scholarship.law.upenn.edu/faculty_scholarship/595

Ross, J. (2018). What the #MeToo campaign teaches about stop and frisk. *Idaho Law Review*, *54*, article 9, 543–61. https://digitalcommons.law.uidaho.edu/idaho-law-review/vol54/iss2/9

Rowbotham, S. (1981). The trouble with "patriarchy." In R. Samuel (Ed.), *People's history and socialist theory* (pp. 364–69). Routledge.

Roy, J., & Marcellus, S. (2019). *Homicide in Canada, 2018* (Catalogue #85-002-XISSN 1209-6393). https://www150.statcan.gc.ca/n1/en/pub/85-002-x/2019001/article/00016-eng.pdf?st=u1mw-tao

Schäfer-Althaus, S. (2014). Painful pleasure: Saintly torture on the verge of pornography. *Mirabilia*, *18*(2014), 151–59. https://www.revistamirabilia.com/sites/default/files/pdfs/18-11_0.pdf

Scott, J.C. (1985). *Weapons of the weak: Everyday forms of peasant resistance*. Yale University Press.

Scott, J.C. (2008). *Against the grain: A deep history of the earliest states*. Yale University Press.

Sedensky, M., & Merchant, N. (2015, October 15). Hundreds of officers lose licenses over sex misconduct. *Associated Press*. https://apnews.com/article/fd1d4d05e561462a85abe50e7eaed4ec

Segal, R. (1995). *The Black diaspora*. Faber and Faber.

Sekyi-Otu, A. (1996). *Fanon's dialectic of experience*. Harvard University Press.

Sharpley-Whiting, T.D. (1996). Anti-Black femininity and mixed-race identity: Engaging Fanon to reread Capecia. In L.R. Gordon, T.D. Sharpley-Whiting, & R.T. White (Eds.), *Fanon: A critical reader* (pp. 155–62). Blackwell.

Shome, R. (2014). *Diana and beyond: White femininity, national identity, and contemporary media culture*. University of Illinois Press.

Sidanius, J., & Pratto, F. (1999). *Social dominance: An intergroup theory of social hierarchy and oppression*. Cambridge University Press.

Sidanius, J., & Veniegas, R.C. (2000). Gender and race discrimination: The interactive nature of disadvantage. In S. Oskamp (Ed.), *Reducing prejudice and discrimination: The Claremont Symposium on Applied Social Psychology* (pp. 47–69). Lawrence Erlbaum Associates.

Sivagurunathana, M., Orchard, T., MacDermid, J.C., & Evans, M. (2019). Barriers and facilitators affecting self-disclosure among male survivors of child sexual abuse: The service providers' perspective. *Child abuse & neglect, 88*, 455–65.

Slim, I. (1969/2011). *Pimp: The story of my life*. Cash Money Content.

Slotkin, J. (2020). California city residents demand answers after Black man found hanging from tree. *NPR*. https://www.npr.org/sections/live-updates-protests-for-racial-justice/2020/06/14/876807835/california-city-residents-demand-answers-after-black-man-found-hanging-from-tree

Smith, W.A., Hung, M., & Franklin, J.D. (2011). Racial battle fatigue and the miseducation of Black men: Racial microaggressions, societal problems, and environmental stress. *The Journal of Negro Education, 80*(1), 63–82. https://www.jstor.org/stable/41341106

Special Investigations Unit. (2013). *SIU concludes strip search investigation in Toronto.* https://www.siu.on.ca/en/news_template.php?nrid=1753

Spillers, H.J. (1987). Mama's baby, papa's maybe: An American grammar book. *Diacritics, 17*(2), 64–81. http://doi.org/10.2307/464747

Spongberg, M. (1997) Are small penises necessary for civilisation? The male body and the body politic. *Australian Feminist Studies*, 12(25), pp. 19–28. https://doi.org/10.1080/08164649.1997.9994838

Stannard, D.E. (1992). *American holocaust: The conquest of the New World*. Oxford University Press.

Stemple, L., & Meyer, I.H. (2014). The sexual victimization of men in America: New data challenge old assumptions. *American Journal of Public Health, 104*(1), 19–26.

Stemple, L., Flores, A., & Meyer, I. H. (2017). Sexual victimization perpetrated by women: Federal data reveal surprising prevalence. *Aggression and Violent Behavior, 34*, 302–11. https://doi.org/10.1016/j.avb.2016.09.007

Stroebe, K., Nijstad, B.A., & Hemelrijk, C.K. (2017). Female dominance in human groups: Effects of sex ratio and conflict level. *Social Psychological and Personality Science, 8*(2), 209–18. https://doi.org/10.1177/1948550616664956

Sweet, J.H. (2003). *Recreating Africa: Culture, kinship and religion in the African-Portuguese world, 1441–1770*. University of North Carolina Press.

Szasz, T. (1997). *The manufacture of madness: A comparative study of the inquisition and the mental health movement*. Syracuse University Press.

Teixeira, M. (2017). The plight of Afghanistan's dancing boys. *Words in a Bucket: Rethinking world thinking*. https://www.wordsinthebucket.com/the-plight-of-afghanistans-dancing-boys

Terkel, S. (1989). An interview with James Baldwin. In F.L. Standley & L.H. Pratt (Eds.), *Conversations with James Baldwin* (pp. 3–23). University Press of Mississippi. (Original interview published 1961)

Thomas, G. (2007). *The sexual demon of colonial power: Pan-African embodiment and erotic schemes of empire*. Indiana University Press.

Trexler, R.C. (1995). *Sex and conquest: Gendered violence, political order, and the European conquest of the Americas*. Cornell University Press.

Trott, D. (2017, July 5). Race play 101: My introduction into the world of racist sex play. *HuffPost*. http://www.huffingtonpost.com/entry/raceplay-101-my-introduction-into-the-world-of-racist_us_595b8fb7e4b0326c0a8d130a

Vilar, E. (1972). *The manipulated man*. Bantam Books.

Wagatsumo, H. (1967). The social perception of skin color in Japan. *Daedalus*, 96(2), 407–43. https://www.jstor.org/stable/20027045

Walker, B. (2010). *Race on trial: Black defendants in Ontario's criminal courts, 1858–1958*. University of Toronto Press.

Wallace, M. (1979). *The Black macho and the myth of the superwoman*. Dial.

Ware, V. (1992). *Beyond the pale: White women, racism, and history*. Verso.

Watkins, D. (2019, April 20). "Straight Black men are trash": Do I have to agree? *Salon*. https://www.salon.com/2019/04/20/straight-black-men-are-trash-do-i-have-to-agree/

Waytz, A., Hoffman, K.M., & Trawalter, S. (2014). A superhumanization bias in Whites' perceptions of Blacks. *Social Psychological and Personality Science*, 6(3), 352–59. https://doi.org/10.1177/1948550614553642

Wells, I.B. (2010). *Ida B. Wells versus Judge Lynch: The anti-lynching trilogy* (J.H. Mitchell, Ed.). CreateSpace Independent Publishing Platform.

Whitehead, Paul. (2019, August 10). Epstein documents: Accuser names powerful elites in alleged sex ring. *NeonNettle.com*. https://neonnettle.com/news/8431-epstein-documents-accuser-names-powerful-elites-in-alleged-sex-ring

Wilford, H. (2008). *The mighty wurlitzer: How the CIA played America*. Harvard University Press.

Williams, J.E., & Carter, D.J. (1967). Connotations of racial concepts and color names in Germany. *The Journal of Social Psychology*, 72(1), 19–26. doi.org/10.1080/00224545.1967.9922295

Winbush, R.A. (2002). *The warrior method: A parents' guide to rearing healthy Black boys*. HarperCollins.

Wong, J.C. (2020, December 27). The year of Karen: how a meme changed the way Americans talked about racism. *The Guardian*. https://www.theguardian.com/world/2020/dec/27/karen-race-white-women-black-americans-racism

Woodard, V. (2014). *The delectable Negro: Human consumption and homoeroticism within U.S. slave culture* (J.A. Joyce, D.A. McBride, & E.P. Johnson, Eds.). New York University Press.

Wynter, S. (1994). "No humans involved": An open letter to my colleagues. *Forum N.H.I.: Knowledge for the 21st Century, 1*(1), 42–73. https://libcom.org/files/Wynter5.pdf

Young, D. (2017, September 19). Straight Black men are the White people of Black people. *The Root*. https://verysmartbrothas.theroot.com/straight-black-men-are-the-white-people-of-black-people-1814157214

Erotic Racism, Tropes, and Interracial Sex

Art, Nations, and Transnationalism

1

Can the Black Man Be Nude in a Culture That Imagines Him as Naked?

A Baldwinian and Fanonian Psychosexual Reading of Black Masculinity in "Western" Art and Cinema

TAMARI KITOSSA

It is so simple a fact and one that is so hard, apparently, to grasp: Whoever debases others is debasing himself.

—JAMES BALDWIN, *The Fire Next Time*

The collective unconscious is not dependent on cerebral heredity; it is the result of what I shall call the unreflected imposition of a culture.

—FRANTZ FANON, *Black Skin, White Masks*

FOR JAMES BALDWIN AND FRANTZ FANON, it takes work for the beneficiaries of colonialist and racist social formations to unknowingly experience sexual innocence. The work of propagating erotic tropes and representations of the Other occurs through language, representation, and symbology—the very essence of culture. The representation of Black[1] men in "Western"[2] art and cinema reifies the hegemonic cultural perception that they are hypersexual, priapic, and prone to be rapists. For James Baldwin and Frantz Fanon, this tripartite trope constitutes a part of the psychosexual furniture of Western (and other Asiatic) cultures.[3]

The central thesis of this chapter is that to explain the material basis for the oppression and endangerment of Black men in the West, we must attend to the persistent recycling of sexual mythologies about them through art and other cultural media such as photography and cinema. Baldwin (1955/1984, 1962/1985a, 1972, 1976) and Fanon (1952/1977) direct attention to the role of cultural media as both crucial agents in the formation of psychologies and as frameworks for practices of erotic and sexual racism. As critical interpreters of culture, Baldwin and Fanon keenly understood the implicit, intuitive, and unconscious role of the sexual principle that channels aggression and makes cooperation among the eligible of a dominative "in-group" possible. Like them, and others they have inspired (Hoch, 1979; Kovel, 1971), I undertake what Walter Abell (1957/1966) calls a "depth psychology" approach to art and representation in a given culture.[4]

I suggest elsewhere that the murder of George Floyd demands a reading that places sexual psychopathology at the centre of explanatory accounts of White police and vigilante murders of Black people (Kitossa, 2020). In this chapter, my argument is that the construction, circulation, and recycling of sexualized representations of Black men in art and cinema provides the ontogenic basis for White psychosexual rationalizations of Black men's ritual degradation and destruction. I tease out how the tripartite trope—which I call the Black Phallic Fantastic—of Black men supposed being hypersexual, priapic, and prone to rape White women is the subtext in the representations of Black men as naked and as forces who undermine social civility. My "data" are representations of the Black Phallic Fantastic in artistic expression from antiquity through to still photography and Hollywood cinema in the contemporary period. I seek to demonstrate that both this trope and the methods of its representation are fertile ground for psychoanalytic meditation on the psychosexual life of the White individual and collective ontology. I suggest a more complex and nuanced understanding of the playing out of desire and fantasy alongside the exercise of power, and how this leads to the breaking of Black men's bodies through a simultaneous fear of and pornographic desire for them. This understanding rests on the recognition of the mundane and persistent nakedness of Black male bodies, even when clothed, in the White cultural imaginary.

After surveying prior iterations of the Black Phallic Fantastic in antiquity, I will apply Baldwin's and Fanon's insights—specifically, those about the cultural utility of erotic racist tropes about Black men and their relevance to hegemonic White masculinity and White supremacy—to examples from contemporary art and cinema. I will centre my attention on the work of Robert Mapplethorpe and on contemporary films such as *Heart Condition* (1990), *Any Given Sunday* (1999), *Hall Pass* (2001), and *The Heartbreak Kid* (2007). Finally, to account for the psychosexual meanings and quotidian reproduction of the tripartite White cultural mythology of Black men as hypersexual, priapic, and prone to rape White women, I will undertake a detailed critique of D.W. Griffith's *Birth of a Nation* (1915), a film adaptation of Thomas Dixon's 1905 novel *The Clansman*.

Historiographic Sketch of the Black Phallic Fantastic in "Western" Culture

To expose the worldview that scripts the psychosexual narratives of the Black Phallic Fantastic in contemporary Western art and cinema as a site for the critical interpretation of hegemonic White masculinity (gay and straight), it is necessary to show that the White fascination[5] with its own construction of Black masculinity has an anterior existence. From Greece and Rome to contemporary European cultures, the tripartite trope that constitutes the Black Phallic Fantastic is what A.A. Roback (1944) called an "ethnophaulism"—a racial stereotype that applies to a single racial group. This is in part because the devil is imagined as a Black man (Baldwin, 1955/1984; Fanon, 1952/1977; Hood, 1994; Lyons, 1975; Washington, 1984). Tying those who are perceived as culturally threatening with the devil has a long history in Western culture. In the late-Medieval period, libels spread of Jews consorting with the devil and Jewish men raping Christian women; these libels were later revived by the Nazis (see Fanon, 1952/1977; Hoch, 1979). But what of the "devil" himself?

While they did not invent the myth of the priapic Black man, third-century rabbinic scholars did invent the curse of Ham—a story that has long been used to explain black skin and to justify slavery—and introduced Black priapism into Judeo-Christian iconography (Brackman, 1977).[6] Note, too, in the story of Ham, how the "shame" of blackness of skin—owing to Ham's reputed sexual impropriety, which further resulted in the curse of an elongated penis—was not only further visited on his descendant Canaan, but centres squarely on males as signifiers for *all* Black people.

Prior to the rabbins, as early as the second century CE, Galen, the Greek and Roman slave physician so highly esteemed by the West and restored to the West by enterprising early Medieval Jewish intellectuals (Brackman, 1977, p. 87), presaged the race "science" of the nineteenth century. Galen, as Chaikh Anta Diop (1991) observes, "reduced the characteristic traits of the Black person to two, 1) inordinate length of his penis, 2) hilarity, strong propensity for laughter" (p. 216). Brackman (1977), paraphrasing Galen, notes:

> In all host countries, Galen concluded, [Black] men suffer from an excess of overheated "black bile"[7] that causes them to grow up "dry, slender, and as it were skeletonized"—and which also accounts for their tendency toward intellectual and emotional instability. The Negro, however, suffers from this debilitating syndrome in its most extreme form. To it are attributable his crinkly hair, meager growth of beard, large nostrils, and thick lips, as well as his frivolous disposition, hypersexuality, and lack of cultural attainments.[8] (p. 86)

Influenced by Galen's "medical" anthropology, Harold Brackman (1977) suggests that it is very likely that the rabbins cast the elements of Ham's physiology (blackness of skin and elongated penis) in terms of religious etiology (p. 87)—but where the rabbins drew on Zoroastrianism and Hinduism and saw immoral essence in "black skin" and sexuality, Galen drew on the anthropological propositions of Pliny the Elder (Washington, 1984, p. 110) and Ptolemy (Jordan, 1977, p. 34). Galen thus saw physical traits as matters of geography that affect morality—a point that would later be developed by Immanuel Kant during the European Enlightenment into "moral geography" (Eze, 1995, p. 214). According to Galen, people in hot environments had hot constitutions, people in cold climates had moral and physical characteristics (i.e., frigidity) that corresponded to the icy temperatures, and those who lived in the "balanced" climes of the Mediterranean were the most even-keeled of all (Brackman, 1979; see also Thompson, 1989). This environmental theory of race would continue hold sway into the twentieth century as countries including Canada sought to exclude African American and African Caribbean migrants on the grounds that their "normal" milieu made them ill-suited for northerly climates (Foster, 2019). While, as noted by Brackman (1977), the "Roman physician [Galen] and the Jewish rabbins shared an aversion to black humanity transcending the differences between the mediums of science and myth in which they chose to express it" (p. 86), this is not really the point. Rather, it is that the "Renaissance" and "Enlightenment" retrieval of Greek and Roman race science amplified the more steady and continuous disparagement of anti-Blackness in Judeo-Christianity. As suggested by Baldwin (1985b) and Fanon (1952/1977), both forms of cultural media—art (understood here as a mode of psychosocial training) and religion—constitute(d) the fundamental dimensions of an erotic epidermal timocracy[9] that mirrored material, hence sexual, dominance of Black men in what has become the "West."

Greeks, the Satyr, and the Black Phallic Fantastic

In fifth and sixth century BCE—earlier than the eras of either Galen or the rabbins—Athenian art began to represent satyrs in plays, effigy, and speculative philosophy explicitly as ithyphallic Africans (Hood, 1994, p. 27). In Greek mythology, the satyr is a beast-man with the head and torso of a man and the four-hoofed body and genitalia of a horse. Dominque Mannoni (cited in Fanon, 1952/1977; see also Baldwin, 1972; Girard, 1989;[10] Szasz,1974/2003) identifies the satyr as an outward projection onto a scapegoat. The actual or ritual sacrifice of this satyr-scapegoat constituted an ancient symbol of expiation for guilt and wrong-doing.[11] However much scapegoating is a sociological process for maintaining order, it is also deeply psychological. As Mannoni (cited in Fanon, 1952/1977) correctly says, it is a as a signifier of neurosis and civilizational crisis, a process that involves projecting the chaos and unruliness within, that ultimately manifests as a method for negotiating difference:

> In his urge to identify the anthropoid apes, Caliban, the Negroes, even the Jews with the mythological figures of the satyr, man[12] reveals there are sensitive spots in the human soul at a level where thought becomes confused and where sexual excitement is strangely linked with violence and aggressiveness. (pp. 165–66)

The very existence of the scapegoat, in the form of targeted groups or individuals marked by some perceived defect that transforms their identity from an "us-like person" into an "animal" or an "Other" (Goffman, 1963), is perceived to be constitutive of a sign or symbol of bad luck or social catastrophe. The subsequent necessity of expiation calls for the everyday cognitive, psychological, and social distancing of the scapegoat, when not their actual murder. The procedure of a "ceremony of ritual degradation" (Garfinkel, 1956), which occurs after an appropriate target has been blamed and selected, sets the stage for morality drama that marks off rightness and wrongness, defenders of order from enemies who endanger it. The end result is the actual or symbolic sacrifice of the scapegoat, a "guarantee" of the restoration of the order of things.

In the Greek context, which took geography as the basis for intelligence and moral sobriety, it was thought that the heat of Africa not only "burned the skin," but also heated the blood to lusty temperatures. Some Greek scholars opined that lusty satyrs originated in the interior of Africa (Hood, 1994, p. 28).[13] Eva Keuls (1985) notes the that the satyr "has a snub-nosed face and a tail and that perennial satyr's attribute, a huge erect penis, which, of course, to the Greeks was a sign not of manhood but of bestiality" (p. 360)—and indeed, on some Greek vases, anticipating the European Medieval bestiary, satyrs sometimes appeared as debauching apes (Beardsley, 1929/1979, p. 59). Frequently, the ithyphallic satyr was

FIGURE 1.1: Head of an Afrioid satyr on an Attic vase. (Reproduced with permission from National Museum of Denmark [Inventory number ChrVIII88].)

represented as molesting, seducing, or raping "maenads" (mad women, apparently sex crazed) or "nymphs" (Keuls, 1985). In short, the chief function of the satyr was to signify the barbarous status of African men *and* to represent a morality tale for disciplining recalcitrant women.[14]

The Greeks valued semen as that which contained wisdom and idealized the penis that transmitted it. Plato, for instance, explicitly understood the penis (and sex, for that matter) as the medium that unifies religion and science (i.e., philosophy). He regarded the spinal marrow—understood as the source of both the brain and of semen—as the site of the divine in humans. The attitude of the Greeks toward the male organ and sex in itself was complex—ambiguous, ambivalent, multivalent. The penis and the sex act were are seen as the source from which generative male creativity and genius "gushed," communicating manly essence, particularly in the pederastic relationship. But they were, simultaneously, means for imposing domination and degradation (Friedman, 2001; Trexler, 1995). Both must be understood in the context that the expansionist and imperialistic Hellenic city states gave them.

On one hand, colossal phallic representations of penises abounded through the various Hellenic city states (Friedman, 2001). They functioned as talismans for protection and prosperity. But David Friedman (2001) notes that "[i]n real life, as opposed to parade floats, Greeks favoured a small thin penis, as on an adolescent exercising at the gymnasium" (p. 22). For aesthetic and ideological reasons (the two cannot be separated) good to them, the Greeks placed a premium on smaller rather than larger penises, preferring them symbolically when not practically. Aristotle, for example, believed that smaller penises were best for procreation, keeping the "seed of wisdom" hot upon ejaculation. A longer penis, it was believed, cooled and therefore diminished the potency of that vital and divine fluid (Friedman, 2001, p. 22; see also Keuls, 1985). Given that pederasty was a rite of passage, often with elites vying to have their sons trained into manhood by responsible, high-status males, smaller penises signified youthfulness in a culture obsessed with looking young (Friedman, 2001, p. 23–25). From an aesthetic perspective, the Greek preoccupation with the beauty of the male form further insisted on representations of "dainty" penises so as to accentuate the symmetry of the ideal masculine form (Keuls, 1985).[15]

On the other hand, in a culture that separated mind and body and emphasized rationality and reason as the hallmarks of civilization and high culture, the penis (both large and enlarged) and sex were understood as inherently unstable. David Friedman (2001) shows that in the *Timaeus*, Plato opined that the divine fluid is elementally unstable—having "a vital impulse to gush forth" (p. 22). Consequently, the penis is potentially an instrument for tragedy. According Plato, the penis—having a mind of its own—can be "disobedient and self-willed" (Friedman, 2001, p. 22). Friedman quotes Albert Henrichs, a historian of Ancient Greece, claiming of the Greeks in general and Plato in particular that "erections are signs of a physiological and mental condition...that Plato identified as 'divine madness'" (p. 21). The danger of the penis is that it threatens constant conspiracy with the irrepressible cosmic force housed in the spinal column. Signifying the moral defect of uncontrolled (sexual) passion, which is unbecoming for "civilized" Greeks trained through pederasty to use rationality and reason to direct the flow of the restive divine force, large penises and uncontrolled sexuality were projected outward onto the barbarous Other.[16] The assignment of demerit for large penises and uncontrolled sexuality are not absolute, however—not least in a militarist social order, as was the case in the 500-year period of Hellenistic imperialism and warmongering. Richard Trexler (1995), for example, reproduces an Attic vase commemorating the 466 BCE Greek defeat of the Persians at the battle of Eurymedon. It depicts a Hellenic victor holding his erect penis thrusted toward the rear of a penniless[17] and defeated Persian. The latter proclaims, "I am Eurymedon, I stand bent over" (p. 15). Citing experts on the topic, Trexler translates this proud claim of the Hellenes into more modern language: "We've fucked the Womanish Persians" (p. 14).

The Roman Black Phallic Fantastic

The phallus, as noted by Thomas DiPiero (2002), is an ancient symbol with multiple connotations from fertility to protection, power, and punishment. The Greeks scorned all who were not Greek using a linguistic epithet—*bar-bar*— meant to ridicule the speech of non-Greeks, but it was sex, sexuality, and the phallus that were the primary media by which civilization and barbarism were determined. For the Greeks—and, subsequently, for the Romans—the projection of large penises onto representations of barbarians signified not only physical ugliness and uncontrolled sexuality, but their subordinate, "animal," enslaveable, and less-than-human status. Unlike the Greeks, however, the Romans loved big dicks—on themselves, anyway. Believing the Greek valorization of the dainty penis to be effete, the Romans valued massive penises in art and on the Roman person.

Aesthetically, axiologically, and physically, Romans loved penises; penile phalluses signified Roman power. Indeed, it was not uncommon for Roman generals to promote soldiers if they had large penises, and at least one Roman emperor, Commodus, elevated a prodigiously endowed soldier to "a special pagan priesthood" (Friedman, 2001, p. 28). Rome was a ribald culture that thrilled to the bigness of the erect penis—not least because the god *Fascinus* (see note 5) was an important deity signifying the potency of imperial Rome (see Friedman, 2001). For Romans, the penis was a principle of power: a sword, a club, a battering ram; a protuberance signalling the pleasure of sexual violence (regardless of the partner's pleasure). For this latter purpose, the bigger the better, because sex, defined by violent entry, manifested virility, twinning Eros (Venus) with militarized violence (Mars), as is dramatically revealed in the Coliseum's orgy of violence (Friedman, 2001). This, of course, did not translate into a respect for the supposedly priapic African male, who continued to be the subject of comedy and disparagement meant to demonstrate their lack the civilizational qualities necessary for the responsible use of such a prodigious member. A large penis on those already considered to be "barbarians" signalled to the Romans not virility and power but deformity and depravity—as well as, paradoxically, also magical totems for fecundity.

The Roman reverence for massive penises, however, had added twists. So prized were large penises, that the term *invidia*—envy of another man's wealth—also connoted jealousy of men with large penises. Whereas Christians made envy one of the deadly sins, for Romans it was the obverse: it was not the person as a whole, but the object of envy itself that could be afflicted with bad luck, illness, or death. Indeed, the *bulla*, a locket worn by elite youth that contained a replica of a penis or an eye, were intended to repel *invidia*. However, Roman baths, as David Friedman (2001) argues, were spaces that allowed men with large penises to strut and expose their personal power; they were also, all across the empire, generously decorated with beautiful frescoes of macrophallic African males. This was not because the Roman's loved African males; rather, like Gothic Churches that position gargoyles on parapets, or like the miniature black, lantern-holding statuary

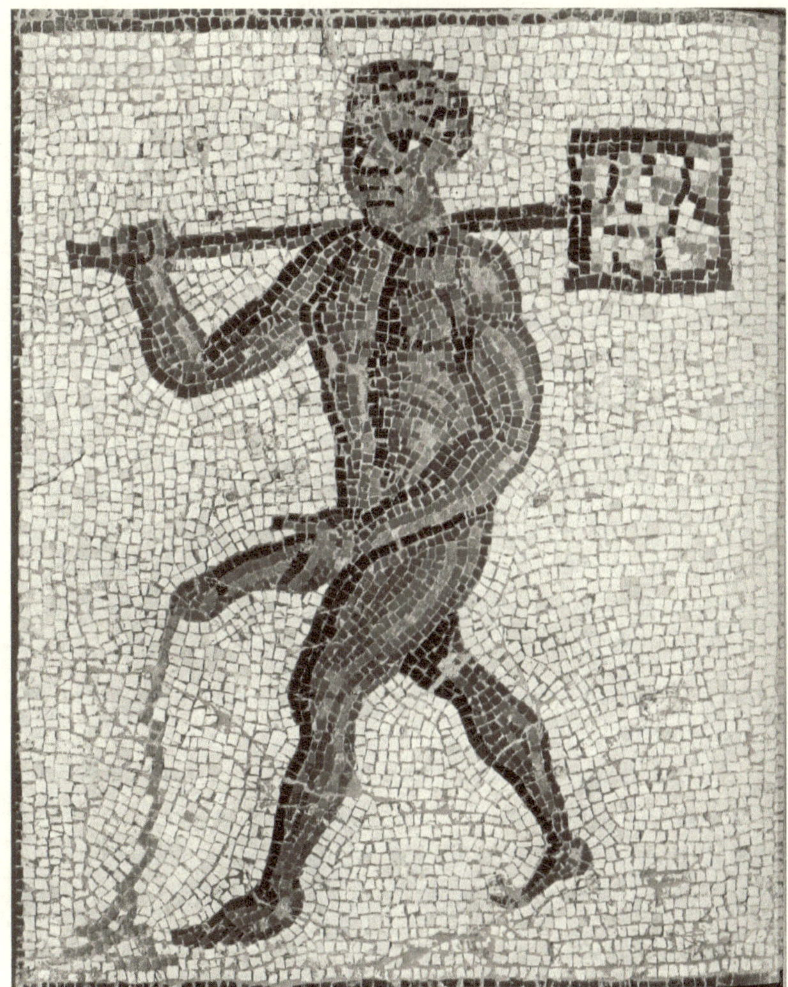

FIGURE 1.2: Tiled image of a Black bath attendant with an enormous penis.

(Reproduced as "black bath attendant" in Snowdon [1976] #347, p. 256, © Centre National de Recherche en Archéologie, Algerie.)

of twentieth-century Canada and the United States, it was a sign of both irony and incantation. Ithyphallic African frescoes were both charms for warding off evil and welcoming fertility, and comedic signifiers of cultural and racial difference: means of psychologically reinforcing the superiority of "balanced" (i.e., *medi*-terranean, middle-earthly) Romans over the frigid Northerners (e.g., Gauls) and over-sexed Southerners (e.g., Western Ethiopians, Africans).

The Black Phallic Fantastic and Christianity

The tripartite construction of African men's sexuality—the Black Phallic Fantastic—was not exclusive to Greeks, Romans, and Talmudists, but was also present in early Christian iconography and theology. The early tutelage of North African and European Christians by rabbinic scholars (Washington, 1984) and the anti-Blackness and sexual asceticism of St. Augustine and other desert fathers (Hood, 1994) merged with the Greco-Roman conception of sexualized moral geography about Africans (or Ethiopians, as they were termed).[18] As noted by African American theologian Richard Hood (1994), "the hierarchy of color in early Christianity enlarged the Greco-Roman aesthetic of blackness and endowed it with a moral disadvantage" (p. 87). Primarily, that "disadvantage" of skin colour connoted sexual impropriety. Where the ancients framed African men as appealing and appalling in the context of their reverence for the penis-as-phallus, early Christian "desert fathers" saw in the conquest of the sexual drive a victory over the Devil and demons. Unsurprisingly, such monstrosities came in the form of Africans boys, girls, men, and women (Brakke, 2001; Byron, 2002; Hood, 1994). The Devil's colour, though sometimes represented as blue or red, was often represented as Black-skinned; he was also often depicted with a two-foot-long penis, and described as having scales (Friedman, 2001).[19] The so-called desert fathers profoundly shaped the deepening of this trope into the sociogenesis of the West (Brakke 2001; Byron 2002; Hood 1994).[20]

Shakespeare and the Elizabethan Black Phallic Fantastic

With Christendom's construction of Europe as a cultural and political entity, ideas of anti-Blackness and its association with sexual opprobrium were suffused throughout the culture. For example, in the theatre—the cinema of its day—one finds the reinforcement of religious iconography and sexual tropes about Black men. Charles Lyons (1975), for example, notes: "In Elizabethan poetry, drama, and common speech the Black man was generally referred to as a lecher, a degenerate, a devil, an animal" (p. 1; see also Hall, Chapter 4 in this volume). In the opening act of *Othello*, for example,

Shakespeare (1975) has the spiteful Iago attempt to incite Desdemona's father, Brabantio, to rage with the taunt:

> Zounds, sir, you're robb'd; for shame, put on your gown;
> Your heart is burst, you have lost half your soul;
> Even now, now, very now, an old black ram
> Is tupping your white ewe. Arise, arise;
> Awake the snoring citizens with the bell,
> Or else the devil will make a gransire of you:
> Arise I say. (p. 1114)

Brabantio is, at first, unmoved by Iago's barb, but Iago has the stopper: "[Y]ou'll have your daughter covered with a Barbary horse," and "your daughter and the Moor are now making the beast with two backs" (1975, p. 114). The imagery of bestial coitus and, most certainly, Desdemona's vaginal rupture from copulation with the horse-like Othello, compels Brabantio to rouse from his casual tolerance of the interracial affair and rescind his consent.[21]

By applying a Fanonian psychoanalytic interpretation to this scene, we see that Shakespeare initially presents Brabantio as a nonneurotic, nonincestuous, nonracist White man, free of the taint of the genital fixation of the Black-man-as-penis. But this is the very possibility that Shakespeare seeks to refuse. Indeed, Shakespeare seeks to establish a different "norm": that Brabantio is pathological *for being* nonracist and nonincestuous. In doing so, Shakespeare establishes for us the (racist) norm by default. A deep psychoanalytic reading reveals Shakespeare's preoccupation with suggesting that nothing good can come of intimacy between a White woman and a Black man.

Here I suggest a turn to Fanon's (1952/1977) *Black Skin, White Masks* is fruitful. What arises is the question of White fathers and the incestuous protection of their daughters, not so much as individuals but as actors in the epidermal reproduction of culture. Fanon seeks to shift the terms of the debate from the entirely speculative presumption of White-father-to-White-daughter incest by asking:

> Granted that unconscious tendencies toward incest exist, why should these tendencies emerge more particularly with respect to the Negro? In what way, taken as an absolute, does a black son-in-law differ from a white son-in-law? In both cases, isn't there an emergence of unconscious tendencies? Is there not a reaction of unconscious tendencies in both cases? Why not, for instance, conclude that the father revolts because in his opinion the Negro will introduce his daughter into a sexual universe for which the father has neither the key, the weapons, or the attributes? (p. 165)

For Fanon, the more plausible and empirically verifiable conclusion draws us toward the evidence of anti-Black-man racist fantasmic psychosexual projection and scapegoating:

> Every intellectual gain requires a loss of sexual potential. The civilized white man retains an irrational longing for unusual eras of sexual license, of orgiastic scenes, of unpunished rapes, of unrepressed incest. In one way these fantasies correspond to Freud's life instinct. Projecting his own desires onto the Negro, the white man behaves "as if" the Negro really had them. (p. 165)

Baldwin (1962/1985a) advances a similar interpretation: "The white man's unadmitted—and apparently, to him, unspeakable—private fears and longings are projected onto the Negro" (p. 129). We shall see that this thesis is also applicable to the makers of contemporary Hollywood films, not least Thomas Dixon and D.W. Griffith, the makers of *The Birth of a Nation*.

Winthrop Jordan (1968/1977) shows that Shakespeare's representations were those, psychologically, of English culture. Early English adventurers merged the religious myth of Ham's sexual opprobrium and priapism with their own commercial and "scientific" justifications for African enslavement. He notes that:

> Elizabethan travelers and literati spoke very explicitly of Negroes as being especially sexual. Othello's embraces were the "gross clasps of a lascivious Moor."...Negro men, reported a seventeenth-century traveler, sported "large propagators." (p. 34).

The Black Phallic Fantastic and the Slave Trade

While the English may have created fanciful stories, their narratives were not made in the context of penis envy and hence the grotesque desire to do violence and to castrate and possess the offending body part. That was reserved for the slave plantation. In a context of *invidia* and of reaction formation in the White male psyche, Jordan (1968/1977) cites portions of a 1718 letter written by an officer of the First Pennsylvania Regiment:

> I am surprized this does not hurt the feelings of the fair Sex to see these young boys of about Fourteen and Fifteen years Old to Attend them. these [*sic*] whole nakedness Expos'd and I can Assure you It would Surprise a person to see these d—d black boys[22] how well they are hung. (p. 159)

It was not unusual for enslaved Black boys, without trousers, to be made to wait the tables of their masters. An embittered Frederick Douglass rued the fact that it was routine for Black boys up to the end of puberty to be made to wander and work on plantations without trousers (Woodard, 2014). Jordan (1968/1977) cites further macabre evidence of this pathological fascination: Johann Blumenbach, founder of craniology, comparative anatomy, modern anthropology and coiner of the term "Caucasian," asserted that:

> It is generally said that the penis in the Negro is very large. And this assertion is so far borne out by the remarkable genitory apparatus of an Aethiopian *which I have in my anatomical collection* [emphasis added]. Whether this prerogative be constant and peculiar to the nation I do not know. It is said that [White] women when eager for venery prefer the embraces of Negroes to those of other men. (n. 46, p. 158–59)

Charles White, member of the Royal Society and a respected authority on midwifery on both sides of the Atlantic (Lyons, 1975, p. 33), commented as follows in his widely read 1799 tract *An Account of the Regular Gradations of Man*: "That the PENIS of an African is larger than that of an European... has, I believe, been shown in every anatomical school in London. Preparations of them are preserved in most anatomical museums; and I have one in mine" (cited in Jordan, 1977, p. 501). And into the twentieth century, one the founding theorists of sexology, Havelock Ellis, opined, as much to disparage Black men as to ridicule the sexual autonomy of White women, that:

> I am informed that the sexual power of Negroes and [their] slower ejaculation are the cause of the favour in which they are viewed by some white women of strong sexual passions in America...At one time there was a special house in New York City to which white women resorted for these "buck lovers." The women came heavily veiled and would inspect the penises of the men before making their selection. (cited in Friedman, 2001, p. 119)

Fanon (1952/1977) notes that so persistent and prevalent is the presumption that Black men are priapic that all credible scientific efforts to refute it have failed. He cites a number of examples of high-profile contemporary (for his time) European intellectuals. One of the most notable was French journalist and screenwriter Michel Cournot, who reflects the pathologic fixation of White men (and women) with the tripartite trope of Black men. Redolent of the satyr in Greek mythology whose double function was to signify the barbarian (as Black man) and to discipline the (White) woman, erotic racism against Black men merges with the murderous, misogynistic desire to punish the White "goddess"/woman[23] in Cournot's writing:

> The black man's sword is a sword. When he has thrust it into your wife, she has really felt something. It is a revelation. In the chasm that is left, your little toy is lost. Pump away until the room is awash with your sweat, you might as well be singing. This is *good-by*....Four Negroes with their

> penises exposed would fill a cathedral. They would be unable to leave the building until their erections had subsided; and in such close quarters that would not be a simple matter.[24] (cited in Fanon, 1952/1977, p. 169)

Inasmuch as Fanon draws attention to the simultaneous elevation and degradation of White women, this is linked to Cournot's deploying the trope of the priapic Black man to ritually degrade the White woman. Inasmuch as the construction of this mythology does multivalent work in the White male imagination, Fanon asserts the White woman is not its victim. Drawing on his personal experience in Lyon, the city in which he lived between 1948 to 1952, Fanon asserts that such imagery stimulates curiosity and erotic terror in young White women:

> When one reads this passage a dozen times and lets oneself go—that is, when one abandons oneself to the movement of its images—one is no longer aware of the Negro but only of a penis; the Negro is eclipsed. He is turned into a penis. It is easy to imagine what such descriptions can stimulate in a young girl in Lyon. Horror? Desire? Not indifference, in any case. So what is the truth? (pp. 169–70)

Fanon takes the trouble to show the ridiculousness of Cournot's claim by citing the empirical research of experts who demolish presumptions that penis size is linked to region, race, or colour. As is shown by John Russell (Chapter 2 of this volume), the mythology that there is a connection between race and penis size remains largely intact. He shows also that scholars such as Philippe Rushton and his ilk have sustained the shameful mythology under the veneer of scholarship.

As Baldwin (1976) shows from his experience, White men, both gay and straight, want to possess African-descended men's penises not just in pickle jars. He writes in *No Name in the Street*, that:

> I have never, for example, written about my unbelieving shock when I realized that I was being groped by one of the most powerful men in one of

the states I visited....drunk... *With his wet eyes staring up at my face, and his wet hands groping for my cock, we were both, abruptly in history's ass-pocket* [emphasis added]. It was very frightening—not the gesture itself, but the abjectness of it, and the assumption of a swift and grim complicity: *as my identity was defined by his power, so was my humanity to be placed at the service of his fantasies...And it is absolutely certain that white men, who invented the nigger's big black prick, are still at the mercy of this nightmare, and are still, for the most part, doomed, in one way or another, to attempt to make this prick their own* [emphasis added]. (p. 61–63)

As I showed in the Introduction to this book, Baldwin notes in works such as "Going To Meet the Man" and *Just Above My Head*, that the colour of a Black man's penis *is* its size. This reductionism of Black men to their penises, and the presumption that the darker their skin the larger their penis, enables both desire and revulsion—a fact which makes sexual authenticity in the White world, whether the Black man is virtual or real, an act of radical resistance.

The Black Phallic Fantastic in Contemporary Western Art and Film

Both James Baldwin (1972) and Frantz Fanon (1952/1977) alert us to the symbolization of the bodies of Black men as reducible to their penises. Deeply embedded in the religion and science of Western culture, sexual mythologies about Black men are both overdetermined and indispensable for White ontological conceptions of civilization, rationality, and reason. Reflecting on the reduction of Black men to their penises as signs of the id in hegemonic White ontology, Kobena Mercer (1994) writes that few are not invested in perpetuating it:

> One might say that despite anatomical evidence to the contrary, the belief symbolized in the fantasy of the big black willy—that black male sexuality is not only "different," but somehow "more"—is a fantasy that many people, black and white, men and women, gay and straight, continue to cling on to and do not wish to give up because it retains currency and force as an

element in the psychic reality of the social relations in which our gendered and racial identities have been historically constructed. (pp. 190–91)

Thus if, as Jacques Le Goff (1985) approvingly cites Ernest Labrousse as saying, "the social changes more slowly than the economic, and the mental more slowly than the social" (p. 167), then it is vital to imagine that the visual arts reflect subconscious workings-out at the core of White hegemonic masculinity—be it gay or straight. In this section, I draw on John Berger's (1973) conceptualization of the distinction between "nakedness" and "nudity," and on Freud's concept of scopophilia (S. Hall, 1997)—concepts vital to the archaeology of a depth psychology of the Black Phallic Fantastic in Western art and cinema—to reinforce Baldwin's and Fanon's critical account of the psychosexual implications of sexualized spectacles of Black men's bodies.

Robert Mapplethorpe

The "high" art of Robert Mapplethorpe is a classic statement on the *re*production and normalizing of the Black penis myth. Mapplethorpe's fascination with the genitalia of Black men is not his alone. He challenges with his representations the guilt of knowing what is knowingly unknown, which is that Black men are reduced to the *sign* of the penis of the enemy. The visceral nature of his work opens up the necessity to think through the many ways that, from slavery to the present, heterosexual, gay, and transgender Black men are sexually exploited by White men, women, and culture in the representational schema of White erotic desire. Mapplethorpe's work reminds us that Baldwin and Fanon already made it impossible to disavow that, a priori, the Black man, as an artifact of White cultural ontology, exists in the mental architecture and field of vision as an erect, dangerous, threatening, and pleasuring penis. There is, in effect, a quality of public display about the body of Black men that eternally fixes on them the sexualized gaze of others. This is a gaze that permanently imagines them as *naked*, even when fully clothed, since there is a snickering secret about him that "everybody" knows, a presumed fact that makes redundant the guilty question, "So, is it true?"

Seeking to account for the ways in which the racial Other is constituted and hegemonic meanings are circulated and reified in the White cultural imaginary, as well as how the foregoing are disrupted and resisted by the Black Other, Stuart Hall (1997) amplifies John Berger's (1973) distinction between *nakedness* and *nudity*, adding to it Sigmund Freud's concept of scopophilia.[25] Hall asserts that the act of looking can have a sexual, erotic aspect to it, suggesting that looking is itself motivated by an unconscious, or at least unacknowledged, search for an unfulfillable, illicit desire. But since fulfillment is multiple, what if "looking" at, or "fixing" the gaze on—which is to say, fetishizing—Black men's genitals, because he *is* his genitals, constitutes, in and of itself, erotic fulfillment? What if the Black Phallic Fantastic is one grand regime of collective voyeurism, where pleasure becomes guilt only upon insisting on the deconstruction of this reductionism?

Here I am seeking to establish the distinction John Berger (1973) established between the concepts of "naked" and "nude." The former unclothedness is for oneself alone, backstage, as it were, where the only other person is the unclothed self in the mirror. The latter is the act of *voluntarily* becoming a subject to be re-presented by another. Between subject-turned-object, representer, and audience is the aesthetics and politics of accommodation, challenge, disruption, play, reification, resistance, and the undermining of the hegemony of taken-for-granted meanings of Black men's bodies-as-penises. Admiring, consuming, gazing at, looking at, and meditating on the "subject"-turned-"object" constitutes the framework for eroticized spectacle, which enables a mélange of affectations—attraction, desire, disgust, revulsion, wonder—whose function is to facilitate a (critical) psychosocial engagement with hegemonic performances of self, demands of the Other, and commitments to the extant social order (Berger, 1973).

A multiplicity of meanings are produced by the violence of the artist's "capturing" and "shooting" of their subject-turned-object for public consumption—meanings that put into question the voluntariness of the contract of consensus between the subject-turned-object and the representer that the Other is nude rather than naked. Baldwin (1955/1984,

1965/1998, 1972) and Fanon (1952/1977) suggest that the representational regime in which Black men are constituted demands, if any of us are to be liberated from it, the acknowledgement and confrontation of the delusions, desires, harms, fulfillment, and manipulation this regime enables. Thus Fanon insists on starting from the vantage point of Black men being enslaved by the gaze that imagines their nakedness, stripping them of the ability to consent to nudity. Here, Richard Philcox's translation of *Black Skin, White Masks* apprehends through visceral metaphors the quality of anguish at one's body being made to serve others:

> Locked in this suffocating reification, I appealed to the Other so that his liberating gaze, gliding over my body suddenly smoothed of rough edges, would give me back the lightness of being I thought I had lost, and taking me out of the world put me back in the world. But just as I get to the other slope I stumble, and the Other fixes me with his gaze, his gestures and attitude, the same way you fix a preparation with a dye. I lose my temper, demand an explanation. Nothing doing. (Fanon, 1952/2008, p. 89)

What representational strategies make it possible for Black men to be human enough to be nude, rather than naked? Can play on the trope of Black priapism and the dangers and desires it elicits for its related condensations of hypersexuality and the presumption of rape propensity be undone?

Mapplethorpe's classic images of African masculinity through his muse Jimmy Freeman seek to make a statement about the very stereotype that disfigures the image of African-descended men in the White imaginary—a stereotype that has cost some, in disproportionate number, their lives and their genitals, their jobs, their health, their sense of themselves. Mapplethorpe's (1980c) *Man in Polyester Suit* is calculated to draw the eyes to a flaccid-yet-pulpy Black man's penis. The model is portrayed in a three-piece suit from the knees up and shoulders down, his fly open, and his penis hanging out. Headless and faceless, Mapplethorpe seems to demand his audience formulate a more sensitive awareness of the fact that Black men are typically seen as *hangers on*, *hanging out* on the streets. Or, it could be that the hanging penis plays on the fact that the Black man is imagined to be *well hung*, and that this same, wild (White) imagination has caused him to be literally hung. The latter of these readings is, however, quite obviously applicable to another of Mapplethorpe's (1980a) portraits of Jimmy Freeman, the *Hooded Man*. Again faceless, the portrait conjures images of Black men's bodies swinging from trees or the bloated, mangled corpse of Emmitt Till. Sanitization of the horror of men about to be lynched, the trauma and suffering of families and communities terrorized is erased to ease the trauma of the White conscience. Finally, Mapplethorpe's (1980b) portrait simply titled *Jimmy Freeman* (see also Hall, 1997, p. 275), depicts an unusually crouched model, head down. Only the pate of his chalk-white-cap-covered head is visible silhouetted against his dark body. His thick, long penis meeting his heels gives the impression that he is defecating. While many readings are possible, we come back to a familiar trope: that Jimmy Freeman is *all* penis

Irrespective of the costs African-descended men have paid for the fantasies and reaction formation of hegemonic White masculinity, the nature of stereotypy generates moral indifference to such facts. In part, we should turn to Mapplethorpe's own fixation with the "big black penis" to understand that *Man in Polyester Suit* more likely signifies the "jungle potentialities" that lurk beneath Black men in polyester suits from the board room to the Oval Office. A friend of Mapplethorpe's reported that Mapplethorpe had "examined" thousands of Black men in a search of "Super Nigger." Mapplethorpe scoured gay clubs and slept with thousands of African American men until he at last found his appropriately measured muse (see Friedman, 2001). A teary-eyed Mapplethorpe, pointing to his muse's penis, said: "Now you know why I love him so" (cited in Friedman, 2001, p. 144). Mapplethorpe's art spoke to a contemporary Eurocentric cultural "truth" about Black men's bodies, but which has a longer historical genealogy than even eighteenth- and nineteenth-century European art and medicine. Consistent with Baldwin and Fanon, Sander Gilman asserts that whether clothed or unclothed, the Black body is effectively naked, signals the danger of and desire for sexual uninhibitedness, and "sexualize[s]...the society in which he or she [is] found" (Gilman 1985, p. 209).

Much ahead of Mapplethorpe, as Thomas A. Foster (2019) shows in his book *Rethinking Rufus*, art circles in London and Paris saw the bodies of Black men as commodities for White male sculptors and painters.[26] Foster recounts the exemplary case of a well-chiselled, early nineteenth-century African American Bostonian, named for posterity only as "Wilson," who was the rage among the circle of White male artists in London at the time. One of these artists, Benjamin Robert Haydon, who referred to Wilson only as "the black," attempted to make a plaster cast of him; Wilson's lungs were nearly crushed as the plaster set. Haydon, on the other hand, was overjoyed at the result, and took care not to damage the cast of Wilson's "hinder part" and genitals (pp. 96–97). Significantly, unlike Haydon, Mapplethorpe successfully killed many of his Black lovers, whom he infected with HIV (Friedman, 2001).

Any Given Sunday

Oliver Stone's *Any Given Sunday* (1999), a forgettable film about the professional culture of US football, contains a scene of interest for us, etitled "Locker room win buzz." This scene brings together the scopophilic specturalization of Black frontal *nakedness*. Christina Pagniacci (played by Cameron Diaz), who recently inherited the football team, enters the locker room unannounced. The only person gratuitously exposed is an African American actor who greets Pagniacci as she enters the dressing room. As Pagniacci makes her way further into the locker room to chat with Jamie Foxx's character, the quarter back, she is sexually leered at by the Black, but not the White, men in the room. On cue, Pagniacci passes a nude White actor and comments, "Don't stiffen up on me." Whether or not he complies we can only guess; there is no genital exposure of the White actor. The careful concealment of White men's genitals throughout the entirety of the scene reveals the "truth" about Black men's penises, but also their consumptive availability.[27] The large, flaccid state of the unnamed Black man's penis is kinetically transformed into a phallus through his invitational exposure and the leering nod-and-wink glances of the other Black men. Indeed, the scene is redolent of the "reckless eyeballing" (see Berry, 2008) for which African men and boys were and continue to be actually, legally and symbolically, lynched (see Kitossa, Introduction to this volume; Moore & Kitossa, Chapter 5 in this volume).

A friend of mine who saw the film in theatres remarked to me the gasps and giggles of four young White women, in the company of a White man, at the sight of the football player's penis. My spouse and I, who saw the film around the same time, noted a different, but no less visceral response: the young White man sitting in front of us with his White female date uttered in disgust, "Aw, come the fuck on!" Desire? Disgust? Envy? Hate? Insecurity? Moral outrage? All in a confused jumble? "Not indifference, in any case," as Fanon (1952/1977, p. 170) would have said of such an instance. Whatever the case may be, Oliver Stone ensured no frontal nudity of White men would dispel the myth he sought to reproduce, since the spectacle of Black men's nakedness marked out the scopophilic domain of the White gaze to constantly fix the Black man as purely genital.

Hall Pass

In spite of the discourse of sexualized and priapic representations of Black men that function as "truth," neither Mapplethorpe's work nor Oliver Stone's *Any Given Sunday* presents contrasting *representations* of Black and White men's penises. The Farrelly brothers' (2011) *Hall Pass*, on the other hand, does offer a visual depiction of the "truth" of the size difference between Black and White men's penises. In an (in)famous scene, Rick, played by Owen Wilson, falls asleep in a hot tub (55:20–56:20). After sleeping for two hours, Rick is awakened by his own drowning and calls for help. Two men, both naked, answer his call, rushing to his rescue: first an African American man, then, right behind him, a White, red-headed man. As the Black man enters the room, the camera zooms in on his large and flaccid penis. The filmmakers do not yet "reveal" the White man's "penis" until Rick is pulled from the hot tub. The White man then enters the room to offer assistance.

As the priapic Black man cradles Rick's head, Rick makes a wincing glance over his shoulder at the Black man's penis. He then says to the White man, "Do me a favour. Hey, Irish, switch places with this guy." Only then does the camera zoom cut from the Black man's penis to the White man's, which is, as might be expected, a micropenis. What audiences are not aware of is that the Farrelly brothers, Bobby and Peter, not only reviewed photos of hundreds of African American men to find their ideal Black penis, but placed a miniaturizing penile prosthetic on the White male character. The Farrelly brothers admitted in an interview that "[t]he other [White] guy is a stand-up comic. For him, the lesser individual, we actually did use a prosthetic. We used it so he could say, 'No, that's not me!' But he was very similar." As the Farrelly brothers describe it, the rationale for this scene and the comparison of Black and White men's penises was meant to "pok[e] fun at men" (cited in Brodie, n.d.)[28] and their preoccupation with their genitalia.

Heart Condition

Like Mappelthorpe, the Farrelly borthers chased the dragon of the big Black dick from casting to representation. Indeed, this is a common Hollywood preoccupation, and one that bubbles up in other ways, as well. In James Parriott's (1990) film *Heart Condition*, for example, Jack Moony, a racist detective played by Bob Hoskins, receives a heart transplant from his recently murdered nemesis, Napoleon Stone, an African American lawyer played by Denzel Washington. Upon waking from the heart transplant in the hospital, Moony's eyes are greeted by a foot-long-plus black dildo planted at the foot of the bed by his giggling, White station house peers (21:12–21:58).[29]

Not coincidentally, in a final act of consumption/possession, Moony becomes partner to Napoleon Stone's White love interest Chloe Webb, played by Crystal Gerrity. The implication is clear. In taking the heart of a Black man in an act of consumption, he, the White man, controls the crossing into forbidden zones of sexual licence, spiritually putting a black face over both his prodigious penis and bestial libido. This is, effectively, transubstantiation.

Jack Moony literally fulfills the ultimate fantasy of hegemonic and civilized White man—he, through the actual appropriation of a heart transplant and ritualized act of gastric internalization, becomes a Black man under the skin. Jack Moony evidently transcended a barrier erected in the hegemonic White imaginary where, as Fanon (1952/1977) notes, "the body of the black man hinders the closure of the white man's postural schema at the moment when the black man emerges into the white man's phenomenal world" (p. 160). The absorption is the resolution. Here, rather than an instance of the Black man as projected fantasy who is responsible for the violence done to him, his reappropriation back into the source from which the nightmare came constitutes a symbolic demonstration that the (Black) beast/id within can be civilized, moderated, tamed.[30] It is notable that the threat to the White goddess/woman is resolved through the process of reabsorption. The myth that "once a White woman goes Black, she never comes back," created by White men to stimulate sexualized conflict with Black men and to control White women (Hernton, 1965/1988), in the context of the film no longer stimulates racialized sexual anxiety. Where, then, does the Black beast go, given that the battle between civilization and barbarism is ongoing at the level of personality? In *Race: The History of an Idea*, Thomas Gossett (1973) is an eloquent interlocutor for a suggestive response: "One still hears the idea expressed by white men in the Deep South that they wish they could be negroes, at least on Saturday nights" (p. 273). It is, however, worth asking why he only mentions the Deep South when across the breadth and depth of what is called Western culture, and indeed in other cultures besides, this motif is constantly repeated?

In *Heart Condition*, the spiritual cannibalization of the Black-man-as-sexual-demon satisfies the psychic demands of negotiating the White man's conception of the burden of civilization's conquest over barbarism. The good/goddess White woman, however, who was once thrown into the abyss of dematerialization both physically because of Napoleon Stone's conjectured priapism, and spiritually because of his libidinous instincts, is restored, made whole again, through Jack Moony's act of consumption.

But there are other strategies and functions that the Black beast can play, especially in the disciplining and degradation of the White goddess.

The Heartbreak Kid

In some films, such as the Farrelly brothers' (2007) *The Heartbreak Kid,* Black men are an absent presence; they exist to intrude on White female/ White male heterosexual encounters to reify the hegemonic gender order on White male terms. In such cases, the tropisitic Black man who is hypersexual, priapic, and prone to rape White women, though physically absent, stands as a metaphor that suggests White male sexual innocence. The Black Phallic Fantastic stands in relation to White men and White women in different ways. First there are two opposing tropes for White women. The first is the bad or fallen White woman whose sexual autonomy, like the Greek Maenads, is imagined to be insatiable, uncontrolled, and uncontrollable. Like the Judeo-Christian Eve or the Zoroastrian Jeh, she threatens disorder from within. She is symbolically restored to her idealized status, as the scapegoat she is, through a ceremony of sacrificial degradation or murder. Noted above, Michel Cournot's remarks about the Black man's penis being a sword of penetrative penality communicates well the erotics of ritualized death. This trope stands against the good/goddess White woman. She is not only imagined as sexually constrained and restrained, but her womb is solely reserved for White racial reproduction and she repudiates Black or other men "of colour" as partners.

Crucially, the playing out of these dynamics does not rely on the force of a visible and disembodied Black man represented by dildos, nor on a naked priapic Black man. Instead, the Black man who sets off these readings is realized in gesture and word, leaving the audience to fill in the gaps with knowledge circulating in the cultural ether. This is a far subtler method of communication that requires a deeper level of psychosexual analysis such as that undertaken by Fanon (1952/1977).

The Farrelly brothers (2007) vapid "romantic comedy" *The Hearbreak Kid* is a good example of the "tacit" playing out of the multiple tropes. The film

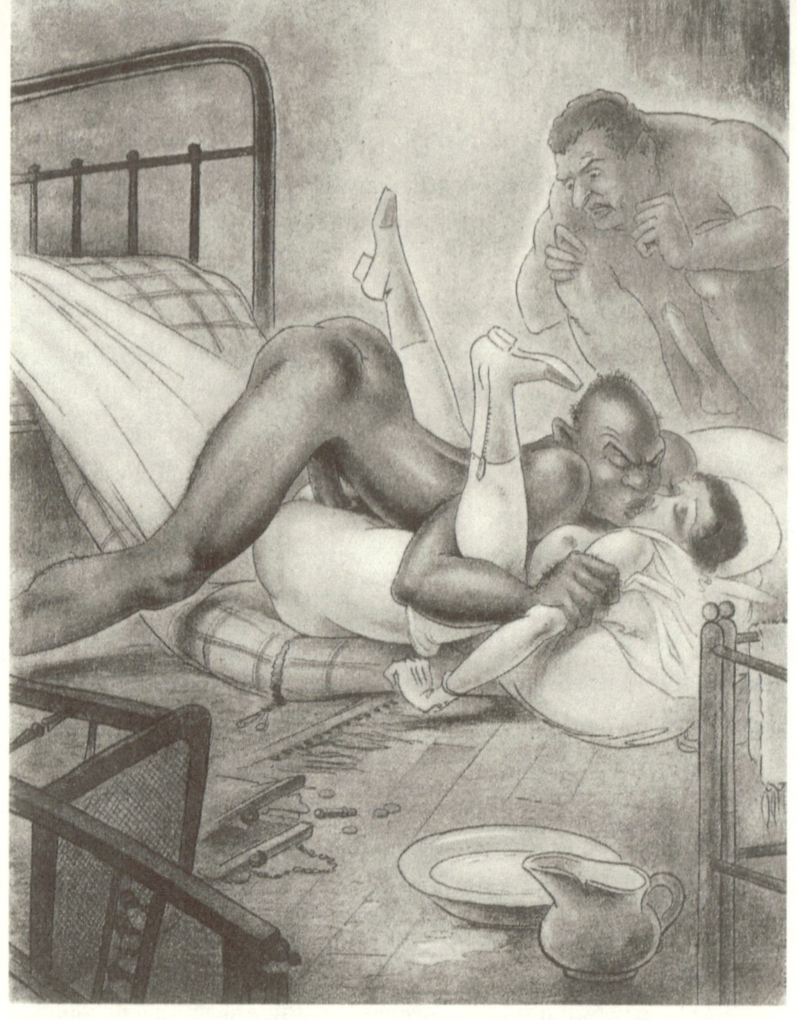

FIGURE 1.3: An untitled, 1925 photo-engraving of voyeuristic and transubstantiative "interracial" cuckolding by Jean Morisot. (Reproduced in Weiermair [1999], p. 177.)

is basically about a hapless, innocent, too-good-for-this-world White guy, Eddie Cantrow (played by Ben Stiller), who finds true love. Eddie is taken in by a vivacious, animal-loving vegan, Lila. She is not as "wholesome" as she seems, though—assuming, that is, that animal-lovers and vegans are wholesome. This is demonstrated during the consummation of their snap wedding, which is punctuated by Lila shouting to Eddie, "Fuck me like a Black guy, Eddie!" (55:27–56:20). Eddie attempts to responds with wild, exaggerated thrusts only to be greeted with Lila's frustrated complaint that "you're not doing it!!!" (44:40–41). The scene ends with a traumatized Eddie muttering incoherently and rocking in a fetal position on a chair in the corner of the room, while Lila sleeps blissfully. Eddie's attempt to obligingly "fuck" Lila "like a Black guy"—and his subsequent failure—is entirely predictable. As a white man, Stiller's character—like Moony in *Heart Condition* before his transubstantiation—cannot hump. To this is added the trope that the wholesome White goddess is, in fact, an untrustworthy, cuckolding vixen who, as Blumenbach claimed, "when eager for venery prefer the embraces of Negroes to those of other [read: White] men" (cited in Jordan, 1977, n. 46, p. 158–59).

Whether an absent presence or represented in the frame of observation, the invocation of the Black man as a prosthetic in white sexual race play is a theme that is recursive in art, pornography, and the swinging lifestyle. The 1925 erotic art of Jean Morisot, for example, depicts a scene of "cuckolding" with a Black man and a White woman and an aroused, yet seemingly traumatized, White man (husband? voyeur?) in the background (Figure 1.3). His pose bears an uncanny resemblance to Ben Stiller's character Eddie Cantrow from the scene in the *The Heartbreak Kid* described above.[31] This sort of labyrinthine erotic and sexual racism was cinematically established in D.W. Griffith's 1915 epic *The Birth of a Nation*.

Exposing D.W. Griffith and *The Birth of a Nation*: Propaganda, Cinematic Innovations, and the Pornography of Desire

Sexualized representations of Black men are now so mundane and repeated so casually as to go without comment. There is simply too much of it, often hidden in five-second takes and casually scripted remarks in random movies and popular television shows from *The Simpsons* to *Curb Your Enthusiasm* to draw much attention. But what is the principal cinematic genealogy of this mundane repetition? And how is it related to hegemonic White psychosexual ontology?

Though not the first racist film, *The Birth of a Nation* is certainly the most infamous, if only for its global reach and the White supremacist hooliganism it promoted, and is central to a sustained identification and criticism of how White psychosexual projections informed subsequent film and popular culture. Unlike contemporary films of its time, where the convergence between mythologies of hegemonic Black masculinity, White masculinity, and White femininity was not disarticulated from explicit ideas of the nation and belonging, *The Birth of a Nation* explicitly mobilized eroticized tropes of heterosexual Black masculinity to accomplish the desires of White scopophilia, centring on the presumed sexual threat of Black masculinity. The worldwide circulation of Hollywood's first major epic launched Hollywood and silent film onto the international scene.[32] More importantly, through its eroticized representations of gender, nation, sex, sexuality, and White supremacy in the triangular asymmetry between Black men, White men, and White women, its novel methods of film technique deepened and globalized sexualized fears of Black men. What I aim to unpack in this discussion is not simply that *The Birth of a Nation* established the framework for contemporary representations of Black men in Hollywood cinema, but that the Southerners Thomas Dixon and D.W. Griffith consciously mobilized erotically charged tropes of Black men and the myth of the good/goddess White woman to effect political propagandic aims tied to hegemonic White male ontology.

The Birth of a Nation, a film Baldwin (1976) critically assessed in detail in *The Devil Finds Work*, was saturated with the trope of the Black Phallic Fantastic and the psychosexual racial pathologies of Thomas Dixon and D.W. Griffith. It was as much loved by White America as it was protested by African Americans and others (Bogle, 2001; Rogin, 1987; Stokes, 2007). *The Birth of a Nation* is ostensibly an account of rapprochement between the North and the South through the coming together of two White families from either region. Besides the "carpet bagger" Northern politicians, the real flies in the ointment of "reunion" are the "Negro" and the "mulatto" offspring of White men. That is about all one needs to know of the plot of this three-hour "epic," of which Baldwin (1976) writes:

> It is impossible to do justice to this story, such story as attempts to make an appearance being immediately submerged by the tidal wave of the plot; and, in Griffith's handling of this fable, anyway, *the key is to be found in the images* [emphasis added]. The film cannot be called dishonest: it has the Niagara force of an *obsession* [emphasis added]. (p. 43)

Indeed, in a world in which moving images were novel, the cinema had a democractizing effect in producing for the first time a mass media and mass culture (Taylor, 1979). Silent film, being a purely visual media, communicated through tropes and metaphors, emotive rather than intellectual content and did so by evoking ideals of common peoplehood and nation, irrespective of class, but certainly not of race (Taylor, 1979, p. 29–30).

There is no doubt that in addition to Baldwin the film has been the object of criticism for its mystification of history (Stokes, 2007; Rogin, 1987) and its offensive mobilization of erotic racism (Dines, 2006). Some critics, including Russell Merritt (1982), gush about the films inaugural technical innovations, editing, lighting, techniques of fade out and flashbacks, and twist themselves to claim "[m]uch of what Griffith filmed is historically accurate, but the illusion of general historical truth and perspective is largely the product of Griffith's art" (p. 168; see also p. 166).[33] But Baldwin (1976) minces few words in centring the results of Griffith's sexual obsession with Black men; he writes, "*The Birth of a Nation*...is really an elaborate justification of mass murder" (1976, p. 45). Baldwin suggests the tawdry plot and its technical wizardry was as effective as it was because the purpose of the film could not be admitted. For him, the film set the trend for others that followed when dealing with representations of Black men. On film, as in life, Baldwin argued that Black men exist "for the sole purpose of perpetuating *the* [emphasis added] legend" (p. 59) that they are hypersexual, priapic rapists. Yet, that *The Birth of a Nation* is outright White supremacist and nationalist propaganda is obfuscated by the competing narrative constituted by the Screen Writers Guild of America's naming its highest award the *D.W. Griffith Award*.

As noted by Baldwin, erotic anti-Black racism and sexual displacement and nationalism are central to the *Birth of a Nation's* propaganda for White supremacy and nationalism. There is no doubt that propaganda is the central objective of the film (Cripps, 1996; Rogin, 1987; C. Taylor, 1996; Williams, 2004). But so as not to prioritize what was being propagandized (nationhood) and to get instead at the depth of *how* the propaganda was effected, it is important to distinguish the propaganda itself from the metaphors and representations that serve its purpose. Edward Bernays (1928/2005),[34] one of the key figures of early nineteenth-century state and advertising propaganda, asserted that

> [t]he conscious and intelligent manipulation of the organized habits and opinions of masses, is an important element in democratic society. Those who manipulate this unseen mechanism of society constitute an invisible government which is the true ruling power of our century. (p. 37)

It is not this in which I am interested. Nor am I interested in propaganda in the sense asserted by Harold Lasswell (1927): "Propaganda is the management of collective attitudes by the manipulation of significant symbols" (p. 627). These definitions are along the lines of indoctrination. Instead, because my focus is the "depth psychology" of the erotic and sexualized tropes of Black men in European culture, I am persuaded by Aldous Huxley's (1936) definition: "Political and religious propaganda is effective, it would seem, only upon those who are already partly or entirely convinced of its truth" (p. 34). And crucially, he adds, "The propagandist is a man who canalizes an already existing stream" (p. 39).

To this end, the "truth" Griffith's canalized, the truth of which White America and global White supremacy was already convinced—that Black men are hypersexual, priapic, and prone to raping White women—needed no persuading, and could all the more effectively be used to achieve the ideological objective of confecting what Benedict Anderson (1991) called an "imagined community." Clyde Taylor (1996) gets to the point of the psychosexual pathology of White male projection working itself out in the film. He writes,

> [Griffith] fashioned a drama of the id in which he could re-enact the deflowering of Nordic nymphs—those virgins who most completely embodied the tribal idea one must live and die for—and then experience the chastisement of this deepest of imaginative sins in the lynching of a Black alter ego who performed the desired sacrilege for his vicarious satisfactions. (p. 27; see also Messerschmidt, 2007; Wiegman, 1993)

In this sense, *The Birth of a Nation* is a work of pornography, most certainly of violence, but also of metaphoric representations of genital significations—specifically black phallic objects, metonyms for Black men. Yet the question of pornography needs to be made out, given that what constitutes pornography or obscenity changes over time. Even so, this fact does not preclude judging the propagandic effect of the film as depending on surreptitious modes of pornographic representation. This is not a judgment against pornography in the sense of accepting manufactured consent about what gets constituted as pornography. Rather, I aim to suggest that sexualized meanings can be communicated to speak a taken-for-granted truth for the express purpose of having a propagandistic objective.

In other words, as noted by Gail Dines (2006), *The Birth of a Nation* achieved the effects of White supremacist propaganda through its pornographic content. Cedric Robinson (1997) argued that to ignore the seemingly pedestrian coincidences of sexual racism in the film, and to focus instead on the richness of technological innovation, as though these were unconnected to African American oppression, is to ignore the thinly disguised political implications of *The Birth of a Nation* as a vehicle for racial, sexual, classist, and nationalist propaganda par excellence in US film history (see also Cripps, 1996; Rogin, 1987; C. Taylor, 1996; Williams, 2004).[35] Thus at the closing of the first screening of *The Birth of a Nation*, "shouts of praise were called across the auditorium" (Cook, 1974, p. 112); Dixon reputedly shouted across to Griffith over the din that *The Clansman* was too tame a title for so "powerful a story; it should be called *Birth of a Nation*" (Cook, 1974, p. 112). And, like any nation, bloodshed is a precondition for its establishment. As the American civil war gave shape to the future conflicts within the nation, these conflicts were not to be resolved, according to Griffith, until "*The Birth of a Nation* began...with Ku Klux Klans" (cited in Rogin, 1987, p. 192). Clearly, in Griffith's vision, binding the nation meant delimiting a historical genesis to the nation that clearly marked the borders of belonging determined by erotic racism.

If we then follow the logic of critics who attended to the psychosexual dimensions of the film (Baldwin, 1976; Dines, 2006, Robinson, 1997; Rogin, 1996; C. Taylor, 1996), then Russell Merritt's (1982) assertion that the "true focal point [of the film] is the Southern [White] woman" (p. 170; see also Merritt, 1990) is incomplete. In reality, the focal point is a triumvirate: the Black man, the White woman, and the White man. While the pornographic nature of the film's propaganda is greater in sum than in its parts, those parts—literally the body parts of the castrated Black man—make the whole possible. It is not the castration of Black Gus's penis near the end of the film (which was edited out of the theatre version) that signifies pornography. It is instead the rarely, if ever, commented-on scene titled "Love's rhapsodies and love's tears" (1:50:29–1:53:25) and its eroticism, which escaped the censors. In it, Elsie Stoneman, played by Lilian Gish, is ecstatic after Ben Cameron professes his love. Signifying fellatio, Griffith has Elsie excitedly and repeatedly caress and kiss the dark mahogany phallic bedpost, against which her white porcelain face is juxtaposed. By this method, Griffith cleverly establishes a visual spectacle that signifies the mythic sexual potency of Black masculinity.

The intentionality of specific cinematic innovations in *Birth of a Nation* had the effect of intensifying the scopophilic field. The method for using lighting in the film produced an abnormal, porcelain look to White women, suggesting fragility and virginity. In a word, the technology of lighting, particularly in black and white film, creates subjects as either "white" or "black." But the framing of subjects is a function of effects the filmmaker seeks to communicate. Since cinematic and photographic lighting was developed with White people in mind, whiteness has become the norm of lighting technology and blackness a problem (Dyer, 1997, pp. 84–89). The unity of lighting technology and its construction of the filmic and social

FIGURE 1.4: "Love's rhapsodies and love's tears" (D.W. Griffith, 1915, The Birth of a Nation*)*

reality of race and gender are most evident in Lilian Gish's own words. She describes the audition that won her the role of Elsie Stoneman, the scene of attempted rape: "During the hysterical chase around the room, the hairpins flew out of my hair, which tumbled below my waist as Lynch held my fainting body in his arms. I was very blonde and fragile-looking. The contrast with the dark man evidently pleased Mr. Griffith" (cited in Lang, 1994, p. 15). Though Griffith claimed that the point of making the film was to speak out against "intolerance," such a scene opens another, and far more likely, reading: that Griffith intended to signify the ever-present danger of the big, Black, and savage penis, ever anxious to despoil the good/goddess White woman who presumably has neither sexual autonomy nor erotic desires for Black men. Griffith's claim that the "The Birth of a Nation began... with Ku Klux Klans" (cited in Rogin, 1987, p. 192) not only repudiated his disingenuous claim, but affirmed the extent to which erotic violence against African American men was central to the nation as he, Thomas Dixon, and Woodrow Wilson understood it.

White Women, Birth, and Nationhood

James Baldwin (1955/1984) asserted that the European and the White American quest for a state of innocence that imagines that Black men do not exist is a denial of their ontological dependence on constructing Black men as folk devils—a deluded pursuit that makes of them monsters. D.W. Griffith and Thomas Dixon would specifically stand out for criticism by Baldwin (1976) in the aptly titled *The Devil Finds Work*. The Southerners D.W. Griffith, Thomas Dixon, and Woodrow Wilson were fully aware that "miscegenation"—in other words, African men and European women *in flagrante delicto*—was the principle obsession in American race politics. *The Birth of a Nation*, as with Thomas Dixon's novel *The Clansman* upon which the film was based, is preoccupied with interracial sex because both Dixon and Griffith were themselves caught up in this obsession. Centring the narrative of "blood and soil" as fundamental to the White supremacist nation-building project, Dixon and Griffith placed anxiety about miscegenation, characterized specifically as the fear of African American men raping White women, at the core of the film.[36] In representing "negro" Gus and "mulatto" Silas Lynch as seeking to defile the "heavenly purity" of the White woman's womb—the incubator of White physical existence—Dixon and Griffith sought to directly enact their vision of the nation through propagandizing the myth of Black rapist terror. For Griffith, it was plain that the chief aim of the film was "to create a feeling of abhorrence in white people, especially white women against colored men" (cited in Rogin, 1987, p. 219).

The mere allusion to miscegenation was enough for enraged White crowds to join in macabre communion of tens to the thousands at picnics to witness the lynching of African men. Photos of the events were made into post cards, and the men's body parts—in particular, their penises—were trophies in the mad scramble for memorabilia. To be clear, "miscegenation" was not a crisis where White men and enslaved or freed African women were concerned. Paul Hoch (1979) articulates the point well by saying that, in the masculine interracial competition of competing group survival, "the most shattering (though rarely admitted) assertion of virility often lay in taking control of the other group's females—most obviously in the institution of slavery—and at all costs excluding them from access to one's own" (p. 47).[37] Victors on behalf of their group exacted genetic punishment by raping the conquered women and castrating, murdering, and controlling, or otherwise preventing conquered men from passing on their genes.

It has been thus noted, with considerable consternation, that White men raped African women both for pleasure and to breed them. With venerables such as Mas' George (Washington) and Mas' Thomas (Jefferson), this was not considered a crisis but an expression of White male virility and a way to increase the enslaved stock[38] (Baldwin, 1961/1989; A. Davis, 1983; Du Bois, 2004; Fanon, 1962/1977; Foster, 2019, 2011; hooks, 1992; Smithers, 2013; Sublette & Sublette, 2016; Wells, 1982/2010). Thomas Dixon, who also happened to be a Christian minister, put the prerogative of the White man as conqueror succinctly: "[T]he surviving polygamous and lawless instincts of the white male [are of] *no social significance,*" but give Negro men access to white women, and they will destroy "the foundation of racial life and of civilization. The South must guard with the flaming sword every avenue of approach to this holy of holies" (cited in Rogin, 1987, p. 220).[39] In terms of challenging White male supremacy, nothing endangered the cause of the Republic more than White women who would not conform to the diktats of White supremacy and economically autonomous and free-moving African American men. The regulation of one meant the control of the other in achieving dominance of Black women.

There were two historically specific convergences that animated the sexual racism and nation-building project from Reconstruction into the early twentieth century. The first is that Whiteness as a demographic and cultural franchise had, necessarily, to be expanded. This meant that hegemonic White femininity was extended beyond upper- and middle-class White women to include poor and working-class White women, though to be sure there was legal and social ambivalence as to whether Italians, Jews, Armenians, and others were to be immediately included (see Brodkin, 1998; Ignatiev, 1995; Jacobson, 1998; Roediger, 1991). Leaders such as Frances Willard not only sought to turn sexual myths about African American men to the advantage of White suffragettes, but also actively collaborated in seeking to produce a paralytic "nameless horror" of Black men among White women (Feimster, 2009; Hodes, 1997; Newman, 1999; Rogin, 1987;

Ware, 1992).[40] Rebecca Latimer Felton of Georgia—who was also the first woman senator in the United States—saw Black men as an obstacle to the progress of White women. She rose to the occasion to incite mobs of White men and women with these words in 1897: "If it takes lynching to protect a woman's [i.e., a White woman's] dearest possession [i.e., her virginity] from drunken, ravening beasts [i.e., Black men], then I say lynch a thousand a week if it becomes necessary" (cited in McGerr, 2003, p. 187; see also D. Davis, 2006, p. 29).[41]

The Beast Within

Fanon (1952/1977) argued that "[t]he civilized white man retains an irrational longing for unusual eras of sexual license, or orgiastic scenes, of unpunished rapes, of unrepressed incest" (p. 165). This thesis is very much applicable to the White men surrounding *The Birth of a Nation*. In constructing African males as well-hung, libidinous beasts, hegemonic White masculinity escape the repressions that are typically associated with "civilization." In a sense, White men get to have their cake and eat it too. They get to be White by the *white daylight* of the conscious mind, and the lurking Black beast by the *darkened night* of the erotic subconscious (Hoch, 1979, p. 54). Through the fantasy of the big, Black buck rooming the countryside ever ready to destroy the White reproductive potential of unwary White women, White men desire the fulfillment of what they abhor—because in the desire itself, the projective force liberates them of the "burden" of civilization. More importantly, they are liberated of the guilt that comes with the projection of desire. Woodrow Wilson (cited in Rogin, 1987) gave the game away when he commented on African Americans in the Postbellum South:

> Some stayed very quietly by their old masters and gave no trouble; but most yielded, as was to have been expected, to the novel impulse and excitement of freedom.... *The country was filled with vagrants looking for pleasure* [emphasis added] and gratuitous fortune....The tasks of ordinary life stood untouched; the idlers grew *insolent, dangerous* [emphasis

added]; nights went anxiously by, for fear of riot and incendiary fire. (p. 193)

To Dixon, Griffith, Wilson, and many others, the pursuit of pleasure, insolent and dangerous in the context of roaming bands of African men, discursively represents the electric pleasure and desire that such horror is supposed to bring. Indeed, at the time of *Birth of a Nation*'s filming, lynching the beast *within* was already a popular pastime that emerged with the simultaneous construction of the Southern White woman as the virgin Mary incarnate in the Postbellum south. As much as *The Birth of a Nation* added pictorial confirmation to the proverbial fire, the governor of South Carolina (the location of Griffith's mythic "black empire") said, "[F]orty to a hundred Southern maidens were annually offered as a sacrifice to the African Minotaur, and no Theseus had arisen to rid the land of this terror" (cited in Lang, 1994, p. 18). When the beast is within, as suggested by Plato and other ancient tales of the demonic, the terror never goes away; it can only find "resolution" in an ongoing process of projections.

In the milieu of the Timocratic epidermal schema in which Dixon and Griffith circulated, "civilization" is marked by the White self while the disordering potentialities of the "barbarian" Other are signified by the presumably hypersexual, priapic, and rapist Black man. As a force registered and reproduced at the subconscious depth of hegemonic culture, the drive for innocence and purity demands a recursive morality play in which both the national culture and the individual psyches that best represent it search for, identify, and slay demons. They do this actually and ritually, as a prophylactic to ward off ontological dissolution. Griffith himself gives a fitting example of the enemy within the nation, as the *shadow* within the White male self. In *The Birth of a Nation*, the pale whiteness of the very women on screen encountering the mythic propensity of the African Minotaur so "evidently pleased Mr. Griffith" that, off-screen, he developed passionate love relationships with them: Lilian Gish, who played Elsie Stoneman, and Mae Marsh, who played Flora, the character who was stalked and raped in the original screen version (Rogin, 1987, p. 208). As though heeding Dixon's injunction that the lawless polygamy of White men is of no consequence, Griffith made of himself in life the sexually promiscuous conqueror who bedded two White goddesses, one of whom had been symbolically sacrificed on screen to the "Black Minotaur."

Conclusion

From Greek and Roman art and science, through to the representation of politics and the politics of representation in the nineteenth and twentieth centuries, the presumption that Black men are hypersexual, priapic, and prone to rape White women has been a central animating theme in Western cultural psychology. These tropes can be found in Hollywood cinema from its foundation to the present and in contemporary art. Drawing on James Baldwin and Frantz Fanon, I have suggested that the cultural preoccupation with the tripartite trope of the Black Phallic Fantastic, rooted in the pornographic scopophilia focused on Black men's bodies and the presumption that they embody sexual licence, demands the treatment of "depth psychology." The mundane repetition and spectacularizing of eroticized representations of the Black Phallic Fantastic trope in contemporary Hollywood, even when as an absent presence, constitutes a quality of fatigue that is yet to be named and critically examined. Yet, until the psychology of White ontological dependence on the routinization and persistence of sexualized representations of Black men is deconstructed with equal persistence, the overwhelming antipathy, antagonism, and objectification of Black men will persist—not least with deadly effects.

Author's Note

The following persons provided helpful perspectives on this essay at varying stages of its development: Patricia Malloy, Charles Simon-Aaron, Cedric Licorish, Katerina Deliovsky, Anita Jack-Davies, and Erica Lawson.

Notes

1. For an explanation of my use of *black/Black* and *white/White*, see Kitossa (Introduction to this volume, n.1).

2. I use the term *Western* as a signifier for *Europe* in the most laconic sense, though both are taken as a transhistorical reality alluded to as "our Western heritage" in work as disparate as Gerda Lerner (1986) and David Brion Davis (2014). Imagined as the "West," what passes for Europe is a raciological construction given birth by the Crusades, Christendom, and nationalistic mythologies. Both Europe and the West, therefore, have no genealogical relationship to Greece and Rome. What elements of Greece and Rome there are, have been expropriated from traces of ideas and representations that serve contemporary and "near-modern" political agendas. In the very real sense of the word, then, "Europe" and the "West" are *invented* categories, largely the work of cultural and political elites over the past 500 years (Bernal, 1987; Diop, 1991; Heng, 2018; MacDougall, 1982; Ousselin, 2009; Poliakov, 1974; Simon-Aaron, 2008). For a discussion of the invention of Africa, see Hountondji (1983) and Mudimbe (1988); for the invention of India, see V.S. Naipaul (1977), Rosalind O'Hanlon & David Washbrook (1992), and Immanuel Wallerstein (1991). None of this, however, precludes a theory of the ontic psychosexual implications for individuals and collectivities in terms of the tripartite ethnophaulic trope of Black men as hypersexual, priapic, and prone to rape White women. For a discussion on this see Kitossa (Introduction to this volume).
3. Europe is fictionally constituted as a separate "continent" from Asia. It is not, in fact, at all separate, but instead the farthest Western reach of that great landmass (see Ousselin, 2009).
4. Fanon's approach to cultural psychology (which is similar to that of Baldwin) is consistent with what Walter Abell (1957/1966) calls "depth history" (p. 30). This is pursuit of social understanding that requires restraining the priority given to the mechanisms of materialist explanations, aiming instead to make explicit that which is tacit and taken-for-granted in a given culture through "depth psychology" (pp. 28–42). Thus, seeking "interpretive comprehension" (p. 29) of the dialectical relationship between materialism and spiritual and psychic forces, depth history implicates a breadth of areas of inquiry—anthropology, economics, sociology, and relevant applications of the sciences such as biology and climatology. Taken together, these modes of inquiry open not to psychology as an area of study about individuals, but as a social practice in the production of that which makes possible human life *as* human life: culture (E. Hall, 1976/1989). As noted by Abell, "[t]he crucial consideration for culture is not the nature of a particular economy, whether urban or rural, but the effect produced by economic and other historical circumstances upon the psychic life of the given society" (p. 41; see also Mumford, 1944/1973, 1967). The key point here is that cultural psychology—constitutive of the hegemony of taken-for-granted ways of feeling and *how* to experience feeling—is selected and reproduced through the "code" (see Ani, 1994, pp. 10–23), or the "field phenomenon of morphic resonance" (see Sheldrake, 2012, pp. 293–310) of a culture, which is contained in that culture's media of expression (its stories and tropes) and communicated by its socially legitimated ideologues (see Ani, 1994, p. 7).
5. The word *fascination* connotes obsession, spectacle, and surprise, but is etymologically related to the political ideology of "fascism." Given the name of Benito Mussolini's National Fascist Party, fascism signifies right-wing political ideology and a modern government administered by an autarch who is supported by an intellectual clerisy that staffs ministries—akin to Plato's

ideal Republic. But Mussolini selected the word *fascist* because of its penetrative and totemic genealogy in a highly erotically militarized Roman culture. Dian Hanson (2012, p. 5) notes that *fascinum*, from the Latin, means "both phallus and magical spirit" (p. 5). Connected to the divinity of the Greek phallic god Priapus, which was borrowed from Eastern cultures, the Romans transformed him into the god Fascinus, who was both protector and (penetrative) conqueror. David Friedman (2003) reminds us that the fascina had wide sociocultural and political meanings for expansionist Rome (see pp. 25–30). Elite young Roman males, yet to become *viri* (virile), wore lockets called bulla containing a replica of a fascinum: a penis. The pride of the peerage, these males only penetrated (female or male), but were never themselves penetrated. Friedman goes on to note that the word *glans*—the tip of the penis—was adopted by the Romans from the Greek word *cinaedus*, which means "head of a bullet." All throughout Rome itself, replicas of pulsating erect penises were everywhere to be seen, much like how in Belgium today there are everywhere replicas of African hands, heads, and feet: totems. Finally, the cult of the penis in Rome was martial, but also crossed into the sport of penetrative violence in the gladiatorial coliseum and into poetry that thrived on priapic cruelty, which hardly bested the Marquis de Sade.

6. Given the significance of the Talmudic gloss linking the presumed hypersexuality of Black men with priapism, I made considerable effort to reach out to Black identified male Jewish professors in North America and Israel, but received no replies. I equally had no success inviting Black Muslim scholars to contribute to this collection (see Chapter 10 this volume, n. 5).
7. The Greeks who imagined themselves superior because they occupied the geographical mean, disparaged northern blond, blue-eyed, and pale skinned peoples as "frigid" (Brackman, 1977).
8. It is little remarked, but the race science of the so-called Enlightenment is directly attributable to the natural and moral philosophers of Greece and Rome, whom were read by the likes Hume, Kant, and others (D. Davis, 2014; Jordan, 1968/1977). We may take as but one source of evidence Benjamin Rush—framer of the US Constitution and so-called father of US psychiatry. At once describing his deadly nostrums and curative devices adapted from inquisitorial torture chambers as "treatments" and "punishments," Thomas Szasz (1970/1997) reminds us that Rush doubted the intelligence of African peoples. More than this, he regarded "blackness" of skin as a disease on par with leprosy. Believing, or at least telling himself he believed, that Africans nerves were insensitive due to the apparent leprosy-like effects of "blackness" of skin, Rush decided Africans could endure medical procedures without difficulty. Above all, Szasz asserts that Rush believed that "so strong were [the sexual] desires in Negroes that even the depressing circumstances of slavery had not prevented their extraordinary fruitfulness" (p. 155).
9. "Timocracy," Orlando Patterson (1982) shows, "is derived from the Greek word for honor" (p. 386; see also Finley, 1980). When Fanon (1952/1977) talks about the "epidermal scheme" of the colonialist and White supremacist context and Baldwin describes the Irish becoming White, both were accounting for the psychology of superiority that lies in the breast of the most down-trodden White person which gives a feeling of superiority over the most well-to-do person of

African descent. W.E.B. Du Bois (1935) famously referred to this as the "psychological wage" (p. 700) of Whiteness.

10. Girard (1989) asserts that the purpose of his study—to discover "the mechanism of the accusation and in the interaction between representation and acts of persecution" (p. 15)—is neither as grand as the Marxist secret will to power nor as totalizing as the unconscious desires that are the preoccupation of psychoanalysis. Assuming that the warding-off of perceived or real catastrophe is essential to the integrity of the personality or to that of maintaining social order, Girard in fact achieves the difficult task of mobilizing both approaches through an account of what Stanley Cohen (1972/2002) called "moral panics" centred on scapegoats constituted as "folk devils."
11. Indicating that the scapegoat is a contemporary as much as an ancient symbol for individual and collective hygienic and psychological "therapeutic" interventions, Thomas Szasz (1974/2003) notes the ancient Greeks called it *pharmakoi* (see pp. 19–20). I suggest below that, particularly with D.W. Griffith's *The Birth of a Nation*, the mythic Black-man-as-rapist was certainly conjured to justify the suppression of economic competition for White men, women, and their families, but was also used as a scapegoat upon whom to project the psychic contradictions of civilization versus barbarism.
12. Mannoni is here obviously referring to White men. This fact has bearing on the problematic assertion of Black feminists that "all the men are Black, all the women are White, but some of us are brave" (see Crenshaw, 1989, p. 139). See Kitossa (Introduction to this volume) for a more detailed discussion of this topic.
13. This presumption, which was a significant change in the attitude of the ancient Greeks toward Africans or Ethiopians in Egypt from whom they previously learned and had tremendous respect, was largely due to imperial dominance of the Grecian city states (Bernal, 1987; Diop 1991).
14. I do not here reify woman as a universal abstraction who is oppressed by universal man. Throughout the ages, in exploitative social formations, elite women have *always* been complicit with hierarchy and status no less than males of their groups (Lerner,1986; see also Patterson, 1982 for copious instances over time of elite women's complicity with domination).
15. Dian Hanson (2012) notes that, even into contemporary times, "female nudes have always been more common than male, and the blame rests with the penis. This graphic and all too obvious sex organ may fascinate, but it also offends delicate temperaments, ruins the graceful flowing lines of the body, and has long marked the dividing line between art and obscenity" (p. 6).
16. Opinions are mixed as to whether pederasty involved anal or intercrural (one partner humping between the thighs of the other) sex, and whether in either case it constituted the stigma "homosexuality." Eva Keuls (1985; see also Trexler, 1995) asserts that the Greeks, like so many others, were "homophobic," but only to the extent that the identity of "active" partner was not spoiled in contradistinction to the stigmatized identity of "dominated," feminized, "passive," and "penetrated" partner. This would imply that anal penetration did not occur in the pederastic relationship. Yet, Friedman (2001) argues that Attic vases depict pederastic intercrural and anal sex. These representations are not pornographic as we would understand them today. Rather, as noted by Friedman, what was being communicated was neither sexual pleasure (which

was secondary) nor "homosexuality" (which was disparaged). Instead, being displayed were primary instantiations of the older male, through emotional and physical intimacy, passing along *arête*—manly virtues such as "courage, strength, fairness, and honesty" (Friedman, 2001, p. 23). In a culture where women were largely a convenience for actual biological reproduction, Aristotle claimed that when an *erastes* (the older male) entered and released the vital principle into the rectum of the *eromenos*, this was not "homosexuality" but a means of giving "birth to other men" (Friedman, 2001, p. 24) without the aid of women. Not all Athenians saw it that way, however. Some regarded "homosexuality," always the act of "receiving" penetration, as unmanly. Friedman records that the famous playwright Aristophanes "mocked those on the receiving end as *europroktos* ['wide assed'] or *katapugon* ['butt fucked']" (p. 24; see also Greenberg, 1984; Hyam, 1991; and Trexler, 1995 describing a similar attitude throughout the history of conquest, establishment of intrahierarchy between males, and state formation).

17. It is no stretch of the imagination that pennilessness has a sexual connotation. The word *penny* is connected to *pawn*, which is connected to the Latin for *pedo*, or foot soldier—a subordinate, who is both expendable and whose life is in the hands of the *dominus*.

18. Augustine, a North African who Richard Hood (1994) notes was likely of Berber heritage, rejected the sexual libertinism of the Eastern-derived Manicheanism upon his conversation to Christianity. Yet Zoroastrianism, which inspired Manicheanism, also divided the world into good/white and bad/black. Augustine's colour-coded anthropomorphism remained untroubled by his Christian theology, which was itself inspired by Zoroastrianism (Stone, 1981). "Black" skin colour, moral impurity, and uncontrollable sexuality, which were one and the same for Augustine because the devil and his minions came in the form of Black men and women, demanded spiritualized racial cleansing. According to Augustine—and he was not alone in thinking so—"those are called to the faith who were black, just they, so that it may be said of them, 'Ye were sometimes darkness but now are ye light in the Lord.' They were indeed called black but let them not remain black, for out of these is made the church to whom it is said: Who is she that cometh up having been made white?" (cited in Hood, 1994, p. 87).

19. It is instructive to note that part of the debasement of women through the trope of witches was the belief that they copulate upon the devil's icy penis. Merlin Stone (1981) shows the antiquity of this trope. She describes how the evil Black lord Ahriman, kissed the first woman, Jeh, and made her menstruate as a consequence.

20. Though beyond the scope of this chapter, under Islamic and Arabic tutelage of Europe in Greco-Roman knowledge prior to the Crusades, both anti-black and anti-Black bias were preserved and mobilized by Arabs, Kurds, Persians, Turks, and other Islamicized groups. See Kitossa et al. (Chapter 10 in this volume, n. 5) for a more detailed discussion.

21. Scholars who should have known better, strain themselves to make an antiracist of Shakespeare (see Jordan, 1968/1977; Lyons, 1975). The plain fact is that Shakespeare, as an investor in the Virginia Company and a committed royalist (Linebaugh & Rediker, 2013), could in his plays hardly but favour disparagement of Africans and affirm the dangers of straying from absolutist authority.

22. It is significant that, as Katerina Deliovsky (Chapter 3 of this volume) shows that Black men who are sex workers in the Caribbean are referred to in slavocratic terms as "boys." This is far from an innocent appellation, particularly in racial honour-bound colonial contexts. It is well known and well recorded in slave narratives, slave manuals, and quotidian practice that, in transatlantic slavocracies, African men and women were not only denied gender designations but, paradoxically, were also constantly referred to as "boys" and "girls," regardless of age (see Tocqueville, 1835/2004; Segal, 1995; Woodard, 2014). In the full-spectrum dominance that was slavery, from children to adults of the White slave-owning caste, anyone could stop a grown "boy" or "girl" to demand, as recounted in the slave narrative of Andrew Jackson: "Where do you belong, nigger?"; "Whose boy are you?"; and "Where are you going, nigger?" (cited in Osofsky, 1969, p. 20). In Jamaica, children of the White slave-owning caste were empowered to assert the "childlike" status of enslaved Africans by beating whichever one of them whenever it pleased them. In *Tacky's Revolt*, Vincent Brown (2020) writes that "Whites trained themselves to discipline slaves at a young age—and learned to enjoy it" (p. 58). He records an observer from 1728 as follows:

> They were pleas'd in the West Indies with Scourging, and the first Play Thing put into their hands is commonly a Whip with which they exercise themselves upon a Post, in imitation of what they see daily perform'd on the naked Bodies of those miserable Creatures, till they are come of an Age that will allow them Strength enough to do it themselves. (p. 58)

Infantilization and animalization of African people during slavery, inculcated into White people across the Americas from childhood onward, normalized the vilest sadism recorded anytime in human history (Brown, 2020; Freyre, 1946/1964; Sweet, 2003). Signifying the special function in slavery to dehumanize males, Victor Ehrenberg (1962) shows that, among the Greeks, "[o]ne of the favourite etymological jokes was to derive the word for 'boy' and 'slave' from the word for 'to strike'; thus even an old slave could be addressed as 'boy' because he was beaten so often'" (p. 187). The point is also established by Moses Finley (1980) who writes: "Yet another dehumanizing device was the habit of addressing or referring to male slaves of any age as 'boy', *païs* in Greek, *puer* in Latin" (p. 96). It was out of this dehumanizing and neutering appellation of "boy" that Black men across the Americas began the practice of referring to each other as "brother," "man," and "brotherman" (see Boyd & Allen, 1996, p. 1). It is in this context, then, that the term *beach boy*, used by White women to describe their male sex work paramours in the Caribbean, revives the connotations and the power of women from the dominant racial caste to assert sexual authority over Black men.

23. The White-woman-as-goddess refers to the nineteenth- to early twentieth-century idealized, saintly, Timocratic representation of what was called in the US South the "cult of true womanhood" (Barnett, 2010; A. Davis, 1981). But this was a relational representation. On one hand, it enabled White men to construct Black women as "fallen" and "Jezebels." This enabled accountable (and forcible) access to their bodies, with that their supposedly inherent sexual

vivaciousness called out for rape (A. Davis, 1983; Jordan, 1977/1968; Wells, 2010). Black men, imagined as competitors to both White men and White people as a whole, were lynched even for the minor infraction of "reckless eyeballing" (Berry, 2008). White women, though they were regarded as victims in this equation, have been demonstrated to have been active agents, resisting the narrative of saintliness as much as seeking their sexual autonomy, often at the expense of Black men's lives (Curry, 2017; Wells, 2010;). But as I discuss below from a Fanonist psychoanalytic positioning, the White-woman-as-goddess also enables her ritualized degradation by hegemonic White masculinity that is both thrilled and exhorted to violence by her defilement.

24. Fanon (1952/1977) cites French novelist René Etiemble's repudiation of Cournot: "M. Cournot applies his talents to the rejuvenation of a fable in which the white man will always be able to find a specious argument: shameful, dubious, and thus doubly effective" (p. 172). Cournot's claims are no doubt specious, not least because he had available to him scientific evidence as to the irrationality of his assertion. Yet, what can be said of Richard Schmitt who, intending to repudiate the myth of Black priapism, concluded nonetheless that the "myth of the Black superpenis may have some basis in fact" (p. 54). How does he know this? Is it possible to know this? Race is a social construction, with only superficial biological significance. A surer conclusion is that of Dian Hanson (2012): "No racial or ethnic group is uniformly large and no group is uniformly small" (p. 5; see also Orakwe & Ebuh, 2007; Poulson-Bryant, 2005).

25. A difficulty with these approaches to representation is that they rely solely on the ableist metaphor of sight rather than vision. The latter recognizes that representations of the world can be made through the word, understood as modalities of signification that convey abstract concepts—referents to other referents—be they aural/vocal, signed/gestured, or conveyed through other sensual cues that go beyond word-as-speech and sight-as-seeing to feeling fields of energy (Sheldrake, 2012).

26. Also discussed by Foster (2019) is Anne-Louis Girodet de Roussy-Trioson's 1797 richly textured painting of the Haitian revolutionary and member of the National Council in France, Jean-Baptiste Belley (see p. 13). Aside from Belley having to share the frame with a bust of the spiritual father of the French Revolution, the Abbé de Raynal, is that fact that his genitals are not only prominently displayed, by his right-hand index finger directs the gaze at his crotch.

27. This scene calls to mind a line from C.L.R. James's (1963) *Black Jacobins*: "Some of the women affected a curiosity, the indulgence of which, with a horse, would have caused them to be kicked 20 yards across the deck. But the slaves had to stand it" (p. 9). James of course means, here, *White* women. Thomas Foster (2019) cites an eighteenth-century visitor to Barbados who commented that White women could be seen at auctions "dispassionately fondling the genitalia of semi-naked black male slaves in order to assess their health and future breeding potential" (p. 21). Gilberto Freyre (1946/1964) and James H. Sweet (2003) similarly document White women in Brazil, even nuns on their plantation cloisters, sexually availing themselves of enslaved Black men.

28. Since accessing the site for this interview on April 22, 2014, the first page containing this response from Bobby Farrelly is no longer available. It is significant that the Farrelly brothers

are responsible for two films cited in this chapter that clearly reflect the homoerotic obsession of White men with Black priapism and the desire for cuckolding and voyeuristic misogyny that pairs "hung" Black men with White women.

29. Without any sense of irony, a young White female university student is depicted with a large chocolate brown dildo hoisted above her head at the 2016 "cocks not glocks" protest against open gun carry on Texas university campuses (Dart, 2016).

30. The archetype of the hero defeating the forces of evil is legion in human history. But the more telling construction of these morality tales, from Enkidu the wild man of Mesopotamia, to Seth in Egypt, to the North American legend of the wendigo/windigo, is that of humans who cannot restrain themselves. The hero is lauded not so much for slaying dragons without, but for rising above base impulses within (Campbell, 1988; Girard, 1989). Paul Hoch (1979) cites Plato to this effect: "[A] lawless, wild Beast [lurks] in all of us, even in good men, [and] peers out in sleep, [when the] reasoning and human and ruling power [is off guard]" (p. 45).

31. Playthell Benjamin (2011), a noted US journalist, asserts that *The Arabian Nights* epic reproduces much the same cuckolding trope.

32. Russell Merritt (1982) cites US newspaper reports published between 1915 and 1917 that indicate the film had a national audience of 5 to 10 million and an international audience of 50 million people. He cites scholarly reports that assert that in its first 50 years, some 200 to 300 million people watched the film (p. 166, n. 2).

33. Merritt's (1990) essay, "D.W. Griffith's The Birth of A Nation: Going After Little Sister" is a descriptive account that avoids any psychosexual analysis. He asserts,"Michael Rogin, I believe, was the first to study *Birth of a Nation* from the perspective of [it's incoherence] and has usefully drawn out the psychoanalytic implications of Griffith's formal obsessions [with rape]" (p. 219).

34. Extraneous though it may seem, Woodrow Wilson relied on Edward Bernays, the nephew of Sigmund Freud, to develop a strategy to justify entering the United States into *The Great War* of 1914. This was after Wilson won the US presidency expressly on a campaign to keep the United States out of the war. It was this very same Woodrow Wilson, a Southerner and a classmate of Thomas Dixon at Johns Hopkins University, who would after a private screening of *The Birth of a Nation* at the White House, reputedly offered exuberant praise, exclaiming, "It is like writing history in lightning. My only regret is that it is all so terribly true" (cited in Merritt, 1982, p. 82). With the controversy surrounding the film, Wilson issued a retraction of his endorsement. Melvyn Stokes (2007) offers a detailed and interesting account of the circle of power in which Dixon moved, involving John D. Rockefeller (see also Merrit, 1982, p. 175), Theodore Roosevelt, and other leading lights of eastcoast power.

35. Theorizing the part played by *The Birth of a Nation* in the reproduction of global White supremacy remains nascent scholarly work. One such recent effort in Canada is by Greg Marquis (2014). Yet, to the extent that the Marquis's essay focuses on the representation of war, he misses the ways that sexual racism saturate the film as *the* cause of war, and thus the *real* significance of why Black people in Canada and the US protested the film will.

36. In the infamous attempted rape scenario, Gus stalks Ben Cameron's sister, Flora. To avoid him after a lengthy chase, she jumps over a cliff. Her brother Ben, searching for her, finds her at the bottom of the cliff. Cradling her dying body in his arms, her last gasp is that Gus had attempted to rape her (2:13:50 – 2:25:26). A despondent Ben returns her body to the house and prepares to ride with the Klan to bring "justice" to his sister. The Klan "apprehend" and "try" Gus for his indiscretion. Finding him "guilty," he is killed, presumably castrated, and his bound body dumped on the steps of Silas Lynch's house (2:25:27 – 2:31:57). Later, as the Klan mobilizes to reclaim the South, Ben holds aloft his sister's Confederate flag, ritually consecrated in a bowl of water, and exclaims, "Brethren, this flag bears the red stain of the life of a Southern woman, a priceless sacrifice on the altar of an outraged civilization." Then more ritual: a cross lit afire is quenched in the bowl to his exclamation, "Here I raise the ancient symbol of an unconquered race of men, the fiery cross of old Scotland's hills...I quench its flames in the sweetest blood that ever stained the sands of Time!" The cross is handed to a Klan sympathizer, who, Paul Revere–style, rides off to raise the posse comitatus (2:31:57–2:33:57).

37. Hoch (1979) overstates the point, since it can be made out that women from the conquering group also engaged in sexual domination of both females and males of the conquered group (Foster, 2011, 2019; Patterson, 1982).

38. David Brion Davis (2014) undertakes a detailed and wider-ranging discussion of the trope of "animalization" in the history of slavery and its specific application to transatlantic enslavement (see pp. 3–44).

39. The question of the rape and sexual abuse of Black men and boys is structurally excluded from thought (see Kitossa, Introduction to this volume; Curry, 2017, 2018; Foster, 2011, 2019; Lemelle, 2010; Sweet, 2003; Woodard, 2014) despite being widely known in Africana communities across the Americas as "buck breaking."

40. Fanon (1952/1977) does not preclude White women from participating in the pornographic scopophilia of Black men: "The Negro is the incarnation of a genital potency beyond all moralities and prohibitions. The women among the whites, by a genuine process of induction, invariably view the Negro as the keeper of the impalpable gate that opens into the realm of orgies, of bacchanals, of delirious sexual sensation" (p. 177).

41. In the United States, "second-wave" feminists such as Shulamith Firestone (1971) and Susan Brownmiller (1993), relied to a considerable extent on the Black-man-as-rapist for its viability and support from the White male economic and political establishment (see Kitossa, Introduction to this volume). Like their counterparts in the United States, "first-wave" feminists in Canada drew on tropes of Black rapists, dangerous Asians, and uncivilized non-Nordic Europeans to assert their right to the vote (Kitossa, 2002). And like his counterparts in the United States, Canada's first prime minister and US Confederate sympathizer Sir John A. Macdonald asserted in 1868 with pride: "We still have retained the punishment of death for rape...[W]e have thought it well...to continue it on account of the frequency of rape committee by negroes, of whom we have too many in Upper Canada. They are very prone to felonious assaults on white women; if the

sentence and imprisonment were not very severe, there would be the great dread of people taking the law into their own hands" (cited in Backhouse, 1991, p. 98).

Bibliography

Abell, W. (1966). *The collective dream in art*. Schocken Books. (Original work published 1957)

Anderson, B. (1991). *Imagined communities: Reflections on the origin and spread of nationalism*. Verso.

Ani, M. (1994). *Yurugu: An African-centered critique of European cultural thought and behaviour*. Africa World Press, Inc.

Backhouse, C. (1991). *Petticoats and prejudice: Women and law in nineteenth-century Canada*. Osgoode Society for Canadian Legal History/ Women's Press.

Baldwin, J. (1972). *No name in the street*. The Dial Press.

Baldwin, J. (1976). *The devil finds work*. The Dial Press.

Baldwin, J. (1984). *Notes of a native son*. Beacon Press. (Original work published 1955)

Baldwin, J. (1985a). *The fire next time*. Dell Publishing. (Original work published 1962)

Baldwin, J. (1985b). *The price of the ticket: Collected nonfiction, 1948–1985*. St. Martin's / Marek.

Baldwin, J. (1998). Going to meet the man. In T. Morrison (Ed.), *Baldwin: Early novels & stories* (pp. 933–50). The Library of America. (Original work published 1965)

Beardsley, G.M.H. (1979). *The Negro in Greek and Roman civilization*. Arno Press. (Original work published 1929)

Benjamin, P. (2011, February 15). On racism and the Arabs! *Commentaries on the Times*. http://commentariesonthetimes.wordpress.com/2011/02/15/on-racism-and-the-arabs/

Berger, J. (1973). *Ways of seeing*. Viking Press

Bernal, M. (1987). *Black Athena: The Afroasiatic roots of classical civilization*. Free Association Books / Rutgers University Press

Bernays, E. (2005). *Propaganda*. Ig Publishing. (Original work published 1928)

Berry, M.F. (2008). "Reckless eyeballing": The Matt Ingram case and the denial of African American sexual freedom. *The Journal of African American History, 93*(2), 223–34. https://doi.org/10.1086/jaahv93n2p223

Bogle, D. (2001). *Toms, coons, mulattoes, mammies, and bucks: An interpretive history of Blacks in American films* (4th ed.). Continuum.

Boyd, H., & Allen, R. (Eds.). (1996). *Brotherman: The odyssey of Black men in America*. Ballantine Books.

Brackman, H.D. (1977). *The ebb and flow of conflict: A history of Black-Jewish relations through 1900* [Doctoral dissertation, University of California, Los Angeles]. WorldCat Libraries.

Brakke, D. (2001). Ethiopian demons: Male sexuality, the Black-skinned other, and the monastic self. *Journal of the History of Sexuality, 10*(3), 501–35. https://doi.org/10.1353/sex.2001.0049

Brodie, A. (n.d.). The Farrelly brothers: "It's a lot easier to poke fun at a guy" [Interview]. In *AskMen*. http://ca.askmen.com/celebs/interview_500/507_farrelly-brothers.html

Brodkin, L. (1998). *How Jews became White folks and what that says about race in America*. Rutgers University Press.

Brown, V. (2020). *Tacky's Revolt: The story of an Atlantic slave war*. The Belknap Press of Harvard University Press.

Brownmiller, S. (1993). *Against our will: Men, women and rape*. Fawcett Columbine.

Byron, G.L. (2002). *Symbolic Blackness and ethnic difference in early Christian literature*. Routledge.

Campbell, J. (1988). *The power of myth*. Doubleday/Broadway

Cohen, S. (2002). *Folk devils and moral panics: The creation of the mods and rockers*. Routledge. (Original work published 1972)

Cook, R.A. (1974). *Thomas Dixon*. Twayne Publishers, Inc.

Crenshaw, K. (1989). Demarginalizing the intersection of race and sex: A Black feminist critique of antidiscrimination doctrine, feminist theory, and antiracist politics. *University of Chicago Legal Forum*, *1*(8), 139–67.

Cripps, T. (1996). The making of *The birth of a race*: The emerging politics of identity in silent movies. In D. Bernardi (Ed.), *The birth of Whiteness: Race and the emergence of U.S. cinema* (pp. 38–55). Rutgers University Press.

Curry, T.J. (2017). *The man-not: Race, class, genre, and the dilemmas of Black manhood*. Temple University Press.

Curry, T.J. (2018). Expendables for whom: Terry Crews and the erasure of Black male victims of sexual assault and rape. *Women's studies in communication*, *42*(3), 287–307. https://doi.org/10.1080/07491409.2019.1641874

Dart, T. (2016, August 25). Cocks not glocks: Texas students carry dildos on campus to protest gun law. *The Guardian*. https://www.theguardian.com/us-news/2016/aug/25/cocks-not-glocks-texas-campus-carry-gun-law-protest

Davis, A.Y. (1983). *Women, race, and class*. Random House.

Davis, D.B. (2006). *Inhuman bondage: The rise and fall of slavery in the New World*. Oxford University Press.

Davis, D.B. (2014). *The problem of slavery in the age of emancipation*. Alfred A. Knopf.

Dines, G. (2006). The White man's burden: Gonzo pornography and the construction of Black masculinity. *Yale Journal of Law and Feminism*, *18*(1), 283–97. https://digitalcommons.law.yale.edu/yjlf/vol18/iss1/12/

Diop, C.A. (1991). *Civilization or barbarism: An authentic anthropology* (H.J. Salemson & M. De Jager, Eds.; Y.-L.M. Ngemi, Trans.). Lawrence Hill Books.

DiPiero, T. (2002). *White men aren't*. Duke University Press.

Dixon, T. (1905). *The clansman: A historical romance of the Ku Klux Klan*. The Country Life Press.

Du Bois, W.E.B. (1835). *Black reconstruction: An essay toward a history of the part which Black folk played in the attempt to reconstruct democracy in America, 1860-1880*. Russell & Russell.

Du Bois, W.E.B. (2004). *Darkwater: Voices from within the veil*. Washington Square Press.

Ehrenberg, V. (1962). *The people of Aristophanes: A sociology of old Attic comedy*. Schocken Books.

Eze, E. (1995). Color of reason: The idea of "race" in Kant's anthropology. In K.M. Faull (Ed.), *Anthropology and the German Enlightenment: Perspectives on humanity* (pp. 103–31). Bucknell University Press.

Fanon, F. (1977). *Black skin, white masks* (C.L. Markmann, Trans.). Grove Press. (Original work published 1952)

Fanon, F. (2008). *Black skin, White masks* (R. Philcox, Trans.). Grove Press. (Original work published 1952)

Farrelly, P., & Farrelly, B. (Directors). (2007). *The heartbreak kid* [Film]. Paramount Pictures.

Farrelly, P., & Farrelly, B. (Directors). (2011). *Hall pass* [Film]. Warner Bros. Pictures.

Feimster, C.N. (2009). *Southern horrors: Women and the politics of rape and lynching*. Harvard University Press.

Finley, M. (1980). *Ancient slavery and modern ideology*. Penguin Books.

Firestone, S. (1971). *The dialectic of sex: The case for feminist revolution*. Bantam Books.

Foster, T.A. (2011). The sexual abuse of Black men under American slavery. *Journal of the History of Sexuality*, *20*, 445–64. https://doi.org/10.1353/sex.2011.0059

Foster, T.A. (2019). *Rethinking Rufus: Sexual violations of enslaved men*. University of Georgia Press.

Freyre, G. (1964). *The masters and the slaves*. Alfred A. Knopf. (Original work published 1946)

Friedman, D.M. (2001). *A mind of its own: A cultural history of the penis*. The Free Press.

Garfinkel, H. (1956). Conditions of successful degradation ceremonies. *American Journal of Sociology*, *61*(5), 420–24. doi.org/10.1086/221800

Gilman, S. (1986). Black bodies, White bodies: Toward an Iconography of female sexuality in late nineteenth-century art, medicine, and literature. In H.L. Gates (Ed.), *"Race," writing, and difference* (pp. 223–61). University of Chicago Press.

Girard, R. (1989). *The scapegoat* (Y. Freccero, Trans.). The Johns Hopkins University Press.

Goffman, E. (1963). *Stigma: Notes on the management of spoiled identity*. Prentice-Hall, Inc.

Goldstein, J.S. (2004). War and gender. In M. Ember & C.R. Ember (Eds.), *Encyclopedia of sex and gender: Men and women in the world's cultures* (pp. 107–16). Kluwer Academic / Plenum Publishers.

Gossett, T.F. (1973). *Race: The history of an idea in America*. Schocken.

Greenberg, D.F., & Bystryn, M. (1984). Capitalism, bureaucracy and male homosexuality. *Contemporary Crises*, *8*, 33–56. doi.org/10.1007/BF00729543

Griffith, D.W. (Director). (1915). *The birth of a nation* [Film]. Gravitas. https://www.youtube.com/watch?v=nGQaAddwjxg

Hall, E.T. (1989). *Beyond culture*. Anchor Books. (Original work published 1976)

Hall, S. (1997). The spectacle of the 'other'. In S. Hall (Ed.), *Representation: Cultural representations and signifying practices* (pp. 283–79). SAGE Publications / The Open University.

Hanson, D. (2012). *The little book of big penis: The compact age of rigid tools*. Taschen GmbH.

Heng, G. (2018). *The Invention of race in the European Middle Ages*. Cambridge University Press.

Hoch, P. (1979). *White hero, Black beast: Racism, sexism and the mask of masculinity*. Pluto Press.

Hodes, M. (1997). *White women, Black men: Illicit sex in the nineteenth-century South*. Yale University Press

Hood, R.E. (1994). *Begrimed and Black: Christian traditions on Blacks and Blackness*. Augsburg Fortress Press.

hooks, b. (1992). *Black looks: Race and representation*. Between The Lines.

Hountondji, P.J. (1983). *African philosophy: Myth and reality*. Hutchinson University Library for Africa.

Huxley, A. (1936, December 1). Notes on propaganda. *Harper's Magazine, 174*, pp. 32–41.

Hyam, R. (1991). *Empire and sexuality: The British experience*. Manchester University Press.

Ignatiev, N. (1995). *How the Irish became White*. Routledge.

Jacobson, M.F. (1998). *Whiteness of a different color: European immigrants and the alchemy of race*. Harvard University Press.

James, C.L.R. (1963). *The Black Jacobins: Tousaint L'Ouverture and the San Domingo Revolution*. Vintage Books.

Jordan, W.D. (1977). *White over Black: American attitudes toward the Negro, 1550-1812*. W.W. Norton. (Original work published 1968)

Keuls, E.C. (1985). *The reign of the phallus: Sexual politics in ancient Athens*. Harper & Row.

Kitossa, T. (2002). Criticism, reconstruction and African-centred feminist historiography. In N. Nathani Wane, K. Deliovsky, & E. Lawson (Eds.), *Back to the drawing board: African-Canadian feminisms* (pp. 85–116). Sumach Press.

Kitossa, T. (2016, November 17). Why the Donald's win might be good for White women—for all the wrong reasons. *Pambazuka News*. https://www.pambazuka.org/gender-minorities/why-donald%E2%80%99s-win-might-be-good-white-women-all-wrong-reasons

Kitossa, T. (2020, December 4). *Anti-Black sexual racism: Linking White police violence, COVID-19, and popular culture* [Symposium paper]. Intervention Symposium—Black Humanity: Bearing Witness to COVID-19, online. https://antipodeonline.org/2020/12/04/black-humanity-bearing-witness-to-covid-19/

Kovel, J. (1971). *White racism: A psychohistory*. Pantheon Books.

Lang, R. (Ed.). (1994). *The birth of a nation: D.W. Griffith, director*. Rutgers University Press.

Lasswell, H. (1927). The theory of political propaganda. *The American Political Science Review, 21*(3), 627–31.

Le Goff, J. (1985). Mentalities: A history of ambiguities. In P. Nora & C. Lucas (Eds.), *Constructing the past: Essays in historical methodology* (pp. 166–81). Cambridge University Press.

Lemelle, A.J. (2010). *Black masculinity and sexual politics*. Routledge.

Lerner, G. (1986). *The creation of patriarchy*. Oxford University Press.

Linebaugh, P., & Rediker, M. (2013). *The many-headed hydra: Sailors, slaves, commoners, and the hidden history of the revolutionary Atlantic*. Beacon Press.

Lyons, C.H. (1975). *To wash an Aethiop White: British ideas about Black African educability, 1530–1960*. Teachers College Press.

MacDougall, H.A. (1982). *Racial myth in English history: Trojans, Teutons, and Anglo-Saxons*. Harvest House / University Press of New England.

Mapplethorpe, R. (1980a). *Hooded Man* [Photograph]. J. Paul Getty Trust and Los Angeles County Museum of Art. https://collections.lacma.org/node/2155810

Mapplethorpe, R. (1980b). *Jimmy Freeman* [Photograph]. J. Paul Getty Trust and Los Angeles County Museum of Art. https://www.getty.edu/art/collection/objects/257191/robert-mapplethorpe-jimmy-freeman-american-negative-1981-print-1991/

Mapplethorpe, R. (1980c). *Man in Polyester Suit* [Photograph]. J. Paul Getty Trust and Los Angeles County Museum of Art. https://www.getty.edu/art/collection/objects/254454/robert-mapplethorpe-man-in-polyester-suit-american-negative-1980-print-1981/

Marquis, G. (2014). A war within a war: Canadian reactions to D.W. Griffith's *The birth of a nation*. *Histoire Sociale / Social History, 47*(94), 421–42. https://doi.org/10.1353/his.2014.0041

McGerr, M.E. (2003). *A fierce discontent: The rise and fall of the progressive movement in America, 1870–1920*. Oxford University Press.

Mercer, K. (1994). *Welcome to the jungle: New positions in Black cultural studies*. Routledge.

Merritt, R. (1982). Dixon, Griffith, and the southern legend: A cultural analysis of *The birth of a nation*. In R.D. MacCann & J.C. Ellis (Eds.), *Cinema examined: Selections from* Cinema Journal (pp. 165–84). E.P. Dutton.

Merritt, R. (1990). D.W. Griffith's *The birth of a nation*: Going after little sister. In P. Lehman (Ed.), *Close viewings: An anthology of new film criticism* (pp. 215–37). Florida State University Press.

Messerschmidt, J. (2007). "We must protect our southern women": On Whiteness, masculinities, and lynching. In M. Bosworth & J. Flavin (Eds.), *Race, gender, and punishment: From colonialism to the war on terror* (pp. 77–94). Rutgers University Press.

Mudimbe, V.Y. (1988). *The invention of Africa*. Indiana University Press.

Mumford, L. (1967). *Technics and human development: The myth of the machine* (Vol. 1). Harvest / HBJ Books.

Mumford, L. (1973). *The condition of man*. Harvest / HBJ Books. (Original work published 1944)

Naipaul, V.S. (1977). *India: A wounded civilization*. Penguin Books

Newman, L.M. (1999). *White women's rights: The racial origins of feminism in the United States*. Oxford University Press.

O'Hanlon, R., & Washbrook, D. (1992). After Orientalism: Culture, criticism, and politics in the Third World. *Comparative Studies in Society and History, 34*(1), 141–67. https://www.jstor.org/stable/178988

Orakwe, J., & Ebuh, G. (2007). "Oversized" penile length in the Black people: Myth or reality. *Tropical Journal of Medical Research, 11*(1), 16–18. https://doi.org/10.4314/tjmr.v11i1.30465

Osofsky, G. (1969). *Puttin' one ole massa: The slave narratives of Henry Bibb, William Wells Brown, and Solomon Northup*. Harper Torchbooks.

Ousselin, E. (2009). *The invention of Europe in French literature and film*. Palgrave MacMillan

Parriott, J.D. (Director). (1990). *Heart condition* [Film]. Sony Pictures Home Entertainment.

Patterson, O. (1982). *Slavery and social death: A comparative study*. Harvard University Press.

Poliakov, L. (1974). *Aryan myth: A history of racist and nationalist ideas in Europe*. Sussex University Press.

Poulson-Bryant, S. (2005). *Hung: A meditation on the measure of Black men in America*. Broadway Books.

Roback, A.A. (1944). *A dictionary of international slurs: Ethnophaulisms, with a supplementary essay on aspects of ethnic prejudice*. Sci-Art Publishers.

Robinson, C.J. (1997). In the year 1915: D.W. Griffith and the Whitening of America. *Social Identities*, *3*(2), 161–92. https://doi.org/10.1080/13504639752041

Roediger, D.R. (1991). *The wages of Whiteness: Race and the making of the American working class*. Verso

Rogin, M.P. (1987). *Ronald Reagan, the movie: And other episodes in political demonology*. University of California Press.

Schmitt, R. (2002). Large propagators: Racism and the domination of women. In N. Tuana & W. Cowling (Eds.), *Revealing male bodies* (pp. 38–55). Indiana University Press.

Sheldrake, R. (2012). *The presence of the past: Morphic resonance and the memory of nature*. Park Street Press.

Shakespeare, W. (1975). *The complete works of William Shakespeare*. Avenel Books.

Simon-Aaron, C. (2008). *The Atlantic slave trade: Empire, enlightenment, and the cult of the unthinking Negro*. Mellen Press.

Smithers, G.D. (2013). *Slave breeding: Sex, violence, and memory in African American history*. University of Florida Press.

Snowden, F., Jr. (1976). Iconographical evidence on the Black populations in Greco-Roman antiquity. In L. Bugner (Ed.), *The image of the Black in Western art* (Vol. 1). Menil Foundation, Inc.

Stokes, M. (2007). *D.W. Griffith's* The birth of a nation*: A history of the most controversial motion picture of all time*. Oxford University Press

Stone, M. (1981). *Three thousand years of racism: Recurring patterns in racism*. Sibylline Books.

Stone, O. (Director). (1999). *Any given Sunday* [Film]. Warner Bros. Pictures.

Sublette, N., & Sublette, C. (2016). *The American slave coast: A history of the slave-breeding industry*. Lawrence Hill Books.

Sweet, J.H. (2003). *Recreating Africa: Culture, kinship and religion in the African-Portuguese world, 1441–1770*. University of North Carolina Press.

Szasz, T. (1997). *The manufacture of madness: A comparative study of the Inquisition and the mental health movement*. Syracuse University Press. (Original work published 1990)

Szasz, T. (2003). *Ceremonial chemistry: The ritual persecution of drugs, addicts, and pushers*. Syracuse University Press. (Original work published 1974)

Taylor, C. (1996). The re-birth of the aesthetic in cinema. In D. Bernardi (Ed.), *The birth of Whiteness: Race and the emergence of U.S. cinema* (pp. 15–37). Rutgers University Press.

Taylor, R. (1979). *Film propaganda: Soviet Russia and Nazi Germany*. Harper and Row, Inc.

Thomas, G. (2007). *The sexual demon of colonial power: Pan-African embodiment and erotic schemes of empire*. Indiana University Press.

Thompson, L.A. (1989). *Romans and Blacks*. Routledge / Oklahoma University Press.

de Tocqueville, A. (2004). *Democracy in America*. Bantam Classic. (Original work published 1835)

Trexler, R.C. (1995). *Sex and conquest: Gendered violence, political order, and the European conquest of the Americas*. Cornell University Press.

Trott, D. (2017, July). Race play 101: My introduction into the world of racist sex play. *HuffPost*. http://www.huffingtonpost.com/entry/raceplay-101-my-introduction-into-the-world-of-racist_us_595b8fb7e4b0326c0a8d130a

Wallerstein, I. (1991). *Unthinking social sciences: The limits of nineteenth-century paradigms*. Polity Press.

Ware, V. (1992). *Beyond the pale: White women, racism, and history*. Verso.

Washington, J.R. (1984). *Anti-Blackness in English religion, 1500–1800*. E. Mellen Press.

Wells, I.B. (2010). *Ida B. Wells versus Judge Lynch: The anti-lynching trilogy* (J.H. Mitchell, Ed.). CreateSpace Independent Publishing Platform.

Weiermair, P. (Ed.). (1999). *Erotic art: From the 17th to the 20th century, The Dopp-Collection*. Edition Stemmle.

Wiegman, R. (1993). The anatomy of lynching. In J.C. Fout & M.S. Tantillo (Eds.), *American sexual politics: Sex, gender, and race since the Civil War* (pp. 223–45). University of Chicago Press.

Williams, L. (2004). Race, melodrama, and *The birth of a nation* (1915). In L. Grieveson & P. Kramer (Eds.), *The silent cinema reader* (pp. 242–53). Routledge.

Woodard, V. (2014). *The delectable Negro: Human consumption and homoeroticism within U.S. slave culture* (J.A. Joyce, D.A. McBride, & J.E. Patrick, Eds.). New York University Press.

2

Anaconda East

Fetishes, Phallacies, Chimbo *Chauvinism, and the Displaced Discourse of Black Male Sexuality in Japan*

JOHN G. RUSSELL

THIS CHAPTER EXPLORES representations of black[1] masculinity in contemporary Japanese popular culture. It presents a descriptive analysis of tropes and memes of black male sexuality in which the black male body is fetishized and constructed as the archetypical hypersexual, pathological, and bestial Other. Specifically, it provides a critical analysis of how transnational tropes of black male sexuality that originate in the West merge with and articulate themselves within local Japanese obsessions and anxieties about power, race, and gender. I suggest that the black male body occupies a distinct space in the Japanese imaginary in and across four discourses: (1) US military power in Japan and Japanese female sexual agency; (2) representations of black men's sexuality in Japanese pornography, (3) the totemic nature of black phallic supremacy as seen in penile enhancement advertisements; and (4) the phenomenological complicity of select expatriate black writers and adult video entertainers who reify gender and racial essentialisms, objectify and fetishize Japanese women, and reduce black men's presence in Japan to a quintessentially phallic and sexually pathological one.

The mainstreaming of the eroticization of the black male body and its depiction as more than just a sexual threat that gained momentum during the so-called *kokujin bōmu* [black boom][2] of the 1990s, a period in which African American film, hip-hop, reggae, and other commercialized forms of global black popular culture began to enjoy popularity in Japan. Visual representations of nude, muscular black men, some apparently inspired by the homoerotic works of Robert Mapplethorpe, were a fixture of Japan's art, media, and, with the rise of the internet, cyberspace landscapes. For example, a black male nude adorns the cover of *Studio Voice* magazine's 1991 special issue *Kokujin-teki* [blackness],[3] in which the object of the voyeuristic Japanese gaze is modestly displaced by the folded hands of the cover's black male model. Similarly, a 1994 flyer for a contemporary black film festival conceals its model's black manhood behind unreeled film (Figure 2.1). Almost a decade later, in 2003, conceptual artist Sakura Yasuyuki[4] initiated his Kabuto Project, which began as a series of photographic and video-captured "power sculptures" of the chiselled musculature of over 80 seminude black male models.[5]

In deconstructing these representations of black masculinity, I situate them as deeply intertwined with Japan's interaction with the West, particularly the United States, and show how they continue to be negotiated and reinscribed through discourses of gender, race, and sexuality. I suggest that these representations are disturbingly familiar to Western observers yet simultaneously particular to Japanese preoccupations and obsessions that are repetitively—and compulsively—articulated within the framework of its mass culture. Specifically, I will first account for the fetishistic preoccupations of the black penis-as-phallus in selected works of Japanese postwar literature that are generally representative of the literary treatment of black masculinity in Japan. I then move to examine how representations of black masculinity in pornography serve to both critique the sexual agency of Japanese women and to channel, mobilize, and—perhaps most importantly—conceal unresolved conflicts concerning the postwar US military presence in Japan, a presence often constructed in the media and popular culture as disruptively and destructively black.

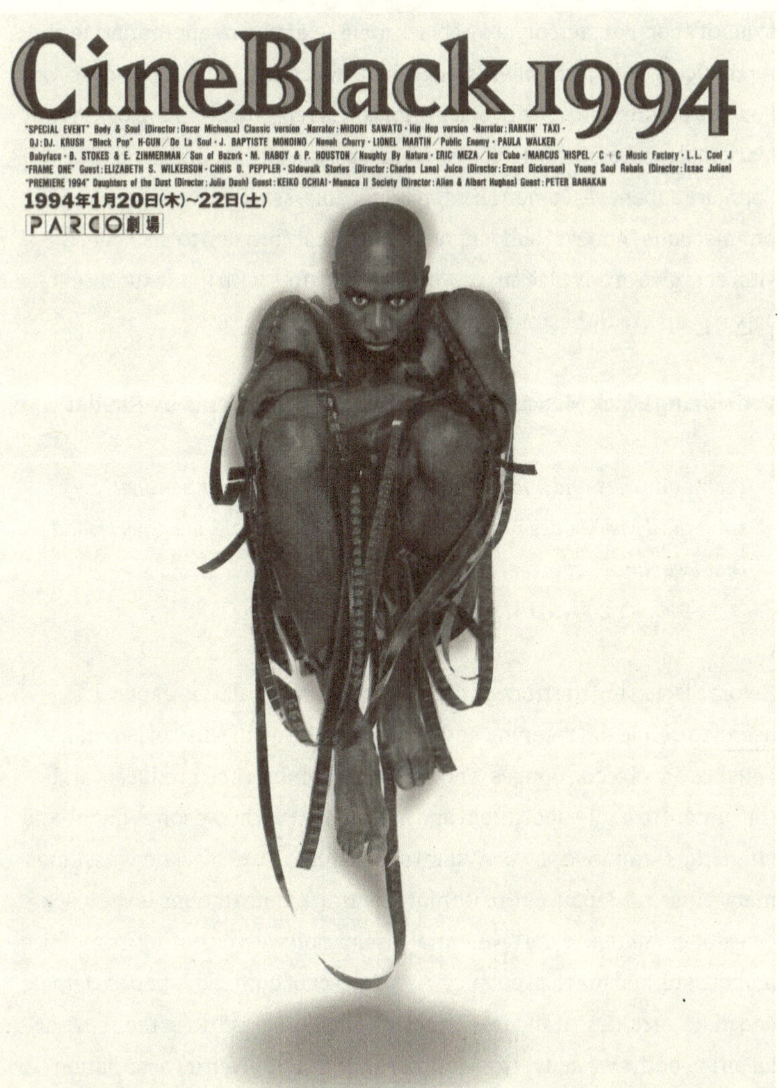

FIGURE 2.1: Black film festival flyer sponsored by Parco department store, 1994. (© Parco Co., Ltd.)

Third, I demonstrate how the identification of black masculinity with hypersexuality and priapism provides an essential prop for a Japanese male sexual enhancement industry and internet discussions that attempt to justify popular stereotypes of black male sexuality by appropriating and reproducing the claims of Western scientific racism. Finally, I discuss how the perdurable trope of black priapism is reproduced in the writings of black male writers who depict Japan as a sexual playground. These writers derogate Japanese women as interchangeable, sex-deprived yet epically promiscuous "honeys" and "sugar mamas" that threaten to dissipate the vital energies of any black man who is too carefree with the sexual licence Japan purportedly bestows upon him.

Fetishizing Black Masculinity: The Totemic Black Penis-as-Phallus

> *I came into the world imbued with the will to find a meaning in things, my spirit filled with the desire to attain the source of the world, and then I found that I was an object in the midst of other objects.*
>
> —FRANTZ FANON, *Black Skin, White Masks*

Before discussing the trope of the black penis-as-phallus in Japan, it is useful to define the meaning and function of the word *fetish* in general. Fetishes are objects, images, and ideas that compel their producers and consumers to fixate upon them and invest them with awesome, awful, and often transformative power. While the fetishization of blackness assumes many guises in Japan, one of its more central manifestations is the black penis-as-phallus and the reverential fascination with narrating its mythical proportions and magical potency. As an object of both the Japanese female and male gaze, desire and fear, the black phallus *transfixes* in the sense of inspiring both awe and terror—or, more accurately given its association with the American military presence in Japan, "shock and awe"—and in the original sense of the Latin root *trānsfixus*, that is, "to pierce through." It is imbued with a phantasmagorical, penetrative power and potency evoked across a wide array of Japanese literary, artistic, pornographic, and commercial texts.

The function of fetishes is to resolve certain threats and contradictions and to manage the chaos of reality. Psychoanalytic theory sees the fetish as a mechanism for the resolution of anxieties primarily centred on castration, where it serves as both "token of triumph over the threat of castration and a protection against it" (Freud, 1927/2001, p. 154). Homi Bhabha (1997) describes fetish as a "a stereotype that gives access to an identity which is predicated as much on mastery and pleasure as it is on anxiety and defence, for it is a form of multiple and contradictory belief in its recognition of difference and disavowal of it" (p. 75). Stuart Hall (1997) has identified the role that substitution, displacement, and disavowal play in fetishization, the last providing a "strategy by means of which a powerful fascination or desire is both *indulged* and at the same time *denied*" (p. 267). Similarly, Anne McClintock (1995) defines fetishization as the

> displacement onto an object (or person) of contradictions that the individual cannot resolve at a person level...The fetish marks a crisis in social meaning as the embodiment of an impossible irresolution. The contradiction is displaced onto and embodied in the fetish object, which is thus destined to recur with *compulsive* [emphasis added] repetition. (p. 184)

It is this last aspect of the fetish—compulsive, ritualistic repetition—that becomes readily apparent when we examine the representation of blackness in a wide variety of media across transnational spaces. I have come to call this repetition the *ricorso*: the cyclical rearticulation of multiple, perdurable, and conflicting tropes of racial alterity that, for all their Bhabhaean fluidity, are fixed in a recursive pattern of opposition and contradiction (Russell, 2011). I employ the term *ricorso* not so much in the Vicoean sense of cyclical historical development as in the Joycean sense of a fluidic repetition and return. That is, in their compulsive repetition, fetishes, particularly racial ones, comprise part of a circular—if paradoxically static—dynamic whose recursive current courses its way across imagined national, ethnic, and "racial" boundaries, its discourse, comprised of insidious implicit assumptions, providing a potent, universal currency of belief. As limned by the ricorso, the black male is construed as a confluence of contradictory oppositions in which cisgender black masculinity is ultimately defined as body: mindless, muscled, pathological, and libidinous. At once beautiful and ugly in its bestiality, wild yet domesticated, powerful yet impotent, it is an object of envy and contempt but seldom of indifference. Ironically, in Japan, despite frequently being redacted and obscured in artistic, photographic, cinematic, and pornographic representation, the black penis-as-phallus is blatantly displayed, examined, measured, and discussed, the putative revulsion that it inspires suspended by the desire it arouses.[6] Still, like all magical exhibitions, misdirection and projection are involved. Fixing the gaze on the black male body, in particular on its genitals, distracts from a more potent, revealing, and conflicted discourse about sexual politics, US military occupation, ambivalent patriarchy, female agency, race, the supremacy of whiteness, and the politics of desire in Japan.

In her pioneering study of the fetishization of the black phallus in Japanese popular culture, Nina Cornyetz (1994) identifies these conflicts and contradictions, observing that Japanese male anxieties and insecurities about the perceived "inferiority" of Japanese men's penis size came to inspire the aforementioned *kokujin bōmu* [black boom] of the 1990s. In that moment of cultural appropriation, "the prewar image of a bestial black man was reconstituted as a sex symbol, and the once threatening black phallus (and suppressed erotic curiosity) was reimaged as overtly desirable, and commodified" (Cornyetz, 1994, p. 125). Nonetheless, this reappraisal of the erotic/exotic worth of the black phallus and the commodification of black masculinity is not as subversive as Cornyetz suggests. For while it is true that the period reconstitutes black men as sexual symbols, they nonetheless remain beasts—sometimes wild, sometimes domesticated. Their raw bestiality, embodied in their ostensibly enormous penises, promises to sate the unsatisfied desires of Japanese women frustrated by the inadequacies of Japanese men, as well as to channel the rage and masturbatory/homoerotic fantasies of those men.

In Japanese literature, the alluring bestiality of the black penis-as-phallus is clearly presented in Ōe Kenzaburō's (1957/1981) prize-winning *Shiiku* [*The Catch*].[7] Although the story depicts the fascination of a group of Japanese boys with their "catch"—a downed black American World War II pilot who is captured and imprisoned by members of their village—it is, ironically, the boys who, enthralled by the awesome, animalistic physicality of their black prisoner, figuratively become *his* admiring captives in a reverse Stockholm Syndrome. Their infatuation is apparent in a scene in which the narrator describes the airman bathing in a stream:

> His naked, wet body, reflecting the strong rays of the sun, shone like the body of a black horse; it was perfect, and beautiful. Suddenly, we noticed that the Negro had a splendid, a heroic, an unbelievably beautiful phallus. We gathered around him clamoring, bumping our naked bodies against each other, and when he grasped it and, taking up a fierce, threatening stance, gave a great bellow, we dashed water on him and laughed till the tears ran down our cheeks.
>
> We looked on him as on some rare, wonderful domestic animal, a genius of an animal. What words now can express the love we felt for the Negro airman, or the richness and rhythm of the sunlight glittering on his wet, heavy skin on that far-off, bright summer afternoon; of the deep shadows on the cobbles; of the smell of the children's and the Negro's bodies; of the voices hoarse with delight? (Ōe, 1957/1981, pp. 47–48)[8]

Since Ōe, each generation of Japanese writers—from Matsumoto Seichō's (1958) *Kuroji no E* [*Painting on Black Cloth*] and Murakami Ryū's (1976) *Kagirinaku Tōmei ni Chikai Blū* [*Almost Transparent Blue*] to the negrophilic oeuvre of Yamada Eimi's *Beddotaimu Eizu* [*Bedtime Eyes*] (1985), *Jeshī no Sebone* [*Jesse's Spine*] (1986), and *Torasshu* [*Trash*] (1991)—have produced transgressive narratives that obsessively—albeit superficially—probe black male sexuality, particularly sexual relationships between Japanese women and black men. This literary treasure trove consistently mobilizes the trope of animalistic, priapic, heterosexual black masculinity, employing it to address fundamental contradictions of power, Japanese racial and sexual identity, and their concomitant anxieties and insecurities.

The spell cast by the black penis-as-phallus in the Japanese imaginary crosses gender boundaries, being as much an overdetermined object of female desire as of male curiosity, envy, and fantasy projection. Affirming the totemic quality of the black penis-as-phallus, the female narrator of Yamada Eimi's (1985) *Beddotaimu eizu* [*Bedtime Eyes*] describes her black lover's penis:

> His dick wasn't the kind of disgusting, red cock that white men have, nor was it the pathetic, infantile thing of Japanese men, the kind that doesn't do a thing for you until it's inside you.
>
> ...
>
> With Spoon, maybe it was just that his pubic hair was the same color as his skin, but I was in awe of his dick. It was gorgeous, like a big chocolate bar, and as I stared at it excitedly I couldn't stop my mouth from watering. (pp. 5–6)[9]

Such salivary phallophilia should not, however, distract from the fact that, regardless of the gender (and race) of those who pursue it, the black penis serves as a formidable weapon in the critical discourse of gender in Japan. Japanese men employ the discourse of the black penis to symbolize their own emasculation and to criticize what they perceived as the promiscuity of Japanese women. On the other hand, when wielded by Japanese women through their domestication of black male lovers, possession of the black penis constitutes an equally effective instrument of resistance in their rejection of Japanese patriarchy and struggle for sexual empowerment (Cornyetz, 1994; Kelsky, 1996, 2001; Russell, 1998).

The fetishization of the black male body in general and the black penis in particular reflects an introjected colonial gaze. Although Japan was never formally colonized by any Western power, its weakened status in relation to the West since the late nineteenth century and particularly under the American occupation (1945–1952) has meant that it has incorporated critical aspects of Western colonial discourse into how it seeks to display itself and nonwhite Others vis-à-vis Western-defined notions of modernity.

Race, gender, and sexuality are dynamic and interactive sites at which are congealed Japanese fears and anxieties about their status relative to an economically and militarily superior white West (Russell, 1993). In Japan, these insecurities are, historically, not overtly expressed, but instead transferred and displaced onto black men's bodies. They are articulated at the intersection of two discourses: the discourse of power and impotence in the asymmetrical United States–Japan relationship and the discourse of black masculinity and phallic mastery. We could add to this pairing, as well, the resentful and sordid critique of sexually autonomous Japanese femininity. Here the fetish of the black penis-as-phallus takes on the weaponized instrumentality of fulfilling the desire of Japanese hegemonic masculinity to objectify and debase Japanese women through their proximity to the phallicized bodies of black men and the desire/repulsion it arouses.

The phallicization of black bodies in the Japanese imaginary is ultimately connected to another, more violent and phantasmagorical construction of black men as physical and sexual supermen. To understand the depth of this fantasy in the minds of Japanese men, it is vital to understand how representations of black men have been deployed by Western powers to signify the real or potential domination of Japanese men. Ever since the sixteenth and seventeenth centuries, when Portuguese and Spanish merchants and missionaries, and later Dutch merchants, arrived on Japanese shores with their African servants and slaves in tow, black bodies have been mobilized by Westerners not only to project their power but to demonstrate the futility of nonwhite resistance against it. Probably the most illustrative example of this harnessing of black masculinity in the service of white domination occurred in 1853, when American Commodore Matthew Calbraith Perry utilized two black crew members as bodyguards during ceremonies to open Japan to Western commerce. Perry's onyx guardians, whom the commodore describes as "a couple of tall jet-black Negroes, completely armed" (Perry, 1968, p. 98), served a role not unlike *niō*, the imposing, muscular guardians of Gautama Buddha that traditionally guard the entrance of Buddhist temples. Indeed, Perry's use of physically powerful blacks as bodyguards served as an extravagant and indelible display of white American power as well as a tacit warning to the Japanese of the futility of any resistance to American demands—for despite being imposing physical specimens, these blacks served a white master (Russell, 2007, pp. 28–29). Emily Roxworthy (2008) cites the official report of the event compiled by Francis L. Hawks in 1856, which describes the dramaturgy of the quite literal power (dis)play involving the strategic exploitation of black masculinity: "All this parade was but for effect. The procession was obliged to make a somewhat circular movement to reach the entrance of the house of reception. This gave a good opportunity for the display of the escort" (p. 28). Roxworthy asserts:

> This self-conscious display of American race relations seemed intent upon reinforcing the notions that the Japanese had been relegated to spectators, cowed by a strange American spectacle of dominance and difference. Indeed, Perry was pleased to see how the black bodyguards fascinated and startled the Japanese audience, not to mention how these tall African Americans—fully armed and bearing American flags—strikingly towered over "*the more effeminate looking*" [emphasis added] Japanese. The passivity of Japan seemed assured by such confident demonstrations of American racialization. (p. 28)

If Western, particularly American, discourse uses black men's bodies to project white Western power, in Japan their bodies serve as totems of desire and revulsion that are used to express repressed fears of powerlessness and emasculation in the form of military domination by and submission to American authority. It finds expression in Takechi Tetsuji's (1965) film *Kuroi Yuki* [*Black Snow*]. In the film, the impotent antihero—a metaphor for a defeated, emasculated postwar Japan—attempts to resolve his inner conflicts and reaffirm his manhood through the symbolically masculine penetrative act of stabbing to death that which most threatens him and, by extension, Japan: a black GI whom he voyeuristically witnessed having sex with his prostitute mother. Some 20 years later, similar male anxieties were reiterated in the discourse of *burasagari-zoku* [literally: Japanese women who "dangle" from the arms of foreign men] and *ierō kyabu* [yellow cabs], both derogatory terms coined by the Japanese media in the 1980s and 1990s and applied to Japanese women who have sexual relations with American, primarily black, men.[10] This time, however, the critique came not only from self-avowed *minzokushugisha* [ethnic nationalists] like Takechi but also from mainstream media that used the phenomenon to criticize both Japanese women and the US military presence in Japan for the emasculation of Japanese men, whom it represented as incapable of competing with black servicemen for the sexual attention of Japanese women.

The black-man-as-sexual-superman finds expression in the perdurable tropistic metonym of the black rapist, where it condenses with the black penis-as-phallus in representations of the black GI as a symbol of (Japan's) rape par excellence. The postwar history of Japan and the United States is marked by repeated acts of sexual violence against Japanese women, with the public face of rape frequently presented as black.[11] Here, construction of the black male as a threat to Japanese women expresses Japanese male fears of powerlessness to protect them against sexual assault. The trope infects virtually all aspects of Japanese popular discourse as chronicled in both fictional and actual incidents of sexual assault. For example, author Matsumoto Seichō's (1958) novel *Kuroji no E* [*Portrait on Black Cloth*] is based on an actual 1950 incident; the story involves members of a black platoon stationed in Kyushu that goes AWOL and rapes a Japanese woman.[12] Black rapists also figure in Okinawan writer Genga Asayoshi's (1975) *Aozameta Machi* [*The Town That Went Pale*] and Saegusa Kazuko's (1989) *Sono Fuyu no Shi* [*A Winter's Death*].[13] In 1995, the rape of a 12-year-old girl in Okinawa by three African American servicemen rekindled these associations.[14]

The real or fictional victims of the "black rapist" need not be Japanese, however. In Tezuka Osamu's (1995) fantasy *Chōjin Daikei* [*Birdman Anthology*],[15] highly evolved birds whose intelligence has been artificially enhanced set out to eliminate the human race. In one tale set in Africa,

Rōdeshia ni te [*In Rhodesia*], we learn that the birds have attacked only whites, sparing blacks who, as was typical in this period, are rendered as stereotypical, bulbous-eyed, thick-lipped coons who brutally kill whites who attempt to escape the birds by fleeing to the black areas. As the story unfolds, a white woman fleeing the bird's attack pleads with a doltish young black man to hide her in his barn. As they huddle inside, the man tells her that the birds attack whites because whites oppress blacks. Suddenly birds flock above the shack. Frantic, the white woman begs the black man to protect her. He demands that she kiss him, but when she refuses, he threatens to throw her to the birds and, helpless, she complies. Wiping his lips afterwards, he escalates his demands, ordering her to strip if she still wants him to continue to protect her. She resists, but as the leader of the birds surreptitiously looks on from a window ledge, the black man rapes her. Suddenly, the barn is engulfed in flames. The leader of the birds, having set the structure afire, leaves the two humans trapped inside, unable to escape. The narrator explains that in their bid to dominate the world, the birds had planned to exterminate the human race starting at its "highest level," but when their leader learned that in the Republic of South Africa whites regarded blacks as inferior and subjugated them, it decided to attack only whites. After witnessing the black man rape the white woman, however, it realized that "*kokujin ga hakujin onna wo okasu no wo mite, sude ni kokujin mo onaji reberu to satotta; kokujin mo onaji unmei ni natta*" [blacks were just as base as whites and deserved the same fate] (p. 83).

Classic and contemporary Japanese manga depict blacks as massively endowed cannibals, baton-dicked basketball players, and witless "*dojin*" [natives] who sport ridiculously oversized penis sheaths. More extreme manga reproduce motifs found in live-action porn, depicting pale-skinned, Bambi-eyed Japanese females violently gangbanged and/or gang raped by throngs of black men with grotesquely huge, thick-veined penises. Such works are not limited to professional manga but also include online fan-produced comics.[16]

In addition to manga, cinema, and literature, the black rapist trope is also a staple of Japanese pornography (Figure 2.2). Ian Buruma (1984) observes

FIGURE 2.2: DVD cover for a film titled The Black Men Rape. *(© Outvision)*

that Japanese pornographic films not only frequently depict American soldiers raping Japanese women, but notes that the fact that the soldiers are often black exacerbates Japanese outrage (p. 57)—and presumably titillation.

In the internet age, this trope has become even more entrenched. For example, as of April 2016, entering the Sino-Japanese term 黒人 [*kokujin,* black person] in the amazon.co.jp DVD search engine automatically generated a list of 10 keywords,[17] including 黒人レイプ [*kokujin reipu,* black rape], which comprised 206 titles.[18] The word *reipu* [rape] and its synonyms *bōkō* and *okasareta* appear in about 18% of these, including one simply called *Black Rape Video Collection*.[19] In contrast, among the 10 keywords generated by 白人 (*hakujin,* white person), 白人レイプ [*hakujin reipu*, white rape] was not one of them.[20]

The association of blacks with rape was on full view on another Japanese online retailer, DMM.com. There, such DVDs form their own pornographic niche[21] and include *Kokujin Shūdan Reipu* [*Black Gang Rape*], a 40-volume series produced between 1998 and 2003; the four-volume, 2012 *Joshi Kōsei Kokujin Reipu* [*High School Girl Black Rape*]; and the English-titled, two-volume *Black Gang-Rape* from 2001 and 2005, to name but a few.[22]

From Cakewalk to Cockwalk

> *[T]o be an American Negro male is also to be a kind of walking phallic symbol: which means that one pays, in one's own personality, for the sexual insecurity of others.*
>
> —JAMES BALDWIN, "The Black Boy Looks at the White Boy"

Discussions of the depiction of black alterity and racial mimesis in popular culture have long grossly exaggerated and caricaturized the black countenance. Other body parts have been appropriated to mark difference but arguably none more than the black penis, which has served both as totem and, often quite literally in the West, as (severed) trophy of racial and sexual otherness. In Japan, as we shall see, disembodied black penises have acquired their own prized, if less physically invasive, status. Many may see blackface for what it is: an offensive, mimetic practice in which certain physiognomic features are mainstreamed as deformed: a dehumanizing caricature for the entertainment of one group at the belittlement of another. And while blackface in Japan has been subject to public censure that has reduced—but not eliminated—its performance, representations of the black penis-as-phallus persist, dominating depictions of black males in Japanese pornography.

Gail Dines (2006) has aptly called American interracial pornography, or IP,[23] "the new minstrel show" (p. 294). Such performances, however, are not confined to America; they are also enacted in Japan where heterosexual male pornography depicting sex between Japanese and non-Asian foreigners occupies a special niche. Although seldom labelled "*ijinshu-kan*" [interracial], these videos fixate on what the American pornographic industry labels "big black cock" (BBC) or, as it is variously and prolifically described in Japan, *kokujin kyokon, kokujin deka mara, kokujin no gokubuto chimbo*, and *kokujin deka chin*. Moreover, Japanese pornography is gendered and raced in ways that further distinguish it from American pornography. Japanese pornography involving foreign performers typically features pale, white (and stereotypically blond) women engaged in sex with men of various pigmentations. Depictions of foreign male sexual engagements, however, tend to obsess on black men and Japanese women. This does not mean that white men's bodies are not subjected to sexual fetishization. White penises are also subject to the Japanese male gaze and their dimensions also serve as objects of speculation, envy, and disdain—yet they do not occupy the cynosure of Japanese male homoerotic speculation and fantasy.

In addition to the "black rapist" trope, something of the nature of Japanese male obsession with the black penis-as-phallus can be seen on Japanese websites. This obsession has expanded exponentially over the decade, judging by the growing number of pornographic DVDs featuring BBCs or, to borrow the initialism of one DVD series, "BDFs" (black dick fucks). In 2006, a search I conducted of the term 黒人 [*kokujin*, black person] in the DVD section of Japan's amazon.co.jp produced 54 thumbnailed titles, all but four of which were pornographic. Another search in 2010 produced 512 titles, all but six of which were pornographic. As of April 26, 2016, the number had almost tripled, growing to 1417 (of which 1386 were nonduplicated listings), all but 21 pornographic. In comparison, a search of the term 白人 [*hakujin*, white person] produced only 487 titles (of which 460 were nonduplicated listings), all but 7 pornographic.[24]

Significantly, while the search term 黒人男優 [*kokujin danyū*, black actor] generated 390 titles (including a few duplicates), all of which were pornographic, 白人男優 [*hakujin danyū*, white actor] produced a scant 26, mostly gay videos featuring Japanese men. Interestingly, although a search of白人巨根 [*hakujin kyokon*, big white cocks] produced 59 discrete titles, only one depicted white male–Japanese female sex; the rest were divided between Japanese gay porn and those featuring white males engaged in sex with non-Japanese (mostly white) women; on none of the covers was a single white penis prominently displayed.[25]

Conversely, a majority of the covers of pornographic DVDs featuring black actors adhere to a metonymic leitmotif that displays a single, petite, nude or seminude Japanese woman flanked on either side by towering, nude or seminude black men who may range in number from two to a half dozen or more. The black men are almost always shaven-headed, typically sporting knit kufis, do-rags, and sunglasses. In many cases, the Japanese woman is framed by two or more enormous, erect black penises, the men themselves upstaged by their tumescent genitalia. The back covers, abandoning the posed discretion of the front covers, graphically portray various sexual acts, each scene captioned with sensationalistic blurbs testifying to the monstrous proportions of the pixelated or redacted appendages and to the spirited efforts of the young women attempting to accommodate them. In a puerile nod to black Hollywood celebrities, one 15-volume DVD series[26] features black actors performing under the stage names Well Smith, Henzel Washington, and Teddy Murphy; silhouettes of their redacted, erect, apparently prosthetic penises are billed as the world's largest, at 40 cm, 39.5 cm, and 38 cm, respectively.

Tellingly, one cover[27] from the series that showcases two of the aforementioned black performers bilingually lists their 10 female costars as "犠牲者 [*giseisha*] Poor victim [*sic*]," suggesting the women are as much victims of predatory black men as of their own masochistic craving for the tumescent object of their desire. The title of another multivolume series, *Ningen Haigyō* [*No Longer Human*], explicitly suggests that the lust of these women for black cocks dehumanizes them, rendering them as monstrously Other as the bantering, swaggering, satyric black brutes who defile them.[28] The cover of the 2016 DVD *Hāremu 3P Special: Bakunyū Kyōgeki* [*Harlem Threesome Special: Dynamite Tits*][29] features two busty, topless Japanese women standing on either side of the Mapplethorpe-esque, headless torso of a naked black man, their fingers stroking the shaft of his massive, up-tilted erection. The sprawling, redundant, English-language word salad beneath the title reads: "AV [adult video] actress of glamorous body pincer with big tits that boast to the world that boasts the black men Japan with the penis of the world's best World Championship multiplied by the penis and horny Japanese women team of pride out of the standard."[30] The cover of another DVD—entitled *Saru no Wakusei de Okasareta Bijo: Saru no Wakusei wa Jitsuzon suru* [*Beautiful Woman Raped on the Planet of the Apes: The Planet of the Apes Actually Exists*] (2016)[31]—combines both the black rapist and black beast tropes. It depicts a black man in an ape mask inspired by the original 1968 film *The Planet of the Apes* sitting behind the titular naked *bijo* [beauty], grasping her left breast with one hand and gripping her throat with the other. Appearing in the upper-left corner of the video cover is a photo of her unmasked, brutish assailant in cornrows and requisite sunglasses.

Verbal descriptions of the black penis-as-phallus use a number of hyperbolic colloquial expressions. Some, combining Japanese with borrowed English loanwords, are no less monotonous in their inflation of the black penis-as-phallus: Tokyo *Tawā-kyū* [Tower-class], *giga-penisu* [giga-penis], *monsutā kyokon* [giant monster dick], and *koku nikubō* [black meat-pole]. Conspicuously absent from these covers and from the videos themselves are Japanese men. For unlike much American so-called interracial/cuckold/breeder pornography, Japanese pornographers appear reluctant to depict Japanese males participating as voyeurs in their own sexual humiliation by black men.

It would be a mistake, however, to conclude that the discourse of black male sexuality in Japan focuses exclusively on the black penis. As the DVD covers suggest, it is not simply the size and colour of the black penis itself that invests it with symbolic potency. Rather, that potency is derived *in relation* to that which surrounds it. Whether the medium is visual or literary, male blackness is consistently juxtaposed against Japanese female whiteness. The Japanese women who stand alongside black men on DVD covers are often described as *bihaku* [white-skinned beauties], their whiteness offering a stark contrast to the dark-skinned brutes with whom they are posed. Black men's bodies are used to evoke a series of binary oppositions in which they are simultaneously desired and saddled with dehumanizing attributes and qualities that signify their repulsiveness. For example, the leashed, naked Japanese woman on the 2014 DVD cover of *Kokujin to Binetsujo* [*Blacks and the Hot Beauty*][32] from the series *Black@ White* is described as a *karisuma bihaku* [charismatic white-skinned beauty]. The woman's "whiteness" is displayed against four naked black men, one of whom is caged. The men are variously described as *yajū* [wild beasts], *kuroi kichiku* [black brutes], and *kokujin gundan* [army of blacks], this latter description evoking black servicemen.

Such contrasts are also invoked in literary pornography, particularly in the work of Chigusa Tadao (2001), whose posthumously published *Hikaru Hebi* [*The Shining Serpent*] recounts sadomasochistic encounters between albescent Japanese women and Niguro Aru (Negro Al). Their contrasting skin colour serves as the basis for a series of polar oppositions that are reiterated throughout the novel.[33] For example, in one scene, the narrator describes the reaction of Tatsuya, a Japanese man who watches an encounter between Al and a Japanese woman:

> The woman whose soft white body lay at the knees of the formidable Negro was being firmly disciplined, his enormous cock stuffed so deep in her mouth that she was gasping for breath. Black and white, strong and weak, hard and soft, such vividly extreme contrasts. How the brilliant whiteness of her skin radiates against the black skin of the Negro. What kind of a face would this haughty female scholar make with the penis of Al, this domesticated sex animal, screwed deep in her mouth? The more vivid the contrast, the more it aroused his sadistic desire. (p. 31)

Mikiko Ashikari (2005) has noted that the Japanese employ white skin as a symbol of "us" that affirms Japanese superiority against negative feelings regarding dark-skinned others (p. 14). In the case of Japanese pornography, however, not only is the colour-coded racial hierarchy affirmed, but the juxtaposition of "white" Japanese women against "black" men accentuates the desirability of the former, while ostensibly intensifying the value of both as objectified masturbatory fodder.

Black Size Matters

> *From the time he was twelve, Kurushima idolized the brave, beautiful phalluses of primitive sculpture. Phalluses like oversized nightsticks: heavy, gleaming, black, hard, glaring provocatively heavenward, brimming with a fearless laughter, as if they had a special connection with some omnipotent god. "Wish I had a cock like that," was the thought that found natural expression in his dreams.*

...

Whenever Kurushima eyed his, he grew depressed. This was his conclusion: "My genitals were made for masturbation."

—SHIMADA MASAHIKO, "Momotaro in a Capsule"[34]

One should not infer that the obsession of Japanese pornography with black penises means that they have accepted their subordination to the foreign phallus quo. Rather, the inundation of such imagery has fuelled insecurities and a desire to compete with and even surpass the object of their obsession. It is not simply the foreign penis that must be transcended, but the black penis in particular. Indeed, a corner of Japanese cyberspace abounds with forums devoted to discursive dissections of black penis size and online advertisements promoting products that promise to enlarge Japanese penises. One particular product, Re:zenoll 100E, couches the legitimacy of its claims on signifiers of "internationally recognized" white male authority. An advertisement taken from the website *Zoudai Penisu*, a website that promotes erectile enhancement supplements, shows a bespectacled, middle-aged, white male "doctor" wearing a lab coat and stethoscope (Figure 2.3).[35] He promotes the product as having received "official recognition" from the "*Kokusai Seishokuki Gakkai*" (translated on the official-looking seal that appears in the upper-left corner of the advertisement as the "International Sexual Organs Society").[36] Directly above and beneath the advertisement, the website asks, "*Amerika kokujin no penisu wa naze ōkii*?" [Why are the penises of American blacks large?] ("Amerika kokujin," 2015). In answer, the website invokes evolutionary scenarios reminiscent of those advanced by real white "authorities," most notably J. Philippe Rushton (1988) and his disciple Richard Lynn (2013), as it expounds on the enigma of the black penis:

The Mystery of Black Penis Size!

The penis size of each race is inherited.

If you are talking about the race that has a big penis, the first image that comes to mind is blacks. Blacks live primarily on the African continent and in America and characteristically have big bodies and larger penises than other races.

> There are hardly any white or Asian men whose penises exceed 20 cm but there are many blacks that do. Why do blacks have naturally large penises? Not only do they have larger penises but also big, muscular bodies. Indeed, blacks are recognized around the world as a race possessing superior musculature. Blacks are like animals that prowl in the jungle.
>
> Penis size is also a barometer of male sexual potency. Men with big penises are more attractive and stimulate female hormones. [A big penis] is a symbol of masculinity. That is, because blacks are genetically superior physically and in sexual potency, they are bigger and stronger than other races, and their penises have become larger. Consequently, the penises of Asians are inferior compared to those of blacks. ("Amerika kokujin," 2015, n.p.).

Another site, *Akuma no Seiten* [*Devil Sex Method*], employs English-language racial taxonomies, comparing the average size and weight of "Negro" (16–20 cm; 50 g), "European" (14–16 cm; 40 g), and "Asian" (10–14 cm; 20 g) penises and testicles to those of chimpanzees (8 cm; 120 g [*sic*]) ("Jinrui no penisu," n.d., n.p.). Reiterating racist evolutionary psychology theories which maintain that black penis size is the result of natural selection, it concludes: "*kokujin penisu ga ijo ni okii no wa afurika no furui shakai ga jiyu renai no rankonjoanko shakai de atta to kangaeraremasu*" [the abnormal size of the black penis is due to the fact that ancient African societies were promiscuous and practised free love] ("Jinrui no penisu," n.d., n.p.).[37] According to the site, the harsh African environment produced physically superior male specimens who will leave behind more progeny than their less endowed competition. Asians, it asserts, born in environments blessed with abundant water and fertile land, produce progeny physically inferior to blacks.

Online penile enhancement advertisements are, nonetheless, ambivalent about the Japanese penis, which, sans herbal intervention, is often presented as failing to measure up:

> Black penises are huge! The penises of whites are also larger than those of Japanese! This is an undeniable fact. Although it may seem we are

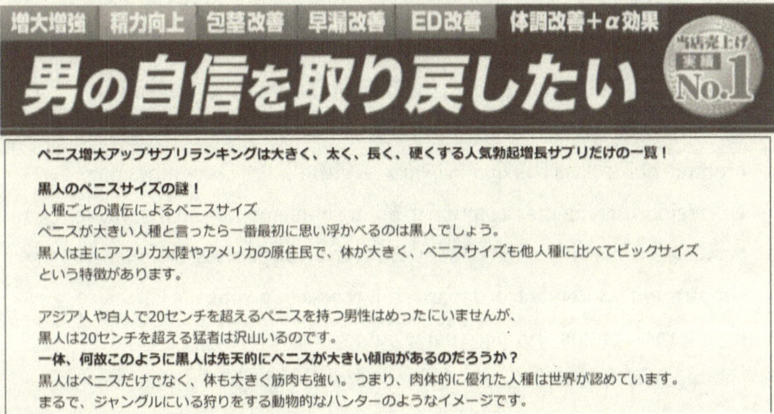

ペニス増大アップサプリランキングは大きく、太く、長く、硬くする人気勃起増長サプリだけの一覧！

黒人のペニスサイズの謎！
人種ごとの遺伝によるペニスサイズ
ペニスが大きい人種と言ったら一番最初に思い浮かべるのは黒人でしょう。
黒人は主にアフリカ大陸やアメリカの原住民で、体が大きく、ペニスサイズも他人種に比べてビックサイズという特徴があります。

アジア人や白人で20センチを超えるペニスを持つ男性はめったにいませんが、
黒人は20センチを超える猛者は沢山いるのです。
一体、何故このように黒人は先天的にペニスが大きい傾向があるのだろうか？
黒人はペニスだけでなく、体も大きく筋肉も強い。つまり、肉体的に優れた人種は世界が認めています。
まるで、ジャングルにいる狩りをする動物的なハンターのようなイメージです。

FIGURE 2.3: *Online advertisement for Re:Zenoll and website text explaining the "mystery of black penis size." (© Zoudai Penisu.com)*

burdened with this inherent handicap, it can be overcome if we make the effort. We must resist despairing that because we are Japanese and are a short race we must throw in the towel and forever lament that we cannot become real men! The fact is we can create a Yamato phallus [*Yamato dankon*] that is as robust as that of any black! ("Kokujin no penisu," 2014, n.p.)

Another site devoted to global comparisons of penis size claims that "*kokujin jitai ga penisu ga ōkii idenshi wo motte iru*" [blacks have big-penis genes] ("Nihonjin no penisu," n.d., n.p.). The site also maintains that cultural factors such as diet influence penis size and that Japanese can improve their penis size by taking supplements ("Kokujin no penisu", 2014, n.p.).

The fragmentary, manically recursive text of an online advertisement for the Asian herbal supplement Triple X (Figure 2.4) promises to provide the consumer with a penis as good as if not better than that of blacks:

> **Triple X Black Supplement:** For penis on par with blacks, bigger than that of blacks and with lasting hardness! One that will shock foreigners. Triple X-class black supplements. Now available for general use. Bigger-than-black Size [*kokujin wo koeru saizu*]. Harder-than-black Hardness [*kokujin ni wa nai kata-sa*]. Porn-Actor Endurance [*danyū nami no jikyūryoku*].[38] Everything a man could want. Triple X: For a Japanese penis size that exceeds even that of blacks. Contains the 3-Ls that promote black-class [*kokujin-kyū*] size: L-citrulline,[39] L-arginine, and L-tyrosine, ingredients not found in other supplements and that make possible a penis larger and stiffer than even black penises. Because the supplement is intended for Japanese, it produces an erectile hardness unique to Orientals [*Tōyōjin*] that is not found in blacks. Because it contains a well-balanced combination of *tongkat ali* [Malaysian ginseng], rhodiolarosea extract, and Korean ginseng, all-natural plant ingredients used in Chinese medicine since ancient times, it restores the staying power of the Japanese penis and provides the vitality necessary to (maintain an erection) no matter how frequent the sex. ("Kokujin nami no penisu," n.d., n.p.)

Significantly, the promises such advertisements dangle before the consumer suggest that these men are not striving to acquire the proverbial

FIGURE 2.4: An online advertisement for Triple X penis supplement promises "greater than black" [黒人以上の] size, hardness, and endurance. (© Girl Q)

"swag" or even the sartorial bling and dark skin that have inspired some young Japanese male "*kokujin ni naritai otoko*" [black wannabes] to appropriate ersatz "black" personae. Their quest instead is to appropriate, through pharmacological and pseudomedical means, a physical attribute inextricably linked to black masculinity. Moreover, it does not appear that these men strive to heighten the sexual pleasure of their partners; rather, their aim is quite literally phallocentric. Ostensibly directed towards overcoming feelings of sexual inadequacy and reappraising not only the sexual worth of Japanese men but also their racial worth, the ultimate outcome is the creation of a new-and-improved Japanese male capable of upsetting the phallus quo in a game of sexual and racial one-upmanship.

This desire is not simply to enhance stunted penises but to create an über-penis whose dimensions spectacularly exceed those of blacks and, in passing, those of whites as well. Reducing black men's penises to tumescent appendages—effectively minimizing the threat those appendages pose to the Japanese male ego—offers Japanese men a subversion of the penile hierarchy and an affirmation of the sexual and racial superiority of Japanese men.

The mantra of black phallic supremacy is repeated on the website *Kamegashira Senin no Chintore Dōjō* [*Glans Wizard Penis Enlargement Training Hall*]. The site claims that the French have the largest penises in Europe, which it attributes to France having a large African immigrant population ("Kamegashira Senin," 2014, para. 11). The site speculates that the reason few African countries appear at the top of international rakings of penis size can be explained by the lack of medical institutions and information networks in Africa. Had African countries been included, the site claims, they would have headed the list ("Kamegashira Senin," 2014, para. 13).

Japanese bloggers, however, are not the only source of such chauvinism. The Japanese-language health blog of a putatively British woman also cites the ubiquitous Mandatory.com / Body Rock survey (see Braham, 2015; "New Study Shows," n.d.). The site essentially fuels Japanese nationalistic arrogance and mollifies insecurities over the popular male stars of imported Korean television dramas while simultaneously recycling stereotypes of black penis size:

> The average Japanese erect penis is 12.5 cm. According to a Canadian survey, this fares pretty well when compared to the 12.7 cm of the average Asian penis. Conversely, the country with the smallest penis is South Korea, where the average length is 9.6 cm. In fact, the penises of those tall, handsome Korean male stars may be mini-sized. Incidentally, average size of American and Canadian penis is 14 cm, and it seems that the "big guys" live in the southern hemisphere, especially Africa and South America. At 17.8 cm, the Congo boasts the world's longest penises. So, all you gals who crave big cocks head over to the Congo, Africa, and South America! (Howard, 2014, para. 6)

Other blogs assert that while black and white penises are larger than those of the Japanese, the latter are superior since they make up in hardness what they lack in size. For example, Kazumoto Iguchi's (2015) blog challenges the masculinist belief that bigger is better. The blog cites the example of the late Japanese professional wrestler and television celebrity Giant Baba who suffered from acromegaly. He claimed that, as a result of his condition, he was so tragically over-endowed that he was unable to find a vagina large enough to accommodate his penis. The blog post maintains that this condition is "*Kokujin no baai mo sō de, tonikaku dekai tosakicchō skikanai. Dakara sakiccho wo masutābēshon shite iru yō na kanji no kaikan shika erarenai*" [also true of blacks, since they are big and can only insert the tip of the penis. Consequently, they can only obtain a physical sensation akin to masturbating the tip] (Kazumoto, 2015, n.p.). On the other hand, the smaller Japanese "*samurai saizu penisu zentai ga nemoto made tsumikomareru yō ni chitsu ni okufukaku maibotsu dekiru. Amaru tokoro ga nai*" [samurai-size penis is capable of being buried deep within the vagina, where its entire length can be accommodated with nothing left to spare] (Kazumoto, 2015, n.p.). The blog further states that "*penisu zentai de chitsuheki no amai shimeri wo mankitsu shite, marude tengoki ni iru kano yō na kibun ni nareru*" [the penis can fully savour the sweet wetness of the vaginal wall and experience its heavenly sensations] (Kazumoto, 2015, n.p.).

Kazumoto's blog also reiterates familiar assertions of a racial phallic hierarchy, noting that blacks have larger penises than whites, who in turn have larger penises than Asians. It goes on to summarize a Japanese-language article from the Canadian men's fitness company Body Rock that references the same Mandatory.com "study" (see "New Study Shows," n.d.). As is the case with many Japanese internet blogs and forums, it should be noted here that an insidious anti-Korean bias taints much of the discourse about race and penis size. In this case, while the blog facetiously points to some of the fallacies of the original English-language article, it claims that its Japanese translation is the work of Western-based "*Zapanēzu*" [Zapanese]—a derogatory term for ethic Koreans—whom it claims have "falsified the (Japanese penis) data" in order to bring "disgrace upon the Japanese people" (Kazumoto, 2015, n.p.). In such instances, Japan's phallic nationalism—or, as I prefer to call it, *chimbo* chauvinism (*chimbo* being Japanese slang for penis)—is aimed not at prodigiously endowed Westerners but rather Japan's Asian rivals, particularly North and South Koreans. The blog pointedly reminds readers that in the 80-nation survey, Japanese penises, at 4.3 in., are tied with Korean and Chinese penises in 73rd place, while North Korea, in 80th place, has the world's smallest at 3.8 in. (Kazumoto, 2015, n.p.). This point is not made in the Body Rock article ("New study shows," 2015), although it is based on data that appears in a graph in the Mandatory.com article (Braham, 2015).

(La) Meme Chose(n)

> *The reason Japanese women...like black men is because the black men, you know, they know what it is. We got swag about us, you know, and we're packin', you know. We...we...you know, we have, uh you know, you know, we have big you-know-what.*
>
> —NATESLION, *The Reason Japanese Women Like Black Men*[40]

As I have shown, the fetishization of black sexuality in Japan plays out across a number of public and discursive fields—Japanese female sexuality, male pornographic iconography, and penis enlargement advertisements—

in which transnational, largely Western-derived images of and "research" on black alterity are adapted to address Japanese obsessions and insecurities. The internal and transnational dynamics of racial commodification under late capitalism ensures that such imagery serves as currency for the Japanese who have introjected Western racial hierarchies—and the stereotypes that infuse and sustain them—and have adapted them toward their own domestic purposes. But in this the Japanese are not alone. I examine below how select, enterprising black men view themselves through the distorted lens of such stereotypes. I show that they are opportunistic in exploiting these stereotypes to their perceived advantage. The ultimate result is twofold. First, they reproduce a belief system that celebrates toxic hypermasculinity and patriarchy, pathologizing their own sexuality in the process. Second, they contribute to the sexual objectification/fetishization of Asian women in general and Japanese women in particular.[41]

To date, three notable books on Japan written by black men present Japan as a land ripe for black men's conquest of Japanese women. These include George Sarratt Jr.'s (1992a) *Nyū Yōku no Kagai Jugyō* [*New York: Extra Lessons*], Wayne Lionel Aponte's (2009) *The Year of No Money in Tokyo,* and Stefhen F.D. Bryan's (2007) *Black Passenger Yellow Cabs: Of Exile and Excess in Japan*. Augustinian in their confessions, each book claims to warn black men against succumbing to the insatiable curiosity of Japanese women who seek to experience well-endowed, indefatigable black lovers. Yet, for all their pretentious soul-bearing, these narratives share a glib, self-confessional tone in which the authors, by pathologizing their own behaviour, become complicit in the fetishization of the black male body, the perpetuation of the trope of pathological male blackness, and the denigration of Japanese women by Japan's patriarchy.

There is, inevitably, the danger that some will (mis)read my critique of these authors as itself complicit in the further pathologization of black men. It may be argued (incorrectly) that I refuse to acknowledge black men as victims of Japanese mythologies of black masculinity. My critique, however, should not be generalized as one against *all* black men. It is, rather, one against those, like the three authors mentioned above, who internalize, project, and propagate stereotypes of black masculinity and sexuality that not only objectify and pathologize black men but also Asian women. Being a victim of an oppressive system (be it slavery, white supremacy, or the patriarchy) does not preclude agency, however constrained the choices. The reality is that *some* people, even as victims, do exploit stereotypes of their own race or gender in order to obtain "success," recognition, or other perceived social and financial rewards. And while victimization is never a "choice," how one acts under the unrelenting weight of oppressive systems, including their resistance to or complicity in them, remains an option. (This critique also applies to Japanese consumers of Western stereotypes of blacks regardless of whether those stereotypes are offered by whites or blacks themselves). Such decisions carry consequences including, on the one hand, the potential of liberation (both mental and physical) and, on the other, the dire prospect of further (and more intense) victimization. To those who would argue that black men are not the authors of their own stereotyping, I would simply respond that some are not above plagiarizing, as it were, the dehumanizing tropes created by their oppressors if they believe it will prove advantageous. In other words, some people chose to cash in on their own oppression, if only because in profiting from it, they do not feel its sting or allow the rewards to serve as an analgesic balm.

To this end, the sexual narratives of these writers in many ways reproduce not only Western stereotypes about black male sexuality but also those that circulated in the Japanese media during the 1980s and 1990s, serving as fodder for news programs and afternoon and late-night talk shows. During the summer in particular, a spate of special programs were regularly aired in which television cameras and reporters pursued so-called *burazagari-zoku* and yellow cabs as they lined up at the gates of US military bases and flocked to nightspots frequented by black men, particularly American servicemen. Noting the phenomenon, the off-camera narrator of one late-night news program, evoking the spectre of Japan's WWII surrender, declares: "*Nihon dansei ni totte makoto, odayakanaranu fuchō de arimasu. Kono goro, 39-nen-me no 8-gatsu 15-nichi, makoto ni motte kanmuryō na no de aru*" [For Japanese men, this is a truly unsettling trend. Now, 39 years since (Japan's surrender on) August 15, 1945, it stirs deep emotion] (Hōdō Desuku, 1984). The narrator then goes on to list the attributes of black men that Japanese women find attractive: *yasashi-sa* [kindness], *seiryoku* [sexual stamina], and *kokujin no sekkusu ga saikō* [terrific sex]. Alas it is not only the warmth of black men's hearts that is the focus of reporters' commentary. The programs also depict black men as "*katamichi kippu Jonīs*" [one-way ticket Johnnys]: lazy, leech-like lotharios who settle in Japan with the sole objective of sponging off their Japanese sugar mamas. Repeating the trope almost a decade later, Tokyo Broadcasting System's (1993) *Ierō Kyabu* [*Yellow Cab*],[42] a 90-minute television documentary, follows five Japanese women, all of whom are involved in failed relationships with black men.

As transacted in Japan, the sex/power dynamic of these black male–Japanese female relations is in some ways similar to that of black male–white female sexual/romantic tourism in the West (see Deliovsky, Chapter 3 of this volume). Japanese media and popular culture present these excursions into sexual tourism as a two-way street, depicting sexually insatiable Japanese women "*muragatte iru*" [flocking] to the United States or to the gates of Japan-based US military bases to have assignations with foreign men, typically represented in the literature as libidinous black men eager to engage in an endless string of entanglements with sexually adventurous, unsatisfied Japanese women (see Ieda, 1991a, 1991b, 1995; Yamada, 1985, 1986, 1991). Significantly, although race emerges as a distinctive feature of these narratives, the issue of racism itself is largely ignored, despite the fact that they exploit perdurable stereotypes of black male sexuality.

The question of racial innocence raised by Deliovsky (Chapter 3 in this volume) acquires new contextual resonance in Japan. The ignoring of racism in Japan is linked to the national myth that it is a "*jinshu sabetsu no nai*" [racism-free] "*tan'itsu minzoku kokka*" [monoracial state]. This race-neutral self-presentation allows the Japanese to perceive themselves as fundamentally ignorant of the phenomenon of racism and, consequently, to claim themselves as racial innocents. One the one hand, the myth suggests that Japanese women's pursuit of foreign male lovers is simply motivated by sexual curiosity, naïveté, and rebellion against Japanese patriarchy rather than a desire to pursue and consummate sexual fantasies based on ubiquitous stereotypes of black masculinity. On the other hand, the narratives of the black men discussed below largely mute the issue of Japanese racism, since the conceptual straightjacket in which racism is conceived in the West seldom permits a sustained interrogation of its articulation beyond the binary of black/white relations to include relations between and among people of colour, nor beyond this to the interrogation of stereotypes of Asian women that reductively fetishize them as sexually and racially naïve exotics. In the end, the conferral of racial innocence upon Japanese women (though, significantly, not necessarily Japanese men) is premised on the belief that, as products of an ostensibly racism-free Japan, such women are naïvely ignorant of the mythologies surrounding black male sexuality or, at best, lack an awareness that these mythologies are racist.

While lacking the historical context of white sexual imperialism, the dynamic shares nonetheless with it the hypersexualization and fetishization of the Other (Woan, 2008). Sexual imperialism in Japan is articulated on multiple intersecting racial registers. Japanese or, if you will, yellow sexual imperialism shares white sexual imperialism's predilection for colonizing nonwhite bodies, while black men's sexual imperialism colonizes Asian female bodies. The narratives of these black men reveal not only how they imagine Japanese women, but also how they, in their perception of themselves as sexual gourmands and voracious consumers of Japanese women, internalize stereotypes of black men.

The nonfiction works of the black expatriate males I reference in this chapter reproduce these tropes, although their own elite backgrounds distinguish them from the black males typically represented in literature and the media. While the authors' phallocentric narratives present their own behaviour as shamefully licentious and abnormal, unlike the Japanese literati's narratives of black men, they occasionally express concerns that their own long tales (tails?) might reinforce stereotypes of black male phallic supremacy and hypersexuality.

In the introduction to his book *Nyū Yōku no Kagai Jugyō* [*New York: Extra Lessons*], George Sarratt Jr. (1992a), a Columbia University graduate, freelance writer, and self-avowed coordinator on Ieda's (1991a) first *Ierō Kyabu* book, describes himself as a "*warui otoko*" [bad man] who wrote his book to confront his "*hajiru-beki kako*" [shameful past] (p. 1). Although he is quick to dissuade his readers from having any lingering doubts that the Japanese women with whom he associated were "*tenshi*" [angels] (p. 1), Sarratt writes that many Japanese women, including those with whom he had sexual relationships in New York, stereotype black men as uneducated and lacking ambition. After completing the book, however, Sarratt (1992a) claims he worried that his sexual exploits would reinforce stereotypes of black men as "*sekkusu animaru*" [sex animals] and that his readers would ignore his privileged background and simply view him as yet another "*nō-nashi no deikku*" [good-for-nothing dick] (p. 2). Sarratt concludes his introduction with the hope that his book will inspire those with similar failings to overcome them. Indeed, the book's titular "extra lessons" are apparently meant to refer to the painful lessons Sarratt confesses to have learned from his licentious past.

Yet in its actual execution, the book presents those lessons less as teachable moments than as guides to the art of female seduction. Indeed, before going on to denounce Ieda's (1991a) *Yellow Cab* as fraudulent, Sarratt (1992b) penned an essay for the men's magazine *Shūkan Pureiboi* [*Weekly Playboy*] in which he boasted of own his sexual prowess (p. 178), although he now maintains that he was "used" by the Japanese media. In fact, in the wake of public criticism of Ieda's book and his involvement with it, Sarratt later contended that "I did not write [the book] as a black man but rather as a human being" (personal communication, February 16, 1993). He blamed the publisher for focusing on black male–Japanese female sex and suggested that he declined to promote his book, lest he be "misquoted or made into a scathing caricature" (personal communication, February 16, 1993).

As a narrative of black male sexual pathology, Sarratt's book provides a template for the books that would follow; all three authors have chosen to reproduce the meme of pathological black male hypersexuality, albeit softening their narratives by framing them as journeys from libertine excess towards personal redemption. At the same time, they hypocritically criticize

Japan as a misogynistic, dysfunctional patriarchy where tradition and modernity are in constant conflict and Japanese women are its ultimate victims while also failing to acknowledge their own smirking paternalism. Sarratt (1992a) adopts a condescending tone towards Japanese women as he urges them not to fear the yellow cab label and to just be themselves, "*Amerika josei wa, Yōroppajin kara 'karukute yasuppoi' to yobareru koto ni, nan ni mo chijoku wo kanjite inai"* [like American women who do not feel shame when Europeans call them "cheap and easy"] (p. 3). It is his hope, he writes, that those Japanese women who once "*gaikoku de sekkusu to doraggu ni oborete ita kuse ni kuchi wo futte Nihon de majime na* kawaiko-chan [emphasis added] *ni fukki shiyō suru"* [wallowed in sex and drugs abroad, wipe their mouths and return to Japan as earnest *honeys* (emphasis added)] (p. 3).

In *Black Passenger Yellow Cabs*, Stefhen F.D. Bryan (2007), a self-described Jamaican "rice king" (p. 9) describes "living everyman's fantasy, at least every sex addicted, yellow fever afflicted [*sic*] man's fantasy [of being] totally immersed in a limitless sea of yellow women" (p. 26). For Bryan, Japan is "an island of sexually frustrated women, especially those in middle age, waiting to be pleasured by foreigners the likes of present company" (p. 32). Bryan plows the same fertile territory as Sarratt, though in more salacious detail. He graphically recounts his sexual conquests and confesses that, after three years of debauchery in Japan, he was plagued by "clear signs of over-ejaculation...semi-flaccid erections, no semen upon ejaculation, and even impotence" (p. 253), all the while paradoxically seeking assurances that he is "more than just my phallus" (p. 255). And yet, Bryan is overtly complicit in reducing both himself and black men in general to precisely that. For example, prior to his fall from grace, Bryan describes a tryst with one of his numerous lovers in which he writes, "My hardened negritude was up to her belly button where she pointed, indicating that's where it felt like it was" (p. 28). At once hedonistic, misogynistic, and negatively masculinist, Bryan manages to strip the term *negritude* of its original Senghorean/Cesairean subversiveness and reduce it to a trite, metonymic measure of priapic invasiveness.

Asian women do not fare much better under Bryan's pen. Bryan (2007) reduces Chinese, Korean, and Japanese women to a collection of rated physical attributes: "small concave noses with a low nose bridge, small upturned eyes with epicanthic fold and milky skin" (p. 24); "small but perfectly shaped breasts" (p. 24) or "large breasts" (p. 27); "extremely steatopygic" (p. 27) and "circular rumps" (p. 44); "long legs" (p. 44); "cellulite-dimpled" (p. 34) and "athletic thighs" (p. 34); a gaggle of "pigeon-toed" honeys, some possessed of "phallus-hardening cello-esque dimensions" capable of "wreaking havoc on my manhood" (p. 44). He grotesquely caricaturizes others as "porcelain complexion[ed]...walking department store mannequin[s]" whose beauty is betrayed by teeth that are too "repulsive a sight to behold" (p. 37). Still others are "butt ugly with apple catchers for teeth, which were the norm in the countryside" (p. 25).

In addition to chronicling his sexual exploits, Bryan's self-styled "erotic ethnography" takes on Japan's "primitive patriarchy" (p. 42). He describes Japan as "without question, the most male chauvinist of all industrialized counties and among the most sexist, female unfriendly [*sic*] societies in the world," where "having internalized their status, the women simply *gaman* or endure" (p. 41). Despite Japan's faults—or perhaps because of them—Bryan finds redemption, and by journey's end writes: "It was in this childish society that I evolved into complete adulthood, it was in this conformist society where I learned to embrace my individuality. And it was in an environment of endless sexual availability that I shook my sexual demons" (p. 360).

Like Bryan, Wayne Lionel Aponte (2009), a former Tokyo-based wire service journalist whose articles have appeared in *The New York Times*, *The Washington Post*, and *The Wall Street Journal*, recounts his sexual exploits and confesses to being "[a]ddicted to hearing women shriek high-pitched praises in bed" (p. 30). Aponte's book *The Year of No Money in Tokyo* is less salacious in its detail than Bryan's work, but retains the confessional tone and requisite redemptive coda. While Bryan's work is self-described an "erotic ethnography," Aponte's, according to front flap of the book's dust jacket, is a work of "creative nonfiction" that "will inspire all people who have encountered personal obstacles by showing them that they can recover, even under the most difficult conditions." Nonetheless, like Bryan, he offers a harsh critique of Japanese society, pointing to a host of issues that he contends have been swept "under the tatami mat of Japanese society: AIDS, homelessness, malicious crime, drugs, teenage pregnancy, alcoholism, child abuse, bullying, poverty, under-education" (p. 64).

Operating in postbubble 1990s Japan, Aponte laments: "I squandered energy, money, and my mid-twenties on perfumed Japanese fantasies" (p. 29), "[e]mbracing whole that figment of the Asian imagination about the Western male's sensuality" (p. 30). Those lean times turned him into a black, male Blanche DuBois who depended on the kindness of Japanese, female strangers. Along the way, as he bemoans his "critical zipper problem—low-minded inclinations" (p. 81), we are treated to perdurable tropes that portray Japanese women as sexually pliant conquests with a weakness for Western men.

Interestingly, as a black man in Japan, Aponte states that he found class rather than race to be more relevant and urges blacks living abroad to "rid themselves of a slave's mentality that robs them of confidence and restricts their lives" (p. 158). But if race does not matter to him, gender and pursuit of sexual gratification do. The book presents Japanese men as castrated, cuckolded husbands and boyfriends, neutered corporate drones who neglect the sexual needs of their partners—who ultimately turn to Aponte to sate their unsatisfied desires. By book's end, however, Aponte has abandoned his profligate ways and recommends temperance, warning his readers that a "pointless life awaits people who devote themselves to immediate gratification and to the pleasures of the flesh" (p. 155). At one point, he cites Proverbs 31:3—"Do not spend your strength on women, your vigor on those who ruin kings" (p. 155)—and touts the benefits of moderation: "Samplings of Japanese erotic love are at the fingertips of all foreign men in Tokyo. You don't exactly have to dedicate yourself to taking full advantage of every single opportunity—potential, actual, and imagined—that comes your way" (pp. 155–56). Having discovered a new spirituality, a contrite, reinvented Aponte writes in favour of celibacy, delayed gratification, and monogamy, offering the reader a series of uplifting bromides that would not feel out of place coming from a pontificating conservative pundit or a pre-scandal Bill Cosby.

There is an intricate and symbolic interplay of competitive and duelling patriarchies here that summarily rejects any prospect of respectful, casual intimacy and genuinely loving relationships between black men and Japanese women. Both Aponte and Bryan criticize Japanese patriarchy for its subjugation of Japanese women and suppression of their sexuality. Ironically, their own, more "enlightened" sensibilities reduce Japanese women to collection of objectified physical attributes—less "yellow cabs" than yellow ATMs. While Japanese patriarchy remains a steady target within their myopic sights, the existence of a black patriarchy that reduces Asian women to sexual fetishes and internalizes cisnormative demands that measure one's ontological worth in phallic centimetres and by the number of one's sexual conquests escapes their critical censure.[43]

Conclusion

And so we come full-circle, like some self-engorging ouroborosian serpent, an anaconda for the ages, an all-devouring, monstrous embodiment of mythic black manhood that feeds hungrily upon itself as it slithers across the globe, leaving behind an insidious, repulsive residue that spans the racial and sexual mythologies of both "East" and "West." The black man-as-ambulatory-penis, a fixture of Western culture, finds itself not only replicated and adapted by Japan, but also by black men themselves who perform the ascribed phallocratic script—one originally written in the West—that awaits them in Japan. In a twenty-first century where black lives matter—despite the perverse and distorted ways in which they are thought to matter and often not to matter at all—it is important to acknowledge the ways fellow human beings are reduced to dehumanized fodder for fetishization and fantasies. On a deeper register, it also matters that some black men legitimate and reify their own fetishization and reduce their sexuality to the sign of the discourses that preexist and (pre)define them. Finally, it matters that this fetishization is transnational in scope, its manifestation in Japan taking place within a cultural, political, and psychological context that has less to do with the mythical satyric sexual potency of black men than with far more potent domestic preoccupations relating to Japan's emergence in world history, how the nation imagines itself, and how it negotiates relations between men and women in the ubiquitous shadow of American presence, both cultural and military.

The transnational nature of fetishes and tropes of black male sexual alterity and their transcription across sites of gender, class, genre, and geography is both ironic and ultimately tragic. Although mobilized toward different purposes depending on the race, gender, and nationality of those who wield them, these "tropic tendencies," to borrow Kevin Adonis Browne's (2013) term, are nonetheless aligned in their representation of black men as objects of desire and dread through which racial and sexual identities are negotiated, reaffirmed, transformed, resisted, and denied, though never fully subverted or transcended. The fundamental humanity of these "objects" of desire and dread is seldom, if ever, acknowledged.

In the end, we are left, in the spirit of Fanon and Baldwin, with the question of the human and the emancipatory radical humanist project to liberate the consciousness of both oppressed and oppressor from the global shackles of gendered racism/racisms and raced patriarchy/patriarchies. The sites of these struggles are not confined to a monolithic "West" and its former colonial or present-day neocolonial possessions but include nations such as Japan—which, although it escaped Western colonization, did not escape the global legacy of the racism that has been produced to justify it. This legacy, combined with Japan's own xenophobic tradition, have coalesced to perpetuate grotesquely distorted and demeaning representations of black masculinity as, to invoke the title of this volume, at once appealing and appalling ambulatory penises—distortions that, as we have seen, are sometimes embraced and performed by those who, letting the "tool possess the man" (Fanon, 1952/1968, p. 231), are its target. It is my hope this chapter has demonstrated that Japan both provides an arena from which to critically interrogate what are essentially global tropes of dehumanized black alterity and serves as an important, though all too often neglected, site of and for radical humanist resistance.

Author's Note

An earlier version of this chapter was presented at the "Blackness and the Asian Century" (BASIC) Conference and Workshop held at the University of California, Irvine, on June 4, 2018. The author would like to thank Nahum Chandler for his encouragement on this project.

Notes

1. In this chapter, except when citing sources in which capitalization is used, I have chosen to use lowercase for racial designations traditionally based on skin colour, while I use uppercase for those derived from geographic regions. I am aware of the philosophical and political issues surrounding such capitalization, particularly in the wake of the endless police murders of black people in the United States and the fact that many media outlets and other institutions following the murder of George Floyd in 2020, now capitalize the word *Black*. The issue of capitalization of racial terminology has been a long standing and recursive one: In the 1920s, W.E.B. Du Bois advocated the capitalization of the *n* in *Negro*, and, in the 1970s, echoing the current moment, there was a movement to capitalize the *b* in *Black*. While these typographic changes have important symbolic resonance, they have had little impact on the implacable reality of systemic anti-black racism in the United States and elsewhere. The victims of police violence are dead; the police who murdered them remain—and will continue to remain—at large whether their police reports describe their victims as "black" or "Black." The same is true for melanated fatalities due to COVID-19, regardless of the typographic style of racial designation on their death certificates. Given these realities, I have decided not to capitalize the term to serve as a typographical reminder that the global pandemic of anti-black racism remains entrenched and will continue to remain so until dismantled. At that point, the adoption of capitalization may then serve to mark the attainment of racial justice and equity—though, ironically, such attainment may render its use unnecessary. But this potential reality lies far ahead of us, perhaps as distant as when Du Bois made his demand, and, as the last century has demonstrated, it will not be realized by the analgesic balm of typographic anodynes.
2. All translations from Japanese in this chapter are my own unless otherwise indicated.
3. See *Studio Voice*, *Kokujin-teki* [Blackness] (October 1991): https://brooklynbook.base.ec/items/19659186. This chapter originally contained 10 figures. Despite efforts to obtain permission to reprint them for this volume, several corporate entities and individuals contacted either did not respond to repeated inquires, denied use of the images, or could not be traced. Consequently, as several of the images can be viewed on the internet, the URLs of those websites have been included in footnotes to enable readers to view the images as originally intended.
4. Japanese names in this chapter are written following the Japanese convention of surname followed by given name.
5. See http://godsmagazine.com/the-power-sculpture-kabuto-project-produced-by-yasuyuki-sakura/. The artist's work was originally on display on two websites (http://www.kabuto-project.com and http://www.sakurayasuyuki.com). Both sites were built with Adobe Flash, which was discontinued on December 31, 2020, rendering the sites unviewable. The first website displayed

photographs of seminude Japanese male bodybuilders in *fundoshi* [traditional Japanese loincloths], as well as other, fully-clothed people of various races, nationalities and genders, all wearing the eponymous *kabuto* [rhinoceros beetle–shaped headwear]. The photos were taken in Tokyo and New York. The second site prominently featured photographs and video images of, primarily, seminude black men wearing black *fundoshi* apparently engaged in battle against one another. The only other group posing seminude was Japanese male rugby players, though they were sporting less revealing athletic shorts. The contrast between the presentation of black men on these sites, as compared to all other groups, is stark.

6. Japanese obscenity laws ban genital displays. Consequently, Japanese pornography redacts such images by blackening them out or obscuring them behind pixilated mosaics. However, there are exceptions in which the phallus is openly displayed, such as the *Kanamara* [Steel Penis] Festival during which a giant, phallus-shaped, portable shrine and life-sized phalluses are used to celebrate fertility.
7. English translations of the title *Shiiku* differ. John Bester (1981) rendered it *The Catch* while John Nathan (1977/1989) went with *Prize Stock*. Nathan's translation further underscores the association of the black pilot with animal domestication.
8. Translation by John Bester (1981).
9. Translation by Yumi Gunji & Marc Jardine (2006).
10. For a discussion of "yellow cabs," see Kelsky (1993, 1996) and Russell (1998).
11. Sexual assaults against women by US personnel constituted a major problem in postwar Japan. According to Dower (1999), in 1945, when Japanese authorities established the *Tokushu Ian Shisetsu Kyōkai* [Recreation Amusement Association], or government-sanctioned "comfort stations" (read: brothels), around 40 Japanese women were raped daily; this reached "an average of 330 a day after it was terminated in early 1946" (p. 579, n. 16). According to Sims (2000) as many as 10,000 Okinawan women may have been raped by US forces after the Battle of Okinawa. Sims reports that "rape was so prevalent that most Okinawans over age 65 either know or have heard of a woman who was raped in the aftermath of the war" (Sims 2000, para. 9). Svoboda (2008) reports that in one prefecture alone, 1300 rapes were reported between August 30 and September 10, 1945. Roberts (2013), noting the disproportionate number of black service personnel charged with committing rape and executed for it in Europe, argues that, particularly in France, incidents of rape were racialized as a result of US military "scapegoating African Americans as the primary perpetrators of the rapes" (p. 10). It is likely that a similar pattern of racialization occurred in Japan. See also Svoboda (2009).
12. See chapter 4 in Bowers et al. (1966, especially pp. 79–81) for a discussion of the Kokura incident. For a discussion of Matsumoto's story, see chapter 3 in Molasky (1999, especially pp. 82–93). The story also parallels the "Katsuyama Incident" that allegedly occurred in 1945 following the Battle of Okinawa in which it is believed that villagers murdered three black marines who had repeatedly returned to their village to rape the local women; it's said that the villagers hid the bodies in a cave, which came to be called *Kuronbo Gama* [Cave of the Niggers]. While the remains

of the soldiers were discovered in 1998, it is not known whether the men were killed by the villagers nor whether they were actually involved in the rapes. See Sims (2000).

13. For a discussion of the black rapist theme in Japanese postwar fiction, see Molasky (1999), chapters 1 and 2.

14. See See (1998) for a discussion of the 1996 rape trial. "Black soldiers," she writes, "are at times oddly invisible and at other times highly visible in a globalized variation on the Myth of the Black Rapist" (p. 73). I would like to thank Ben Crossan for pointing me to the article.

15. Tezuka's *Birdman* stories were originally serialized in *S-F Magajin* [*SF Magazine*] between 1971 and 1975.

16. For examples of fan-produced works of this sort, see http://eroproject.com/?p=73257y and http://www.erojima2.com/archives/2013/1120_203000.html.

17. The 10 keywords were: (1) 黒人 [*kokujin*]; (2) 黒人アドルトDVD [*kokujin adoruto* DVD, black adult DVDs]; (3) 黒人巨大マラ v [*kokujin kyodai mara vs.*, big black cock vs.; the absence of an object following *vs.* is meant to imply Japanese women in general or the specific pornographic actress(es) featured in the DVD]; (4) *kokujin onna* [blacks and women/black women]; (5)黒人中出し [*kokujin nakadashi*, black creampies]; (6) 黒人女性 [*kokujin josei*, black women/blacks and women]; (7) 黒人レイプ [*kokujin reipu*, black rape]; (8) 黒人美女 [*kokujin bijo*, black beautiful women / blacks and beautiful women]; (9) 黒人巨大 [*kokujin kyodai*, big black cocks]; and (10) 黒人美女１５人 [*kokujin bijo 15-nin*, 15 beautiful black women]. Significantly, despite *kokujin josei* having two possible meanings, of the 21 thumbnails it produced, 19 featured black men and Japanese women; only two included black women. The same ambiguity was true of *kokujin bijo*, which produced 59 titles (54 featuring black males and Japanese women and only five featuring black women) and *kokujin onna (*472 titles, only nine featuring black women).

18. See, for example, https://www.amazon.co.jp/s?k=%E9%BB%92%E4%BA%BA%E3%83%AC%E3%82%A4%E3%83%97&i=dvd&__mk_ja_JP=%E3%82%AB%E3%82%BF%E3%82%AB%E3%83%8A&crid=2UEGPJLOGVFSM&sprefix=%E9%BB%92%E4%BA%BA%2Caps%2C331&ref=nb_sb_ss_ts-a-p_4_2.

19. See https://www.amazon.co.jp/gp/product/B06XHH33VL?ie=UTF8&redirect=true to view this DVD cover. Note, too, that the term *kokujin reipu* does not always appear in the titles of the DVDs that come up as hits under these keywords. Moreover, although the term refers to the rape of women (usually but not always Japanese) by black men, it may also refer to the rape of black women by men of any race.

20. The 10 keywords generated by 白人 [*hakujin*] were: (1)白人 [*hakujin*] ; (2) 白人AV [*hakujin* AV, white adult videos]; (3) 白人女優 [*hakujin joyū*, white actresses]; (4)白人桃太郎映像 [*hakujin Momotarō eizō*, white Momotarō videos; *Momotarō* here refers not to the Japanese folktale figure but the name of the DVD company]; (5) 白人男優 [*hakujin danyū*, white actors]; (6) 白人セックス [*hakujin sekkusu*, sex with whites]; (7) 白人黒人 [*hakujin kokujin*, white and black]; (8) 白人女性 [*hakujin josei*, white women]; (9) 白人巨根 [*hakujin kyokon*, big white cocks]; and (10) 白人ナンパ [*hakujin nanpa*, white seduction]. While *hakujin* did not automatically produce an association with rape, entering *hakujin reipu* [白人レイプ, white rape] did produce 53 thumbnails. The term

reipu itself appeared in only three titles, though significantly the act was not linked to the race of either of the victim or the victimizer: in one, white women are raped by white men, in another, Japanese women are raped by black men, and in the third, blond white women are raped by Japanese men. Of the 53 titles, six featured white women, 16 featured Japanese women, 30 were gay male porn titles, and one was a nonpornographic video game unrelated to the search term. The results suggest that rape, particularly the rape of Japanese women, is associated with black men or with Japanese men when the victim is a black woman, since *kokujin reipu* produced four DVDs advertising the rape of black women by Japanese men. See https://www.amazon.co.jp/s?k=黒人+レイプ&i=dvd&__mk_ja_JP=カタカナ&crid=21DEZU695TF8X&sprefix=kokujin%2Caps%2C278&ref=nb_sb_ss_ts-do-p_4_7.

A similar search of *hakujin reipu* on DMM.com, another online retailer, produced 126 thumbnails, including 37 nonduplicates, almost all of which featured white women being raped by Japanese men. Significantly, none of the thumbnails featured white men. In contrast, *kokujin reipu* produced 239 titles, including 51 nonduplicates, all depicting the rapists as black men.

21. See http://www.dmm.co.jp/search/=/searchstr=黒人集団レ●プ/ and https://tv.rakuten.co.jp/adult/search/?sub_genre_id=all&keyword=女子高性黒人&frm=1.
22. For example, see *Kokujin Shūdan Reipu* [Black Gang Rape], Vol. 32, https://www.dmm.co.jp/monthly/premium/-/detail/=/cid=usa032/?dmmref=recomend1.
23. Interracial pornography, or IP, is a commercial term designating a subgenre within the pornography industry that refers to works that depict sex acts between black male and white female performers. The term is rarely applied to works that depict sex between other racial groups. See Dines (2006) and Snow (2017).
24. It should be noted that entering *kokujin* in romaji in the DVD search engine of online retailers produces a different result from the Sino-Japanese compound 黒人. For example, during this same period, a search using the former term on https://www.amazon.co.jp generated 241 titles of books, audio CDs, and MP3 downloads about black (primarily African American) music, literature, history, and culture—but, oddly, not a single DVD! See Russell (2011, pp 134–35).
25. A similar search of the adult DVD section of DMM.com produced 10,322 thumbnails for *kokujin* and 13,050 for *hakujin*, although these numbers include duplicates. While *hakujin* DVDs outnumbered *kokujin* DVDs, black men/penises adorn the majority of *kokujin* covers. Images of black women were few. In contrast, white, primarily blond, women dominated *hakujin* DVD covers; displays of white men and their penises were rare.
26. Generally sold under the extravagant title *Sekai Ichi to Sekai Ni no Chimbo ni Kusuri Tsukesarete Shirome Muku made Gantsuki* FUCK [*Power Fuck: Overdosing on the World's Largest and Second Largest Dicks Until One Faints*], the series covers' monotonously recursive imagery is evident in the thumbnails. See https://www.hmv.co.jp/en/artist_Tsubomi_000000000443101/item_世界一と世界二のチ●ポで白目むくまでガン突きfuck!!!-つぼみ_4122319.
27. See http://www.dmm.co.jp/monthly/premium/-/detail/=/cid=h_127ynb00003/?i3_ref=search&i3_ord=29.

28. See https://www.amazon.co.jp/s?k=人間廃業+黒人&i=dvd&crid=2VWOoGNKIIHVS&sprefix=人間廃業%2Caps%2C294&ref=nb_sb_ss_ts-a-p_2_4.

29. See https://www.amazon.co.jp/最強の黒人巨根で絶頂-ハーレム3P爆乳挟撃SPECIAL-風間ゆみ-千乃あずみ-Fitch/dp/B018U33XNE/ref=sr_1_2?__mk_ja_JP=カタカナ&dchild=1&keywords=黒人+ハーレム&qid=1586315642&s=dvd&sr=1-2.

30. See http://www.dmm.co.jp/digital/videoa/-/detail/=/cid=jux00276/?i3_ref=list&i3_ord=3.

31. See https:hbox.jp/content/89258/.

32. See http://www.dmm.co.jp/digital/videoa/-/detail/=/cid=jux00276/?i3_ref=list&i3_ord=3.

33. Chigusa's (2001) fetishization of blackness is not confined to black skin. It also includes articles of clothing—bras, panties, garter belts, negligees, and other items of lingerie—that are contrasted with the whiteness of his Japanese female characters.

34. Translation by Terry Gallagher (Shimada, 1991).

35. The trope of authoritative, white, male physicians is a staple of Japanese penile enlargement supplement advertisements. See also, for example, https://www.0105.net/ed_s/boltecex.html; http://blog.livedoor.jp/strong40/ http://web.archive.org/web/20160312081342/http://bechnoll.com/; and http://zenofarex.main.jp/zoudai_penis_supliment.html.

36. With the exception of links to websites that advertise penile enhancement products, an internet search for the *Kokusai Seishokuki Gakkai* [International Sexual Organs Society] produced no results. The same was true for a search for Dr. Richard Neisthtatt, who is pictured in Figure 2.3 and whom some ads describe as the "private New York clinician" who developed the product Re:zenoll 100E.

37. When one compares the conclusion of *"Jinrui no penisu"* (n.d.) to Rushton's (1988, pp. 1014–15) and Lynn's (2013, p. 262) comments on sexual fidelity and penis size, one is reminded of Fanon's (1968) summary of the medical profession's view of blacks: "[T]he Negroes have tremendous sexual powers. What do you expect, with all the freedom they have in their jungles! They copulate at all times and in all places. They are really genital" (p. 157).

38. While the text of the advertisement uses the racially neutral term *danyū* [male performer, 男優], the graphic beneath it promises "*kokujin ijō no jikyūryoku*" [greater-than-black endurance, 黒人以上の持久力] ("Kokujin nami no penisu," n.d., n.p.).

39. In an ironic coincidence, the name of this organic compound, an amino acid used to treat erectile dysfunction, derives from the Latin *citrullus* (watermelon), from which it was isolated by Japanese scientists in 1914.

40. This epigraph was transcribed from a YouTube video by nate5lion (2014, 0:26–0:51). This YouTube account no longer exists.

41. For different contexts and analyses of Self and Other commodification and objectification/fetishization, see Deliovsky (Chapter 3 in this volume) and Rehal (Chapter 9 in this volume).

42. The term "yellow cab" refers to Japanese women living in America who have sexual relationships with foreign men, particularly (but not exclusively) African Americans. The term implies that, like their namesakes, these women are "easy rides" who will "stop for anyone." The Japanese media began to use the term in the 1990s after it was popularized by erstwhile journalist, author, and

former actress Ieda Shoko in her bestselling books *Ierō Kyabu* (1991a) and *Ierō Kyabu 2* (1995). Ieda's books are purportedly nonfiction exposés of relationships between Japanese women and black men living in New York and Los Angeles. Japanese media claim that, while the term is used by Americans, Japanese women in the United States report that it is of Japanese—not American—origin. With its implication of easy (sexual) access, the term is thought to have originated among blacks, though this is highly suspect given the difficulty blacks regularly experience hailing the real thing. Although the term itself was new, Japanese fascination with black male sexuality and sexual relationship between them and Japanese women was not (see Covert & Wada, 1993; Toyoda, 1994).

In the mid-1980s, Ieda had previously made a name for herself with series of articles on *burazagari-zoku* that were later published in book form (Ieda, 1991b). Prize-winning author Yamada Eimi has continued to write best-selling and award-winning novels and short stories on the theme (see Yamada, 1985, 1986, 1991). Takeda Mayumi, a hearing-impaired former sex-trade worker who used her earnings to come to the United States, has written four books documenting her attraction to and failed relationships with black men (see Takeda 1999, 2000, 2002, 2004). As with Japanese male depictions of black men, these narratives generally present the black body as diseased and dangerous, portraying the black men with whom these women become involved as outlaws, gang members, drug-addicts, and HIV/AIDS–infected lowlifes.

43. Public discourse in both countries tends to reduce the black encounter with Japan to a sexual one between black men and Japanese women. Encounters between black women and Japanese men are seldom discussed, although recently Japanese television programs have begun to feature segments on Japanese men married to African women and the internet has seen the emergence of several English-language sites and YouTube vlogs devoted to discussions of relationships between black women and Japanese/Asian men. See, for example, the now defunct *The Blasian Narrative* (2010–2015; http://blasiannarrative.blogspot.jp/2015/06/this-is-still-ambw-blog.html); *This is a BW/AM Blog* (https://www.pinterest.jp/pin/521502831832811733/) and *Black Women Who Love Asian Men* (http://www.tagged.com/blackwomenwholoveasianmen). Significantly, mainstream Japanese media treats these relationships as successful, focusing almost exclusively on married couples, while its coverage of black male–Japanese female relationships tends to portray them as "illicit," ultimately doomed trysts.

Bibliography

Amerika kokujin no penisu wa naze ōkii? Ōbeijin no yō na ōki na chino ni naritai [Why are black American penises large? Want a big dick like Westerners]. (2015, December 9). *ZoudaiPenisu*. http://zoudaipenisu.com/zoudaisapuri.html

Aponte, W.L. (2009). *The year of no money in Tokyo*. Watkins & McKay.

Ashikari, M. (2005). Cultivating Japanese whiteness. *Journal of Material Culture*, *10*(1), 73–91. https://doi.org/10.1177/1359183505050095

Baldwin, J. (1961). The black boy looks at the white boy. In *Nobody knows my name* (pp. 171–90). Dell Publishing.

Bester, J. (Trans.). (1981). *The catch and other war stories* (by K. Ōe). Kōdansha.

Bhabha, H.K. (1997). *The location of culture*. Routledge.

Bowers, W.T., Hammond, W.H., & MacGarrigle, G.L. (1996). *Black soldier, white army: The 24th army regiment in Korea*. United States Army Center for Military History.

Branham, M. (2015, February 26). Which country has the biggest dicks in the world? *Mandatory.com*. Retrieved December 27, 2015, from https://www.mandatory.com/living/1057233-which-country-has-the-biggest-dicks-in-the-world

Browne, K.A. (2013). *Tropic tendencies: Rhetoric, popular culture, and the Anglophone Caribbean*. University of Pittsburgh Press.

Bryan, S.F.D. (2008). *Black passenger yellow cabs: Of exile and excess in Japan*. Kimama Press.

Buruma, I. (1984). *Behind the mask: On sexual demons, sacred mothers, transvestites, gangsters, drifters, and other Japanese cultural heroes*. New American Library.

Chigusa, T. (2001). *Hikaru hebi [The shining serpent]*. Nihon Shuppansha.

Cornyetz, N. (1994). Fetishized blackness: Hip hop and racial desire in contemporary Japan. *Social Text, 41*, 113–39. https://doi.org/10.2307/466835

Covert, B., & Wada, H. (1993, June 8). New York residents call 'Yellow Cab' author a fraud. *Mainichi Daily News*. Retrieved May 15, 2015 from https://www.inochi-life.net/archives_author_fraud.html

Dines, G. (2006). The white man's burden: Gonzo pornography and the construction of black masculinity. *Yale Journal of Law and Feminism, 18*(1), 283–97. https://digitalcommons.law.yale.edu/yjlf/vol18/iss1/12/

Dower, J.W. (1999). *Embracing defeat: Japan in the wake of World War II*. W.W. Norton.

Fanon, F. (1968). *Black skin, white masks*. (C.L. Markmann, Trans.). Grove Press. (Original work published 1952)

Freud, S. (2001). Fetishism. In J. Breuer & A. Richards (Eds.), & J. Strachey (Trans.), *The standard edition of the complete psychological works of Sigmund Freud, Vol. XXI* (pp. 152–58). Vintage. (Original work published 1927)

Genga, A. (1975, November 7). Aozameta machi [The town went pale]. *Ryūkyū Shimpō*, Sx.

Hall, S. (Ed.). (1997). *Representation: Cultural representation and signifying practices*. SAGE Publications.

Hawks, F.L. (2005). *Commodore Perry and the opening of Japan: Narrative of the expedition of an American Squadron to the China seas and Japan, 1852-1854: The official report of the expedition to Japan* (F.L. Hawks, Ed.). Nonsuch. (Origianl work published 1856)

Hōdō Desuku. (Producer). (1984, August 14). *Totsugeki no natsu: Gaijin punku ōkōhimo-zoku [Summer blitz: Foreign punk pimp gang infestation]* [Film]. Tokyo Broadcasting System.

Howard, M. (2014, April 8). Ōkii? Chiisai? Hito ni kikenai danjo no asoko no heikin-chi [Big? Small? Average size of male and female genitalia]. *Hot Pink Health and Beauty* via *Web Archive*. https://web.archive.org/web/20141229062717/http://sex.co.jp/the-average-value-of-the-size-of-the-genital/

Ieda, S. (1991a). *Ierō kyabu [Yellow cab]*. Kōyū Shuppan.

Ieda, S. (1991b). *Ore no hada ni muragatta onna-tachi [The women who flock to my skin]*. Shōdensha.

Ieda, S. (1995). *Ierō kyabu 2 [Yellow cab 2]*. Kōyū Shuppan.

Jinrui no penisu wa kiwamete kyokon?? [Is the human penis extremely large??]. (2014, May 25). *Akuma No Seiten [Devil Sex Method]*. http://sex.devil- method.com/humankind-penis/#i

Kazumoto, I. (2015, March 5). Jōku: "Sekai penisu saizu ranking" Nihon 73-i: nagasa yori kamara-do ga daiji!?" [Joke: World penis size ranking: Japan ranks 73rd place; hardness more important than length!?]. *Kazumoto Iguchi's Blog*. Retrieved December 23, 2015, from http://quasimoto.exblog.jp/22854086

Kelsky, K. (1993, October 17). *Thoughts on yellow cabs* [Transcript of talk]. Afro-American Friendship Association.

Kelsky, K. (1996). Flirting with the foreign: Interracial sex in Japan's international age. In W. Dissanayake & R. Wilson (Eds.), *Global/Local: Cultural production and the transnational imaginary* (pp. 173–92). Duke University Press.

Kelsky, K. (2001). *Women on the verge: Japanese women, Western dreams*. Duke University Press.

Kokujin nami no penisu e Toripuru Ekksu Burakku kokujin ijō no saizu & orenai katasa! [Triple X black for a penis on par with blacks, bigger than blacks', with lasting hardness!]. (n.d.). Retrieved December 23, 2015 from *Girl Q*. girlq.jp/?pid=62709680

Kokujin no penisu wa naze ōkii? [Why are black penises large?]. (2014, November 25). *Kamegashira Senin No Chintore Dōjō [Glans Wizard Penis Enlargement Training Hall]*. Retrieved December 15, 2015, from http://チントレ道場.com/チントレコラム/黒人や白人もチントレでペニスを大きくしている

Kokujin Shūdan Reipu [Black gang rape] Vol. 32 [Film]. (2016). FANZA. https://www.dmm.co.jp/monthly/premium/-/detail/=/cid=usa032/?dmmref=recomend1

Kokujin-teki [Blackness] [Magazine issue]. (1991, October). *Studio Voice*, Vol. 190. https://brooklynbook.base.ec/items/19659186

Kokujin to binetsujo [Blacks and the passionate white beauty] [Film]. (2014). FANZA. http://www.dmm.co.jp/digital/videoa/-/detail/=/cid=jux00276/?i3_ref=list&i3_ord=3

Lynn, R. (2013). Rushton's r–K life history theory of race differences in penis length and circumference examined in 113 populations. *Personality and Individual Differences*, *55*(3), 261–66. https://doi.org/10.1016/j.paid.2012.02.016

Matsumoto, S. (1958). *Kuroji no e [Painting on black cloth]*. Kōbunsha.

McClintock, A. (1995). *Imperial leather: Race, gender and sexuality in the colonial contest*. Routledge.

Molasky, M.S. (1999). *The American occupation of Japan and Okinawa: Literature and memory*. Routledge.

Murakami, R. (1976). *Kagirinaku tōmei ni chikai blū [Almost transparent blue]*. Kōdansha.

NABE. (Producer). (2016). *Hāremu 3P Special [Harlem Threesome Special]* [Film]. Fitch. https://www.amazon.co.jp/最強の黒人巨根で絶頂-ハーレム3P爆乳挟撃SPECIAL-風間ゆみ-千乃あずみ-Fitch/dp/B018U33XNE/ref=sr_1_2?__mk_ja_JP=カタカナ&dchild=1&keywords=黒人+ハーレム&qid=1586315642&s=dvd&sr=1-2

nate5lion. (2014, June 20). *The reason Japanese women like black men.* [Video file]. YouTube. Retrieved December 18, 2015, from https://www.youtube.com/watch?v=l4ITCHYWk-A

Nathan, J. (Trans.). (1989). *Prize stock* (by K. Ōe). In K. Ōe (Author), *Teach us to outgrow our madness.* Grove Press. (Original work published 1977)

New study shows which country has the biggest penises in the world. (2015, February 27). *Body Rock.* http://www.bodyrock.tv/life/new-study-shows-country-biggest-penises-world

Nihonjin no penisu no ōki-sa wa sekai de nanban-me!? Kuni ni yotte chigau saizu no chigai wo tettei kaimei!! [Where does Japanese penis size rank in the world!? An exhaustive elucidation of differences in penis size by country!!]. (n.d.). *Urban-Heartbeat.* Retrieved December 27, 2015, from http://www.urban-heartbeat.com/size.php

Perry, M.C. (1968). *The Japan expedition 1852–1854: The personal journal of Commodore Matthew C. Perry* (R. Pineau, Ed.). Smithsonian Institution Press.

Roberts, M.L. (2013). *What soldiers do: Sex and the American GI in World War II France.* University of Chicago Press.

Roxworthy, E. (2008). *The spectacle of Japanese American trauma: Racial performativity and World War II.* University of Hawai'i Press.

Rushton, J.P. (1988). Race differences in behaviour: A review and evolutionary analysis. *Personality and Individual Differences,* 9(6), 1009–24. https://doi.org/10.1016/0191-8869(88)90135-3

Russell, J.G. (1993). Amerika no chiteki Nihon senryō [The intellectual occupation of Japan]. In I. Henshū (Ed.), *Senryō to Bungaku [War and literature]* (pp. 60–73). Orijin Shuppan Sentā.

Russell, J.G. (1998). Consuming passions: Spectacle, self-transformation, and the commodification of blackness in Japan. *Positions: East Asia Cultures Critique,* 6(1), 113–77. https://doi.org/10.1215/10679847-6-1-113

Russell, J.G. (2007). Excluded presence: Shoguns, minstrels, bodyguards, and Japan's encounter with the black other. *Zinbun: Annals of the Institute for Research in Humanities, 40,* 15–51. https://repository.kulib.kyoto-u.ac.jp/dspace/bitstream/2433/71097/1/40_15.pdf

Russell, J.G. (2011). Race as ricorso: Blackface(s), racial representation and the transnational apologetics of historical amnesia in the United States and Japan. In Y.I. Takezawa (Ed.), *Racial representations in Asia* (pp. 124–47). Kyoto University Press and TransPacific Press.

Russell, J.G. (2017). Replicating the white self and other: Skin color, racelessness, gynoids, and the construction of whiteness in Japan. *Japanese Studies,* 37(1), 23–48. https://doi.org/10.1080/10371397.2017.1297183

Saegusa, K. (1989). *Sono fuyu no shi [A winter's death].* Kōdansha.

Sakura, Y. (n.d.). *Kabuto Project: A group of semi-naked black men don rhinoceros beetle headgear.* Yasuyuki Sakura Official Website. http://www.sakurayasuyuki.com

Sarratt, G. Jr. (1992a). *Nyū Yōku no kagai jugyō [New York: Extra lessons].* Kōyū Shuppan.

Sarratt, G. Jr. (1992b, July 28). Nichi-Bei sukebe samitto: NY ierō kyabu wa konna sex wo shite iru. *Shūkan Pureiboi [Weekly Playboy],* 178.

See, S.E. (1998). Trying whiteness: Media representations of the 1996 Okinawa rape trial. *Hitting Critical Mass: A Journal of Asian American Cultural Criticism,* 5(2), 57–78. https://www.

academia.edu/1999587/Trying_Whiteness_Media_Representations_of_the_1996_Okinawa_Rape_Trial

Sekai Ichi no Chimpo wo motsu Weru Sumisu-shi to sekai ni no chimpo wo motsu Henzeru Washinton-shi no Shiro-me muku made gan-totsuki kushidashi 10 FUCK!! [10 fucks with Mr. Well Smith who has the world's largest dick and Mr. Henzel Washington who has the world's second largest as they skewer (their victims) until they faint] [Film]. (2011). FANZA. http://www.dmm.co.jp/monthly/premium/-/detail/=/cid=h_127ynb00003/?i3_ref=search&i3_ord=29

Shimada, M. (1991). Momotaro in a capsule. In A. Birnbaum (Ed.), & T. Gallagher (Trans.), *Monkey brain sushi: New tastes in Japanese fiction* (pp. 122–46). Kōdansha.

Sims, C. (2000, June 1). 3 dead marines and a secret of wartime Okinawa. *The New York Times*, A12. https://www.nytimes.com/2000/06/01/world/3-dead-marines-and-a-secret-of-wartime-okinawa.html?pagewanted=print

Snow, A. (2017, April 14). Why porn's interracial label is racist. *The Daily Beast*. https://www.thedailybeast.com/why-porns-interracial-label-is-racist

Svoboda, T. (2008). Race and American military justice: Rape, murder, and execution in occupied Japan. *The Asia Pacific Journal/Japan Focus*, 6(5). https://apjjf.org/-Terese-Svoboda/2737/article.pdf

Svoboda, T. (2009). U.S. courts-martial in occupation Japan: Rape, race, and censorship. *The Asia Pacific Journal/Japan Focus*, 7(21), 2–10. https://apjjf.org/-Terese-Svoboda/3148/article.pdf

Takechi, T. (Director). (1965). *Kuroi yuki [Black snow]* [Film]. Dai-san Production..

Takeda, M. (1999). *Faito! [Fight!]*. Gentosha.

Takeda, M. (2000). *Issho ni faito!* [*Let's fight together!*]. Gentosha.

Takeda, M. (2002). *Itsumademo faito* [*Fight forever*]. Gentosha.

Takeda, M. (2004). *Faito nikki [Fight diary]*. Gentosha.

Tezuka, O. (1995). Rōdeshia ni te [In Rhodesia]. In *Chōjin daikei 1: Tezuka Osamu manga zenshū* [*Birdman anthology, vol. 1: The complete Tezuka Osama manga collection*]. Kōdansha.

TMA. (Producer). (2017). 黒人レイプ *[Black rape]* [Film]. Amazon. https://www.amazon.co.jp/gp/product/B06XHH33VL?ie=UTF8&redirect=true

Tokyo Broadcasting System. (1993, January 29). *Ierō Kyabu* [Television documentary]. Tokyo Broadcasting System.

Toyoda, M. (1994). *Kokuhatsu! ierō kyabu [Yellow cab exposed!]*. Sairyūsha.

Woan, S. (2008). White sexual imperialism: A theory of Asian feminist jurisprudence. *Washington and Lee Journal of Civil Rights and Social Justice*, *14*(2), 275–301. https://scholarlycommons.law.wlu.edu/cgi/viewcontent.cgi?article=1243&context=crsj

Yamada, E. (1985). *Beddotaimu eizu [Bedtime eyes]*. Kawade Shobō Shinsha.

Yamada, E. (1986). *Jeshī no sebone [Jesse's spine]*. Kawade Shobō Shinsha.

Yamada, E. (1991). *Torasshu [Trash]*. Bunkei Shunjun.

Yamada, E. (2006). *Bedtime eyes* (Y. Gunji & M. Jardine, Trans.). St. Martin's Press.

3

White Femininity, Black Masculinity, Sex/Romance Tourism, and the Politics of Feminist Theory

Theorizing Desire and Erotic Racism

KATERINA DELIOVSKY

> *The national bourgeoisie organizes centers of rest and relaxation and pleasure resorts to meet the wishes of the Western bourgeoisie. Such activity is given the name of tourism, and for the occasion will be built up as a national industry...[T]he beaches of Rio, the little Brazilian and Mexican girls, the half-breed thirteen-year-olds, the ports of Acapulco and Copacabana—all these are the stigma of depravation of the national middle class...[They] will have nothing better to do than to take on the role of manager of Western enterprise, and it will in practice set up its country as the brothel of Europe.*
>
> —FRANTZ FANON, *The Wretched of the Earth*

> *The funny thing about this story of hypocrisy and brutality is not just that you can't stop people fancying each other across any kind of racial barrier. The real irony is that the myths could almost have been designed to spark off some of the most intense sexual experiences ever. No fruit has ever been quite so forbidden. What person of spirit could fail to crave such a taste? And how sweet is this poem of contrasts between gleaming black skin and creamy pink flesh. How tender the refuge from the terror and rage of the world. How piercing the intrusions of apprehension and guilt.*
>
> —MIKE PHILLIPS[1]

AS EARLY AS THE 1960S, Frantz Fanon observed the development of male sex tourism in the Caribbean and South America that catered to (white) males from the European metropoles. Fanon (1961/1968) noted that elites, craven and lacking imagination to rebuild their societies from the ashes of colonialism, would instead maintain that ruinous enterprise by "prostituting" their nation's wealth and even the bodies of their people for the sexual gratification of their former masters (see also Thomas, 2007). Given the colonial patterns of power and dominance embedded in global tourism, Fanon (1961/1968) discerned very early on that the region was becoming "the brothel of Europe" (p. 1154; see also Kempadoo, 2004).

Since Fanon's trenchant observation, anthropologists and sociologists have examined the sexual tourism of European American men who seek sex with Latin American, Caribbean, and Asian men and women (Cabezas, 2009; Cincone, 1988; Kempadoo, 1999; Truong, 1990) and sometimes children. Given the considerable attention Fanon (1952/1977) pays to "the man of colour and the white woman" (p. 63) in *Black Skin, White Masks*, and that he is also unsparing of white women's participation in the mythologizing of black men, it is interesting that white women tourists' sexual/social practices are not only less well known, but often less nuanced and less vigorously theorized.

While the body of scholarly work that explores (primarily white) tourist women's social/sexual behaviour in transnational contexts is growing, it still remains small. Suggestive of key epistemological differences in examining gender, race, sexuality, and power, this behaviour variously goes by innocuous nomenclature such as "cross-border desires and encounters" (Frohlick, 2013, p. 7), "romance tourism" (Pruitt & LaFont, 1995, p. 423), and, more penetratingly, "sex tourism" (Taylor, 2006, p. 42). For the purposes of this examination, I will call it *sex/romance tourism* to signal that there is considerable complexity going on in the traffic between subjectivities, history, and social structure.

This chapter parses what I believe are representative samples of the sex/romance tourism literature into two broad approaches: (1) the gender/feminism approach[2] and (2) the political economy approach. Feeling frustrated primarily with the former and more sympathetic to the latter, I sketch an alternative approach grounded in both Fanonist epistemology and antiracist and critical race feminism. This sketch includes examining the two opposing approaches for the possibility of opening new vistas of inquiry for (a) exploring emerging raced, gendered, and classed configurations of white femininity, black masculinity, whiteness, and Otherness; and (b) rethinking how white femininity's sexual autonomy moves globally on the dynamics of empire while simultaneously reifying and transforming colonialist tropes of black masculinity. I contend that while the gender/feminism approach presents a "thick description" of white women involved in sex/romance tourism, it is at the expense of counter-colonial theorizations for how race and whiteness saturate[3] gender, femininity, and class to produce complex and paradoxical forms of racialized gender power.

Before diving into the development of this alternative approach, however, it is important to set the stage with two brief discussions: one of racialized gender power, and another of the phenomenon of sex/romance tourism in the Caribbean.

Beyond White Innocence: Rethinking Loci of Racialized Gender Power

Race and gender, as it connects to other sites of inequity and privilege, are key elements in sex/romance tourism. Yet the gender/feminism approach, as I will demonstrate, is not able to legibly reconcile the fact that white women are positively racialized beings, nor that, by virtue of race, whiteness (and to some degree class), and the renewed afterlife of colonialism and slavery, they are constituted within the realm of racialized gender power. I suggest that the gender/feminism approach is animated by a gender-essentialist model that draws on monistic and unproblematized conceptualizations of femininity, sexuality, and patriarchy. Here, I am making a fine point: the gender/feminism account of race in white women's sex/romance tourism in the Caribbean is primarily focused on how black men are racially imagined by the white women and the larger Western society from which their imaginations are inscribed or socialized. White women's whiteness and economic power, as a superior(ized) *racial* position, is omitted. Within these accounts, white women, in the final analysis, are victims of (white) patriarchal relations (from which they are "liberated" in these sex/romance encounters). At the same time, there is a downplaying of the economic privilege they enjoy. As a consequence of circumventing questions of racialized gender power within the histories of colonialism and slavery, white women are granted "innocence" (Wekker, 2016) and are imagined to be *without power* in these sex/romance encounters. Black heterosexual masculinity, however, is perceived and theorized in the Western imagination in pathological ways that follow predictable tropes. But more than this, black masculinity is imagined to be inherently complicit in patriarchy if not conferred the status of patriarchy[4] itself (see Kitossa, Introduction to this volume).

Here, I borrow Gloria Wekker's (2016) concept of innocence to capture the "denial and disavowal of the continuities between colonial sexuality and contemporary sexual modalities" (p. 18) that permeate the reproduction of contemporary erotic racism in sex/romance tourism. Innocence in this context is a classic Sartrean conception of bad faith: it is "connected to practices of knowing and not-knowing [continuities that are elided and]...defended" (Wekker, 2016, p. 18) and reified by both the researchers studying and writing about it and the women and men who participate in sex/romance tourism.[5] In this sense, a Fanonist psychoanalytic approach leads us to consider that there is a continuum between innocence and ignorance—a continuum that, supported by the ethos of whiteness as property (see Harris, 1993), is constituted as the exclusive property of white femininity. Thus, on one end of the continuum, white women's claims that "they didn't know" and that "it just happened," despite the obvious prevalence of mythologies about black men's endowment, unflagging virility, and the supposed uninhibitedness spurred on by the sultry climes of equatorial regions, produces a presumption of innocence that creates the possibility of revelation, discovery, and surprise. On the other hand, "white ignorance" (Mills, 2007), which grants the presumption of white (female) naïveté—enables white women to experience the liberating effects of their sexual agency through the projection of moral responsibility onto a black man who, "naturally," is as beguiling and unyielding as he is irresistible and repugnant—*appealing* and *appalling*—for his lack of "civilized" restraint. In this context, white women's participation in erotic racism is "not-known" (Wekker, 2016), glossed over by an avoidance of white women's "positional superiority" (Said, 1979)[6] and reproduction of white dominance.

I suggest the political economy approach (represented by Jacqueline Sanchez Taylor's scholarship) is far more sensitive to the contradictions, complexities, compromises, and nuances of power, privilege, and subordination that are endemic to the contexts and situations of white women's sex/romance tourist interactions with black men. I, therefore, follow Taylor's (2011) definition of sex tourism as

> [a] phenomenon involving sexual-economic exchange between tourists and locals/migrants in less economically developed countries [in the Global South] ranging from straightforward prostitution contracts to more diffuse short- or long-term sexual relationships that have some economic element to them. (p. 64)

The following is by no means exhaustive and does not constitute an intellectual genealogy of white women's sex/romance tourism. I have, instead, chosen select articles and monographs that seem to me generally representative of the two approaches that specifically focus on white tourist women's social-sexual behaviour with black men in the Caribbean.[7] Additionally, the scholars included in my examination may not necessarily agree with my analysis[8] and categorization of their works. In contrasting and making judgments about this scholarship, it should be noted that my aim is not to be polemical or demeaning of any approach, but to seriously engage with and build on them.

In a conversation with Tamari Kitossa (editor of this collection) about the challenges of such an engagement, he stated:

> There is a lot at stake in the lives of many people—tourists, locals, governments and researchers alike and struggling to "getting it right" [*sic*]

is important to achieving the radical humanism Fanon believed in and worked for. (personal communication, May 28, 2020).

For Kitossa, achieving Fanon's vision of a radical humanism[9] requires that researchers position the people under study "not simply as 'categories' for analysis, but real human beings meeting under definite terms and conditions informed by history" (personal communication, May 16, 2020). They "invest their bodies, minds, hearts and souls," he states, "in and through conceptions and mythologies from which they derive meaning, satisfaction and a sense of their humanity, no matter how contradictory, convoluted and paradoxical" (personal communication, May 28, 2020). It is in the spirt of "getting it right" and honouring Fanon's radical humanism, then, that I write this chapter.

White Women, Tourism, Sex, and "Romance": An Overview

While the majority of sex tourists are men, ethnographic research shows that it is routine to see "foreign" women on the arms of local men in the resort areas of the Caribbean and Central America (Frohlick, 2013; Pruitt & LaFont, 1995; Taylor, 2001, 2006).[10] Marked by growing economic independence at home, the increase in women travelling as tourists abroad signifies a change in social and cultural norms and historical patterns of sex tourism. While this scholarly work, alongside journalistic accounts, has increased public awareness of these relationships, the phenomenon of sex tourism is certainly not new. Since the 1970s, the Caribbean (as well as southern Europe, Turkey, Thailand, and destinations in North, East, and West Africa) has been a tourist destination for white women who seek sex or "romance" with local men (Bauer, 2013). Many of these women travel from the United States, Canada, Britain, and Germany; a smaller number come from other European countries such as France and Italy (Davidson & Taylor, 1999).[11] Beyond tourism, wide-scale involvement of white women in global sex/romance tourism is connected to a range of government and private philanthropic initiatives such as the US government's Peace Corps and similar programs by other Western governments as well as study-abroad scholarships inaugurated in response to the 1960s' Cold War. Significantly, in the post–Cold War world, these initiatives morphed into the government-aid/humanitarian industrial complex in which white women play a prominent role (see Cook, 2007; Heron, 2007). The role of white women as power-brokers, and in some cases power-holders, over the funding of "aid" projects (i.e., neocolonialism), principally designed by male Western policy makers, is largely unrecognized (Del Zotto & Jones, 2002). All of this is suggestive of the complicated and nuanced ways in which white women are not, in fact, objects/victims of "patriarchy," but agents of desire and power. All of this remains open for critical empirical studies and theorizing.

In the context of Global North–Global South sex/romance intimacies, white women tourists come from various ethnicities, ages, socioeconomic backgrounds, professions, and body morphologies; contrary to common mythologies, there is no type of white woman "most likely to." Most sex/romance tourism relationships are interracial and intercultural because the vast majority of tourist women are "white" while the majority of Caribbean men are "black" (of African descent) or "mixed" (of Latino and African ancestry). White female sex/romance tourists tend to stay anywhere from a few weeks to a few months. Many are repeat visitors (Pruitt & LaFont, 1995) and a few ultimately migrate as semipermanent or permanent residents. The local men who participate in sex/romance tourism and transnational relationships are generally poor, working-class, and most often internal migrants to beach areas. They often have little formal education and are referred to by a number of common and disparaging monikers in the local vernacular. These include *gigolo*, *hustler*, *player*, *beach boy*, and *rent-a-dread*. On occasion, a small minority are educated and middle class. Some scholars report that darker-skinned men are more highly valued and generally preferred by sex/romance tourists because they are perceived to represent the tropistic, hypersexual black stud: the embodiment of "an insatiable sexual [appetite] and a large, ever-hard penis, both of which are continually in need of expression and can tirelessly sustain multiple sexual partners" (Kempadoo, 2004, p. 134; see also Philips, 1999). The assumption is, then, that black men not only sell their sexual labour power, but also rationally bring to market their presumed "biological gifts."

Significantly, the scholarly works examined here note that neither party considers their sexual interaction to be prostitution or to fit the label "sex tourism," even though others may label it so. Suggestive of a conceptual identity crisis (Carr, 2016), sex/romance tourism scholars themselves debate whether the tourist women's and local men's behaviours should be conceptualized as prostitution, sex tourism, or something entirely different—romance tourism, for example, or companion tourism (Cabezas, 2004; Herold et al., 2001).

Regardless of the tensions involved, I believe that both gender/feminist approaches and political economy approaches refer to the same phenomenon of tourist women engaging in transnational sex/intimacies with local/migrant men in Global South countries. In most cases, some degree of socioeconomic exchange takes place, but in other instances the exchange is symbolic. As Taylor (2011) explains,

> sexual-economic relationships between tourist and local/migrant persons range from brief and explicit cash-for-sex exchanges that both parties understand as "prostitution," through to more open-ended, diffuse exchanges, to relationships that are understood by both parties to be "romantic" despite the asymmetry of economic power between them. It is actually very difficult to draw a sharp line between tourists' experience of commercial and non-commercial sex. (p. 63)

My intent here is not to downplay the importance of naming this phenomenon, for this naming is indeed conceptually, theoretically, and politically important for understanding the multidimensionality of the experience (Oppermann, 1999). However, correctly naming the phenomenon is not all that is involved in, as Kitossa says, "getting it right." My focus, instead, is to develop an alternative way, beyond both gender/feminist approaches and straightforward political economy approaches, of understanding this phenomenon. This alternative way offers, through Fanonist as well as antiracist and critical race feminist lenses, a deeper understanding of how the "articulated categories" (McClintock, 1995) of class, gender, and race differentially situate black men and white women within structures and relations of power. Before laying out my own approach, it is first necessary to understand what I identify as the two leading approaches in the literature: the gender/feminism approach and the political economy approach.

The Gender/Feminism Approach

The first scholars situated in the gender/feminism approach to focus on the phenomenon of white women's sex/romance tourism with black men are Pruitt and LaFont (1995) in their article "For Love and Money: Romance Tourism in Jamaica." To distinguish heterosexual male sex tourism from other tourist sexual encounters in the Caribbean, they name this phenomenon "romance tourism."[12] They argue that, contrary to male sex tourism, the encounters between primarily (European American) white women and Jamaican men are potentially transformative of gender relations. Pruitt and LaFont (1995) maintain that

> [w]hereas sex tourism serves to perpetuate gender roles and reinforce power relations of male dominance and female subordination, romance tourism in Jamaica provides an arena for change...Each of them are engaged in manipulating and expanding their gender repertoires. (p. 423)

As such, they further argue that "gender is constitutive of the relationship, not ancillary to it" (p. 423). It is travel/tourism, Pruitt and LaFont say, that creates the social space whereby these "romantic" relationships are able "to transform traditional gender roles across cultural boundaries, creating power relationships distinctive from those existing in either native society" (p. 436). In this context, Pruitt and LaFont argue that white women are accorded "new opportunities...to liberate themselves from patriarchal authority [read: *white male* patriarchal authority] relations and redefine 'woman'" (p. 437).

Redefining "woman" rests on the socioeconomic disparity between the tourist women and the local men because, according to Pruitt and LaFont

(1995), it affords the women the ability to explore a "more dominant role in the tourism relationship" (p. 427). In fact, Pruitt and LaFont maintain the "racial, educational and economic differences that constrain tourist women at home are often diminished or ignored as part of the necessity of having a 'freeing' experience" (p. 427). Thus, for example, a young, poor, rural, African Jamaican man can be the "companion" of a much older European Canadian professional woman. For some of these women, Pruitt and LaFont argue, the socioeconomic control they have in these relationships, as a result of these differences, is preferred because it keeps the men dependent on them and "fully available to meet [their] needs" (p. 427). They explain that the Jamaican Caribbean man, however, is not just "a sexual object, but [also] the woman's personal cultural broker. He serves to ease her experience in [Jamaican] society and provide her with increased access to the local culture" (p. 426). Although this locates the men in a subordinate position to the tourist women, Pruitt and Lafont maintain that it also "acts as a catalyst for these men to manipulate gender identity as a strategy for economic access" (p. 429).

As such, Pruitt and LaFont (1995) conclude that power in romance tourism is fluid between the (male and female) parties involved: "rather than the purview of men, dominance is rooted in various attributes such as economic power, physical strength, and personality characteristics that may reside with the man or the woman" (p. 437). To buttress their conclusion, they argue that, given this fluidity,

> dominance and power are not static, but are shifting and situational, constantly negotiated and contested. As the partners in these relationships play off traditional social and gender repertoires, as well as the immediate circumstances of finance and cultural capital, the power in the relationships fluctuate between them. (p. 437)

Susan Frohlick's (2013) work *Sexuality, Women, and Tourism: Cross-Border Desires Through Contemporary Travel*, a recent addition to the literature on sex/romance tourism, has some thematic overlap with Pruitt and LaFont's (1995) analysis. Frohlick's anthropological account, by her own declaration, attempts to paint a more nuanced picture of these "heterosexual cross-border relations" (p. 179). She does so to challenge what she believes is a predominant political economy framework that situates sex tourism

> as a unidimensional exertion of power where, in their pursuit of racialized exotica and erotic experiences, heterosexual Western women (often stereotyped as older, unattractive and desperate women) are seen to wield...extraordinary economic power over disenfranchised non-Western men. (p. 180)

Frohlick's feminist ethnography in Costa Rica (specifically, Puerto Viejo) challenges this so-called "unidimensional exertion of power" that constructs the white tourist women as "despicable" and tries to offer a more complicated account by asking the question, "Who's using who[m]?" (p. 180). Frohlick's answer is, "[A] mix of exploitation and instrumentality [exists] on *both* [emphasis added] sides" (p. 180).

Frohlick (2013) contends that the asymmetries of political economy place white tourist women in positions of relative power over local black Costa Rican men because their financial resources "and also crucially, their mobility...related to their passports and citizenship in [Global North] countries grant them the access to go almost anywhere in the world they can afford to go" (p. 179). She maintains that gender discourses, however, allow local men masculinized power *regardless* of socioeconomic standing that enable them to "control the town's public and semi-public spaces of leisure and informal economies and engage in performances of hyper-masculinity." (p. 179). This hypermasculinity grants these men, according to Frohlick, "physical and symbolic power over heterosexual (and bisexual) tourist women for whom being desired by men is highly seductive and valued" (p. 179). In this context, she maintains that "[i]nternational travel engenders eroticism through exoticism" but stresses that it is "locality and actual corporeal gendered beings that shape the outcomes of sexual exchange" (p. 172).

Frohlick (2013) asserts that, rather than the desire for "liminality, transgression or carnivalesgue [*sic*], as tourism is sometimes conceptualized" (p. 181), the cross-border experiences of European American and Canadian women are embedded in a complex desire for personal growth and mid-life transformations. It is "about the start of a new life post-divorce or post-university, or carrying out work as a yoga teacher in a different locale" (p. 181). Attempting to capture the contradictory social and interpersonal relations that inform the outcome of these relationships, Frohlick concludes:

> The gender politics of heterosexual hook ups, relationships, and marriages [are] played out in a complex multicultural site rapidly changing due to globalization and tourism. Men...[use] foreign women to chase their own dreams, just as women's fantasies [are] expected to be fulfilled by men; both parties [are], in different ways, *naïve* [emphasis added] about a mutuality of these dreams and aspirations, which, as it [becomes] clearly evident over time, [are] not shared. (p. 181)

Limitations of the Gender/Feminism Approach

As I critique some aspects of the gender/feminism approach, I wish to reiterate that my intent is not to diminish or condemn the scholarship on "romance tourism" or "cross-border sex." Both Frohick (2013) and Pruitt and LaFont (1995) labour to bring complexity to a social phenomenon that has been given little in-depth scholarly attention. Frohlick, in fact, discloses that she endeavoured to create a careful and respectful portrait that gives "specificity to how transnational sex happens from the perspectives of women involved in the relationships...so that the line between 'us' and 'them' and between 'sex tourism' and 'ordinary sex'...is ruptured" (p. 191). Her intent is to be applauded. By providing a "thick description" of white women's "cross-border" intimacies, she challenges simplistic and scintillating generalizations and stereotypes that circulate in the media, popular culture, and academic literature, and which represent the women as insecure, sex-crazed, and despicable sexual exploiters. I believe, however, in the final analysis and contrary to their good intentions, both Frohlick (2013) and Pruitt and LaFont (1995) do a disservice to a deeper understanding of how racialized gender systems and identities are inextricably intertwined, given the colonialist and white supremacist contexts of transnational dominance. They also miss that white women *qua* white women are invested *in* and *with* white racialized superiority and, therefore, that the gender/feminism script—which assumes universal patriarchal domination over all women—does not in fact comport with the reality of men who are black, poor, and immobilized in the Global South.

Their assertions of mutual exploitation (i.e., Frohlick, 2013) or a mutually imbricating cycle of exploitation (i.e., Pruitt & LaFont, 1995) suggest an equivalent partnership of sorts through the checks and balances of their respective class, gender, and race locations. It assumes the hypermasculinity of the local men counters the economic power and mobility of the tourist women and, consequently, both parties are positioned on an equivalent terrain of power. Such over-determinations of the microdimensional aspects of these relations elide the ways the white women's embodiment within colonial, imperial, and racist contexts mobilize the political and economic power of the Global North *and* the racialized gender power accessible to the women in these transnational locations. Indeed, if we follow Frohlick's (2013) line of reasoning regarding the "physical and symbolic power" of the local men and Pruitt and LaFont's (1995) argument of gender/power fluidity in romance tourism to their ends, we are left with an uncomfortable conclusion: that the gender/feminist approach to women and sex/romance tourism is an instrumental methodology that appropriates for white women the best of all worlds. On one hand, they are powerless as victims of a white heteropatriarchy that constrains and restricts their autonomy at home and, therefore, they are granted *innocence* in the practising of power. On the other hand, they get to exercise racialized gender power and transcend "heteropatriarchy" vis-à-vis cross-border travel and sex/romance with poor black men in the Caribbean who have "physical and symbolic power" over them. The evasions and elisions of white women's racialized gender power—and consequently black men's racialized gender disempowerment—reflect a pervasive lacuna in "whitestream" feminist (Grande, 2003; see also Thomas,

2007) understandings of race, gender, and power and allow for these seemingly contradictory conclusions. As such, the black male sex/romance worker becomes the straw horse for white women's sexual and personal liberation.

Also of significance here is the fact that these evasions and elisions go beyond Frohlick's (2013) and Pruitt and LaFont's (1995) research; they can also be found in other sex/romance tourist scholarship that draw on traditional feminist constructions of patriarchal power relations. Herold et al. (2001), for example, argue that, while the women they call "female travellers" enjoy more economic power than the local men, this power "is counter-balanced by the interpersonal social skills of the 'beach boys'[13] who are very adept in using this knowledge to their advantage in manipulating the female tourist [for their economic gain]" (p. 996). Remarkably, the researchers position the interpersonal skills of the "beach boys" on equal footing with the economic power of the white women.

These gender-focused, race-absent (with a splash of class) analyses are troubling for the reasons highlighted. But they are also disconcerting because they diminish and/or erase the actual vulnerabilities and traumas experienced by black men who are sex/romance tourist workers. These erasures are made possible because gender-racialized evasions and elisions provide the analytical space for tropes of black masculinity to easily slip into the theoretical void and function as what Tommy Curry (2017) calls "a cog in a conceptual scheme that reduces black male life to the examples, or proof, of a predetermined abstraction" (p. 203). This abstraction reduces the black men in such sex/romance tourist configurations to unsavoury, licentious, and manipulating "beach boys" who are perceived and theorized, as Richards and Ried (2015) argue, as "free agents in [these] sexual relationships" (p. 424) and who "unlike women, have total control over their labor, relationships, and their bodies" (p. 424; see also Dennis, 2008; Jones, 2010). From a Fanonist perspective, black men are overdetermined in such arguments as "sociogenic" a prioris in the white cultural imaginary, from which not even researchers are immune. As a result, capturing the full humanity of the men as complex material beings made in and by history who are vulnerable to sexual exploitation in these sex/romance tourist contexts (and beyond) is rendered a conceptual and, therefore, a material impossibility.

I am not arguing that race is ignored in the researchers' accounts. To the contrary, Frohlick (2013) and Pruitt and LaFont (1995), for example, acknowledge that race plays a role in these cross-border sexual relationships. They do so, however, by exploring the essentializing prism of the racial difference of the black men and not the gendered racial power of the white women. As a consequence, the meanings and implications of whiteness as a positively racialized position and the power of structures and relations in which it is embedded—for example, anti-blackness and neocolonialism in the Caribbean—are not fully developed and extrapolated (Wekker, 2016) toward understanding white women's sex/romance tourism *with* black men. In the end, gender/feminist researchers ultimately disavow the significance of race (and class) and overdetermine gender (as it relates to women) in their framings of power and subjectivity by claiming either that both parties engage in mutual exploitation or that power fluctuates between them.

In the section that follows, I advance my critique through the political economy approach represented by Jacqueline Taylor's (2001, 2006) scholarship on sex/romance tourism. Drawing on her research in the Caribbean, Taylor alerts us to some of the political and analytical dangers of theorizing power and subjectivity in sex/romance tourism. In particular, she offers a sustained critique of accounts that give primacy to feminist conceptions of patriarchal power relations.

Political Economy Approach

Highlighting some of the conceptual and theoretical problems associated with existing analyses, Taylor (2001, 2006) makes a trenchant and, to my mind, compelling critique of the literature on sex/romance tourism.[14] She points out that the distinction between romance tourism and sex tourism is often split along gendered lines. Sexual and romantic encounters between tourist women and local men are more likely to be categorized as "romance tourism" while similar encounters between tourist men and local women are often referred to as "sex tourism." Taylor's (2006) ethnographic research suggests that sexual-economic exchanges between tourist women and local men in Jamaica and the Dominican Republic map onto and are "predicated upon the same global economic and social inequalities [of structural adjustment managed by the World Bank, the International Monetary Fund, and the World Trade Organization] that underpin the phenomenon of male sex tourism" (p. 44). As such, any distinction on the structuring dynamics that inform both processes is problematic. Furthermore, male and female sex tourists may exhibit similar "sex tourist" behaviour, yet are conceptualized differently.[15]

It is in this context that Taylor (2006) launches a criticism of the "overlooked" similarities between men and women tourists from the "overdeveloped" Global North. She argues that the overlooked similarities "between male and female sex tourism [reflect] and [reproduce] weaknesses in existing theoretical and common-sense understandings of gendered power, sexual exploitation, prostitution and sex tourism" (p. 42). The failure to see these similarities largely rests on the fact that the "North American and European feminist" (Taylor, 2006, p. 45) discussion on sex work, informed by a radical feminist approach, largely ignores male sex workers, and instead focuses on female sex workers as "victim[s] of male sexual violence." It questions "whether [female sex workers] are engaging in 'free choice' prostitution wherein female prostitutes are autonomous agents choosing to sell their sexual labour" (Taylor, 2006, p. 45). Male prostitution, according to Taylor, has been overlooked because victimization in this tradition is a "gendered" concept (see Lamb, 1999) that constructs women as victims and men as victimizers, making it difficult to conceptualize the ways men might be sexually exploited by women (Taylor, 2006, p. 45; see also Curry, 2017). Taylor explains that radical feminist theory, for example, posits sexuality as a fundamental location of male power. According to this theory, it is in the heterosexual sex act that

> women submit to men, and men affirm their masculinity and patriarchal power by penetrating the female body...This model of gender power as

domination constructs relations between men and women as a master-slave relation. (Taylor, 2006, p. 47)

This theorization treats both men and women as undifferentiated social groups and consequently, Taylor (2006) argues, it obscures the importance of age, class, and race "for an individual's social power and life chances" (p. 47). This is a crucial point because much of the research and analyses of sex tourism generally begin from the premise "that it represents a form of prostitute use and can, therefore, be primarily explained in terms of patriarchal power relations" (Taylor, 2006, p. 45). In this framework, women *cannot* actually be sex tourists (and men cannot be prostitutes), hence the term *romance tourism*. These essentialist conceptualizations of gender, sexuality, and patriarchy "preclude the possibility that a woman can sexually exploit a man" (Taylor, 2006, p. 44), especially if racialized power dynamics are obscured or ignored (Taylor, 2001).

As a result of such taken-for-granted configurations, we have limited insight into how gender within these sex tourist relationships is varied and complex and that "in some circumstances, women can pursue a social ideal of heterosexuality without automatically placing themselves in a subordinate position" (Taylor, 2006, p. 52). Importantly, Taylor (2006) emphasizes, "if [white] women are not necessarily subordinated by the heterosexual sex act, then it becomes possible to recognize that they too can, in certain circumstances, sexually exploit [black] men" (p. 52). This recognition necessitates an epistemic project that rejects claims of mutual exploitation and the "theoretical privileging of gender power over questions of racism and racialised power" (Taylor, 2001, p. 759).

The Alternative Approach: Anchoring Sex/Romance Tourist Relationships in a Diverse Politics and Analytics of Agency and Power

The necessity of the epistemic project to which Taylor alerts us requires an alternative approach beyond the gender/feminism and political economy approaches. This approach must seriously engage with Taylor's anticolonial insights by anchoring the "thick descriptions" of the gender/feminist approach into the political economy of sex/romance tourism. Additionally, and more importantly for me, it requires an epistemological anchoring of Fanon's radical humanism and antiracist and critical race feminism's analytics and politics of agency and power. The objective is to open up new possibilities for epistemological and methodological (re)framings that neither evade and obscure complex racialized gender power dimensions through essentializing analytic categories, nor pathologize the people involved in these sex/romance tourist relationships. This is important because, as Tamari Kitossa affirms, "these men and women are not simply 'categories' of analysis, but are real human beings meeting under definite terms and conditions informed by history" (personal communication, May 28, 2020).

Fanon (1952/1977) contends, referring to the deeply embedded and pervasive narratives about the black man as solely determined by his precocious genitalia (which is the mark of his unalterable negation demanded by white "civilization"), there are "legends, stories, and above all historicity" (p. 112). *Historicity* in these sex/romance tourist contexts refers to an a priori "field of racial and sexual visibility" (Deliovsky, 2002b; see also Butler, 1993; Fanon, 1952/1977) forged in colonial violence that profoundly affects all aspects of these relationships, from how tourist women and local men themselves experience the sex/romance tourist relationship, to how the media takes up these relationships, to how scholars and nonscholars conceptualize and interpret them. These factors make it all the more important to "get right" the radical humanism Fanon believed in and worked for. I assert that researchers and scholars—white, feminist, and otherwise—attend to this historicity as the backdrop and source of the drama and of their studies. As such, they must reckon with how their fields of study and their work are implicated in epistemic violence of defining—from their position in the Global North—the Global South.

I believe Anne McClintock's (1995) "articulated categories"[16] can offer a fruitful way to attend to these issues.[17] Describing the conceptual framework that informed her examination of power and Western imperialism, she explains that

> race, gender and class are not distinct realms of experience, existing in splendid isolation from each other; nor can they be simply yoked together retrospectively like armatures of Lego. Rather they come into existence *in and through* relation to each other...In this sense, gender, race and class can be called articulated categories. (p. 5)

These articulated categories of gender, race, and class, she argues, are not "reducible to, or identical with, each other; instead, they exist in intimate, reciprocal and contradictory relations" (p. 5). For example, gender, race, and class placed colonial women "ambiguously" (McClintock, 1995, p. 6) in the imperial process. As McClintock explains, while marital, property, land laws, and "the intractable violence of male decree bound [colonial white women] in gendered patterns of disadvantage and frustration" (p. 6), the women nonetheless experienced "the rationed privileges of race" that located them "in positions of decided—if borrowed—power" (p. 6) over both colonized women *and* men. As such, and central to the alternative approach I am proposing here, McClintock underscores that white women were and are not unfortunate "onlookers of empire" but "complicit both as colonizers and colonized, privileged and restricted, acted upon and acting" (p. 6; see also Kitossa, 2002; Ware, 1997)—all in relation to a degraded colonized Other. It is through this understanding of articulated categories that we can examine white women's sex/romance tourism with black men as a site for the reproduction of relations of dominance through which the historicity of empire articulates itself.

A side note is needed here. Articulated categories certainly alert us to the insidiousness of white imperial tourist[18] encounters (Alexander, 1997) and make it difficult to establish equivalencies that then perpetuate neat framings whereby white women are rescued from degrading and pathological appellations. But, given the limits of knowledge, it should be understood that the concept of articulated categories is just one conceptual potentiality among others. There are several possible strands of analysis in the alternative approach; however, attention to historicity and the development and/or mobilization of complex theorizations of race, gender, and power are the only ways (at least for me) to disrupt the racialized gender evasions and elisions in gender/feminist discourses (Thomas, 2007). Again, these lacunae result in the tropistic default position of white female powerlessness and innocence and the reproduction of white domination and black male primitive and "savage heterosexualism" (Curry, 2017, p. 198)—all in the pursuit of sex, money, and power.

I do not believe the political and epistemological necessity for this alternative approach can be overstated. Nor do I believe an (over)emphasis will contribute to a "unidimensional exertion of power" (Frohlick, 2013, p. 180) that situates the white sex/romance tourist women as wielding inordinate economic power over black men. As McClintock's (1995) work suggests, white women are not the policy makers who structure imperial relations of domination,[19] but their exercise in personal/sexual agency implicates them, irrespective of whether they are "good" or "bad" people, in reproducing the power inequities of white imperial tourism—a term I borrow from M.J. Alexander (1997) to signify the commodified tourist space for the consumption of sexualized and eroticized black bodies. These points cannot be ignored or diminished to eschew disparaging appellations of white women (i.e., sex-crazed N... lovers, etc.) who cross racial and national boundaries to experience "intimacy" that they control. We know that white women who have transgressed tropes of white femininity[20] have been historically subjected to scrutiny and salacious voyeurism, if not punitive regulation. But antiracist and anticolonial practice demands that we not be precluded from examining the broader structural and relational inequities and colonial violences in which these relationships exist. It is precisely because white women's intimate relations are open to surveillance due to the gendering processes that are bound up with ability, age, class, race, and sexuality that their ostensibly intimate, reciprocal, and contradictory relations can be theorized without evading uncomfortable truths.

White Imperial Tourism: Commodification and Exoticization

This section mobilizes the conceptual logic of articulated categories in order to develop connections between white imperial tourism and the commodification and exoticization of black racialized bodies through a Fanonist as well as antiracist and critical race feminist examination of existing narratives of white women involved in sex/romance tourism. Before turning to this examination, it bears repeating here that white women's striving for autonomy and sovereignty in these sex/romance tourism contexts occurs within and is made possible by the very structuration of contemporary white imperial tourism. As members of a group who are allocated the "rationed privileges of race" (McClintock, 1995, p. 6), gender, and class, white women (unlike any female member of a racialized group) are granted a particular kind of mobility in these imperial spaces, which allows them to participate in the commodification and consumption of black racialized bodies. This mobility is not allowed for negatively racialized women who are always and already coded as objects of sexuality for "white" masculine desire.

I do not want to suggest here that all white women who travel to the Caribbean will or want to partake in the "pleasures" of sex/romance tourism. My argument, rather, is that, for those who *do* travel for sex/romance, the violent legacies of colonialism and slavery in the Caribbean and the ongoing neocolonial processes of globalization and tourism are such that no one travels for sex/romance innocently. What I, therefore, suggest is that white imperial tourism creates the place, space, and conditions for white women to pursue personal growth and mid-life transformations on and through the locations, cultures, and bodies of black local men (and women). As such, these sex/romance tourist relations can never be intimate and erotic spaces of mutual exploitation, nor of romance, companionship, and personal transformation outside of the inequities of white imperial tourism.

Be that as it may, "practices of knowing and not-knowing" (Wekker, 2016, p. 18) ignore, minimize, or obscure how sex/romance tourism in the Global South is located within profound asymmetries of power. These asymmetries position both the white male and female tourist as "a king and queen" (Davidson & Taylor, 2005, p. 87) in these sex/romance tourist contexts (even though they may not be a king and queen in their home countries). Davidson and Taylor (2005) point out:

> In the [Global South], neocolonial relations of power equip Western sex tourists with an extremely high level of control over themselves and others as sexual beings and, as a result, with the power to realize the fantasy of their choosing. (p. 52)

In this way, black men, as the sex/romance tourism providers, are what John Russell (Chapter 2 of this volume) calls "the dehumanized fodder for fetishization and fantasies." Yet, recognition of the processes and structures instrumental to this dehumanization is denied through the theoretical evasions and elisions of gendered, racialized power that construct colonized black men as complicit and/or active in their own sexual/racial exploitation and white women as innocent and/or ignorant of the process.

My emphasis on the inseparable role of white imperial tourism and the racialized, gendered dimensions that shape the men's and women's sexual, erotic exchange is not manufactured for dramatic effect, nor is it simply theoretic conjecture; it is actually demonstrated in the narratives of female sex/romance tourists themselves. Such narratives, for example, can be found in Frohlick's ethnography. In one representative narrative, Frohlick (2013) recounts her research participant Carolyn's description of her two sexual encounters with a "really beautiful rasta" and "a pretty rasta":

> They are really amazing in bed. Not in a giving way at all. Not like they're going to perform oral sex for an hour to you. No. They're in really good shape most of them. A lot of them surf so they're strong through the middle. Powerful, passionate, crazy sex. Crazy wild *jungle sex* [emphasis added]. (p. 144)

In prodding Carolyn to expand on the notion of "jungle sex," Frohlick asks, "How different are they as lovers from Canadian guys?" (read: most likely "white guys," since these were her first sexual encounters with black men) (p. 144). Carolyn responds:

> A lot of women don't like to admit it, but I think they like to be manhandled, not have to be in charge, not have to initiate things. It's macho...The two that I had sex with, they're just powerful. More animalistic. None of this "Are you okay?" None of them are ever going to give you a massage. None of them are ever going to give you oral sex. It's just powerful. (p. 144)

Indeed, perceiving the sex with black men as "not giving," and the men being perceived as "macho," "powerful," and "more animalistic" than (white) Canadian men, resulted in "crazy wild jungle sex" that was intensely pleasurable for Carolyn. Note, too, that the perception of the men's disregard for the women's sexual pleasure and safety also designated the sex as more powerful and animalistic. Nevertheless, we can certainly extrapolate from this narrative that sex with the black racial Other amplified Carolyn's erotic excitement, but this is only one possibility for what made her experience of the sex so "powerful and animalistic."

Pointing to another possibility, Gargi Bhattacharyya (2002) argues, in her Fanonist-inspired analysis of power disparities and erotic racism, that "without the sense that the object of desire is lesser, dangerous and forbidden—alluringly other and beyond any everyday social contact—there is no exoticist dynamic" (p. 106). In this context, Carolyn's designation of the sex as more powerful and animalistic is precisely because the black man is imagined not as a fully formed human being but as an *animal*. Bhattacharyya explains that "there is something about being socially disadvantaged, or even degraded, that makes for exoticization" (p. 104). The power inequity between the exoticist (white women) and the exoticized (black men) "heightens the sexual hit" (p. 102). Bhattacharyya further states:

> When we examine the cultural products of exoticism, each instance comes from a very tangible set of political relations. Although the stories are dressed up in fantasy, it is not difficult to see the geopolitics that informs [*sic*] the desire. In exoticism the desired object is your slave, your enemy, your absolute other—the desire may fixate on the anticipation of danger of the pleasure of dominating the weak or the adventure of an alien and

forbidden experience, but each scenario demands that the object has less agency and access to mainstream power than the one who desires. (p. 107)

Pointing to the uneven positionality of the one who desires versus the one who is desired, Bhattacharyya speaks tangentially to the inequities of "exoticism" in white imperial tourism. These inequities clearly challenge notions of exploitation as "mutual" or conceptions of power as "fluid" and "shifting." They also illuminate that gendered, racialized power structures and relations in sex/romance tourism are not only dictated by history, culture, and material relations, but are also shaped at the interpersonal-dynamic level by the actions and discursive practices of the parties involved.

The narratives of the sex/romance tourists themselves are, again, particularly illuminating when it comes to these complexities and connections (local, national, and global). In another narrative taken from Frohlick's (2013) ethnography, a research participant attempts to articulate what "mysteriously" draws white women tourists to Puerto Viejo, Costa Rica:[21]

> Something draws women here that we don't even understand. For me, it was just word of mouth [spread by other white women]—"You've got to come down here. You would so like it"...So something brings us women here to, I call it, the "twilight zone." It transforms us. It transforms, most women do not leave this place unaffected. (p. 83)

A serious Fanonist engagement with sex as a site that manifests the dead weight of white historicity's myths and mythologies would here reveal that this transformation is not separate from their intimate relations with the local men nor, properly speaking, of their imaginings of them. Fanon (1952/1977) notes:

> There is one expression that through time has become singularly eroticized: the black athlete. There is something in the mere idea, one [white] young woman confided to me, that it makes her heart skip a beat.

> A prostitute told me that in her early days the mere thought of going to bed with a Negro brought on an orgasm. She went in search of Negroes and never asked for money. But, she added, "going to bed with them was no more remarkable than going to bed with white men. It was before I did it that I had the orgasm. I used to think about (imagine) all the things they might do to me: and that was what was so terrific." (pp. 158–59)

The desire for, in Bhattacharyya's (2002) words, that alien and forbidden erotic adventure with a poor, young, athletic, racialized Other (and at times "thingified" nonbeing) whose "black afro-Caribbean masculinity" (Frohlick, 2013, p. 131) is especially valued by the white women, is grafted onto the "primitive" and "wild" physical and social landscape of this transformative "twilight zone" (i.e., jungle sex). Speaking to this intertwining of erotic adventure/pleasure and the physical/social landscape, Frohlick (2013) recounts another participant's twilight experience. She writes:

> [Linda's] sexual pleasure derived not simply from the dark-skinned virile body of a local black young man but the physical-sensual space in which their bodies interacted...The dwelling space with its chickens and tin roof, along with the sounds of children playing in the yard, were iconic "Caribbean roots" to her and she was pleased to have been able to cross a number of boundaries (racial, cultural, sexual) to acquire that experience. (p. 145)

The rustic poverty of this wild, unsettled, and primal setting—which could just as well be imagined as stolen sex in a thatch-roofed, earthen-floored slave shack (see Foster, 2019; Wells, 2010)—jarringly reveals Bhattacharyya's conception of the sexual high that derives from power imbalances in these transnational intimacies.

The body and the physical space of the exotic Other, enveloped in notions of romanticized poverty, are intertwined and inseparable in the generation of erotic pleasure. As bell hooks (1992) argues in Fanonist terms, this longing for erotic pleasure has led "the white west to sustain a romantic fantasy of the 'primitive' and the concrete search for a real primitive paradise" (p. 27). Not represented solely by geography, this real primitive paradise can be, hooks says, "a country or a body, a dark continent or dark flesh, perceived as the perfect embodiment of that possibility" (p. 27). The sex/romance tourist relationship reflects the "perfect" embodiment of this primitive paradise: It literally provides both the body and the country from which "imperial tourists" (Alexander, 1997) get to pursue their self-interests yet elide how their erotic and emotional desires are "irrevocably link[ed] to collective white domination" and erotic racism (hooks, 1992, p. 24; see also Davidson & Taylor, 2005).

It is for these reasons that Annabelle, another research participant from Frohlick's (2013) ethnography, can "unabashedly" express her desire to have sexual relations with any local man that appealed to her. Frohlick recounts Annabelle's narrative: "'I want this one and this one!' she exclaimed, referring to the 'hot' bodies of local men who were, in her eyes, 'gorgeous,' 'hard' and 'beautiful' [i.e., 'exotic']" (p. 128). Racial overtones are evident in Annabelle's narratives of cross-border sex, Frohlick reports, "including stereotypes about 'black guys' as naturally skilled dancers and athletes" (p.128). As Annabelle and her friends "go out on their nightly jaunts to the town's hot spots to seek out the sexiest local 'hotties'," Frohlick explains, "the local men are objectified as hers for the picking" (p. 128).

It is within the context of white imperial tourism that white women can invert the traditional white heteropatriarchal gender script and objectify these men as theirs "for the picking."[22] White women's positional superiority,[23] their whiteness—their racial and to some degree class assignment relative to the black men's—grants them the social/racial mobility to engage in these sex/romance tourist encounters.[24] But, more importantly in some ways, the construction of the women as innocent and without power (and thus victimizable by rapacious Black men) disguises the extent and quality of their participation in white domination. Kate Davy (1995) explains that, paradoxically, white women can never "fully embody the unembodied dimension of white masculinity, for to 'embody' is still [their] definition and destiny" (p. 197). And while they can never fully embody white masculinity, sex/romance tourism in the Global South positions these women, even white working-class women, to enact masculinized power conferred by their whiteness. These sex/romance tourist relationships rely on "explicit and comprehensible power disparity" (Bhattacharya, 1997, p. 106) to fulfill their erotically charged potential, but white women's role as *the subjects who desire* (rather than objects of desire) gets muddied by arguments of mutual exploitation. And this is made possible precisely because it is the disenfranchised hypersexual black male Other who plays the role of the object of her desire.[25] Bhattacharya (1997) argues:[26]

> Whether or not the exoticist wields real-world power, making someone your exotic object demands a fantasy of power...Therefore...exoticism transfers the contradictions of certain power structures into the realm of the sexual in order to rework discomfort. Sex promises to allow room for terror and desire and to conciliate the two. In this telling, exoticism performs a certain therapeutic function for the powerful—reworks cruelty and unfounded privilege as the more ambivalent position of desire, as if all this conflicted emotion was a product of psychic contradictions as opposed to class [gender, and race] contradictions. (p. 106)

Conclusion

I want to close this chapter by briefly encapsulating and reiterating the problems with the gender/feminism approach's epistemic and discursive race-neutral account of gender, which is transcended by political economy's open engagement with colonialism, imperialism, and racism. More than this, I want to briefly demonstrate that in as much as the political economy approach channels Fanon, it would greatly benefit from a substantive engagement with his psychosexual analytics in the immediacy of social interaction, which is possible in a "thick description" of the type offered by the gender/feminism approach.

The gender/feminism approach to white women's transnational intimacies abstracts the women out of racialized power relations and structures. Doing so obscures the positional superiority (Said, 1979) of white women relative to the racialized Other and colludes with white women's self-construction as either, or at one and the same time, *innocent* or *ignorant*. Implicit or explicit, this results in pathological constructions of local heterosexual black men whose commodity is their complicity in selling back to white women the fantasies and mythologies white culture produces of them. As Russell (Chapter 2 of this volume) argues, "The transnational nature of fetishes and tropes of black male sexual alterity and their transcription across sites of gender, class, genre, and geography is both ironic and ultimately tragic." The irony and tragedy lie in the commodification of "beach boys" and "rent-a-dreads" as objects that "fascinate and repel" (Davidson & Taylor, 1999, p. 50) in sex/romance tourist contexts and other contexts where race, gender, and sexual identities "are negotiated, reaffirmed, transformed, resisted, and denied, though never fully subverted or transcended. The fundamental humanity of these 'objects' of desire and dread is seldom, if ever, acknowledged" (Russell, Chapter 2 in this volume).

This latter point is particularly important to stress because it is the "historico-racial schema" (Fanon, 1952/1977, p. 111) of satyr-like black masculinity that allows for their dehumanization and construction as beneficiaries, if not predators and/or exploiters, in the sex tourist relationship. Myths about the black man are irrational, but as Fanon (1952/1977) notes "that is not what matters" (p. 159), since they are rationally believed. Sometimes with all the fears of rape that attach themselves to black men in the white imaginary, sex/romance tourism flirts with all the presumed dangers, especially that of the rapist (however "domesticated" and "pacified" by the safety of white imperial tourism) that black men represent.[27]

But for the white woman so involved, their experience with white patriarchal oppression subordinates the pervasiveness of racism to ensure that sex with the Other takes on the character of liberation. Fanon (1952/1977) explains that for white women, the black man is "the keeper of the impalpable gate that opens into the realm of orgies, of bacchanals, of delirious sexual sensations" (p. 177). Where carnality is imagined as the exclusive domain of the black man, Fanon observes that "there are sensitive spots in the [white] human soul at a level where thought becomes confused and where sexual excitement is strangely linked with violence and aggressiveness" (p. 166). The black man becomes an end, an instrument in white women's sexual liberation and personal sovereignty; but in this way, the black man is literally a scapegoat, sacrifice, prop, and prophylactic that is necessary to avoid self-implication and moral responsibility for guilt and shame where white women pursue sexual freedom. The power of the black man as a totemic scapegoat is that he can never pass any judgment on white women's sexual agency because he is not a white man and because he, too, is subject to white heteropatriarchy.

A Fanonist psychoanalytic approach suggests that, given both the correlation of whiteness with civility and sexual repression and the gender dynamic of sex with a subordinate male racial Other, these sex/romance relationships can produce a definite sexual catharsis. The very opportunity for sexual liberation is made possible in this way by white women's channelling and following of colonial roots and routes of sexual desire. White women, in some ways aided and abetted by white researchers, can experience the fruits promised by feminism and Western culture—agency and autonomy within those sex/romance tourist contexts—but with the benefit of projecting blame and moral responsibility onto the socially powerless black men who ply Caribbean beaches. Transformed by the evasions, elisions, and essentialisms of the gender/feminist scholarship, they become the archetypical patriarchal monster and "lords of the polis"[28] (Kitossa, Introduction to this volume) desiring sexual domination and power over others, despite their actual political, social, and economic vulnerabilities (Curry, 2017). As Bhattacharyya (2002) tells us, "making someone your exotic object demands a fantasy of power" (p. 106). How else can white women be made innocent and ignorant for desiring a man of whom white culture has made a perdurable sexual demon?

A Fanonist psychoanalytic approach, at both the individual and collective cultural levels of race discourse, enables the political economy approach to more trenchantly elaborate the contradictions and paradoxes of the transnational sex/romance tourism intimacies of white women with black Caribbean men. It is through this epistemological anchoring that the goal of developing an alternative way becomes possible.

Author's Note

I must acknowledge Tamari Kitossa's contribution to the writing of this paper. His intellectual depth and breadth coupled with his brilliant editorial skills proved invaluable in helping me to capture some of the complex power dynamics and the Fanonist-inspired radical humanism of these sex/romance tourist arrangements.

Notes

1. Cited in Ware (1997), p. 133.
2. Class is theorized within the gender/feminism approach. The analysis, however, is superficial and disconnected from racialized gendered contexts.
3. See Hortense Spillers (1987) and Robyn Wiegman (1994) for discussions on how identity categories saturate one another.
4. As a concept, patriarchy rests on the notion that all men are privileged by gender relative to all women. In the context of black men, this notion is questionable given, for example, the disproportionately punitive treatment black men experience. As Athena Mutua (2013) points out, this occurs "not only in the context of anonymous public space that often characterize racial profiling, but also in terms of higher rates of hyper incarceration, death by homicide and certain diseases, suicide rates, and high unemployment as compared to black women" (p. 346). Mutua points out that these experiences negate the idea that black men have any patriarchal (gender) privilege as posited by feminist theorizing.
5. This knowing and not-knowing includes instances where: (1) scholars argue that the term *romance tourism* more aptly describes what these tourist women do; and (2) some of the research participants themselves argue their relationships are not sex tourist relationships. They "just happened" (see Frohlick, 2013).
6. Borrowing from Edward Said (1979), positional superiority is a privileged location that arises from having structural advantage within systems of white supremacy.
7. There is a larger body of scholarship that explores women's sex/romance tourism but it is part of a broader examination of sex work as a whole, including men's sex tourism. There is also research that examines women's sex/romance tourism with Asian, Southeast Asian, and African men. While I do not analyze this large body of scholarship, I do sometimes refer to it.
8. For example, Taylor (2001) takes the position that Fanon was "so heavily invested in the idea of gender difference [that he] failed to critique gender hierarchies in the same way he critiqued hierarchies of race" (p. 54). She argues, as such, that this ideological leaning can all too easily translate "into a celebration of the Black phallus" (p. 54). Since I argue for a Fanonist

epistemology, I clearly do not agree with her argument; however, with due respect, I also believe it is based on a misreading of Fanon.

9. As he spells out in *A Dying Colonialism* and *Wretched of the Earth*, Fanon (1959/1967, 1961/1968) insisted the fundamental principle of individual, cultural, material, and social egalitarianism are the minimum standard for all human beings.

10. Interestingly, this reading ignores the possibility that the couple may be an interracial tourist couple on holiday.

11. A small number of the women are African American and Japanese.

12. See also Bras and Dahles (1999) for a discussion of romance tourism in Indonesia.

13. See Kitossa (Chapter 1 in this volume, n. 21) for a discussion on the disparaging connotations of referring to black men as "boy."

14. Taylor's (2001, 2006) critiques predate Frohlick's (2013) monograph; nonetheless, some of the critiques can be applied to Frohlick's research.

15. Taylor (2001, 2006) acknowledges that there are differences between male and female sex tourism, but these differences should not preclude an analysis of the similarities in sexual experiences and associated privileges given that the reproduction of colonial relations of power through sex is what is at stake.

16. Stuart Hall (1980) developed and elaborated "articulations" as a mode for theorizing the multiplicity and saliency of one identity as the articulation of others in his essay "Race, Articulation and Societies Structured in Dominance." Troublingly, McClintock (1995) does not cite Hall in *Imperial Leather*. See Kitossa (Introduction to this volume, n. 25) for a discussion of McClintock's interpretation of Fanon.

17. Some may offer "intersectionality" (Crenshaw, 1989) as the way to understand the class, gender, and race dimensions of these relationships. I, however, agree with Tommy Curry's (2017) argument that although intersectionality is perceived and popularized as an antiessentialist paradigm, there are essentialist notions operating within its theorization. Curry argues that "[u]nder intersectionality, the disadvantages of Black men are conceptualized as consequences of the racial category, not the gendered subordinate male category, since 'male' is thought of only as a designation of privilege" (p. 215). As a result, black male disadvantage and vulnerability is obscured.

18. Referring to Bahamas, Jacqui Alexander (1997) argues that tourism has been the major economic strategy of modernization for the state. It has been "transformed from its tentative beginnings of a leisure activity of a white-imperial elite...to a mass-based tourism" (p. 67). She explains that the significance of tourism for the neocolonial nation state "lies in its ability to draw together powerful processes of (sexual) commodification and (sexual) citizenship" to create a population in service of "both the imperial tourist (the invisible subject of colonial law) and for a presumably 'servile' population whom the state is bent on renativizing" (p. 68). Central to this process is the eroticization of black bodies. As Alexander argues, "white imperial tourism would not be complete without eroticized blackness" (p. 96).

19. I would like to note that where women are themselves involved in the policy making process (i.e., Margaret Thatcher, Golda Meir, Indira Gandhi, Madeleine Albright, Condoleeza Rice, Susan Rice, Hilary Clinton, etc.), there is little evidence to support the idea that they, too, will not conform, like male policy makers, to the protection of interests of capital and all other ruling forces of domination.
20. See McIntosh (2019) for a contemporary discussion on tropes of white femininity.
21. The fact that Frohlick's (2013) interlocutor simultaneously mobilizes white innocence and white ignorance escapes Frohlick's critical scrutiny. This theorization is much needed.
22. Frohlick (2013) does not apply the connections between white imperial tourism and white women's positional superiority to the narratives.
23. White femininity, as a trope, never occurs outside a process of racial domination and the negation of black women (and men), women of colour, and Indigenous women who are constructed as fallen women denigrated by their racial assignment.
24. Within a gendered and racialized hierarchy, white tourist women are positioned aprioristically as innocent, benevolent, life-transforming, adventuring-seeking tourists until they form permanent or semipermanent relations with these men and choose to stay in these locations. These permanent or semipermanent relations signal a more permanent transgression of white womanhood (Deliovsky 2002b, 2010; Taylor, 2001). Ironically, while they are punished and lose status for transgressing the rules of white femininity when they enter a permanent or semipermanent relationship with the black men, it is their whiteness, "the rationed privileges of race" (McClintock, 1995, p. 6), that permits them this transgression in the first place.
25. Whiteness, as positional superiority, allows the women a space to enact sexual agency, particularly in these transnational contexts; however, it is confined in some important ways by their gender, class, and ethnic locations, which have yet to be fully explored in the context of these transnational intimacies.
26. It is important to emphasize here that these very points were developed in both Fanon's and Baldwin's works.
27. There is no place for its consideration in this chapter, nor is it examined by any researchers of sex/tourism that I am aware of, but it is worth noting here the subculture of "cuckolding" in which white heterosexual couples contract black men, both in the Caribbean and in Canada and the United States, to "play" with the script of the black rapist.
28. Kitossa (Introduction to this volume) signals the irony of this transformation of poor, marginalized black men into "lords of the polis"—patriarchs with masculinized power regardless of socioeconomic standing to "control the town's public and semipublic spaces of leisure and informal economies and engage in performances of hypermasculinity" (Frohlick, 2013, p. 179).

Bibliography

Alexander, M.J. (1997). Erotic autonomy as a politics of decolonization: An anatomy of feminist and state practice in the Bahamas tourist economy. In M.J. Alexander and C.T. Mohanty (Eds.), *Feminist genealogies, colonial legacies, democratic futures* (pp. 63–100). Routledge.

Baldwin. J. (1972). *No name in the street*. The Dial Press.

Bauer, I.L. (2013). Romance tourism or female sex tourism? *Travel Medicine and Infectious Disease, 12*(1), 1–9. https://doi.org/10.1016/j.tmaid.2013.09.003

Bhattacharyya, G. (2002). The exotic. In G. Bhattacharyya (Ed.), *Sexuality and society: An introduction* (pp. 102–97). Routledge.

Bras, C.H., & Dahles, H. (1999). Entrepreneurs in romance tourism in Indonesia. *Annals of Tourism Research, 26*(2), 267–93. https://doi.org/10.1016/S0160-7383(98)00098-X

Butler, J. (1993). Endangered/endangering: Schematic racism and white paranoia. In R. Gooding-Williams (Ed.), *Reading Rodney King, reading urban uprising* (pp. 15–22). Routledge.

Cabezas, A.L. (2004). Between love and money: Sex, tourism, and citizenship in Cuba and the Dominican Republic. *Signs: Journal of Women in Culture and Society, 29*(4), 987–1015. https://doi.org/10.1086/382627

Cabezas, A.L. (2009). *Economies of desire: Sex and tourism in Cuba and the Dominican Republic*. Temple University Press.

Cincone, L. (1988). *The role of development in the exploitation of Southeast Asian women: Sex tourism in Thailand*. Women's International Resource Exchange.

Carr, N. (2016). Sex in tourism: Reflections and potential future research directions. *Tourism Recreation Research, 41*(2), 188–98. https://doi.org/10.1080/02508281.2016.1168566

Cook, N. (2007). *Gender, identity and imperialism: Western women development workers in Pakistan*. Macmillan.

Crenshaw, K. (1989). Demarginalizing the intersection of race and sex: A black feminist critique of antidiscrimination doctrine, feminist theory, and antiracist politics. *University of Chicago Legal Forum, 1*(8), 139–67.

Curry, T.J. (2017). *The man-not: Race, class, genre, and the dilemmas of black manhood*. Temple University Press.

Davidson, J.O.C., & Taylor, J.S. (1999). Fantasy islands: Exploring the demand for sex tourism. In K. Kempadoo (Ed.), *Sun, sex, and gold: Tourism and sex work in the Caribbean* (pp. 37–54). Rowman & Littlefield Publishers.

Davidson, J.O.C., & Taylor, J.S. (2005). Travel and taboo: Heterosexual sex tourism to the Caribbean. In E. Bernstein and L. Schaffner (Eds.), *Regulating sex: The politics of intimacy and identity* (pp. 83–99). Routledge.

Davy, K. (1995). Outing whiteness: A feminist/lesbian project. *Theatre Journal, 47*(2), 189–205. http://doi.org/10.2307/3208483

Deliovsky, K. (2002a). The more things change...rethinking mainstream feminism. In N. Wane, K. Deliovsky & E. Lawson (Eds.), *Back to the drawing board: African Canadian feminisms* (pp. 234–61). Sumach Press.

Deliovsky, K. (2002b). Transgressive whiteness: The social construction of white women involved in interracial relationships with black men. In N. Wane, K. Deliovsky, & E. Lawson (Eds.), *Back to the drawing board: African Canadian feminisms* (pp. 54–84). Sumach Press.

Deliovsky, K. (2010). *White femininity: Race, gender and power*. Fernwood Publishing.

Del Zotto, A., & Jones, A. (2002, March 23–27). *Male-on-male sexual violence in wartime: Human rights' last taboo?* [Paper presentation]. Annual Convention of the International Studies Association (ISA), New Orleans, LA, United States. http://adamjones.freeservers.com/malerape.htm

Dennis, J.P. (2008). Women are victims, men make choices: The invisibility of men and boys in the global sex trade. *Gender Issues, 25*(1), 11–25. https://link.springer.com/article/10.1007/s12147-008-9051-y

Fanon, F. (1967). *A dying colonialism*. Grove Press. (Original work published 1959)

Fanon, F. (1968). *The wretched of the earth*. Grove Press. (Original work published 1961)

Fanon, F. (1977). *Black skin, white masks*. Grove Press. (Original work published 1952)

Foster, T.A. (2019). *Rethinking Rufus: Sexual violations of enslaved men*. University of Georgia Press.

Frohlick, S. (2013). *Sexuality, women, and tourism: Cross-border desires through contemporary travel.* Routledge.

Grande, S. (2003). Whitestream feminism and the colonialist project: A review of contemporary feminist pedagogy and praxis. *Educational Theory, 53*(3), 329–46.

Hall, S. (1980). Race, articulation and societies structured in dominance. In United Nations Educational Scientific and Cultural Organization (Ed.), *Sociological theories: Race and colonialism* (pp. 305–45). UNESCO.

Herold, E., Garcia, R., & DeMoya, T. (2001). Female tourists and beach boys: Romance or sex tourism? *Annals of Tourism Research, 28*(4), 978–97. https://doi.org/10.1016/S0160-7383(01)00003-2

Heron, B. (2007). *Desire for development: Whiteness, gender and the helping imperative*. Wilfrid Laurier University Press.

Harris, C. (1993). Whiteness as property. *Harvard Law Review, 106*(8), 1707–52. https://doi.org/10.2307/1341787

hooks, b. (1992). *Black looks: Race and representation*. South End Press.

Jones, S.V. (2010). The invisible man: The conscious neglect of men and boys in the war on human trafficking. *Utah Law Review, 2010*(4): 1143–88. https://heinonline.org/HOL/Page?handle=hein.journals/utahlr2010&div=49&g_sent=1&casa_token=EGMdurCYxjoAAAAA:EnPAu9mJy-_s-x94rf1oj6DKFr6y-vIQ_p4xZUzBi8T-pXv5wU1kZvomLA3Aij_5p8ZJvSo_&collection=journals

Kempadoo, K. (1999). *Sun, sex, and gold: Tourism and sex work in the Caribbean*. Rowman & Littlefield Publishers.

Kempadoo, K. (2004). *Sexing the Caribbean: Gender, race and sexual labour*. Routledge.

Kitossa, T. (2002). Criticism, reconstruction and African-centred feminist historiography. In N. Nathani Wane, K. Deliovsky, & E. Lawson (Eds.), *Back to the drawing board: African-Canadian feminisms* (pp. 85–116). Sumach Press.

Lamb, S. (1999). *New versions of victims: Feminist struggle with the concept*. New York University Press.

McClintock, A. (1995). *Imperial leather: Race, gender and sexuality in the colonial contest.* Routledge.

McIntosh, D.M.M. (2018). From white ladies to white trash mamas: (Re)locating the performances of white femininity. In D.M.M. McIntosh, D. Moon, & T. Nakaya (Eds.), *Interrogating the communicative power of whiteness* (pp. 94–116). Routledge.

Mills, C. (2007). White ignorance. In S. Sullivan & N. Tuana (Eds.), *Race and epistemologies of ignorance* (pp. 11–38). SUNY Press.

Mutua, A.D. (2013). Masculinities studies and multidimensional masculinities: Origins and theory: Multidimensionality is to masculinities what intersectionality is to feminism. *Nevada Law Journal, 13*(2), 341–67.

Oppermann, M. (1999). Sex tourism. *Annals of Tourism Research, 26*(2), 259–66. https://doi.org/10.1016/S0160-7383(98)00081-4

Philips, J.L. (1999). Tourist-oriented prostitution in Barbados: The case of the beach boy and the white female tourist. In K. Kempadoo (Ed.), *Sun, sex, and gold: Tourism and sex work in the Caribbean* (pp. 183–200). Rowman & Littlefield Publishers.

Pruitt, D., & LaFont, S. (1995). For love and money: Romance tourism in Jamaica. *Annals of Tourism Research, 22*(2), 422–40. https://doi.org/10.1016/0160-7383(94)00084-0

Richards, T.N., & Ried, J.A. (2015). Gender stereotyping and sex trafficking: Comparative review of research on male and female sex tourism. *Journal of Crime and Justice, 38*(3), 414–33. https://doi.org/10.1080/0735648X.2014.1000560

Said, E. (1979). *Orientalism*. Vintage Books.

Spillers, H.J. (1987). Mama's baby, papa's maybe: An American grammar book. *Diacritics, 17*(2), 65–81. http://doi.org/10.2307/464747

Taylor, J.S. (2001). Dollars are a girl's best friend? Female tourists' sexual behaviour in the Caribbean. *Sociology, 35*(3), 749–64. https://doi.org/10.1017/S0038038501000384

Taylor, J.S. (2006). Female sex tourism: A contradiction in terms? *Feminist Review, 83*(1), 42–59. https://doi.org/10.1057/palgrave.fr.9400280

Taylor, J.S. (2011). Sex tourism and inequalities. In S. Cole & N. Morgan (Eds.), *Tourism and inequality: Problems and prospects* (pp. 49–66). CABI.

Thomas, G. (2007). *The sexual demon of empire: Pan-African embodiment and the erotic schemes of empire*. Indian University Press.

Truong, T. (1990). *Sex, money and morality: Prostitution and tourism in Southeast Asia*. Zed Books.

Ware, V. (1997). Purity and danger: Race, gender and tales of sex tourism. In A. Mcrobbie (Ed.), *Back to reality? Social experience and cultural studies* (pp. 133–51). Manchester University Press.

Wells, I.B. (2010). *Ida B. Wells versus Judge Lynch: The anti-lynching trilogy* (J.H. Mitchell, Ed.). CreateSpace Independent Publishing Platform.

Wekker, G. (2016). *White innocence: Paradoxes of colonialism and race*. Duke University Press.

Wiegman, R. (1994). Introduction: Mapping the lesbian postmodern. In L.L. Doan (Ed.), *The lesbian postmodern* (pp. 1–20). Columbia University Press.

What Does a Black Man Want?

Situating the Lives of Black Men

4

Beyond the Exotic and the Grotesque

Toward a Theology of Black Men and Radical Self-Love in the United Kingdom

DELROY HALL

> *The children, having seen the spectacular defeat of their fathers—having seen what happens to any bad nigger and, still more, what happens to the good ones—cannot listen to their fathers and certainly will not listen to the society which is responsible for their orphaned condition.*
>
> —JAMES BALDWIN, "A Report From Occupied Territory"

> *Poverty creates conditions that make young, uneducated, and unemployed Black [men] into scavengers. They are forced to live or die by chance. It is this peculiar reality where criminality, the denial of work, poverty, and Black maleness puts Black men and boys toward the prison and ultimately toward death at the hands of the police or other Black [men] forced to scavenge for survival...This class bias from which Black people generally, but Black [men] particularly, are observed is saturated with condemnation, not earnestness or understanding.*
>
> —TOMMY J. CURRY, *The Man-Not: Race, Class, Genre, and the Dilemmas of Black Manhood*

LONG GIVEN TO RACIAL DELUSIONS about the ancientness of their origins (McDougall, 1982) and purity of their stock (Poliakov, 1974), white men of the English Isles have imposed presumed danger, devilishness, threat, and aesthetic and moral otherworldliness of the black man in their midst. But strikingly, the black man has also been an object of desire: the homosocial, homosexual, and evil doppelganger to the "civilized" Englishman. He is, in short, desired as much as despised, which is how he is conjured in the white man's (and woman's) imagination. The average countryside Tudor-and-Stuart English person of the sixteenth century heard about black men through lore and myth in quotidian exclamations from the pulpit about black devils and everyday speech about blackamoors used to scare children into obedience. They were also a common sight in the royal court, in the homes of nobles, and in London and nearby towns, if not farther afield (Kauffman, 2017; Onyeka, 2013; Wood, 2012). Elizabeth I, herself an investor in the slave-raiding ventures of the reverend Sir John Hawkins, sought to rid London, and England altogether, of Africans. Five hundred years before Enoch Powell's infamous "rivers of blood" speech—that is, Powell's harsh criticism of racial quotas, immigration, and multiculturism—Elizabeth I, in 1596, "said to the lord mayor of London and mayors and sheriffs of other towns in the following terms: Her Majesty understanding that several blackamoors have lately been brought into this realm, of which kind there are already too many here...her Majesty's pleasure therefore is that those kind of people should be expelled from the land" (Fryer, 1984). Alarmed by the growth of the black population—a growth that was due to her own actions and those of other elites like Shakespeare who invested in colonialism and slavery—an *exasperated* Elizabeth, being "highly discontented" hired a German slave dealer to abduct black people and sell them into slavery in the Caribbean (Linebaugh & Rediker, 2013). Indeed, Shakespeare's plays, making good on his own anti-black racism and that of other Englishmen, electrified commoner and noble alike with sordid tales of hypersexual, obtuse, priapic, potential rapists, and savage black men, who variously threatened wholesale violence and racial degradation through, almost always, forced miscegenation (Jordan, 1977; Lyons, 1975).

History, as noted by the likes of James Baldwin (1962/1990), Frantz Fanon (1967), John Henrick Clarke (1974), Malcolm X (1970), and Carter G. Woodson (2009), among others, demonstrates that the black man lives in a complex and uncompromising space in which he has been forced, literally and symbolically, to battle, hog tied, on the white man's terms. He is in this sense but a metaphorical, when not actual, prisoner to the actual ontological, psychosexual workings-out of white men's self-conscious anxieties and insecurities through the projection of their cultural complexes' patriarchal necessity for a demonic other. As John Henrick Clarke (1974) notes, "Black people must always remember that Western civilisation was not created with them in mind." Fanon (1952/1986) extends the point in splendid detail:

> From within the metaphor of vision complicit with a Western metaphysic of Man emerges the displacement of the colonial relation. The black presence ruins the representative narrative of Western personhood: its past tethered to treacherous stereotypes of primitivism and degeneracy will not produce a history of civil progress, a space for the socius; its presence, dismembered and dislocated, will not contain the image of identity that is questioned in the dialectic of the mind/body and resolved in the epistemology of "appearance and reality." The white man's eyes break up the black man's body and in that act of epistemic violence its own frame of reference is transgressed, its field of vision disturbed. (p. xii)

Fanon's comments underline the commonly known fact that it is not only the oppressed that need liberating, but the oppressors too.

As a black Christian pastoral theologian, minister, and registered counsellor, born and socialized in Britain, who is aware of the wreckage of British racism in and on the lives of black men, I do not purport to proselytize in this instance. It is only proper early on in this effort to sketch a theory of radical black men's love of self that the history I present above offer us the turn signals on the road to a moral philosophy grounded in a secularization of the Christian gospels. I want to take Christian ministry seriously as a site for resistance against anti-black racism and as a space from which to tentatively sketch a biblical and moral philosophy of self-inquiry—one that uplifts the black man who is being downtrodden by pernicious, pervasive, and longstanding psychosexual anxieties and projections as a grotesque stain on the "Anglo-Saxon" nation. The black man, along with his family and community, is facing a dire situation in the United Kingdom. While advocates struggle to effect change in policies and the state makes nominal efforts to make and enforce laws to, as Martin Luther King Jr. (cited in Goodman, 2017) said in 1964, "restrain the heartless," the existence and spiritual life of the black man is being ignored. No amount of formal equality can simply wipe away 500 hundred years of deeply ingrained contempt, denigration, hatred, and negation directed towards the black man without a corresponding need for his material uplift and psychological and spiritual renewal. It is evident that the white man must look to himself to discover love in himself without the error of determining his worth by denigrating others—but this is neither my concern or responsibility nor that of black men. As Marcus Garvey (1986) has articulated, "Hear all, but attend only to that which concerns you" (p. 320), for in reality, the black man, being the object of domination by white men for 500 years can neither expect his oppressor to lend him a helping hand nor to imagine him as his equal. My concern in this chapter is, rather, to put forward a perspective that squarely addresses the two central questions that organize Frantz Fanon's (1952/1986) *Black Skin, White Masks*: first, "What does a man want?"; and second, "What does the black man want?" (p. 10). The former question is not the latter and vice versa, since the latter is imagined and treated by the former as a nonbeing, a veritable thing. This leads me to ask (and this is the focus of this chapter), What does the black man *mean* to himself in a white world that denies him the status of being human? With such a tortured ontology in mind, Ta-Nehisi Coates (2015), like James Baldwin and Frantz Fanon before him, insists that the black man make a world for himself against and within a world defined by others. Coates writes: "This is your country, this is your world, this is your body, and you must find some way to live within the all of it" (p. 12).

Having laid down the historical context of this chapter, I will explore three other major themes for further reflection. The first section considers the social determinants of the black male highlighting discrimination faced in health, employment, education, and other areas of life within the UK context including the dichotomy of how the black male is potentially viewed as exotic while simultaneously grotesque. The second section examines the black man's continual struggle within a harmful and dangerous context for survival which includes his innate desire for self-acceptance or self-love. Here, the distinction is made between self-love and narcissism. The final section examines this desire for self-love through a black theobiblical-centred lens, concentrating on the fact that at one point in history, Africa was the centre of Christianity; thus the black man is able to draw from this aspect of the rich reservoir of his history to develop the facets of self-love. This chapter then is a meditation on how the black man can live and learn love to himself again.

Social Determinants of Health and Anti-Black Misandry in the United Kingdom

The remnants of the anti-black, Elizabethan histories earlier described still resonate today. This resonance manifests in a variety of statistically measurable ways in the lives of black men. In patriarchal societies, it is axiomatic, especially where state policies are favourable to intergenerational inequity and transfers of wealth, that children's social attainments are strongly correlated to their father's social status. This much was admitted in the United States by Senator Daniel Patrick Moynihan's (1965) infamous report *The Negro Family: The Case for National Action*, commonly known as the Moynihan Report—though Senator Moynihan blamed the problem of the black family on single-parent mother households and, by extension, absentee fathers, rather than on government policies and anti-black racism in the corporate sector and civil society.

More than 50 years on from Moynihan's report on US American soil, the black man in the United Kingdom—particularly the African Caribbean man—is in serious trouble. Overall, unemployment in Britain in 2018 was 4%; when broken down, this figure translates to 6.3% unemployment among African Caribbean men and 3.6% among white men. For contrast, during the 2008 global financial crash, unemployment for those from white backgrounds averaged around 7.8% in the United Kingdom—but around 14.7% for people from the black and Asian minority ethnic (BAME) groups (Foley, 2020). In 2020, during the coronavirus pandemic, unemployment in the United Kingdom was 5% overall: 4.5% in white populations, and 8.5% for people BAME populations. Unpublished government statistics provide a bleak picture for young black men in general: "Unemployment among young black men has doubled in three years, rising from 28.8 percent in 2008 to 55.9 percent in the last three months of 2011" (Ball et al., 2012). Admittedly, unemployment in the United Kingdom is highest among Pakistani and Bangladeshi communities, but unemployment is not the only issue at play here. Due to the unique valences of anti-black racism, for example, African and Caribbean Britons experience disproportionate levels of violence from the criminal justice system and experience inordinate mental health crises.

The picture of black Briton's mental wellbeing is sorrowful. Black people make up 3% of the British population, with black men and boys making up around half of that 3%. While mental illness among minority groups is a complex matter, "a black man in the UK is 17 times more likely than a white man to be diagnosed with a serious mental health condition such as schizophrenia or bipolar. Black people are also four times more likely to be sectioned under the Mental Health Act" (Fanin, 2017, para. 12).

(Un)employment and mental health challenges—both social determinants of health—come to a head in the racism of the UK criminal justice system. Hayden Smith (2017) notes that, according to a Ministry of Justice report, 9 out of every 10,000 black Britons spend time in youth custody compared to only one white youth in 10,000. Smith's commentary identifies the fact that, while there has been a substantial decrease in custody across all ethnicities, the rate of decrease for ethnic minority groups has been much slower. Thus, the custodial rates for the BAME communities has increased over the last decade. Adding to this already troubling picture, the arrest rates for young black men is three times higher than their white counterparts. This situation is worsened when we recognize that, relative to white youth, black youth serve longer periods in custody with longer "sentence lengths for violence against the person, theft and possession of weapons" (Smith, 2017, para. 12).

The commonly expressed sentiment that "if you cannot do the time, don't do the crime" is irrefutably irrelevant. What is at stake here is not whether or not someone is innocent; it is the fact that black men and boys are treated more harshly within the British criminal justice system than their white counterparts, often for the same or lesser crimes. Given these facts, one could safely assume that the myth of black men as a dangerous threat to the wellbeing of white people is still played out in the psyche and lives of white people.

That black men are seen as dangerous threats that need to be controlled and surveilled is evidenced by the frightening disproportionality of DNA from black men that has been gathered by Scotland Yard. Dorothy Roberts (2011) argues in *Fatal Invention* that "[t]he targeted imprisonment of black men is translated into the disproportionate storage of their genetic profiles in state and federal databases" (p. 277). Citing the United Kingdom as a bellwether for ill-portent in the United States, Roberts (2011) reports that 41% of African Americans are registered in the Combined DNA Index System (CODIS); in the United Kingdom, 40% of all black men and 77% of all young black men (aged 15 to 35) have their genetic profiles stored in the Scotland Yard's DNA database. By comparison, the same is true of only 6% of white men in the United Kingdom. This genetic encircling is of a piece with the criminalization of black men and boys in the United Kingdom, which ultimately marks them off for the possibility of genocide.

Because employment and financial security generally increases one's access to resources that can help in assisting the wellbeing of oneself, one's family, and one's community, it is important in analyzing this dilemma to look again at employment—and, specifically, remuneration—statistics for black men compared with those of their white colleagues.

As Croxford (2018) summarizes, the Russell Group revealed that, in the United Kingdom, "black and Arab academics at the UK's top universities earn an average 26 percent less than white colleagues and female academics fare even worse, with an ethnicity pay gap on top of the gender pay gap" (para. 9). Other studies, including a recent St. George's University Hospital (2018) report for the National Health Service, demonstrate that there is an increasing income gap between "ethnic" (a term that includes BAME populations) workers compared to their white counterparts doing the same type of work (Therrin, 2018). Given these two great institutions in the United Kingdom—universities and the National Health Service—one can only imagine what might be occurring in other industries where ethnic workers are employed.

There are two final notes on ethnic and racial pay gaps worth mentioning. The 2018 Human Rights and Equality Commission's Report concludes that pay was determined by several factors including whether someone was born abroad or in the United Kingdom. The implication is that "language and cultural barriers, confronted by immigrants, had an effect on pay" (Longhi & Brinin, 2017). It has futher been found that black African and black Caribbean male employees, whether born overseas or the United Kingdom, when compared to their white colleagues, "experience[d] a pay gap" of anywhere from 3.5% to over 6.4% (Longhi & Brinin, 2017). The second aspect of note with respect to the ethnicity pay gap is that ethnic or migrant workers reported significantly higher levels of stress as a part of their daily lives. The resultant effect on health correlates with lower earnings. That is a serious pastoral issue. Robert Beckford (2001), cultural critic, has written in *God of the Rahtid* that even when black people are somewhat successful in their jobs, there is an ensuing "low-level rage" experienced by many black Christians who, refusing to vent their feelings in violent protest, are denied any channel of expression. The impact of stress due to discrimination in the workplace is still an under-researched area of the UK employment market (Giga et al., 2008).

The intensification of the foregoing crises experienced by black men in the United Kingdom mires them in a struggle for survival and a mad scramble to make the best of crumbs loosely fallen from the trickle-downism of the United Kingdom's elites. These crises are, in real and concrete terms, attributable to Thatcherite neoliberal policies which have been continued by successive Conservative and Labour regimes. But to be sure, Thatcherism did not originate black social exclusion in the United Kingdom. The roots of the present crisis are deeply endemic in the country; they are economic and predicated on governmental exclusionary policies as much as they are the result of deeply engrained attitudes and discriminatory racist practices of white Britons. Stuart Hall and Bill Schwarz (2017) and Paul Gilroy (2002/2013) notably identified the contemporary branches of racism in British culture in the tree of Britain's colonial afterlife: policing, media practices, and political culture. Much of what Hall, Schwarz, and Gilroy describe in their works is still at play. Recently, for example, the regime of the Conservative Party led by David Cameron and, subsequently, Theresa May sought to "transport" criminal offenders of Jamaican origin back to Jamaica. One who is lively to history cannot help but notice that this type of governmental action is far from new. It is the habit of English governments to shovel the problems of marginality arising from public policies at home onto "their" colonies. Take, for just one example, Cromwell and his ilk (and subsequent administrations) who transported the Irish religious heretics, criminal offenders, sex workers, vagrants, sturdy beggars, and other assorted undesirables to Britain's American and Caribbean colonies throughout the eighteenth century, and to Australia and South Africa in the nineteenth century. Adding insult to indignity, the generation of Caribbean peoples known as the Windrush generation, now in their twilight years, are shamelessly threatened with deportation after making significant contributions to the United Kingdom.

However, the effects of the hatred of black people in the United Kingdom and the wreckage against which black men heroically struggle to transcend, is not limited to that generation; it extends to their families and their yet unborn children. The field of epigenetics—the study of how genes are read by cells and, subsequently, how these readings produce particular proteins—has opened a new way of thinking about the interactive relationships of trauma, the family, the social environment, and the body. To develop an in-depth understanding of the recently discovered phenomenon of epigenetics is beyond the scope of this chapter. Yet, it is worth noting that new insights gleaned from the field of epigenetics is helping us to understand and appreciate the complexity of humanity and, in particular, what happens when people encounter life-threatening and traumatic experiences. Epigenetics has shown that existential and ontological traumas (such as those experienced through racial violence) impact not only parents and adults but their offspring as well. What has been felt by the offspring of those previously traumatized is as though they experience the trauma firsthand. These epigenetic impacts may contribute to poor social outcomes that are compounded by problematic responses to irrational social conditions. Teen Vogue journalist Lincoln Anthony Blades (2016) starkly outlines this interplay between epigenetics and intergenerational trauma. He states that "[i]f the Holocaust caused immense emotional, physical, and psychological effects intense enough to cause trauma to survivors, then the abject horrors and brutality suffered by slaves is more than likely to have the same effects on black slavery descendants worldwide" (para. 5).

Blades capitalizes on the work of Dr. Rachel Yehuda, professor of psychiatry at Icahn School of Medicine at Mount Sinai. Examining trauma from a psychiatric and neuroscientific perspective, Yehuda (2015) first tested a small control group of her neighbours who had survived the Jewish Holocaust. She found that the Holocaust survivors had a similar hormonal profile to Vietnam veterans suffering from post-traumatic stress disorder (PTSD). Years later, studying the offspring of Holocaust survivors, Yehuda (2015) discovered the following, which confirmed her speculation: "Holocaust offspring had the same neuroendocrine or hormonal abnormalities that we were viewing in Holocaust survivors and persons with post-traumatic stress disorder" (para. 44). In a later study, psychiatrist John Krystal (cited in Bugno, 2016), contended that "[t]he observation that the same genes might be affected in parents and children suggests that something specific, perhaps related to stress response, is being conveyed from parent to child" (para. 11).

The fact that survivors from remote historical traumas should have similar physiological traces in the present is odd but worth investigating.

Yehuda's and Krystal's research only confirms earlier psychosocial conceptualizations articulated in social scientist J.D. Leary's (2005) work on what she calls *post-traumatic slave syndrome*. Leary asks nuanced questions: "Isn't it likely that many slaves were severely traumatized? Furthermore, did the trauma and the effects of such horrific abuse end with the abolition of slavery?" (cover copy). As argued by James H. Sweet (2003), routinized starvation, whippings, amputations, rapes (of men and women), and brutal work regimes from cradle to grave left no enslaved African physically or psychologically whole. Sweet writes:

> As...young slaves grew into mature adults, they reacted to their childhood traumas in a variety of ways. Some were most certainly broken by the accumulation of suffering that they were forced to endure. We can never be sure about the rate of psychological disorder among slaves, but it must have been high. Notations of "crazy" (*louco/a*) slaves in property inventories are not unusual. (p. 81)

The brutality of enslavement—the capturing and torturing of bodies, the colonial rule, the enslaving of one's mind and disrupting of one's culture in the Caribbean, followed by Jim Crow and lynching in the United States—is protracted. There has, since enslavement, been a normalized regime of objectification and violence. One must bear in mind that it has not been long since many Caribbean islands won independence from their colonizers, or since the 1960s Civil Rights victories in the United States. In the context of nation-building, let alone that of developing an infrastructure to address the severe traumas black people experienced and have passed along to subsequent generations, it has been no time at all.

The Exotic and the Grotesque

From a psychosocial perspective, the root of the black man's current situation in the West lies in the white man's imagination, where he is enduringly portrayed as both exotic and grotesque. We can take the roots of anti-black racism and antipathy toward black men even further. Going back to the fifteenth century at the very least, we see the genesis of our contemporary ambivalent mix of desire and exoticization along with the imagined repulsiveness of black men. All around us are associations with black men's and boy's presumed hypersexuality and sexual misconduct that run deep in the sinews of English culture. In *To Wash an Aethopian White,* Charles Lyons (1975) charts around 170 years of Eurocentric creation of an ideology dismissing black people as being equals. This history reinforces the notion that the perception of the black body in a negative light has its origins, in part, in the Elizabethan period. Lyons (1975) comments, "In Elizabethan poetry, drama, and common speech of the day, the black man was generally referred to as a lecher, a degenerate, a devil, an animal" (p. 1). When British travellers arrived in Africa, they transported and then simply projected these beliefs—which were already entrenched in their conscious and unconscious minds—on to the unsuspecting but ready-made African. As is commonly known, ideas carry, and what is *believed* to be real is *taken as* real. The racial fantasies and ideologies, reinforced by the scientific mores during the time of the Tudors and the Stuarts, that black people are biologically and psychologically inferior and insensible to pain and suffering have taken deep root (Lyons, 1975).

The Exotic

The exotic, as a concept, carries its own intricacies. Examining the etymology of the word *exotic* is important. At its most primal, the word means "belonging to another country, foreign" (Oxford English Dictionary, n.d.). Demonstrating the complexity of the term, Graham Huggan (2001), professor of English, emphasizes that "[w]e need to go back to the history of exoticist representation and trace exoticism's development from a privileged mode of aesthetic representation to its contemporary status as a global mode of mass consumption" (p. 13). Huggan further writes that

> exotic is not, as is often supposed, an inherent *quality* to be found "in" certain people, distinctive objects, or specific places; exotic describes, rather, a particular mode of aesthetic perception—one which renders

> people, objects and places strange even as it tries to domesticate them, and which effectively manufactures otherness even as it claims to surrender to its immanent mystery. (p. 13)

The exotic, then, is something that is other, odd, and different. In other words, the person who observes the exotic Other simultaneously sees them as beautiful and attempts to dominate them.

In a similar vein, Dorothy Matilda Figueira (1994), professor of comparative religion, argues that the exotic has a tinge of "foreignness." Figueira advances the concept that the "exotic has a special force which can be strangely beautiful and unfamiliarly enticing. This physical and (meta)physical identification at the heart of the exotic, accounts for the tension it often presents between extraneity and the erotic" (p. 1). The interpretations of Huggan and Figueira depict the exotic as a mystical-like and desirable quality that is difficult to describe while remaining unquantifiable.

Ronald Jackson (2006), cultural scholar, offers another perspective of the exotic. Jackson conceptualizes the black male body as problematic by categorizing it as simultaneously visible and peripheral. In defining the African American black man's body, Jackson concludes by stating that "the Black [man's] body is exotic and strange, violent, incompetent and uneducated, sexual, exploitable and innately incapacitated" (p. 75). This understanding is also articulated by Maurice Hall (2011), professor of communication, who employs it in describing the Jamaican black man's body. Hall challenges the alleged low status of the black man and asserts that Jamaica and the Caribbean have produced world leaders in a range of disciplines. He admits, however, that "there are still enduring Western caricatures of the Caribbean male as breezily self-assertive, yet devoid of substance, exotic, and anti-intellectual" (p. 35).

This notion of the exotic was earlier derided by James Baldwin (1955) in his seminal work "Stranger in the Village." Reflecting on his experience of being a visitor in a Swiss village that had never seen a black man walk through their streets, Baldwin, at times filled with rage and astonishment at his apparent oddity in the eyes of the locals, writes the following: "The black man insists, by whatever means he finds at his disposal, that the white man cease to regard him as an exotic rarity and recognize him as a human being" (p. 8).

The point is that the exoticized and negative tropes of the black man produced and reproduced in the psychosexual reality of the white collective imaginary has real consequences for the white "subject" and the black "object." First, such tropes are calculated to shield the white self from (a) the moral responsibility of *passively* obfuscating and refusing to acknowledge the humanity of the black man (that is, implicit bias); and (b) actively and rationally securing white self-interests by discriminating against the black man through acts of physical violence (e.g., the murder of Stephen Lawrence), degradation (i.e., dehumanization), and social exclusion (e.g., imprisonment and unemployment).

From a feminist perspective, Rachel Kuo further problematizes the exotic. Kuo (2015) argues that although there may be good intention in calling a woman of colour "exotic," what white men are doing is giving us, all people of colour, a backhanded "reminder that in a white society, we are less normal, less human, and less real than white people" (sect. 5, para. 1). Kuo's (2016) analysis stresses that, "[b]eing called exotic is rooted and entrenched in violence. While on the surface, it seems complimentary, and at worse [*sic*], a casual faux pas, the historical and current impact of exotifying women of colour has targeted us for sexual violence" (sect. 4, para. 6). This unconscious expression of mystique and sensual definition directed at women of colour dehumanizes them as Others for the ones describing them. The notion of the exotic thus leads to its antagonistic bedfellow: the grotesque.

The Grotesque

Being labelled as grotesque is complicated and demeaning. The term means "[c]haracterized by distortion or unnatural combinations; fantastically extravagant; bizarre" as well as "fantastically absurd" (Oxford English Dictionary, n.d.). Leonard Cassuto (1996), professor of English and American literature, asserts that "[h]uman objectification can result from all kinds of perceived differences, but in [white] American culture it happens most readily to people with dark skin" (p. 3). Cassuto illustrates that "racial objectification was institutionalized by slavery, but (as the colonial experience demonstrates) it has never been limited to that practice" (p. 3).

With this convoluted lived experience of the exotic and the grotesque in mind, the black man finds himself in a difficult position. Frantz Fanon (1952/1986) refers to this existential dilemma. He writes:

> The black man has no ontological resistance in the eyes of the white man. Overnight the Negro has been given two frames of reference within which he has had to place himself. His metaphysics, or, less pretentiously, his customs and the sources on which they were based, were wiped out because they were in conflict with a civilization that he did not know and that imposed itself on him. (p. 110)

Fanon theorizes that, on the one hand, from the eyes of the oppressor, the black man is paradoxically unimportant. This is why his existence has been erased from the pages of Western history. In one sense, he and his people are no more; he has been given another existence, an anaemic whisper of his former self. He is now the bogeyman of the West, another scapegoat who has been given ill-fitting, unkempt clothes to hide him. On the other hand, however, this erasure requires the recognition that the black man is an overwhelmingly large, absent *presence*. While the black man's body is seen as splayed out, grotesque, Fanon (1952/1986) suggests that, in reality, this perception is a process of reaction formation in which the black-man-as-grotesque is an unconscious projection of the white male: a sort of cathartic releasing of primal repression and suppression in which the black man's body is appropriated as the convenient receptacle for the fractious inner machinations of the white man's psyche. The white man, in short, becomes whole through fantasy projections onto the black man who, mysteriously and without any effort or physiological change, is morphed into another being occupying an imposed exotic and grotesque identity.

From these descriptions, the plight of the black man is a harrowing existence filled with complications, conflicts, and convolution, much of which he has consumed—to his detriment. Underpinning the terms *blackness*, *exotic*, and *grotesque* is a deep-seated repulsion mainly by the white male other. This repulsion, this fear, views and treats the black man with a level of hatred that mirrors its other: desire. I would be remiss to ignore, however, the valid influence of the black male body, albeit through a black religious lens, described by Anthony Pinn (2003), professor of religion. While Pinn's contribution is based in the American context, it is equally applicable throughout the diaspora. His following comments are noteworthy:

> I am just as interested in the body lived as I am as the body as metaphor. Therefore, I am not suggesting that experience is simple physiological data: rather, I understand the body as complex. Because of this, I make no attempt to talk in terms of the body as a universal symbol or representing a universally lived history. Hence, the body may mean something different in each cultural and historical context. (p. 236).

Pinn's assertion bucks the notion that the black male experience is homogenous; each location, while there are similarities, will have nuanced expressions of a lived oppression. Although I am presenting a general picture of the experience of living in a black, male body, it is crucial to keep the importance of the subjective experience, too, at the front of mind.

Having established a Fanonist psychosocial history of black men in the United Kingdom, and having explored their paradoxical location as both exotic and grotesque, I now turn to theorizing the psychological effects of such an imposed, distorted humanity on the burden bearer. To this end, I aim to develop the lineaments of a radical black self-love through which the black man does not just *exist for* the white man, but is a *being:* a consciously resilient person, an existence for himself and in service of his own humanity.

Black Men and the Struggle for Survival

This point of view is reflected in Bob Marley's (1980) classic "Redemption Song," where he makes it clear that it is the task of the black man alone to free himself from mental slavery. Listen to the lyrics: "Emancipate yourself from mental slavery, none but ourselves can free our minds" (Marley, 1980). Using black theology as a lens for analysis, I suggest, following Cone (1970/2020), that Marley's lyrics are a "theology of survival" that "refuses to accept conditions as they are" nor to accept conditions as "being the will of God" (p. 17). Furthermore, Cone fiercely contends that black people must strive "to make sense of their existence in a white society whose suffering and humiliation is beyond rational explanation" (p. 17).

Self-love, then, is difficult within an environment where one is made to struggle for survival, but that survival and, ultimately, thriving must be the black man's responsibility as he intentionally reworks his psychosocial position—something he cannot rely on the white man to give him. If one takes the history of the black man with any seriousness, one wonders how he has survived, given the continual destructive effort expended for his annihilation. This matter of survival is explored by Naim Akbar (1992), African American clinical psychologist, in *Visions for Black Men*. Akbar states, "Given all the odds; given the almost impossible circumstances we have faced; given these barriers which would have devastated any other human breed a long time ago—the simple question is: Why are we still here anyway?" (cover copy).

Given the brutality to which black men have been exposed, and given their relentless mistreatment, one can only assume that they are seen in the eyes of the perpetrators as being "nonhuman" (Curry, 2017). Tommy Curry's following descriptions makes for frightening and dismal reading. He writes:

> Popular categories of analysis such as class, gender, and even race suppose a universal human template upon which they imprint. But what is the applicability of human categories on the nonhuman? The black male is negated not from an origin (human) being, but from nihility... [N]onbeing expresses the condition of black male being—the nihility from which he is birthed. (p. 6)

From Curry's position, the image of the black man is hard to categorize; from earlier cited descriptions of the black man, his imposed plight, social construct, and distorted labelling highlight the fact that he alone can create a life for himself that is worth living. He is left with no other alternative but to remove the mental shackles of his life, imposed by the imagination of the white man and to forge for himself an image of self-love alone, a self-image that does not require any acceptance or validation from any white person. This self-sculpting is a painful, lifelong endeavour toward liberation and freedom and bears no relation to any off-the-shelf packages of self-love we find in our local bookstores or online shops. For me, biblical narrative provides the ideal milieu for this kind of self-development in authentic self-love.

Towards Self-Love: Creating a Life Worth Living

To give some context to an understanding of the use of the biblical narrative in helping black men, I will draw on some generalizations from numerous scenarios in which I have been involved. Given my role as a minister and community leader, I have, on many occasions, been asked to conduct the funerals of individuals who have taken their own lives. It is always an honour to be asked by the family to undertake such a service at a sensitive time in the life of the deceased's family.

All the men whose funerals I have officiated were at one level jovial individuals, sociable, and full of life; but they all carried a darker side, as well, struggling with bouts of various forms of mental ill health. Many, despite their sociability, struggled with living life. Most of these men had similar life traits. First, many black men are raised by a single parent and are either unsure of who their father is or have never met him. Secondly, many black men have not learned how to talk about their emotions or what troubles them; this affects their mental and emotional wellbeing. Third, as a means of anaesthetizing excruciating existential pain, it is not uncommon for individuals to use alcohol and other drugs. Fourth, negative life events may be emotionally and psychologically suppressed and internalized, often leading to mental illness, suicidal ideation, or other self-destructive behaviours that are vented onto loved ones and others.

How is it possible to begin the healing process of black men? I suggest it is important to turn to the biblical text to help in developing a way of dealing with the current plight of black men. It is here that we can reflect on the story of Jesus encountering Pharisees and Sadducees who question him on a variety of issues to which Jesus responds through a variety of parables. A scribe—a religious writer of the ancient text—in overhearing Jesus condemnation of temple administrators, challenges him by asking, "Which is the first commandment of all?" (Mark 12:28 New King James Version). And Jesus answers him:

> [T]he first of all the commandments is, Hear, O Israel; The Lord our God is one Lord: And thou shalt love the Lord thy God with all thy heart, and with all thy soul, and with all thy mind, and with all thy strength: this is the first commandment. And the second is like, namely this, Thou shalt love thy neighbour as thyself. There is none other commandment greater than these. (Mark 12:29–31 New King James Version)

Jesus's teaching was uttered during a time of Roman oppression on the Jewish people and an imposed limit on how they practised their faith, while the Roman Empire obsessed with global expansion, imperialism, and violence. It is in this similar context that the black man exists and somehow must transcend his current context if he is going to have a worthy existence in the future—that is, an existence in which he does not find himself at the bottom of the ladder while the West continues to exert oppression as it displays an insatiable thirst for world domination.

Arguably, even if a black man has risen quite far in, for example, his profession today, he can still be perceived as being at the bottom of the ladder. George Yancy (2018) further explores this notion in his article "The Ugly Truth about Being a Black Professor in America," highlighting the continual racial incongruence in which he lives. For example, in recent years, racial tensions have increased globally, currently with the Black Lives Matter protests and demonstrations, but beginning in more recent times with the rants of former American President Donald Trump; Michelle LePen, the leader of the far-right in France; other right-wing groups in Europe; Brexit in the United Kingdom; and the most recent results of a long-term study within the UK National Health Service exposing the fact that the BAME groups are paid significantly less than their peers for doing the same work (Campbell, 2018).

Jesus's comments are profound. The scribe asks one question, but Jesus challenges him further. As a practising clergyman, theologian, and someone who has spent all his years being involved in the life of church, I have heard countless sermons on the importance of loving God and many sermons on loving thy neighbour. To this date, as a mature man, I have never heard a sermon on self-love, ever. In contrast, one must not dismiss the fact that a good deal of the crisis experienced by black men is the monumental internalization of self-loathing that often finds its outlet in harm to themselves and to others.

Self-Love Versus Narcissism

Some psychologists use the term self-love and self-care interchangeably; the term self-compassion is equally applicable. At this juncture, it is important to make the distinction between the self-love taught by Jesus and narcissistic love, which focuses on the self to the point of total self-centredness. The self-love taught by Jesus is love that treats oneself healthily and manifests itself in helping others, ultimately leading to a healthy understanding of and relationship with God. Another definition of self-love is: "Self-love is not simply a state of feeling good. It is a state of appreciation for oneself that *grows from actions* that support our physical, psychological and spiritual growth. Self-love is dynamic; it grows through actions that mature us" (Khoshaba, 2012, para. 4). We are able to accept ourselves, warts and all.

Given the plight of many black men, it is apparent that they have not learned to appreciate themselves in a deep and meaningful way in order to cope with life's problems. It must be stressed that appreciating oneself with loving action transcends contemplation, doing fulfilling labour, eating healthily, exercising, reading, wearing good clothes, and looking good. Loving oneself is all of these and more, for it is not an end result, but a constant striving: the struggle to constantly assess, reassess, and, with equanimity, forgive oneself, and then to forgive and live in peace with others.

The black man learning to love himself, if he has not grown up in an environment where he has been so taught, is more than a three-step plan. It is a lifelong journey, beginning quite often with the pain of acknowledging one's blackness, then continuing on an excursion of discovery, deconstruction, and reconstruction in communion with likeminded sojourners; we are, after all, the company we keep. One way for black men to begin the process of self-love is to discover their black selfhood by finding an appropriate person to talk with as means of self-exploration. One of the crises of masculinity, after all, is that men rarely talk about their emotional life. In other words, all men, but black men in particular, need, quite literally, to learn a new language and vocabulary that enables them to explore their hearts, minds, and souls. To the black men reading this: Pay a professional, if necessary, to assist you in discovering who you are and to assist you in finding your purpose, place, and God-given potential. The epigram over Egyptian temples was, after all, "Man, Know Thyself!"

It is ironic that something as crucial as knowing oneself is not invested in, but often only given lip service, while at the same time many will spend exorbitant amounts of money on consumer products which ultimately reduce in value and fade with age (Burrell, 2010). In other words, many black men will spend thousands of British pounds or American dollars on flashy cars but will balk at the idea of spending a few hundred dollars or pounds to help themselves develop a better and more wholesome sense of self. This is, however, no more than the priorities of a consumption-driven social order that assigns worth, however fleeting, to material goods.

Reclaiming History as a Portal for Loving the Self

Another way to learn self-love is to combat the communal pandemic of self-loathing common in the black man. The challenge is to discover facts about African people, to recognize their achievements prior to the European onslaught and before conscious attempts were made to obliterate the African past from the pages of history and from those to whom it would matter most—black men (Clarke, 1974; Malcolm X, 1970; Woodson, 2009).

One may wonder what history has to do with self-love and self-care. To understand this, one needs to understand how vital history is for people who have been repeatedly told they have no history and that they have made little or no contribution to the development of the planet. Reclaiming history can, for the black man, demonstrate the vitality and strength his ancestors possessed as a people. It will allow him to recognize and identify with black people, despite the attempts to stymie his inner strength. John Clarke (cited in Ubani, 2011) endorses history's importance in this context, asserting that:

> [h]istory is not everything, but it is a starting point. History is a clock that people use to tell their political and cultural time of day. It is a compass they use to find themselves on the map of human geography. It tells them where they are but, more importantly, what they must be. (p. 405)

Knowing one's history is pivotal in gaining self-knowledge, self-respect, and self-love. It gives one a sense of communal and human belonging.

Radical self-love for the black man cannot wait. It does not require validation, approval, or legitimization from white people. There is little in the Western social fabric reflecting positive black men other than images that are often disturbing to his wellbeing and existence. Black men have learned, and have been conditioned, not to love themselves. But what is learned can be unlearned with guidance, education, enlightenment, and a willingness to change while making allies with a community of like-minded people.

The Bible and Human Freedom

Undeniably, the Bible has been used as a tool of oppression, and is therefore, for some black people, problematic. It has, however, also been used to bring liberation. Indeed, the resistance to, and forbearance of, slavery is, in some cases, directly linked to the discourses of the biblical text. However, Susan Buck-Morss (2009) contends that while a minority of enslaved Africans in the Americas were Muslim, Boukman (i.e., Book Man, so named because he was literate), who was formerly enslaved in Jamaica before being sold into slavery in Haiti, is considered the actual and spiritual founder of the Haitian Revolution. Caribbean diaspora theologian Delroy Reid-Salmon (2012) cogently argues that the Jamaican Baptist War of 1831 was led by Baptist deacon Sam Sharpe, who used the Bible to mobilize the enslaved to confront the evils of slavery. Garnett Roper (2015) argues a similar point when he states that Sharpe was most influenced by his religious faith which was assisted by his reading strategies of the Jewish and Christian scriptures.

Similarly, in United States, African American author, philosopher, theologian, educator, and civil rights leader Howard Thurman (1996) writes:

> The basic fact is that Christianity as it was born in the mind of this Jewish teacher and thinker [Jesus] appears as a technique of survival of the oppressed. That it became, through the intervening years, a religion of the powerful and the dominant, sometimes used as an instrument of oppression, must not tempt us into believing it was thus in the mind of Jesus. "In Him was life, and the life was the light of men." Wherever his spirit appears, the oppressed gather fresh courage; for he announced the good news that fear, hypocrisy and hatred, the three hounds of hell that tracked the trail of the disinherited, need have no dominion over them. (p. 29)

Thurman argues that Jesus's agenda was never for the entrapment or the exploitation of people. Again, from the Caribbean context, William David Spencer (1999), in *Dread Jesus* quotes a well-known saying by Marcus Garvey, the Jamaican political activist and philosopher. Spencer cites the following words:

> I believe in God the Father, God the Son, and God the Holy Spirit. I endorse the Nicene Creed. I believe that Jesus died for me. I believe that God lives for me as for all men, and no condition you can impose upon me by deceiving me about Christianity will cause me to doubt Jesus Christ and to doubt God. I shall never hold Christ responsible for the commercialization of Christianity by the heartless men who adopt it as the easiest means of fooling and robbing other people out of their land and country. (p. 134)

Marcus Garvey was resolute in the true nature of the Christian religion and recognized that his own work, the liberation of humanity, was in keeping with the agenda of Jesus.

John Mbiti (1990), African theologian, stresses that Christianity had deep African roots going back many centuries. Though there are many others, it is worthwhile to recall the biblical narrative of the Ethiopian eunuch, who, travelling home to Ethiopia from Jerusalem, met Philip, a follower of Jesus. The nameless, eminent Ethiopian, reading the scriptures, recognizes something of value, but struggles to understand what he is reading. Meeting Philip, he enters a conversation with him concerning the scriptures. Having the text explained to him, he accepts the message and asks to be baptized. After his baptism, the Bible states that Philip continued his unknown mission and the eunuch returned home rejoicing (Acts 8:32 New King James Version).

The story of the eunuch has him returning home and sharing the great news he has heard and experienced (Cole-Rous, n.d.). Later in history, Christianity also had an influence on Alexandria in Egypt (Griggs, 1990). Christianity has had a long and enduring history in Africa and in the lives of black people. Indeed, it was Egypt where the infant Jesus was sent for protection against the infanticidal Herod; it was North Africa (Numidia) where St. Augustine was born, raised, and converted, and where many "Church Fathers" sought isolation and contemplation. Moreover, in the Old Testament, it was Egypt to which Abram sojourned before being renamed Abraham; where Joseph rose to high status in Pharaoh's household; and where Moses, like Osiris before him, was saved by a maidservant from drowning in the Nile. According to John Mbiti (2015), Christianity became problematic in Africa during the eighteenth century with the arrival of European missionaries who, in sharing the gospel, thought they were bringing something new to Africa. The Christian faith had been alive in Africa long before the arrival of European or American missionaries. On this matter, Mbiti (2015) emphasizes:

> For Africans, the whole existence is a religious phenomenon; man is a deeply religious being living in a religious universe. Failure to realize and understand this starting point, has led missionaries, anthropologists, colonial administrators, and other foreign writers on African religions to misunderstand not only the religious as such but the peoples of Africa. (p. 15)

From these examples, it is evident that the Christian faith has been at the core of African sensibility and was a life force in the lives of Africans. Thus, in relation to the biblical narrative, crypto-Islam and subsequent Islamic conversions notwithstanding, the Bible was, during slavery, used as a code for ensuring the survival of the black man here in the West. I now turn to the biblical text—taken as either a religious or secular meditation on self-love—for a similar reason: to help develop a way of dealing with the plight of black men and the psychological implications of their being marginalized.

The Biblical Text and Black Psychology

From the perspective of Christian theology, the black man is challenged to engage with how Jesus's teaching can be applied to himself and his community. This call ought not to be read as an advocation of conversion to Christianity. Certainly, as a pastor, I encourage it—but the theologian in me, the pragmatist in me, believes that the Bible is a profound text, a meditation on the meaning of life and how to live the good life. As such, a secular approach to the Jesus's injunction to love oneself accepts the seriousness of this teaching as an antidote to the crises in which black men are mired. Such an approach argues that loving oneself is more than an act of positive psychology and positive mental attitude, though such disciplines have their place. Rather, self-love requires, as is taught within the African cosmology of which the black church is a part, coming to terms with spirituality a nonmaterial force that permeates all affairs, human and nonhuman. This aspect of spirituality is expounded by Joseph Cervantes and Thomas Parham's (2005) "Toward a Meaningful Spirituality for People of Color: Lessons for the Counseling Practitioner." They emphasize that spirituality is anchored in, and affects, every facet of life. One must remember that, although the West compartmentalizes existence, the same is not true in so-called developing countries, in which, often, material and immaterial aspects of life are viewed as inseparable.

The journey of self-love begins in the mind and must have a deep, piercing, and honest acknowledgement of how the black man views himself—not as the other sees him, but how he views *himself*—as an individual and as belonging to a collective. This must be a candid process of introspection, but it must also involve a mode of extrospection. Loving oneself, and radically so, might prove too much of a painful chasm to cross for some black men and they might wish not to begin the journey towards self-love. On many occasions, I, in sharing Caribbean history or black literature with other black men, have been faced with such a response. Many black men, as they are invited to negotiate and discover themselves, are faced with a deep-seated fear that they will end up hating white people. Black men have suffered at the hands of white male hegemony, yet in gaining the rei(g)ns of their life, they fear hating the one who has oppressed them. They are held back by an intense anxiety over their own self-understanding. This reaction gives some indication of how much black men have been made impotent by the tyranny of white supremacy, and how unconsciously and repeatedly many are willing defer to hegemonic white masculinity while harbouring the mountains of anger, doubt, and self-hate that are among its consequences.

Erica McInnis (2018), clinical psychologist, expounds and writes persuasively about the benefits of an African psychology in *Understanding African Beingness and Becoming*. For McInnis, the goal of this work is to

> envision what black people's optimal self would look like if it had not been colonized and overlaid by a Eurocentric framework of normality, and to pursue the trajectory that enslavement and colonization interrupted, with advances then far superior to those in the West in healing, and economic and spiritual wellbeing. (p. 28)

McInnis makes it clear that black psychology is not anti-white even though white psychology is anti-black. McInnis is informed by Wade Nobles (1986), an African American psychologist, who asserts that what is essential for black people is the reclamation, reascension, revitalization, and affirmation of "African Beingness" and African culture. Nobles also stresses the importance of issuing a corrective challenge to Eurocentric psychology. McInnis (2018) describes her use of African symbols and artifacts in her sessions to connect with her clients of African descent. For the African-centred model of the African self, McInnis develops, for example, the divine self as a spiritual self that has a purpose in life. Within the Christian context, one is seen as being created in the image of God, but adorned in black skin. As God created humankind in his image, so too must black people's *representation* of God be black, for "God has created man in such a way that man's own destiny is inseparable from his relation to the creator" (Cone, 1997, p. 156).

Practical Black Self-Love

While McInnis makes pivotal strides to employ an African-centred model to help in conscientizing and healing black people, there remains a problem for many African Caribbean people. Because of the transatlantic *Maafa* (a Kiswahili word meaning "great tragedy"), many are so far removed from Africa that there is little direct cultural connection with anything African. Similarly, some African Caribbean people who were born and raised in the United Kingdom and alienated by British culture, find that their connections to the Caribbean are figurative and tangential, despite the tenacious historical memory contained in reggae, calypso, and various patois.

As a counsellor, psychologist, pastor, theologian, and a black man myself, I want to speak directly to black men about six practical things they can do to take charge of their wellbeing, in line with some of the recommendations of Deborah Khosaba (2012):

1. It would be prudent for you to live your life for yourself and your relations, rather than for the anxieties, insecurities, and stereotypes white men have of you. After all, as noted by both Baldwin

(1955) and Fanon (1952/1986), the white man's psychopathology is neither your responsibility nor your problem, but his own. Thus, to consciously reject his negative commentaries and stereotypes is to give yourself a quality of power and to live a conscious life that affirms your humanity for yourself and relations.

2. As a black man, act on what you know you need, and resist those things in a consumerist, demoralized, despiritualized white society that you know to be harmful to you.
3. Practice good self-care. This is achieved by exercise, having a good and balanced diet, getting enough sleep, and being with likeminded people. If you love yourself as your neighbour, treat yourself like you matter.
4. Set boundaries, not for others, but for yourself, by being mindful of those people, situations, and environment that deplete you of good energy. After all, as Jesus admonished, "should you throw your pearls before swines" (Matthew 6:7 New King James Version).
5. Learn to forgive yourself. The traits of self-loathing are absolutisms of all forms—perfectionism, for example, and self-contempt when things go wrong. One way to work on self-loathing is to develop the skills of journaling or self-reflection that enable you to learn from what has just happened in your life. Such lessons, well learned, increase maturity and develop a strong sense of self and depth of value about life and living.
6. Live with focus and intention. In other words, let self-discipline not give way to ascetism as you continually discover the love and joy in all things, large and small—the things that bring joy, happiness, and a sense of responsibility to your life.

Conclusion

Within a society that continues to wrestle with race, racialization, and racism, the black man's body remains a property, an object of sexual fantasy, a site upon which violence is visited, and a "thing" presumed to be void of feelings and sensibility. After all these years, the black man is still

considered, by society at large, to be "less than" and "other than" the full range of his humanity. The black man's being has become a straw horse in the tribal conflict between white men and women who are locked in a struggle over and between class, pay, and gender. In addition, there is, it seems, a form of Eurocentric blindness, an inability or resistance to see the black man as human. While the black male is caught in this imposed vice, hundreds of years of conditioning have left a psychological and emotional keloid that is difficult to hide and even more difficult to remove.

There is no shortcut to accepting oneself, but one must recognize that, after all that the black man has experienced since his forcible confinement in the West, we are still here. Our existence testifies to the fact that while we are highly resilient, we have, as noted by Baldwin (1955) and Fanon (1952/1986), paid a steep price for living and for aspiring toward a future where we are autonomous and take willful, intentional action toward our wellbeing. Since no one else will, this is, this must be, our burden and responsibility.

Bibliography

Akbar, N. (1992). *Visions for black men*. Mind Productions.

Allen, T., Jackson, K. (Producers), & Bourne, S.C. (Director). (1996). *John Henrik Clarke: A great and mighty walk* [Documentary]. Black Dot Media.

The Assembly of the British Council of Churches. (1976). *The new black presence in Britain: A Christian scrutiny*. Community and Race Relations Unit of the British Council of Churches.

Baldwin, J. (1955). Stranger in the village. In J. Baldwin, *Notes of a native son* (pp. 159–75). Beacon Press.

Baldwin, J. (1961). *No one knows my name: More notes of a native son*. Knopf Doubleday Publishing Group.

Baldwin, J. (1966). A report from occupied territory. *The Nation*. https://www.thenation.com/article/report-occupied-territory/

Baldwin, J. (1990). *Another country*. Penguin Books. (Original work published 1962)

Ball, J., Milmo, D., & Ferguson, B. (2012, March 9). Half of UK's young black males are unemployed. *The Guardian*. https://www.theguardian.com/society/2012/mar/09/half-uk-young-black-men-unemployed

Beckford, R. (2000). *Dread and Pentecostal: A political theology for the black church in Britain*. Wifp and Stock Publishers.

Beckford, R. (2001). *God of the Rahtid: Redeeming rage.* Darton, Longman and Todd.

Blades, L.A. (2016). Trauma from slavery can actually be passed down through your genes. *Teen Vogue.* https://www.teenvogue.com/story/slavery-trauma-inherited-genetics

Buck-Morss, S. (2009). *Hegel, Haiti, and universal history.* University of Pittsburgh Press.

Burrell, T. (2010). *Brainwashed: Challenging the myth of black inferiority.* Smiley Books.

Campbell, D. (2008, September 27). Black medics in NHS paid less than white medics. *The Guardian.* https://www.theguardian.com/society/2018/sep/27/black-medics-in-nhs-paid-thousands-less-than-white-medics

Cassuto, L. (1996). *The inhuman race: The racial grotesque in African American literature and culture.* Columbia University Press.

Cervantes, J., & Parham, T.A. (2005). Toward a meaningful spirituality for people of color: Lessons for the counselling practitioner. In *Cultural Diversity and Ethnic Minority Psychology, 11*(1), 69–81. https://doi.org/10.1037/1099-9809.11.1.69

Clarke, J.H. (1974). *Black Americans, immigrants against their will.* Atlanta University Press.

Coates, T. (2015). *Between the world and me.* The Text Publishing Company.

Coleman, A. (2017, September 25). Stealing eternity: The black conscious movement's dangerous misrepresentation of Christianity. *The K.I.N.G. Movement.* http://www.kingmovement.com/stealing-eternity-black-conscious-movements-dangerous-misrepresentation-christianity/

Cole-Rous, J. (n.d.). The eunuch of Ethiopia. *Journey Online.* http://globalchristiancenter.com/christian-living/lesser-known-bible-people/31308-the-eunuch-of-ethiopia

Cone, J. (1997). *Black theology and black power.* Orbis Books.

Cone, J. (2020). *The black theology of liberation* (50th Anniversary ed.). Orbis Books. (Original work published 1970)

Cox, O. (2001). Class, caste and race: A study in social dynamics. In E. Cashmore & J. Jennings (Eds.), *Racism: Essential readings* (pp. 49–74). SAGE Publications.

Croxford, R. (2018, December 7). Ethnic minority academics earn less than white colleagues. *BBC.* https://www.bbc.co.uk/news/education-46473269

Curry, T. (2017). *The man-not: Race, class, genre, and the dilemmas of black manhood.* Temple University Press.

Exum, J.C. (2002). *Lethal woman 2*: Reflections on Delilah and her incarnation as Liz Hurley. In M. O'Kane (Ed.), *Borders, boundaries and the Bible* (pp. 254–73). Sheffield University Press.

Fanin, I. (2017, July 5). Is there institutional racism in mental health care? *BBC.* https://www.bbc.co.uk/news/health-40495539

Fanon, F. (1967). *The wretched of the Earth.* (C. Farrington, Trans.). Penguin Books.

Fanon, F. (1986). *Black skin, white masks.* (C.L. Markmann, Trans.). Pluto Press. (Original work published 1952)

Figueira, D.M. (1994). *The exotic: A decadent quest.* New York Press.

Foley, N. (2020). *Unemployment by ethnic background* (Briefing paper No. 6385). Retrieved from the UK Parliament House of Commons Library website: https://commonslibrary.parliament.uk/research-briefings/sn06385/

Fredrickson, G. (1987). *The black image in the white mind: The debate on Afro-American character and destiny, 1817–1914*. Wesleyan University Press.

Hill, R, (Ed.). (1990). *The Marcus Garvey and Universal Negro Improvement Association papers, Vol. VII: November 1927–August 1940*. University of California Press.

Garvey, M. (1986). *The philosophy and opinions of Marcus Garvey, or, Africa for the Africans* (Vol. 1). The Majority Press.

Giga, S., Hoel, H, & Lewis, D. (2008). *A review of black and minority ethnic (BME) employee experiences of workplace bullying*. University of Bradford. https://www.researchgate.net/publication/260246604_A_Review_of_Black_and_Minority_Ethnic_BME_Employee_Experiences_of_Workplace_Bullying

Gilroy, P. (2013). *There ain't no black in the Union Jack: The politics of race and the nation*. Routledge. (Original work published 2002)

Goodman, A. (2017, January 16). Newly discovered 1964 MLK speech on civil rights, segregation & Apartheid South Africa. *Democracy Now.* https://www.democracynow.org/2017/1/16/newly_discovered_1964_mlk_speech_on

Griggs, C. (1990). *Early Egyptian Christianity: From its origins to 451 C.E.* Brill.

Hall, M. (2011). Negotiating Jamaican masculinities. In R. Jackson III and M. Balaji (Eds.), *Global masculinities and manhood* (pp. 31–51). University of Illinois Press.

Hall, S., & Schwarz, B. (2017). *Familiar stranger: A life between two islands (Stuart Hall: Selected writings)*. Penguin Books.

Huggan, G. (2001). *The postcolonial exotic: Marketing the margins*. Routledge.

Jackson, R., III. (2011). *Scripting the black masculine body: Identity, discourse, and racial politics in popular media.* State University of New York.

Jordan, W. (1977). *White over black: American attitudes toward the Negro, 1550–1812*. W.W. Norton.

Kauffman, M. (2017). *Black Tudors: The untold story.* Oneworld Publications.

Khoshaba, D. (2012, March 27). A seven-step prescription for self-love. *Psychology Today*. https://www.psychologytoday.com/gb/blog/get-hardy/201203/seven-step-prescription-self-love

Krystal, J. (2016, September 1). Trauma's epigenetic fingerprint observed in children of Holocaust survivors. *Elsevier*. https://www.elsevier.com/about/press-releases/research-and-journals/traumas-epigenetic-fingerprint-observed-in-children-of-holocaust-survivors

Kuo, R. (2015, November 28). 6 reasons why 'bad Asians' rock and 'positive' racial stereotypes need to go. *Everyday Feminism*. http://everydayfeminism.com/2015/11/positive-stereotypes-still-bad/

Kuo, R. (2016, January 26). 4 reasons why calling a woman of color 'exotic' is racist. *Everyday Feminism*. http://everydayfeminism.com/2016/01/calling-woc-exotic-is-racist/

Leary, J.D. (2005). *Post traumatic slave syndrome.* Uptone Press.

Linebaugh, P., & Rediker, M. (2013). *The many-headed hydra: Sailors, slaves, commoners, and the hidden history of the revolutionary Atlantic.* Beacon Press.

Longhi, S., & Brynin, M. (2017). *The ethnicity pay gap.* Institute of Social and Economic Research. University of Essex. https://www.equalityhumanrights.com/sites/default/files/research-report-108-the-ethnicity-pay-gap.pdf

Lyons, C.H. (1975). *To wash an Aethiop white: British ideas about black African educability, 1530–1960.* Teachers College Press.

Malcolm X. (1970). *By any means necessary.* Pathfinder Press.

Mbiti, J. (1990). *African religions and philosophy*. Heineman Publishers.

Mbiti, J. (2015). *Introduction to African religion: Second Edition*. Waveland Press.

McDougall, H. (1982). *Racial myth in English history: Trojans, Teutons, and Anglo-Saxons.* University Press of New England.

McInnis, E.M. (2018). Understanding African beingness and becoming. *Therapy Today*, *29*(8), 28–31. https://library.laredo.edu/eds/detail?db=a9h&an=132445483&isbn=17487846

Moynihan, D.P. (1965). *The Negro family: The case for national action*. US Government Printing Office.

Nobles, W. (1986). *African psychology: Toward its reclamation, reascension and revitalization.* Institute for the Advanced Study of Black Family Life and Culture.

Oyeka, N. (2013). *Blackamoores: Africans in Tudor England*. Narrative Eye.

Oxford English Dictionary. (n.d.) *Oxford English dictionary.* Oxford University Press. Retrieved November 26, 2020, from www.oed.com

Pinn, A. (2003). *Terror and triumph: The nature of black religion.* Fortress Books.

Poliakov, L. (1974). *Aryan myth: A history of racist and nationalist ideas in Europe*. Sussex University Press.

Reid-Salmon, D. (2012). *Burning for freedom: A theology for the black Atlantic struggle for liberation.* Ian Randle Publishers.

Roberts, D. (2011). *Fatal invention: How science, politics, and big business re-create race in the twenty-first century.* New Press.

Roper, G. (2015). Sam Sharpe in the context of the struggle for freedom and equality in the Caribbean: Freedom, innate desire or acquired appetite. *American Baptist Quarterly*, *34*(1), 86–97. https://ixtheo.de/Record/1647196590

Russell Group. (2018). *Our universities*. https://russellgroup.ac.uk/about/our-universities/

Said, E. (1979). *Orientalism*. Vintage Books.

Smith, H. (2017, September 1). Nine in every 10,000 black Britons spend time in youth custody, says Ministry of Justice report. *The Independent*. https://www.independent.co.uk/news/uk/crime/young-offenders-black-british-people-more-likely-prison-time-nine-10000-ministry-justice-report-a7924156.html

Spencer, W.D. (1999). *Dread Jesus*. SPCK Publishing.

St. George's University Hospital. (2018). *Ethnicity pay gap 2018/19*. https://www.stgeorges.nhs.uk/wp-content/uploads/2020/03/Ethnicity-Pay-Gap-2018-19.pdf

Sweet, J.H. (2003). *Recreating Africa: Culture, kinship, and religion in the African-Portuguese world, 1441–1770*. University of North Carolina Press.

Therrin, A. (2018). Ethnic minority consultants "paid less" than white colleagues. *BBC*. https://www.bbc.co.uk/news/health-45421437

Thurman, H. (1996). *Jesus and the disinherited.* Boston Press Books.

Topping, A., Barr, C., & Duncan, P. (2018). Gender pay gap figures reveal eight in 10 UK firms pay men more. *The Guardian*. https://www.theguardian.com/money/2018/apr/04/gender-pay-gap-figures-reveal-eight-in-10-uk-firms-pay-men-more

Ubani, L. (2011). *Afrikan mind reconnection & spiritual re-awakening* (Vol. 1). Xlibris Corporation.

Wood, M. (2012). Britain's first black community in Elizabethan London. *BBC*. https://www.bbc.com/news/magazine-18903391

Woodson, C.G. (2009). *The mis-education of the Negro.* CreateSpace Independent Publishing.

Yancy, G. (2018). The ugly truth about being a black professor in America. *The Chronicle.* https://www.chronicle.com/article/The-Ugly-Truth-of-Being-a/243234

Yehuda, R. (2015). How trauma and resilience cross generations. *On Being*. https://onbeing.org/programs/rachel-yehuda-how-trauma-and-resilience-cross-generations-nov2017/

5

A Krip-Hop Theory of Disabled Black Men

Challenging the Disabling of Black America, Resisting Killing and Erasure Through the Arts and Self-Empowerment

LEROY F. MOORE JR. & TAMARI KITOSSA

> *Mutilations were common, limbs, ears, and sometimes private parts, to deprive them of pleasures which they could indulge in without expense.*
>
> —C.L.R. JAMES, *The Black Jacobins: Tousaint L'Ouverture and the San Domingo Revolution*

> *Good & healthy, and not blind Lame or Blemished...Defects to be avoided: Dwarfish, or Gigantick Size wch are equally disagreeable; Ugly faces; Long Tripeish Breasts wch ye Spaniards mortally hate; Yellow Skins; Livid Spots in ye Skin wch turns to an incureable evil; Films in ye Eyes; Loss of Fingers, Toes, or Teeth; Navells sticking out; Ruptures wch ye Gambia Slaves are very Subject to; Bandy legs; Sharp Shins; Lunaticks; Idiots; Lethargicks.*
>
> —HUMPHRY MORICE[1]

WITH A FOCUS ON James Baldwin and Frantz Fanon's early interventions in theorizing disabilities, this chapter further works with Leroy Moore Jr's Krip-hop theory (Moore, 2019; Robertson, 2017) to contribute to disabilities studies. We draw on the work of critical Black[2] disabilities scholar Christopher M. Bell (2011) and the contributors to his edited collection *Blackness and Disabilities: Critical Examinations and Cultural Interventions*, Tommy J. Curry (2017) and Josh Lukin (2013) to bridge the gap between theorizing Black disabilities and Black disablement. In this regard, this chapter contributes to critical disabilities studies (Couser, 2017; Haisman & Davis, 2009; Kuppers, 2015; Rioux, 2009) in broad strokes.

Bell (2011) calls for a radical politics of Black disabilities to speak to commonplace and taken-for-granted production of disabilities among African Americans. Throughout this chapter, we mobilize the work of critical theorists of Blackness and disabilities to explore the experiences of Black disabled men and the ways in which the political disablement of Black America promotes disabilities. We do so to recognize the genealogy of the functional role of "structural violence" and of concrete, sadistic violence slavery through to contemporary spectacles and spectacularization of (White) police violence and the murderous White vigilantes of Black men (see Kitossa, Introduction to this volume). But we also want to disrupt tolerance for the production of disabilities and the refusal of Black American communities to develop a language of cognition for the role and power of disabilities, which are at the centre of their identities as Black people living in the afterlife of chattel slavery (Hartman, 2003; Nunn, 2008). We demonstrate the centrality of disabilities in resistance, arts and culture, and political organizing. Indeed, we suggest that from slavery to the present the vital contribution of disabled people to African American culture, life, and resistance is beyond question. As noted by Dea Boster (2013), enslaved Africans, born with disabilities or acquiring them as a result of the violence of enslavement, crafted spaces of autonomy and resistance for themselves and their community in ways that undermined "the delicate illusion of control and stability white authority figures had constructed about...race, deviance, defect" (p. 3; see also Dusinberre, 2000).

In this chapter, we meditate on *being* Black, disabled, and male through and within an account of slavery and its afterlife in and beyond Jim Crow: segregation to the criminal industrial complex (i.e., police and prisons).

We begin with an account of disabilities in the work of Frantz Fanon and James Baldwin. Then we move to examine how Black men's disabilities contributes to their brutalization and murder, while we argue that the disabling of Black America produces disabilities in Black men. We elaborate how *Krip-Hop Theory* helps to formulate through the arts and spoken word, ways of coming to terms with vital contribution of Black disabled men to culture in the United States.

Frantz Fanon, James Baldwin, and the Case for Disabilities

Neither James Baldwin nor Frantz Fanon wrote explicitly of disabilities—at least not as the concept is currently understood in terms of an identity or field of study. Nor did they provide elaborated theorizing of the dignity and humanity of persons whose embodiment and mental states do not conform with hegemonic conceptions of "normalcy." If one looks closely enough, however, there are tantalizing clues that disabilities and disabling are effects, if not the intentions, of colonialism and racism.

Fanon (1952/1977, 1959/1965) describes in detail the mental and physical disabilities produced by colonial exploitation, rape, and quotidian military and police torture and violence in France's Algerian colony. It is not merely a well-placed literary allusion when, in *The Wretched of the Earth*, Fanon (1963/1968) states that "[t]he colonial world is *cut* [emphasis added] in two" (p. 38). Evoking images of blood-stained knives bullets tearing into flesh, bodies as a topographic site for the doing of power, violence, and resistance abound. These representations are not only metaphors; he means them literally, as force is the only arbitrator that the colonizer knows: "[T]he policeman and the soldier, by their immediate presence and their frequent and direct action maintain contact with the native and advise him by means of rifle butts and napalm not to budge. It is obvious here that the agents of government speak the language of pure force" (Fanon, 1963/1968, p. 38). Fanon had occasion, both as soldier-in-training in Algeria in 1943 and later, from 1953 to 1956, as head of the psychiatric unit at Blida-Joinville Hospital, to see the amputated, broken, debilitated, and disfigured bodies of Algerians—

those who survived casual beatings by settlers, the police, and soldiers, as well as strafing villages and torture.

Hospitals, too, were no respite from the breaking of bodies that Michel Foucault (1979) thought ended with the "birth" of the prison.[3] Just as well, Foucault who detailed the discovery of madness and its quarantining in the "mental hospital," had nothing to say of the psychological trauma caused by slavery and its afterlife.[4] Fanon (1959/1965) notes that in colonial hospitals, the minds *and* bodies of the colonized were intentionally disabled by actual and biochemical scalpels:

> French soldiers hospitalized in the psychiatric services of the French Army in Algeria have all seen the experimental epileptic fits produced in Algerians and in infantrymen from south of the Sahara, for the purpose of estimating the specific threshold of each of the different races. (p. 124)

As is evident from *A Dying Colonialism*, Fanon (1959/1965) the psychiatrist is concerned with mental trauma. He observes that the alienation and neurosis of the colonized—both the individuals and the collective—was a dynamic produced by the fact of colonialism itself, which was calculated to wreck the mind and spirit. And this is true not only of the colonized, but also of the colonizer whose erotic sadism fed itself, producing a maddening and boundless desire for flesh. After his resignation at Blida-Joinville—by then, he was already highly lauded in the anticolonial world—Fanon gave a presentation at the 1956 Congress of Negro-African Writers and Artists. (Baldwin was also in attendance.) In his presentation, Fanon observed that the racist culture of the colonizer was designed to sicken the colonized: "Racism is a necessary ideological weapon which accompanies domination...Since the weapon must be flexible in order to retain its effectiveness,
it undergoes many metamorphoses" (cited in Adi & Sherwood, 2003, p. 65). That Algerian patients would complain of pain in fantom limbs, and other psychosomatic pains, signified for Fanon the disabilities of colonialism. Disabilities were not only evidence of the power of colonialism. It seemed to

Fanon, as in medieval times when bodily stigmata were imagined as signs of grace, disability signified both resistance and forbearance. Our thesis in this chapter—that ontological and political disablement are twinned and constitute sites of resistance—leads Fanon (1952/1977), in *Black Skin, White Masks*, to make two opposing but mutually inclusive claims. On one hand, he notes that, for the colonized, "consciousness of the body is a solely negating activity" (p. 110); but on the other he writes: "The crippled veteran of the Pacific war says to my brother, 'Resign yourself to your color the way I got used to my stump; we're both victims.' Nevertheless with all my strength I refuse to accept amputation" (p. 140). Refusing to accept amputation does not mean that colonialism is not amputizing—literally and metaphysically—only that the resultant disability is the colonizers' problem, since it is not a self-definition the colonized give themselves.

It is to be expected that Fanon, being a physician, would attend to disabilities and the disabling fact of colonialism. But reading Baldwin, too, through the prism of disabilities turns up a wealth of concrete references to disability and political disablement—especially among the poor, ghetto occupants, working-class, and rural share-cropping African Americans. Like Fanon, Baldwin pays special attention to the ways that colonial occupation and the keeping of the "natives" in their place through abject and sadistic police violence produced psychological dread and physical disability. Growing up in the ghetto, and subsequently as an adult travelling to the Southern United States as a "witness" for African Americans, Baldwin describes irrepressible resistance to abject and debilitating degradation. Throughout the South and the Northern ghetto colonies Baldwin (1955/1984, 1963, 1967, 1972) chronicles a litany of morbidities that are a part of African American life. These include: madness, particularly that of family, friends, and strangers in the streets of Harlem; the warping of mental horizons from crushing poverty; diseases from unsanitary and dilapidated housing; cognitive impairments and malformations in children from lead toxicity and malnourishment; escapism through alcohol, chemical dependency, and religion; asthma and other respiratory infections; diabetes and related amputations; and disease from rats and insect infestations.[5]

Akin to Fanon's colonial police whose only language is that of grunts and riffle buts, Baldwin, in a number of places, describes disabling encounters and consequences with the occupiers of the ghettos. In one account, Baldwin (1962/1985) describes that when he was 10, "two policemen amused themselves with me by frisking me, making comic (and terrifying) speculations concerning my ancestry and probable sexual prowess, and for good measure, leaving me flat on my back in one of Harlem's empty lots" (p. 32). How little things have changed from the auction block when Black men's genitals were cupped and lifted to test their weight; now, it is the mass sexual assault that is stop-and-frisk. The psychological costs of the dread at being publicly fondled and the terror it has spread far and deep in Black American culture has yet to be fully appreciated. This is a calculated, psychological terror: one that stalks *all* African Americans, *all* their lives, because it could end their lives or leave them scarred for life.[6] Baldwin called attention to the torture that Whiteness signified, and notably the emasculation that accompanied the bludgeoning, crushing, breaking of bones, and loss of body parts when the police undertook their favoured method: billy-clubbing and pistol-whipping African American males about the head. Baldwin (1966) describes one such account:

> The [black] salesman had been so badly beaten around one eye that it was found necessary to hospitalize him...For fourteen days, the doctors at Harlem Hospital told him that they could do nothing for his eye, and he was removed to Bellevue Hospital, where for fourteen days, the doctors tried to save the eye. At the end of fourteen days it was clear that the bad eye could not be saved and was endangering the good eye. (para. 4)

The offence of this man was to intervene in White police officers' random billy-clubbing of 14-, 15-, and 16-year-old boys on the streets of Harlem. Though Baldwin does not explicitly call attention to the Black veterans disabled from fighting wars on behalf of the US military (another neglected area of concern in disabilities studies [Drazen, 2012]), it is important that he alludes to Black veterans victimized in violent confrontation with the police.

Interestingly, Baldwin called attention to the disabling of the Black family by the assault on the authority of Black fathers (and men), whose sons were compelled to watch them either be psychologically broken by colonialism and racism (like Baldwin's father) or physically beaten or murdered by police and soldiers, as well as, on top of it all, stoically do with what they had to support their families.[7] For Baldwin, as it was for Fanon with the colonized, when Black men resisted disablement—even at the price of being disabled—disability became not only a recovering of manhood and an act of communal love, but also evidence of the bankruptcy of the liberal project.

Baldwin and Fanon, it seems to us, offer an approach to the Black experience that de-essentializes disabilities as solely ontological, while repositioning ontological disabilities at the centre of Blackness. In their accounts of colonialism and forcible confinement in ghettos, they incorporate an analysis of contexts that amplify, devalue, and produce cultural, ontological, and political disabilities. They also offer ways to resist disfigurations of the material and symbolic life-world of the colonized and of the objects of racism. Their work suggests ways to theorize and engage, through activism and the arts and culture resistance, "normalcy"—to recuperate and value the disabled body by placing disability at the centre of Black life as a nurturing and vibrant site for culture, politics, and philosophy.

Emmett Till: What's Disabilities and Boyhood Got to Do With It

The torture and brutal murder of Chicagoan 14-year-old Emmett Till in Mississippi in 1955 occurred at a critical juncture in the early stages of the Cold War and was crucial in galvanizing African Americans. Emmett Till was brutally tortured, disfigured, and tossed in the Tallahatchie River. His bloated, pulverized, and decomposed corpse washed ashore. When still alive, Till was disabled: he badly stuttered and his mother taught him to whistle to help him to calm himself to form his words (Bell, 2011).[8] This fact is lost to history, overwhelmed by the no less important imposition of disablement and the breaking of his body—but what killed Emmett Till is as important as who killed him. A love of hatred inspired by the projected anxieties, desires, fantasies, and neuroses of White men: this is what both

Baldwin and Fanon sought for people to understand about the psychology of sexual desire in the context of colonialism and White supremacy. In Fanonian terms, the physical "thingness" of Till's Black body transcended into the metaphysical: it became a spectre that could not die because it lived in the White man's imagination—a neurotic self that could only exist through negation of the Other rather than affirmative relation with the Other. This negation of Black life as a condition for the existence of White ontology demands that each blow and bullet mark be a reminder that killing the Black body is a "necessity," a precondition of the more central task of what Patricia Williams (1987) calls "spirit murder" or what Nell Irvin Painter (1995), in the context of slavery, calls "soul murder."

In a superadded way, the killing of Till was not only anti-Black spirit murder, it also demanded transformation of another site of temporary social death: childhood. To unman a Black boy demanded first that he be transformed from a child into a man. Nadera Shalhoub-Kevorkian (2019), Palestinian legal theorist, has developed the concept of "unchilding" to describe this phenomenon. It accounts for the ways that Palestinian children, especially boys, are transformed in the imagination of Israeli soldiers into adults in miniature. In much the same way, young Black boys from Trayvon Martin to Tamir Rice are denied the innocence of childhood because they are not only unchilded, but also superhumanized. They become objects for erotic desire and have projected onto them qualities that are deemed threatening to the ontology of Whiteness. As objects of desire, they are appropriate and consumed; as threats, they *must* be broken, disabled (literally), or killed (when expedient, for the erotic pleasure of it) (Goff et al., 2014; Henning, 2017; Wynter, 1994).

From a Fanonian point of view, racism, the ideology and practice of degrading the Other predicated on the imputation of inferiorization, affirms material and psychic drives where opposites unify the whole. First, White ontology, in order to be, depends on the negation of Blackness. The White self does not simply know itself by what it is not, it must constantly, consistently, *know* that which it does not know. This is Sartre's famous "bad faith" (see Fanon, 1952/1977, p.41), which is effectively a recursive performance of spectacle and spectacularization through rituals of degradation of the Other. It is to be found, Fanon (1952/1977) asserts, in the singular instance of the appellation: "Look, a Negro" (p.112); "Mama, see the Negro! I am frightened!" (p.112). Second, since "[c]onsciousness is a solely negating activity" (Fanon, 1952/1977, p.112), the Black Other is nature, the "stickiness" of the world that demands the symbolic construction of dirt and its opposite, purity, from which Whiteness must work to separate itself (see Douglas, 1970). Ritual procedures for cleansing, purification, washing away the "stick," demand sacrifice: a scapegoat (Baldwin, 1955/1984; Girard, 1989; Goffman, 1963).[9] To maintain the White self then, demands not *only* actual violence, but also epistemic violence. This violence demands two opposing yet complementary procedures. It confects the Black Other "out of a thousand details, anecdotes, and stories" (Fanon, 1952/1977, p. 111); then by this process of overdetermination from without, the Black Other is a "slave not of the 'idea' that others have of me but of my own appearance" (p.116). This constitutes the basic conditions for the production of Black ontological disabilities, the denial of the humanity of the Black disabled and the determination of Black disablement.[10]

Centring Emmett Till in life and death as exemplar and metaphor for the disabling of Black America, we aim to provide a theoretical appraisal of Black men as desired but also as monstrous in the White imagination. They exist as apparitions, objects, and things toward the ends of White ontology. With the police and vigilantes as the embodiment of the state and collective White ontology, the hegemonic White personality experiences their life through the parasitic destruction of Black life and the breaking of their bodies. In this context, Till's maleness transformed him from a child into a being whose existence transcended the male gender. He was made into a superhuman, and this demanded that he be acted upon not only in order to assert the manhood of White hegemonic ontology, but also because the act of eroticized murder affirmed the feminization and powerlessness of Blackness. Because Till's maleness was inseparable from his blackness, Till, like Rodney King, Michael Brown, Walter Scott, Freddie Gray, and others, was (and is) imagined as superhuman: a force that can be controlled only by being killed. But in all this, with Till as a point of departure for thinking about disability, masculinity, and the Black community, we want to suggest that though he was, indeed, killed *because* he was Black, he was also killed *because* he was disabled (he stuttered) and *because* his mother taught him to manage his disability by whistling.

Our contention is that, in as much as Black disabled boys and men (and girls and women) are the objects of class and racial violence, we want also to draw on critical disability studies to resist the erasure of Black disabled men within the Black community. We want to recognize the necessity of their sovereignty to experience, not least, their sexual freedom. Finally, we want to show that the disabling of Black America must be countered, and that we must confront and struggle to resist Black ableism. It is vital to come to terms with the role that ontological disability plays as a site for cultural articulation and political resistance. In this regard, we now turn to ontological disabilities theorized through Krip-Hop activism.

Krip-Hop Activism, the Arts, and Recentring Masculinity

In this chapter, we build on the work of Leroy F. Moore Jr.: one of the chapter authors and founder of Krip-Hop Nation. Krip-Hop Nation is an international movement that critically examines, with the aim of understanding and addressing the discrimination disabled Black people—and Black people in general—face at the intersections of racism and ableism. This chapter aims to articulate a theory of Krip-Hop that resists the erasure of disability in Black communities and addresses connections between disability and gender-based sexual violence, with a specific focus on Black men.

To fully understand Krip-Hop theory, however, it is first important to understand Krip-Hop Nation and the experiences from which it sprung. We now turn, therefore, to Leroy F. Moore Jr.'s personal experiences with disability, activism, Black masculinity, and how his arts-based organization, Krip-Hop Nation, moves disabilities from the margins to the centre of collective experience. We begin with a few simple questions: To whom and where do

Black, disabled young men turn to be proud of who they are? What are their conceptions of masculinities? And how do they perform these masculinities?

Reflecting on his experiences as a young Black man in grade school, high school, and college, where almost every door was closed to him, Moore thought, like Carter G. Woodson, to cut his own door. Krip-Hop Nation was the result. Its mission, theory, and politics of radical love and inclusiveness are what its members live by and spread, especially within the Black community. As a leader in the disabilities community, Moore grew into being "the change he wanted to see," and is now as an elder who inspires Black disabled youth to reach their fullest potential. Just as with the birth of hip-hop, when the Black community took back its power to represent itself, its talents, its voices, and its art, Krip-Hop Nation follows this tradition to produce music and organize events to advance the agenda for persons with disabilities. These events include the first public conference at UC Berkeley in 2009, entitled Diversifying Hip-Hop: Krip-Hop & Homo-Hop. The conference challenged ableism and homophobia in hip-hop. The inclusion of homophobia as a topic tested many of Krip-Hop Nation's supporters, resulting in the loss, following the announcement of the conference's theme, of many of its male supporters.

James Baldwin's 1954 essay "Gide as a Husband and Homosexual," subsequently republished as "The Male Prison" (1993), challenged men not to aspire to the unattainable goal of a hegemonic masculine identity. Baldwin understood that masculinity and patriarchy were not in and of themselves about men dominating women, but about racial domination in the context of gender relations in which dominant men (and women) dominated subordinate males in order to dominate the whole group. Because of this, Baldwin (1972) opined that masculinity constitutes a site for disabilities, writing that "[e]very black man, whatever his style, had been scarred, as in some tribal rite; and every white man, though men, mostly, had no style, had been maimed" (p. 69). Baldwin asserted it was necessary to resist striving towards a way of being a man that was delusional at best and harmful at worst. Without ever equalizing Black men and White men, Baldwin argued for men to liberate themselves from the prison of masculinity, as with gay men who are trapped in the performance of heteronormativity. He suggested that all men, but especially White men, confront the inhumanity inherent to their tribal conflict in order to find a more compassionate way not only of being, but of being men.

Now, Baldwin was especially sensitive to the plight of Black men, knowing well the dreadful paradox of their existence. In a lengthy and wide-ranging conversation with Nikki Giovanni in 1971, at a key moment Baldwin asserts that the defining criteria for manhood have been denied Black men—a fact that positions them precariously in relation to Black women and their families (thepostarchive, 2019, 49:05–57:07). Even able-bodied straight and straight-performing Black men struggle to define themselves in an ableist White man's (and woman's) world that has no use for them; the struggle of how to define oneself is all the more excruciating for disabled young Black men. As objects of pity rather than individuals recognized, in solidarity and appreciation, for the central role of disabilities in the African American experience, disabled young Black men are feared and shunned as if their disability were a contagious disease. For those with supportive families who do not lock them away and who have access to inclusive peers and programs, the lives of disabled African American youth, both male and female, are substantially enriched; but of course, challenges remain. For other Black disabled young males whose lives are marked by exclusion and invisibility, however, the problems are more intense; they are driven even harder to play bit parts on the stage of what Baldwin called the masculine prison.

Since its beginning in 2007, Moore has always imagined Krip-Hop Nation to be about more than calling out the hip-hop industry and the underground about their discrimination toward hip-hop artists with disabilities. Krip-Hop Nation aims to bring back to prominence the incredible contributions of Black and Brown disabled musicians from the blues, jazz, and other genres that are the bedrock for contemporary hip-hop. The goal is to facilitate the empowerment of disabled communities of colour and to validate the identities of disabled peoples. Krip-Hop politics, theory, and art have the potential to bring disabilities from the margins to the centre of Black cultural, economic, social, and political life. So, what is Krip-Hop Nation and what are its politics? Krip-Hop Nation is an international network of hip-hop and other musicians with disabilities, working with artists they call MCs With Disabilities (MWD). This is worldwide: in Germany, the United Kingdom, and several countries in Africa. These artists *own* their disability, not as a badge of pride, but as a statement and a celebration of the fullness of their humanity. More than a style of music, Krip-Hop is also a community, an artistic space where people with disabilities can speak out, about, and back to the social structures that exclude people based on disability, race, sexuality, and a host of other marginalized identities.

Why Krip-Hop Nation? If we go back to slavery—not as a starting point, but in keeping with the politics of slavery's afterlife, including the experience of post-traumatic slave syndrome (discussed below)—artists and musicians with disabilities have always been in the Black community. We can think here also of Beethoven—deaf, but also descended from Black people in Brandenburg, Germany—to signify how race and disability articulate themselves. Interestingly, Brandenburg was one of the German principalities that profited, for a time, from the disability-producing transatlantic slave trade (Weindl, 2008). The historical example of Beethoven demonstrates the sort of cultural and social activism that is possible with Krip-Hop. It aims for a disability justice that takes advocacy seriously, but also displays the talents of musicians with disabilities. At the same time, Krip-Hop celebrates the history of disabled people across cultural, national, local, and linguistic differences since art, like math, is a universal language.

A Krip-Hop *theory*, based on the values and principles of Krip-Hop Nation, is one that recentres disability within Black communities, and within the larger context of Black history. The theory we present in this chapter focuses on how disability and the disabling effects of colonialism and racism affects Black populations. We focus, in particular, on the experiences of Black men in this regard, in part because of the ways in which these dynamics are tied to sexuality and gender-based sexual violence—a topic on which much literature and popular discourse tends to be silent.

Krip-Hop Theory and Black Masculinities

Though there is much talk and mockery of Black men as hypermasculine, these discussions of masculinity either erase or do not include Black straight and queer disabled men. Our ultimate goal is to think about other possibilities for Black masculinity and to centre disabilities at the heart of African American existence and the Black Atlantic more generally.

There is a Pan-Africanist side to Krip-Hop theory, given that Moore's Krip-Hop Nation redefines language to recognize disabled people in the African disapora by using terms like *Afro-Krip*. The African diaspora in the West refers to communities that derive from post-sixteenth century, principally forced migration from Africa. The term has been historically applied in particular to the descendants of the West and Central Africans who were enslaved and shipped to the Americas in the Atlantic slave trade, with their largest populations in Brazil, followed by the United States and other countries of the Americas. Krip-Hop Nation argues for *Afro-Krip*, a term "to help united Afro disabled people around the African diaspora associate to Krip-Hop during and after becoming politicized" (Moore, 2019, para. 2). Moore (2019) has noted that "as a Black disabled activist/artist living in America having a need and vision of connecting with other disabled artists/activists in the African diaspora [I] realized there must be terminology that speaks to our experiences" (para. 2). So, it makes sense that disabled people, their culture, and their activism are also a part of this African diaspora in their shared stories and the realities they create today. The term *Afro-Krip*, in other words, speaks to an aspect of African diaspora culture with a focus on disability through its activism, art, music, culture writ large.

In part, the objective of the term *Afro-Krip* is meant less to invent or bring such utopian possibilities into being and more to recover prior and concurrent realities, as well as to enlarge the long tradition of disabled Black masculinities that have contributed to and nurtured Black communities over time and across the United States. Black men confront the "toxic masculinity" of their White oppressors in all its stratified gradation (a fact that is beneficial to White communities). As noted by Tommy J. Curry (2017) there is considerable evidence that Black men have and continue to resist "toxic masculinity," which is a particular relation of domination in service to White group interests (pp. 19–25).[11] For instance, contrary to the hegemonic discourse of Black hypermasculinity propagated by capitalistic popular culture and largely accepted as given by both Black and White feminisms (which treat these representations as expressing a norm that marks Black men as atavistic boars), the past and current reality of Black men is more varied and sensitive, and more supportive of Black (and all) femininity and women's aspirations than is generally assumed (Curry, 2017; Mutua, 2006a, 2006b; Newman, 1999). A critical issue in this chapter, then, is the question: What does this all mean for disabled Black men in the United States?

It is important, therefore, at the start to try and understand what disabilities are and what they are not. For too long, disability has been thought of as a condition to overcome by faith or medical cure. In the Black communities where we struggle and resist indignities that question our humanity, some Black families often regard disabled family members as a sign of their failure and shame. The combination of social genocidal approaches in the form of eugenics, the dominance of experts over defining the meaning of "disabilities," and the general stigma toward people with disabilities means that Black communities must struggle to rethink how disabilities are defined within the Black experience.

Because Black and White people in the United States have, in general, very different life conditions and opportunities, the Black disabled experience in America has different roots from those of White disabled people. Historically, in Black communities across the United States, through art, music, and political activism, Black disabled people have been at the heart of the community experience; this makes it all the more hurtful that they are now often excluded and erased. Furthermore, the recognition of this exclusion and erasure demands renewed disabilities activism to heal the wounds inflicted on Black disabled people by their families and by their own Black communities. It is imperative, therefore, that Black disabled people's stories are (re)collected and (re)defined to provide education and resources for Black communities.

We can begin by resisting prejudices and labels that deny disabled people dignity, respect, and the fundamentals of life solely based on their difference. There are stereotypes, largely inaccurate, associated either with disability in general or with certain disabilities in particular. The presumption that disabled people are "dependents" leads to the presumption that all disabled people want to be cured, that wheelchair users necessarily have an intellectual disability, and/or that blind people have some special form of insight. These stereotypes in turn serve as a justification for ableist practices and reinforce discriminatory attitudes and behaviours toward people who are disabled. Ableism in Black communities and outside of them imagines persons with disabilities as less valuable or even less than human. And if it is the case that presumably able-bodied Black people are, as shown above and below, "killable," it is more so the case for persons with disabilities. To better understand this, we turn to a Krip-Hop-informed account of Black disabilities, disablement, and masculinities from slavery to the criminal industrial complex.

Slavery, Black Disablement, Disability, and the Quest for Manhood

In the ableist, capitalist, heteropatriarchal, White-supremacist social order of the United States, disabled Black masculinity seems a self-evident contradiction. So much of what it means to be a Black man, from slavery, to abolition, to Reconstruction, through Jim Crow, to the present, has been a quest for sovereignty of self, community, and others (Baldwin, 1972; Curry, 2017; Douglass, 1845/2009; Foner, 1986; Foster, 2019; Garvey, 1992; Lemelle, 2010; Perry, 2009; Thomas, 2007; Walker, 1830/2001; Woodard, 2014). In both slavery and emancipation, aside from contributing to the making of viable communities along with Black children and women, Black men had to find ways to constitute their *being* against what was denied them: the sense and prerogative of manhood as the right to self-possession. The reasons are not hard to find. In slavery, Black men and women were genderless, even if their sexes were used to exploit them in different ways (Curry, 2017). For African women, their reproductive capacities made them what economists call "perfect commodities"—they produced value through their labour, but also through their sexual reproductive capacity, which was itself a means of adding value. Thomas Jefferson knew this well and gloated in letters to the other slave-owning president, George Washington, that his plantation annually increased its value by 4%, in part due to slave births exceeding deaths (Wiencek, 2012). Thus, enslaved women endured rape and repeated childbearing starting as young as 14 and 15; these experiences contributed to the disabilities and the disabling of Black women.

It is undeniably true that enslaved women were considered to be "perfect commodities" because of the double value of their forced physical and reproductive labour (Smithers, 2012; Sublette & Sublette, 2016). They were also subject to extraordinary tortures, often by their female owners (Bush, 1990; Jones-Rogers, 2019). Yet, the sex essentialism in hegemonic Black and non-Black feminist theory and scholarship on transatlantic slavery has led to the taken-for-granted "truth" that sexual exploitation was a unique reality *only* for enslaved females (Davis, 1983; hooks, 1981/1990; J. James, 1996; Spillers, 1987). This female-specific biological essentialism is plainly contradicted factually and theoretically, since, by its very nature, slavery sexually exploits both females and males through "penetrative penality," forced reproduction, sadistic sport, and as sexual playthings (Patterson, 1982; Trexler, 1995).

Throughout the Americas, enslaved Black men were particularly susceptible to sexual exploitation *because* they were, in the eyes of White men, males (not men) to be feared (not least because of the many desperate attempts at liberty they mounted, from slave ship to plantation). White men thus felt it necessary to defeat Black men; this required not only sadistic physical torture by corporal punishment, but also psychological terror and degrading penetrative penality to demean them in the eyes of slave women and their communities in general as a means of control.[12] (This dynamic continues today. One need only think here of Abner Louima, anally brutalized with a broom stick by White New York City police officers; or Théo, the 22-year-old African-descended youth worker in France, anally savaged in 2017 by a White French police officer who claimed it was an "accident" [Saad, 2017].) To imagine the scale and scope of sexual degradation and the physical injuries that were involved in "buck breaking" and "seasoning"—means of terrorizing enslaved communities by processes intended to *neuter* Black men in relation to *all* White people—is to rethink all we think we know about slavery and Black men (Curry, 2017; Foster, 2011; Kitossa, Introduction to this volume; Lemelle, 2010; Woodard, 2014).

Vincent Woodard's (2014) *The Delectable Negro: Human Consumption and Homoeroticism within US Slave Culture* details the disabilities produced by the actual and symbolic consumption of Black flesh in plantation culture. "Buck breaking" and "seasoning" were of a piece. The former, according to Aristotelian logic, transformed African males into anthropoda (human-footed beasts), while the latter signified the parasitism of consuming human flesh in the literal and symbolic senses (Woodard, 2014). Throughout antiquity to the present, slavery signified sexual domination and the penetrability of the degraded and fungible Other (Patterson, 1982). In addition, the metaphorical grounds for cognition reflected practices of cutting, amputating, and dissecting the Other in a culinary sense. Richard Trexler (1995) observes that "slaughter house vocabulary and practice is part of the broad human tendency first to emasculate or desexualize, consequently to dehumanize, and thus finally to treat our enemies as dirt" (p. 17). In the transatlantic of the "Middle Passage" and plantation culture, Woodard (2014) explores Frederick Douglass's descriptions of "breaking," "seasoning," and human consumption—all of which are consistent with Trexler's connection between sexual domination, penetrative penality, and slavery. It is not simply that the range of disabilities inflected on enslaved Black people is numerically stunning, but that these numbers have been normalized to the point of, for many, not being stunning at all.

A most cogent statement of the "normalization" of Black disability can be read in Theodore Dwight Weld's (1839) *American Slavery as It Is: Testimony of a Thousand Witnesses*. One of the principal architects of the American slavery abolitionist movement during its formative years from 1830 through 1844, Weld is best known for drawing attention to the strategies of euthanasia and eugenics inherent to the capital-intensiveness of chattel slavery. In his antislavery tome, Theodore Dwight Weld dryly writes that in respect to large classes of slaves, it is for the *interest* of their masters to treat them with barbarous inhumanity.

1. *Old slaves*. It would be for the interest of masters to shorten their days.
2. *Worn out slaves*. Multitude of slaves by being overworked, have their constitutions broken in middle life. It would be *economical* for masters to starve or flog such to death.
3. *The incurably diseased maimed*. In such cases it would be *cheaper* for masters to buy poison than medicine.
4. *The blind, lunatics, and idiots*. All such would be a tax on him, it would be for his interest to shorten their days.
5. *The deaf and dumb and persons greatly deformed*. Such might or might not be serviceable to him; many of them would at least be a burden, and few men carry burdens when they can throw them off.
6. *Feeble infants*. As such would require much nursing, the time, trouble and expense necessary to raise them, would generally be more than they would be worth as *working animals*...
7. *Incorrigible slaves*...It is for the *interest* of the masters...to put upon such slaves iron collars and chains, to brand and crop them; to disfigure, lacerate, starve and torture them—in a word, to inflict upon them such vengeance as shall strike terror into the other slaves...
7. [*sic*] *Runaways*...It is for the interest of the master to make an example of him, by the greatest privations and inflictions .
8. [*sic*] *Hired slaves*. It is for the interest of those who hire slaves to get as much out of them as they can; the temptation to overwork them is powerful...
9. [*sic*] *Slaves under overseers whose wages are proportioned to the crop which they raise*. This is an arrangement common in the slaves states, and in its practical operation is equivalent to a bounty on *hard driving*—a virtual premium offered to overseers to keep the slaves whipped up to the top of their strength. (pp. 132–33)

FIGURE 5.1: Illustration by Jean-Michel Moreau from chapter 19 of Candide *(Voltaire, 1787), "Le nègre de Surinam." The caption reads: "It is at this price that you eat sugar in Europe." (Jean-Michel Moreau, public domain)*

Weld's account of the routine ways in which Black Americans were drained of their vitality for capitalist consumption, and the extent to which that very process demanded sadistic corporal, penetrative, and psychological terror brings new urgency to theorizing the implications of slavery and its afterlife for Black American culture, politics, and self-understanding.

There is a paucity of research on Black Americans and disabilities, especially connected to slavery (Bell, 2011; Boster, 2013; Mustakeem, 2016). But given the centrality of slavery and its afterlife to Black America, rigorous attention is needed on the role of disabilities in cultural idioms such as "the dozens" and expressions that attend to psychic recuperation from dismemberment in the form of gospel, the blues, jazz, rock'n'roll, soul, R&B, and hip-hop. It is not that these expressions were either for the sake of art or for articulating modes of resistance to domination. Nor are they in some racialist sense akin to the soul of Black folk. They are statements of joy, irony, freedom, and the insistence that, in the face of the most awful and quotidian tyranny, change is going to come because Black resistance will persist. Reflecting on recuperating what he fled when he left Harlem for Paris in 1948, James Baldwin (1962/1985) writes, without any nostalgia:

> In spite of everything, there was in the life I fled a zest and a joy and a capacity for facing and surviving disaster that are very moving and very rare. Perhaps we were, all of us—pimps, whores, racketeers, church members, and children—bound together by the nature of our oppression, the specific and peculiar complex of risks we had to run; if so, within these limits we sometimes achieved with each other a freedom that was close to love...This is the freedom that one hears in some gospel songs, for example, and in jazz. In all jazz, and especially in the blues, there is something tart and ironic, authoritative and double-edged. (pp. 59–60)

Baldwin's pragmatic recuperation makes it possible to rethink binary approaches to disabilities as either transcending or enduring (Bailey, 2005). Here we turn to the lyrical foundation of hip-hop—coded speech in slave songs and the Dozens—as well as lock and pop and breaking—the "buck dance" or, alternatively, the "bulk dance." These latter forms of dance, which continue to articulate themselves in contemporary choreography and popular dance, were clandestine, expressive movements that spoke to the joy of existence in the midst of White terror.

Disability and the Dozens

Between those killed during capture to "Middle Passage," anywhere from 12 to 50 million Africans were trafficked to the Americas (Allen, 1997, p. 297), and of that number, approximately two-thirds were males (Blackburn, 1998; Segal, 2001). Fatalities varied by "carrier," but, as a rule, were exceedingly high. James H. Sweet (2003), drawing on Joseph Miller's *Way of Death: Merchant Capitalism and the Angolan Slave Trade, 1730–1830*, observes that "from capture in the interior of Africa until fully seasoned in Brazil, only about 30 percent of Africans survived" (n. 8, p. 241). Coming from of a variety of ethnicities, tribes, and nations, enslaved Africans varied in the local cultures of their homelands, including their folklore, foodways, gender arrangements, inheritance patterns, language, music, and sexual and marriage practices (see Ipsen, 2015). Still, especially given that many came from the same regions of Western Africa, there were also a great many commonalities including shared cosmologies.

In forging new lives with one another, as well as with neighbouring Europeans and Native Americans, the rich variety of African diaspora culture took root in a "New World" decidedly shaped by the cultural innovations of Africans and their descendants. Through folklore, music, dance, and more, all people had connection to disability, but very few know about this connection. For example, the tale/song "Follow the Drinkin' Gourd" is connected to the Underground Railroad. In this tale, the main character, Peg Leg Joe,[13] sings to an elder disabled man, Jim Crow, about the direction to freedom for Africans. There is also the "bulk dance," in which people shackled themselves at the ankles, causing "disabilities," and were then made to dance. The dance derived from the slave ship practice of forcing Africans—often while still chained to each other, because slavers learned not to unshackle

FIGURE 5.2: Alillia Johnson's painting "Blues/Activist Elders Looking Out of Windows!" depicts two elders, Rec. Cecil Ivory, an activist and regional NAACP director, and Johnnie Mae Dunson, a blues singer and drummer. They are unable to warn the next generation of the pit falls they may face because that generation has locked them away in nursing homes (Moore, 2018). (© Alillia Johnson, Krip-Hop Nation, 2017)

them—to dance jigs with sailors cracking whips at their ankles. This was to "exercise them" (Mustakeem, 2016). At other times on plantations, males were encouraged to engage in controlled bouts of boxing, racing, wrestling and other physical sport to "burn off steam." They were encouraged at specific periods to engage in "frolics" where they played music and danced (Douglass, 1845/2009).

There is one area of research on Black disabilities during slavery that is proving itself to be particularly important in establishing a link between slavery and contemporary African American culture: the Dozens! Research on the meaning and origins of the Dozens, its wordplay, and its continuity in African folklore, for example, suggests that disabilities were key to these expressive developments, which would ultimately shape the blues, jazz, and, later, hip-hop (see Figure 5.2). As with dance, the story of the Dozens has been pivotal to African American vernacular, word play, and, currently, hip-hop and African American comedy. The Dozens—also called "snapping" and "crackin'"—is a Black oral tradition that involves trading insults back and forth. It predates transatlantic slavery but took root in Mississippi and Louisiana. *The Dozens*, the name of this verbal exchange, refers to the sale of slaves who had been overworked and were disabled or beaten-down. Their physical (and often mental) conditions affected their value and they were sold by the dozen. Being sold in this way was considered by slaves to be the lowest position within the community. From this, the term evolved to mean a competition between two people in a contest of wit, mental agility, verbal ability, and self-control. It is believed that the Dozens developed as an outlet for slaves who were depressed and served as a creative outlet for pent-up aggression. Since it was nearly impossible for slaves to display aggression towards their oppressors except in open revolt, aggression toward each other was encouraged by masters and overseers. In this context, the Dozens served as a creative means of managing aggression and, at the same time, of resisting the slave masters' expectations that Africans would turn on each other—although this certainly also occurred, as can be seen in Frederick Douglass's (1845/2009) autobiography. The Dozens became a practice for nearly all slaves, male and female, young and old. As explained in Susan Hadley and George Yancy's (2012) anthology *Therapeutic Uses of Rap and Hip-Hop*, the Dozens also played out in early hip-hop, with MCs battling each other in a cipher (see also Vervaet, n.d.).

Hip-hop, despite drawing on the legacy of the Dozens, is stereotyped as ableist, homophobic, and misogynist. Certainly, some performers do fit these categories, but that does not justify smearing the whole art form. This broad-stroke stigmatization of hip-hop ironically erases the tradition of narrating and living with disabilities that lead to the much-celebrated spoken word forms that we have today. Significantly, the hypersexuality associated with hip-hop, a linear descendant of the Dozens, ironically invisiblizes Black disabled men (and women) as sexual agents.

On Black Disability and Sexual Sovereignty

As a matter of course, persons without disabilities take it for granted that sex and sexual reproduction is their right, though they may not make the same assumption for disabled persons. Sexual autonomy in the Black experience has a political significance not found in other communities for the simple reason that, during slavery, Black females and males could not control their sexuality: castration and gelding, forced breeding and rape were routine (Foster, 2011, 2019; Smithers, 2012; Sublette & Sublette, 2016). Yet, in spite of the prevalence of disabilities among Black Americans, there is considerable internalized stigma and fear around disabled people and sex and sexuality.

A significant challenge to ableist assumptions of sex and sexual desire took place on the stage in 1935. One of the earliest and most profound explorations of sexuality and disability among African Americans—an affirming representation of Black disabled persons and their right to sexual sovereignty—is George and Ira Gershwin's *Porgy and Bess*, an operatic adaptation of DuBose Heyward's[14] 1925 novel *Porgy.*

It was at a 1970s production of this very opera that Leroy F. Moore Jr. first encountered the image of a Black disabled man exploring his sexuality. *Porgy and Bess* tells the story of a Black disabled man (Porgy) who falls in love with a sex worker (Bess). Moore saw himself in Porgy and realized how important it is that people see complex and life-affirming reflections of themselves in mass media. Since that time, however, less than a handful of similar real-life situations concerning disabled people, sexual desire, and intimacy—much less Black experiences at these intersections—have been represented in mainstream media.

For Moore, being a Black and physically disabled boy in a White suburb in the 1970s and '80s was like being Ralph Ellison's invisible man: a character who is seen, not seen, and surrounded by the benign indifference and patronization that enables the able-bodied to feel good about themselves.

But alongside watching *Porgy and Bess*, Moore was also exposed to artists with disabilities in the Black music arena. Through them he saw himself as a historical and social agent. In his parents' basement, with his father's huge record collection, he discovered albums by Robert Winters and Walter Jackson, both Black men with polio who performed on crutches. He listened to their smooth, soulful love songs as they sang about women and making love. This gave him a positive image of the possibilities for Black disabled men to experience their sexuality. Teddy Pendergrass and Curtis Mayfield, who were paralyzed in accidents in 1982 and 1990 respectively, also provided a mirror; through their struggles to live their lives as disabled men, they demonstrate possibilities for disabled people. The Black community's embrace of both men, each of whom stood for different experiences of Black masculinity—one a disciplined master of the sensual arts and the other the embodiment of a radical politics that merged Malcolm and Martin—reignited a lost awareness in Black America of the role of disabled people in their communities and in US popular culture. While Moore had some awareness of Black disabled men who were on TV and in the music industry in the early 1980s and 1990s, awareness of the prominence of Black artists with disabilities, many of whom were foundations in the blues, soul, R&B, and rock'n'roll, did not reach the whole Black community.

The hidden aspects of the lives of disabled people include not only their contributions, which are too often denied, but how their personal lives are ones of sexual trauma. Disabled women, for example, have been noted to have one of the highest rates of sexual assault. Moreover, the United States has a long and continuing history of forced sterilization of girls and women with disabilities. Feminists and others have been instrumental in bringing the quotidian sexual abuses of disabled girls into the public arena (Boyd, 2004; Roberts, 1993), as have students of the politics of race-as-science such as Stephen J. Gould (1984) in his essay "Carrie Buck's Daughter." More recently, Tarana Burke's hashtag #MeToo has spurred a deepening awareness of women's and girls' sexual harassment and assault. In particular, Burke (2017) aims to broaden the scope of constituencies impacted by sexual violence:

> What history has shown us time and again is that if marginalized voices—those of people of color, queer people, disabled people, poor people—aren't centered in our movements then they tend to become no more than a footnote. I often say that sexual violence knows no race, class or gender, but the response to it does. "Me too." [*sic*] is a response to the spectrum of gender-based sexual violence that comes directly from survivors—all survivors. We can't afford a racialized, gendered or classist response. Ending sexual violence will require every voice from every corner of the world and it will require those whose voices are most often heard to find ways to amplify those voices that often go unheard. (para. 11)

It is an open question, however, whether #MeToo in its present configuration speaks only and exclusively to women's and girls' experiences with sexual assault or, in fact, has room to contemplate men's and boys' experiences with sexual harassment and assault. We go on to suggest that, once again, if we take transatlantic slavery and its urban- and rural-plantation guises, it becomes possible to imagine how the sexual exploitation of Black men is invisiblized by the mask of masculinity. Indeed, we show that not only are disabled Black boys and men exposed to a high prevalence of sexual abuse, policing and mass incarceration ensure that Black men have higher incidence of being sexually assaulted than Black women in "free" society. Thus, though disabled Black men (and women) are stigmatized and invisiblized as sexual subjects with desire, they are at the same time objects of sexual abuse.

At the Intersections of Disability: Masculinity, Sexual Assault, Prisons, and Police

Disabilities among prisoners are exceptionally higher than in the general population. The American Bureau of Justice Statistics (2015) estimated that "32% of state and federal prisoners and 40% of local jail inmates reported having at least one disability in the 2011–12 National Inmate Survey." This is significant since sexual violence is prevalent in policing and rampant in female and male prisons. As demonstrated by the exposure of sexual scandals implicating police officers and prison guards across the country (Sedensky, 2015), it is clear that safety for women—especially poor, undocumented, Asian, Black, Brown, and Indigenous women—is not assured anywhere in the United States. Quite literally, being female is a risk factor for sexual assault. However, the absence of a language to talk about boys and men as victims of sexual assault and harassment leaves little room to explore boys' and men's survival of sexual assault and harassment (Del Zotto & Jones, 2002; Trexler, 1995; Valente, 2005).

It is well established that women in prisons in the United States are routinely the objects of sexual assault, even to the point of lawsuits demonstrating that guards are responsible for impregnating prisoners and coercing them to have abortions (Parenti, 1999). Angela Y. Davis (2003) argues the prison is a gendered space that legitimates, promotes, and invisiblizes sexual violence against women (2003). As much as the sexual assault of women is made invisible by incarceration, the scale and extent of sexual assault against male prisoners is an open and tolerated public secret (Del Zotto & Jones, 2002; Smith, 2015; Sykes, 1956/2007), the extent of public knowledge being the grounds for ribald jokes like "don't drop the soap." Rape in men's prisons is, indeed, implicitly encouraged as one more way to teach "criminals" a lesson. Jeff Smith (2015) cites a 1993 *New York Times* report indicating there are 300,000 rapes in men's prisons annually, while there are 135,000 reported rapes of women in "free" society (pp. 181–82). Citing different data from anti-prison-rape groups and scholarly sources, Christian Parenti (1999) reports there are anywhere from 200,000 to 290,000 men raped in US carceral facilities on an annual basis (p. 185). Parenti draws on one scholarly paper that asserts that the chances of a young prisoner entering prison being raped is 100% within 24 to 48 hours. To be sure, the rape of women in free society is grossly underreported, but there remains a strong possibility that the prevalence of men in prison being raped is higher than the official number of women in "free" society (Filipovic, 2012).

The prevalence of rape in men's prisons demands reconsideration of the implications for disabilities (Curry, 2017). On one hand, men experience the exact same sorts of mental, physical, self-blaming, and post-traumatic stress effects from sexual assault that women do (Del Zotto & Jones, 2002). But because of their socialization and limited public support, boys and men are at even higher risk for depression, suicide, and acting out than girls and women, in part because there is little public support available to them as victims of sexual assault (Del Zotto & Jones, 2002; Trexler, 1995). As a result, male prisoners develop crises of mental wellbeing, PTSD, and increased violence.

The risk of narrating rape in men's prisons as an organized, administratively encouraged and sanctioned regime of jailhouse discipline runs the risk of reproducing homophobia, heteronormativity, and gender-based misogyny. Even among prisoners, the refusal to acknowledge that men can love men is unhinged by the discourse of situationality or "gay for the stay" (Smith, 2015, p. 184). But the reality, as determined by the Thirteenth Amendment, is that all prisoners are slaves of the state (McHugh, 1978, pp. 46–47). Consensual commitment to sexual intimacy is therefore an impossibility in prisons. It is, thus, highly problematic to launch an affirming discourse around men-loving-men without also advocating for abolition of the prison and the disabilities it produces as much as the way it exploits the disabled. For a principled stand, the necessity for protection against abuses, exploitation, and rape makes consent, if one can find a willing protector, itself a myth. Rather, the critical issue in resisting the right of prisons to exist is in itself to criticize how rape in prison "creates a gender and, therefore, a division of labor and a set of class relations" (Parenti, 1999, p. 188) where some males perform feminine labour and others occupy privileged positions of social parasitism. Drawing attention to the paradox that prison slaves enslave others, Parenti (1999) shows that some "punks" (a willing or coerced sexually subordinate male) "are loaned, traded, pimped, and outright *sold* as property" (p. 188). In the words of one "punk":

> It is not uncommon for a Man to develop a genuine concern and affection for his punk and passionate love affairs are common in prison. Some couples even go through imitation marriage ceremonies...the one

difference that stands out is that most men feel comfortable letting other men have access to their sexual partners. (cited in Parenti, 2008, p. 188)

We cannot meaningfully understand the disabling of Black men and Black men's disabilities with respect to prison without getting a grasp on the numbers of Black men under lock and key. In 2018, for state and federal prisoners, excluding municipal lockups, 2027 out of every 100,000 Black men were under lock and key; the number for Black women was 88 per 100,000 (Sawyer, 2020). Given that disparity, we return to the impairment of Black families and the associated mental and physical disabilities that go along with it when so many fathers, brothers, uncles, and sons—all potential income earners—are removed from families. The effects are not only financial, but have direct bearing on the social determinants of health for Black families and communities. Significantly, that prisoners have higher exposure to sexually transmitted infections, liver and respiratory diseases, outright physical violence, and psychological traumas, the catch-and-release revolving door not only means that infectious disease, physical violence, and mental traumas circulate from prison to families and community, but also that Black men are disproportionately living with illnesses that are preventable and treatable (Curry, 2017, p. 110).[15]

The trauma of rape, disease, and ill health for men in prisons is amplified by the fact that prisoners tend to have higher incidences of cognitive and physical disabilities than the general population. In the United States, between local, state, and federal facilities, Black men comprise about 37% of all prisoners. In US carceral facilities, at least 50% of prisoners live with physical disabilities, compared to 15% of the general population (Fels, n.d.). Those with a mental health issue comprise 45% of federal, 55% of state, and 65% of local institution populations (Khazan, 2015). In addition, 32% of those in prison and 40% of those in jail report at least one cognitive and physical disability that impairs their capacity to care for themselves (Bureau of Justice Statistics, 2015; Morgan, 2017). While the incidence of disability is about eight points higher for women than for men, men comprise 95% of all prisoners.

The question of the relationship between disability and sexual assault so far suggests that having a disability in prison is a risk factor for sexual assault, though as a percentage of prisoners with disabilities, women are more frequently victimized than men (Wolff et al., 2007). Still, the sheer aggregate numbers suggests that Black incarcerated men, with and without disabilities, experience considerable trauma from sexual violence and other disability-producing factors.

That prisons are a weapon for the social debilitation of Black men is incontrovertible. That prisons are spaces for the production and amplification of disabilities is not well considered, despite all the talk about the visibility of Black men versus Black women. The challenge of the abolition of the prison is to reposition the narrative to place disabilities and disablement at its centre. But this must be in such a way as not to erase and silence the physical and psychological disabilities prison produces, not least those disabilities that result from sexual violence that Black prisoners experience. But how do so many Black men end up in prison? What is the relationship between Black men, disabilities, fatalities, and policing?

At every stage of the criminal legal system, beginning with police, Black American men are disproportionately targeted (Sawyer, 2020). Too often, however, police targeting of Black men is not framed in such as a way as to apprehend the ways police produce disabilities of the sort described by James Baldwin above, nor the fact that Black men with disabilities are also disproportionately the objects of police violence and murders. While there is justified outrage at the murders of Black people by the police, less attention is paid to police beatings that result not in death, but in the cognitive, physical, and psychological impairment of thousands of Black men annually. Both should be taken as a whole. Take Rodney King, for example. He lived with traumatic brain injury, permanent physical disablement, and psychological scars so deep that he turned to self-medicating his pain with alcohol. The extent of King's injuries was not due simply to the brutality of the beating, but to the decision of police administrators to equip LAPD officers with bone-crushing batons in the first place (Cannon, 1997). The language of "disabling" is a key justification when police forces such as the LAPD used nonhuman animal imagery to refer to African American males (Wynter, 1994). The savaging of Rodney King was not simply an issue of physical violence; it was also, as Judith Butler (1993) noted, an act of sexual violence. Utterances of sodomization, sexual domination, and objectification accompanied each blow, as Butler observes, thus linking buck breaking during slavery to lynchings and, ultimately, to contemporary police violence against African Americans.

How many more Rodney Kings are there? What is the full range of the impact on their families and communities? The exposure of the torture chambers at the Homan police station in Chicago's South Side, in operation between 1971 and 1992, gives us an inkling of an idea. Not unlike the practice of buck breaking during slavery, Vietnam veteran John Burge and his underlings at Homan beat, attacked the genitals of, and sodomized at least 118 (a conservative estimate) mostly African and Latino American men, ostensibly to gain confessions (Curry, 2017; Guarino, 2013). It was the malign neglect of politicians and police administrators who allowed Burge and his subordinates to continue their not-so-secret reign of terror for 20 years. This sort of neglect allowed and allows for the disabling physical and psychological trauma that reverberates among the Black community and is central to the continued production of disabilities in Black America by White America. Tommy Curry (2017) provides examples of a litany of African American men sodomized and sexually assaulted by police. One, a 17-year-old African American honours student from Philadelphia, fundamentally had one of his testicles castrated by a White female police officer who, in frisking him, squeezed his crotch so hard his testicle ruptured with the sound of a busted paper bag. Castration and eugenics meet in quotidian police interactions as stop-and-frisks, using the police as a means of legitimating the state's attack on the sexual reproduction of Black men.

More recently, the police maiming of more and more Black men and the murders of Black men with disabilities has slowly begun to register in scholarly research, policy institutes, and press stories (DeVylder et al., 2017; Edwards et al., 2019; Eunjung, 2020; Laurencin, 2020; McLeod et al., 2020).[16]

Here, both public policy and corporate profiteering—plundering tax dollars by hocking destructive weapons to the police—are at the heart of the disablement of Black America and the killing of Black disabled men (and women). Whether the Baltimore police used bone-crushing batons or not, the sight of Freddie Gray's mangled body being dragged into a "paddy wagon" (originally a slave term for the carts into which freshly whipped, clubbed, and manacled freedom-seekers were tied up) reveals the tip of the iceberg of the systematic disabling of Black men in their encounters with police. Unfortunately, the issue of Black disablement is generally met with the indifference of researchers. Indeed, at the time of this writing, the authors are not able to find any estimates of the financial and social costs borne by impacted Black men (and women), nor the costs borne by their families, and, not least, their caregivers, particularly their mothers.

These historical facts can help us think about and question why the majority of men on death row are not only African American, but also men and boys who live with mental disabilities. Black men with disabilities are the predominant population not only on death row, but for school expulsions and in that other carceral enterprise from which they are dispatched—the public prison (Ramey, 2015). Death row and expulsion both reflect—one actually, the other symbolically—the brutal end for which Black men are prepared by their encounters with school resource officers, police, and prisons. Take, for instance, Kalief Browder: framed and brutalized by police, then further brutalized by guards and other prisoners at Riker's Island. Sadly we know what became of Browder: deeply depressed and experiencing post-traumatic stress and psychological disablement from a lifetime of brutality by police and prisons, he committed suicide. How many Kalief Browders are there? At this point, the research is limited, but scholars are beginning to address this void. What researchers are finding is that depression, suicidal ideation, and general malaise is considerably amplified by both the physical injury and disempowerment implicated in police abuses and violence. These despairing effects of police violence are most pronounced for African Americans.

Related to disabilities arising from state repression in the everyday lives of African Americans, we must also consider how racist ideologies of medicine disable Black people. The impact is evident, for example, in the education system. There is considerable evidence that Black children with disabilities are the ones most likely to be expelled from school (National Centre for Learning Disabilities, 2014; Ramey, 2015). Children of colour, particularly Black children, with manifest and less obvious disabilities are seen as having the full range of abilities as able-bodied children, treated harshly, and presumed guilty until proven innocent (Goff et al., 2014; Lawyers' Committee, 2014). African American children—boys in particular—are presumed to "suffer" a cultural or even genetic "predisposition" to violence. This belief, held by lawmakers, the news media, academics, and scientists, has led to policies and practices not dissimilar to those of the Nazis. As shown by Harriet Washington (2006) in *Medical Apartheid*, African American boys are widely believed by White America to be genetically unfit for civilized existence. The result has been an array of practices from actual to chemical lobotomy, most notably in regimes of drug cocktails aimed to make Black boys docile and manageable. With the idea that Black childhood is a disease, and "crime" its manifestation, eugenics is implied by some academicians to be a method for controlling "criminal behaviour." In reality, since "crime" is seen as a symptom of blackness, such research uses the supposed abortion–crime connection as a euphemism for the eugenic control of African American boys (Donahue & Levitt, 2019).[17]

Over five decades ago, James Baldwin and Frantz Fanon drew attention to the problem of policing and the production of disabilities among colonized groups in the context of White supremacy. It is something of a surprise that so little attention has been paid to this issue by policy makers, scholars, research institutes, and the news media. Surprisingly, disabilities studies scholars themselves seem not to have noticed that these elements of the state coercive apparatus disproportionately produce disabilities in Black men, but also disproportionately target Black boys and men with preexisting disabilities (which are, anyway, very often the products of Black political disablement). The historical continuity of the production of disabilities during slavery, through Jim Crow to the present raises important questions as to what it is about Black men that is the source of this disinterest. In part, the indifference to disabilities, slavery, and Black men is a legacy of indifference to Black humanity, which is at the heart of research about slavery. James H. Sweet (2003) notes:

> Many of the works on American slavery written in the past twenty-five years provide a sanitized view of the institution. Slaves have been depicted as overwhelmingly resilient in withstanding the pain and cruelty of slavery. These works have stressed the vibrancy of slave culture, economy, and society, largely neglecting the physical and psychological tolls that the institution took on the majority of the enslaved...Several recent works have begun to assault the idea of "teflon-coated" slaves who used culture to defend themselves from the brutalities of slavery.
> (pp. 245–46)

But, if a certain inherited indifference toward the dehumanization of Black people predominates among academic work about slavery, what accounts for the lack of interest in both Black men and disabled Black men as victimized by the enduring afterlife of slavery's production of disabilities and Black disablement?

Since the 1970s, a Black feminist discourse has emerged around the phrase "all the men are Black, all the women are White, but some us [i.e., Black women] are brave"—this alongside the thesis that the stereotyped Black nationalist "patriarchy" was the archetype for Black (heterosexual) masculinities. In addition to feminist theoreticians, this perspective has had currency in disabilities studies (see Lukin, 2013). As noted by scholars critical of the standard pathologizing framing of Black men (Curry, 2017; Lemelle, 2010; Thomas, 2007), the problem with this trope is that it avoids the overwhelming evidence that the hypervisibility of Black men is in fact deleterious to their mental, physical, and economic wellbeing, and that of Black women, children, and the broader community as well. The harms and injuries inflicted on (provisionally) able-bodied Black men is related to, but amplified for, Black disabled men. From our perspective, any serious criticism about the abolition of police and prisons must place at its centre disabilities, being fully cognizant that the humanity of disabled Black men hangs in the balance.

Sexual Agency and Disability

While mass incarceration and police violence reveal the problematic convergence of gender-based violence, disabilities, and the disabling of Black America, people with disabilities are now beginning to explore what their sexual agency might look like. For example, the short documentary *Double the Trouble, Twice the Fun* (Hillenbrand & Hillenbrand, 1992) explores queer sex and desire among disabled persons. More recently, Patty Berne,[18] a disabled queer woman of colour, and Leroy F. Moore Jr. started the Sins Invalid (www.sinsinvalid.org) project in 2006. This film and performance project incubates and celebrates artists with disabilities. It centralizes artists of colour and queer and gender-variant artists as communities that historically have been marginalized. Sins Invalid explores the themes of sexuality, embodiment, and the disabled body. Conceived of and led by disabled people of colour, the project develops and presents cutting-edge work where normative perspectives of sex and sexiness are challenged. The documentary offers a different vision of beauty and sexuality that is inclusive of all individuals and communities. Sins Invalid recognizes that people with disabilities will be liberated as whole beings—as disabled, queer, gender-non-conforming, trans, women, men, and non-binary of any and every race and colour. The project challenges us to recognize that we are far greater whole than partitioned. It ultimately recognizes that allies emerge from many communities and that demographic identity alone does not determine one's commitment to liberation.

A cofounder and contributor to the development of Sins Invalid, Moore is nonetheless concerned that there remains a lack of Black and other men of colour among the disabled men in the project. His concern centres around the fact that there are few spaces for disabled men to talk about sex, sexuality, and other topics. The lack of avenues for disabled Black men to explore these issues led Moore and Krip-Hop Nation to organize an informal gathering in 2014 titled Black Disabled Men Get Together. Moore and Krip-Hop Nation continue to promote the value of men's circles, especially young Black men's programs, and advocate for these to be more inclusive. The aim is to facilitate future conversations and build networks that resist the isolation of Black disabled men. The programs further aim to demonstrate that ableism, racism, and the fear of Black disabled people increase the risk of state violence, sexual assault, and killings by strangers, friends, family members, and personal attendants. Until we come to terms with the ways that ableism, ageism, classism, homophobia, racism, and sexism enable predators to assault and exploit persons with disabilities, the sexual rights of persons with disabilities will continue to be a vibrant site for political struggle.

Toward a Krip-Hop Resistance to Anti-Ableist Respectability Politics in Black America

We concur with Dr. Joy DeGruy Leary's (2005) proposition that African Americans experience *post-traumatic slave syndrome* (PTSS). Her thesis holds that the exploitation, pain, and trauma that endure in "slavery's afterlife" (Hartman, 2003) were produced by White society's pervasive dehumanization of Black people and indifference to the harms it caused them. Black people have never received acknowledgement, apology, compensation, or therapeutic treatment that would enable them either to cope with or make sense of the abuses of slavery and the White supremacy that replaced it. From a Krip-Hop perspective, the implications of PTSS in part involve Black people's own repression of disability. We think this repression, which can be seen in the exclusion and shunning of children with disabilities, is the result of Black people playing into the respectability politics of ableism. On the one hand (though in an absurd way), this makes sense. African Americans are so despised as appallingly defective citizens that ableism, though it mirrors a generalized anti-Black racism, becomes a way for Black people to experience a sense of "normality" in White-dominated American culture. But we think, also, that this type of ableist respectability politics has serious consequences for Black communities to mobilize a politics of resistance that would bring tangible benefits to all, especially in poor Black communities exposed to environmental racism, aggressive policing, and other social determinants of ill health.

Ableist respectability politics has led Black America to treat disability as a condition that ought to be overcome. Of course, well-known personalities such as Ray Charles and Stevie Wonder reveal something of the incredible capacities of people with disabilities, but because of our current ableist bias, we know very little of the extent and range of the abilities of Black people in the United States from slavery to the present. What if we can know something of the determination of Black disabled people as leaders of rebellions, revolts, and operations like the Underground Railroad? Indeed, one of prime figures of the Underground Railroad was Harriet Tubman, a woman who lived with seizures due to head trauma from her slave master throwing a metal weight at another enslaved person, striking Tubman instead.

PTSS describes a set of behaviours, beliefs, and actions associated with or related to the multigenerational trauma experienced by African Americans. This sort of trauma is not limited to undiagnosed and untreated PTSD in enslaved Africans and their descendants. Similar to what was noted by Du Bois's (1899/1967) Philadelphia study, PTSS posits that centuries of slavery in the United States, followed by systemic and structural racism and oppression—including lynching, Jim Crow laws, and unwarranted mass incarceration—have resulted in multigenerational maladaptive behaviours. The syndrome continues because children, whose families and communities endure structural violence amplified by PTSS, must live as best they can with "maladaptive conditions," as Martin Luther King Jr. (1968) called the exploitative conditions of African American life.

From the perspective of a Krip-Hop theory of disabilities, PTSS is important for helping us to think about disabilities differently in the African American context. Rather than disabilities being seen as a sign of a moral stigma (Goffman, 1963) or a signifier of the projected anxieties and fears that able-bodied people project onto people with disabilities, a Krip-Hop theory says that African Americans should place disabilities at the heart of their economic, cultural, social, and political lives.

It is possible that a radical rethinking of Blackness and disabilities—not as separate, but as a holistic reality—will do two things. First, it will, in an affirming sense, "normalize" disabilities to enable Black persons with disabilities to experience life to the fullest of their potentialities. To deny Black disabled people the human essential of achieving in an ongoing way their actual realization of their potentialities[19] is to deny them their humanity and membership in the Black community. It is necessary to reject Black respectability politics around disabilities that conform with the hegemonic norm to exclude, oppress, and stigmatize persons on the spectrum of disabilities. Here we draw on Carter G. Woodson's (1933/2009) Negro History Week, which was built on the idea that if only Black people could imagine themselves as agents of history, *with* history, and with contributions to humanity, they will transform themselves beyond the limitations on their self-concept imposed and constantly reinforced by the myths of White America. In this sense, central to Black people's liberation is a project of refusal and resistance to hegemonic norms.

We suggest a public pedagogy that centres awareness of disabilities in Black people's lives through histories that name, reclaim, and represent Black disabled people in all their variety *as* Black people *with* disabilities. At the same time, holding Black people with ontological disabilities at the centre of a Black politics insists that justice and fairness are human deserts; it is a project that recognizes that the essence of Black politics is to resist the social determinants of disablement that both produces and oppresses the Black disabled in particular and the Black community in general. This, to us, is a necessary and minimum condition for rethinking exclusionary practices and the discourse of respectability politics, which assumes that Black disabled people need to be "integrated" and "rehabilitated" into the burning house that is the hegemonic myth of a stable "ability" and "normality" (see Lukin, 2013, pp. 312–13).

This approach will be important for the politics of representation to facilitate disabled Black people, especially children, to come out from the shadows and see that people with disabilities are central to Black life in the United States. Centring disabilities this way will also open up space to expose and resist hierarchies among and within Black disabled people. The point is not to excuse (provisionally) abled persons from ableism, but to resist the performance of hegemonic "normality" among disabled Black people. Particularly for Black disabled children, this helps them resist internalized shame; for provisionally abled children, a critical and inclusive disabilities education will help them to understand that abilities are a spectrum and that ableness is a social construction. And for provisionally abled adults who may be in denial about the salience of disabilities, which are so much a part of Black existence in the United States since slavery, they will be more able to develop a language, narrative, and practice that takes up activism and resistance from a sociopolitical perspective in which disablement is ontological, political, and multiple (i.e., age, classe, gender, race, and sexuality all translate to increased incidence of ontological disabilities).

We believe that with this sort of psychocultural shift in representation and political practice there will be a strengthening of abled and disabled Black Americans better positioned to engage in communal activism. To prioritize the strength of the community is to ensure that accessibility for disabled Black people is as much a priority as eliminating the social determinants that produce disabilities. It is important, then, to recognize what is already a fact: disabilities are *already* at the centre of African American life. It is just as important to provide a language to make this explicit. If we recognize that, in both concrete and ritualized ways, capitalism and White supremacy are built upon a moral philosophy that justifies the practice of subjecting African Americans to what Orlando Patterson (1982) calls "social death" (see pp. 38–45), then disabilities can be seen in a different way. As Black people are subject to ritualized social death through poverty, police violence, mass incarceration, pollution, and chronic illness, all of which result from White America's regime of anti-Black structural violence, we can say that central to achieving the fullness of Black humanity in the United States of America is resistance to ableism in general, as well as internalized ableism and external political disablement.

So, what does this look like? We need to see that the disabling of Black America runs on a spectrum. At one end are "acquired" disabilities. These are wholly preventable forms of traumatic disablement caused by structural violence such as poisoned water in Flint, Michigan, hog farms around African American communities in North Carolina, chemical plants in coastal Texas, and so many other Black American majority counties and municipalities. Recent data indicates that of the 9% of the US population with disabilities, there is a swath of the United States, descending from the east coast (Pennsylvania and New York) and then curving toward the southern states (to Texas, Oklahoma, and Arizona) called the "disability belt" (Ross & Bateman, 2017). While there are vast variations in regional incidence of disabilities with the result of significant racial variation, among Americans with disabilities 30% are Native Americans and Native Alaskans, 25% are African Americans, 20% White Americans, and 16% Latinx (Centre for Disease Control, 2020). While in some states such as Florida, North Carolina, and Connecticut, Black Americans have lower rates of disabilities than White Americans, in most other regions, census metropolitan data reveals that "blacks have higher disability rates than whites, up to 2.5 times greater" (Ross & Bateman, 2017). Irrespective of the general impression of this data, there has been a mountain of evidence from the late 1960s to the present demonstrating that the exposure of African Americans to lead and other toxins has a direct impact on morbidity, mortality, and cognitive impairments that lead to interpersonal violence (Drum, 2016; Masters, 2007; Masters, et al., 2007; Newfield, 1971). Quite aside from the massive health costs foisted onto Black America from official negligence and corporate malfeasance, African Americans must also cope with the disabling effects of the interpersonal violence that is correlated with White America's chemical warfare on them. Further, interpersonal violence in Black America, especially among the youth, contributes to the production of ontological disabilities; this, too, must be understood as a symptom of the organized disabling of Black America.

Conclusion

Krip-Hop Nation continues to be a work in progress. Its very existence is evidence that people with disabilities, especially Black people, can make the leap from decades of abuse, erasure, hiding, and exploitation toward Black disabilities as a site of empowerment. For Moore and Krip-Hop Nation, there are three avenues to self-empowerment and correcting history. The first seeks out and brings to presence Black disabled people who have challenged the ableism in our Black communities across the nation and around the world. The second promotes self-education of the disabled as a robust and coherent politics that challenges structures of inequality. The third supports Black mothers, but does not exclude fathers, because they are the first advocates and activists for equitable services, education, and accessibility for disabled children and youth.

In 2008, Moore was involved in The Men's Story Project (MSP), a replicable storytelling and community dialogue project that invites critical exploration of social ideas about masculinity in the public eye around the world through the less-often-heard voices and stories of men. In the MSP, boys, men, and folks who identify in any way with maleness publicly share personal stories that help transform social ideas about masculinity. The aim is to support healthy masculinities and social justice for all people. The MSP is rooted in an antiracist, intersectional feminist framework. The mission of the MSP is to strengthen social norms around the world that support healthy masculinities and gender justice.

As a contribution to MSP, Krip-Hop members like Moore and Rob Da' Noize Temple composed a song in the radical tradition of progressive Black masculinity described by Tommy J. Curry (2017) and Athena Mutua (2006b) and her anthology's contributors. The song draws us in important ways to recognize that, when disabilities and masculinities are viewed through the antiracist and anticolonial theories of James Baldwin and Frantz Fanon, new vistas are opened to reflect on the ways that disabilities are at the centre of resistance and struggles for justice. Focusing on Black masculinity and sexuality, the song—"Man to Man Talk"—is offered here, less as a conclusion to this essay than an invitation to continue a dialogue that places disabilities at the heart of African American arts, culture, and politics, and that promotes and enlarges our experience of progressive Black masculinities.

Man to Man Talk

LEROY F. MOORE JR. & ROB DA' NOIZE TEMPLE

Hey you stop stop I'm right behind you
I'm Black like you my brother
Yeah the Black Kripple
Look at me look at me
Hear this hear this

But let's go back born DOA, Dead On Arrival
Caused lack of oxygen to the brain
CP Cerebral Palsy POC Person Of Color
Big Black Football player, my dad
In the waiting room didn't like the doctor's news
Men in white suites pumping my chest, eyes opened
Welcome to the living Leroy

My life
Black and disabled
Home was stable
Adults thought I was unable
Like a penny I have been
Flipped dual identities—

My two communities don't want me
Felt like I was homeless

My childhood haunts me
Children were ruthless
Racism & Ableism created a mask
I continue to see single Black mothers with their disabled sons
Husbands gone could not deal
Mothers strong had to be real
Black disabled boys from broken homes
Lingering questions, did Dad leave because of me
Girlfriends not a reality
Women want my advice but can't see me as a mate
Black disabled men are in a stalemate
Will I die a single man?

But it's another cold night
The Isley Brothers singing *Between the Sheets*
While Black disabled men sleeping on the streets
Sex education came from the Lusty Lady
It's a lonely world

Self-employment, self-love putting society's attitudes on the shelf
Black sisters don't know what they are missing
She, a Black woman
Me, a Black disabled man
We were trained to fear, compete and not talk to one another
Is this why all my intimate relationships are with White women?

Race + Disability divided by Sexuality = uh uh
I was 3/5 of a person
With a disability I'm not even on the scale
Disability & Masculinity? Can we talk?

Black Masculinity has to make room for my body
Ask Teddy Pendergrass
The Black Stallion of the '70s & '80s
Regained his sexuality as a wheelchair user
Now that is the true strength of a man
Black Disabled and Masculine
Morris Day, What Time Is It? Somebody Bring me a mirror
Cause I know I'm fine

Masculine mixing with feminine
Like all of us I came from a woman and a man
My sexuality goes deeper than what you see
But you treat me like Ralph Ellison's invisible man
Bumping up against our shadows

It took forty years to walk with my head up
Saying Black is beautiful and
Disability is gorgeous
Too sexy for society's straight jacket
Wearing my sexuality on my sleeves
My body, mind and soul stepping into the spotlight

You see society tries to put me down
But you can't keep a good man down
This is a message to all my black disabled brothers
Feel your masculinity and step into your sexuality
Brothers, it's time we ALL had a man-to-man talk

Authors' Note

We are indebted to Maureen Connolly, Christopher Lytle, and Delores Mullings for commenting on earlier iterations of this paper.

Notes

1. Cited in Rediker (2007), pp. 34–35.
2. For an explanation of our use of *black/Black* and *white/White*, Kitossa (Introduction to this volume, n. 1).
3. Joy James (1996) undertakes a succinct critique of Foucault's eliding of the spectacle of anti-Black state (e.g., death penalty, incarceration, and police violence) and vigilante violence (e.g., lynching and rape) in the United States (see pp. 124–43).
4. Similar to Foucault's avoidance of the violence of transatlantic slavery and its enduring afterlife in public spectacles of tortured Black people's bodies in South Africa and the Southern United States, his avoidance of the relationship between early psychiatry and medical experimentation on enslaved Africans, too, raises questions of selective historical engagement. Alerting us to slavery and the production of madness among enslaved Africans arising from the madness of quotidian sadism of the West, La Marr J. Bruce (2017) colourfully demonstrates that Foucault's "ship of fools" was more than an isolated space of containment—that the ship of madness was metaphorically and literally a multidimensional, ideological, and spatial reality in which slave labour, including the broken bodies and minds it creates, "commandeers the ship of fools, tows the ship of fools, orients Western notions of madness and Reason, and helps propel this process we call modernity" (p. 304). Psychiatry—another area of Foucault's specialization—also played a key role in promoting anti-Black sanist tropes. Harriet Washington (2006) details that, in 1851, William Cartwright concocted a range of "uniquely" African psychiatric "diseases": *drapetomania* for running-away madness; *dysthesia Aethopica* for the Luddite-like tendency to destroy "productive" property; *hebetude* for "laziness"; and *cachexia Africana* for eating (mineral rich) clay, chalk, and dirt owing to starvation diets (see p. 36). To be clear about all this, it is not that Foucault never addressed race. It is that this address was never in relation or reference to an exogenous Other. Focused solely on Europe, Foucault, imagined racism as an endogenous development arising from the project of "normalization" that demonized difference, as evidenced by the imagining of disabilities as monstrous and sexualities as abnormal and deviant (Taylor, 2011). Foucault's evasion and furtive approach to race and racism in the midst of France's dying colonial empire has not gone without comment and puzzlement (Young, 1995).
5. (Un)health, as both question and problem in the United States, is all too apparent in the 2020 COVID-19 pandemic. Among the poorest of citizens in mainland United States, African Americans have been devastated by the virus in large measure because they suffer from preexisting diseases that make them more susceptible in the first instance—diabetes being chief among them. Much prior to COVID-19, which has already carried off so many, diabetes was already ravaging the bodies of African Americans. Lizzie Presser (2020) exposes the many-decade-long, diabetes-related amputation crisis confronting African Americans, showcasing the story of Dr. Foluso Fakorede who has challenged the routinization of amputation of African Americans in the Delta region of Mississippi. Fakorede notes that it is not only genetics, lifestyle, poverty, and food that contribute to diabetes, but overwhelmed physicians, physician ignorance about the angiograms, and the prosurgery reward structure of American hospitals and insurance

companies that literally promote amputations. Fakorede notes that the regional distribution of amputations in Mississippi exactly maps onto the highest density of enslaved African Americans in the Antebellum South. He notes the irony that back then, too, African Americans were subject to amputations. Whether past or present, the preventability and disproportionality of amputations raises serious concerns for the capacity of African Americans to support themselves as well as the increased and debilitating financial and emotional costs on relatives, thereby deepening and extending the disabling of African Americans.

6. Baldwin (1972) notes that: "Then, as now, a Northern policeman, black or white...introduce[s] into one's life the stunning realization that...life can be ended at any moment" (p. 58). Baldwin's words today evoke images of Eric Garner, Freddie Gray, and George Floyd; we apprehend the still-current dreadful carnage that police produce.
7. Baldwin (1972) notes that it was not only sons who indicted their fathers, it was also daughters. On visiting a long-time friend, he describes the reaction of his friend's step-daughter to the man eschewing any activism:

> I and a black militant could possibly disagree about anything. But what was most striking about our brief exchange was that it obliquely revealed how little the girl respected him at all. This was not revealed by anything she said to him, but by the fact that she said nothing to him. She barely looked at him. He didn't count. I always think that it is a terrible thing to happen to a man, especially in his own house, and I am always terribly humiliated for the man to whom it happens. Then of course you get angry at the man for allowing it to happen. (pp. 16–17)

8. Bell takes for granted that Emmett Till whistled at Carolyn Bryant. In 2007, Bryant admitted that her testimony that Till whistled was false—a fact only disclosed in 2017 (Carroll, 2017).
9. Baldwin (1972) understands the need for a scapegoat as a crisis of personality produced by an ethically and morally bankrupt civilizational complex the ontology of which depends on the negation of the Other—or, in other words, the refusal of its own responsibility. It is worth citing him at length to grasp how ontologically impaired the White self is in its dependence on what it negates:

> [The] failure of the private life has always had the devastating effect on American public conduct, and on black–white relations. If Americans were not so terrified of their private selves, they would never have needed to invent and could never have become so dependent on what they still call "the Negro problem." This problem, which they invented in order to safeguard their purity, has made of them criminals and monsters, and it is destroying them; and this is not from anything blacks may or may not be doing but because of the role a guilty and constricted white imagination has assigned to the blacks. That the scapegoat pays for the sins of others is well known, but this is only legend, and a revealing one at that. In fact, however the scapegoat may be made to suffer, his suffering

> cannot purify the sinner; it merely incriminates him the more, and it seals damnation. The scapegoat, eventually, is released, to death: his murderer continues to live. The suffering of the scapegoat has resulted in seas of blood, and yet not one sinner has been saved, or changed, by this despairing ritual...People pay for what they do, and, still more, for what they have allowed themselves to become. And they pay for it very simply: by the lives they lead. (pp. 54–55)

10. The US government's COINTELPRO is a case in point. Designed to destroy the movement for Black liberation, it relied upon clandestine communicative deception and spectularization of state-sanctioned murder and breaking of Black people's bodies (see Thomas, 2007). Arguably, the quotidian realities of police violence against the Black disabled—realities that produce mental and physical disabilities and murders—constitute the White racial state's performative reaffirmation of White collective ontological negation of Blackness.
11. See Kitossa (Introduction to this volume) for a critique of "patriarchy."
12. For those enslaved Black men already "broken," the routine degradation of genital exposure from being underclothed from childhood through to adulthood, was a ritualized form of castration, which had as much psychological trauma for the men as for their reputation before the women and children of the slave community. Enslaved men fulminated at the implications. Anticipating James Baldwin's concern about the destruction of Black fathers' esteem, one formerly enslaved man wrote, "Fathers! Think of being tied up and stripped before our wife and children" (cited in Foster, 2019, p. 24). This was not merely a matter of pride. In one instance noted by Theodore Weld (1839), two White men "named Wilson found a fine looking [*sic*] negro man at 'Danbridge Quarter,' without a pass; and flogged him so that he died in a short time. They were not punished" (p. 47). Of course, as also cited by Weld, enslaved women were not spared wanton floggings to death and outright murder. Yet, for the males who were especially targeted for "buck breaking," the enduring trauma at not being able to eat, defecate, lie down, urinate, walk, or wear clothes were constant reminders to enslaved men and their communities that the "negro [man] has no family; [and] woman is merely the temporary companion of his pleasures, and his children are upon an equal footing with himself from the moment of their birth" (de Tocqueville, 1835/2004, p. 386). Even White children, any White child, be they in the public or private domain, could command enslaved Black men to their bidding (Osofsky, 1969).
13. Such references were not merely metaphorical. They recalled those who lived with amputations. Metaphorically, however, terms such as *peg leg* alluded to the coffles of enslaved African men and women who were forced marched from purchase in Virginia and the Carolinas to the Deep South. Whereas females and children were loosely tied with rope, males were chained, 30 or more at a time, in rows of two by heavy metal chains, manacles on hands and feet with each man carrying a heavy metal ball (Baptist, 2014, pp. 1–6). Lacerations on ankles frequently lead to infections and sepsis with either prolonged periods of infection or gangrene leading to amputations.
14. Heyward was an elite White South Carolinian descended from the plantocracy. He spent considerable time in his late teens working on the Charleston waterfront with African

Americans. He himself contracted polio in his late teens and subsequently contracted a number of respiratory ailments.

15. The circulation of disease and ill health in Black communities arising from mass incarceration of Black men is akin to the Tuskeegee experiment (1939–1970) in which, as Harriet Washington (2006) documents, the US federal government allowed some 400 poor Black men to go untreated for syphilis. Many of the infected men were never tracked and thus were allowed to infect their male and female sex partners. Similarly, prisons in the United States are rife with experimentation for corporate, military, pharmaceutical, and prison control purposes (Mitford, 1973; Washington, 2006).

16. Over the past 5 years there have been a number of high-profile instances of police murders of disabled Black men: Marcus-David Peters, March 14, 2018; Miles Hall, June 2, 2019; Daniel Prude, March 22, 2020; Steven Taylor, April 18, 2020; Kurt Andras Reinhold, September 25, 2020; Walter Wallace Jr, October 26, 2020...

17. For a critique of this research, see Harriet Washington (2006) and Foote and Goetz (2008).

18. Patty Berne is Cofounder and Director of Sins Invalid. She currently chairs the Board of Directors at San Francisco Women Against Rape and is the 2009 recipient of the Empress I Jose Sarria Award for Uncommon Leadership in the field of LGBTQI and disability rights by the National Gay and Lesbian Task Force.

19. For a discussion of the moral philosophy of actual and potential realizations, see Johan Galtung's (1969) highly original article on the point.

Bibliography

Adi, H., & Sherwood, M. (2003). *Pan-African history: Political figures from Africa and the diaspora since 1787*. Routledge.

Allen, T.W. (1997). *The invention of the White race: The origin of racial oppression in Anglo-America*. Verso.

Bailey, M. (2011). "The illest": Disability as metaphor in hip hop music. In C. Bell (Ed.), *Blackness and disability: Critical examinations and cultural interventions* (pp. 141–61). LIT Verlag Münster.

Baldwin, J. (1963). *The fire next time*. Laurel.

Baldwin, J. (1966). A report from occupied territory. *The Nation*. https://www.thenation.com/article/report-occupied-territory/

Baldwin, J. (1967, April 9). Negroes are anti-Semitic because they're anti-White. *New York Times*. https://www.nytimes.com/1967/04/09/archives/negroes-are-antisemitic-because-theyre-antiwhite-why-negroes-are.html

Baldwin, J. (1972). *No name in the street*. The Dial Press.

Baldwin, J. (1984). *Notes of a native son*. Beacon Press. (Original work published 1955)

Baldwin, J. (1993). The male prison. In J. Baldwin, *Nobody knows my name: More notes of a native son*. Vintage Books. (Original work published 1954)

Baptist, E.E. (2014). *The half has never been told: Slavery and the making of American capitalism*. Basic Books.

Bell, C.M. (Ed.). (2011). *Blackness and disability: Critical examinations and cultural interventions*. LIT Verlag Münster.

Blackburn, R. (1998). *The making of New World slavery: From the Baroque to the modern, 1492–1800*. Verso.

Boster, D. (2013). *African American slavery and disability: Bodies, property and power in the Antebellum South, 1800–1860*. Routledge.

Boyd, S.C. (2004). *From witches to crack moms: Women, drug law, and policy*. Carolina Academic Press.

Bruce, L.J. (2017). Mad is a place, or, the slave ship tows the ship of fools. *American Quarterly*, 69(2), 303–08.

Bureau of Justice Statistics. (2015). *Disabilities among prison and jail inmates*. https://www.bjs.gov/content/pub/pdf/dpji1112_sum.pdf

Burke, T. (2017, November 9). #MeToo was started for Black and Brown women and girls. They're still being ignored. *Washington Post*. https://www.washingtonpost.com/news/post-nation/wp/2017/11/09/the-waitress-who-works-in-the-diner-needs-to-know-that-the-issue-of-sexual-harassment-is-about-her-too/?utm_term=.35adcf0e5eb0

Bush, B. (1990). *Slave women in Caribbean society, 1650–1832*. Indiana University Press.

Butler, J. (1993). Endangered/endangering: Schematic racism and White paranoia. In R. Gooding-Williams (Ed.), *Reading Rodney King, reading urban uprising* (pp. 15–22). Routledge.

Cannon, L. (1997). *Official negligence: How Rodney King and the riots changed Los Angeles and the LAPD*. Times Books / Random House.

Carroll, R. (2017, January 27). Woman at centre of Emmitt Till case tells author she fabricated testimony. *The Guardian*. https://www.theguardian.com/us-news/2017/jan/27/emmett-till-book-carolyn-bryant-confession

Centre for Disease Control. (2020). *Adults with disabilities: Ethnicity and race*. https://www.cdc.gov/ncbddd/disabilityandhealth/materials/infographic-disabilities-ethnicity-race.html

Couser, G.T. (2017). Disability, life narrative and representation. In L. Davis (Ed.), *The disability studies reader* (5th ed.; pp. 531–34). Routledge.

Curry, T. (2017). *The man-not: Race, class, genre, and the dilemmas of Black manhood*. Temple University Press.

Davis, A.Y. (1971). The Black woman's role in the community of slaves. *The Black Scholar, 3*(4), 1–14.

Davis, A.Y. (1983). *Women, race, and class*. Random House.

Davis, A.Y. (2003). *Are prisons obsolete?* Seven Stories Press.

Del Zotto, A., & Jones, A. (2002, March 23–27). *Male-on-male sexual violence in wartime: Human rights' last taboo?* [Paper presentation]. Annual Convention of the International Studies Association (ISA), New Orleans, LA, United States. http://adamjones.freeservers.com/malerape.htm

DeVylder, J.E., Frey, J.J., Cogburn, C.D., Wilcox, H.C., Sharpe, T.L., Oh, H.Y., Nam, B., & Link, B.G. (2017). Elevated prevalence of suicide attempts among victims of police violence in the USA. *Journal of Urban Health*, 94(5), 629–36. http://doi.org/10.1007/s11524-017-0160-3

DiPiero, T. (2002). *White men aren't*. Duke University Press.

Donahue, J.J. & Levitt, S.D. (2019, May). *The impact of legalized abortion on crime over the last two decades* (Working Paper no. 25863). National Bureau of Economic Research. https://doi.org/10.3386/w25863

Douglas, M. (1970). *Natural symbols: Explorations in cosmology*. Pantheon Books.

Douglass, F. (2009). *Narrative of the life of Frederick Douglass, an American slave, written by himself*. Belknap Press. (Original work published 1845)

Drazen, C.C. (2012). Both sides of the two-sided coin: Rehabilitation of African American disabled veterans. In C.M. Bell (Ed.), *Blackness and disabilities: Critical examinations and cultural interventions* (pp. 149–62). LIT Verlag Münster.

Drum, K. (2016). Lead: America's real criminal element. *Mother Jones*. https://www.motherjones.com/environment/2016/02/lead-exposure-gasoline-crime-increase-children-health/

Du Bois, W.E.B. (1967). *The Philadelphia Negro: A social study*. Schocken Books. (Original work published 1899)

Dusinberre, W. (2000). *Them dark days: Slavery in the American rice swamps*. University of Georgia Press

Edwards, F., Lee, H., & Esposito, M. (2019). Risk of being killed by police use of force in the United States by age, race–ethnicity, and sex. *Proceedings of the National Academy of Sciences, 116*(34), 16793–98. https://doi.org/10.1073/pnas.1821204116

Eunjung, A. (2020, 5 July). Quadriplegic man's death from COVID-19 spotlights questions of disability, race and family. *Washington Post*. https://www.washingtonpost.com/health/2020/07/05/coronavirus-disability-death/

Fanon, F. (1965). *A dying colonialism* (H. Chevalier, Trans.). Grove Press. (Original work published 1959)

Fanon, F. (1968). *The wretched of the earth* (C. Farrington, Trans.). Grove Press. (Original work published 1963)

Fanon, F. (1977). *Black skin, white masks* (R. Philcox, Trans.). Grove Press. (Original work published 1952)

Fels, H. (n.d.). Learning disabilities in prison [PowerPoint slides]. *The University of California San Francisco School of Medicine*. http://odpc.ucsf.edu/sites/odpc.ucsf.edu/files/pdf_docs/REVISEDforensicpsychSQ.pdf

Filipovic, J. (2012, February 21). Is the US the only country where more men are raped than women? *The Guardian*. https://www.theguardian.com/commentisfree/cifamerica/2012/feb/21/us-more-men-raped-than-women

Foner, E. (Ed). (1986). *W.E.B. Du Bois speaks: Speeches and addresses 1920–1963, with a tribute to Dr. Kwame Nkrumah*. Pathfinder.

Foote, C.L., & Goetz, C.F. (2008). The impact of legalized abortion on crime: Comment. *The Quarterly Journal of Economics, 123*(1), 407–23. https://doi.org/10.1162/qjec.2008.123.1.407

Foster, T.A. (2011). The sexual abuse of Black men under American slavery. *Journal of History of Sexuality, 20*(3), 445–64. https://www.utexaspressjournals.org/doi/abs/10.5555/jhs.2011.20.3.445

Foster, T.A. (2019). *Rethinking Rufus: Sexual violations of enslaved men*. University of Georgia Press.

Foucault, M. (1979). *Discipline and punish: The birth of the prison*. Vintage Books.

Galtung, J. (1969). Violence, peace, and peace research. *Journal of Peace Research, 6*(3), 167–91. https://www.jstor.org/stable/422690

Garvey, M. (1992). *Philosophy and opinions of Marcus Garvey*. Atheneum.

Girard, R. (1989). *The scapegoat* (Y. Freccero, Trans.). The Johns Hopkins Press.

Goff, P.A., Jackson, M.C., Di Leone, B.A.L., Culotta, C.M., & DiTomasso, N.A. (2014). The essence of innocence: Consequences of dehumanizing Black children. *Journal of Personality and Social Psychology, 106*(4), 526–45. http://doi.org/10.1037/a0035663

Goffman, E. (1963). *Stigma: Notes on the management of spoiled identity*. Prentice-Hall.

Gould, S.J. (1984). Carrie Buck's daughter. *Natural History, 93*(7), 14–18.

Guarino, M. (2013). Chicago mayor Rahm Emanuel apologizes for two decades of police torture. *Christian Science Monitor*. https://www.csmonitor.com/USA/Justice/2013/0912/Chicago-Mayor-Rahm-Emanuel-apologizes-for-two-decades-of-police-torture

Hadley, S., & Yancy, G. (Eds.). (2012). *Therapeutic uses of rap and hip-hop*. Routledge.

Haisman, A., & L.J. Davis. (2009). Normal and normalcy. In S. Burch (Ed.), *Encyclopedia of American disability history* (pp. 662–64). Facts on File. https://www.handicapcenter.com/wp-content/uploads/2014/05/Encyclopedia-of-American-Disability-History.pdf

Hartman, S.V. (2003). *Scenes of subjection: Terror, slavery, and self-making in nineteenth-century America*. Oxford University Press.

Henning, K. (2017). Boys to men: The role of policing in the socialization of Black boys. In A.J. Davis (Ed.), *Policing the Black man: Arrest, prosecution, and imprisonment* (pp. 57–94). Vintage Books.

Hillenbrand, D., & Hillenbrand, S. (Directors). (1992). *Double the trouble, twice the fun* [Film]. Hillenbrand Holdings.

hooks, bell. (1990). *Ain't I a woman? Black women and feminism*. South End Press. (Original work published 1981)

Ipsen, P. (2015). *Atlantic slavers and intermarriage on the Gold Coast*. University of Pennsylvania Press.

Isaacs, H.R. (1967). Group identity and political change: The role of color and physical characteristics. *Daedalus, 96*(2), 353–75.

James, C.L.R. (1963). *The Black Jacobins: Tousaint L'Ouverture and the San Domingo revolution*. Vintage Books.

James, J. (1996). *Resisting state violence: Radicalism, gender & race in U.S. culture*. University of Minnesota Press. http://wrap.warwick.ac.uk/596/1/WRAP_Jones_If_this_be_living.pdf

Jones-Rogers, S.E. (2019). *They were her property: White women as slave owners in the American South*. Yale University Press.

Khazan, O. (2015). Most prisoners are mentally ill. *The Atlantic*. https://www.theatlantic.com/health/archive/2015/04/more-than-half-of-prisoners-are-mentally-ill/389682/

King, M.L., Jr. (1968). The role of the behavioral scientist in the civil rights movement. *Journal of Social Issues, 24*(1), 1–12. https://doi.org/10.1111/j.1540-4560.1968.tb01465.x

Kuppers, P. (2015). Performance. In R. Adams, B. Reiss, & D. Serlin (Eds.), *Keywords for disability studies* (pp. 390–95). New York University Press.

Laurencin, C.T. (2020). Unconscious bias, racism, and trauma-informed policing: An address and message to the Connecticut Racial Profiling Prohibition Project advisory board. *Journal of Racial and Ethnic Health Disparities, 7*, 590–91. https://doi.org/10.1007/s40615-020-00794-8

Lawyers' Committee for Civil Rights and Economic Justice. (2014). *Not measuring up: The state of school discipline in Massachusetts*. http://lawyerscom.org/wp-content/uploads/2014/11/Not-Measuring-up_-The-State-of-School-Discipline-in-Massachusetts.pdf

Leary, J.D. (2005). *Post traumatic slave syndrome: America's legacy of enduring injury and healing*. Uptone Press.

Lemelle, A. (2010). *Black masculinity and sexual politics*. Routledge.

Lukin, J. (2013). Disability and Blackness. In D.J. Lennard (Ed.), *The disability studies reader* (4th ed.; pp. 308–15). Routledge.

Masters, R.D. (2007). Heavy metal pollution and race as factors in hypertension and heart disease. *Scientific American*. https://static.scientificamerican.com/sciam/assets/media/pdf/Mn_Pb_HypertenFinal.pdf

Masters, R., Hone, B., & Doshi, A. (2003). *Environmental pollution, neurotoxicity, and criminal violence*. In J. Rose (Ed.), *Environmental toxicology: Current developments* (pp. 13–48). CRC Press.

McHugh, G.A. (1978). *Christian faith and criminal justice: Toward a Christian response to crime and punishment*. Paulist Press.

McLeod, M., Heller, D., Manze, M., & Echeverria, S.E. (2020). Police interactions and the mental health of Black Americans: A systematic review. *Journal of Racial and Ethnic Health Disparities, 7*(1), 10–27. https://doi.org/10.1007/s40615-019-00629-1

Mitford, J. (1973). *Kind and unusual punishment: The prison business*. Alfred A. Knopf.

Moore, L.F., Jr. (2018, February 19). Separation from the Black community since slavery: Black disabled folks. *POOR Magazine*. https://www.poormagazine.org/node/5734

Moore, L.F., Jr. (2019, May 19). Afro-Krip original terminology/theory by Krip-Hop Nation. *Krip-Hop Nation*. https://kriphopnation.com/afro-krip-original-terminologytheory-by-krip-hop-nation/

Morgan, J. (2017). Prisoners with physical disabilities are forgotten and neglected in America. *ACLU*. https://www.aclu.org/blog/prisoners-rights/solitary-confinement/prisoners-physical-disabilities-are-forgotten-and

Mustakeem, S.M. (2016). *Slavery at sea: Terror, sex, and sickness in the Middle Passage*. University of Chicago Press.

Munford, C.J. (1996). *Race and reparations: A Black perspective for the 21st century*. Africa World Press.

Mutua, A. (2006a). Introduction. In A.D. Mutua (Ed.), *Progressive Black masculinities* (pp. xi–xvii). Routledge.

Mutua, A. (2006b). Theorizing progressive Black masculinities. In A.D. Mutua (Ed.)., *Progressive Black masculinities* (pp. 3–42). Routledge.

National Centre for Learning Disabilities. (2014). *The state of learning disabilities*. https://www.ncld.org/wp-content/uploads/2014/11/2014-State-of-LD.pdf

Newfield, J. (1971, June 16). Let them eat lead. *New York Times*. https://www.nytimes.com/1971/06/16/archives/let-them-eat-lead.html

Newman, L.M. (1999). *White women's rights: The racial origins of feminism in the United States*. Oxford University Press.

Nunn, N. (2008). The long-term effects of Africa's slave trades. *The Quarterly Journal of Economics, 123*(1), 139–76. https://doi.org/10.1162/qjec.2008.123.1.139

Osofsky, G. (1969). *Puttin' on ole massa: The slave narratives of Henry Bibb, William Wells Brown, and Solomon Northup*. Harper Torchbooks.

Painter, N.I. (1995). *Soul murder and slavery*. Baylor University Press.

Parenti, C. (1999). *Lockdown America: Police and prisons in the age of crisis*. Verso.

Patterson, O. (1982). *Slavery and social death: A comparative study*. Harvard University Press.

Perry, J.B. (2009). *Hubert Harrison: The voice of the Harlem radicalism, 1883–1918*. Columbia University Press.

Presser, L. (2020, May 19). The Black American amputation epidemic. *ProPublica*. https://features.propublica.org/diabetes-amputations/black-american-amputation-epidemic/

Ramey, D. (2015). The social structure of criminalized and medicalized school discipline. *Sociology of Education, 88*(3), 181–201. http://www.jstor.org/stable/43743450

Rediker, M. (2007). *The slave ship: A human history*. Penguin Books.

Rioux, M. (2009). Bending towards justice. In T. Titchkosky & R. Michalko (Eds.), *Re-thinking normalcy: A disability studies reader* (pp. 201–16). Scholar's Press.

Roberts, D.E. (1993). Crime, race, and reproduction. *Tulane Law Review, 67*(6), 1945–77.

Robertson, D. (2017, July 1). Hip hop and disability: An interview with Leroy Moore Jr. *Black Perspectives*. https://www.aaihs.org/hip-hop-and-disability-an-interview-with-leroy-moore-jr/

Ross, M., & Bateman, N. (2018, May 15). Disability rates among working-age adults are shaped by race, place, and education. *Brookings Institute*. https://www.brookings.edu/blog/the-avenue/2018/05/15/disability-rates-among-working-age-adults-are-shaped-by-race-place-and-education/

Saad, A. (2017, February 16). Justice for Theo: Who can protect us from the police? *Al Jazeera*. https://www.aljazeera.com/opinions/2017/2/16/justice-for-theo-who-can-protect-us-from-the-police/

Sawyer, W. (2020, July 27). Visualizing the racial disparities in mass incarceration. *Prison Policy Initiative*. https://www.prisonpolicy.org/blog/2020/07/27/disparities/

Sedensky, M. (2015, October 31). Hundreds of officers lose licenses over sex misconduct. *Associated Press*. https://apnews.com/article/fd1d4d05e561462a85abe50e7eaed4ec

Segal, R. (1995). *The Black diaspora*. Faber and Faber.

Segal, R. (2001). *Islam's Black slaves: The other Black diaspora*. Farrar, Straus and Giroux.

Shalhoub-Kevorkian, N. (2019). *Incarcerated childhood and the politics of unchilding*. Cambridge University Press.

Smith, J. (2015). *Mr. Smith goes to prison: What my year behind bars taught me about America's prison crisis*. St. Martin's Press.

Smithers, G.D. (2012). *Save breeding: Sex, violence, and memory in African American history*. University of Florida Press.

Spillers, H.J. (1987). Mama's baby, papa's maybe: An American grammar book. *Diacritics, 17*(2), 64–81. https://doi.org/10.2307/464747

Sublette, N., & Sublette, C. (2016). *The American slave coast: A history of the slave-breeding industry.* Lawrence Hill Books.

Sweet, J.H. (2003). *Recreating Africa: Culture, kinship, and religion in the African-Portuguese world, 1441–1770.* University of North Carolina Press.

Sykes, G. (2007). *The society of captives: A study of a maximum security prison.* Princeton University Press. (Original work published 1956)

Taylor, C. (2011). Race and racism in Foucault's Collège de France lectures. *Philosophy Compass, 6*(11), 746–56.

thepostarchive. (2019). *James Baldwin & Nikki Giovanni, a conversation [FULL]* [Video]. YouTube. https://youtu.be/eZmBy7C9gHQ

Thomas, G. (2007). *The sexual demon of colonial power: Pan-African embodiment and erotic schemes of empire.* Indiana University Press

Trexler, R.C. (1995). *Sex and conquest: Gendered violence, political order, and the European conquest of the Americas.* Cornell University Press.

Valente, S.M. (2005). Sexual abuse of boys. *Journal of Child and Adolescent and Psychiatric Nursing, 18*(1), 10–16. https://doi.org/10.1111/j.1744-6171.2005.00005.x

Vervaet, E. (2012, December 25). *KRS-One about the origin of the dozens* [Video]. YouTube. https://www.youtube.com/watch?v=Uu-FaOmcSso

Walker, D. (2001). *Walker's appeal, in four articles; Together with a preamble, to the coloured citizens of the world, but in particular, and very expressly, to those of the United States of America, Written in Boston, State of Massachusetts, September 28, 1829.* Academic Affairs Library, UNC-CH. https://docsouth.unc.edu/nc/walker/walker.html (Original work published 1830)

Washington, H. (2006). *Medical apartheid: The dark history of medical experimentation on Black Americans from colonial times to the present.* Doubleday.

Weld, T.W. (1839). *American slavery as it is: Testimony of a thousand witnesses.* American Anti-Slavery Society.

Weindl, A. (2008). The slave trade of northern Germany from the seventeenth to the nineteenth centuries. In D. Eltis & D. Richardson (Eds.), *Extending the frontiers: Essays on the new Transatlantic Slave Trade Database* (pp. 250–72). Yale University Press.

Wiencek, H. (2012, October). *The dark side of Thomas Jefferson: A new portrait of the founding father challenges the long-held perception of Thomas Jefferson as a benevolent slaveholder.* https://www.smithsonianmag.com/history/the-dark-side-of-thomas-jefferson-35976004/

Williams, P. (1987). Spirit-murdering the messenger: The discourse of fingerpointing as the law's response to racism. *University of Miami Law Review, 42,* 127–56.

Wolff, N., Blitz, C., & Shi, J. (2007). Rates of sexual victimization in prison for inmates with and without mental disorders. *Psychiatric Services, 58*(8), 1087–94. https://www.ncbi.nlm.nih.gov/pmc/articles/PMC2811043/

Woodard, V. (2014). *The delectable Negro: Human consumption and homoeroticism within US slave culture.* New York University Press.

Woodson, C.G. (2009). *The miseducation of the Negro.* Journal of Pan African Studies eBooks. http://www.jpanafrican.org/ebooks/3.4eBookThe%20Mis-Education.pdf (Original work published 1933)

Wynter, S. (1994). "No humans involved": An open letter to my colleagues. *Forum N.H.I.: Knowledge for the 21st Century, 1*(1), 42–73.

Young, R.J.C. (2007). *Foucault on race and colonialism* [PDF]. http://robertjcyoung.com/Foucault.pdf

III

National Culture, Transqueering Black Masculinities, and Challenging Hegemonic Masculinity

Carrying Corporeal Narratives

Weighing the Burden of Antiqueer Representations in Jamaica

KEMAR MCINTOSH

EMPLOYING INTERSECTIONAL THEORY (Crenshaw, 1989), this chapter explores the psychosocial effects of antiqueer visual representations encountered by a group that I refer to in this chapter with the hyphenated compound *lower-class-black-queer-male* for reasons that will become clear below. In particular, I will be focusing on lower-class-black-queer males in Jamaica to address the politics and aesthetics of antiqueer representations in Jamaica as a means to build upon Fanon's work on violence, madness, and the challenges of postcolonial national identity. This chapter presents a critical assessment of antiqueer caricatures and visual narratives in the *Jamaica Obeserver*, a renowned newspaper stationed in Kingston, Jamaica. Specifically, it will focus on the caricature work of Clovis Brown, a seasoned caricaturist at the paper. The chapter asks how Brown's antiqueer representations serve to reinforce the marginalization and hypervisibility of lower-class-black-queer-male bodies in Jamaica. I suggest that queer Jamaicans, particularly lower-class-black-queer males, experience antiqueer visual narratives as anxiety provoking. I posit that Brown's caricatures and antiqueer representations help to reify the perceived vice or sociocultural pathology of lower-class-black-queer-male bodies situated in Jamaica, thereby normalizing bias and violence toward Jamaican queers.

Jamaica's hostile, antiqueer culture is deeply connected to national identity and expressed through various forms of violence. Within this context, the bodies of lower-class-black-queer males are made to carry the psychosomatic burden of queerphobia, which is facilitated and mediated by visual antiqueer representations of their bodies being threatened or, conversely, scripted as socially threatening. In other words, I propose that Jamaica's mainstream media contributes to the imposition of certain restrictive corporeal narratives on queer black men, which they are subsequently forced to "carry." I argue that "carrying corporeal narratives" means interpellating (Althusser, 1971) the Jamaican queer body as a prepolitical site that is embroiled in social discourse. Social discourse, it must be noted, itself never escapes historically mediated heteronormative and culturally cultivated discourses around masculinity and nationhood. Hence, the bodies of queers, being psychologically distanced from the mainstream imagination of what it means to be Jamaican, are forced to take on, interpellate, or carry narratives involving their embodiment ready to suit heteronormative and nationalist discourses.

This chapter is organized around the discussion and deconstruction of Brown's caricature work and its place and power within Jamaican (queerphobic) nationalism, and the ways in which Brown's work (re)creates and upholds the dominant narratives around queer identities in Jamaica. In this regard, it asks three central questions: (1) Do Brown's antiqueer representations of lower-class-black-queer-male persons in Jamaica remain relevant because he is the sole caricaturist making such representations visible? (2) Would Brown betray the heteronormative aesthetic education of Jamaicans if he were to visually represent gender-transgressive, lower-class-black-queer males as nonthreatening and belonging to Jamaica's sociocultural and political landscape? And (3) If so, why would this be perceived as betrayal?

But before we jump into answering these questions, it is important to develop a deeper understanding of some of the theoretical bases of this discussion: the dynamics of normative and "Other" visual narratives, and what it means to "carry" such narratives about and within one's body.

Othered Images: The Cultural Weight of Visual Narratives

> *If the same motif is not treated a hundredfold by different masters, the public does not learn to get beyond its interest in the content; but the public will itself ultimately grasp and enjoy the nuances, the delicate new inventions in the treatment of a motif, if it has long known it in many adaptations and no longer experiences the charm of novelty or suspense.*
>
> —FRIEDRICH NIETZSCHE, *Human, All Too Human: A Book for Free Spirits*

When tasked with conservative political intents, visual narratives tend to portray homogenizing stories by way of excluding marginalized experiences and unseen realities. Also, these visual narratives usually represent cultural and sociopolitical thematics through conservative or confined singular imagery. It is, however, critical to note that singular images do not complete the story, but instead create the illusion of completion by erasing the visual narratives of those that they deem to be Other. Nonetheless, the political thingification and concomitant systemic erasure of marginalized visual narratives can indirectly serve to demonstrate the vulnerability of hegemonic visual narratology. Images that are Othered by this narratology, when they are resurrected in the public gaze, can work to challenge and disrupt the singularity of conservative political imagery. Othered images allow us to interrogate the illusive homogeneity of hegemonic visual narration, as they exhibit and expose hidden cultural realities that more mainstream visual narratives often omit. This discursive display of visual narratives conceptualizes the dialectics of visual culture, wherein political images clash to create visualscapes of inclusion and exclusion.

Carrying Corporeal Narratives

We must also examine the corporeality of lower-class-black-queer-male bodies that psychosomatically carry harmful antiqueer visual narratives with them, never quite gaining respite from queerphobia in Jamaica. I will discuss the process of weighing and the consequent weight of antiqueer representations carried by lower-class-black-queer-male bodies themselves.[1]

As mentioned above, the "carrying of corporeal narratives" refers to the myriad ways in which lower-class-black-queer-male bodies in Jamaica are made to carry the psychosomatic burden of queerphobia imposed on them, facilitated and mediated by both visual and nonvisual antiqueer representations of their bodies being threatened or scripted as socially threatening. The carrying of corporeal narratives means the body, as the primordial site embroiled in social discourse, never escapes historically mediated discourse and culturally cultivated discourse; hence, the body is forced to take on, interpellate, and carry narratives involving the negation of its authentic embodiment (Chen, 2012; Foucault, 1977/1995, 1978/1990). Visual antiqueer representations in Jamaica are clearly biopolitical, as such visual narratives are premised on the sort of bodies prefigured to encounter violation, dehumanization, and processes of exclusion. Weighing the carrying of corporeal narratives by lower-class-black-queer-male Jamaicans results in detecting episodes of anxiety and corollary feelings of depression and existential despair (Kristeva, 1982). In clinical terms, Frantz Fanon (1963) diagnoses this weight as manifestations of "reactional psychoses" (p. 251). He goes on to explain this weight as "psychosomatic [since the] pathology is considered as a means whereby the organism responds to, in other words adapts itself to, the conflict it is faced with, the disorder being at the same time a symptom and a cure" (p. 290). Though largely silent on queerness save for sexuality implied by Freudian psychoanalysis, Fanon may have concurred that this weight, manifested as affective or psychosomatic symptoms, creates a concrete epistemology of burden wherein quotidian queerphobic encounters experienced by lower-class-black-queer-male Jamaicans come together to inform a unique social ontology, deemed separate, but nonetheless connected to divergent ontologies produced through encounters with systems of oppression.

Clovis Brown: Visually Creating the Other

Clovis Brown, a seasoned caricaturist at the *Jamaica Observer*, is known for the creation and dissemination of several such narratives about a variety of different social groups in Jamaica. Here, I will focus specifically on Brown's antiqueer narratives—in particular, the ridiculing and recurring dehumanization of lower-class-black-queer-male persons in his caricature work. Brown's satirical antiqueer visual narratives are meant to make comical the quotidian marginalization of queer bodies in Jamaica. He uses these images to enhance the visibility of dominant cultural themes surrounding race, class, and gender dynamics in Jamaica. Brown's antiqueer caricatures customarily represent lower-class-black-queer-male persons as gender transgressive (Alturi, 2001; Brand, 1998; Butler, 2006; Narain, 2012) and as valorizing feminine whiteness through acts of skin bleaching (Fanon, 1952/2008; Gordon, 2000). Brown also extends his caricatures to make visible the operation of classism in Jamaica through depicting lower-class-black-queer-male bodies as performing dress codes associated with lower-class expressions of femininity. It is worth mentioning that such dress codes not only serve to codify a lower-class distinction, but also work to play on the upper-class presumption that lower-class feminine performativity is vulgar (Cooper, 1993).

In relation to gender and race, Brown's visual representations serve to reinforce colonial and postcolonial stigmas (Bleys, 1995; Cliff, 1989) about the black male body and femininity. These stigmas have to do with the perceived feminization that occurs through serial encounters with white supremacy; the implication is that failing to resist these feminizing moments of white supremacy translates into embracing the aberrational queerness associated with whiteness (though I must, here, acknowledge that serial encounters with white supremacy encountered by black men, in both colonial and postcolonial contexts, are processual and evoke dissonant ontologies). In other words, white supremacy, despite being a global phenomenon, produced different colonial realities, possibilities for revolution, and steps toward nationalist liberation; hence, lived colonial and postcolonial realities for black men in Jamaica are often materially different from the lives of black men situated in, say, the United States. Still, there is a common thread between colonial and postcolonial realities for Black men in both of these locations and beyond: Black subjugation and political forms of effeminization under white regimes of power.

The intersectionality of race, class, and gender present in Brown's caricatures is rehearsed through *hyphenization*: the making of singular bodies into discursive identities, making clear the conjunctive layers of identity formation. These identities, when linked through hyphenization, produce particular standpoint epistemologies. Hyphenization, like intersectionality, must be employed when assessing experiences, as they allow the dynamism lodged in identity formation and politics to be grasped. For this reason, I understand the term *gay* to be a reductionist term that contributes to both the simplification and erasure of the other identities contained within any individual. *All* of these identities are necessary for a full appreciation of the nuances and linkages found in identity politics. Nevertheless, I am cognizant that the term *gay* is politically deployed as a form of "strategic essentialism" (Spivak, 2006).

Questioning Artistic Conservatism in a Queerphobic Culture

Brown plays a role in visually reinforcing harmful stigmas around the vice or social pathology of lower-class-black-queer-male bodies in Jamaica. To this end, my concern is the political power (Rancière, 2000/2004) Brown holds in aiding the heteromasculinity of the polity and society to serially marginalize queer identities. It is also my position that Brown's antiqueer visual narratives work to reify the marginalized and oppressed positionality of lower-class-black-queer-male persons; he has yet to caricature queers as either meandering or transcending essentialist images of vice, threat, and social pathology recycled in Jamaica's popular visual culture. That is, he has yet to depict their positive contributions. It would be a form of artistic radicalism—disrupting Jamaica's queerphobic status quo—if Brown were to caricature the unseen positive contributions of lower-class-black-queer-male subjectivities to local Jamaican culture and cultural contributions appropriated transnationally. Such caricatures would be radical and counterhegemonic (Chivallon, 2002; Wright, 2015; Zeleza, 2010) as they would visually restore erased positive queer contributions made and silently distributed within and beyond Jamaica's borders through, for example, Jamaica's dancehall culture (Moore, 2014). Although not stemming from Jamaica's lower-class, Marlon James, a black-queer-male author who won the prestigious Man Booker Prize, positively highlighting Jamaica's presence on the literary world stage, was proudly featured and introduced in the *Jamaica Observer* in an article by the London Associated Press (2015) as follows: "Marlon James became the first Jamaican winner of the prestigious Man Booker Prize for fiction...with a vivid, violent, exuberant, and expletive-laden novel based on the attempted assassination of Bob Marley." But months before the *Observer's* adulatory publication, James (2015) wrote a piece for *New York Times Magazine* entitled "From Jamaica to Minnesota to Myself," which chronicled traumatic encounters with homophobia, his gender negotiations, and his inevitable escape from Jamaica to Minnesota where he could be his queer self. Notably, at no point in the article published in the *Observer* was there mention of James's queerness; the narrative was set on including him and his contribution as uniquely Jamaican.

Like the *Observer* more broadly, Brown has long preserved and organized this form of political erasure in his own work. Such erasure stems from Brown's conscious effort to maintain, without disruption, his own visual narratives constructed around the social pathology of black-queer-male sexuality and, moreover, the acutely threatening position of lower-class-black-queer-male Jamaicans. Although James is an openly queer Jamaican man, Brown did *not* include him in his caricature work. Caricaturing James's pioneering contribution to Jamaica's image on the literary world stage, *qua* his queerness, would have been tantamount to linking James's textual affirmations of his queer sexuality with Jamaican national pride. This would have served to disrupt stereotypical tropes of immoral contagion and vice associated with male queers in Jamaica. This is not because Brown shies away from depictions of Jamaican national pride in general. Without negating the fact that Brown's caricatures are seasoned instruments of political satire, Brown still employs his artistic power (Rancière, 2000/2004)

FIGURE 6.1: "Sartorial Transgressions" by Clovis Brown.

(Reproduced with permission from the Jamaica Observer.*)*

to recognize and represent the achievements of nonqueer, gender conforming Jamaicans. The direct erasure of queers reveals Brown's artistic conservatism; his work implies that nonqueer, gender conforming Jamaicans are the only bodies worthy of positive celebrity. Visibly queer Jamaicans, on the other hand, are excluded from positive recognition, routinely visualized or caricatured instead as a social contagion.

It is fair to conjecture that Brown does not disrupt his own conservative distribution of antiqueer visual narratives, as he is neither willing nor able to transcend his own queerphobic anxieties; queerphobia remains central to Jamaican identity. The argument could also be made, however, that Brown does not caricature James because of James's cisgender appearance. In other words, James's queerness does not fit Brown's concept of "queer." This concept, represented in his antiqueer caricatures, is characteristically lower-class, black, and male, and remains normatively gender transgressive.

Thus, the heteronormative and nationalized appropriation of James's contributions are perhaps not visualized as "authentically" queer, slipping past Brown's usually scrutinizing heterosexist gaze.

To illustrate some of these points, let's unpack the messages implicit in one of Brown's cartoons (Figure 6.1). In the cartoon, we see three concerned women, apparently heterosexual and presumably representing Jamaica's upper or middle class. One is lamenting her frustration, articulated in salt-of-the-earth Patois calculated to erase class differences among the reading audience: "*Lawd wi ah suffa, because ah dem wi cyaan get nuh clothes fi wear*" [Lord we are suffering, because of them, we don't have clothes to wear]. These words depict the imagined scarcity of female clothing due to the hoarding of those garments, once exclusively secured for women, by the gender-transgressive, lower-class-black-queer-male bodies in the cartoon. The cartoon further implies that the woman's agitation is due not just to the clothing scarcity, but also the conspicuously visible gender transgression at work. This reinforcement and preservation of the woman's acceptance of Jamaica's heterosexist patriarchy while simultaneously rendering the gender-transgressive, lower-class-black-queer-male subjects as objects for her antiqueer spectacle, is a clear articulation of antiqueer antagonism. Her eyes, accompanied by the antiqueer stares of others in the cartoon, visualize those two queer bodies as socially deviant, deserving of hostility and ridicule. The cartoon also shows us that even female subjects are capable of reproducing and preserving colonial heteropatriarchy.

Alluded to earlier, the theme of race is at play in the cartoon via the pale facial complexions of both lower-class-black-queer-male bodies, signifying skin bleaching. This melanin manipulation of black faces not only serves to address the postcolonial phenomenon of skin bleaching but seeks to resuscitate discourse concerning the connection between race and class consciousness in Jamaica. Treviene A. Harris's (2014) thesis *Bleaching to Reach* certainly encapsulates the message Brown seeks to provide surrounding the dialectical relationship between privileged white- or light-skinned upper- and middle-class Jamaicans, and the usually poor, black (darker-skinned), lower-class Jamaicans pushed to the margins. Brown's cartoon engages what I conceptualize as triple marginality: the cartoon works to display Jamaican queer bodies as marginalized along not just racially conservative lines, but conservative class and gender lines as well.

Visual Power: Clovis Brown and Jamaica's Visual Culture

Brown's role as an artist and his political positionality in Jamaica's visual culture will be analyzed through Jacques Rancière's (2000/2004) work *The Politics of Aesthetics: Distribution of the Sensible*. Rancière's work addresses the politics behind aesthetic formations, since what is produced, becomes art, and is distributed within any given culture rests on bodies of elites who hold economic, social, and political power. Brown's antiqueer cartoons are ordinarily distributed through a popular newspaper and reinforce queerphobic sensibilities, as members of Jamaica's polity and the larger cultural landscape work to reinscribe Jamaica as essentially queerphobic.

Rancière (2000/2004) posits that "art consists in constructing spaces and relations to reconfigure materially and symbolically the territory of the common" (p. 22). Brown's antiqueer representations of lower-class-black-queer-male bodies serve to demarcate three core interactive and overlapping "spaces" (race, class, and gender politics) in Jamaican society. It is apparent that, separate from the queerphobia shaping Brown's visual narratives, other interwoven social forces of inclusion and exclusion are made visible. Lower-class-black-queer-male bodies are excluded from upper- and middle-class privileges, barred from protections enmeshed in whiteness, and violently ridiculed for not performing and conforming to hegemonic heterosexism in Jamaica (Chrisman, 2003; Glave, 2008).

Why Is Brown Still Relevant?

Let's turn, now, to the first central question to be answered by this paper: Do Brown's antiqueer representations of lower-class-black-queer-male persons in Jamaica remain relevant because he is the sole caricaturist making such representations visible? I argue that, indeed, Brown's antiqueer visual narratives remain relevant owing to his virtual monopoly over the production of such cartoons, made possible by the illusory apolitical position he holds as an artist representing delicate social affairs. I suggest that his position is "illusory" because no artistic production is ever politically neutral or apolitical. Brown nevertheless is bestowed artistic immunity—and "neutrality"—by normalizing hegemonies of race, class, and gender. His position allows him to distance himself from those who he portrays, as many Jamaicans perceive him to be a mere spectator and visual *reporter*—not interpreter—of cultural politics. Thus, as the cartoons serve to create voyeuristic distance, he too becomes politically distant, elusively detached from the violence distributed through antiqueer cartoons of which he is both producer and hegemonic interlocutor.

Rancière (2000/2004) informs us that

> [art] is not, in the first instance, political because of the messages and sentiments it conveys concerning the state of the world. Neither is it political because of the manner in which it might choose to represent society's structures, or social groups, their conflicts or identities. It is political because of the very distance it takes with respect to the functions, because of the type of space and time that it institutes, and the manner in which it frames this time and peoples this space. (p. 23)

Here, Rancière would concur that Brown's work creates "space": the "space" between his antiqueer cartoons, his social position as an unaffected artist, the traumatic visualizing of his antiqueer representations of lower-class-black-queer-male Jamaicans, and the amusement-turned-queerphobic-intolerance projected by many Jamaicans (Cameron, 2006; Murray, 2007).

Another Rancierian (2011/2013) work, *Aisthesis: Scenes From the Aesthetic Regime of Art*, allows for another interpretation: that Brown's relevance in Jamaica, separate from this creation of "space" through creatively keeping lower-class-black-queer-male bodies at the margins of society ("in their place"), is maintained through the way in which his work regenerates queerphobic sentimentalities. Rancière informs us that "art... is not merely the production of works through technique. It is the power

FIGURE 6.2: "Spectacular Fear" by Clovis Brown.

(Reproduced with permission from the Jamaica Observer.*)*

of ordering forms of individual life and those in which the community expresses itself as such within the same spiritual unity" (p. 148). This suggests that Jamaica's cultural zeitgeist of queerphobia is revived and reified through Brown's antiqueer representations, causing heterosexual fears and anxieties to be violently projected against and to target lower-class-black-queer-male subjectivities in Jamaica. According to Peter de Bolla (2000), "the artwork is not a fact, nor is it knowable in the sense of knowing a person. Our knowing the artwork or knowledge of it, is precisely contained in and by our response to it. Thus, the limits of what can be known to us of the artwork are identical to our affective response...because affective experiences tell us about ourselves" (p. 213). The fears, anxieties and moral alarms, represented and reinforced in Brown's antiqueer cartoons, ordinarily discharged from heterosexualized bodies and heteronormative political institutions in Jamaica, set up "affective" spaces of *différance* (Derrida, 1972) where heterosexuals are encouraged to defend their identity through ridiculing, dehumanizing, and, specific to Brown's antiqueer cartoons, enacting exclusions of lower-class-black-queer-male bodies.

Again, let's turn to one of Brown's caricatures (Figure 6.2) to unpack some of these ideas. The traditional Jamaican street festival known as Jankunu (also known as John Canoe, Jonkonnu, John Kuner, Junkanoo) features Jamaica's cultural connection to the African Igbo tradition of masking "spirits" (Rommen, 2011)—a holdover of creole adaptations that arose during plantation slavery. In it, performers festooned as other-worldly beings make gestures calculated to inspire fear among spectators (Carrol, 2007). Kenneth Bilby (2010), affirming the festive production of fear as a necessary and authentic feature of Jankunu, posits that

> [a successful Jankunu] evokes strong emotional response, which cannot be replaced by intellectual rationale, even concerning so-called "artistic excellence." If the commitment to judgement is made, then a concurrent commitment must be made to find a way to judge emotional response [when judging Jankunu festivities]. "It scared the hell out of me" is a more successful response than "it was nice..." (p. 186)

No longer harkening to slaves scaring away the demonic presence of their white slave masters, Brown's cartoon (mis)appropriates Jankunu to represent the threat queer culture poses to (hetero)normative Jamaican culture, when, in fact, the opposite is true. In the cartoon, Brown clearly makes a direct connection to the generative, fear-producing spectacle (i.e., Jankunu) and the presence of a lower-class-black-queer-male body. In other words, Brown signifies this body as an object to be feared. This almost existential repulsion is mirrored in the child's flight, leaving his mother equally fearful and alarmed. This cartoon serves to show the intensity of queerphobia in Jamaica, with mother and son represented as bodies encountering the highest risk of being harmed: the presence of a queer male in Jamaica. One other effect of Brown's misappropriation of Jankunu is that it erases the reality of queerness among enslaved Africans in Jamaica—a reality that Watufani M. Poe (Chapter 7 in this volume) unambiguously demonstrates was the case for "New World" Latin countries.

While invisibilizing the authoritative role of heteropatriarchy that Brown and his ilk inhabit, Brown portrays mothers as responsible for "preventing" homosexuality. On another register, it is clear that the child in the cartoon is a young boy. Since it is believed that male homosexuality can be imprinted onto the impressionable young and is closely correlated with pedophilia in Jamaica, the boy's flight implies a flight from the imagined risk of being sexually molested, and potentially becoming infested with the sociosexual vice of homosexuality. It also shows the mother's fear in response to her son fleeing the imagined pernicious threat posed by the lower-class-black-queer-male body's presence. The revulsion of lower-class-black-queer-male embodiment is synonymous with other political actions deployed and ideologies calculated to dehumanize queers. Schemes of dehumanization begin with excommunication, wherein select bodies are made hypervisible and thereafter forcefully displaced or stripped from belonging to a human community. It is through excommunication—moments of recurring exile—that lower-class-black-queer-male bodies become dehumanized.

Betrayal? Reproducing Conservative Norms as Hegemonic Cultural Solidarity

Brown's cartoons work to reify an aesthetic public education about what is and is not Jamaican. His cartoons are as nationalistic as they are queerphobic. Subordinated by the International Monetary Fund (IMF) and the World Bank, exaggerated heteronormativity and queerphobia become substitutes for anticolonial resistance to the imperialistic predations of geofinance capitalism. Brown's cartoons reintroduce into Jamaica's consciousness the queerphobia employed to distinguish Jamaica from other politicocultural landscapes working towards accommodating and including queer bodies into the modern nationalist order (Cooper, 1993, 2004; Thomas, 2004).

I must acknowledge that my work does not cover both domestic and international structural adjustment policies for Jamaica, though it is equally important to situate Jamaican lower-class-black-queer-male bodies as socially threatening in relation to Jamaica's post-independence anxieties around geopolitical and economic feminization effectuated through international financial institutions such as IMF and World Bank. Still, while geofinancial politics are important to articulations of local and national culture in Jamaica, this is a concern farther afield than this chapter's central motif: the burden of certain corporeal narratives imposed on black, queer Jamaican men by the cultural pedagogy and social semantics of queerphobic visual representations in Jamaican media.

With that in mind, let's turn to the second and third central questions of this chapter: First, would Brown betray the heteronormative aesthetic education of Jamaicans if he were to visually represent gender-transgressive, lower-class-black-queer males as nonthreatening and belonging to Jamaica's sociocultural and political landscape? And second, if it would, why would this be so? I argue that, indeed, this would constitute a betrayal, as it would divert attention from *reproducing* queerphobic visual narratives, instead shaping Jamaican nationalism towards equity and inclusion of queers. This, as I have already shown, is at odds with Jamaica's self-concept, insofar as queerness is understood in connection with whiteness, and Jamaican identity is positioned against white colonialism.

Brown's cartoons not only represent Jamaica's opposition to queer identities but also display the exilic modes of violence enacted against vulnerable lower-class-black-queer-male bodies in Jamaica. In part, the presumption is that queerness has no tradition in Jamaica's prior plantocratic slave and indenture society, but is a degenerative import from the West. Thus, violence against queers *qua* queers has a sanctimonious ring of defending Jamaica's cultural and social autonomy. Here, Brown helps to annex antiqueer sentiments, ideologies, and violence to dogmatic expressions of Jamaican nationalism. Therefore, if Brown were to challenge Jamaica's queerphobic status quo, he would compromise his allegiance to defending Jamaica's national borders against the perceived foreign infestation of queer sexual identities as much as Jamaica's economic and political subordination to imperial powers. To be Jamaican is to defend and privilege the moral position of heterosexuality and render queer sexualities deviant.

David Carrol (2000) informs us that

> the aesthetic dimension of nationalism could be argued to be essential to its conceptualization and implementation, the poetics of nationalism serving as the foundation for its highly coherent and often dogmatic politics, its aesthetics not just illustrative of nationalist themes or providing emotive examples when analytical argumentation [is] lacking, but rather the very basis of the "systematic logic" of nationalism. (p. 114)

Carrol's work can be taken to imply that Brown's cartoons present a "poetics of nationalism" predicated on excommunicating queer bodies from Jamaica's heterosexist landscape. Brown's visual narratives represent the excommunication of lower-class-black-queer-male bodies in Jamaica, speaking to the hegemonic feature of nationalism (Chivallon & Fields, 2002; Gilroy, 1995; Wright, 2015) by which, for homogeneity's sake, different identities are deemed deviant and thus excluded, along with their ontologies.

The tight maintenance and border protections were invented as nationalism worked to reduce anxieties surrounding intrusion, literally imagined in the context of the homophobic imagination as "penetration." These imaginary borders become real through acts of exclusion. Brown's antiqueer cartoons serve to protect Jamaica's bordered heterosexual community by reinforcing images of bodies violently positioned against its border. Jamaican queers become imagined as displaced persons invading the body politic, implying a schema of social closure necessitating exclusion, excommunication, and quarantine. Brown's cartoons are, therefore, representative of Carrol's (2000) claim that nationalism "would have to be considered one of the most important of the political names given to such a projection of community, the one that in modernity could be argued to have been the most frequently institutionalized" (p. 133). Thus, being Jamaican, according to the immutable construction of national identity tied to heterosexuality, naturally means being heterosexual and antiqueer.

Maurice Hall's (2011) work "Negotiating Jamaican Masculinities" provides a comprehensive historical genealogy detailing the evolution of Jamaica's antiqueer culture. Hall helps us to better understand both the historical and cultural complexities informing antiqueer practices and sentiments in Jamaica, framing them within the context of a postcolonial nation-building enterprise that was orchestrated by elite men who occupied Jamaica's polity during and after British colonialism. Hall discusses the post-independence compensatory hypermasculinity (Cooper, 2004; Hirsch et al, 2010; Thomas, 2004) performed by black, lower-class Jamaican men, mobilized to protect their manhood and protest residual structural inequalities produced under British colonialism. Historically, the generation of Jamaica's antiqueer culture, analogous to America's heteropatriarchal Black Power movement in the 1950s and early 1960s (see Poe, Chapter 7 in this volume), was to challenge the effeminizing prowess of white supremacist patriarchy. Postcolonial black phallicism (black heteropatriarchy), in Jamaica, collectively meant and continues to mean protecting the masculine heteronormalized nation-state from perverted feminization perceived as present in male homosexuality.

Speaking about Jamaican masculinity and how it dominates Jamaican popular culture, Hall (2011) informs us that "[as] a culture with a history of colonialism that has also had a sustained culture of patriarchy (Lewis, 2003), constructions of what Jamaican male identity means, then, in postcolonial Jamaica have everything to do with understanding the intersecting discourses of race, class, and gender and to the extent to which white maleness became the construct against which blackness was constituted and defined" (p. 33). Hall's analysis shows Jamaica's popular postcolonial landscape, in response to both white colonial and neocolonial patriarchy, to be built on a misogynistic patriarchy predicated on defending against myriad vulnerabilities encountered by ordinarily black, lower-class male subjectivities; therefore, the black-male-as-feminine or -feminized remains aberrational and produces violent postcolonial anxieties. Hall (2011) reminds us that "[black] men were not just infantilized by the systems of slavery and colonialism; they were also gendered as feminine to the extent that they were reduced to dependence on the white slave and then colonial master" (p. 36). Therefore, the postcolonial erection of phallic energy that dominated black nationalist movements transnationally embedded its presence in Jamaica as a way of reinstating, particularly among disenfranchised Jamaican men, manhood, which had been systematically stripped from both them and their once-enslaved transatlantic ancestors. Jamaica's homophobic culture—like other postcolonial geographies formerly imbricated with plantation slavery and the systematized subjugation of African bodies—reproduces patriarchal violence inherent to white colonialism as a way of wholly controlling, possessing, and hegemonically maintaining the masculine appearance rooted in securing the political cohesion of the nation-state. Therefore, the potential subversiveness of male homosexuality in postcolonial Jamaica is the feminization of the black male body: simultaneously feminized erotically (through rape) and materially under Western imperialism. It is clear, then, Jamaica's Offences Against the Person Act (OAPA) (1864)—which includes a buggery law (section 76) that criminalizes anal sex—acts as a disciplinary technique (Foucault, 1977/1995) not solely against homoerotic desires but as a strategic juridical bulwark against the feminization (i.e., symbolic penetration) of Jamaica's idealized masculine body politic.

Drawing upon diverse literary materials surrounding America's Black Power movement and black nationalisms globally, Rolland Murray's (2007) *Our Living Manhood* tells us that "[black] heteronormative nationalisms maintain their hegemony through the abjection and negation of the homosexual subject. Black Power nationalisms routine hostility toward the homosexual [is] an assault on the 'scapegoat, the sign of chaos and crisis' in order to 'return the community to normality to create boundaries around blackness, rights that white men are obliged to recognize'" (p. 85). Jamaica's sexual politics concerning queer sexualities, and more apparent antagonisms against male homosexuality, works to position the nation-state as being under existential threat—threatened, that is, by a Western, almost neocolonial enterprise destined to distort and infect the postcolonial body politic with a sexual "chaos" perceived in male homosexuality.

Jamaican popular culture, fashioned and promulgated by working-class Jamaicans, is an easily accessible site wherein raw antiqueer sentiments and peculiarly masculinist antiqueer sentiments are pronounced through local parlance, restrictive masculine dress codes, and lethal dancehall lyrics such as Buju Banton's (1992/2001) "Boom Bye Bye" (resembling the sound of gun shots), which begins: "*World is in trouble anytime Buju Banton come Batty bwoy get up and run*" [The world is in trouble, and anytime Buju Banton comes around, a gay man (Batty bwoy) must quickly flee for his life] (track 13, 3:49). Banton's lyrics, released in 1992, received numerous criticisms from both domestic and international human rights organizations. The lyrics were appropriately labelled "murder music," as they lucidly advocate the mass extermination of queer male Jamaicans. However, without rehearsing heated debates surrounding Banton's vulnerable class position and his constitutionally provided right to pursue and release contentious artistic expressions, his lyrics speak to a culturally imagined threat of male homosexuality against Jamaica's heteronational identity: an identity that imagines itself to warrant protection through lethally eliminating queer male Jamaicans.

To corporealize the violence of Jamaica's antiqueer culture, instigated and promulgated through black nationalist patriarchy, I turn to Lenford "Steve" Harvey, a former outreach worker for Jamaica AIDS Support for Life (JASL). Harvey was a self-affirming gay man who was robbed and murdered on November 30th, 2004, ironically on the eve of World AIDS Day (Young, 2006). Harvey's murder, initially permitted through the nation-state's complicity in violating and exterminating queer bodies, is demonstrative of antiqueer postcolonial anxieties. Jamaica's quotidian protectionism against homosexuality—and more viscerally against phallic (male) homosexuality—reflects longstanding postcolonial insecurities emerging from Jamaica's anticipated "crisis of masculinity" (Mbembe, 2001) or, in other words, Jamaica's failure to maintain a racially driven postcolonial imaginary grounded on a black or Africanized heteronormative identity.

Brown's antiqueer representations certainly work to reaffirm the national ideology of hegemonic heterosexuality; queers are visualized as foreign to the nation, caricatured as abject outsiders. Brown's antiqueer visual narratives, therefore, evoke questions and concerns surrounding the politics of citizenship and belonging (Alexander, 1991), as his antiqueer cartoons elaborate the assumption that queer bodies can neither be constituted as Jamaican citizens nor as the product of its culture. However, Fanon's (1963) postcolonial formulation, set on inspiring an assemblage of human energies charged with inventing new and collectively beneficial social relations, rejects any form of nationalism propped on articulating neocolonial dogmas of exclusion. To ferment this point, Fanon (1963) imparts that "[the] living expression of the nation is the moving consciousness of the whole of the people; it is the coherent, enlightened action of [the people]. The collective building up of a destiny is the assumption of responsibility on the historical scale" (p. 204). Therefore, Fanon, presenting a humanist politics of inclusion, a "whole of the people" anticolonial politics, would reject dehumanizing praxes of discrimination (e.g., queers as noncitizens) and neocolonial exclusions ordinarily encountered by queers situated in postcolonial Jamaica.

The Burden of Queerphobia

The carrying of corporeal narratives implies the epistemic and existential burden of queerphobia imposed on Jamaican queers. Properly situated in the social psychology of scapegoating and victim-blaming, the weighing and resultant weight of queerphobia can be assessed through the symptoms it produces. These symptoms include episodes of anxiety and corollary feelings of depression and existential despair (Parr, 2005; Radstone, 2007; Sheppard, 2003). These symptoms reflect hostilities projected against queer bodies in Jamaica. Specific to Brown's cartoons, they reflect the aesthetic dehumanization of lower-class-black-queer-male bodies. In addressing the weight of neurotic anxieties experienced by hypervulnerable lower-class-black-queer bodies as a consequence of how they are represented in Brown's cartoons, we can fruitfully turn to Ruth Ronen's (2009) *Aesthetics of Anxiety*.

Ronen informs us that

> [anxiety] signifies the entry of certainty into subjectivity by suffering. The anxious subject is hence facing something that knowledge cannot relieve, and that presentation cannot screen out. Anxiety is the connection of the subject to the Real, not a way of camouflaging the Real with an image [or] sign. (p. 96)

Here, Ronen's theorizing points to the ways that "presentation(s)" of black-queer bodies become "real," and enter the realm of Jamaican queerphobic reality by being projected onto queers as "consequences" for which they are themselves responsible. Brown's antiqueer representations engage and denigrate the embodied existence of lower-class-black-queer-male Jamaican bodies, imposing the burden of existential anxiety. The cartoons intrinsically enact antiqueer violence as they serve to remind readers across class, gender, and racial lines of the aberrational positionality of queer subjectivities in Jamaica. In such an epistemic configuration of psychosexual projection, which works to absolve heterosexuals of violence against queers by deeming that violence to be inherently justified, queers are presumed to be *born fi dead* [born to be killed].

The anxieties experienced by queer bodies are always in relationship to heterosexual hostilities, subtle or covert, articulated in antiqueer spaces. Marilyn Charles (2015) thus posits that "[human] beings are born into meaning structures that are utterly embodied, assimilated through attempts at 'reading' the nonverbal communications that assail us through sound, image, touch, taste and smell" (p. 29). This reading makes possible a critique of the ways that Brown's cartoons or visual narratives certainly "assail" the presence of lower-class-black-queer-male bodies and broadly signals Jamaica's wholesale, ultimately murderous, rejection of queer identities and subjectivities.

The politics of rejecting queer identities in Jamaica is articulated through legal codes as the state transparently secures Jamaica's national identity as queerphobic. For example, the OAPA buggery law (section 76), shared by

FIGURE 6.3: "Embodied Guilt" by Clovis Brown.
(Reproduced with permission from the Jamaica Observer.*)*

neighbouring postcolonial Anglophone geographies in the Caribbean, is a direct articulation of the state's aversion to male homosexuality and, more broadly, other nonheteronormative and non-gender-eroticized identities.

Brown, like most Jamaicans, is conscious of juridical prohibitions against male homosexuality, as can be seen in another of his cartoons (Figure 6.3). The character in the right of the panel clearly visualizes the self-indictment of a gender-transgressive lower-class-black-queer-male Jamaican. This banal self-indictment demonstrates an awareness most male queer citizens have about their relationship with antiqueer juridical codes that criminalize their existence in Jamaica. The gender-transgressive lower-class-black-queer male appears nonchalant about the self-pronouncement of "guilty" in this visual narrative. This cartoon dramatizes the banal reality of entrenched queerphobia in Jamaica, where male queer subjects are familiar with the active stigmatization and criminalization of their bodies by the state. The defiant self-pronouncement of "guilty" by the queer subject in the cartoon affirms the uselessness of the state's legal prohibition against male homosexuality. To the anxiousness of heteropatriarchy, the speech act (Searle, 1969) of self-criminalization (Foucault, 1977/1995) signifies that the state has failed to subjugate male queers in Jamaica despite their de facto deviantization in the broader culture. The cartoon shows the judge, clearly perplexed by the lower-class-black-queer male's gender transgression, staring down in disapproval while simultaneously approving a culturally reinforced legal tone of antiqueer politics practised in Jamaica. Heightening the repudiation of gender nonconformity through the presumption of skin bleaching, the lower-class-black-queer-male body is imagined as a transgressive mimesis of the "whiteness that is cultural property" (C. Harris, 1993) of Jamaica's upper- and middle-class whites and near whites. This move, I argue, also illustrates the elites' and the state's aversion to lower-class, black bodies striving to mimic whiteness, hence the pervasiveness of public health discourses around regulating skin-lightening elements, ordinarily, however nonexclusively, used by lower-class, darker-hued Jamaicans (Charles, 2011; London Associated Press, 2011).

Another dimension to this cartoon is the social reality of hypermasculine admonition and the unwavering heterosexist gaze encountered by visibly queer Jamaicans. Brown's cartoon shows the state-sanctioned male figure exerting his antiqueer masculine authority, supported by the judge's dissenting stare. Both figures, I argue, serve to reinforce the hegemonic patriarchy operationalized and normalized through the marginalization of queer subjectivities in Jamaica.

Certainly, the political significance in emphasizing the corporeality of antiqueer aesthetic experiences encountered by lower-class-black-queer-male bodies is that such work acknowledges the objectivity of those bodies. Brown's cartoons are not abstract; they clearly represent the cultural stigmatization and, as in "Embodied Guilt" (Figure 6.3), the criminalization of lower-class-black-queer-male bodies in Jamaica. Rehearsing the corporeality or the carrying of corporeal narratives by lower-class-black-queer-male bodies situated in Jamaica, Max Dessoir's (1970) work *Aesthetics and Theory of Art* reminds us that

> [to] speak of aesthetic objects would have no meaning if the aesthetic consisted merely of mental processes. Of course, even an aesthetic [object] is fashioned subject to conditions imposed by the evaluating person and according to a cognitive rule. [And] these suppose objectivity... not subjectivity. (p. 62)

Supported by Dessoir's contention, anxieties routinely experienced by lower-class-black-queer-male Jamaicans are closely linked to the "objectivity" of their bodies being subjected to hostile heterosexist threats—threats vividly pronounced in Brown's antiqueer visual narratives.

Rollo May's (1977) *The Meaning of Anxiety* tells us that

> [anxiety] and hostility are interrelated; one usually generates the other... [A]nxiety gives rise to hostility. This can be understood in its simplest form in the fact that anxiety, which its concomitant feelings of helplessness, isolation, and conflict, is an exceedingly painful experience. (p. 230)

Many would agree that a key symptom of carrying corporeal narratives, as is done by lower-class-black-queer-male bodies in Jamaica, is existential anxiety, discharged in response to antiqueer anxieties generating heterosexist hostilities. In other words, the carrying of corporeal narratives translates into lower-class-black-queer-male bodies introjecting the violence present in Brown's antiqueer visual narratives. Such introjection produces ontological anxieties.

Carrying corporeal narratives also leads to abjection. In line with Fanon's conception of "thingification," Derek Hook (2012) tells us that

> [in] speaking of the abject, one refers to the contemptible, the repugnant, wretched, that which is unwanted, unclean, viewed as contaminating, a danger to the moral order. Abjection then, as a verb, should be understood

> as an operation: the powerful visceral reaction toward a given object that is then denigrated, reviled. (p. 68)

Hook's definition is helpful in defining the social reality of lower-class-black-queer-male bodies in Jamaica, and in showing how Brown's cartoons work to represent and reify the active abjection of said bodies.

Conclusion

In this chapter, I have argued that Clovis Brown's cartoons are visual narratives that work to further ridicule and marginalize lower-class-black-queer-male bodies in Jamaica. His visual narratives are often premised on making singular the representation of lower-class-black-queer-male bodies as pernicious to Jamaica's political and sociocultural landscape. Brown's visual narratives are as nationalistic as they are queerphobic, since they serve to represent Jamaica's intolerance toward male homosexuality and other queer sexual identities. I also claim that since Brown is the sole caricaturist producing antiqueer visual narratives in Jamaica, he remains culturally relevant because of this, and is also perceived by many Jamaicans as merely an artistic reporter of Jamaican cultural affairs. This perception, I claim, is illusory; Brown's cartoons are, in fact, political insofar as they aid in furthering the marginalization of lower-class-black-queer-male Jamaicans along race-, class-, and gender-conservative lines. Additionally, I argued that Brown's cartoons facilitate a collective retraumatization of queer Jamaicans across racial, class, and gendered lines insofar as his visual representations work to excommunicate and consequently dehumanize the social presence of queer Jamaicans.

I also posited that existential anxieties experienced by lower-class-black-queer-male bodies are responses to antiqueer hostilities prevalent in Jamaican queerphobic culture. Such existential and ontological anxieties are connected to the phenomenological condition of queer embodiment in Jamaica. Antiqueer hostilities in Jamaica being known to be lethal, these anxieties are linked to ever-present concerns around being physically eliminated. Such social knowledge produces an epistemology of burden, wherein quotidian queerphobic encounters ordinarily experienced by lower-class-black-queer Jamaicans inform their unique social ontology, deemed separate, however connected to divergent ontologies generated from encountering systems of oppression. Finally, this chapter served to cover the politics of aesthetic representations by demonstrating the asymmetrical power relations that emerge in Brown's antiqueer visual narratives. In this regard, it aimed to complicate the illusive apolitical position of visual artistic expressions; the artist is never neutral in constructing visual narratives aimed at representing sociopolitical realities.

Note

1. Antiqueer representations are similarly perpetrated against and perniciously affect black-queer-female bodies and black transgender bodies in Jamaica (King, 2014). The focus of this discourse, however, is "homosocial" (Sedgwick, 1985).

Bibliography

Alexander, M.J. (1991). Redrafting morality: The postcolonial state and the sexual offences bill of Trinidad and Tobago. In C.T. Mohanty, A. Russo, & L. Torres (Eds.), *Third world women and the politics of feminism* (pp. 134–40). Indiana Press University.

Alturi, T.L. (2001). When the closet is a region: Homophobia, heterosexism and nationalism in the Commonwealth Caribbean. *Caribbean Review of Gender Studies*, 9, 287–326.

Armstrong, I. (2000). *The radical aesthetic*. Blackwell Publishers.

Banton, B. (2001). Boom bye bye. On *The Early Years: 1990–1995* [CD]. VP Records. (Original work published 1992)

Bilby, K. (2010). Surviving secularization: Masking the spirit in the Jankunu (John Canoe) festivals of the Caribbean. *New West Indian Guide, 84*(3–4), 179–223.

Bleys, R.C. (1995). *The geography of perversion: Male-to-male sexual behaviour outside the West and the ethnographic imagination*. New York University Press.

Brand, D. (1998). *No language is neutral*. McClelland & Stewart Press.

Butler, J. (2006). *Gender trouble: Feminism and the subversion of identity*. Routledge.

Cameron, D. (2006). *On language and sexual politics*. Routledge.

Carrol, D. (2000). The aesthetics of nationalism and the limits of culture. In S. Kemal & I. Gaskell (Eds.), *Politics and aesthetics in the arts* (pp. 112–39). Cambridge University Press.

Carroll, A.B. (2007). *The history of Junkanoo part two: The individual Junkanoo participants and performers 1940–2005*. AuthorHouse Press.

Charles, M. (2015) *Psychoanalysis and literature: The stories we live*. Rowman & Littlefield.

Chen, M.Y. (2012). *Animacies: Biopolitics, racial mattering, and queer affect*. Duke University Press.

Chivallon, C., & Fields, K.E. (2002). Beyond Gilroy's black Atlantic: The experience of the African Diaspora. *Diaspora: A Journal of Transnational Studies, 11*(3), 359–82. http://doi.org/10.1353/dsp.2011.0055

Chrisman, L. (2003). *Postcolonial contraventions: Cultural readings of race, imperialism and transnationalism*. Manchester University Press.

Cliff, M. (1989). *No telephone to heaven*. Vintage Press.

Cooper, C. (1993). *Noises in the blood: Orality, gender and the "vulgar" body of Jamaican popular culture*. Macmillan Caribbean.

Cooper, C. (2004). *Sound clash: Jamaican dancehall culture at large*. Palgrave Macmillan.

Crenshaw, K. (1989). Demarginalizing the intersection of race and sex: A black feminist critique of antidiscrimination doctrine, feminist theory and antiracist politics. *University of Chicago Legal Forum, 1*(8), 139–67.

Crowther, P. (1996). *Critical aesthetics and postmodernism*. Oxford University Press.

De Bolla, P. (2000). The discomfort of strangeness and beauty: Art, politics and aesthetics. In S. Kemal & I. Gaskell (Eds.), *Politics and aesthetics in the arts* (pp. 204–19). Cambridge University Press.

Derrida, J. (1972). *Positions*. University of Chicago Press.

Dessoir, M. (1970). *Aesthetics and theory of art*. Wayne State University Press.

Fanon, F. (1963). *The wretched of the earth* (C. Farrington, Trans.). Grove Press.

Fanon, F. (2008). *Black skin, white masks* (R. Philcox, Trans.). Grove Press. (Original work published 1952)

Foucault, M. (1990). *The history of sexuality: An introduction* (Vol. 1; R. Hurley, Trans.). Vintage Books. (Original work published 1978)

Foucault, M. (1995). *Discipline and punish: The birth of the prison* (A Sheridan, Trans.). Vintage Books. (Original work published 1977)

Gilroy, P. (1995). *The black Atlantic: Modernity and double consciousness*. Harvard University Press.

Glave, T. (2008) *Our Caribbean: A gathering of lesbian and gay writing from the Antilles*. Duke University Press.

Gordon, L.R. (2000). *Existentia Africana: Understanding Africana existential thought*. Routledge.

Hall, M. (2011). Negotiating Jamaican masculinities. In R.L. Jackson & M. Balaji (Eds.), *Global masculinities and manhood* (pp. 31–51). University of Illinois Press.

Harris, C.L. (1993). Whiteness as property. *Harvard Law Review, 106*(8), 1710–91.

Harris, T.A. (2014). Bleaching to reach: Skin bleaching as a performance of embodied resistance in Jamaican dancehall culture [Master's thesis, Florida International University]. FIU Institutional Repository. https://digitalcommons.fiu.edu/etd/1129/

Hirsch, J.S., Wardlow, H., Smith, D.J., Phinney, H.M., Parikh, S., & Nathanson, C.A. (2010). *The secret: Love, marriage, and HIV*. Vanderbilt University Press.

Hook, D. (2012) *A critical psychology of the postcolonial: The mind of Apartheid*. Routledge.

James, M. (2015, March 10). From Jamaica to Minnesota to myself. *New York Times*. https://www.nytimes.com/2015/03/15/magazine/from-jamaica-to-minnesota-to-myself.html

King, R.S. (2014). *Island bodies: Transgressive sexualities in the Caribbean imagination*. University Press of Florida.

Kristeva, J. (1982). *The powers of horror* (L.S. Roudiez, Trans.). Columbia University Press.

London Associated Press. (2015, October 13). Jamaica's Marlon James wins Booker Prize. *Jamaica Observer.* http://www.jamaicaobserver.com/NEWS/Jamaica-s-Marlon-James-wins-Booker-Prize_19233483

May, R. (1977). *The meaning of anxiety*. The Ronald Press Company.

Mbembe, A. (2001). *On the postcolony*. University of California Press.

Millet, K. (2000). *Sexual politics*. University of Illinois Press.

Moore, C. (2014). Wah eye nuh see heart nuh leap: Queer marronage in the Jamaican dancehall. [Master's thesis, Queen's University]. QSpace. https://qspace.library.queensu.ca/handle/1974/8599

Murray, R. (2007). Dark intimacies: Sex, nationalism and forgetting. *Our living manhood: Literature, Black Power, and masculine ideology*. University of Pennsylvania Press.

Narain, D. (2012). Naming same-sex desire in Caribbean women's texts: Toward a creolizing hermeneutics. *Contemporary Women's Writing*, 6(3), 194–22. https://doi.org/10.1093/cww/vps027

Offences Against the Person Act, Cap. 268. (1864). https://moj.gov.jm/laws/offences-against-person-act

Parr, H., & Butler, R. (2005). New geographies of illness, impairment, and disability. In R. Butler and H. Parr (Eds.), *Mind and body spaces: Geographies of illness, impairment and disability* (pp. 1–24). Taylor and Francis Group.

Radstone, S. (2007). Trauma theory: Contexts, politics, ethics. *Paragraph, 30*(1), 9–29. http://dx.doi.org/10.3366/prg.2007.0015

Rancière, J. (2004). *The politics of aesthetics: The distribution of the sensible* (G. Rockhill, Trans.). Continuum. (Original work published 2000)

Rancière, J. (2013). *Aisthesis: Scenes from the aesthetic regime of art* (Z. Paul, Trans.). Verso Press. (Original work published 2011)

Rommen, T. (2011). *Funky Nassau: Roots, routes, and representation in Bahamian popular music*. University of California Press.

Ronen, R. (2009). *Aesthetics of anxiety*. State University of New York Press.

Searle, J. (1969). *Speech acts: An essay on the philosophy of language*. Cambridge University Press.

Sedgewick, E. (1985). *Between men: English literature and male homosocial desire*. Columbia University Press.

Sheppard. M. (2003). *Mental health work in the community: Theory and practice in the social work and community psychiatric nursing*. Taylor and Francis Group.

Spivak, G.C. (2006). *In other worlds: Essays in cultural politics*. Taylor and Francis Group.

Thomas, D.A. (2004). *Modern blackness: Nationalism, globalization, and the politics of culture in Jamaica*. Duke University Press.

Wright, M.M. (2015). *Physics of blackness: Beyond the middle passage epistemology*. University of Minnesota Press.

Younge, G. (2006, December 6). Jamaican gay activist shot dead after being abducted. *The Guardian*. https://www.theguardian.com/world/2005/dec/06/gayrights.garyyounge

Zeleza, P.T. (2010). Reconceptualizing African diasporas: Notes from a historian. *Transforming Anthropology*, *18*(1), 70–73.

7

A Quare Eye to Slavery

Black Homoerotic Encounters in Brazil and Cuba

WATUFANI M. POE

The sexual question and the racial question have always been entwined.

—JAMES BALDWIN, *The Last Interview*

[M]en have been sleeping with men for thousands of years—and raising tribes...Men will be sleeping with each other when the trumpet sounds. It's only this infantile culture which has made such a big deal of it.

—JAMES BALDWIN, *The Last Interview*

BOTH ERASURE AND SILENCE fall on historicizing the desire, the horrors, and the sociospatial materiality of same-sex relations among the enslaved and between them and their masters over the 500 years of transatlantic slavery. It helps little that the terms of discourse by which same-sex pairing were narrated over the long arc of this time have changed, nor that the capacity to decode their cultural referents have, like an extinct language, also been lost (Woodard, 2014).

To this must be added two other factors, each of which leads, in different ways, to the pall of scholarly inquiry into male same-sex desire and the sexual exploitation of Black men during transatlantic slavery. The first involves the ongoing emergence since the 1960s of a lesbian, gay, bisexual, transgender, and queer (LGBTQ) aesthetic, identity, and politic. This cultural emergence is one that takes the present as a historically continuous fact, and has created a specific (and contested) narrative of what it means to locate one's identity in counter-heterosexual ideology and practice (Johnson, 2005). This narrative has in turn led to a lack of nuance in the historical memory of the intersection of slavery and homosexuality, and, in particular, the view that homosexuality is largely a construction of the nineteenth century (Aldrich, 2003; Foucault, 1978/1990). The second (and opposing) factor is that the post-1960s culture of Black Power and radical hegemonic Black masculinity theory has treated same-sex pairings as both distinctly "modern" and as internalizations of Eurocentric indulgences.

Centred on colonial and plantation Cuba and Brazil, which abolished slavery in 1886 and 1888 respectively, this chapter contributes to the still-emerging examination of Black men and same-sex relationships during transatlantic slavery. Given the contradictions and paradoxes—and at times the necessity—of transhistoricism in recuperating Black identities formed in the crucibles of slavery and colonialism, my task is to expose the complex interactions between systems of anti-Black racism, heteropatriarchy, capitalism, and slavery to come to an understanding of homoerotic desire and racism.

I draw on James Baldwin's (2014) assertion that men loving and having sex with men is ancient, generative of life, and, when reviled, is held out as a projective anxiety of danger and fear of the responsibility of loving another person as much as an ascetic "terror of the flesh" (p. 64). Also, using E. Patrick Johnson's (2005) notion of *quare* as a lens through which to approach same-sex desiring among Black men, I examine the intertwining of race and sexuality through three textual exegeses of sex and sexuality in Brazil and Cuba. The first two sections centre Brazil and Cuba in the preabolition periods through two texts: João Silvério Trevisan's (1986) social history of sexuality, *Perverts in Paradise*; and the slave narrative of Esteban Montejo, recorded and written by anthropologist Miguel Barnet (Montejo & Barnet, 1968) in *The Autobiography of a Runaway Slave*. Third,

I turn to interracial and same-sex male desire, love, obsession, and tragedy in one of the earliest novels of post-abolition Brazil, Adolfo Caminha's (1895/1982) *Bom-Crioulo: The Black Man and the Cabin Boy*.

With these materials as my empirical data, this chapter presents an alternative queering, or "quaring" of Black men's stories in slavery that centres questions of both sexuality and race. Such a quaring is in line with Baldwin's frequent and critical exegeses on love, which encourage us to rethink the sensual—particularly among Black people—if we are to struggle to attain the radical possibilities of a humanism that resists alienation and oppression. I argue that rethinking the realities of same-sex desire in the context of colonialist slavocracies—systems built on the exploitation of Black physical and sexual labour in which Black people's bodies, male and female, were the vehicles through which white (male) desires were articulated and realized, and through which white (male) wealth was built—provides an opportunity to rethink Black sexualities today. When thinking through sexual intimacy in the context of slavery, James Baldwin's (2014) aphorism that the sexual question is inseparable from the race question is most apt. Baldwin's point is that subjectivities and identitarian categories of analysis—even those often thought to be separate—are constantly in conversation. Black men's same-sex relationships with one another, as well as with their white masters, were defined by their Blackness, their slave status, their sexualities, and the African cultural traits brought with them across the Atlantic. This opens up the opportunity for nuanced accounts, analyses, reflections, and articulations of ability, class, gender, and sexuality from slavery through to emancipation and beyond to today. In conversation with Black feminist thought and Afrocentric scholarship, I propose an expansion of our understandings of Blackness, Africanity, and sexuality during the period of slavery in the colonial Americas.

Sexual Violence

The horrors enslaved Africans faced across the Americas were innumerable. On top of the painstaking physical labour required of enslaved Africans, many were also required to partake in sexual labour, fulfilling the wants of their masters. Black women experienced this exploitation of their sexual labour to an extreme. This super-exploitation of Black women (Davies, 2007, p. 2) is particularly evident in Latin America where notions of *mestizaje* and racial mixture seeped into the dominant rhetoric of society to mask and excuse the large-scale rape of enslaved African women. Black women, however, were not only forced into sexual relationships with their white masters, but also subject to sexual violence by being forced into relationships with Black men. As bell hooks (1981) says in her work *Ain't I a Woman: Black Women and Feminism*, "While institutionalized sexism was a social system that protected Black male sexuality, it (socially) legitimized sexual exploitation of Black females" (p. 24). She argues that although both Black women and Black men were disadvantaged under a slave system that survived on forced Black labour, Black men and white men were privileged above Black women through a patriarchal system. In fact, earlier in her work, hooks (1981) claims that "[t]he sexism of colonial white male patriarchs spared enslaved Black males the humiliation of homosexual rape and other forms of sexual assault" (p. 24).

The existence of multiple sexualities, however, complicates the sexual violence experienced by enslaved Black people in slavery across the diaspora. As Hortense Spillers (1987) argues in her work "Mama's Baby, Papa's Maybe: An American Grammar Book," the state of captivity in which Black people's bodies were kept blurred the lines of gender in slave societies. Spillers states, "Under these conditions, we lose at least gender difference in the outcome, and the female body and the male body become a territory of cultural and political maneuver, not at all gender-related, gender-specific" (p. 67). The complete availability of Black people's bodies under a slave system requires us to look at the ways in which Black men have also been subjected to sexual violence by white men, and how this complicates how heteropatriarchy relates to Black communities (Foster, 2011; Woodard, 2014). While hooks's (1981) statement—that is, that white colonial sexism "spared enslaved Black males the humiliation of homosexual rape and other forms of sexual assault" (p. 24)—represents one possible understanding of US slave society, it is important to analyze her statement diasporically and unpack colonial sexism in other contexts. I argue that white male (and female) entitlement over Black people's bodies ensured that heteropatriarchal norms did not, in fact, protect all Black men from sexual violence by their white masters.

Depending on their economies, development vis-à-vis contending imperial powers, topography, and method for conquering and displacing the Indigenous peoples, different slave systems in the Americas operated distinctly in each colony. These systems were all linked, however, by racial ideologies and the extreme oppression they enacted against Black people's bodies. Brazil—a country to which more than 4 million enslaved Africans were brought between 1531 and 1853, a number larger than any other colony in the Americas—is an extremely important space for examining the particularities of chattel slavery in the colonial Americas (Klein, 1987, p. 132). Cuba is another important site of study. After the success of the Haitian Revolution and the fall of Saint Domingue, Cuba became the centre of sugar production and was heavily reliant on slave labour (Ferrer, 2008, p. 269). While Cuba became the centre of sugar production, Brazil became the centre of coffee production, and both depended on Black people's bodies to produce their main export. The countries reliance on and prevalence of slavery practices also makes them important areas of study for thinking about and rethinking homosexuality and slavery.

In João Silvério Trevisan's (1986) *Perverts in Paradise*, which chronicles the history of homoeroticism in Brazil, Trevisan revisits Catholic confessions in Bahia, Brazil from 1591 to 1592. Throughout the records of the confessions, there are numerous accounts of rape and sexual encounters between enslaved Black men and their white masters. Trevisan (1986) recounts one account of these situations as follows:

> Pero Garcia, the owner of a large sugar-mill in Bahia..."overcome by the appetite of the flesh"...commit[ed] the sin of sodom with four partners, among them a free mulatto and two slaves. It was said that his relationship with Joseph, the mulatto, was so well-known and steadfast, that the other servants called Joseph "the master's concubine." (p. 53)

This case clearly shows an instance of sexual coercion and violence. As the owner of a large sugar mill in the centre of Brazil's slavocracy at the time, Garcia's entitlement over Black people's bodies is especially apparent. Although there is no information on the specifics of the encounter from the viewpoint of the two enslaved Blacks or the free mulatto, evidence suggests that his want for "flesh" and the feeling of ownership over Black people's bodies made Garcia feel that he was entitled to rape three of the four men. Even the free person mentioned was referred to as Garcia's concubine—which leads us to ask whether, for Garcia, a truly free Black (or mulatto) body existed or could exist that was beyond his sense of possession. Garcia's interaction with the men and other repeated sexual encounters suggests that in Garcia's mind, and within the confines of a slave society, it did not.

Trevisan (1986) describes another account from the confessions between two white, teenage brothers, Bastião and Antonio Aguia, and their slave Marcos:

> One night, as all three were sleeping in the same bed, the penitent lying face down, [Marcos] lay over him and placed his dishonest member in the back passage of the penitent, performed in him from behind as with a woman from the front, committing and effecting the sin of sodomy. By the same method he, the penitent, placed himself upon him and behind him, sleeping with him carnally as a man with a woman and this happened each of them some fifteen or twenty times in the space of a month. (p. 52)

This confession presents the complexity of sexual encounters between master and slave. Through this confession it would appear that the slave, Marcos, began a "consensual" sexual interaction. With no account of Marcos's side of the story, we are only left with the words of the young white masters. The power dynamics between young white slave masters and an enslaved Black person, however, call into question the "consent" of the enslaved. There might have been some want or desire from Marcos to engage sexually with his two young masters, and there might have been a kind of sexual or even romantic relationship between them. Within a slave society, however, Marcos's two young white masters had absolute control over his *being*, whereas Marcos could exert no power over his masters. As Saidiya Hartman (1997) says in *Scenes of Subjection*, "The opportunity for nonconsent is required to establish consent, for consent is meaningless if refusal is not an option" (p. 111). Marcos, as the property of his two white young masters, is owned in "its" entirety. The opportunity, therefore, to refuse advances by his white masters, even if he wanted to, is unavailable to Marcos as an enslaved person, rendering consent impossible. This doesn't mean that want or desire is not involved, but rather that complete agency is not possible, inherently complicating the ability to consent.

In his opening to the chapter that details these confessions, Trevisan chooses to begin on a comedic note, telling the story of a musical comedy by Hermilo Borba Filho. Trevisan says:

> A youth enters and confesses to having experienced "unparalleled delight" on sodomising a delicate slave. When the inquisitor asks if he has done it often, the boy immediately confesses: "More than a thousand times." Afterwards a group of men sings the "Buggers Anthem," which claims that it is much better to take it up the backside than to go to war or obey the government. (p. 40)

Trevisan's choice to include this story is strange, but deeply telling about the interaction between Brazil's slave society and Black humanity. Just as with a large majority of the confessions, the focus in this play is only on the "sin" and pleasure of the white men, and neglects the effect of sexual violence inflicted upon enslaved Black men. In addition, the treatment of the rape of enslaved Black men in the format of comedy suggests there is disregard for the traumas enslaved Black men experienced. They are simply objects for white men to use. Since their trauma is of no value, it is ripe for comedic retelling. The callousness of this musical comedy is reflective of the harsh realities of a slavocracy.

Why, then, is it important to acknowledge the realities of sexual violence perpetrated by white men[1] on Black men during slavery, regardless of how often or seldom it occurred? The instances of rape experienced by Black men show the complete ownership over Black people's bodies that white people claimed within slave societies. For white people, Black people's bodies were objects to fulfill all of their needs and desires, whatever those desires might be. These desires, however, did not always follow the norms of hegemonic society. The claim that heteropatriarchal norms protected Black men from any advances from their white male masters doesn't acknowledge that human desires do not follow such norms. Human desires are complex, and white men in a slave society were allowed to explore their desires—including those that departed from the beaten path of socially normative desire—using Black people's bodies, male and female, children and adults. But while both Black women and Black men were subjected to the sexual violence of their white masters, the freedom for Black people to explore their desires in a slave society, regardless of whether they had "free" or "slave" status, were severely restricted.

"Quare" Relations

As many scholars of the Black queer world have noted, queerness is commonly mapped as "foreign" or outside the cosmologies of a Black and African world (Beam, 1991; McBride, 2005; Pinho, 2004; Reid-Pharr, 2001). Investments in heteronormativity from within the Black world have attempted to paint a simplified image of histories of sex and sexuality in the Black diaspora that have ignored evidence that states otherwise (Aidoo, 2018; Woodard, 2014). Archival materials from colonial periods, as well as fiction writing, provide this contrary evidence. Same-sex desire among Africans appear in various records from colonial periods. These relations between Black men come across as foreign to our current day understandings of what "gay" or "lesbian" relations are. Homoerotic relations of Black people during slavery required a clever navigation of a system that profits from the dehumanization of Black people. Relations between Black men at the time also synthesized multiple cultures that were brought across the Atlantic from Africa through the slave trade. All of these factors make sexual and romantic same-sex relationships of Black men somewhat incompatible with our current language of sexuality. E. Patrick Johnson (2005), in his article "'Quare' Studies, Or (Almost) Everything I Know About Queer Studies I Learned From My Grandmother," provides helpful language for understanding this construction of sexuality. Johnson writes:

> "Quare"...not only speaks across identities, it *articulates* identities as well. "Quare" offers a way to critique stable notions of identity and, at the same time, to locate racialized and class knowledges...This reconceptualization foregrounds the ways in which lesbians, bisexuals, gays, and transgendered people of color come to sexual and racial knowledge...[T]he different "standpoints" found among lesbian, bisexual, gay, and transgendered people of color...are also conditioned by class and gender. (p. 127)

Applying the term *quare* to describe the complex sexualities of Black men within slavery is important to understanding their situation. The particular "class" situation of Blacks during slavery, whether free or enslaved, is one of disadvantage. In addition, the culture brought with them from before their arrival in the Americas complicates the translation of their gender and sexuality into a heteropatriarchal colonial American society. The intersectional approach provided by quareness gives an alternative lens through which to view Black men's sexuality.

In contrast to its Anglo-Protestant counterpart, the Latin-Catholic transatlantic slave regime provides the most fresh and abundant evidentiary possibilities for a meditation on homoerotic desire, homosexuality, and anti-Black racism. This is possibly due to its Catholic confessional culture and that the Inquisition provides unadorned evidence of intimate relations. I now turn to the example of Esteban Montejo, a Black Cuban man who lived through slavery and freedom in Cuba from 1860 to 1965. His story was recorded by anthropologist Miguel Barnet and published in 1968 as *The Autobiography of a Runaway Slave*. Barnet recounts Montejo's life in slavery, his escape, and his life post-slavery. Throughout Montejo's account of his enslaved life, he also mentions moments of witnessing quareness. At one point, Montejo, speaking about men on the plantation, says:

> Others had sex between themselves and did not want to know anything of women. This was their life-sodomy. The effeminate men washed the clothes and did the cooking too, if they had a "husband." They were good workers and occupied themselves with their plots of land, giving the produce to their "husbands" to sell to the white farmers. It was after Abolition that the term "effeminate" came into use, for the practice persisted. (Montejo & Barnet, 1986, p. 41)

Unlike complex situations of sexual violence between master and slave, the relationships described by Montejo are consensual and drawn from the desire of both parties. As Montejo understands it, there are social norms set up for these relationships. Such an account implies that these relationships are not isolated incidents; rather, they were common in Cuba, both during and after slavery.

Through Montejo's description, these relationships suggest multiple sites of negotiation with a heteropatriarchal society. The men defined roles for one another similar to those of "normal" heterosexual relationships seen on the island: husband and wife. This definition of roles suggests that these quare men are not only mimicking the social roles defined for men and women in society, but also the "active" sexual role defined for the husband and the "passive" sexual role defined for the wife. This mirrors roles in quare relationships in Brazil at the turn of the twentieth century and before, as outlined in James Green's (1999) work *Beyond Carnival: Male Homosexuality in Twentieth Century Brazil*. Green's juxtaposition of the roles of men who identified as more "masculine" and those who identified as more "feminine" applies to Montejo's explanation of the gendered roles in quare relationships in Cuba. Green (1999) says:

> While gendered roles are present in the representation of the *puto* and the *fanchono*, both have same-sex desires that differentiate them from other

> men. Moreover, the *fanchono* is not merely a married man or a sexually frustrated bachelor out on the town picking up boys because women are not available. His sexual object of choice is someone who, while feminized and younger, is not female. (p. 14)

Green's explanation of the masculinized *fanchono* and the feminized *puto* provide a framework for understanding the relationships Montejo outlines. This framework situates the relationship between quare men in a dichotomous masculine/feminine relationship, following the relationships between men and women dictated by society. Thus, same-sex desiring and performing Black men in Cuba and Brazil attempted to negotiate their desires within the rigid constructs of heterosexual and heteropatriarchal society.

A question arises, however, of how to explain Montejo's antipathy toward homosexual unions among enslaved men. Of relationships between enslaved men, Montejo says, "I don't think it can have come from Africa, because the old men hated it. They would have nothing to do with queers" (Montejo & Barnet, 1986, p. 41). Montejo's assertion, however, rests on entirely different foundations from that of historians and scholars who write sexual diversity out of African and African-diasporic history. Born into slavery in Cuba and having little interaction with his parents and others with memory of sexual diversity in "precontact" Africa, Montejo can only assume same-sex relationships arose in colonial and plantation culture. But when we compare Montejo's account with the Bahia confessions cited earlier (Trevisan, 1986), the supposition that quare relationships are antithetical to African identity appears to be specious. Trevisan (1986) says:

> Among blacks there were interesting cases such as that of Francisco Manicongo, a cobbler's apprentice known among the slaves as a sodomite for "performing the duty of a female" and for refusing to "wear the men's clothes which his master gave him." Francisco's accuser added "that in Angola and the Congo, in which lands he had wandered much and of which he had much experience, it is customary among the pagan negroes

> to wear a loincloth with the ends in which leave an opening in the rear... [T]his custom [is] adopted by those sodomitic negros who serve as passive women in the abominable sin. These passives are called *jimbandaa* in the language of Angola and the Congo, which means passive sodomite." The accuser claimed to have seen Francisco Manicongo "wearing a loin-cloth such as passive sodomites wear in his land of the Congo and he immediately rebuked him." (p. 55)

This account complicates the idea of same-sex desire not being rooted in Africanity, as well as the gendered roles within same-sex relationships being rooted solely in norms of colonial American society. The passage notes that the tradition of male homoerotic sex is not foreign to some communities from which enslaved Africans were stolen. The passage also suggests that in these cultures, there were those who desired to be the penetrated partner during sex. The existence of this cultural trait shows a possible root outside of colonial influence in the construction of quare relationships in Cuba and Brazil with such defined "active" and "passive" sexual roles.

In Trevisan's (1986) account, Manicongo's resistance to "men's" clothing of colonial Brazil suggests that norms of masculinity, gender, and sexuality were different than the Black African non-Creole societies, and that the process of negotiating their identity into colonial slave society was a violent one. Some Black men resisted violently imposed norms that insisted upon conformity with colonial European constructions of gender and sexuality. Yet it seems plausible that Black men could have found ways to maintain their African sexualities by blending conflicting traditions of masculinity and femininity in the colonial Americas. Indeed, there is plenty of evidence of this happening in other contexts. Take the religious and cultural traditions of Candomble, Capoeira, and Santeria, for example. All of these traditions are hybridization of African and European cultures—a means of hiding, protecting, and continuing the African cultures within them.

Representations of Interracial Desire and Intimacy Among Men in Early Brazilian Literature

Relationships between Black men and white men in slave societies were complex and harken back to the questions of Black agency and the possibility of consent mentioned before. Dealing with the complexities of societies that reduced Black people's bodies to property caused complications even for Black and white people who shared the same "free" legal and lower economic class status—even though racial difference is a permanent marker of differential aesthetic and symbolic status. Adolfo Caminha's (1895/1982) novel *Bom-Crioulo* [*Good Negro*] represents just this situation. First published in 1895, *Bom-Crioulo* was one of the first books to openly discuss homoerotic and homosexual relationships in Latin America. It tells the story of a formerly enslaved Black man, Amaro (also called Bom-Crioulo), who runs away and enrols in the navy in Rio de Janeiro. There, he meets a young white boy, Alexio, and falls deeply in love. At the end of the novel, Amaro's obsessive love for Alexio leads him to tragically murder his would-be lover. Although this is a work of fiction, it shows important historical trends of the time about which it was written. Peter Beattie (2001), in his historical account of the Brazilian army *The Tribute of Blood: Army, Honor, Race and Nation in Brazil 1864–1945*, explains that during the second half of the nineteenth century the Brazilian army, which was mostly constituted of Black and poor white men, dealt with multiple court cases suggesting the prevalence of homoerotic sexual relations amongst soldiers (p. 277). Caminha himself, a former lieutenant in the military, would have had firsthand knowledge of homosexual encounters within the military.

Caminha's construction of Amaro and Alexio's relationship in *Bom-Crioulo* is rooted in a mimesis of the gender norms of heteropatriarchal Brazilian society. When Amaro begins to feel deeply for Alexio, Caminha describes his feelings saying, "He was very fond of the cabin-boy, and he was sure that now he could win him over completely, the way one conquers a beautiful woman, a virgin wilderness, a land of gold" (p. 35). Articulated in the connotations and lexical codes of his time, the audience is able to apprehend Caminha's account of desire between the two men because it is presented in the form of a relationship between a man or *fanchono* (masculine) and woman or *puto* (feminine). Quareness is foundational to Alexio and Amaro's relationship. Amaro is the masculine "husband" and Alexio is the feminine "wife." Caminha draws on this dynamic further in describing Amaro's seemingly gallant defence of Alexio, saying that Amaro was a "true, unselfish protector" (p. 46) of Alexio, who goes so far as to attack other soldiers who intimidate Alexio. Amaro's "masculine" defence of Alexio shows a strong desire to uphold colonial constructs of hegemonic masculine and feminine roles. In addition, analyzing the racial aspect of Amaro and Alexio's relationship, it is possible to read Amaro's "unselfish" protection of Alexio as the desire of Caminha, and of colonial Brazilian elites more generally, to imagine protection and reconciliation rather than retaliation and retribution from enslaved Brazilians.

Raised enslaved in a slave society, Amaro would have understood that Black subjectivity, relative to white objectivity, is an impossibility. This system sets up a hierarchy of value on human life, placing Black lives at the bottom and white lives at the top. In addition, Beattie's (2001) work also discusses how the military was used to protect the white elite of Brazil from the largely African and mixed-race masses. Amaro's naval training would have, in other words, indoctrinated him into a practice of protecting whiteness in Brazilian society. Within this context, we must ask whether the budding love and protectiveness Amaro—a Black man raised in a society that places little value on Black life—feels for Alexio—a white young man who, despite his status as poor, lives in a society that largely values his whiteness—is rooted in authentic desire or an unconscious upholding of white supremacy.

Alexio's eventual murder at the hands of Amaro is foreshadowed throughout the novel by descriptions of Amaro's uncontrollable passion and rage. This event is one example of a literary trope that depicts the African man as animal, ruled by sexual passion rather than reason and civility. Like his portrayal of Amaro as a protector of white people, Caminha's portrayal of Amaro as dangerous could also be rooted in white fear of rebellion from runaways and other "freed" Black people. Caminha (1895/1982) narrates, "In those days the 'runaway Negro' terrified the whole population to an unbelievably extent...Doors were locked and bolted in fear and trembling" (p. 37). The irrational fear of Amaro and other runaways highlights the fear of "free" Blackness in colonial Brazil. Revolts like the *Malê* Rebellion[2] struck fear in the hearts of white Brazilians that their Black and mixed-race majority might rise up against them (Reis, 1995). Whites might have also feared backlash in the form of Black mimetic violence that would recompense the horrors of slavery upon whites.

Caminha's portrayal of Amaro may well also be signalling that that no good comes of an interracial union in which Blackness occupies the dominant gender position and whiteness the subordinate. Indeed, when Amaro and Alexio move into an apartment in Rio de Janeiro together and begin to regularly consummate their desire for one another, Amaro's passion is portrayed as disproportionately intense. At the sight of Alexio's naked body, Caminha (1895/1982) writes, "[a]ll the raging desire of the bull when he senses the presence of the female roared within the black man" (p. 75). Equating Amaro's lust for Alexio to a bull calls forth a violent image of a man waiting to charge. Amaro's feelings are filled with intensity, while Alexio gently shows fondness for Amaro. Caminha's bestial portrayal of Amaro's blind desire for his young white lover conveys dangerousness, not only that which African men represent in general, but also unrestrained passion that they symbolize in particular.

Whereas Caminha's *Bom-Crioulo* rehearses deep-seated anxieties about Black men dominating white men, Trevisan's research shows documented historical instances of interracial same-sex encounters in which a Black man was imagined to have deflowered and feminized adonic white masculinity. Trevisan (1986) retells the story of an African-descended man accused of raping a white boy in the Bahian confessions:

> And let us not forget Mateus Duarte, a 50-year-old free mulatto who "has been held in prison in Salvador for a year and a half, accused of having committed the abominable sin of sodomy, according to public knowledge, which says that he attacked a white boy of seventeen and that the said boy did not consent and cried out." (p. 53)

This instance is the only time a rape by an African-descended man of a white man is mentioned in Trevisan's account of the confessions. It is also one of the few times Trevisan tells of an imprisonment resulting from a case of sexual violence, despite the numerous accounts of sexual violence from white men towards Black men and women.

In the context of the fear of Black compensatory violence, revolts, and freedom, this pederastic incident raises a range of possibilities about which the archive is silent, likely because knowing that sexual desire transcends racial difference would have felt particularly threatening. Did the story happen as the boy told it? There is no question this is a possibility, but it is at least as possible that context has been erased from the archives that could have given us other ways of understanding the situation and the reaction to it. Given the age of consent as we understand it today did not apply to the colonial period (Aldrich, 2003), we might ask what prior knowledge or relation these two had with each other. We might also wonder about the context in which this incident was constituted as an act of rape. Were the two caught in a willing embrace and the boy feigned rape, clearly signalling the vulnerability of enslaved and free Black men to act with sexual sovereignty? Did the boy not cry out at all, but his father and the white magistrates prosecuted the case because same-sex penetration was understood to be a perversion that white men were allowed to exercise on Black men and boys—not the other way around? What if the case were reversed and it were a 50-year-old white male pederast who debauched a 17-year-old Black boy, willing or unwilling, known or unknown? Would such a situation ever give rise to the protection of Black boyhood, prosecution of the pederast, and mobilization of the discourse of rape? To be sure, these are empirical questions that are abstract only to the extent the archives are silent about details that would make explicit the playing out of the deeper meanings of homoerotic desire, homosexuality, and racism in both Cuban and Brazilian slave plantocracies.

Conclusion

As evidenced by the stories of Montejo (Montejo & Barnet, 1986), Caminha (1895/1982), and Trevisan (1986), Black men practising same-sex desire had to translate their desire to fit in as best they could with an anti-Black heteropatriarchal society. At the same time, these men offer their loving as a site of African cultural reclamation. A common dismissal of quareness by Black men invested in heteropatriarchy is the argument that "homosexuality" is not an African cultural trait. Homosexuality, as communicated through Eurocentric societies, might be "un-African" (although this is up for debate), but quareness, a same-sex desire rooted in the complex histories of African and African-descended people, is not. Through these stories, it is clear that Black quare men's expression of their sexuality during slavery is linked to the colonial systems they inhabited. Moreover, it is clear that these practices are also rooted in cultures of same-sex desire in which some Africans lived before their journey across the Atlantic. For Black quare men in colonial Latin America, negotiating between their past and present contexts became a constant necessity.

The stories mentioned throughout this chapter highlight the complex histories of sexuality within Afro-Latin America, and root this sexuality not only in the colonial cultures is which Africans were enslaved, but also in the African cultures they brought with them. Constant negotiation was necessary for these relationships, which contradicted the norms of colonial slave societies, to continue to survive. The acknowledgement of these histories is important to understanding not only the histories of the African diasporas, but their current realities. The negation of queer Black sexualities during slavery erases an important history. This erasure then contributes to the erasure of contemporary Black quare communities and questions the nature of Black quare love and desire. There must be a full telling of the complex histories of the African diaspora to ensure that the complex lives of Black people throughout the diaspora can embrace all of their complexities. Only then will the full humanity of African, Afro-Latin, and African American lives be acknowledged.

But there is more work to do than simply telling the story of these complexities. What love, loving, sex, and sexuality looked like in slavery, a regime of horror, is not a matter of the past. Rather, it is a matter of recuperating—now, today—complexities and simplicities that challenge us to transcend the horrors of ascetism and the recoil from love and the flesh. In other words, it is a matter of the sort of radical humanism espoused by Baldwin—one that sees beyond binarism in sexual identity. It also speaks to the dangers of ascetic power, fear of love and pleasure, that exceeds the parameters of singular identitarian politics. As Baldwin (2014) recounts,

> [coming to terms with my sexuality]...frightened me so much...But the so-called straight person is no safer than I am really. Loving anybody and being loved by anybody is a tremendous danger, a tremendous responsibility. Loving of children, raising of children. The terrors homosexuals go through in this society would not be so great if the society itself did not go through so many terrors which it doesn't want to admit. The discovery of one's sexual preference doesn't have to be a trauma. It's a trauma because it's a traumatized society. (p. 63)[3]

Author's Note

A huge thanks to Tamari Kitossa for his dedicated help editing and thinking through my ideas. Thanks, too, to my adviser Keisha-Khan Perry for her detailed workshopping of the chapter with me in her class; to Lamonte Aidoo and Jafari Allen for their scholarship and mentorship, which helped fuel my interest in the subject; and my parents Evelyn and Zizwe Poe, whose Pan-Africanist mentalities always pushed me to think about the diverse histories of the African Diaspora.

Notes

1. Thomas Foster (2011) shows that, despite its occurrence, the fact that white women, be they masters or not, also sexually abused enslaved Black men is an area of inquiry that has been little explored.
2. The *Malê* Rebellion was a rebellion organized by Black enslaved Muslims in 1835 in Salvador da Bahia, Brazil. Inspired by the Haitian Revolution nearly 40 years earlier, the rebellion was planned for Sunday, January 25, 1835. The day before, however, police received tips that the rebellion would happen the next day, and in a day-long confrontation with the police authorities, the fighting rebels were captured or killed. The rebellion served as a catalyst for an adoption of stricter laws governing enslaved people in Brazil, as fear of rebellion struck through the minds of slave owners throughout Brazil.
3. In his classic work on sex, sexuality, and the British empire, Ronald Hyam (1991) noted that venereal disease and sexual license of all sorts, including pioneering the development and traffic in pornography, were spread by an imperial order whose soldier's and official's libidos found

ample opportunity for release. Paradoxically, official discourse was not far from practice: "One of the worst results of the expansion of Britain was the introduction of its guilty inhibitions about sex into societies previously much better sexually adjusted than perhaps any in the west" (Hyam, 1991, p. 3). As I have demonstrated in this chapter, Iberian colonies in the Americas, along with the efforts of the Catholic Church's puritanical forays, are entwined in a similar paradox.

Bibliography

Aidoo, L. (2018). *Slavery unseen: Sex, power, and violence in Brazilian history*. Duke University Press.

Aldrich, R. (2003). *Colonialism and homosexuality*. Routledge.

Allen, J.S. (2011). *Venceremos? The erotics of Black self-making in Cuba*. Duke University Press.

Allen, J.S. (2012). Black/queer/diaspora at the current conjuncture. *GLQ: A Journal of Lesbian and Gay Studies*, *18*(2–3), 211–48. https://doi.org/10.1215/10642684-1472872

Asante, M.K. (2009). *Encyclopedia of African religion*. SAGE.

Baldwin, J. (2014). *James Baldwin: The last interview and other conversations*. Melville House Publishing.

Beam, J. (1991). *Brother to brother: New writings by Black gay men*. E. Hemphill (Ed.). Alyson Publications.

Beattie, P.M. (2001). *The tribute of blood: Army, honor, race, and nation in Brazil, 1864–1945*. Duke University Press.

Caminha, A. (1982). *Bom-crioulo: The Black man and the cabin boy*. Gay Sunshine. (Original work published 1895)

Davies, C. (2007). *Left of Karl Marx: The political life of Black communist Claudia Jones*. Duke University Press.

Dos Santos, G.A. (2002). *A invenção do "ser negro": um percurso das idéias que naturalizaram a inferioridade dos negros [The invention of "being Black": A journey of ideas that naturalized the inferiority of Blacks]*. Universidad Pontificia Comillas.

Ferrer, A. (2008). Cuban slavery and Atlantic antislavery. *Review (Fernand Braudel Center)*, *31*(3), 267–95. https://www.jstor.org/stable/40241721

Foster, T. (2011). The sexual abuse of Black men under American slavery. *Jounral of the History of Sexuality*, *20*(3), 445–64.

Foucault, M. (1990). *The history of sexuality: An introduction* (Vol. 1; R. Hurley, Trans.). Vintage Books. (Original work published 1978)

Green, J.N. (1999). *Beyond carnival: Male homosexuality in twentieth-century Brazil*. University of Chicago Press.

Hartman, S.V. (1997). *Scenes of subjection: Terror, slavery, and self-making in nineteenth-century America*. Oxford University Press.

Hartman, S., & Wilderson, F. (2003). The position of the unthought. *Qui Parle*, *13*(2), 183–201. https://www.jstor.org/stable/20686156

hooks, b. (1981). *Ain't I a woman: Black women and feminism*. South End.

Hyam, R. (1991). *Empire and sexuality: The British experience*. University of Manchester Press.

Johnson, E.P. (2005). "Quare" studies, or almost everything I know about queer studies I learned from my grandmother. In E.P. Johnson (Ed.), *Black queer studies: A critical anthology* (p. 124–57). Duke University Press.

Klein, H.S. (1987). A demografia do tráficoatlântico de escravos para o Brasil [The demographics of the Atlantic slave trade to Brazil]. *EstudosEconômicos*, *17*(2), 129–49. http://www.revistas.usp.br/ee/article/view/157390

McBride, D. (2005). *Why I hate Abercrombie & Fitch: Essays on race and sexuality*. NYU Press.

Montejo, E., & Barnet, M. (1968). *The autobiography of a runaway slave*. Pantheon.

Pang, E.S. (1979). Modernization and slavocracy in nineteenth-century Brazil. *The Journal of Interdisciplinary History*, 9(4), 667–88. http://doi.org/10.2307/203379

Pinho, O. (2004). A guerra dos mundos homossexuais: Resistência e contra-hegemonias de raça e gênero [The war of the homosexual worlds: Resistance and counterhegemony of race and gender]. In Rios, L.F., de Almeida, V., Parker, R., Pimenta, C., & Terto, V., Jr. (Eds.), *Homossexualidade: Produção Cultural, Cidadania e Saúde* (pp. 127–33). ABIA: Associação Brasileira Interdisciplinar de AIDS.

Reid-Pharr, R.F. (2001). *Black gay man: Essays*. NYU Press.

Reis, J.J. (1995). *Slave rebellion in Brazil: The Muslim uprising of 1835 in Bahia*. Taylor & Francis.

Spillers, H.J. (1987). Mama's baby, papa's maybe: An American grammar book. *Diacritics*, *17*(2), 64–81. http://doi.org/10.2307/464747

Trevisan, J.S. (1986). *Perverts in paradise*. Alyson Publications.

Tinsley, O.E.N. (2008). Black Atlantic, queer Atlantic: Queer imaginings of the middle passage. *GLQ: A Journal of Lesbian and Gay Studies*, *14*(2–3), 191–215. https://doi.org/10.1215/10642684-2007-030

Woodard, V. (2014). *The delectable Negro: Human consumption and homoeroticism within US slave culture*. NYU Press.

"7 Eleven"

Dialectics of Jamaican Popular Music Culture and Hegemonic Masculinity

DENNIS O. HOWARD

> *It is worth observing, too, that when men can no longer love women they also cease to love or respect or trust each other, which makes their isolation complete. Nothing is more dangerous than this isolation, for men will commit any crimes whatever rather than endure it.*
>
> —JAMES BALDWIN, "The Male Prison"

> *Overnight the Negro has been given two frames of reference within which he has to place himself... [H]is customs and the sources on which they are based, were wiped out because they were in conflict with a civilization that he did not know and that imposed itself on him.*
>
> —FRANTZ FANON, "The Fact of Blackness"

THIS CHAPTER IS A MEDITATION on the ambivalence, contradictions, and fragilities of poor, working-class men in Jamaica's garrison communities in their resistance and transcendence of what has come to be termed "toxic masculinities" (Knuttila, 2016). I draw on James Baldwin's and Frantz Fanon's approaches to culture, gender, eroticism, and critique of masculinity to describe the context in which trend-setting artists such as Dexta Daps resist both the official morality of middle-class Jamaican sexual mores and hegemonic heteropatriarchal norms. But while it is vital to resist "uptown people's" and foreign imperialist's anti-Black racism that stigmatizes garrison communities[1]—especially the men in these communities—as the ultimate embodiments of the worst that heteropatriarchy has to offer, I take seriously the prospects and possibilities, and ultimately the failings, of garrison-based artists to fully embody what Athena Mutua (2006) calls "progressive Black masculinity" (p. xi). I aim to show that in Jamaica, popular music culture has long been a site at which the liberating impulses of desire, gender, and sexuality have been a vehicle to reproduce, reify, and challenge upper- and middle-class values and hegemonic masculinities.

I will begin this chapter by outlining the theoretical and methodological foundations on which my research and analysis is based. In line with this groundwork, I will then present the cultural context of Jamaican popular music and garrison music culture; in particular, I will examine the gender norms and hegemonic masculinity at work there. The stage being set, I will then dive into an analysis of Dexta Daps's (2015) controversial song "7 Eleven," and how it both challenges and plays into these gender norms. Finally, I will examine this challenge through both a biblical lens and the lens of gender performativity.

Theory and Method

My research and analysis in this chapter rests on several theoretical considerations, which should be kept in mind throughout. It is my aim to uncover the apparent conflict between the aggressive, male-dominated ethos of Jamaican popular culture that privileges misogynistic tendencies as normative behaviours that are articulated through cultural texts such as popular music recordings. Popular culture in Jamaica is now grappling with a serious challenge to the prevalent male-centred hegemonic worldview that fetishizes the female body and sexuality. This challenge questions the established norm of relegating the female body to the male gaze an object of male sexual gratification. The interrogation of this phenomenon through the lyrics of Dexta Daps's (2015) song "7 Eleven," and its manifestation on popular culture will rely on a cultural studies theoretical perspective.

The ostensible emancipation of female sexuality and female empowerment and the rejection of male stereotyping of the female body marks the metamorphosis of a new millennial female body politic. This politic is free of the puritanical restrictions, Victorian values, sexual continence, and propriety imposed on working-class Jamaicans by the colonial metanarratives that have been adopted by Jamaica's elite from our imperial colonizers.

The chapter will, however, also draw on discourses of Caribbean male identity and hegemonic masculinity. There seem to be variations in the established notions of masculinity within popular culture as the effects of globalization take hold of cultural negotiations in the urban space. Masculinity and gender identity, it appears, are being blurred in a world linked by megabytes rather than by real human interaction. Donna Hope (2015) makes the point that "the core issues that underscore Caribbean masculinity are those of power and control, and historical shifts in Afro-Caribbean masculinities are informed by the concept of hegemony" (p. 107). If there is, in fact, a cultural shift in male/female interaction and politics, what are these new hegemonic considerations?

One answer involves the concept of progressive Black masculinity of the sort heralded by James Baldwin's (1976) critique of hegemonic masculinity. The term *progressive Black masculinity* as used by Athena Mutua (2006) refers to

> the unique and innovative performances of the masculine self that on the one hand personally eschew and ethically and actively stand against social structures of domination. On the other hand, they validate and empower black humanity, in all its variety, as part of the diverse and multicultural humanity of others in the global family. (p. 4)

Progressive Black masculinities provide a countervailing critique to the hegemonic tendencies of Afro-Caribbean masculinity mentioned beforehand. As Mutua (2006) notes, progressive masculinity "centers its efforts on reorienting men's concepts and practices away from ideal masculinity, which, by definition, requires the domination of men over women, children, and, yes, other subordinate or 'weaker' men" (p. 5). Progressive Black masculinity will provide an explanation for the way in which Dexta Daps's "7 Eleven" ostensibly upended the hegemonic tendencies of the patriarchal colonial domination of Caribbean society. It does this, I argue, by virtue of its pro-Black, antiracist, profeminist, and antisexist stance (see Mutua, 2006).

With these theoretical ground stones in place, I must also make a few preliminary comments about the methods according to which I undertook this research and analysis. This chapter will rely heavily on content analysis and ethnography, two qualitative tools that have a long tradition in analyzing cultural text. Qualitative content analysis is one of the numerous research methods used to analyze text data. As Hsieh and Shannon (2005) note, "research using qualitative content analysis focuses on the characteristics of language as communication with attention to the content or contextual meaning of the text" (p. 1278). They do not refer here to language in the abstract, but to a fully sociological examination that conforms with C. Wright Mills's (2000) conception of the "sociological imagination," which takes in hand both personal troubles and their agglomeration into social issues. In other words, decoding culture into the manifest and latent dynamics operative in the social experience of actors is vital to the exploration of textual meaning. Making sense of social experience also requires an appreciation of social participants as historical actors who are free-willing agents of their own making, with the power to shape their lives and the events around them. But as Marx has said, we ought not to confuse the abstract principle of individual sovereignty with the concrete reality that, by virtue of *being*, we are ontologically compelled (i.e., coerced) by the fact of being embedded in contemporary and historical relations not of our choosing. In other words, when theorizing social reality, we must grapple with the Marxist dialectic of agency and structure. That is, we must understand that all persons and groups are a constellation of prior and contemporary relations of domination and interaction that mutually inform each other and that have concrete effects beyond the control of any one person (Hoffman, 1988). Language, because it is a currency that stores meaning and is the principal medium in the making of social reality, is therefore not simply a loose collection of words bound by grammar and syntax. It is, instead, "a totality of determined notions and concepts" (Gramsci & Buttigieg, 1992), which therefore identifies it as an artifact of political expression.

Taking language as both the site and medium of political expression positions us to (re)consider political "discourse" as more than simply coherent speech and writing. On one hand, discourse is a way for social actors to *represent* social experience. On the other, it constitutes an object that researchers subject to critical scrutiny to expose the interests of social actors in relation to hegemonic constructions of reality (Hall, 1996). Thus, Hall (1996) argues:

> A discourse is a group of statements which provide a language for talking about—i.e., a way of representing—a particular kind of knowledge about a topic. When statements about a topic are made within a discourse, the discourse makes it possible to construct the topic in a certain way. It also limits the other ways in which the topic can be constructed. (p. 201)

Where text, talk, and representation constitute the raw materials of cultural studies, qualitative content analysis corresponds to critical discourse analysis (CDA): a rigorous process of identifying and deconstructing what seem to be self-evident, taken-for-granted ideologies. CDA demonstrates that such ideologies in fact constitute "the mental frameworks—the languages, the concepts, categories, imagery of thought and the systems of representation—which different classes and social groups deploy in order to make sense of, define, figure out and render intelligible the ways society works" (Hall, 1996 p. 26). CDA, then, is "a study of the relations between discourse, power, dominance, social inequality and the position of discourse analyst in such social relations" (van Dijk, 1993, p. 249). As such, "critical discourse analysts want to know [and demonstrate] what structures, strategies or other properties of text, talk, verbal interaction or communicative events play a role in modes of reproduction [i.e., affect, cognition, psychology]" (van Dijk, 1993, p. 250) and, it should be added, in production.

CDA, as a methodology, implies that researchers must understand themselves to be always already entangled in the relations of accommodation, dominance, subordination, and resistance manifest in the discourses they wish to study. CDA researchers must, therefore, situate themselves ethnographically within the study. According to Scott Reeves et al. (2008), "ethnography is the study of social interactions, behaviours, and perceptions that occur within groups, teams, organizations, and communities" (p. 512). The study of this recording and its cultural destabilization of traditional perception of maleness in Jamaican society lends itself to utilizing this methodological tool. As Reeves et al. (2008) note, "[t]he central aim of ethnography is to provide rich, holistic insights into people's views and actions, as well as the nature (that is, sights, sounds) of the location they inhabit, through the collection of detailed observations and interviews" (p. 512).

I will unpack the mentalities, performances, and representations of garrison cultural production in Jamaica using the methods and modes of discourse analysis described above. In line with Reeves et al.'s (2008) ethnographic approach, I conducted unstructured interviews for this chapter. These interviews targeted key participants in Kingston's popular music scene. The research also takes into account my own position as an industry insider. My personal observations of individuals' reactions to Dexta Daps's "7 Eleven" are also considered to be data, and are included in the data analysis. Following a CDA model, my analysis will involve, in particular, centring the fact that cultural texts signify competing social and political narratives and practices in the life worlds of social actors who are engaged in making meaning of their existence.

Jamaican Popular Music Culture and Social Forces in the Garrison

My claim in this chapter is that Dexta Daps's song "7 Eleven" challenges conservative Jamaican heteropatriarchy within the context of Jamaican popular music culture. Before I deconstruct Daps's song, however, I want to make some preliminary observations that situate garrison communities as cultural and sociopolitical spaces in which class, global, and neoliberal forces shape manifestations, performances, and understandings of gender relations. I also want to explain my choice of certain specific terminology within this context.

I use the term *popular music culture* in the title of this chapter intentionally. It indicates my deliberate departure from the use of the term *dancehall* in referring to the current Jamaican reality within the Jamaican music scene and popular cultural movement. I will argue that as evidence of a Victorian bourgeois class mentality, those referred to by garrison residents and working-class Jamaicans as "uptown people" are a distinct cultural articulation of capitalist social relations of production in Jamaica that reinforces the social distance between the middle- and working-class and marginalized populations. Despite the sharpness of their class privileges and spatial distance, however, "uptown youth" have embraced and appropriated aspects of downtown or garrison culture. It may well be that, as with White youth in the 1950s and 1960s in relation to rock and roll and more recently ghetto African forms such as trap, Jamaican uptown youth relate to garrison culture as their point of resistance to the empty materialism of bourgeois culture.

In many ways, garrison culture is to uptown culture as privileged planation culture was to the culture of the disenfranchised. Even though the uptown youth appropriation of garrison culture is not likely to transform itself into a substantive politics of transclass solidarity toward the development of a socialist national culture, it is suggestive of such a possibility.[2] The existence of two distinctive class structures within popular culture in Jamaica is not new, but we need to acknowledge this phenomenon and find ways to engage with it to gain a comprehensive understanding of the realities of youth culture in Jamaica and the Caribbean today. My discomfort with the continued use of the dancehall label is rooted in the fact that this label does not adequately describe the new realities of urban popular culture in Jamaica. As part of an ongoing class warfare in Jamaica that registers itself in cultural expression, the word *dancehall* has increasingly been used as a pejorative by Jamaica's uptown middle class and national elites. The aim of this uptown move is to devalue poor, disenfranchised, working-class youngsters, with the net effect of relegating and maintaining them to the lowest rungs of Jamaica's pigmentocratic socioeconomic ladder (see McIntosh, Chapter 6 in this volume).

Representatives of official state morality and moral entrepreneurs alike have generated moral panics and scapegoated popular culture and garrison-driven music as evidence of the moral failings of poor youths, painting them as sexual deviants and gun-toting criminals who are making Jamaica an unsafe country. While popular culture may be viewed as contributing factor to social problems, it in reality cannot be isolated as the cause of social problems when there are so many forces of structural violence (e.g., poverty, structural adjustment, official corruption, police violence, etc.) at play. These forces of structural violence denote illegal and illicit conduct from the government and elites on down. I have, therefore, abandoned the use of the term *dancehall* both as signifier of the current idiomatic creative output in popular music and the sociopolitical and cultural environment (i.e., popular cultural spaces within which cultural norms, lifestyle, and texts are produced). For the purposes of this discussion on class, gender, and heteropatriarchy, I will instead use the terms *garrison culture*, *uptown culture*, *Jamaican popular music* and *popular music culture* to denote and describe the current cultural and sociopolitical milieu in which Jamaican recordings are being produced and cultural trends created and negotiated. I believe these descriptors will allow for a clearer, deeper, and multilayered exploration of the ambiguities, ambivalences, and contradictions of Dexta Daps's ostensible critique of hegemonic patriarchy.

Garrison culture[3] can be defined as the current styles, behaviour, trends, slangs, and social interactions that permeate the pop culture space of most urban, working-class areas of Jamaica. Some of these areas have been immortalized in popular recordings. Garrisons like Rema, Arnett Gardens, Tivoli Gardens, Waterford, Canterbury, Flankers, Tel Aviv, Dunkirk, and Water House were called into being by the post-1980s pauperization of structural adjustment and the political clientelism of the Jamaica Labour Party (of Seaga fame) and the People's National Party (of Michael Manley fame) which welcomed in an era of "dons"—gang leaders—who act as both enforcers and disbursers of party handouts. Garrison communities—well-armed and hostile to other territories—are cultural, social, special, and political configurations that nonetheless reflect internalized class conflicts and the sentiments of political parties. Yet for all this, garrison culture is the source of all the latest slangs, dance moves, and fashion statements, and an intense site of gender negotiations in Jamaican society. Trends start in the garrisons and radiate outward through the process of legitimization and acceptance under the auspices of the sound system culture and social media. From there, garrison cultural trends and products move into the mainstream through mass media to shape Jamaican popular culture.

Inasmuch as garrison culture is the product of colonialism, the afterlife of plantation slavery, globalization, and neoliberal capitalism, it can be argued that uptown culture is equally the result of the same dynamics and forces that have engulfed the Caribbean. According to George Monbiot (2016),

> neoliberalism sees competition as the defining characteristic of human relations. It redefines citizens as consumers, whose democratic choices are best exercised by buying and selling, a process that rewards merit and punishes inefficiency. It maintains that "the market" delivers benefits that could never be achieved by planning. (p. 2–3)

In the post-structural-adjustment era, Jamaica is explicitly a society of haves and have nots, and this situation it is worsening. Due to these dynamics, Jamaica is now a highly competitive and consumer driven society in which the majority of the working- and under-classes are victims of low wages and under- and unemployment. They have limited and deficient health care and no social welfare system to speak of. These are arguably the inevitable consequences of deregulation and state–corporate collusion. At the same time, however, there are those who cannot engage in the formal economy but must instead depend on a mix of remittances and participate in a vibrant and thriving informal economy. Any effort to make sense of garrison culture, particularly the ways in which masculinities articulate themselves, must recognize the deepening and widening of the ways the informal economy is structured both by capitalism and as a site of resistance to wage-labour corporate–state discipline. The privileged class in Jamaica is keen to emulate the grand lifestyle of the rich in North America and Europe—a lifestyle that economists have suggested the country can neither afford nor sustain. But the garrison stands as a rich site of cultural production and resistance to official morality. At the same time, however, it takes part in the dominant discourse of masculinity. It is, then, both a unique challenge to and an accommodation of heteropatriarchy.

Dexta Daps and Jamaican Popular Music Culture: Locating the Problematic

The controversial lyrics of the 2015 hit "7 Eleven" from Jamaican popular music artist Dexta Daps are unparalleled. No other song has in recent times created such a stir in the Jamaican society. To be sure, the controversy raised by Daps is not a first. Popular music from mento to dancehall to one beat[4] has been the site of controversy and excitement for music fans and the broader society from as far back as the start of recorded sound in Jamaica. Mento songs of the 1950s such as "Night Food"[5] by Alerth Bedasse (1958), 1960s ska songs such as "Push Wood" by Jackie Opel (1965) and rock steady classics such as "Fatty Fatty" by the Heptones (1967) and "Wet Dream"[6] by Max Romeo (1968) created their fair share of concern, censorship, and controversy. They openly celebrated the liberating pleasures of desire and heterosexual sex, though problematically within a framework that centred the autonomy of men to objectify women and their bodies. Such songs affected and reflected attitudes and perceptions both about sex and sexuality and about the most appropriate purposes to which popular music should be put.

Dexta Daps follows in the tradition of pushing the envelope established by his musical forebears in Kingston's garrison enclaves, which are persistently the crucible of popular music and creative expression in Jamaica (Howard, 2016). Daps's (2015) song "7 Eleven" is a meditation on gender and heterosexual relations that challenges traditional norms and gendered relations of power. The lyrics suggest a rewriting of the power relationship between male hegemony and the normalization of female sexuality and sexual continence.

Let's now take a closer look at the lyrics of Dexta Daps's (2015) controversial song "7 Eleven":

Patois	**English Translation**
[Intro]	**[Intro]**
Troyton	Troyton[7]
Me nuh know who she gi' it to	I don't who she had sex with
But me hear say she gi' it weh	But I heard she was unfaithful
Natalie say, he say, she say, she gi' it weh True	Natalie reported he reported she reported that She was unfaithful
But a good ting me naan fools	Thankfully I'm not a fool
Cah me almost believe it	And I don't believe it
Now me see it say	Now I realize
Natalie did a pree me	That Natalie likes me
[Chorus]	**[Chorus]**
So all when you have ten man me haffi be Eleven	So even if she has ten men I will make Eleven
Me neva ask dem fi watch your body fi me	I don't ask anyone to watch your activities
Dat me a tell dem	That's what I'm trying to tell them
All when dem say six man go deh	Even if you had sex with six men
Guess who mek seven	Guess who will make it seven
Gal your body still feel right	Girl your body feels perfect
Me feel like me deh in heaven	I feel like I'm in heaven
Yeaahhh	Yes!

The controversy surrounding the song stems from its apparent endorsement of that which is reprehensible to conservative and heteropatriarchal morality: women's "promiscuity." Dexta Daps is apparently saying that he does not care about his lover's alleged infidelity and promiscuity. He even disregards the reports he's receiving from both females and males as to her undesirability. His response to his news-carrying friends is to declare that he did not ask anyone to watch his girl. In essence, he rejects the news he's receiving about her infidelity and "looseness."

The narrative of the song clearly shows that Dexta Daps is rejecting the stories that are being communicated to him about his lover. The story establishes that she is not the virtuous woman that roots singer Warrior King extols in his 2002 hit song of the same name, nor the virtuous woman of Proverbs 31 in the King James Bible. Despite receiving reports from both men and women about her infidelity, Dexta declares first that he is not sure who his woman has slept with or, in his words, "who she gave it to," as if her body is separate from her soul or identity, devoid of emotions, feelings, and, worse, the ability to make an intelligent decision. Despite the whisperings, however, Daps declares that his love and confidence in her is resolute and his presumption of her bodily sovereignty so absolute that even if she had dated 10 men, he would gladly accept the status of the eleventh man. Significantly, however, Daps makes a clear distinction between the number of men his lover has dated and those she has slept with.

The number of men dated is more than she has, allegedly, slept with, which is an important signal. It suggests that despite her "looseness," she has not slept with all the men she has dated. In popular culture, a woman who sleeps with everyone is not someone with whom one should be associated. A discreet liaison with such a girl would not, however, be beyond the realms of possibility. He continues by stating that, even if she has slept with six men, he will accept being the seventh. This is new territory in the hypermasculine terrain that exists in all sections of popular culture in Jamaica. Admitting allegiance to or association with an unvirtuous woman is taboo and not normally accepted by either males or females. As they say in the streets, "*nuh loose gal caan stay roun yah so, dem fi guh wey*" [no loose girl can stay around here, they must go away].

According to one of my informants, however, this has been changing for some time. Men are now showing no displeasure with women who have adopted a *mani mani* stance—that is, women who have multiple male sexual partners simultaneously (personal communication, February 15, 2016). Women for some time now have been having multiple men, each serving a different purpose in their lives: men for modelling and display in social settings; men to pay bills; men to provide comfort; men to be advisers and life coaches; and, most importantly, the *worka man*—the studs to satisfy them sexually. This informant suggested that Dexta Daps has found a way to articulate a realistic and nonstigmatizing interpretation of the socioeconomic forces shaping heterosexual women's negotiation of heteropatriarchy without offending men's territorial sensibilities. In short, in the vernacular of the garrison, Daps is "keeping it real" (personal communication, February 15, 2016).

By even casting doubt on the validity of the news-carrying about his woman's promiscuous ways, the lyrics do not emasculate men. At the same time the lyrics do not degrade women, as Daps declares that he will not leave his lover because of her infidelity, be it alleged or real.

Another informant, appreciating this realistic portrayal, contended:

Patois	**English Translation**
It deh deh long time man but him put it in a way whe him know sey de girl dem a excited and the man dem a excited same way. Cuz the ghetto girl dem like to sey a seven man mi have you know. So, the girl dem wey have seven man a it the gal dem wan hear.	It's around for a long time he wrote the lyrics in order to excite the women and also please the men. In the ghetto, girls boasts about having up to seven men at the same time, so the girl who has multiple men are pleased with those lyrics.

(personal communication, February 15, 2016)

When asked why some men would accept the proposition of a so-called unvirtuous and promiscuous woman, this informant stated that "*according to how the woman a deal with it* [i.e., the song] *dem just feel happy bout it said way*" (personal communication, February 15, 2016).

In other words, Daps song simultaneously exposes, legitimizes, and reinforces a phenomenon in the lives of garrison men and women that has been implicit, tolerated, and unnamed, principally to protect men's egos. From my experience as a Jamaican music insider, the wild popularity of the song, especially its whole-hearted embrace among women, indicates that it is taken at face value as a celebration of women's empowerment.

Jamaican heteropatriarchy holds that a woman's power is her mouth. A close second, if not preceding that, is her sexuality. Contrary to the appearance of respect for his lover's sovereignty, Daps (2015) declares one of the reasons for not wanting to abandon her is because her body conforms to Afro-Jamaican heteropatriarchal aesthetics of a fecund appearance: "*Gal your body still feel right. Me feel like me deh in heaven.*"

Much like the French who describe a good orgasm as a *petite mort*, Daps signals that sex with his African goddess is like being in heaven. Again, the words indicate a reduction of the female to a body or tool reserved merely for the gratification of male desire and lust. It is not her brain or personality that is important here; it's her sexuality that is central. When asked if it all rests on her body, my informant told me that Dexta Daps placed the lyrics about her vagina in the song "*to get deh support deh.*" In other words, his lyrics were meant to get further support from his female fans, who may see the lyrics as a validation of the powerful female body. I'm suggesting, however, that Daps uses the bait of sexual conquest and the construction of woman's Eve-like sexual siren song to reaffirm, through a veil of progressive sexual relations, the positional superiority of men to women. In a real sense, then, this gendered debate about the meaning of the song comes down to the woman's vagina, sexual attractiveness, and allure.

In much the same way that baroque masters relied on the ancient representations of the fecund and voluptuous form of woman to represent the liberated libido, Daps calls attention to women's vagina as a site both of desire and pleasure for men and of power for the self-possessed woman. As I will argue below, I have reason to suspect that, for Daps, the possibility that women can and do enjoy sex for the sake of self-pleasure and also (at times) for communion with another (significant or otherwise) does not enter his heteropatriarchal dream.

Further in the song, Daps registers surprise that other women are reporting to him about his lover. He rationalizes their actions as being pretexts to be with him; as he states, "*dem want to climb up on the pinnacle*" (i.e., these women want to climb on his penis). He reiterates that he will not listen to their reports and affirms his love for his lover and her body. Multiple readings are possible at this point. It may be that Daps is casting aspersions on duplicitous and flirtations women who betray their girlfriends by seeking to have sex with her lover, and who probably have a man at home themselves. Maybe Daps is parodying men's preoccupation with their penises as the core site of their identity. And, in an act of open-mindedness and generosity, it may be that Daps is modelling a monogamous and stoic man who is so above it all that he accepts his lover's ostensible polygamy.

Consistent with this reading, Daps states that he will not hurt his woman for sleeping around, since "*mi neva ever kill nobody so dapa don naw go damage yuh. But if you give weh the loving me a go malice you*" [I will never kill anyone, so dapper Dan is not going to hurt you]. The fly in the heteropatriarchal ointment of forbearance, then, is if "she gives away her body"; only then will he "malice" her (i.e., cease speaking with her). One can read Daps's overall acceptance as making a clear distinction between his lover having sex with another man, which is after all only a transient experience, versus giving away her love, which would transgress a deeper and abiding spiritual communion that joins two hearts. The very idea that a man can love this way seriously challenges normative conceptions of heteropatriarchy and masculinity.

Nonetheless, speaking of "malice," or hurt, in this way has potentially violent gendered undertones. One could read Daps's rejection of malice in most circumstances as a condemnation of violence against women. However, Garrison culture dictates that *bad man* [strong men] and *gyallis* [read: lotharios], the ultimate alpha males, are not in the habit of engaging in malice because that is the tendency of women; real men beat their women for their infractions.

Virtuous Woman: Daps, Warrior King, and the Exposure of Cultural Tensions

In contrast to Dexta Daps's (2015) "7 Eleven," Warrior King's (2002) "Virtuous Woman" reflects the heteropatriarchal demand for women to essentially "know their place." As the lyrics to "Virtuous Woman" show, it also insists that men define themselves in relation to the performances of heteronormative patriarchy:

> Now, no real man can live without a woman
> Like night to day, is a woman to her man (woman to her man)
> She's essential to his purpose and his mission
> A good woman, is a glory to her man
> She'll never take the power, she'll just make him a better man
> Every great man, has a virtuous woman
> Woman, you say you love me and never leave me lonely
> You'll always be there for me, so need not worry.

Warrior King taps into and reinforces the belief that a woman's place is behind her man; she is subjugated by his whims and must support him at the expense of any independent thought. Warrior King continues along this line when he states, "she never takes the power, she'll just make him a better man / Every great man, has a virtuous woman." The term *virtuous* in this context translates to obedience, loyalty, sexual subjugation, and unimpeachable morality. In other words, a virtuous woman is a "lady" who is the "glory of her man." Warrior King's song, transparent as it is, is interesting to the extent that it conforms with the dominant hegemonic narrative—but it lacks the rich layers of subtext that have caused Dexta Daps's "7 Eleven" to inspire so much controversy.

Compared with Warrior King's "Virtuous Woman," Dexta Daps's "7 Eleven" seems to be a paragon of progressive Black masculinity. Daps appears to stand against the rules of engagement in the garrison culture which dictates that the women should be beaten for sexual indiscretions.

"7 Eleven" is rich in ambiguity, ambivalence, and contradictions in laying bare the possibility of a man accepting a woman's autonomy.

From a popular music production perspective, the contradictions inherent in the song lay bare the dilemma faced by male recording artists from the garrison, as they are held to impossible standards. In the general context of Jamaica's hypermasculine culture, Dexta Daps's declaration and apparent acceptance of his lover's bodily and sexual autonomy is supposed to be taboo. But the condemnation of garrison male artists like Daps breaks in different ways. In the conflict between garrison and uptown culture, Daps persona in the song cannot win for losing. On one hand, by the rules of garrison culture, Daps's character is imagined as "soft" and lacks the machismo that is expected of a heterosexual alpha male who dominates women and lesser men equally. In the class war against the uptown and foreign forces that represent the moral decadence of "Babylon," masculinity is a site of resistance. Thus, men who even give the appearance of recognizing the autonomy and free will of women within the framework of progressive masculinity are imagined as bad representatives of the garrison culture whose defenders must wear the aura of warrior. An authentically progressive masculinity that "centers its efforts on reorienting men's concepts and practices away from ideal masculinity, which, by definition, requires the domination of men over women, children, and, yes, other subordinate, or 'weaker' men" (Mutua, 2006, p. 5) becomes a threat to be shouted down, if not eliminated. On the other hand, whether progressive or patriarchal, garrison men in the imagination are painted with the same classist, moralistic, and pigmentocratic brush of the uptown people. The social Darwinian standards of uptown morality, which need little justification to cast aspersions on men in the garrison as nothing short of brutes, assert that garrison men are sexually incontinent and heteropatriarchal, "heathen" throwbacks to their "savage" African ancestors who were held on the plantation (see McIntosh, Chapter 6 in this volume).

Criticism of garrison artists such as Dexta Daps reflects a class warfare of sorts in which the artist (who usually stems primarily from the disenfranchised Black underclass) is constantly bombarded by Victorian moral values. In many instances, middle- and upper-class values are in contradiction with the tone, tenor, and difficult realities of garrison life. Conflict arises when upper-class values of sexual propriety and appropriate male behaviour are promoted through the mass media and institutions such and the schools and church in a way that casts harsh judgments on garrison cultural norms around gender and sexuality.

"Love Punany Bad": Situating Male Dominance in Jamaican Popular Music

Hegemonic masculinity is "the dominant form of masculinity in any given society" (Collins, 2006, p. 78). In Caribbean societies hypermasculine tendencies identify "real men" in sharp juxtaposition to women, weak men, and gay men (see McIntosh, Chapter 6 in this volume). In theory, this sharp dichotomy recognizes a hegemonic ideal, but does not give scope to the fluidity in the real experience of men's lives. In contrast, there are contending versions of masculinity in Caribbean society that are classified as "marginalized and subordinated masculinities."

Problematically, the "soft" male or masculine persona is not explicitly included in Donna Hope's theorizing on Caribbean masculinities. Consistent with hegemonic masculinity, the masculine archetypes described are *ole dawg* and *gyallis*—the polygamous male and the bad man, who are chief among males and who rigorously police the borders of masculinity. The "soft" male has not found a space to fit comfortably among these various hardcore representations of masculinities in garrison cultural space, nor in theory. The soft man persona, however, has been a part of Jamaican and Caribbean gender discourse for a very long time. Linden Lewis (n.d.) clearly identifies this type of masculinity in the 1983 calypso song by calypsonian Penguin, entitled "Soft Man." Lewis argues that the song "'Soft Man' is in effect a manifesto of a narrowly constructed hegemonic masculinity...Soft man is a play on words in which the idea of a spineless and wimpy man merges with the image of a firm erection" (p. 29).[8]

Though not as stringently guarded against as male homosexuality, the soft male, the *maama* man, and the effeminate male are all transgressors of theories of masculinity and are reviled by hegemonic masculinity. While, as noted by Crichlow et al. (2014), the Caribbean is no stranger to the study of men, this study is, of course, still open to new perspectives. The recognizing and theorizing of men as gendered beings, as well as the explorations of how they experience hegemonic masculinity in its idealized and unattainable form and how some resist and articulate alternate ways of being men remains open for development, as demonstrated by this chapter. Thus, I turn now to theorizing the limits of Dexta Daps's engagement with a progressive masculinity. I will then provide an account of the ways in which men in the garrisons of Jamaica struggle to define themselves in meaningful ways that enable them to cope with poverty and social exclusion, for instance by valorizing their mothers in an effort to articulate a different masculinity that refuses the *ole dog* and *gyallis* images that they associate with their fathers. I suggest the rehabilitation of their mothers' reputations from that of the sexually autonomous woman suggested by Dexta Daps (2015) to a Madonna's is a vital tactic to hold up the survivability of garrison women as the glue and focal point of garrison life. What this means for the *gyallis* reputation and performances is, however, unclear.

Daps's apparent acceptance of his girlfriend's infidelity is viewed by the popular culture as being "soft." Although this "soft male" is accused of promoting/allowing female promiscuity and the emasculation of normative maleness, Daps still upholds and supports hegemonic masculinity as it relates to control over women's bodies, sexual autonomy through his ability to judge a "good *punany*"[9] (see Hope, 2010, 21). The tactic of objectification which reduces women to the multiple signs of the vagina—fearsome, habitable, humbling, mysterious sign of wonders (i.e., childbirth), penetrable, and soft enough to "break steel" (Hope, 2010)—is a direct transposition of Baldwin's (1976) and Fanon's (1952/1977) critiques of the signification of the Black man's cock in the White imaginary. Thus in "7 Eleven" when Daps (2015) says, "*yu body still feel right, mi feel like say me deh in heaven*" [your body still feels right, I feel like I'm in heaven], he is in fact reproducing the dominant masculine narrative in garrison culture of a real man who has control over his woman. Such a man is purportedly endowed with the innate ability to tell if his woman has been unfaithful. He can feel the difference in the "muscular agility, tightness, fatness, flexibility, elasticity and suppleness" (Hope, 2010, 21) that should characterize a good and faithful vagina. In reality, however, the metric for the love of *punany* is also about penis size and performance anxiety should a bigger and better lover also "go there."

Other readings of Daps's text are also possible. For one, Daps's (2015) incredulity at the accusations against his woman is, by a reading of hegemonic masculinity, not grounded in respect for her autonomy and good judgment. Instead, it is his supreme confidence that his lover, like Warrior King's (2002) "Virtuous Woman," will prioritize his image as a man who is in control and can satisfy his woman. Another reading suggests a coded and strategic deployment of heteronormativity and homophobia that does not run the risk of contradicting the official discourse of tolerance for homosexuality. The "love *punany* bad" narrative achieves the same end by coding itself in heterosexual desire. Furthermore, Daps's refusal of the sexual advances of his lover's accusers who may attempt to get impregnated by him because of his celebrity, not only proves Daps's self-discipline but also confirms his *gyallis* status: women seem to throw themselves at his feet.

On the face of it, Daps's justifications of his lover's actions are unacceptable in a culture that accepts promiscuity (see Beenie Man, 1996/2000a) and polygamous (see Beenie Man, 1996/2000b) relationships from males but condemns and frowns upon any such conduct from women, especially in the form of infidelity to one man. At one level, then, I have suggested that Daps has broken the cardinal rule of hypermasculine heteropatriarchy. By supporting his woman's "promiscuity," he is departing from the traditional doctrine of condemnation of sexually autonomous women. Under hegemonic patriarchy, such women are figuratively, when not literally, tortured, battered, burned, or killed. What is worse is the apparent betrayal of maleness within the popular culture by accepting this bad behaviour and declaring that his unfaithful and loose woman lets him feel like he's in heaven. His pitiful acceptance of her promiscuity is exposed when he states that even if six men had sex with his girl he would stay around and be the seventh man to make love to her.

However, female "promiscuity," as signified by Dexta Daps's (2015) song "7 Eleven," can also be seen as a production of the celebrated *ole dawg/gyallis* masculinity. As a result of competitive patriarchies, the male is encouraged to have many female partners, provide proof of this through several offspring, and finally to be crowned king in completing the task of having all his women live harmoniously (Hope, 2010, p. 19). This masculinity is evidence that female promiscuity and infidelity is tacitly encouraged and tolerated whether through willful ignorance or denial. Feminists, according to Storey (1998), purport that patriarchy as an ideology is expressed in "how it operates to conceal, mask or distort gender relations...in presenting half-truths as whole truths" (p. 3). For example, masculinity is constructed and presented as natural while femininity is misrepresented, defined by or subjugated to masculinity, or omitted from cultural and historical texts entirely. Saying that a female's polygamous behaviour or robust sexual appetite is deviant is a patriarchal idea that sets out to misrepresent and distort femininity, and is only a half-truth. According to Derrick Aarons (2014):

> As much as 70 per cent of families across Jamaica are single-parent, matriarchal families, and while some mothers have a visiting relationship with their children's fathers, many children grow up without any significant relationship with their fathers. Many irresponsible fathers prefer to live alone or away from the mother or mothers of their children since that allows them the freedom to date new women, proffering themselves as single and available. (para. 5)

One could think that single-parent matriarchal homes are a direct result of competitive patriarchies in which one *gyallis* courts a female to the point of sexual activity and reproduction, then becomes absent from that woman and family, making himself appear free and single to another woman and family, repeating the cycle. But it is not just the male that appears single and available; the female now has a vacancy that needs to be filled. This will either be filled by another form of masculinity, which oftentimes is another *ole dawg* or *gyallis* that is just seeking to rack up points on the masculinity chart (Hope, 2010, p. 19).

In social relationships within garrison culture, huge points are said to be scored if a man can *tek wey*—that is, if he can take away or have relationship with another man's woman while the woman is still involved with her man. This behaviour can be interpreted as encouraging infidelity and promiscuity among females. While this discussion does not find reasons to explain female promiscuity, it is important to take a realistic look at female-male-female relationships. There is also a more concrete, materialistic explanation to explain this cultural tendency. Women in a rigidly patriarchal culture and social formation without a robust welfare system are exposed to poverty and want that may make them dependent on others. This dependency creates and facilitates a certain cultural style. This is played out with men of material means having as many partners as they can afford or, in some cases, more than they can afford. According to the theories of traditional hegemonic masculinity promoted by upper- and middle-class Jamaicans and even within garrison culture, a good woman or virtuous woman is satisfied with and is faithful to one man, regardless of her situation.

Although the popular cultural space may seem to be a site of contestation of traditional values, it often is "covertly recreating and re-enforcing these structures" (Hope, 2010, p. 12). So, while "7 Eleven" is about a promiscuous woman, the problematic is more about the celebration of her by a male. Hegemonic masculinity finds that situation totally unacceptable, as it diminishes the male identity with regard to his ability to satisfy and control female bodies through sexual acts. Progressive Black masculinity, conversely, would view this through a more sympathetic lens.

From Mary Magdalene to Virgin Mary

These are sentiments and declarations that feel forbidden in Jamaican's heteropatriarchal popular culture. But is it *really* forbidden and, if so, forbidden by whom? According to Carolyn Cooper (2004) it is the "airy fairy

Judeo-Christian definition of appropriate female behaviour" (p. 99). It's this same Judeo-Christian caveat that the traditional Jamaican upper and middle classes impose on African working-class women. It is from this highly religious and patriarchal space that Jamaican masculinity and femininity has been engendered. I am proposing that a culture that promotes promiscuity and sexual prowess for males while rejecting similar behaviour by females is either in denial or oblivious to its own encouragement of this so-called female promiscuity, if not the creation of it. Such is the case of Jamaican popular music orthodoxy. Further, at the expense of supporting theory and fantasies, a lived reality is being willfully ignored.

In the New Testament, as in much of the rest of the text of the Bible, there are two types of women: fallen women and virtuous women. This stark duality is also at work in garrison popular music culture. In the case of Dexta Daps's "7 Eleven," Daps (2015) has brought to the fore the complexities, dynamics, and realities of the male/female relationships in the popular cultural space, especially as they play out among men and women in garrison communities. Here, I will argue that a new sort of masculinity is attempting to work itself out by confronting the limits of hegemonic masculinity, since many of the youth in the garrisons are the products of men who have to cope with material degradation and economic uselessness. They have virtually no other way to mark their passing in this life than to have numerous offspring to carry their names.

Let us examine this Judeo-Christian stance. Was it not Jesus the Christ, who offered himself the living water to the Samaritan woman at the well (John 4:4–26 New International Version), forgave the adulterous woman who was about to be stoned (John 8:1–11 New International Version), documented the prostitute Rahab among his genealogy (Matthew 1:5 New International Version). Were not all of these women labelled promiscuous? It would seem that Daps, like Jesus Christ, although going against the traditional normative masculinity, are more understanding and nonjudgmental of reality and human behaviour—even the feminine gender.

So, what is wrong with the message of "7 Eleven"? It could be said that Dexta Daps is "wifing up" this allegedly unfaithful and promiscuous woman.

He is "wifing her up" in that he's elevating her to wife status—making her his number-one woman without reprimand. The *wifey*, though not technically a married woman (Hope, 2006), is rated very highly on the female chart of femininity in popular music culture. The only woman than outshines her is "mama," mother, who is deified in garrison culture and the Jamaican society at large. Dexta Daps (2015), instead of rebuking his woman, rebukes her accusers: "*mi neva ask dem fi watch yu body fi mi*" [I don't ask anyone to watch your activities]. His willingness to overlook the accusations and freely accept her is a behaviour that I believe is typically reserved only for mothers, in garrison culture and Jamaican context.

The prevalence of single mother homes—a part of our colonial history—has resulted in the deification of Jamaican single mothers. "Loose ladies," *skettels*, and *maties* are not taken home to meet mothers—who, by the way, may well have led a similar life in their younger days, but who, through the sanctity of time, have been redeemed and become the queen in the eyes of their male children. These children, for their part, often display a type of Freudian appreciation for their mothers (see Worthen & Harrison, 2005). That is, mothers who have singlehandedly raised their several children, whom they had by several absent fathers, are not regarded as promiscuous by their sons. They become the epitome of heroic figures. Especially when contrasted against the wicked and careless father, they are seen as a Madonna, a pure mother, sacred and to be revered. The mother becomes the ultimate measurement for any woman whom her son thinks may have the potential to be his wife or wifey. This measurement, however, is only in relation to the endless support, nurturing, and acceptance of the male at all times, regardless of his faithfulness. It is not farfetched or counter to the norms of garrison culture that promiscuity and looseness—and what sometimes is viewed through the patriarchal lens as unvirtuous behaviour—among women can be rationalized as normative and without recrimination, in particular when the exigencies of the family economics demand it. Besides, in this culture a male cannot be unfaithful; he can only be masculine.

Performing Gender in Garrison Popular Music Culture

According to Judith Butler (1990), gender is not something we are automatically born with, but something we continually "perform." How gender is acted out or performed determines our perception of gender and how these perceptions determine the rules of engagement as to what is appropriate behaviour. However, Butler also notes that performance cannot be the sole determinant of gender identity. Butler (1990) concludes:

> It would not be enough to say that gender is only performed or that the meaning of gender can be derived from its performance, whether or not one rethinks performance as a compulsory social ritual. For there are clearly workings of gender that do not "show" in what is performed as gender, and the reduction of the psychic workings of gender to the literal performance of gender would be a mistake. (p. 31)

I, therefore, conclude that what constitutes masculinity in Jamaican popular music is a preoccupation with certain sociosexual notions of performance. This explains the dominance of male narratives about female subjugation and reduction. Female performance, is, however alive and well in garrison culture, too. Female artists have been at the forefront of gender bending and asserting their right to be heard and recognized as equals and not as sexualized bodies. The irony is that the tool of engagement is the very same sexuality that has fixated the male gaze. Cooper (2004) argues that the

> culture at home and in the diaspora is best understood as a potentially liberating space in which working-class women and their more timid middle-class sisters assert the freedom to play out eroticized role that may not ordinarily be available to them in the rigid social conventions of the everyday. (p. 17)

Cooper (2004), however, posits that erotic performances in garrison culture by women can be recontextualized through an "African diasporic discourse as a manifestation of the spirit of female fertility figures such as the Yoruba Oshin" (p. 103). Of the many powers attributed to her, she has numerous lovers and is known by many praise-names.

From the cultural perspective, some see Daps's "7 Eleven" as reinforcing a situation in which the female body is breaking free from the sexual straitjacket imposed by society that encourages different standards for sexual male and female behaviour. From a popular cultural perspective, however, Jamaican men from the inner city, such as Daps, "often articulate their masculine ethos by inflating and/or ritualistically performing particular heterosexual masculine characteristics that may tighten their slippery grasp of masculine status" (Hope, 2010, p. 14). In performing "7 Eleven," Daps essentially let go of these traditional reins and succumbed to a subversive performance that privileges the femme fatale, who is known in the Eastern Caribbean as the *mamaguy* and in Jamaica as the Delilah.

Daps's rejection of traditional notions of masculinity suggest a rethinking of cultural norms. As Patricia Hill Collins (2006) notes, "rejecting views of black masculinity grounded in dominance would enable black men to question troublesome behaviour by themselves and others that hurts black women, black children, and each other" (p. 93).

Cooper's (2004) invocation of slackness is useful at this juncture. She observes that slackness can be articulated and critiqued through a conservative sexual political prism. Slackness "can be much more permissively theorized as a radical, underground confrontation with the patriarchal gender ideology and the duplicitous morality of fundamentalist Judeo-Christian Jamaican society" (p. 3).

In hegemonic terms, uptown people's sensibilities are constantly at odds with the actions of their actors. These people promote enlightenment, propriety, and neoliberal notions of success and prosperity on the one hand while, on the other, engaging in "loose and degrading" behaviour; in other words, acting like *gyallis*, *mamaguys*, and *skettels*. Additionally, they are victims of the debt trap that the neoliberal philosophy has unleashed on the world, resulting in "epidemics of self-harm, eating disorders, depression, loneliness, performance anxiety and social phobia" (Monbiot, 2016, para. 6). Cooper (2004) continues her treatise: "slackness is not merely sexual looseness, though it certainly is that. Slackness is a contestation of conventional definitions of law and order; an undermining of consensual standards of decency" (pp. 3–4).

Conclusion

Garrison culture and the Kingston music scene reinforce and perpetuate misogynist tendencies that relegate females to sexual beings to be objectified by the male gaze and imagination. Jamaican popular music output reflects this concept through recordings such as Beenie Man's "Nuff Gal" (1996/2000b) and Vybz Kartel's "Unfaithful" (2010) and "Tek Buddy Gal" (2009). These popular songs are examples of the hypermasculine modality of Jamaican popular culture in which men are lauded and lionized for their ability to have multiple relationships and boast about their sexual prowess while, simultaneously, females are held to puritanical standards. The fact that women are often viewed as sexual objects for the express purpose of male sexual satisfaction exacerbates this problem. The male-dominated performance of such testosterone-laden songs collides at the intersection of masculinity and the garrison and uptown cultures of popular music culture.

The popular cultural environments of Jamaica and many other places in the Caribbean have been sites of censorship, marginalization, and distorted representation of gender identities. Garrison culture continues to provoke, excite, and destabilize perceptions of Jamaican upper- and middle-class discourses of sexual continence and propriety. Its imposition on working-class popular culture represents a milieu of moral regulation. This is done with the aim of promoting "proper" behaviour and exerting hegemonic control over a primarily African-descended population struggling with its dark colonial past. This condition is ripe for the class warfare that is ensuing in Jamaican society due to the effects of slavery, colonialism, globalism, and neoliberalism. Daps's "7 Eleven" epitomizes the gender crisis and competitive patriarchies that are being played out in popular culture.

As Butler (1990) argues, "Gender is the repeated stylization of the body, a set of repeated acts within a highly rigid regulatory framework that congeal over time to produce the appearance of substance, of a natural sort of being" (p. 33). The song and its declarations have clearly substantiated the proposition of Daniel J. Kruger et al. (2014), who conclude that "[p]atriarchy may be in part a product of our evolutionary heritage, yet the cross-national and historical variation in women's social empowerment indicates that highly biased social conditions are not inevitable" (p. 10).

The song "7 Eleven" and its creators *seem* to have turned garrison culture taboos, Jamaican popular music performance, and gender identity on their heads. Whatever the case, popular music culture in Jamaica continues to be a site in which, yes, middle- and working-class values and hegemonic masculinities are performed—but they are also reworked, reexamined, and challenged.

Author's Note

Special acknowledgement to Georgette McGlashen for her tireless fieldwork, research efforts, and contribution to this chapter.

Notes

1. Garrison communities are the result of colonial rule, structural adjustment, and neoliberal policies. Bad policies have intensified poverty in these small enclaves, which are generally aligned with one of the major political parties and are led by gang leaders referred to as "dons."
2. This suggests that transclass solidarities are being built by and between youth, which results in some in the social elite casting aspersions on dancehall culture: dividing and conquering maintains class distinctions through a racialized discourse about music.
3. Initially, the term *garrison* was used to describe only specific communities associated with armed political thugs who represented opposing political parties in Jamaica.
4. I believe that we have reached the post-dancehall period in Kingston's music scene. Dancehall is no longer the main genre; it has been replaced by a new genre I call "one beat."
5. The lyrics to Bedasse's (1958) "Night Food" are full of sexual innuendos:

   The room is dark, She said, "Come and eat,
   This night food is very warm and sweet."
   I said, "Lady, there's no knife and fork,
   And how can I eat food in the dark?"

She said, "This food needs no knife and fork
How can a human be so dark?
The food is right here in the bed.
Come here, man, make me scratch your head."

6. Again, sexual innuendo is the foundation of Max Romeo's "Wet Dream":

Every night mi go to sleep mi have wet dreams
Every night mi go to sleep mi have wet dreams
Lie down gal let me push it up push it up lie down
Lie down gal let me push it up push it up lie down
Lie down gal let me push it up push it up lie down
Lie down gal let me push it up push it up lie down.

7. Troyton is the name of the producer of the song. It is customary in Jamaican music to call the name of the producer or a popular musician or team member in the introduction of a song.
8. This has also played out at the level of national politics in Jamaica with former Prime Minister Edward Seaga, who called the then–Prime Minster P.J. Patterson a *chi chi man*, a local descriptor for homosexual.
9. The Patois word *punany* is slang for vagina.

Bibliography

Aarons, D. (2014, July 13). Considering the welfare of fatherless kids. *Jamaica Observer*. http://www.jamaicaobserver.com/news/Considering-the-welfare-of-fatherless-kids

Badesse, A. (1958). Night food. On *Chin's calypso, Vol. 6: 1955–2007* [CD]. Kaylypso.

Baldwin, J. (1976). *The devil finds work*. The Dial Press.

Beenie Man. (2000a). Ole dawg. On *Best of Beenie Man* [CD]. VP Records. (Original work published 1996)

Beenie Man. (2000b). Nuff gal. On *Best of Beenie Man* [CD]. VP Records. (Original work published 1996)

Boyne, I. (2017, July 9). Crime, corruption and culture. *Jamaica Gleaner*. http://jamaica-gleaner.com/article/focus/20170709/ian-boyne-crime-corruption-and-culture

Butler, J. (1990). *Gender trouble: Feminism and the subversion of identity*. Routledge.

Collins, P.H. (2006). A telling difference: Dominance, strength, and Black masculinities. In A. Mutua (Ed.), *Progressive Black masculinities* (pp. 73–98). Routledge.

Cooper, C. (2004). *Sound clash: Jamaican dancehall culture at large*. Palgrave Macmillan.

Crichlow, W., DeShong, H., & Lewis, L. (2014). Vulnerability, persistence and destabilization of dominant masculinities: An introduction. *Caribbean Review of Gender Studies, 8*, 1–14. https://sta.uwi.edu/crgs/december2014/journals/CRGS_8_Pgs001-14_EditorialVulnerability_CrichlowDeShongLewis.pdf

Daps, D. (2015). 7 Eleven. On *Street shots* (Vol. 11) [CD]. 21st-Hapilos Digital Distribution.

Dawes, K.S. (1999). *Natural mysticism: Towards a new reggae aesthetic in Caribbean writing*. Peepal Tree Press.

Fanon, F. (1977). *Black skin, White masks*. (C.L. Markmann, Trans.). Grove Press. (Original work published 1952)

Gramsci, A., & Buttigieg, J.A. (1992). *Prison notebooks*. Columbia University Press.

Hall, S. (1996). The west and the rest: Discourse and power. In S. Hall, D. Held, D. Hubert & K. Thompson (Eds.), *Modernity: An introduction to modern societies* (pp. 184–227). Blackwell Publishers.

The Heptones. (1968). Fatty fatty. On *Fatty fatty* [CD]. Coxsone Records.

Hoffman, J. (1988). *State, power, and democracy: Contentious concepts in practical political theory*. Wheatsheat Books.

Hope, D.P. (2006). *Inna di dancehall: Popular culture and the politics of identity in Jamaica*. University of the West Indies Press.

Hope, D.P. (2010). *Man vibes: Masculinities in the Jamaican dancehall*. Ian Randle.

Howard, D.O. (2012). *Rantin from inside the dancehall*. Jahmento Publishing.

Howard, D.O. (2016). *The creative echo chamber: Contemporary music production in Kingston, Jamaica*. Ian Randle.

Hsieh, H., & Shannon, S.E. (2005). Three approaches to qualitative content analysis. *Qualitative Health Research, 15*(9), 1277–88. http://doi.org/10.1177/1049732305276687

Knuttila, M. (2016). *Paying for masculinity: Boys, men and the patriarchal dividend*. Fernwood Publishing.

Kruger, D.J., Fisher, M.L., & Wright, P. (2014). Patriarchy, male competition, and excess male mortality. *Evolutionary Behavioral Sciences, 8*(1), 3–11. http://doi.org/10.1037/h0097244

Lewis, L. (2014). Gender and performativity: Calypso and the culture of masculinity. *Caribbean Review of Gender Studies, a Journal of Caribbean Perspectives on Gender and Feminism, 8*, 15–42. https://sta.uwi.edu/crgs/december2014/journals/CRGS_8_Pgs015-42_GenderPerformativityCalypso_LLewisx.pdf

Mills, C.W. (2000). *C. Wright Mills: Letters and autobiographical writings*. University of California Press.

Monbiot, G. (2016). Neoliberalism—The ideology at the root of all our problems. *The Guardian*. https://www.theguardian.com/books/2016/apr/15/neoliberalism-ideology-problem-george-monbiot

Mutua, A.D. (Ed.). (2006). *Progressive Black masculinities*. Routledge.

Opel, J. (1965). Push wood. On *The best of Jackie Opel* [CD]. Coxsone Records.

Penguin. (1983). Soft man. On *Touch it* [CD]. Bs Records.

Peterson, R.A., & Berger, D.G. (1971). Entrepreneurship in organizations: Evidence from the popular music industry. *Administrative Science Quarterly, 16*(1), 97. http://doi.org/10.2307/2391293

Reeves, S., Kuper, A., & Hodges, B.D. (2008). Qualitative research methodologies: Ethnography. *BMJ*, 337, a1020. http://doi.org/10.1136/bmj.a1020

Romeo, M. (1968). Wet dream. On *Best of Max Romeo* [CD]. Unity.

Samuel, J. (1997). The fact of Blackness: Franz Fanon and visual representation [Book review]. *Race and Class*, *39*(2), 101–04.

Stolzoff, N.C. (2000). *Wake the town and tell the people: Dancehall culture in Jamaica*. Duke University Press.

Storey, J. (1998). *Cultural theory and popular culture: A reader*. University of Georgia Press.

Van Dijk, T.A. (1993). Principles of critical discourse analysis. *Discourse and Society*, *4*(2), 249–83. https://doi.org/10.1177/0957926593004002006

Warrior King. (2002). Virtuous woman. On *Virtuous woman* [CD]. VP Records.

Worthen, J., & Harrison, A. (2005). *D.H. Lawrence's Sons and lovers: A casebook*. Oxford University Press.

Zeilig, L. (2016). *Voices of liberation: Frantz Fanon*. Haymarket Books.

IV

The *Other* Other and the Black Man

Hot Sex and the Black Man in the Global South

9

Sila ay Malaki

Anti-African Racism, the "Filipino Gaze," and the Paradox of Black Masculinity in Collegiate Basketball in the Philippines

SATWINDER SINGH REHAL

IMAGES OF MASCULINITIES are core features of advertisements in television, movies, and billboards in the Philippines. Fetishized representations of masculine virility mesh with the culture of consumption and objectification of women on the panoply of images evoking beauty and nostalgia. Sport in the Philippines, particularly basketball, constitutes a crucial site through which masculine hegemony is constructed and reconstructed and national identity reified. This chapter focuses on the negotiations of Filipino[1] male masculinities against African student-athletes in collegiate basketball in the Philippines. I focus on the media scripting and reproduction of Eurocentric and Filipino nativist patriarchal tropes of Africans as opposed to African American hypermasculinity and visibility. The paper mainly draws upon Frantz Fanon's (1952/1967) *Black Skin, White Masks* as a framework to theorize the double entendre of *sila ay malaki* [they are big]—a phrase commonly used in sports discourse in the Philippines—as a productive site for the homoerotic "reproduction" of stereotyped Black[2] masculinities in collegiate basketball in the Philippines, vital to structuring a nativist hegemonic Filipino masculinity set against the long arc of Spanish and US colonization. The term *malaki* is commonly used in the Filipino language in reference to a large size, stature, or attribute, such as vast experience or beauty (see Pascasio, 1961; Samonte & Sconras, 2019). For example, after losing to Mongolia in a FIBA 3-on-3 World Cup match in 2018, the national coach of the Philippines' basketball team, Ronnie Magsanoc, used the term *malaki* in reference to Mongolia's vast experience over his players (Go, 2018). The coach is captured saying the following:

> It's all about knowing how to win in the end, and I think *malaki 'yung experience factor ng team ng Mongolia* [Mongolia's experience was a big factor]. (Go, 2018)

The term *malaki* has nonetheless become strongly associated with Black African physicality and hypermasculinity in the Philippines. Over the past decade, Black African basketball players from the African continent have come to dominate intercollegiate basketball competitions in the Philippines. Both their presence and success have given rise to gendered and racial discourses from Filipino commentators who deploy anti-African colonialist tropes as a foil to recuperate an imagined hegemonic Filipino masculinity trammeled by a history of colonialism and military occupation. This chapter makes reference to concepts of Black and White with regard to their social construction rather than to a biophysiological marker of skin colour. The chapter centres the construction of Blackness in a colonial history of White anti-Black racism and the resultant suffering of the Black body "in the making of Blackness" (Tafira, 2016, p.139). From a Fanonian lens, the Black subject is made to feel inferior and nonexistent. As Fanon (1952/1967) argues, "the black man's being is experienced through others; his blackness is in relation to whiteness and its gaze, and the black body becomes a curse, attacked severally, thus giving way to an epidermal racial schema" (p. 192).

Drawing on Fanon's insights about the implications of sexual mythologies in the colonial context, the chapter ends with a call for developing the field of intra-Global South masculinity studies in the era of neoliberalism. As Besnier et al. (2018) argue, in a neoliberal system, masculinity is hinged on the possibility of participating in "a global system of mobility, work and glory"

(p. 864). The chapter thus makes this call based on the entangled relationship between sport, neoliberalism, and masculinities characterized by increased mediatization, corporatization, and commoditization of sports emerging in the Global South as evidenced in the context of collegiate basketball in the Philippines. In a neoliberally organized sporting sphere, masculinity becomes organized as embedded in contemporary economic and social structures, as products of global and local forces, and in locating men in relations of sameness and otherness. I situate the presence of Black African athletes in the Philippines within intra-Global South migration where professional sport becomes a desirable way out of poverty caused by the impacts of neoliberalism and resultant economic downturn in most African countries best illustrated by the following two media scripts:

> "I came from Africa, and Africa is pretty far from Asia, so that was something tough for me, to leave my family and everything," said Clement Leutcheu from Cameroonian [*sic*] who went to the Philippines to pursue a hotel and restaurant management course at the De La Salle College of St. Benilde. In exchange for his scholarship, his 6-foot-7 frame came in handy as he manned the paint for the Blazers in the NCAA [Philippines National College Athletic Association] men's basketball tournament. It wasn't easy, Leutcheu admitted, but such sacrifices are needed if you to go anywhere in life. (Leongson, 2020, para. 7)

> Most of them are of African variety—from Nigeria to Cameroon to Sierra Leone, to Congo (the former Zaire) to Ghana—for the simple reason that they are as athletic as African-Americans but come in cheaper in recruitment payoffs to sports agents and monthly allowances to players.
>
> Regardless, the foreign recruits are paid handsomely, if not royally. There's free tuition and tutorship, a rented condo unit, a high-end vehicle for their transport, tutorship for the academically-challenged and, of course, a monthly allowance. All these benefits are courtesy of the rich businessmen among their alumni communities. (Liao, 2014, paras. 4–5)

As Besnier et al. (2018) argue, a career in sport was a desirable strategy "because of its glamour, celebration of masculinity, potential as a conduit to mobility, and promises of millennial returns" (p. 843). To make sense of the scripting of the Black athlete's body, I will also tie in contemporary theoretical reflections on men and masculinity by Connell (1995, 1998, 2000; Connell & Messerschmidt, 2005) and Messner (1992, 2002; Messner et al., 1990) along with Stuart Halls's (1990, 1993, 1996) account of how Blackness is deployed as a discursive formation within the messy flows and motion of dynamic social interaction. With this multilayered theoretical platform, I focus on media scripting and Filipino nativist reproduction and deployment of Eurocentric patriarchal tropes of Africans. I centre the discussion by departing from Besnier et al. (2018) who contend that professional sport is one institution that is "deeply entangled in the production of masculinity" (p. 841) in that it exacerbates the tension between the physical performance of masculinity through sporting prowess and masculinity as imagined in the fulfillment of certain social expectations. As Besnier et al. argue, masculinity in a neoliberal system enables the "the possibility of participating in a global system of mobility, work, and glory that may resurrect one's ability to provide for others" (p. 864). In a neoliberal configuration, they argue that athletes become repacked, starting with their bodies, as a product of a complex array of factors including the surveillance of their exercise regimens, their everyday lives, as well as sport recruiters increasing global searches for athletic talent. The resultant outcome of this form of sporting governance for the migrant athlete is "their precarious belonging, dependence on work contracts for legal residence, and vulnerability to racism and xenophobia" (Besnier et al., 2018, p. 853). I suggest that basketball—widely accepted as the national obsession in the Philippines—and African Blackness are metaphorical spaces in and through which grand narratives of an imagined restoration of Filipino hegemonic masculinity and cultural and racial superiority play out. I make this suggestion on Connell and Messerschmidt's (2005) argument that masculinity and gender inequalities are not a matter of just men dominating women, but also of structures of domination within genders—what Connell

(1995) termed "hegemonic masculinity" in reference to "the combination of the plurality of masculinities and the hierarchy of masculinities" (Connell & Messerschmidt, 2005, p. 846). As objects of homoerotic desire, imagined as prodigiously hypersexual and repudiated as culturally and physiologically "foreign," the African Black athlete in the Philippines becomes an interesting case study for new thinking about men and masculinities in intra-Global South migration in a neoliberal world.

In the first part of this chapter, I lay the theoretical ground for thinking about the implications of nativist anticolonial discourse about African athletes by developing an account of men and masculinity that reflects Fanon's early interventions with contemporary gender and masculinity theorists. I then move on to provide an account of the role of sport in popular culture in the Philippines and as a creative space in which nativist hegemonic masculinity crafts imaginings of resistance to hundreds of years of foreign domination and occupation.[3] The chapter then moves to account for how intercollegiate male recruits from Africa are imagined and represented as threats to hegemonic Filipino masculinity. Finally, I draw the foregoing themes into a critical examination of how on-court anti-Black scripts and off-court hegemonic masculine social performances by African athletes are seen to conform to masculine African stereotypes that mutually reinforce grand narratives of hegemonic Filipino masculinity.

Toward an Intra-Global South Theory of Men and Masculinity

Neoliberalism and the emergence South–South trading blocs are increasing intra-Global South interactions by facilitating flows of people, ideas, and cultural dynamics. Besnier et al. (2018) note that the phenomenon of global migration was primarily situated in the face of economic downturns in many countries of the Global South following the impacts of global neoliberal politics since the 1980s characterized by structural adjustment and austerity measures.[4] A number of scholars contend that young men in many societies in the Global South were most affected by the new neoliberal condition instituted by the Bretton Woods system in the 1980s (Cornwall, 2016; Perry, 2005; Yang, 2010). In response, various strategies were mooted to mitigate the economic downturns, including developing entrepreneurial livelihood strategies such as petty trade and informal work (Newell, 2012). Migration also accords opportunities for social and economic mobility through professional sport caused by the impacts of neoliberalism and resultant economic downturn in most countries of the Global South (Besnier et al., 2018). Akindes (2013) exemplified this phenomenon by highlighting the pathways of African footballers to South and South-East Asia since the mid-1990s "hoping for a football career unreachable in Europe or unavailable in their home country" (p. 698). Adepoju (2018) argues that the intensification of South–South migration is a key manifestation in the twenty-first century attributed to the general economic decline in most countries in the Global North, on the one hand, and improved economic prospects in trading blocs characterized by countries mostly from the Global South on the other, including BRICS (Brazil, India, China, and South Africa) and CIVETS (Colombia, Indonesia, Vietnam, Egypt, Turkey, and South Africa).

Adepoju (2018) hypothesizes that since emerging economies in the Global South have generally stable economies, low inflation, and low debt, global migration will likely be directed towards these Southern economic nodes. Trends in migration attest to Adepoju's (2018) hypothesis. In 2017, 38% of all international migrants were from the South and residing in another country in the South (South–South migrants) compared to 35% of migrants who were born in the South but residing in the North (South–North migrants) (UNDESA, 2017). Lombaerde et al. (2014) argue that new patterns of South–South migration have not only developed intraregionally, evidenced by African migrants to South Africa (Adepoju, 2006), but also interregionally. Lombaerde et al. (2014) cite the "Asian factor" (p. 105) playing an increasingly significant role in South–South migration flows. The role of China in this intra-South migration has been significant factor (Egbula & Zheng, 2011; Taylor, 2009; Tull, 2006).

But disparities among different regions in the Global South do, of course, exist. Akindes (2013) illustrates these intra-South disparities in the phenomenon of Black African footballer migration to South and South-East Asia, which risks rendering Africa to be "rooted at the periphery of the football world system with an export-oriented culture" (p. 698).

Intra-Global South interactions are therefore occurring in important and much more intensive and unequal ways than imagined by nonaligned states parties to the 1955 Bandung Conference in Indonesia. At that time, in the first wave of the Third World independence movement, the Bandung Conference formalized Cold War nonalignment, mutual exchange in knowledge and technology, and (especially) fraternal culturo-racial solidarity among Third World peoples. Gerits (2016) contends, however, that calls for Afro-Asian Third World racial solidarity as a unifying dynamic were limited and threatened by the cultural paternalism of Asian anti-African racial stereotyping (see also Russell, Chapter 2 in this volume; Kitossa et al., Chapter 10 in this volume). The racial dimension of the Bandung Conference was not simply an issue of White versus non-White. Rather, it was *intra*racial. Kwame Nkrumah (1961, 1963) explicitly pointed towards Asian leaders' condescending views of Africa and Africans at the Bandung Conference, and how these views were buttressed and amplified by, among other things, the uneven pace of development and integration of the newly independent African states into the postcolonial world system. Walter Rodney (1973) and Frantz Fanon (1963) had indeed theorized that Africa's uneven development was attributed to the legacy of colonialism coupled by what Makki (2015) argues was the inability of postcolonial African leaders to restructure the colonial systems and institutions they inherited.[5]

The cultural paternalism of Asian anti-African racial stereotyping led Ghana's Kwame Nkrumah to perceive Asian leaders as harbouring condescending views of Africa and Africans. At the Conference of Independent African States held in Accra, Ghana in April 1958, Nkrumah subtly explained that anti-African remarks were not only coming from Europe and the United States, but also from India. Gerits (2016) notes that Nkrumah presented a "rivers of the world" analogy to "avoid a scenario in which European guidance would be supplanted by Asian paternalism" (p. 270). In this story, Nkrumah noted that the Thames, the Ganges, and the Mississippi laughed and cried out, "Africa! Africa! Why? Nile why don't you go to some place worthwhile? Why don't you stay at home where you belong?" (cited in Legum, 1958, p. 13). Gerits (2016) argued that Nkrumah's "rivers of the world" analogy essentially reflected his Pan-African project, which envisioned Africa's problems endogenously solved. Taking his cue from Nkrumah's vision, George Padmore proposed a "conference to match Bandung on an African scale where Asians would be observers and Africans would take the lead" (cited in Gerits, 2016, p. 270). This led to Ghana hosting the Conference of Independent African States in April 1958, where Nkrumah envisioned the image of an "African personality": one who self-constructs his own identity and destiny, and who "will have a chance of making its proper impact and will let the world know it through the voices of Africa's own sons" (Nkrumah, 1963, p. 125).

Nkrumah's vision of an African personality was in relation to his proclamation that for "too long in our history, Africa has spoken through the voices of others" (Nkrumah, 1963, p. 125; see also Nkrumah, 1961; Biney, 2011). Nkrumah's perception about the Asian leaders' condescending views of Africa and Africans at the Bandung Conference typifies Fanon's insights on colonialism and intraracial competition among men and masculinities. As noted by Françoise Vergès (1997), "The body of the black man is at the centre of *Black Skin, White Masks*—a humiliated, mocked, beaten, raped, assaulted, tortured, murdered body" (p. 582). The fact of Blackness, therefore, was little addressed at the Bandung Conference. Asian paternalism toward Africa becomes constructed in a process by which "Black identity [formation] is shaped by the oppressive sociopolitical structure of colonial culture" (Bergner, 1995, p. 76). The Black man's body is, however, not only Black in relation to the White man's body but also in relation to the Japanese and the Indian/South Asian man (see Russell, Chapter 2 in this volume; Kitossa et al., Chapter 10 in this volume). And, as I argue in this essay, hegemonic Filipino masculinity, too, demands that the Black man be Black in relation to the

Filipino. As a result, Blackness in Asia and Southeast Asia today continues to animate a range of neurotic responses.

Agathangelou (2016) contends that, for Fanon, the beginning of the modern colonial practice of politics and theorizing presupposes a con-figuration of Africa as an anarchical space in which African bodies and lands are constituted as fungible and prepolitical. Though this is a fiction, Agathangelou (2016) illustrates that Fanon's *Black Skin, White Masks* outlined how dichotomies of civilized/savage, flesh/body, and body/mind still play a role in the disorder of the neoliberal world. As Frank Wilderson (2011) argues, slavery is a "condition that anyone can be subjected to, to a world which reconfigures the African body into Black flesh as the African's access to, or banishment from, ontology" (p. 18). From a Fanonian standpoint, the assumption that Black = slave and non-Black = free is the establishment of an ontology in which the *being* of the African is not *nothingness* but a *non-being*. This assumption of a Black nonbeing, according to Marriott (2012), is a fiction that presumes the material life, or "destiny" of the African (or "Negro") is about sites and bodies that are ahistorical since they "fall outside of time" (p. 51). Such racial ahistoricization of Black civility as well extends to the racialization of Black masculinity.

A gendered view of men stereotypically characterizes them as having agentic authority or instrumental traits. That is, men are conceptualized as valuing the self and as having unfettered potential for action (i.e., self-assertiveness, self-interestedness, self-protection, etc.). Men imagine themselves and are imagined as being concerned with adapting to critical physical and social conditions in order to "provide" food, protection, and shelter (Bakan, 1966; Valledor-Lukey, 2012). Women on the other hand are imagined to have traits that emphasize communion or expressiveness (Spence & Helmreich, 1978), with particular emphasis on selflessness and the ability to address the emotional needs of others. Valledor-Lukey (2012) opines, in this regard, that while these are clearly archetypal and are not true of all individuals or cultures, gender traits have often been used as a guide for defining hegemonic femininity and masculinity. A unidimensional theoretical approach tends to place masculinity and femininity on opposite ends of a single spectrum; that is, being masculine means being the polar opposite of being feminine (Spence & Helmreich, 1978). Connell and Messerschmidt (2005) define hegemonic masculinity, in contradistinction to subordinate and othered masculinities, as the dominant form of masculinity in which (some) men come to dominate women and, crucially, other men.

From a social constructionist perspective of hegemonic masculinity theory, two social processes are articulated. The first concerns how all men benefit from patriarchy (Burton-Nelson, 1995; Connell, 1995, 1998; Messner, 2002; Messner & Sabo, 1990). The second is the process by which an intramasculine hierarchy is created and legitimized.[6] Anderson (2011) cites Connell's (1995) conceptualization of intramasculine domination in which one hegemonic archetype of masculinity is esteemed above all others, such that boys and men who most closely embody this standard are accorded the most social capital. Theories of hegemonic masculinity and constructed intramasculine hierarchies precede more recent work from Connell and Messerschmidt (2005) and others in the works of Frantz Fanon and James Baldwin, who explained the hypermasculinization of the Black man as the result of projecting onto the uncontrollable Black body the (repressed) impulses of the White man.

In *Another Country*, James Baldwin (1960) illustrates the plight of an urban African American man, Rufus, who struggles to reconcile his homosexual desire with the Black hypermasculine "cool pose" he dons as overcompensation and protective shield from the White world. Baldwin demonstrates Rufus's desire to prove his Black hypermasculinity to other White men. After he sexually brutalizes a White woman, Leona, Rufus presents himself to White men not simply to gloat but to also witness their judgment of him as a man. Benson (2012) asserts that Rufus's behaviour stems not only from his desire to guard his hypermasculine persona, but also from a desire to punish, fuck, and own that which White men ostensibly cherish—White women. But Rufus rapes Leona not out of genuine desire for the White woman but as a deferred, neurotic, homoerotic desire for the hegemonic White man. In Rufus, Baldwin is drawing attention to the irony, impossibility, and limits not only of Black "hypermasculinity" but of any sense of solidarity between Black men and White men under these conditions. Fanon (1952/1967), who himself drew on novelists such as Richard Wright and Chester Himes to theorize not only the Black man as a rapist but also White women's and men's desire *for* the Black rapist, dramatizes the foundations of deep and distinct intergender, intragender, and interracial psychopathologies. Fanon shows that the creation of the rapist Black man stereotype was more and other than White men's justifications for protecting the White woman by oppressing and torturing the Black man. A critical reading of Baldwin's tragic Rufus character suggests that this character is, in fact, not meant to evoke sympathy for Rufus, but instead provoke the reader to confront White society's libidinal investment in Black bodies.

As Fanon's (1952/1967) *Black Skin, White Masks* suggests, readers do not see Rufus as a person; they instead see only a penis. As Fanon argued in the book, the Black man is reduced to his biological essence: "one is no longer aware of the Negro but only of a penis; the Negro is [therefore] eclipsed. He is turned into a penis. He *is* a penis" (p. 170). In such symbolism, Jackson (2006) illustrates how scripting Black masculinity explicates a dialectic of Black sexuality in the White imagination. Anticipated by Baldwin and Fanon, McPhail (2008) therefore asserts that inscriptions of Black people as dystopic are projections of a hegemonic White mind incapable of reconciling its own moral and rational incoherence. Scripting, in effect, illuminates a range of symbolic and ideological impulses and implications of popular depictions of Black bodies. On the whole, scripted masculinity is an ideal as opposed to a realized actuality (Park, 2015): "a goal to strive towards, but [one that is] not ultimately attainable" (MacKinnon, 2003, p. 7). However anticipatory *Black Skin, White Masks* was, Fanon's theory was less theoretically explicit than Connell, Messner, and others in teasing out the relationship between gender, men, and masculinity as mutually imbricating dynamics.

Masculinity is socially constructed in that it "exist[s] impersonally in culture as a subject position in the process of representation, in the structures of language and other symbol systems" (Connell, 2000, p. 30). This fundamental fact throws us back to Baldwin and Fanon, who both show that Black men are not imagined as men in the eyes of White men; this is not only because of the White man's "bad faith" refusal of I/Thou sense (Gordon, 1995), but also in the capricious representations of Black men as nonhuman *untermenschen* and superhumans. In this regard, Fanon (1952/1967) has encouraged us to think of the possibilities for theorizing the neuroses and psychopathologies of intergroup and intermasculine competition and hatred informed by colonialism and capitalism:

> Some years ago we were astonished to see for ourselves that the North Africans despised black men. We found it impossible to have any contact with the native Arab population. We left Africa for France without understanding the reason for this animosity. Certain facts, however, were food for thought. The Frenchman does not like the Jew, who does not like the Arab, who does not like the black man. (pp. 82–83)

Within the circulating and toxic brew of hatred and scapegoating, the material basis of horizontally stratified oppressions that rob Black men and women of their collective humanity and capacity to see that their liberation from the strictures that enchain most people of colour, demands a new theory of man(kind). We are only now on the cusp of developing a uniquely intra-Global South viewpoint on men and masculinity. However, Kwame Nkrumah's complaint of intracolonized racism remains largely ignored. An illustrative example of this is the anti-Black racism in Philippine collegiate basketball.

Colonialism, Masculinity, and the Culture of Sports in the Philippines

Having sketched the outlines of an intra-Global South theory of men and masculinities from a Fanonian humanistic viewpoint, I now move to explore how basketball constitutes a site through which masculinist and nationalist discourses of Filipino hegemonic masculinity mobilize anti-Black colonialist erotic tropes. The history of basketball in the Philippines cannot, thus, be divorced from the colonial politics that institutionalized the deployment of the physical education curriculum in the country. At its inception, basketball in the Philippines was introduced in the educational system as a women's sport. It was, essentially, used to enhance their education and health as a means to meet a female stereotype: "ideal white American women [as] nurturers of civilization" (Halili, 2006, p. 186). Sport was thus used by the American imperialists in the Philippines as a medium of "soft power" to distinguish themselves from the former Spanish colonial rulers in the country.[7] To manage the tension between colonizer and colonized, the United States was keen to present itself as a benevolent liberator of Filipinos (Lizada, 2015). Antolihao (2010) notes that, in the context of colonialism, sport would become the site of American imperialist pedagogical indoctrination policies in the Philippines.[8]

There may, however, have been a more sinister motive behind introducing physical education through sports like basketball in the Philippines. Antolihao (2009) notes that basketball was used to affirm the colonial American racial ideology, projecting Filipinos as a "weak race" (p. 62) and therefore justifying American "benevolent" colonialism in the Philippines. The distinctive bodily attributes of the local inhabitants became an integral aspect of what Kramer (2006) terms the "racial politics of [American] empire" (p. 2) in reference to the ways in which the racial hierarchical structure was generated and mobilized in order to legitimate and organize the colonial administration.

Basketball later transitioned from being a "sport for the skirt" to a "guy thing" rooted in the role the Catholic Church played as a major organizing force (Lizada, 2015, p. 200). In this role, basketball became the interlocutor of an emerging hegemonic male in Philippine culture, thanks in large part to the Young Men's Christian Association's (YMCA) Play for All program. This program was initially established after the arrival in 1910 of Elwood S. Brown, the first Physical Director of the YMCA in the Philippines. It was first introduced as school-based physical education program (Antolihao, 2010). The program led the Society of Jesus fraternity in the Philippines to coordinate intercollegiate athletic competitions through the Philippines NCAA (De La Costa, 1959). This paved the way for the gendered nature of the sport to shift from feminine ideals to masculine ones, such that Catholic boys were seen to be "as manly as anyone around them" (Arcilla, 2009, p. 65).

In Filipino culture, the patriarchal system organizes gender in a manner that promotes hegemonic masculinity. According to some authors, Filipino masculinity is organized around the *barkada* [gang] phenomenon, which is both an expression of homosociality and masculine solidarity and a form of escape from the daily grind of work and family (Angeles, 2001). As such, core desirable masculine traits among Filipinos include showing bravery, strength, elegance, and affinity with others (Valledor-Lukey, 2012). A man who does not conform to stereotypical masculine traits is therefore "at risk" of being labelled as gay or feminine, regardless of his actual sexual orientation or gender identity (Valledor-Lukey, 2012). Men in Filipino society are thus encouraged to prove and practice their power and virility such that being a man has stereotypically been associated with overcoming obstacles, losing one's virginity at a young age, and having a "healthy" libido (De Castro, 1995). Bartholomew (2010), in this regard, illustrates how basketball teaches Filipino adolescents masculine virtues such as teamwork and aggression. Indeed, Bryson (1987) described sport as a crucial arena in which masculinity is constructed and reconstructed, and, in turn, directly supports male dominance via the association of males and maleness with valued skills and the sanctioned use of aggression, force, and violence (Lizada, 2015).

In acknowledgement of sport as a site in which masculinity is performed, Lizada (2015) illustrates the masculinized narratives in the psyche of Filipinos exemplified by the Ateneo de Manila University and the De La Salle University basketball rivalries that have sustained an imaginary of the ideal Filipino alpha male. Another study by Rubio and Green (2011) explored how men involved in sports in the Philippines reproduced hegemonic constructs of masculinity and gender roles that reflected the hypermasculine image of the Filipino male (Aguiling-Dalisay et al., 2000). As Devilles (2013) contends, images of masculinities are core features in Filipino television, movies, advertisements, and billboards where hegemonic masculinity is on display. Such images, in turn, feed on the fetishism of masculine virility, which is exemplified in on-court basketball performances.

Basketball in the Philippines is, therefore, a site where Filipino masculinity is significantly at play. This has given the sport a more country-wide attention, as well as a masculine complexion as a site of performance of masculine hegemony. However, this site of Filipino hypermasculinity has come to perceive the presence of Black Africans as a threat. I argue that hegemonic Filipino masculinity seeks to control and reclaim itself through the use of othering lenses and practices used to effectively eliminating the perceived threat of Black Africans. It does so by deploying, in both forms and scripts, the White gaze that, according to Barthes (1999), actively extends a repository of stereotyped attitudes that not only forms the basis of signification, but also applies meaning to the hypervisible Black bodies on which it gazes, thus affixing meaning to them in the public arena through the processes of representation.

The Black African Athletic Body and Its Threat to Filipino Masculinity and National Culture

The "foreign" continental Black African male collegiate athlete in the Philippines has been constructed in the Filipino media as a threat to Filipino hegemonic masculinity. A thematic construction of some illustrative media representations of African student-athletes in collegiate basketball in the Philippines, presented below, reinforces what Hobermann (2007) notes are certain racialized scripts that subject the bodies of Black athletes to disciplinary scrutiny. All emphasis in the following examples has been added to highlight the scripts being used in each case.

> They *easily stand out* due to *their physique, appearance, names and of course, skill and talent*. Hence, they are usually at the forefront of the campaign of colleges and universities to dominate the opposition and capture one tournament championship after another. They are the *muscle-bound, athletically gifted behemoths* lured from halfway around the world in Africa to the sizzling basketball competitions of the UAAP [University Athletic

Association of the Philippines], [Philippines'] NCAA, CESAFI [Cebu Schools Athletic Foundation, Inc.] in Cebu and other collegiate basketball hotbeds in the country. (Toledo, 2017, n.p.)

He's a big (forward) who can run, he's fast, *he's agile, physically strong and mentally he's sharp*, and he has a good attitude. (Agence France-Presse, 2017, para. 7)

The *size and dominance* of the Africans in our college game is *jarring* for those accustomed to watching *graceful, high-flying and sharp shooting* Filipino players. (Sarmenta, 2016, para. 6)

Ben Mbala Goes *Beast Mode* Against Chibueze Ikeh And Gian Mamuyac! (ABS-CN Sport, 2018, headline)

[S]ome of the players begin with *very limited basketball know-how* and end up being *schooled by patient Filipino coaches* and as a result improve and sharpen skills *beyond snaring rebounds or clogging the lane*. (Sarmenta, 2016, para. 4)

The Archers did not *spear* Mbala in Africa. No. They *snared* him in Cebu, where he was enrolled in a university. (Mendoza, 2016, para. 9)

The [Philippines'] NCAA, like the UAAP, is also peopled by *Africans manning key positions* in literally every member school of the league. Usually, the key positions are the *center, or No. 5*. (Mendoza, 2016, para. 4)

African players in [Filipino] colleges [are] *hurting* [Filipino] basketball. (Tempo Online, 2017, para. 1)

CdSL [Colegio de San Lorenzo], Diliman College ride African *reinforcements' heroics* in MBL Open. (The Wires, 2017, para. 1)

African *power* in UAAP is even worse. (Mendoza, 2016, p. 1)

These illustrative anti-African representations in media in the Philippines mobilize long-held Western-propagated "scientific" racist myths regarding natural Black athleticism, "which have underpinned the institutional routine of transferring black students more into sporting competition" (Cashmore, 1982, p. 98). The Black athletic body in Philippine collegiate sport in effect recalls Fanon's (1952/1967) metaphoric illustration of the Black man becoming an object of voyeurism: "[T]he people in the theatre are watching me, examining me, waiting for me" (p. 140). In the scene that Fanon describes, the Black viewing subject becomes the object being looked at and interpolated into a system of representations, signs, and symbols. In the context of the Philippines, media scripts "interpolate" the Black subject (the athlete) as an object to be gazed upon into a system of (stereotyped) representation of "Blackness." Filipino media is, in other words, deploying the White gaze in an effort "to explore the Black body within the context of whiteness" (Yancy, 2017, p. xv), effectively transposing White objectification of the Black Other to Filipino objectification of the Black Other. Ultimately, this "powerful use of stereotypes [and] images... provides the language and interpretations that help structure, normalize, and make sense out of [a racially structured] society"" (Feagin, 2009, p. 11). As Bonilla-Silva (2003) argues, racist ideologies are not "free-floating" (p. 469); rather, they have structural foundations that involve some form of hierarchy that produces definite social relations between the races. In the Philippines, as earlier noted, the racialized structure and inherent ideologies are rooted in the imperial Spanish and American race politics—what Kramer (2006) refers to as "the ways in which the racial hierarchical structure was generated and mobilized in order to legitimate and organize the colonial administration in the Philippines" (p. 2).

Media scripts in the Philippines come to extend a stereotypical impression of continental Africans that uses a race-logic grounded in White-held imperialist worldviews, which held the assumption that Black people are physically advanced because of some genetic predisposition toward athleticism (Sailes, 1998). The thematic representations of continental Black physicality in the media in the Philippines therefore deploy White frames which tend to orient heavily toward the rhetoric of "animalistic" representations of the Black male body, which in other contexts has "long been the site of white fascination, consumption, and fear" (Guzzio, 2005, pp. 223–24). As Bonilla-Silva (2003) contends, this racialized lens, rooted in American racial history against enslaved Black people, not only comes to explain and interpret the everyday world, but also implies or offers an explanatory perspective to structure racial relations. In employing the White frame, Black lived experiences are erased by prototypical conceptualizations of the Black body in the White imaginary. In this gaze, Black and other colonized peoples have been cast as the opposite of the White colonizer, typically framed as "uncivilized, subhuman, infantile, even bestial" (King & Springwood, 2001, p. 104). These tropes become seen as the "normal reality of common-sense" (hooks, 1992, p. 75). Indeed, they are taken as normalized "representations of events relating to race that have premises inscribed into them as a set of unquestionable assumptions" (Hall, 1990, p. 13). In such normalized representations, Wellard (2009) notes that the Black person's sporting presence is "a masculine prowess which can [only] be presented through bodily performance" (p. 59). That is, it is reduced to their athletic muscular body and, notably, not about the human behind the athletic performance.

Thus, anti-African representation in media scripts in the Philippines come to represent what King and Springwood (2001) conceptualize as "mass-mediated spectacles that return the White gaze back onto the black body" (p. 106). The mass media's representation of Black Africans in the Philippines reifies White racial ideology that Black athletes are physically superior and are specifically recruited for their athletic ability. Once rooted in colonialist and imperialist doctrines and discourses, a form of "new racism" against continent Africans seems to reemerge in the contemporary world where the salience of "race" appears as both opaque and ubiquitous. As Fanon (1952/1967) wrote on anti-Black racism, the White gaze makes of the Black body an object, "in the midst of other objects" (p. 82)—that was historicized based on a racial epidermal schema residing within the purview of the White gaze. Fanon's racial epidermal schema translates into a racial muscular schema in Filipino narratives of Black hypermasculinities. This reinforces an ideology of common-sense racial articulation that, as Yancy (2017) notes, seems to profess specific kinds of meanings on Black people. Fanon termed these as the "fact of blackness," (p. 89) in reference to the lived experience of the Black man whose identity is constructed by others purely on the basis his skin colour. As Fanon states, "ontology does not allow us to understand the being of the black man, since it ignores the lived experience. For not only must the black man be black; he must be black in relation to the white man" (p. 90). The Black college athlete in the Philippines is no longer marked by an "invisibility" within the public sphere (Carrington, 2002). Basketball in the Philippines is, therefore, a site in which continental Black African bodies are gazed upon; basketball provides Filipinos a legitimate space for racialized ideologies on Black bodies within homosocial encounters. In Hawkins's (2010) view, the mass media discourse fluctuates between celebrating cultural diversity and reinforcing dominant racialized Black ideologies. Therefore, the on-court performances of Black African masculinity are to be checked.

A proposal to ban foreign students, specifically targeted at African student-athletes, in future intercollegiate basketball events is seen as a move to guard against Black African masculine performances. The exceptions to this rule are foreigners of Filipino descent (or *Fil-foreigners*) in reference to their being mixed-race and mostly from the diaspora. Their inclusion, at the expense of African students, is argued on the basis that they, the Fil-foreigners, can be part of the pool for selection in the national team and can presumably assimilate into Filipino society. Amid the COVID-19 pandemic which has severely impacted the Philippines (WHO, 2020),[9] the Philippines' NCAA Management Committee (Mancom) issued a directive that the ban on foreign players will remain as the competition plans to resume for Season 96 in early 2021 (Atencio, 2020). The ban on foreign student-athletes is grounded on the alleged "negative impact" these players have on the "development" of collegiate basketball competition in the Philippines. This sentiment was reiterated by the current Chair of the Mancom, Fr. Vic Calvo of the Colegio de San Juan de Letran:

> *Sa open discussion* [in open discussion], we realized that the presence of foreign players has done more harm than good in basketball. As of the moment, majority of the NCAA schools agree, *na mas maraming negative na nadudulot yung presence ng imports* [the presence of imports causes more negative outcomes]. (Fr. Vic Calvo, cited in Verzosa, 2020)

The directive to sustain the ban on foreign student-athletes means that there will be no more recruitment of non-Filipino foreign student-athletes after Season 95 of the 2019–2020 academic year, which inadvertently got disrupted by the COVID-19 outbreak in the Philippines (Yumol, 2020). This means that the last batch of African student-athletes recruited in 2013, consisting of Donald Tankoua, Eugen Toba ,and Arnaud Noah of San Beda University; Prince Eze of University of Perpetual Help; Eli Ongolo-Ongolo of Arellano University; Hamadu Laminou of Emilio Aguinaldo College; Clement Leutcheu of De La Salle College of Saint Benilde; and Mike Nzeusseu of Lyceum of the Philippines University, played their last competitive collegiate games of Season 95 in the NCAA (Verzosa, 2020). This decision provides a veiled attempt to protect Filipino masculinity in collegiate basketball conceived in an ideology of nationalism reflected in the following media report:

> Imports get benefits that are not given to Filipinos; we must appeal to the good sense and the nationalistic inclinations of those who run the schools, says Nathanielsz.[10] (Gasgonia, 2013)

From a Fanonian lens, the decision to ban Black Africans in future collegiate sports events in the Philippines is a move to appropriate the imagined Black phallic power to Filipino males. In order to perform the social function of appropriating Blackness, Filipino masculinity must first be seen to be under threat of being overwhelmed by Black bodies. Awareness of the presumed threats posed by African basketball players

FIGURE 9.1: Jun Manzo (left) of the University of the Philippines' Maroons, and Angelo Kouame (right) of the Ateneo de Manila University Blue Eagles in Game 1 of the UAAP *Season 81 Finals on December 1, 2018.* (Philippine Daily Inquirer, *Sunday, December 2, 2018. Reproduced with permission from Sherwin Marion Vardeleon [photographer] and the* Philippine Daily Inquirer.)

is aptly captured in the following quote by Cameroonian student-athlete Moustapha Arafat of the University of the East:

> When my teammates go up against me and (Charles) Mamie, they get challenged physically because you know, we are larger than they are. But

> as they progress and maybe even move onto professional leagues, they won't be too scared to go up against someone so big. (cited in Alejandrino, 2016)

The same presumed threats are also captured in an iconic David/Filipino versus Goliath/African image, originally printed in the *Philippine Daily Inquirer* (Figure 9.1). Barthes's (1977) theory of the photograph can help us better understand this image. For Barthes, the photograph is a code of cultural knowledge and ideas: a way in which society communicates certain cultural biases. According to Barthes (1977), a photograph in a newspaper "transmit[s]...the scene itself, the literal reality" (p. 17) by representing both its denoted message (that is, the direct representation of the image itself) and its connoted message (that is, the extent to which the society communicates what it thinks of the image). It is alongside such projected media images, and in the same vein, that Sarmenta (2016) portrays African student-athletes as "tall and beefy" (para. 4) and suggests that their recruitment only boosts a college team's prospect of winning games and trophies. Media scripts in the Philippines therefore come to embellish Black skin with what Farley (1997) notes are "ideologies and satire" (p. 464) in order to distinguish, separate, and create Filipinos as distinct from the negative image of Blackness. This is best captured when media texts describe the role of foreign African "imports" as being only to "lend colour to the tournaments [whereas] games are won and lost by the local boys" (Micua, 1976).

As King (2004) notes, the historic objectification of Black men's bodies during the period of slavery in the West reduced the Black man to "a body and then reduc[ed] this body to a thing, ultimately dehumanizing the slave and making him a quantifiable object that could be traded as a commodity" (p. 24). In the current neoliberal era, the commodification of Black bodies continues, exemplified in the world of sport, where "there is a mystified image of the black athlete enacted through a biological obsession with his body" (King, 2004, p. 19). Such commodification is a form of contemporary slavery in which the Black man is "caged" within a notion of Black masculinity, which, as Guzzio (2005) suggests, has long been the site of White fascination, consumption, and fear. This obsession with the perceived physical advantages of Black men is "the same obsession that maintains the pathology of black bodies in the forms of paranoia and suspicion" (Guzzio, 2005, p. 229). Thus, basketball as a homosocial space interpolates Black Africans into a system that produces a psychological fragmentation within Black African men—an aspect that Fanon (1952/1967) calls "the black man's dimension of being-for-others" (p. 1). Such interpolations occur because mainstream competitive sport is inherently homoerotic (as much as homophobic), with its codes of domination and penetration. It is also governed by strict rules that emphasize a system of masculinist heteronormativity (Messner & Sabo, 1990). In effect, the appalling and simultaneously desired Black African body, by virtue of its "thingness," serves to reinforce the performance of hypermasculine Filipino identity on the basketball court.

Therefore, the Filipino male attempts to "reclaim" his masculinity from African athletes by rendering continental Black bodies as Others—but herein lies a paradox. Although Filipinos are objects of a long history of racist imperial colonial domination, first from the Spanish then the Americans, they are now (ironically) drawing on colonial, anti-African representations to narrate their own symbolic resistance to threats posed by Black African athletes in the sporting sphere of collegiate basketball. In other words, by disseminating representations of Black African athletes as threats to Filipino hegemonic masculinity, Filipinos are attempting not only to recuperate their masculinities, but also their culture and identity.

Reclaiming the Basketball Court in the Philippines as a Site for the Performance of Filipino Hypermasculinity

As has already been discussed, though basketball was initially introduced as a girls-only sport in the Philippines, it is now seen as an essential homosocial space for the performance and display of Filipino masculinity (Lizada, 2015). The homosocial hypermasculine nature of men's intercollegiate sport has served to counter Filipino men's fears of feminization rooted in an imperial American racialized ideology against the Filipino race (Antolihao, 2009) through an overt emphasis on their collective gendered role in society. In the contemporary setting, Filipino masculine performance in the homosocial basketball space has once again become threatened by Black African masculinity. In this homosocial space, Fanon (1952/1967) contends that the Black male was the repository of White fears, fantasies, desires, and, above all else, "the singular eroticization of the black athlete" (p. 158). Inherent in this threat are both fears of and desires for the "tough" Black athlete among Filipino males—a situation that is in line with Connell's (1995) contention that "black sporting stars become exemplars of masculine toughness" (p. 80).

The basketball court, in Filipino popular culture, allows a context in which Filipino men "can safely articulate and experience their desire for black men" (Alexander, 1996, p. 170). That is, the continental Black male athlete in the Philippines has been placed in a position of subordination through a representational practice that Hortense Spillers (1987) calls "pornotroping." In reference to a hypersexualized figure, pornotroping is "a kind of fetishistic practice that the black body is subjected to; a suspended identity where African peoples were divested of cultural and sexual identity, a site where they were 'culturally unmade'" (Spillers 1987, p. 74). In the realm of sport, Pronger (1990) notes that male athletes tend to be compared to a pumped-up penis, which symbolically presents the hypersexualized imagery that shapes masculinity in homosocial environments. It is in this understanding I use the term *sila ay malaki* [they are big] in reference to the physical attributes, athleticism, and hypermasculine images that African Black athletes in collegiate basketball in the Philippines come to symbolically represent. As noted at the beginning of the chapter, the term *malaki* in the sports discourse in the media in the Philippines is strongly associated with the physical and masculine attributes of Black athletes. For example, a Filipino basketball website makes reference to Houston Rockets' James Harden (an African American) and his condescending view on Milwaukee Bucks' Giannis Antetokounmpo (a Greek) in the American NBA (Fastbreak, 2020). The headline, which reads "*Malaki lang, walang skills! Harden claps back at Antetokounmpo,*" metaphorically captures Harden's reference to Antetokounmpo's height while downplaying the latter's skills. In collegiate basketball in the Philippines, reference to the use of the term *malaki* is commonly made to the physical stature or hypermasculine attributes of Black African student-athletes. For example, in a statement made by the University of the Philippines' Fighting Maroons coach Rickey Dandan to his team during a match versus the University of Santo Thomas (UST) Growling Tigers in the UAAP Season 74 in 2011–2012, Dandan makes reference to the physical size of Karim Abdul, a student-athlete from Cameroon representing UST:

> *Malaki 'yan, isang ganito lang sa inyo 'yan* [He's big. He can create with a single motion]. Initiate contact, hold your ground. (cited in Silvestre, 2012, p. 67)

Another example comes from an opinion expressed by a former coach of the national men's basketball team at the 29th Southeast Asian Games about his opposition to the preferential recruitment of tall Africans in collegiate leagues in the Philippines at the expense of equally tall Filipinos:

> *Kung may malaki kang African, bakit ka pa kukuha ng mga 6-5 or 6-6 na Pinoy?* [If you have a big (tall) African, why would you get a 6'5" or 6'6" Filipino?] (cited in Tempo Online, 2017, para. 5)

Thus, pornotroping African Black athletes in the Philippines subjects them to the control of the institutions governing their performance and future participation. Such a form of governmentality is captured in the words of Cameroonian player Mike Nzeusseu: "We have to abide by whatever decision they're making" (cited in Leongson, 2020, para. 35).

Fetishizing Black men while seeking to domesticate and manage the impact of their representation requires a symbolic act of castration. Fanon (1952/1967) utilizes the idea of castration to describe racial disempowerment, investing social power with relevance to skin colour. Punishing continental African student-athletes by taking from them their due recognition, opportunity, reward, and—the very thing for which they were initially recruited—their athleticism (Verora, 2018; Velasco, 2015) is constitutive of a symbolic castration of the Black man's symbolic power in the Filipino hegemonic masculine imaginary. Filipino masculinity accomplishes by other means what was once done, actually and symbolically, to the Black man by the White man.

Black African college basketball players resist anti-Black rhetoric they face in collegiate basketball in the Philippines. For example, Cameroonian Donald Tankoua, winner of the 2019 Philippines NCAA Best Foreign Player MVP, noted the following as a parting shot:

> Again, we thank the NCAA for letting us play. We gained experience as well and helped Filipino basketball players. We still have a life to live. Thank you for letting us play in the Philippines. (cited in Leongson, 2020, para. 39)

Tankoua's comment demonstrates a sense of freedom from the Filipino gaze. It draws in Fanon's (1952/1967) analysis of the Black subject's desire to break free from White subjugation within a dualist relationship characterized between "'freedom and space', 'escape and movement', 'violence', which can be either real and symbolic, and lastly, 'embodied emancipation'" (p. 50). In this regard, Tankoua's comment reflects a form of Black resistance, or reaction, that aligns with Carrington's (2010) description of the Black athlete claiming their freedom by transgressing some of the racial constraints imposed on their lives. This form of reaction draws on Fanon's reference to a liberation movement that disrupts the idea that the masculine "property owners are [the] only human[s]" (Agathangelou, 2016, p. 125). It is a sense of an imagined Pan-Africanism that visualizes itself as "one great body refusing any mutilation" (Fanon, 1952/1967, p. 151), once again reigniting Nkrumah's (1963) call for Africans to autonomously speak for themselves in reaction to Asian leaders' condescending views of Africa and about Africans. This "voice" draws on Fanon's (1952/1967) "prayer" for the Black man to constantly raise his consciousness over his body by "making me always a [black] man who questions" (p. 232). Thus by regaining a sense of freedom, specifically in response to their proposed ban in collegiate sport in the Philippines (Alejandrino, 2016), African student-athletes are effectively talking back to the Filipino scripting of an idealized and totemic representation of African hypermasculine men—a representation that is, itself, a riff on White constructions of African men as anticivilized "libidinous beasts" (Meisenhelder, 2003, p. 103).

Conclusion

This chapter highlights the predicament of Black African male student-athletes in the Philippines. I principally drew on Frantz Fanon (1952/1967) conceptual framework in *Black Skin, White Masks*, the very title of which encapsulates the "split" or "divided" self at the heart of the colonialist objectification of Black men. Such a divided self is reflected in Fanon's reference to the Black man being "perpetuated by alienated psyches" (p. 59). This remark reference the White female lover who offers the Black man a form of recognition that is, in the condition of colonialism, nonetheless mired in a sexual myth about the quest for White female flesh. Hall (1996) articulates Fanon's argument "that the black man can only exist in relation to himself through the alienating presence of the white 'Other'" (p. 18). Herein lie questions of desire and envy, and the sexualized nature of the relationship between the hegemonic "Filipino man" and his opposite, the "continental Black athletic man." I demonstrated that anti-Black media scripts, coupled with exclusionary practices in a homosocial sporting space, have, in effect, mutually reinforced grand narratives of hegemonic Filipino masculinity. These findings reflect Fanon's insights on colonialism and intraracial competition among men and masculinities.

This chapter further illustrates how basketball in the Philippines allows for Filipino hegemonic masculinity to be performed against a colonial stereotype that constructs Filipinos as a physically small people in contrast to the White, mostly American colonial masters (Antolihao, 2012). The presence of African athletes once again rekindles the colonial construction of a weak Filipino masculinity. The presence and on-court dominance of Black African athletes has in effect led to another struggle for the Filipino male to once again seek to regain their masculinity through a negotiated process with these foreign Black bodies. These negotiations include processes of exclusion, the deployment of stereotypical media scripts borrowed from the White colonial gaze, and homoerotic representations of continental Africans that Hortense Spillers (1987) calls "pornotroping."

Media scripting of Black athletic bodes in the Philippines has reproduced Eurocentric and Filipino nativist patriarchal tropes of continental African hypermasculinity and visibility. As Stuart Hall (1993) suggests in his essay "What Is this 'Black' in Black Popular Culture" (p. 104), identities are inextricably linked to and shaped by both contemporary social positioning and self-constructed narratives set within the messy flows and motion of dynamic social interaction with others. Collegiate basketball in the Philippines in effect has "transferred and appropriated phallic [Filipino] power" (Lizada, 2015, p. 201) that, in order to perform its social function, must first be seen to be under severe threat from emerging Black African bodies. Such racial profiling brings to the fore what Fanon termed the "Fact of Blackness" (p. 82): a "fact" that Carrington (2002) argues no longer renders Black people "invisible" within the public sphere. Thus, within a homosocial space that is the basketball court, excluding and/or scripting Black foreign bodies allows Filipino males to reify a hegemonic and heterosexual imagination in order to produce and sustain their markers of manhood.

Reflecting on the racialized media scripts, the pornotroping of Black African athletes, and the Black man *qua* penis in the homosocial collegiate basketball space in the Philippines, *sila ay malaki* [they are big], a phrase commonly used in sports discourse in the Philippines, is a discursive double entendre, a productive site for the homoerotic (re)production of stereotyped Black masculinities in structuring a nativist hegemonic Filipino masculinity set against the long arc of Spanish and US colonization of the Philippines. The fear of the continental Black athlete, whether praised or vilified, is a powerful reminder of the continuance and efficacy of a once-colonial racist discourse that has, in the contemporary global setting, expanded from the West to the East. An interrogation of contemporary forms of race relations and masculinity in non-White geographical spaces requires a departure from White ideological frames and towards those which situate these relations in neoliberal structural arrangements which unravel "hierarchical relations between the races in those systems" (Bonila-Silva, 1997, p. 476). As Hawkins (2010) argues, these discourses can only be challenged once we begin to recognize and deconstruct the normalizing power inscribed in the spectacle of the Black body, which increasingly serves to shift attention away from everyday forms of racial inequality in the Global South context.

Notes

1. *Filipino* is the Hispanized (or Anglicized) way of referring to both the people and the language in the Philippines. Locals call the country *Pilipinas*, a name derived from the old Spanish name of the country during colonial occupation, *Las Islas Filipinas* (The Philippine Islands). This name is derived from the Spanish King Felipe II (or, in English, King Philip II, whence the *Ph* in *Philippine*) (Center for Philippine Studies, 2020).
2. The terms *Black* and *Blackness* have been used in the discourse on race in reference to both the external and internal characteristics (such as character or mental ability) of "the so-called Black group" (Hrabovský, 2013, p. 65). Hrabovský (2013) contends that the black skin came to be regarded as "damned" (p. 66) and one of the reasons of enslavement since the launch of slave trade in 1441. Such characterisation has resulted in a wide range of prejudices and stereotypes assuming an immediately "lower" status for persons with black skin. In effect, Black and Blackness, Hrabovský (2013) argues, became the basis for a long-lasting prejudice and at the same time "constantly abused 'argument' for the humiliation of [Black] human beings on the basis of their external appearance" (p. 67). This chapter uses the term *Black* as a reference to the social construction rather than as a biological reference to skin colour.
3. The Philippines was a Spanish colony from 1565 to 1898, when Spain ceded the colony to the Americans following Spain's defeat in the Spanish–American War of 1898. As part of Spain's administration of the colony, the Spanish colonial policy of divisiveness was enacted. This promoted and encouraged regional isolation and ethnic distinctions. Duka (2008) illustrates how the Spanish introduced the term *Filipino* in reference to the Spanish *Insulares*, or those of Spanish descent born in the Philippines. These were distinguished from those who born in the Iberian peninsula (*Peninsulares*). These two social groups, despite their definitional distinction, wielded immense authority and power over the rest of the Indigenous population composed of the black-skinned Atea, and the brown-skinned Malays of Indo-Asia extraction. With Spanish colonialism, a system of racial hierarchy was established which privileged those of White Spanish descent over the local non-White population (Rodriguez, 2006). This racially-organized system polarized the society in that "locally born (non-White) Filipinos began to see the country as rightfully theirs

and the *peninsulares* as alien rulers" (Steinberg 1982, p. 39). During the American colonial reign, the central role of racism and race prejudice was exhibited in the genocide of non-White Filipinos during the Philippine–American War (1899–1902), coupled by institutional and cultural racism of US officials and magistrates throughout the early decades of US colonial rule, putting into question the "benevolent" aims of US institutions and the "positive" effects of the US colonial legacy (Blanco, 2011). Antolihao (2009) further illustrates the colonial cultural project in which the Americans introduced physical education in schools, where Filipino students were required to incorporate aspects of American values and culture. In the US colonial project, the Filipino physique was perceived as an inferior racial category that, in effect, established the hierarchy of racial difference used to justify American colonialism.

4. Neoliberalism is rooted in the policy and ideological orientation of the International Monetary Fund (IMF) and the World Bank which premised that political and social problems should be solved primarily through market-based mechanisms as opposed to state intervention. Soederberg (2005) observes that neoliberalism in effect became a dominant policy that is also referred to as the Washington Consensus. This policy espoused a raft of structural adjustment programs (SAPs) which included debtor nations in the Global South adopting export-led industrialization strategies, minimal restrictions on the activities of private-market participants, along with austerity measures that reduced spending on social welfare. The SAPs resulted in massive resource transfers from the debtor countries to the developed world (Bienefeld, 1993) which according to Soederberg (2005) "assisted in creating a greater, not lesser, dependency of Third World governments on global capital markets as opposed to bilateral aid, not to mention higher poverty rates than before the debt crises of the early 1980s" (p. 330).

5. The colonial political economic system in Africa varied across regions. Samir Amin (1972) suggested three distinctive regional patterns: the labour reserves for the extractive sector in the gold, copper, and diamond mines in southern Africa, or the coffee, tea, and sisal estates in East Africa; the colonial trading sector in parts of West Africa and North Africa, characterized by the production of agricultural commodities for metropolitan industries; and lastly, the commercial sector for concession companies in central and equatorial Africa where chartered companies used forced labour in quasi-plantation-like systems. These systems were essentially sustained by the newly independent states of Africa that in part extended an extraverted economy and the gatekeeper functions of the colonial state. An extraverted economy, according to Bayart and Ellis (2000), theoretically presumes that African elites deliberately create and sustain a dependency role with the West albeit at their own interest (Cheeseman et al., 2019). Gatekeeper functions refers to a system in which colonies served as administrative centres of the beneficiary colonial master where the apparatus of power was centralised and directly felt at certain strategic nodes. These nodes, connected by railway lines, where specifically areas of raw material production and the points of connection with the world market served by ports which served as centres for revenue collection from duties imposed on imports and exports. As Makki (2015) notes, "colonial states were in this sense "gatekeeper states" situated astride the junction of the world market and

the colonial territory and primarily engaged in *rentier* activities and control over the movement of people and goods in and out of the colony" (p. 130).

6. For an alternative view that draws on Baldwinian and Fanonian conceptions of men, masculinity, and patriarchy as interracial group competition and social contract, see Kitossa's Introduction in this volume.
7. Spanish occupation of the Philippines spanned from 1521 to 1898 which ended with the signing of the Treaty of Paris on December 10, 1898. Following the end of the Spanish–American War, Spain ceded its overseas territories to the United States, including the Philippines (Duka, 2008).
8. The first phase of US rule was from 1898 to 1935, during which time Washington defined its colonial mission as one of tutelage and preparing the Philippines for eventual independence. The second period of United States rule—from 1936 to 1946—was characterized by the establishment of the Commonwealth of the Philippines and occupation by Japan during World War II (Tagalog Lang, 2002).
9. The Philippines is among the countries most impacted by COVID-19 in the Southeast Asian region, with over 344,000 confirmed cases of COVID-19, and 6,372 deaths recorded in the month of October, 2020, alone (WHO, 2020). All sports events, including collegiate sports, were effectively banned following the outbreak of COVID-19 in the Philippines. Plans are afoot to resume some sports events in 2021 (Asis, 2020).
10. Ronald "Ronnie" Nathanielsz is a former Filipino sportswriter and broadcast journalist of Sri Lankan descent who lived in the Philippines for five decades until is passing in 2016. Nathanielsz was best known for analyzing boxing matches and once served as Muhammad Ali's media liaison officer when the legendary boxer fought Joe Frazier in Manila in 1975 for the heavyweight championship (Basco, 2016).

Bibliography

ABS-CBN Sport. (2018). Ben Mbala goes beast mode against Chibueze Ikeh and Gian Mamuyac! *ABS-CBN Sport*. Retrieved October 3, 2020, from https://sports.abs-cbn.com/uaap/videos/2017/12/03/ben-mbala-goes-beast-mode-chibueze-ikeh-17537

Adepoju, A. (2006). Internal and international migration within Africa. In Kok, P., Oucho, J., Gelderblom, D., & Van Zyl, J. (Eds.), *Migration in South and southern Africa: Dynamics and determinants* (pp. 26–46). Human Sciences Research Council.

Agathangelou, A.M. (2016). Fanon on decolonization and revolution: Bodies and dialectics. *Globalizations, 13*(1), 110–28. https://doi.org/10.1080/14747731.2014.981056

Agence France-Presse. (2017, March 2). Big Ben towers in basketball-mad Philippines. *Philippine Daily Inquirer*. Retrieved September 26, 2020, from https://sports.inquirer.net/239726/big-ben-towers-basketball-mad-philippines

Aguiling-Dalisay, G., Mendoza, R., Mirafelix, E., Yacat, J., Sto. Domingo, M., & Bambico, F. (2000). *Pagkalalake [masculinity]: Men in control? Filipino male views on love, sex and women*. Pambansang Samahan ng Sikolohiyang Pilipino.

Akindes, G.A. (2013). South Asia and South-East Asia: new paths of African footballer migration. *Soccer and Society, 14*(5), 684–701. https://doi.org/10.1080/14660970.2013.792486.

Alejandrino, A. (2016, December 9). Foreigners speak up on UAAP's move to ban foreign student-athletes. *Sports Illustrated*. Retrieved September 26, 2020, from http://www.sportsillustrated.com.ph/College/2016/12/09/Foreigners-speak-up-on-UAAPs-move-to-ban-foreign-studentathletes

Alexander, E. (1996). "We're gonna deconstruct your life!": The making and un-making of the Black bourgeois patriarch in *Ricochet*. In M. Blount & G. Cunningham (Eds.), *Representing Black men* (pp. 157–72). Routledge.

Amin, S. (1972). Underdevelopment and dependence in Black Africa-origins and contemporary forms. *The Journal of Modern African Studies, 10*(4), 503–24.

Anderson, E. (2011). Masculinities and sexualities in sport and physical cultures: Three decades of evolving research. *Journal of Homosexuality, 58*(5), 565–78. https://doi.org/10.1080/00918369.2011.563652

Angeles, L.C. (2001). The Filipino male as "macho-machunurin": Men and masculinities in gender and development studies. *Kasarinlan Journal of Third World Issues, 16*(1), 9–30. https://www.journals.upd.edu.ph/index.php/kasarinlan/article/view/1073

Antolihao, L. (2009). *Can the subaltern play? Postcolonial transition and the making of basketball as the national sports in the Philippines*. [Doctoral dissertation, National University of Singapore]. ScholarBank@NUS. http://scholarbank.nus.edu.sg/bitstream/10635/17351/1/AntolihaoLA.pdf

Antolihao, L. (2010). Rooting for the underdog: Spectatorship and subalternity in Philippine basketball. *Philippine Studies, 58*(4), 449–80. https://www.jstor.org/stable/42634651

Antolihao, L. (2012). From baseball colony to basketball republic: Post-colonial transition and the making of a national sport in the Philippines, *Sport in Society, 15*(10), 1396–412. https://doi.org/10.1080/17430437.2012.744209

Arcilla, S.J. (2009). *150: The Ateneo way*. Muse Books.

Asis, M.A. (2020, November 15). Philippine college sports challenged by COVID-19. *Manila Times*. Retrieved November 20, 2020, from https://www.manilatimes.net/2020/10/12/122nd-anniversary/philippine-college-sports-challenged-by-covid-19/779239/

Atencio, P. (2020, June 11). NCAA season 96 to start early months of 2021. *Manila Standard*. https://manilastandard.net/sports/sports-plus/325820/ncaa-season-96-to-start-early-months-of-2021.html

Bakan, D. (1966). *The quality of human existence*. Beacon Press.

Baldwin, J. (1960). *Another country*. Vintage.

Barthes, R. (1977). The rhetoric of the image. (S. Heath, Trans.). In *Image, music, text* (pp. 32–51). Hill and Wang.

Barthes, R. (1999). Myth today. In J. Evans & S. Hall (Eds.), *Visual culture: The reader* (pp. 33–40). SAGE.

Bartholomew, R. (2010). *Pacific rims: Beermen ballin' in flip-flops and the Philippines' unlikely love affair with Basketball*. New American Library.

Basco, K.C. (2016, November 12). Ronnie Nathanielsz dies at 81. *ABS-CBN News*. Retrieved September 26, 2020, from https://news.abs-cbn.com/sports/11/11/16/ronnie-nathanielsz-dies-at-81

Bayart, J. & Ellis, S. (2000). Africa in the world: A history of extraversion. *African Affairs, 99*(395), 217–67. http://doi.org/10.1093/afraf/99.395.217

Benson, J.D. (2012). *Failed heroes: Hypermasculinity in the contemporary American novel.* [Doctoral dissertation, University of South Florida]. ScholarCommons, University of South Florida Libraries. http://scholarcommons.usf.edu/etd/3975

Bergner, G. (1995). Who is that masked woman? Or, the role of gender in Fanon's *Black skin, White masks*. *PMLA*, *110*(1), 75–88. http://doi.org/10.2307/463196

Besnier, N., Guinness, D., Hann, M., & Kovač, U. (2018). Rethinking masculinity in the neoliberal order: Cameroonian footballers, Fijian rugby players, and Senegalese wrestlers. *Comparative Studies in Society and History, 60*(4), 839–72. http://doi.org/10.1017/S0010417518000312

Bienefeld, M. (1993, November 24–25). *Structural adjustment: Debt collection device or development policy?* [Conference paper]. Structural Adjustment: Past, Present, and Future, Sophia University, Tokyo. https://carleton.ca/africanstudies/wp-content/uploads/Bienefeld-2000-Review-Structural-Adjustment-as-Debt-Collection-Device.pdf

Biney, A. (2011). *The political and social thought of Kwame Nkrumah*. Palgrave MacMillan.

Blanco, J.D. (2011). Race as praxis in the Philippines at the turn of the twentieth century. *Southeast Asian Studies*, *49*(3), 356–94. https://doi.org/10.20495/tak.49.3_356

Bonilla-Silva, E. (1997). Rethinking racism: Toward a structural interpretation. *American Sociological Review, 62*(3), 465–83.

Bonilla-Silva, E. (2003). *Racism without racists: Color-blind racism and the persistence of racial inequality in the United States*. Rowman & Littlefield Publishers.

Bryson, L. (1987). Sport and the maintenance of masculine hegemony. *Women's Studies International Forum*, *10*(4), 349–60. https://doi.org/10.1016/0277-5395(87)90052-5

Burton-Nelson, M. (1995). *The stronger women get the more men love football: Sexism and the American culture of sports*. Avon Books.

Carrington, B. (2002). *"Race," representation and the sporting body* [Paper submitted to the CUCR's Occasional Paper Series, Goldsmiths College, University of London]. https://www.gold.ac.uk/media/documents-by-section/departments/research-centres-and-units/research-centres/centre-for-urban-and-comm/carrington.pdf

Carrington, B. (2010). *Race, sport and politics: The sporting Black diaspora.* SAGE.

Cashmore, E. (1982) *Black sportsmen*. Routledge.

Center for Philippine Studies (2020). *Filipino, Pilipino, Pinoy, Pilipinas, Philippines—What's the difference?* University of Hawaii-Manoa. http://www.hawaii.edu/cps/filipino.html

Cheeseman, N., Bertrand, E., & Husaini, S. (2019). *A dictionary of African politics*. Oxford University Press.

Connell, R.W. (1995). *Masculinities*. Polity Press.

Connell, R.W. (1998). Masculinities and globalization. *Men and masculinities*, *1*(1): 3–23.

Connell, R.W. (2000). *The men and the boys*. University of California Press.

Connell, R.W., & Messerschmidt, J. (2005). Hegemonic masculinity: Rethinking the concept. *Gender & Society, 19*(6), 829–59. http://www.jstor.org/stable/27640853

De Castro, L.D. (1995). Pagiging lalaki, pagkalalaki at pagkamaginoo [Being a man, masculinity and being a gentleman]. In M.C. Gastardo-Conaco (Ed.), *Gender issues in Philippine society* (pp. 127–42). University of the Philippines College of Social Science and Philosophy.

De La Costa, H. (1959). The Jesuits in the Philippines 1581–1959. *Philippine Studies, 7*(1), 68–97.

Devilles, G. (2013). Performing hypermasculinity in billboard ads and malls in Manila. *Asian Perspectives in the Arts and Humanities, 3*(1), 61–77. https://pdfs.semanticscholar.org/a693/8bd2172cacbe847548e357660116867f49cf.pdf

Duka, C.D. (2008). *Struggle for freedom: A textbook on Philippine history*. Rex Book Store.

Egbula, M., & Zheng, Q. (2011). China and Nigeria: A powerful south–south alliance. *West African Challenges, 5*, 1–20. http://www.oecd.org/swac/publications/49814032.pdf

Evans, M. (1996). Languages of racism within contemporary Europe. In B. Jenkins & S.A. Sofos (Eds.), *Nation & identity in contemporary Europe* (pp. 33–53). Routledge.

Fanon, F. (1963). *The wretched of the earth* (C. Farrington, Trans.). Grove Press.

Fanon, F. (1967). *Black skin, White masks* (C.L. Markmann, Trans.). Pluto Press. (Original work published 1952)

Farley, A.P. (1997). The Black body as fetish object. *Oregon Law Review, 76*(3), 457–535. https://ssrn.com/abstract=1518415

Fastbreak. (2020, February 29). Malaki lang, walang skills! Harden claps back at Antetokounmpo. *Fastbreak.com.ph*. Retrieved October 26, 2020, from https://fastbreak.com.ph/malaki-lang-walang-skills-harden-claps-back-at-antetokounmpo/

Feagin, J.R. (2009). *The White racial frame: Centuries of racial framing and counter-framing*. Routledge.

Gasgonia, D. (2013). Imports in UAAP, NCAA bad for PH basketball. *ABS-CBN*. Retrieved September 26, 2020, from http://news.abs-cbn.com/sports/01/04/13/imports-uaap-ncaa-bad-ph-basketball

Gerits, F. (2016). Bandung as the call for a better development project: US, British, French and Gold Coast perceptions of the Afro-Asian Conference (1955). *Cold War History, 16*(3), 255–72. https://doi.org/10.1080/14682745.2016.1189412

Go, B. (2018, June 9). PH surrenders early lead, bows to Mongolia in 3x3 World Cup. *Rappler*. Retrieved September 26, 2020, https://www.rappler.com/sports/gilas-pilipinas/results-philippines-mongolia-fiba-3x3-june-2018

Gordon, L.R. (1995). *Bad faith and antiblack racism*. Humanities Press.

Guzzio, T.C. (2005). Courtside: Race and basketball in the works of John Edgar Wideman. In A. Bass (Ed.), *In the game: Race, identity and sports in the twentieth century* (pp. 221–36). Palgrave MacMillan.

Halili, S.D. (2006). *Iconography of the New Empire: Race and gender images and the American colonization of the Philippines*. University of the Philippines Press.

Hall, S. (1990). The Whites of their eyes: Racist ideologies and the media. In M. Alvarado & J.O. Thompson (Eds.), *The media reader* (pp. 7–23). British Film Institute.

Hall, S. (1993). What is this "Black" in Black popular culture? *Social Justice, 20*(1–2), 104–14. https://www.jstor.org/stable/29766735

Hall, S. (1996). The after-life of Frantz Fanon: Why Fanon? Why now? Why *Black skin, White masks*? In A. Read (Ed.), *The fact of Blackness: Frantz Fanon and visual representation* (pp. 12–37). Bay Press, Institute of Contemporary Arts, Institute of International Arts.

Hawkins, B. (2010) *The new plantation: Black athletes, college sports, and predominantly White NCAA Institutions*. Palgrave MacMillan.

Hobermann, J. (2007). Race and athletics in the twenty-first century. In J.A. Hargreaves & P. Vertinsky (Eds.), *Physical culture, power, and the body* (pp. 208–31). Routledge.

hooks, b. (1992). *Black looks: Race and representation*. South End Press.

Hrabovský, M. (2013). The concept of "blackness" in theories of race. *Asian and African Studies, 22*(1), 65–88.

Jackson, R. (2006). *Scripting the Black masculine body: Identity, discourse, and racial politics in popular media*. State University of New York Press.

King, C. (2004). *Offside racism: Playing the White man*. Berg Publishers.

King, R.C., & Springwood, C.F. (2001). *Beyond the cheer: Race as spectacle in college sport*. State University of New York Press.

Kramer, P.A. (2006). *The blood of government: Race, empire, the United States, and the Philippines*. Ateneo de Manila University Press.

Legum, C. (1958). *Bandung, Cairo and Accra: A report on the first conference of independent African states*. Africa Bureau.

Leonard, W.M. (1986). Stacking in college basketball: A neglected analysis. *Sociology of Sport Journal, 4*(1), 403–09. https://doi.org/10.1123/ssj.4.4.403

Leongson, R.B. (2020, January 24). Last word from final batch of NCAA foreign players: 'We're not mercenaries'. *Spin.ph*. Retrieved September 26, 2020, from https://www.spin.ph/basketball/ncaa-men/end-of-an-era-last-batch-of-ncaa-foreign-student-athletes-express-gratitude-despite-mercenary-claims-a2437-20200124-lfrm

Liao, H. (2014, July 24). Foreign student players. *Bandera*. Retrieved August 29, 2020, from https://bandera.inquirer.net/68151/foreign-student-players.

Lizada, M.A.N. (2015). Masculinity, patronage politics, and the feminization of school spirit in the Ateneo-La Salle UAAP Rivalry. *Philippine Sociological Review, 63*(1), 191–216. https://www.jstor.org/stable/24717165

Lombaerde, P.D., Guo, F., & Neto, H.P. (2014). Introduction to the special collection: South–south migrations: What is (still) on the research agenda? *The International Migration Review, 48*(1), 103–12. http://doi.org/10.1111/imre.12083

MacKinnon, K. (2003). *Representing men: Maleness and masculinity in the media*. Arnold.

Makki, F. (2015). Post-colonial Africa and the world economy: The long waves of uneven development. *Journal of World-Systems Research, 21*(1), 124–46. https://doi.org/10.5195/jwsr.2015.546

Marriott, D. (2012). Inventions of existence: Sylvia Wynter, Frantz Fanon, sociogeny, and the "damned." *CR: The New Centennial Review, 11*(3), 45–89. https://www.jstor.org/stable/41949756

McPhail, M. (2008). [Review of the book *Scripting the Black masculine body: Identity, discourse, and racial popular media*, by Ronald L. Jackson II]. *Howard Journal of Communications 19*(3), 273–75. https://doi.org/10.1080/10646170802218388

Meisenhelder, T. (2003). African bodies: "Othering" the African in precolonial Europe. *Race, Gender & Class, 10*(3), 100–13. https://www.jstor.org/stable/41675090

Mendoza, A.S. (2016). Mendoza: African power in UAAP is even worse. *The Sun Star*. Retrieved September 26, 2020, https://www.sunstar.com.ph/article/104274

Messner, M.A. (1992). *Power at play: Sports and the problem of masculinity*. Beacon Press.

Messner, M.A. (2002). *Taking the field: Women, men, and sport*. University of Minnesota Press.

Messner, M.A., & D. Sabo (Eds.) (1990). *Sport, men, and the gender order: Critical feminist perspectives*. Human Kinetics Books.

Micua. L.V. (1976). No longer brittle...The Noritake festival. *Sports Weekly Magazine, 2*(65), 20.

Naredo, C. (2013). Imports in college hoops will hurt local big men. *ABS-CBN*. Retrieved September 26, 2020, http://news.abs-cbn.com/sports/08/15/13/imports-college-hoops-will-hurt-local-big-men

Nkrumah, K. (1961). *I speak of freedom: A statement of African ideology*. William Heinemann.

Nkrumah, K. (1963, September 4). Africa had scholars before Europe. *Evening News*, n.p.

Park, M.K. (2015). Race, hegemonic masculinity, and the "Linpossible!": An analysis of media representations of Jeremy Lin. *Communication & Sport, 3*(4), 367–89. https://doi.org/10.1177/2167479513516854

Pascasio, E.M. (1961). Comparative study: Predicting interference and facilitation for Tagalog speakers in learning English noun-head modification patterns. *Language Learning, 11*(1–2), 77–84. http://doi.org/10.1111/j.1467-1770.1961.tb00742.x

Patterson, O. (1982). *Slavery and social death: A comparative study*. Harvard University Press.

Pronger, B. (1990). *The arena of masculinity: Sports, homosexuality and the meaning of sex*. GMP Publishers.

Rodney, R.R. (1973). *How Europe underdeveloped Africa*. Bogle-L'Ouverture Publications.

Rodriguez, E., I. (2006). Primerang bituin: Philippines-Mexico relations at the dawn of the Pacific Rim century. *Asia Pacific Perspectives*, 6 (1), 4–12.

Rubio, R.J., & Green, R. (2011). Filipino men's roles and their correlates: Development of the Filipino adherence to masculinity expectations Scale. *Culture, Society & Masculinities, 3*(2), 77–102.

Sailes, G.A. (1998). The African-American athlete: Social myths and stereotypes. In G. Sailes (Ed.), *African-Americans in Sport* (pp. 183–98). Transaction Publishers.

Samonte, S., & Sconras, G. (2019). Adjective ordering in Tagalog: A cross-linguistic comparison of subjectivity-based preferences. *Proceedings of the Linguistic Society of America, 4*(1), 1–13. http://doi.org/10.3765/plsa.v4i1.4511

Sarmenta, S. (2016). Quo vadis, collegiate "imports"? *Sports Inquirer*. Retrieved September 26, 2020, from http://sports.inquirer.net/226220/quo-vadis-collegiate-imports

Silvestre, J.D.P. (2012). *An ethnography of communicating motivation in the University of the Philippines men's basketball team* [Bachelor's thesis, University of the Philippines]. Iskomunidad. https://

iskwiki.upd.edu.ph/images/9/9b/Silvestre,_Julio_Danilo_Perez_10-12_Driven_By_Words_An_Ethnography_of_Communicating_Motivation....pdf

Soederberg, S. (2005). Recasting neoliberal dominance in the global south? A critique of the Monterrey consensus. *Alternatives: Global, Local, Political, 30*(3), 325–64. http://doi.org/10.1177/030437540503000304

Spence, J.T. & Helmreich, R.L. (1978). *Masculinity & femininity: Their psychological dimensions, correlates, & antecedents*. University of Texas Press.

Spillers, H.J. (1987). Mama's baby, papa's maybe: An American grammar book. *Diacritics, 17*(2), 64–81. http://doi.org/10.2307/464747

Steinberg, D.J. (1982). The Philippines, a singular and a plural place. Westview Press.

Tafira, H.K. (2016). The social construction of Blackness in Azania. In H.K. Tafira (Ed.), *Black nationalist thought in South Africa: African histories and modernities* (pp. 139–81). Palgrave Macmillan.

Tagalog Lang. (2002). *Summary of the American colonial period*. Retrieved September 26, 2020, from https://www.tagaloglang.com/summary-of-the-american-colonial-period/

Taylor, I. (2009). *China's new role in Africa*. Lynne Rienner Publishers.

Tempo Online. (2018). African players in colleges hurting PH basketball—Jong. *Tempo*. Retrieved October 20, 2020, from http://tempo.com.ph/2017/08/28/african-players-in-colleges-hurting-ph-basketball-jong/

Toledo, N. (2017). Memorable imports in the collegiate ranks. *FHM*. Retrieved June 17, 2018, from https://www.fhm.com.ph/pop-culture/sports/16-memorable-imports-in-the-collegiate-ranks-a1548-20170902-lfrm

Tull, D. M. (2006). China's engagement in Africa: Scope, significance and consequences. *Journal of Modern African Studies, 44*(3), 459–79. http://doi.org/10.1017/S0022278X06001856

United Nations Department of Economic and Social Affairs [UNDESA]. (2017). *Population facts*. Retrieved October 20, 2020, https://www.un.org/en/development/desa/population/migration/publications/populationfacts/docs/MigrationPopFacts20175.pdf

Valledor-Lukey, V.V. (2012). *Pagkababae at pagkalalake [Femininity and masculinity]: Developing a Filipino gender trait inventory and predicting self-esteem and sexism*. [Doctoral dissertation, Syracuse University]. Syracuse University Libraries. https://surface.syr.edu/cfs_etd/66/

Velasco, B. (2015, Feb 14). Lessons from African athletes. *Philstar*. Accessed September 20, 2020 https://www.philstar.com/sports/2015/02/14/1423585/lessons-african-athletes

Vergès, F. (1997). Creole skin, Black mask: Fanon and disavowal. *Critical Inquiry, 23*(3), 578–95. https://doi.org/10.1086/448844

Verora, L., Jr. (2018). In basketball-crazy Philippines, Africans live their hoop dreams https://medium.com/@leviverorajr/in-basketball-crazy-philippines-africans-live-their-hoop-dreams-4ce7085ca564

Verzosa, P. (2020, June 23). NCAA keeps doors closed to foreign players. *CNN Philippines*. Retrieved October 20, 2020, from https://www.cnn.ph/sports/2020/6/23/NCAA-doors-closed-foreign-athletes-.html

Wellard, I. (2009). *Port, masculinities, and the body.* Routledge.

Wilderson, F. (2011). *Red, White & Black: Cinema and the structure of U.S. antagonisms*. Duke University Press.

The Wires. (2017). CdSL, Diliman College ride African reinforcements' heroics in MBL *Open*. *Spin.ph*. Retrieved October 20, 2020, from http://www.spin.ph/basketball/news/cdsl-diliman-college-ride-african-reinforcements-heroics-in-mbl-op

World Health Organization [WHO]. (2020, October 13). COVID-19 *in the Philippines* [Situation report No. 57]. Retrieved October 20, 2020, from https://www.who.int/philippines/internal-publications-detail/covid-19-in-the-philippines-situation-report-57

Yancy, G. (2017). *Black bodies, White gazes: The continuing significance of race*. Rowman & Littlefield Publishers.

Yumol, D.T. (2020, March 19). NCAA cancels remainder of season 95 due to COVID-19 threat. *CNN Philippines*. Retrieved October 20, 2020, from https://www.cnnphilippines.com/sports/2020/3/19/NCAA-season-95-cancelled-coronavirus.html

10

A Fanonist Reading of Anti-Black Sexual Racism in the Indian Imaginary

Siddis, African Students, Anti-Blackness, and Psychosexual Politics in the Indian Ocean World and Its Diaspora

TAMARI KITOSSA, ELISHMA NOEL KHOKHAR, & MOHAN SIDDI

> *Ontology...does not permit us to understand the being of the black man. For not only must the black man be black; he must be black in relation to the... [hegemonic Indian][1]...man.*
>
> —FRANTZ FANON, *Black Skin, White Masks*

THE CONTINUAL REDISCOVERY of Siddi people in India (and South Asia generally), the exclusion and oppression many of them encounter, the growing exposure of Indian mobs attacking African students, and the general indifference to anti-Black racism in India and its diaspora have found a new basis for awareness: the murders of George Floyd and Breonna Taylor. Unlike no other instance of Black men openly lynched by White police and vigilantes, the murder of George Floyd has tripped a switch that has led some to seek cognitive understanding of the necrotic affectivity of anti-Blackness. As though discovering it for the first time, with a posture of innocence (which is, in effect, an act of "bad faith anti-blackness"[2] [L. Gordon, 1995]), the world has been forced to confront, on an arbitrary level, the transnational significance of anti-blackness (aesthetic and axiological negation) and anti-Blackness (hatred of people defined, imagined, or marked as culturally distinct and having African physiognomy and are epidermally "black"). In *Black Skin, White Masks*, Frantz Fanon (1952/2008) suggests that to make any headway in understanding concrete and epistemic violence toward Black people and the negative axiology of anthropomorphic colour coding, primacy must be given to the sexual dimension (see also Kitossa, 2020). Fanon restrained his analysis to the West. In this chapter, we take Fanon seriously in a radical application of his thesis to contexts that he, himself, refused: the "Third World," with a specific focus on India. Our aim is to sketch an interpretation of the sexual dynamic of anti-blackness and anti-Blackness[3] by exploring how nineteenth-century Hindu nationalism and the myth of Indo-Aryan racial superiority bequeathed the mobilization tropes of sexual incivility and impropriety to two different African diasporas in India: the Siddi and African students.

Beginning where Fanon ended—the Arab world—we first undertake a critique of Fanon's failure to take his own theory of psychosexual theorizing about Black men to its logical application in non-European contexts. We then undertake a historico-ethnographic sketch of Siddi men and populations in India and the Indian Ocean World. The latter is followed by attention on African male students to expose how Hindu nationalism and Indo-Aryan fetishism from Gandhi and Nehru through to the present mobilizes sexualized tropes of Africa and Black men as foils to mark off Indian "civilized" hetero-normative masculinity. We suggest, finally, that the sexualization of anti-blackness and anti-Blackness in India and its diaspora are reified and reaffirmed through the dominant Bollywood industry and upper-caste elite culture and their representations of a "timeless India" and Indian identity. We suggest further research should centre on the multiplication of endogenous and exogenous psychosexual discourses of anti-blackness and anti-Blackness in India, the Indian Ocean World, and its diaspora's normalization of sexual mythologies about Black men to mark off the exceptionality of South Asian identities. However uncompromising our mobilization of Fanon's thesis of anti-Black-man erotic racism is, we suggest that the radical humanism

Fanon advocated demands that in defence of humanity, researchers and activists draw on and extend these insights to resist both anti-blackness and anti-Blackness the world over.

Fanon's Failure to Launch

In spite of evidence to the contrary, about which he was well aware, Fanon assumed there was an organic solidarity among "Third World" peoples that transcended the lateral racial prejudices that could only divide and conquer. Thus, prior to throwing himself into and being accepted by Algerian anticolonial revolutionists in 1953, Fanon, in 1943, first had to deal with anti-Black racism from the French and Arabs alike while in Algeria training as a volunteer for the Free French Forces. Fanon (1952/2008) reports in *Black Skin, White Masks*:

> Some ten years ago I was astonished to learn that the North Africans [i.e., Arabs and others] despised [black] men of color.[4] It was absolutely impossible for me to make any contact with the local population. I left Africa and went back to France without having fathomed the reason for this hostility. (pp. 102–03)

Fanon assumes that Arab antipathy was a healthy, generic repudiation of all who represented the French colonial regime, not epidermally determined by anti-blackness and anti-Blackness. That it may have been otherwise—that, for instance, it was the Arabs who first entered and then remained in Africa as enslavers and colonizers, and had, prior to European colonialism, developed a well-articulated anti-African cultural psychology—is obfuscated by Fanon.

The irony is that Arab anti-Blackness is suppressed, though Fanon's account of the circulation of racism and prejudice that protects the capitalist class and colonialist elites shows a slippage in this lack of recognition:

> [T]he Frenchman does like the Jew, who does not like the Arab, *who does not like the Negro* [emphasis added]....[T]he Arab is told: "If you are poor, it

> is because the Jew has bled you and taken everything from you..." The Jew is told: "You are not of the same class as the Arab because you are really white and because you have Einstein and Bergson." The Negro is told: "You are the best soldiers in the French Empire; the Arabs think they are better than you, but they are wrong." But that is not true; the Negro is told nothing because no one has anything to tell him...the brave fellow-who only-know-how-to-obey. (p. 103)[5]

This is the last instance of a quotation in this chapter that focuses on Black masculinities in the upper-caste Indian imaginary.[6] Our concern is the application of Fanon's psychosexual thesis for both the liberation struggles of non-African societies and the application, therein, of the tripartite trope of the Black Phallic Fantastic: that is, the imagining of Black men as hypersexual, priapic, and prone to commit rape (see Kitossa, Chapter 1 in this volume). What is to be made of representations of the Black man, Blackness and blackness among non-Black people preceding, during, and after Western colonialism, where anti-blackness, and thus anti-Blackness, are multiplied in "non-European" aesthetic, axiological, and moral registers?

Answering this question will be the focus of this chapter. We will do this, specifically, by applying Fanon's underdeveloped elaboration on this matter in *Black Skin, White Masks* to the African experience in India. Our aim is to uncover the psychosexual dimensions of mythologies around Black masculinities in the Indian, and, more specifically, the Hindu nationalistic imaginary. Our exemplars will be the Siddi community and African university students in India.

We aim to show that the popularization of sexual tropes about these groups is a consequence of three specific historical dynamics. First, while the role of Africans as soldiers and administrators in the Muslim conquests of India from the twelfth through to the nineteenth century gave Siddis unprecedented scope for political influence and rulership—which was impossible in the transatlantic African experience—both Islam and nativist Hinduism furnish discourses of anti-blackness and anti-Blackness in which sexual stereotypes are pervasive. Second, European colonialism, bringing discourses of barbarism and sexual impropriety along with the traffic in African peoples in the Indian Ocean World, established an ethnophaulic link between blackness, incivility, sexual endangerment, and sexual impropriety. And third, we want to show that Indian independence, informed by Brahmanical cultural, racial, and religious superiority, reified anti-blackness and anti-Blackness. We draw attention to Nehruvian and nationalistic Indian elites, patronizing presumption of tutelage for a benighted Africa. This view of Africa and Africans as "backwards" and licentious nourishes continued antipathy and promotes violence toward African students studying in India (Andre, 2016; Soumya, 2013; Prabhu, 2017). We also elaborate how anti-Blackness, centred on tropes of Black men, has played a part in highlighting assertions of a "pure" Indian essence, that itself involved rummaging through the Orientalist racial trash heap of Europe. There, upper-caste Hindus such as Gandhi found a pure "Aryan" origin, borrowed from the likes of Blumenbach, which they used as the basis for a "timeless India." While there was much chatter of nonaligned solidarity between Africa and India, the Indian elite and middle class imagined Africans as their intellectually infantile and physically overdeveloped brothers who must be led into political maturity and responsibility. Sexual continence, the mark of civilization, would be a discursive mode through which Indian elites would police African "development," the moral regulation of Siddis, and the disciplining of African migrants and students.

In exposing the fusion of these ideological and historic forces for Siddi men and their communities, and for African male students to India, we think it is urgent to confront sexual anxieties and mythologies about African men in the Indian cultural imaginary. While we seek to expose the roots of the psychosexual-based violence toward Black men in India, our aim is not to establish a state of moral innocence for Black men; nothing could be more non-Fanonian than this. It is, rather, to emphasize that, if we are to achieve the radical humanism to which Fanon (1952/2008, 1963, 1964/1967, 1959/1965) aspired, we must admit, confront, and defuse the explosive psychosexual and raciological dynamite that constitutes one of the pitfalls of post-independence Indian national culture.[7]

The Siddi of India: Toward an Ethnographic Sketch

Commercial, cultural, and genetic exchanges and interchanges between Africa and the Indian Ocean World have been continuous from the first stirrings of humans out of Africa to the present. To speak of the African presence in India, then, is to speak of the earliest migratory stirring of hominids out of Africa. In spite of ongoing dispute, evidence errs on the side of a Paleolithic African migratory peopling of India (Chauhan, 2010; cf. Dennell, 2010; Karmwar 2010). To this day, one finds on the Andaman, Nicobar, and Sentinel Islands off the southern coast of India remnant stone-age populations of ancient migratory Africans once called by the derogatory Spanish term *Negritos* (Getzels, 2013; Man, 1883; Rogers, 1952).[8] Different from the Paleolithic peoples are southern Indian descendants of the ancient indigenous Dravidian cultures of Harappa and Mohenjo Daro called Dalits and Afro-Dalits.[9] By many thousands of years, these indigenous peoples predate the third millennium "Aryan" invaders who either established the caste system or positioned themselves as the superior caste within a preexisting hierarchical social order (Ghose, 2003; Mason, 1971; Prashad, 2000a, 2001; Rajeshkar, 1988; Rogers, 1952/1967).[10] These outcasts, upon whom so much of India's crushing exclusion, poverty, and revulsion bears, have as part of their political activism since the 1870s, and with B.R. Ambedkar and W.E.B. Du Bois, extended arms of mutual friendship to African Americans and other people of the West (Ghose, 2003; Prashad, 2000a).[11] In particular, among their intellectuals and political activists, this relationship led to a deeper connection with the Black Power Movement, and young Dalit called themselves Panthers in homage to the Black Panther Party (Slate, 2012b).

The story of the African presence in India is a story of the movement and settlement of ideas and people set against the backdrop of the post-nineteenth-century discourse of "eternal India" that continues to position Blackness as foreign to India. By a combination and accumulation of factors, there is an intensification of transatlantic and trans–Indian Ocean World interchange. This requires a more open-ended grammar and an attention to contemporary and historical nuances that link Africa, the transatlantic, and the Indian Ocean World as spaces of Blackness (Burton & Hofmeyr, 2016; Ghose, 2003; Harris, 1971; Jayawardene, 2016, 2013; Raghavan & Pavithra, 2019; Prashad, 2000a, 2000b; Siddi, 2014a, 2014b; The Sidi Project, 2020; Van Sertima & Rashidi, 1988).[12] In developing a grammar by which to sketch the African presence in India, we are informed by Vijay Prashad (2000a). He argues that we should accept as arbitrary the terms we apply at present to who and what count as "African" and "Indian"; these terms should be understood as mutable. Prashad points out that one example of this complexity of cultural crossings is that KiSwahili is a linguistic amalgamation "comprised of Bantu, Arabic, and Gujarati" (p. 195). Prashad adds that several other coastal languages viewed in historical context—Goan Konkani, Sri Lankan, Moorish, Arabic, and languages of Gujarat among them—are the results of human exchange and interchange between Africa and the Indian Ocean World over thousands of years. He goes on to argue that, when one considers that "[i]n Sudan, Egypt, and in the interior of East Africa, Indian merchants made their homes from early modern times [to the present]" (p. 195), India has long been in Africa too. Indeed, the Siddi themselves, in India and elsewhere in the Indian Ocean World, are enmeshed in regional languages and linguistic valences that manifest distinct and evolving languages reflecting the multiplicity of their amalgamated African and Indian cultural and national heritages.

Keeping in mind the historical complexity of Africans and Blackness in India, we turn to an ethnographic sketch of African populations in India. We first discuss ethnographic and sociological dimensions of Siddi experiences with exclusion and racial stereotypes. We then move to examine anti-Black-man erotic racism in the context of Gandhi's 20-year sojourn in Africa (Naipaul, 1977)[13] and the post-Jawaharlal Nehru period with its hypersexual imaginings of African men. We suggest that Gandhi's Hindu- and Indo-Aryan-supremacist sensibilities, as well as his obsequious love of British imperialists, complicated his wounded Brahmin pride in South Africa and informed his anti-Blackness. We explore in broad terms how Nehru and middle-class Indian (inter)nationalists cultivated India's paternalistic orientation to Africa. Central to that imagining were the ways that the projection of sexual fantasies played a vital role in the contemporary Hindu imaginary of Black masculinities and of hegemonic South Asian masculinity. To understand this dynamic, we follow V.S. Naipaul's (1990, 1977) assertion that Indian/Hindu nationalism rests on a sedimented view of a "timeless" India in which the barbarism and parasitism of caste is intensified by the class imperatives of neoliberalism. But we add a dimension hinted at by Naipaul and which is made possible by a Fanonist criticism of a Brown skin, White mask that hinges on both anti-blackness and anti-Blackness as modifiers of Indo-Aryan "racial" pride with the social distancing emblem and condensation symbol of a virile heterosexual African man who endangers the purity of the Hindu nation. The latter is imagined as the inviolable body and womb of the idealized, upper-caste and -class, light-skinned, Indo-Aryan woman who is reserved for the idealized, upper-caste, Hindu/Indo-Aryan man. In a context driven by tropes of Hindu and Indo-Aryan supremacy, a disciplinary regime of public spectacle and spectacularized erotics of gendered/sexualized violence meshes with nationalism, religiosity, racism, colourism, and casteism. The effect is to routinize the practice of "penetrative penality,"[14] which constitutes a technology of discipline to mark off the exalted status of the idealized Hindu and Indo-Aryan subject from the eroticized exclusion, objectification, and thingification of Dalit women (and men),[15] lower-caste Indian women, African international students, outcastes, and racialized and tribalized Others.[16]

The Siddi

There is significant variation in ethnographic nomenclature and meaning in the appellations for creole Africans in the Indian Ocean World. In India, where they are designated as a "Scheduled Tribe," the most common terms of reference are *Siddi*, *Sidi*,[17] and *Cafrees* (Obeng, 2011; Yimene, 2007). While recognizing different significant historic settlement patterns, class, and ethnographic distinctions, some scholars appear to use both *Siddi* and *Sidi* interchangeably (Karmwar, 2010). Some scholars, such as Beheroze Shroff (2007), claim a specified spelling as a methodological tool of categorization rather than as an endogenous nomenclature of the group. Shroff asserts: "I have chosen to spell Sidi with a single 'd' in all of my writing on Gujarati speaking Sidis. This spelling differentiates Sidis of Gujarat and Mumbai from Karnataka and Hyderabad Siddis" (p. 305). In other instances, whether *Sidi* or *Siddi*, these are terms of epithet for elite creole descendants of African elites and "Anglo-Indians" (the descendants of British soldiers with either Hindu mothers or Christian or Muslim Siddi and non-Siddi mothers) (Yimene, 2007). *Sheedi*, *Habshi*, *Habishi*, and *Habashi*—derived from the word *Abyssinia*—are terms used mostly in Pakistan (Luedi, 2018) and to a lesser extent in India (Rao, 1973; Segal, 2001). In Sri Lanka, *Kaffir* is the term of designation (Jayawardene, 2016). Though at time confounding, the takeaway is this: the creole African diaspora in the Indian Ocean World ranges from India, to Bangladesh, Goa, Java, Maldives, and Sri Lanka. While these different appellations are not insignificant, for simplicity in this chapter, we use the term *Siddi* to refer to all of these communitites.

There is little consensus on the sociohistorical origins of the name *Siddi*.[18] Some scholars suggest the term was likely founded on a distinction of infamy and irony. Others, including the Siddi themselves, suggest differently—and for good reason, given the profound and illustrious influence Africans had in shaping various pre-independence Indian states, not least of which Gujurat (Harris, 1971; Rao, 1973; Segal, 2001). While he is not specific about the time-period, Richard Pankhurst (2003) suggests the nomenclature *Siddi* has its origins in a parody of the Arabic word *saiyid*, meaning "master." This is evident in his citation of an early nineteenth-century English source: "The word, as Edwardes notes, had 'an honourable import' when first assumed, but in common parlance, had become 'rather an appellation of reproach than distinction'" (Pankhurst, 2003, p. 190). Consistent with a derisive conception that linked blackness with slave status, Pankhurst (2003) also cites a comment from a 1607 report by French traveller Francois Pyrard, who notes that, in Maldives, "'[t]he greatest insult that can be passed upon a man is to call him a Cisdy', i.e., Sidi" (p. 190). Segal (2001) gives a different account. He indicates that enslaved Africans were freed if they converted and fought for the invading Islamic armies from the seventh through to the thirteenth centuries. According to Segal, *Siddi* derives from *Sayyad*, meaning "descendants of Muhammad" (p. 71). Vijay Prashad (2000a) asserts alternatively that "[s]ince the captains of the African and Arab vessels bore the title 'Sidi' (from Sayyid), the settlers on the Indian mainland came to be called 'Siddis' (or 'habshis,' from Al Habish, for Abyssinia)" (p. 195).

Nevertheless, from the second through to the nineteenth century, these creole Africans, particularly the post-Islamic invasion aristocracy among them, mixed with ancient and contemporaneous subcontinent creoles (i.e., Afghans/Pathans, Arabs, Greeks, Huns, Mongols/Khans, Persians, and Turkic peoples).[19] Since the Islamic invasion of the eighth century, in which Arabs brought larger numbers of both forced and voluntary East Africans and Malagasies as labourers, soldiers, and administrators, the Siddi have been a presence in the Indian Ocean World outside of the Hindu caste system. The Portuguese also scattered enslaved Africans, mostly from Mozambique, throughout its Indian Ocean World colonial empire, not least in India (Cardoso, 2010). Siddi communities, because of the cultural mixing involved in the creation of these communities, tend to be Christian or Muslim; due to marriage rules within the Hindu caste system, they are rarely Hindu. Over time, as suggested above, Siddis have forged an ethnographically complex identity given their regional distinctions, their exposure to endogenous languages, and their own agglomeration from a mixture of East African and Malagasy peoples (Yimene, 2010).

What is the origin of post-second-century African migrants who contributed to the establishment of the Siddi and its variant nomenclature in the Indian Ocean World? Joseph Harris (1971) and Richard Pankhurst (2003) note that the first-century Graeco-Roman trading manual *The Periplus of the Erythraean Sea* reveals bustling trade between the Aksumite and Somali ports with Arabs, trading goods and enslaved peoples into what is now India and Sri Lanka (formerly Ceylon). The Ethiopians exchanged ivory, rhinoceros horn, and, to a lesser extent, enslaved persons (to be used as status symbols) for spices. The expansion by the sword of Islam into

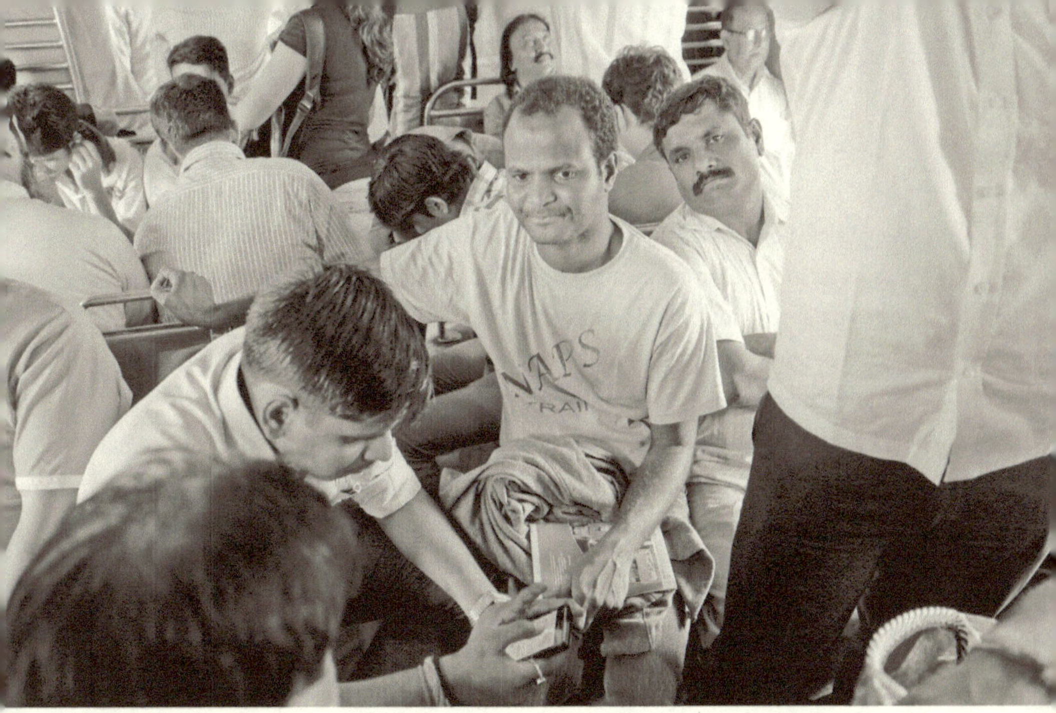

FIGURE 10.1: Mohan Siddi on a train, facing centre. (© Luke Duggleby, The Sidi Project, 2020)

FIGURE 10.2: Mohan Siddi in classroom, facing centre. (© Luke Duggleby, The Sidi Project,

the Sindh (in the eighth century) and the Punjab (in the tenth century), followed by the Moghul (i.e., Mongol) invasions and consolidation of political power in the subcontinent from the thirteenth century onward, saw an increase in the number of Africans in various capacities. In addition to enslaved soldiers and labourers, Africans were also high administrators and majordomos who installed kings or were kings themselves. One such notable figure was the seventeenth century Malik Ambar (Harris, 1971; Pankhurst, 2003; Segal, 2001). Ronald Segal (2001) reminds us that even before Ambar—indeed, as early as the 1100s—Africans "established kingdoms of their own in Janjira and Jaffrabad in western India" (p. 71).

Hardened soldiers from their home countries, the Ethiopian or Habashi played important roles in the fighting forces of various Khanates' and Sultanates' land and marine forces. Chroniclers like Ibn Battuta, the twelfth-century Arab anthropologist, chronicler, and geographer who was well known for his unfavourable characterizations of Africa and Africans, crowed about the bravery, competence, fearsomeness, and stature of Habashi soldiers and sailors (Segal, 2001). It was not uncommon for Moghul potentates have 5000, 8000, or even upwards of 10,000 African men at arms in their forces. In the fourteenth century, Delhi alone boasted 40,000 soldiers and 12,000 artisans of immediate African origin (Yimene, 2007, p. 323). These slave soldiers in the employ of Moghuls, Omanis, and Yemenis, adopted their masters' sect of Islam, which tended toward Sunni rather than Shiite. From the fourteenth century onward, these soldiers played important roles in the consolidation, extension, and formation of sultanates all across the subcontinent. The absorption of "princely states" into Indian, and subsequently Pakistani, independence saw a sudden reversal in the fortunes of Siddi communities across the subcontinent. Even Siddi men who were intergenerationally employed and felt dignified as soldiers were let go with small pensions and a corresponding diminution in individual and communal esteem. Particularly for Muslim Siddis in the urban areas of southern India (i.e., Hyderabad), as compared to Siddis in rural areas, this change in communal fortunes has led to downward mobility. Muslim Siddis tend, by cultural norms, to have larger families. On top of this, they face exclusion and anti-Muslim bias and experience lower educational attainment and more poverty than Christian Siddis (Yimene, 2007).

At independence and with the theoretical abolition of bonded labour, some Siddis took asylum in the forests of the Western Ghats in India. For them, the forest of Western Ghats provided ample resources of food and shelter. In the later periods, they also came in contact with the neighbouring communities and provided agricultural and menial labour for them. Given the near-feudal nature of land ownership and tenure in India, Siddi men's major means of livelihood was labouring for their landlords. In these remote and agricultural contexts, as opposed to their urban counterparts, they shifted from one landlord to another, invariably establishing a seminomadic character that has only become permanent in the past 40 to 50 years. But with land as the basis for wealth and social status, they remain, like the Dalits, highly marginal peoples.

Though the numbers are not precise, it is estimated that more than 250,000 Siddis live in India (Segal, 1995; The Sidi Project, 2020), dispersed throughout cities, states, and provinces such as Andhra Pradesh, Bengal, the Bombay region, Daman and Diu Gujurath, Goa, Karnataka, Kerala, and Maharashtra (Jayawardene, 2016; Karmwar, 2010; Obeng, 2011). Across the regions Siddis speak a range of distinct languages such as Konakani, Kannada, Gujurathi, and Marathi, as well as languages uniquely their own, including Bantu/KiSwahili and local dialects. Siddis are predominantly Muslim with a minority of Christians. Ritual practices of elder worship are common. In various parts of India, most notably in Karnataka, Siddis have unique cultural practices including Damai and Damal music and dance performance and street theatre (Obeng, 2011).

Though constitutive of an agglomeration of dispersed creole Africans with identities rooted in countries of the Indian Ocean World, the Siddi now constitute a distinctive, disparate, "tribal," and "racial" agglomeration in India. Some Siddis have an emergent conception of themselves as part of an East African and the worldwide African diaspora (Yimene, 2007). Until recently, non-Siddi scholars and anthropologists have documented the Siddi people. Now, however, Siddi in India and across the Indian Ocean World are beginning to document and assess their own realities. For example, Mohan Siddi (2014a, 2014b), coauthor of this chapter, is among this emerging body of Siddi scholars and cultural interlocutors connecting Indian Siddis with the pan-African world, and their Black and non-Black allies at home and abroad (see Figures 10.1 and 10.2).

Endogamy, Exogamy, and Siddi Identity: Caste, Class, and Race

The Siddi and other creole Africans in the Indian Ocean World today identify with their nation-states and a cultural memory of Africa. With the exception of Anglo-Indian Siddis and those directly descended from the Siddi aristocracy (Karmwar, 2010; Shroff, 2007) as "Scheduled Tribes," peasant and working-class Siddis in rural and urban areas encounter considerable racial discrimination and often struggle to survive. As a result of their historical specificity and racial distinctiveness, Siddis occupy a socially ambivalent space simultaneously between, outside, and within what Sureshi Jayawardene (2016) calls India's "racialized-caste" relations of ruling. In specific cities and regions such as Gujurat and Hyderabad, however, Siddis are honoured societal members occupying socially valued roles such as healers, seers, and keepers of Siddi ancestral and saint shrines that attract South Asian Hindu and Muslim newlyweds and other devotees (Basu, 2003; Shroff, 2007). But they are in every sense Indians, even if this national identity is questioned and dismissed by their fellow Indians who, because of their hair texture and skin colour, insist on asking, "Where are you from?" (Jayawardene, 2016; Shroff, 2007; Yimene, 2007). It is clear that in the hegemonic imagination of the Indian nation, blackness is imagined as "foreign matter" in the body politic, to be either expelled or marked as a sign of eternal difference—a negation—that thus, conversely, confers a "natural belonging" to upper-caste South Asian Indians.

While many Siddis have retained physiognomic features that distinguish them from the South Asian Indian population, this is so because Siddis have a long history of marrying within and across Christian, Muslim, and, though to an almost negligible extent, Hindu communities. (Due to *jati*, endogamous caste-based Hindu marriage rules, Siddis are all but precluded from marrying Hindus, as such a marriage would lead the Hindu individual to be excommunicated.) Moreover, in the caustic mix of ongoing conflict between a deepening and widening Hindu nationalistic tendency and Muslim communities clearly on the defensive, there is increasing pressure to racially assimilate into the contending non-African Indian religious communities—notably Christian and Muslim. Importantly, Siddi identity in exogamy is conferred patrilineally or matrilineally, depending on the gender of the Siddi spouse and the gender of the children. Thus, in all cases when Siddi women marry non-Siddi men, their children are not Siddi. When Siddi men marry non-Siddi women, only their sons are Siddi (Yimene, 2007). Some researchers suggest exogamy into Christian and Muslim communities raises the prospect of a loss of Siddi identity reflecting the religious and regional cleavages in the nation (Basu, 2003; Yimene, 2007). Yimene (2007), indicating another dynamic of internalized and socially propagated anti-Blackness, claims that urbanized young Siddi men in Hyderabad "are not willing at all to marry a Siddi girl of a darker complexion because of the prevalent colour prejudice" (p. 341). Yimene (2007) reports that these prefer instead to marry Arabs, Patans (i.e., Afghani descendants), and Khans (i.e., Islamized Indians). Interestingly, Yimene (2007) notes that high levels of poverty militate against exogamy, particularly in the case of daughters. It is likely that racial discrimination is at play in that there seems to be a premium for Siddi families who seek to marry their daughters to Arabs and Muslim Indians. Yimene notes that "Siddi parents unable to pay the dowry to marry off their daughters to Indians or Arabs find it relatively easier to get them husbands among their 'own' people because Siddi men do not demand a large dowry" (p. 342).

There is good reason, however, to doubt Yimene's (2007) claim. Given that, as Yimene himself points out, many Siddis in Hyderabad are phenotypically indistinct from Arabs and Indians, the persistence of "racial discrimination [against Siddis]...will be a driving force for many Siddis to further intermarry with the Yemeni Arabs and other Indians" (p. 341). Even in this case, however, there are at least three reasons to suspect that Yimene (2007) extrapolates from the particularity of urban, Muslim, Siddi men in Hyderabad to all of Siddis in India. First, in the absence of more robust data, it cannot be assumed that the interactional dynamics and social pressures toward integration is the same among Siddis across India. In the more rural areas of the Western Ghats, for example, where the Siddi have acquired tribal status, it is more than likely that patrilineal endogamy will be prevalent as a means of retaining their tribal status. Thus, there will be an imperative toward the retention and strengthening of Siddi identity in those contexts, which includes a growing consciousness of their origins as African creoles in India.

Erotic Anti-Black Racism in the Hindu Imaginary: The Siddi and African Male Students as Threats to the Imagined Nation

Although research into the historical contributions and presence of Siddis in the prenational Indian state has yet to fully flower, scholars are belatedly turning attention to the sociological dimensions of Siddi life and experience. What is notable is not only discrimination against Siddis, but the increasing virulence of anti-Blackness with rationalizing tropes and representations that Hindu nationalists and Arab bigots are culling from the West—the United States in particular. This is, in effect, an amplifying dynamic on top of the preexisting, low-level, anti-Black bias in the cultures of the subcontinent. Yimene (2007) reports that in the gentrifying Siddi neighbourhood of African Cavalry Guards in Hyderabad, which was bequeathed by the Nizam to his Siddi troops who were stationed there, "[t]he local Moslems often accuse [Siddi men] of religious leniency, drunkenness, homosexuality, adultery, sexual indulgence, excessive appetite, idolatry, notoriety, laziness, untidiness, begging and immorality" (p. 332). Adding to this compendium of all-inclusive and apparently racially specific improprieties, Yimene (2007) adds that even the state-owned news organ *Express Newsline* published a 1996 story that stated: "The Siddi, brought from Africa centuries ago, are in the web of illiteracy, alcoholism and poverty'" (p. 332). This stock-in-trade, tropistic stigmatization can be separated neither from the growing caste-race-religious factionalism nor from the growing class divide which, as Yimene (2007) notes, is seeing the African Cavalry Guards area coveted for gentrification by government and real estate developers alike.

Others also document anti-Black stereotyping that relies on discourses of sexual racism. In Sureshi Jayawardene's (2016) examination of "the cleavages created by hierarchies of race, caste, and colorism"—hierarchies that shape the diasporic experience in the Indian Ocean World—she reveals a circuit of European colonialist anti-Black tropes that were imposed on South Asians (p. 326). Positioned between and outside the "traditional" caste system but within an aesthetic and moral privileging of whiteness, Jayawardene reports that the "public awareness of Siddis and Kaffirs is limited to the principally negative ideas in circulation about these communities and the deep-seated sense of caste ideology, even in remnant form, that distinguishes between groups" (p. 329). In particular, a recurring theme that signifies non-Indianness and marks the African as foreign is the issue of hypersexuality.

Jaywardene notes that "Siddis are generally considered lazy, socially and culturally backward, unintelligent, and sexually promiscuous" (p. 339). Set against the backdrop of these tropes, the religio-casteist ideology sustaining the reproduction strategies of Muslim Siddi men seems coherent with and reifying of these disparaging mythologies. Yimene (2007) notes that Muslim Siddi men in the community he studies in African Cavalry Guards regard having a multitude of children as "a divine blessing" (p. 336). While having many children satisfies religious doctrine, it also saddles the men with larger families. The men, confronted with economic-racial discrimination and low levels of education, are unable to channel their meagre earnings into the education and maintenance of their children. The result is a downward spiral in which Siddi Muslim girls, as compared to Siddi Christian girls, marry and bear children early, thus hindering their education, earning capacity, and independence. This state of affairs is linked with the intensification of poverty among Muslim Siddis, but it also comes with derogatory imputations for Siddi Muslim men being more interested in sex than work.

Taken together, tropes of African Otherness, hypersexuality, sloth, and intellectual incompetency distill and merge in the experience of Siddi men and African international students. The key pressure points are Hindu nationalist anti-black and anti-Black animosity and Indo-Arab and Indo-Aryan Muslim anti-Siddi bigotry. Especially within the larger framing of Hindu nationalism, myths of Hindu caste and race purity and "civilization" stand in relation to the polluting signification of the "foreign" African and Black Other. African male students are imagined as a threat to the nation, which is metaphorically represented as the body of the idealized Bollywoodesque, light-skinned, young, upper-middle-class, traditionally "beautiful" woman. Fantasy overtakes reality, and the time-worn tripartite trope of hypersexuality, rape propensity, and priapism—the Black Phallic Fantastic—is imagined to connote danger to this idealized Indian woman, who is almost always imagined as upper caste and Hindu.[20]

This convergence of anti-Black sexual racism with Hindu nationalism is a grammar for the explosive and well-publicized erotic violence directed toward African students studying abroad. For example, in Delhi, Mumbai, and other parts of India, African international students, both male and female, have been attacked by mobs and are routinely racially profiled by police and bar owners. They are, furthermore, routinely subject to epithets and discrimination by run-of-the-mill South Asian Indians. In one telling case in 2014, as the Indian Prime Minister attended the Martin Luther King Jr. Memorial with President Barack Obama, a mob of about 75 young Indian men assailed three Gabonese and Burkinabi male students at a Delhi subway station. The African students were subject to racial epithets and beaten with sticks and pieces of metal bar while the mob chanted, "*Bharat Mata Ki Jai*" [Victory for Mother India] (Mackey, 2014). Participants in the attack accused the students of "'misbehaving with female passengers' [and] making lewd comments to a woman on a train" as well as making an "'anti-India' comment" (Mackey, 2014, para. 7). As we show below, the projection of sexual violence onto African men both conceals and legitimates Hindu men's quotidian misogyny and spectacular instances of sexual violence against Indian women (both Hindu and Muslim).

Blackness in India: The African Fly in the Ointment of a "Timeless" Hindu and Indo-Aryan India

Edward Said notes Orientalism is an epistemic project of the Western colonial imagination to construct an undifferentiated "Oriental" mass personality,[21] an arrested civilization (i.e., Marx's "Asiatic Mode of Production"), and a specific geographical terrain. As a discursive formation, it is both mirror and enabler of Western colonial domination of the "Orient." Given that Africa is not in the "Orient," but "Orientals" (i.e., Arabs) have and continue to hold dominance in North Africa (not as Africans, but as Arabs), we ask: Is there a place for the African between the competing larger (i.e., European) and lesser (i.e., Arab, Hindu, and other Asiatic) proprietary claims to the origin of human "civilization"?[22] Is Orientalism, both as a discursive formation and a site for mobilizing criticism of colonialism, imperialism, and racial superiority, a form of "bad faith anti-blackness" (L. Gordon, 1995)? These are vital questions given that, as supposed by Hegel (1956), the African continent nowhere furnishes evidence of civilization and history save that which the Arabs, as "Orientals" and through the beneficence of slavery, conferred upon the continent prior to European conquests (Deliovsky & Kitossa, 2013).[23] How are we to think about the construction of Africa and Africans in the hegemonic Indian "imagination" without reproducing the very problematics under consideration? That is, how does one offer criticism of anti-African racism inherent in the discursive formations of Orientalism and Indo-Aryan Hindu myths of superiority without reifying the latter two?

Though we will not answer them in a point-by-point chronological manner, these are not rhetorical questions. We set out to answer the foregoing questions in broad conceptual and historically specific terms, and offer the questions themselves as signifiers of a theory about how to imagine the Black Phallic Fantastic in the context of intra-Global South relations. This approach to theory follows from Gunnar Myrdal's thesis that researchers in the social disciplines, quick to provide an abundance of answers, do not tarry long enough to ask questions that facilitate a deeper engagement with theory—for theory, he asserted, is "no more than a correlated set of questions to the social reality under study" (cited in

Wallerstein, 1991, p. 80). Working from questions of theoretical import, then, we set out to *describe*. Here we assert the possibility of a radical application of Fanon's thesis of anti-Black erotic racism to the non-Black "Third World," which is a possibility that Fanon himself refused. We therefore draw on V.J. Prashad's (2000b, 2001) effort to navigate an alternative between the essentialisms of nation and race without refuting the salience of, nor fetishizing, anti-blackness and anti-Blackness in the "Global South." Finally, we draw on Dhruba Gupta's (1991) argument that, inasmuch as we must avoid *Oriental* Orientalism, it is vital to engage in critical and decolonialist reflexivity to expose the anti-blackness and anti-Blackness in the social psychology of hegemonic Indo-Aryan and Hindu supremacy. To avoid *mentalities* altogether would be to deny a general tendency, produced by Hindu nationalism, to imagine an Indian "self" that, "in its conscious and unconscious confrontation and contact with the African 'other'" tends to conform to a certain paradigm of perception "of Africa [that is] largely shaped by what we are [as Indians]" (Gupta, 1991, p. 158). Indeed, the very proposition of an undifferentiated South Asian subject vis-à-vis the African subject must itself be categorically rejected since the Indian Ocean World has always been a site of cultural, ethnic, linguistic, racial, and religious *masala*. Consistent with the theme of this book, then, we seek in the next section to sketch the roles accorded to gender, nationalism, sex, and sexuality in the constitution of Africa and Blackness, both in the context of Indian imagination.

Creating "Timeless" India: Gandhi, Nonviolence, and Anti-Black Racism

V.S. Naipaul (1977) launched a sustained critique of Hindu nationalism's retreat to a mystical past as the basis for, paradoxically, the forward motion of the Indian state. While Naipaul was not in error about the facts of how this discourse for the nation arose even before the British quit India in 1947, his criticism did not trouble that past enough. He tended to assume, be it in the past or at the time of his writing, that the Indian masses were inert, blank tableaus, written on and about but rarely themselves speaking and resisting, except in rare instances.[24] That the British had to suppress the

Indian Mutiny in 1857 and other smaller acts of resistance suggests otherwise. Indeed, Kathleen Gough (1976) counts that between 1765 and 1857, there were at least 77 revolts by peasants both against the colonizers and at times comprador elites in the areas controlled by Britain and the Dutch East India Company. Others, such as Rosalind O'Hanlon and David Washbrook (1992) remind us that far too many poststructural historians of India, even in resisting their resistance to Orientalism, slip and "put forward timeless or undifferentiated conceptions of the Indian past, often in a glaring way" (p. 147). *This* India, an Orientalist India, emerged as a historically specific coproduction of the colonizer (i.e., the British) and the nationalistic Brahmanical elite who sought to constrict and constrain Muslim elites, traders, and the assorted huge mass of the peasantry (Ghose, 2003; Gough, 1976; Mason, 1971; O'Hanlan & Washbrook, 1992; Prashad, 2000a). Caste and Aryanism took on concrete meanings and a quality of rigidity to ensure colonial governance, where it was once more ambiguous and fluid prior to the East India Company and the British Raj. Thus, O'Hanlan and Washbrook (1992) note that most histories and counter-histories of colonial Orientalism in India are written by the elites—both British and Brahmanical—and that through the fragments of their records, which are the most visible material available to counterhegemonic historians, these oppositional scholars very often reproduce the sort of nondynamic stereotypes of social forces which are purportedly to be rejected.[25]

O'Hanlon's and Washbrook's point is that there is a multiplicity of complicities. Because the British colonizers and the imposition of their (mis)conceptions of Indian culture as collectivist and static (while theirs was individual and dynamic) found fertile ground among a comprador Brahmanic Hindu caste antagonistic to Muslim rule, a notion of India was born through the self-representation of the latter, which reproduces the Orientalism that is to be rejected. Thus, grounding counter-Orientalism in eighteenth- and nineteenth-century Brahmanical discourse

> look[s] disturbingly similar to those of East Indian Company officials, who also thought of culture as "collectively constituted difference" in

early colonial India. When [East Indian Company officials] wished to elucidate the major principles of what they assumed to be a composite Hindu culture they turned to the Brahman pandits who were deemed to be experts and authorities in the matter. The result of this privileging of particular informants was the longer-term emergence of an all-India Hindu tradition very much the image of Brahmanic religious values. These values, now embodied written legal codes and disseminated in a wide range of social contexts, gradually eroded what had previously been a much more heterogeneous collection of local social and religious practices. (O'Hanlon & Washbrook, 1992, pp. 161–62)

What is of consequence here is that the construction of a "timeless" India is the discursive production of practical collusion between the colonizer and an aspiring "oppressed" fraction of colonized elites, who found common cause in the idea of an undifferentiated and "timeless" India.

The British astutely recruited and cultivated Brahmanic elitism and Hindu superiority. As noted by V.S. Naipaul (1977), "In the British time, a period of bitter subjection which was yet for India a period of intellectual recruitment, Indian nationalism proclaimed the Indian past; and religion was inextricably mixed with political awakening" (p.18). In the hands of the Brahmanical elites, caste, as part of the concretizing nationalistic impulses among Hindus, was politically mobilized to manifest concrete and transcendent understanding of Hinduism as the arbiter of the place of Muslims (to be expunged) and Untouchables, forever beyond the pale (see Jayawardene, 2016). To everyone a place and a place for everyone. This discourse read back into the mists of time, especially a time without Muslims and in which the Siddi and Blackness are imagined as foreign or consigned to invisibility.[26] Brahmanical elites, therefore, not only colluded with the British against the Muslim Nawabs and Nizams, but used colonialism to gain a greater share of economic and political power by concocting a puritanical ideology of Brahmanism. They would be aided in this endeavour by the anthropological, legal, and linguistic mania over Aryanism and Sanskrit that swept intellectual circles in Europe and its colonial off-shoots from the 1880s through to the 1940s.[27] Set against the ideological and intellectual moves of colonial empire, mythologizing of a "timeless" Indo-Aryan and Hindu India were seeds that would later bear fruit in M.K. Gandhi,[28] Jawaharlal Nehru, and others of the post-independence elites and state functionaries. Not only would there be a strengthening of Brahmanical and Indo-Aryan ideology with the secular state (Naipaul, 1977), but following Gandhi's and Nehru's derogatory and paternalistic vision of Africa and Blackness, India's middle class and state-bureaucracy would follow suit in continually reinventing a pure India against a sexually depraved Africa.

Especially with M.K. Gandhi, because of his formative experience of racial wounding in South Africa, his Brahmanism, his mimesis of a fetishistic Aryanism, and his enduring commitment to British supremacy, the social construction of civilized India was as much contingent on imagining Africa as backward and sexually incontinent. David Caute (1970), a biographer of Frantz Fanon, observed that "Fanon did not admire Gandhi" (p. 69). Hakim Adi and Sherika Sherwood (2003) equally assert that "Fanon...argued against Gandhian non-violence" (2003, p. 67). When Fanon said that, in the pursuit of national liberation, "[a]ll forms of struggle must be adopted, not excluding violence" (cited in Adi & Sherwood, 2003, p. 145), he was not rejecting nonlethal counter-force, only that this ought not to be the only method.[29] Fanon's commitment to liberatory counter-violence as a necessary means for ejecting colonizers or at least compelling their absorption into the indigenous culture was at odds with Gandhi's obsequiousness to White supremacy and India's colonizers. Paradoxically, Gandhi did not renounce the violence of the European colonizers and imperialists. His all-too-willing complicity with militarism while in South Africa and then England on the eve of World War I set him at odds with many an English, Irish, and White South African admirer. All this despite Gandhi's experimental philosophy of *Satyagraha* [weapon of the truthful], which was born in Africa, not India, and which preceded Gandhi's nonviolent, "go slow" approach to pushing the British out of India (Gandhi, 1927/1996, see pp. 261–64, 289–93).[30]

Gandhi's Indian compatriots in England and Ireland, and his White devotees and fellow *Satyagraha* experimentalists in South Africa, condemned his cheery insistence that Indian students should follow the example of their White English peers and volunteer to do "their bit" for the British war effort during World War I. Gandhi was unmoved by suggestions that the Raj made "slaves" of the Indians and "masters" of the White British. He rejected the criticism that he was contradicting *Satyagraha* in his support of military volunteerism in defence of his beloved British Empire. From the perspective of Gandhi's detractors, fighting on behalf of their "masters" (i.e., the British) in their hour of need would be tantamount to ensuring their continued enslavement (i.e., colonization). Rejecting this counsel, Gandhi states, "I knew the difference between the status of an Indian and an Englishman, but I did not believe we had been quite reduced to slavery. I felt it was more the fault of individual British officials than of the British system, and that we could convert them with *love* [emphasis added]" (p. 290). If Gandhi knew the difference between an Indian and Englishman, did he know the difference between a master and an enslaved person? He does not say. Ever a man of the "system," Gandhi stood in solidarity with the English colonialists of both India and South Africa, rather than with Indian students who saw Britain's distraction with the "Great War" as a weakness and an opportunity to strike a death blow to the Raj. Gandhi (1927/1996) was not only undeterred by these suggestions of action, but more determined to counter them:

> [Their] argument failed to appeal to me then...If we would improve our status through the help and co-operation of the British, it was our duty to win their help by standing by them in their hour of need....I thought that England's need should not be turned into our opportunity, and that it was more becoming and far-sighted not to press our demands while the war lasted. (p. 290)

It hardly needs to be said that both Gandhi's Brahmanic elitism and his anti-Blackness assured his demurring to the allusion between the Indians as "slaves" and the British, the lords of civilization, their "masters."

Ultimately, Gandhi, in Socrates-like fashion, demonstrated great ethical, mental, and moral flexibility to reconcile *Satyagraha* with the duty to maintain social order (however maladaptive), and, not least, with his love of the British Empire.

On the face of it, it may seem unlikely that Gandhi would be a major link between Indian independence and modernist discourses of anti-Blackness. This is especially so given that his 21 years in South Africa (1893–1914), principally in Durban, exposed him to the violence of colonialism and the virulence of White supremacy. All of these experiences ostensibly laid the basis for *Satyagraha*, which he developed 15 years into his sojourn in South Africa (Gandhi, 1927/1996; Naipaul, 1990). Yet, according to exhaustive research by Singh and Watson (2009), Gandhi's principal angst with colonialism and White supremacy, notably in South Africa, was that Indians were forced to be on the same footing as, in Gandhi's words, the "natives" (cited in Singh & Watson, 2009, p. 19).[31] Gandhi, for example, railed against a Durban bylaw requiring the registration of Indians as "coloured servants." For Gandhi, this was an intolerable affront. Singh and Watson (2009) cite Gandhi as saying, "The Santhals of Assam will be as useless in South Africa as the natives of that country" (p. 16).[32] As far as he saw it, whether in Africa or later upon his return to India, indigenous people were savages without the guiding light of civilization and must be rigorously instructed into that competency. Gandhi left no doubt in this regard, saying, "This rule may be, and perhaps is, necessary for the Kaffirs who would not work,[33] but absolutely useless with regard to the Indians" (cited in Singh & Watson, 2009, p. 16). And while on a trip to Gujurat, Gandhi sent a letter to Durban opposing the registration law as follows:

> There is...a bylaw in Durban which provides for the registration of native servants and "others belonging to the uncivilized race of Asia." This presupposes that the Indian is a barbarian. There is good reason for requiring registration of a native in that he is yet being taught the dignity and necessity of labour. The Indian knows it and he is imported because he knows it. (cited in Singh & Watson, 2009, pp.16–17)

For Gandhi, Singh and Watson (2009) assert, equality among all people was not his ultimate goal. Instead, he aspired to have the British recognize "that both the Anglo-Saxon and the Indians races...have sprung from the same Aryan stock, or rather the Indo-European as may call it [*sic*]" (p. 18). But, more than a discourse of shared origins between the Anglo-Saxons and Indians, Gandhi conceded that the British are *primus inter pares*: "We believe as much in the purity of race as we think they [the British] do...We believe also that the white race in South Africa should be the predominating race" (cited in Singh & Watson, 2009, p. 14). Ghandi was, then, not just the leading fount of Hindu nationalism and Indo-Aryan racial supremacy; he also helped to entrench the erasure of the Siddi and install anti-African racism in post-independence Indian culture. In this he helped to add to what was already a tendency in Gujurat.

Nehru's India: Systematizing Anti-Black Erotic Racism and Anti-African Paternalism

While Gandhi had sought to distance the Indian identity from Africa and Africans, Jawharlal Nehru (who would become the first Prime Minister of India) and other architects of Indian independence, took an altogether different approach, leading to the same result. Here, patronage and strategic closeness, especially in terms of the exploitation of African resources, were centrepieces of India's national policy toward its benighted "postcolonial" African brethren (see Russell, Chapter 2 in this volume). In all this, and in the context of the Cold War, the 1955 Bandung Conference in Indonesia (see Rehal, Chapter 9 in this volume, for a discussion of the racial paradox of the Bandung Conference) represented a genuine effort to accomplish the radical humanism between countries, nation-states, and peoples that Fanon (1963) subsequently advised in *Wretched of the Earth*. Here Prashad's (2000b) conception of "weak bad faith" anti-blackness reveals how the Manichean discourse of barbarism and civilization centred on psychosexual tropes.

At the Bandung Conference, India sought not only to establish a neocolonial position between the superpowers, but also to maintain a paternalistic relationship with the entire African continent (Burton & Hofmeyr, 2016). In the mid-1950s for instance, the government of India enrolled African students in 55 Indian universities to "cultivate African capabilities" for postcolonial self-government (Burton & Hofmeyr, 2016, p. 92).[34] Undertones of racist European enlightenment that once guided the European relationship with India can be heard echoing in Nehruvian ideology. While European philosophers imagined India to be producing some worthy ideas and artifacts, they conceived of Africa as a "dark continent," a place with "no history" (Said, 1979; Prashad, 2000b). It is not incidental, then, that Nehru and Mohammad Ali Jinnah (the first Governor General of Pakistan), assumed paternalistic postures of "gentlemanly... statesmanship" toward their African contemporaries who, contrarily, imagined relationships of full equality (Burton & Hofmeyr, 2016).

Nehru, a man of biting wit with a flair for pen portraiture, drew representations of two delegates from the Gold Coast as "helftly and giantly persons" (cited in J. Brown, 2003, p. 261). Nehru, as early as the 1920s, eyed Africa as a repository of raw minerals and a market for finished Indian manufactures (J. Brown, 2003). As part of India's Africa policy, Nehru established a number of "technical" and "goodwill" programs manifested by a one-way exchange that saw an initial cohort of 600 African (mostly male) students attend Indian universities in 1965 (J. Brown, 2003). At the same time, in line with his policy of "economic diplomacy," Nehru dispatched 4700 Indian troops to Congo between 1961 and 1963 under the banner of UN Peace Keeping, much to the displeasure of many African leaders, in an attempt to wrest control of the mineral-rich Katanga region from rebels. Interestingly, that operation was dubbed "Operation Morthor" (Raghavan, 2016), *Morthor* being a Hindi word meaning "twist and break." The name, at least, truthfully abandoned all pretenses of Indo–African equality.

After Nehru deployed troops to Congo, tensions that had already been building between African Ugandans and Indo-Ugandans broiled into open conflict in 1972. Idi Amin, then President of Uganda, responded by expelling almost all Asians from the country (though some remained, even in high administrative and political posts [S. Rehal, personal communication,

May, 20, 2019]). Amin accused Indo-Ugandans, most of whom were, interestingly, Gujurati, of a range of impieties such as commercial exploitation, cultural hubris in refusing to mix with Africans, and loyalty to foreigners (i.e., the British). While Amin indeed made a scapegoat of Indo-Ugandans (although Kenyan and other non-Ugandan Africans were also expelled), it is true also that the British aided and incubated Indian economic achievements expressly as a buffer against the economic independence of indigenous Ugandans.

Amin's expulsion of 80,000 people amidst the jingoism of Indian political impieties struck chords in India and with Indians in Kenya and Tanzania. It had the effect of reifying preconceived biases about Africans as blood-thirsty savages. Antoinette Burton and Isabel Hofmeyr (2016) point out that just one year after Amin launched the expulsion, Indian novelist Chanakya Sen published his 1973 Afro-Asian competitive patriarchy novel, *The Morning After*, in the spirit of Nehru's policy of "economic diplomacy" toward Africa. Burton and Hofmeyr interpret Sen's novel as a radical working-out of the gender, race, and political self-understanding of India during the Cold War world. They suggest that the desire for, and the threat of, African male sexuality is used in the novel to juxtapose Indian civility and Black man's licentiousness. Both middle-class/upper-caste Hindus and low-status sex workers are attracted and simultaneously repulsed by African men. In the book, Sen brings questions of barbarism (i.e., Africans) and civilization (i.e., Indians) into sharp relief. For example, Burton and Hofmeyr note that "the scene of sex with an Indian prostitute [and a male African university student] reproduces stereotypes about the size and power of his 'manhood' with nary a trace of self-consciousness [by Sen] about the stereotypes entailed by such images" (p. 110). Much like Gandhi, who circulated unflattering representations of Africans in his communications between South Africa and India, post-independence Indian literati exploited tropes of African men's supposed sexual incontinence, which threatened "virtuous Indian womanhood," be it in East Africa or in post-Nehru India. The circulation and popularity and of Sen's novel among Indian literati in India and East Africa relied heavily on homoerotic imaginings. This depiction, in psychosexual terms, served to cultivate a sense of Indian civilizational distinctiveness and racial superiority through normalizing representations of a "fear of marauding African [men's] sexuality in Indian cities" (Burton & Hofmeyr, 2016, p. 115).[35]

It is more than ironic that Siddi men and male African students in India should be the ones tarred with the brush of sexual impropriety given recent, high-profile incidents of South Asian Indian men raping women in public. In 2012, three Indian men raped and murdered a 23-year-old woman, beating her male companion in the process ("India court upholds," 2017). In 2014, in separate incidents occurring within the span of a single week, an 18-year-old German aid worker was raped on a Chennai-bound train and a 51-year-old Danish woman was robbed and gang raped by at least 15 Indian men in New Delhi ("Teenage German tourist," 2014). In 2015, aboard an Amritsar-bound train, a 14-year-old girl was forcibly intoxicated and raped by three Indian soldiers ("Indian army men," 2015). The world was shocked in 2017 by the reported abduction in India of a 16-year-old girl who was then raped repeatedly and thrown from a moving train by five men ("India girl," 2017). And while not a case of rape, a 21-year-old Tanzanian woman attending university in Bangalore was publicly stripped of her clothing and beaten by a mob of men in retaliation for an unrelated incident in which a Sudanese student allegedly ran over an indigent woman while driving drunk ("India mob," 2016).[36] These instances suggest a complex alchemy of caste and race at work in the establishment and maintenance of erotic anti-Black racism in India, to be sure. More specifically, they call attention to the ways that casteism, gender, femininity, masculinity, patriarchy, sex, and racism are implicated in essentialist and nationalist conceptions of the African body as a fly in the Indian ointment of Indo-Aryan and Hindu purity.

Playing at Difference: Bollywood, Anti-Blackness, Minstrelsy, and the South Asian Diaspora

We suggest in this chapter that Indian Siddi men and African male students in India provide an interesting case study of interracial competitive masculinities. In this case, we have shown that in India, Hindus particularly rely on tropes of African male sexuality. Yet, in the larger context the circuits of anti-Blackness and its eroticization cuts across South Asian communities in India, Africa, and the Caribbean. At play are Brahmanical ideologies of Hindu/Indo-Aryan racial superiority, a "timeless India," mythologies from British colonialism and US popular culture, and the inducement of the "model minority" thesis. Film is a central site for making these convergences across the South Asian diaspora legible (Desai, 2004; S. Singh, 2001). Depending on context, place, and space, South Asians negotiate their own identities through hegemonic class and gendered race constructs and the experiences of African Americans and White Americans through the so-called black/white binary paradigm (Thangaraj, 2012). In addition, the South Asian diaspora's "ideologies of return," without ever returning, particularly in the Caribbean, are based on civilizational discourses evoked in Bollywood and other modes of racial literacy, which construct India as a "great and ancient civilization" (S. Singh, 2001). Though it is beyond the scope of this chapter to examine it in detail, postcolonial racial antagonism between Africans and Indians in Guyana and Trinidad manifest in quotidian conflicts over interracial sex. There is at times pronounced antipathy by Indo-Guyanese and Indo-Trinidadian men, be they Hindu or Muslim, toward Afro-Caribbean men and Indo-Caribbean women (see Mason, 1971; Segal, 1995). Not surprisingly, this antagonism has not only survived immigration processes to Canada, the Netherlands, the United Kingdom, and the United States, but has sharpened precisely because of it, as immigrant groups police their borders (Deliovsky & Kitossa, 2018). Tragically, beyond mutual group antagonism articulated through conflicts over interracial sex, it is notable in both Guyana and Trinidad that interracial rape by men of both groups has, since independence, become a method of expressing economic, social, and political grievances (Segal, 1995). In South Africa, a hegemonic "India-centric" approach to forging a Hindu collective identity elided the subordination of Zulu and other African indigenous peoples under apartheid (Burton, 2011). Cross-racial tensions resulted in the violent encounter of the Durban Riots of 1949. More recently, in the aftermath of the first democratic elections in 1994, some Indian

South Africans complained against affirmative action because they felt that "unqualified and inefficient Blacks" had taken over jobs, schools, and suburbs (Ramdass, 2017, p. 128).

To account for tropes of African male sexuality in the Indian and other Indian Ocean World anti-Black imaginaries, we suggest that European narratives of anti-Blackness inform how South Asian Indians imagine Africa, Africans, and blackness. Within that psychosexual imaginary, there are also inescapable, pre-European-colonialism, endogenous anti-blackness and anti-Blackness that inform both colourism and caste (Gupta, 1991). In the Indian subcontinent, as we noted earlier, both colonial propaganda and early Hindu nationalism injected and projected an Aryan myth into upper-caste Brahmanical thinking. It thereby created a racially charged element between Hindus and Muslims and non-Hindu lower-caste populations (Van Der Veer, 1999). The consequence was that darkness and blackness, along with ideas of purity and pollution, came to be associated with poorer, dark-skinned people and indigenous African populations (L. Gordon, 1995; Rajeshkar, 2004). As Sureshi Jayawardene (2016) observes, caste, class, and colour don't just merge in the fluid and solid reality of existence—they are inherent in that dialectic, continually mobilized in accommodation, amplification, and resistance to social inequality. Currently, in parts of India and Pakistan, the descendants of African Siddis are relegated as perpetual foreigners because they phenotypically "look African" (The Sidi Project, 2020). Although the black/white Manicheanism is historically associated with European culture, it is also prevalent in everyday lexical terminologies in South Asia that underpin racial and caste-based subtexts (see Russell, Chapter 2 this volume). Terms including *kalu* [black], and *Habshi* have gradually evolved to become racial slurs used liberally by South Asian Indians, Pakistanis, and diaspora groups to describe darker-skinned groups and Black people (Andre, 2016; Majeed, 2017; Qamar, 2016). More specifically, Stanley Thangaraj (2012) observes that the term *kalu* underscores how South Asian American masculinity is understood in relation to Black American masculinity: Blackness as much as Whiteness is embedded in the pre- and postcolonial South Asian imagination.

The caste–race nexus is especially complex as caste works as a smokescreen for anti-Black racism. Vishal Bhardwaj's (2006) movie *Omkara*, an adaptation of Shakespeare's Othello for Indian cinema, displays the insidious racialization of caste in popular culture and Bollywood cinema. Although Bhardwaj proposes that the film substitutes caste for race in that it follows the interracial union of "half-Brahmin/half-kanjar" Omkara (Othello) and Brahmin Dolly (Desdemona), Omkara is dark-skinned while Dolly and the characters of his nemesis Ishwar (Iago) and Kesu (Cassio) are light skinned. In addition, Omkara is positioned as both a (sexual) outsider/foreigner in opposition to Kesu, who is not only light skinned but also "civilized and educated" (Sharda, 2017, p. 615) underscoring the anti-black and anti-African tropes encircling the casteist narrative in the film. Saksham Sharda (2017) importantly notes that by assuming a colour-blind posture over the "caste-ification of race," the film elides that the actor Ajay Devgan who plays the character of Omkara, is in blackface. Sharda further elaborates that the film's anti-black overtures with respect to caste exogamy were imperative to its success amongst Western and savarna audiences.

In a similar vein, Mira Nair's (1991) *Mississippi Masala* explores the tensions between caste, culture, and race through the negative reception of Mina and Demetrius's union. When Mina's father Jay finds out about their relationship, he asserts that by dating Demetrius, Mina has let down not only her family and community, but also her "entire race." In using caste and race interchangeably, Jay secures not only his family and community's boundaries, but also their position as non-black subjects in the American racial hierarchy. Based on prior mentioned incidents of violence toward Siddi and African-descended men in India in relation to Indian women, we can confer that future inquires on Siddi interracial unions, both with Savarna Indians and Dalit, Bahujan, and Adivasi communities, will further reveal the "consciousness of racial superiority (brown over black) and its correlative, sexual purity (fear of miscegenation)" (Burton & Hofymeyr, 2016, p. 92).

Conclusion

In tracing the African contours of anti-blackness and anti-Blackness as these connect to sexual tropes about Black men in the context of Hindu superiority and Indian nationalism, we have argued that these are dynamics both endogenous and exogamous to India and elsewhere in the Indian Ocean World. In particular, the invention of a "timeless" India mobilized by Gandhi and Nehru both denied the presence of Blackness in India as much as constituted the Indian "self" in juxtaposition to a heterosexual Black masculinity at once appealing and appalling. We have suggested that Bollywood film and cultural production of a "timeless," civilized India extend these narratives and discourses to reinforce antagonistic African and Indian descent dynamics in the Caribbean and anti-Black-dependent tropes of Indians in the West as "model minorities." We suggest that Fanon's (1952/2008) thesis of erotic racism applies not only to the West, but also to an imagined South Asia and its diaspora.[37] Such inquiry should explore the experiences and lives of Siddis, African students, and immigrants to India who must contend with a virulent nationalism that promotes violence by recursively dramatizing the sexual objectification of the Black-man-as-Other who stands against a civilized, Hindu and Indo-Aryan national culture.

Authors' Note

We wish to thank Biko Agozino, Antje Deckert, Charles Simon-Aaron, and the confidential reviewers for their feedback on prior iterations of this chapter. We thank also Luke Duggleby, founder of the Sidi Project (http://www.lukeduggleby.com/the-sidi-project), for facilitating the introduction between Mohan Siddi and Tamari Kitossa.

Notes

1. Our focus on India does not preclude other countries of the Indian subcontinent and Ocean World such as the Andaman and Nicobar Islands, Bangladesh, Pakistan, Sri Lanka and Maldives to which the epigram from Fanon may apply. In these countries are three distinct accretions of Africoid peoples. First are pre-"Aryan" indigenous Africoid peoples most evident on the Andaman and Nicobar Islands. Second, from the second to the nineteenth centuries are

episodic voluntary and involuntary settlement communities of peoples now referred to as Siddi and its variant nomenclature. Finally, from post-independence India to the present, India has been a venue for students (and, more recently, economic immigrants) from sub-Saharan African countries. In sum, endogenous anti-blackness and anti-Blackness in Hinduism and Islam has now fused with Western anti-blackness and pro-whiteness to create a complex and entangled layering of psychosocial and psychosexual anti-black and anti-Black bias that implicates caste, class, nationalism, outcastes and non-castes, racialized aesthetics, and "tribes." It is beyond the scope of this chapter to write a fully elaborated contemporary and social history of aesthetic and normative anti-blackness and the adjectival noun form of anti-Blackness in the Indian Ocean World. We sketch an outline of such a broader inquiry with a focus on India and occasional references to other countries.

2. Throughout his text, L. Gordon (1995) uses the lowercase *b* to signify a globally inclusive designation for people designated as black.
3. For an explanation of our use of black/Black and white/White, Kitossa (Introduction to this volume, n. 1).
4. The term *men of colour* was a nineteenth- to mid-twentieth-century euphemism for African-descended or Black men, whereas today that term is an inclusive reference to non-White people.
5. It must be said that Fanon would not likely approve of his analysis of the erotic tropes of Black men elaborated in *Black Skin, White Masks* being applied to the psychosexual imaginary in non-European cultural configurations (see Russell, Chapter 2 in this volume; Rehal, Chapter 9 in this volume). As a staunch Third World internationalist who was an implacable foe of European colonialism and psychosexual mythologizing of Black men, Fanonism precludes the very possibility of sexualized tropes of Black men being applied to non-Black, "Third World" cultures or societies (Fanon, 1952/2008, 1959/1965, 1963).

   There are problems with Fanon's position. First, seeing as he makes the ontoepistemic claim that "Marxist analysis should always be slightly stretched every time we have to do with the colonial problem" (Fanon, 1963, p. 40), why should Fanon refuse to stretch his thesis of racism beyond warning pro-independence leaders against incorporating racial hatred as a plank in revolutionary violence? Fanon (1964/1967) could have stretched his own analysis without losing the effect of this warning nor violating his principle that "[r]acism is...not a constant of the human spirit" (p. 41). In tethering racism to colonialism, Fanon (1963) obviates the possibility that, in the colonial context, racism is not only one of the "pitfalls of national consciousness" (p. 149) and a mimesis of colonialist racial ideology, but that it also has endogenous roots that precede Western colonialism. The truth of this proposition is that Europeans were the first ever colonizers, thus any prior historical phase of colonialism must have mobilized some equivalent discourse of race to produce racism. Second, and relatedly, Fanon saw colonialism and racism in Africa from a strictly modernist viewpoint. Thus, the prior existence of Arab colonialism in Africa and the continued anti-Black racism and oppression of Africans in North Africa by Arabs is erased in the name of a supranational continental African unity—which, paradoxically, ignored vast distinctions in regional valences of culture, race, and religion. In *Wretched of the Earth*,

Fanon (1963) dismisses any possibility of deep and persistent anti-Black animus of Arabs, both past and present. For him, calling attention to Arab anti-Blackness was no more than invigorating "'spiritual' rivalries" (p. 160) that served Western colonialist troublemakers and self-interested comprador elites. Fanon says, to whit: "In Senegal, it is the newspaper *New Africa* which week by week distills hatred toward Islam and of the Arabs...The missionaries find it opportune to remind the masses that long before the advent of European colonialism the great African empires were disrupted by Arab invasion" (p. 160). Well, if racial Arab superiority and anti-Blackness persist, why should Africans not call attention to it? Given that Fanon himself called attention to Arab animus toward Black men, could it not be that, in admonishing Africans to be silent on Arab anti-Blackness, he contributed to the erasure of anti-Blackness all about him in Algeria and Tunisia? How is it possible for Fanon to assert that "[r]acism is a necessary ideological weapon which accompanies domination...since the weapon must be flexible in order to retain its effectiveness, it undergoes many metamorphosis" (cited in Adi & Sherwood, 2003, p. 65)? Strangely then, imagining himself as though he were a Frenchman, Fanon (1964/1967) believed that, by virtue of being in Algeria working in the Blida-Joinville Hospital in 1953, he was a racist toward North African Arabs. Shaken from this apparent stupor, as an antiracist purgative, he throws himself into the Algerian Revolution. The reality of anti-Blackness and the colour-caste Timocratic legacies of anti-Blackness in Tunis, where for a time he was stationed by the FLN (National Liberation Front), should have been obvious to him (see Menin, 2018; Scaglioni, 2016). No less should it have been obvious in Algeria.

Despite Fanon's (1959/1965) excellent cultural anthropology of Algeria and his advocacy of minority rights in Algeria in *A Dying Colonialism*, he has nothing to say of Black North Africans or the realities of anti-Black racism and African enslavement among North Africa's Arab, Tuareg, Berber, and others (Armah, 1979; Benjamin, 2011; C.L. Brown, 1967; Diop, 1974; M. Gordon, 1992; Laffin, 1982; Lewis, 1971, 1986; Patterson, 1982; Rediker, 2007; Segal, 2001; C. Williams, 1972). The heretical question should be asked: Was Fanon an Arabized bourgeois subject rather than a Pan-Africanist? If Fanon's biographer David Caute (1970) could rightly expose the bourgeois complicity of Malcolm X, who, in his travels in Africa and the Middle East, "moved from airport to palace and palace to airport...[without] turn[ing] his head or his mind to the peasants hawking yams by the roadside" (p. 97), can we not also imagine a similar complicity for Fanon, but with Arab anti-Blackness? According to Faizal Slisli (2012), Fanon converted to Islam, adopting the name Ibrahim Fanon. Might this explain, more or less, his erasure of the Black presence in Algeria and North Africa? If so, it is a bitter irony, given Fanon's criticism of blood and soil types of anticolonial revolutionary action. For it turns out that the very racialism he decried may account for why he was overlooked for a post in the interim Algerian independence government. It may also explain, starting a decade after the revolution, why Fanon was effectively written out of the national narrative of the revolution (see Gendzier, 1973).

If the argument above has any merit, Afrocentrists, Black Nationalists, and Pan-Africanists should reconsider propagating the myth that Fanon in any way a Black revolutionaries' revolutionary. A revolutionary he was, just not a Black one. As noted by David Caute (1970),

"Fanon regarded Negro-ism as a transitional cult which was already obsolescent. There is no sign or trace of any 'African cultural heritage' in Fanon's own writings" (p. 96). Should any of this critical commentary on Arab anti-Blackness and Fanon's evasiveness be in doubt, the tragedy that is Libya says otherwise (see Allegra, 2019; Ditz, 2013; Ford, 2011; Johnson, 2000; Khalid, 2011; "Libyan government," 2017).

Parallel to "everyday" Arabs and militants is the "everyday" anti-Black racism of the Arab and Afro-Arab intelligentsia. They, as noted by Mona Kareem (2019), construct in their literature Black characters who occupy stations of degradation and "seem at ease when othering Africa—the bordered continent is harder for them to grasp than an imaginary 'Arab world' made up by the French and later appropriated by Arab nationalism" (para. 8). Significantly, Tamari Kitossa, the editor of this volume, contacted numerous Pan-African and Black Muslim scholars to contribute to this book. Troublingly, one West African male scholar declined contributing to a Fanonist analytic of Arab anti-Black erotic racism on grounds of not wanting to "antagonize Arabs." No Black Muslim male scholar contacted for a contribution responded.

6. Readers may rightly dispute the suggestion that there is an Indian imaginary since, after all, India is an invention (Naipaul, 1977). We do not disagree with this statement. It could have been other than what it is and what it could be in the future will certainly be other than what it is now, even to the point of dissolution into some other configuration. But we are not here dealing with hypotheticals. There is a real India, produced by real historical forces within and without and it is constantly being (re)imagined as part of the political reality of human dynamics (Burton & Hofmeyr, 2016; Naipaul, 1977; Wallerstein, 1991).
7. Naipaul's (1977) *India: A Wounded Civilization* is a profound statement on the limits of M.K. Gandhi, Nehru, and subsequent politicians establishing a national state grounded in the stultifying mysticism of the "Aryan" conquest, Hindu superiority, and the brutality of caste.
8. Aside from asserting the great antiquity of the Andaman Islanders, E.H. Man's (1883) account is interesting for two other reasons. First, he cites Graeco-Egyptian knowledge of the Bay of Bengal and Ptolemy's reference to the islanders. Second, he draws on Arab travelers and Marco Polo to verify the existence of the Islanders. Finally, he notes an ethnographic affinity between the Andaman "Negritos" and other related groups in Indonesia and the Philippines. J.A. Rogers (1952/1967) provides photographic evidence of the Andaman but also textual account of "Negritos" in various parts of the Indian Ocean World, Indonesia, and through to the Philippines and Japan (pp. 67–72).
9. Some 150 million in number, Dalits are the "untouchables" of India—or, as Gandhi patronizingly called them, harijans, the "children of God" (Ghose, 2003). The term *pariah* in fact derives from the Hindi word *paRaiyar*, meaning "those of the drum" or alternatively "the leather people" (Ghose, 2003, p. 84). Degraded and disparaged, Ghose (2003) notes that

> [Dalits] are the main targets of what are termed "caste-related crimes." Over 2000 Dalits died in the three years between 1989 and 1991 as a result of "atrocities against harijans" (Memorandum of Dalit Writers Forum, 1996, p. 9). In the rural countryside, stripping,

hacking to death, massacres, and lopping off heads are the marks of a horrific bestiality inspired by the unshakeable taint of dirtiness. The dalit [*sic*] body, powerful, suppressed, and perennially dirty from such tasks as removal of dead cattle and waste, tanning, or toddy tapping (collecting juice from the bud of palm tree flowers) is to be violently exorcised, ritually cleansed, from the pure "Aryan" body of the Hindu caste system. (p. 86)

V.S. Naipaul (1977) states that "to the ancient Aryans the untouchables were 'walking carrion'. Their descendants, or at least who imagine themselves as such, maintained the untouchables in a constant state of 'terror and sometimes by deliberate starvation'" (p. 47). Naipaul also reports the burning of their villages, quotidian sadistic and wanton floggings, and even outright murders were so much the norm and so much the prerogatives of Hindu mobs in cities and of the "great" landholders in the rural areas, that these went without much outrage or concern of the police.

10. Whether or the "Aryans" established caste or not, it is certainly the case that racism, via varna (colour), which was absorbed into caste, was institutionalized into the social order. V.S. Naipaul (1977) gives eloquent testimony to both the antiquity and deep resonance in the mentality of Indians: "Kali, 'the black one', the coal-black aboriginal goddess, surviving in Hinduism as the emblem of female destructiveness, garlanded with human skulls, tongue forever out for fresh blood, eternally sacrificed to but insatiable" (p. 92). Describing the horror of high-caste Hindu opposition politicians who, during Indira Gandhi's 22-month state of emergency in 1975, regarded the punishment of their faces being blackened as "torture," Naipaul quips on the painfulness of it all: "Black is a colour horrible to the Indo-Aryan" (p. 115).
11. Vivek Bald (2013) shows that, in the late 1800s and into the 1940s, Bengali men (mostly Muslim) who laboured in the British merchant marine jumped ship and melted into African American communities in New York City, Detroit, and elsewhere. Thus, much in advance of Kamala Harris, some of the first South Asian and African American children were those born to Bengali fathers and African American mothers. It is notable that this mixing, merging, and modification of cultures and races occurred at key moments such as the rise of Garveyism, the birth of the NAACP, anticolonial solidarism, and the momentous migration of African Americans from the rural South to cities in the North. This sort of history is important to counter contemporary anti-Black racism of South Asian immigrants to the United States.
12. In what amounts to a Mary Lefkowitz-like attack on Afrocentrism and pan-Africanism, Gwyn Campbell (2006) asserts the Siddi are so totally integrated into local and national Indian Ocean World communities that they cannot be considered an African "diaspora." His dubious argument is presumably based on scholarly criteria that characterize the trans-Atlantic African diaspora. As a result, he disqualifies the Siddi as part of an Indian Ocean World African diaspora. The assumption that the amorphousness of the scattered Siddi and other such creoles indicates that they are not "victims" of forced migration both is simplistic and contradicts historical facts. Campbell asserts that the construction of a diasporic consciousness among the Siddi is an imposition by African American scholars such as Joseph Harris (1971). Such a view neglects

that pre-independence "Indian" academics wrote about the Siddi as early as the 1930s. It also assumes that ethnic, national, and racial identities are fixed and unchanging rather than malleable, mutable, and responsive to, as much as making a contribution to, social dynamism. Significantly, Campbell's assertion that the Siddi do not have an African-centred consciousness as a diaspora is not based on first-hand ethnography. His disqualification of Siddis as having diasporic consciousness is not only itself an imposition on the Siddi, it seems a thinly veiled ideological attack against Afrocentrism and pan-Africanism. If nothing else, his work places urgency on the training of Siddi scholars who can contribute to scholarly discourse about their communities.

13. Naipaul (1977) gives the impression that Gandhi's 20 years abroad in South Africa were absolute. As noted by G.B. Singh and Tim Watson (2009), this is not the case and it has explicit bearing on Gandhi's role as a Hindu nationalist leader.
14. This term is drawn from Richard Trexler's (1995) *Sex and Conquest*.
15. Noted Dalit lawyer and activist Kiruba Munusamy (2020) explains that the contemporary sexual violence of upper caste Hindu men toward Dalit women is part of a historical process of generalized exploitation of the bodies of Dalit people.
16. There is a striking parallel to the hegemonic exaltation of Hindu and Indo-Aryan upper caste women to the white supremacist cult of "true womanhood" in the southern United States in the nineteenth and twentieth centuries (see Davis, 1981; Wells, 2010). This enables the spectacle of sexual violence toward Dalit women, but also permits sexualized violence against Dalit men. This tends, however, to have neither a language nor compelling discourse because gender-based violence is imagined in biologically essentialized terms as that which is done to female bodies. Nevertheless, however privileged upper-caste Hindu women may be by this idealization, it remains a gilded cage, insuperably linked to eroticized and sadistic degradation of assorted gendered and nonbinary Others imagined as *manu* [polluted]. From this vantage point, grounding our work in Jayawardene's (2016) conception of "racialized casteism," we specify that sexual violence toward these marginalized communities in India is informed by the complex relationality between casteism, colourism, and anti-Black racism that create the necessary grounds for pigmentocracy and the related casteist conceptions of purity and pollution. We assert that this analysis may very well be extended to the experiences of marginalized and indigenous communities in other South Asian contexts including Pakistan, where "outcasted" groups like Christians, Hindus, and the Sheedi community experience similar genocidal patterns of sexual violence and racism including, but not limited to, trafficking, forced conversions, and violent, often mob-initiated, sexual assault, enslavement, and hereditary bondage (see Bhaiwala et al., 2020; Chaudhry, 2016; De Lauri, 2015; Husain, 2020; World Sindh Congress, 2017).
17. The word Sidi with a single d connotes specific regional, class, and status ethnographic valences but also national difference among this creole diasporic African population. Thus, Sidi with a single d, is sometimes used as a term of ethnological distinction. It is also a term of ethno-class distinction for the African descendants of the administrators and rulers, who often mixed with Afghans and others and are very light-skinned. At other times, Sidi is a term of ethnographic

distinction used by scholars to categorize regional distinctions. There is significant variability in ethnographic nomenclature, and it is a matter of ethical concern where scholars impose labels on these creole communities for their convenience.

18. Totally unrelated to the African creoles in the Indian Ocean World who call themselves Siddi, the term is also used in contemporary Morocco in a gendered- and racialized-caste "Timocratic" way (see Patterson, 1982). Marta Scaglioni (2016) notes that "even today black people in rural areas refer to their former white masters as 'sidi' and 'lella' (master and mistress)" (para. 3).

19. As noted by Vasant Rao (1974), as a result of marriage alliances with various elites from the Levantine and northwest regions of Asia, elite Siddis of Janjir and Sachan tend to be very light-skinned. To some extent, the darker the skin of Siddi people the more it signifies class and differences among Siddi groups.

20. In other contexts, such as in Pakistan where casteist notions undergird the religio-cultural practices of the imagined Muslim (primarily Sunni) nation, we theorize that a similar dynamic would hold in relation to the upper-caste South Asian Pakistani Muslim woman (see "Anger over 'blackface'," 2018).

21. Our use and implicit criticism of the term *knowable psychology* does not in any way refute a Marxist-Gramscian reading of "mentalities" as theorized by Jacques Le Goff (1974) or Norbert Elias (1939/2000). In this instance, mentalities refers to the ideas and feelings corresponding to the emergence, entrenchment, and resistance to discourses, training, and practical innovations that reflect contests for dominance and hegemony in a given social order. In our use of concepts such as the "Indian imagination," we are not reifying one counter-discursive formation for the hegemonic norm. Instead, we recognize that "national" feeling is a hegemonic formation of cultural reproduction (however much it may be contested and resisted within nation states) that is akin Marx's and Engels's (1847/1978) dictum that "[t]he ruling ideas of each age have ever been the ideas of the ruling class" (p. 489).

22. Fanon's (1952/2008, 1964/1967) oeuvre criticizes national cultures that rely on a racialized romanticism of "great" civilizations of the past as the grounding for independence, resistance, and post-independence national pride. Regarding the "educated classes," mimesis of their colonizer's own penchant for raciological myth-making, their "lack of practical links between them and the mass of people, their laziness, and...cowardice at the decisive moment of struggle will give rise to tragic mishaps" (Fanon, 1963, p. 148). The masses, Fanon (1952/2008) would say, cannot eat their racial pride at past glories nor experience the fullness of their humanity by such means. Yet Fanon does not give the "educated classes" enough credit. To train the masses into obedience to the authority of the "educated classes," what better ideological training can there be than to naturalize a timeless hierarchy of command. Consistent with Fanon's criticism of the "educated classes" in Africa, V.S. Naipaul (1977) undertakes an equally withering criticism of M.K. Gandhi's embedding into Indian nationalism the "gift" of Hindu caste-religio-racial superiority. Yet in the African context, as shown by Paulin Hountondji (1983), the likes of Cheikh Anta Diop and Theophile Obenga take a counter-nationalistic and pan-African approach to refute the claims of both Occidentalism and Orientalism as the founts of human civilization. Hountondji asserts,

however, that these approaches do not refute mimesis. For Hountondji, the most important point is not whether Egypt, before Persian, Greek, and Roman conquest, was African, nor that one finds scripts and science signifying abstract philosophy through pre-Arab and European colonial invasions. Instead, inspired by Fanon, his concern is whether arts, letters, and science were democratized or "were they monopolized by a tiny class of [kings, nobles, and] priests who made them instruments of domination" (p. 100). To this end, Hountondji shows that Diop and Obenga, as well as the "young" versus the "mature" Nkrumah, refused the possibility for a more radical present and future humanistic African independence implicit in rejecting culturalism.

23. Our criticism of Orientalism as anti-African would reject neither that V.Y. Mudimbe's (1988) thesis is an invention of the European colonial mind nor Ali Mazrui's (2005) contention that there have been multiple inventions of Africa internal and external to Africa since Egypt and other state formations. Yet we agree with Deliovsky and Kitossa's (2013) contention that Orientalism, as discourse and criticism, is fundamentally negating of Africa and/or Blackness, whatever the content of either appellation.

24. One of the more intriguing instances of resistance that Naipaul (1977) cites is that of the reversal of reverence some Indians showed Gandhi on the eve of independence and at the end of his life. Seventeen years before, in 1930, some of the Hindu poor covered the ground with green leaves to symbolically elevate the Mahatma on his great Salt March protest. But in 1947, on what Naipaul called Gandhi's "[s]ad last march," Gandhi went to Bengal to staunch the flow of blood between Hindus and Muslims, stoked, indeed, by Indian nationalism, of which Gandhi himself was the chief spokesperson. Instead of leaves, "embittered people scatter broken glass on the roads he is to walk" (p. 111). Obviously disgusted by Hindu nationalists who would have them meekly accept blows and bullets from the British but raise hatchets to each other, Gandhi was obviously held as the lead malefactor in the internecine conflict that would lead, quickly, to the birth of Pakistan by Muhammad Ali Jinnah and others. The luckless and friendly "harijans," without an international ummah [supportive community of Muslims] to come to their aid, remained under the boot of the Hindus.

25. This is not merely bias that favours elite, official, and state-sanctified discourses in scholarly research; it is the ongoing consequence of the humanities and social "sciences" being expressly created by the state. It is no accident, then, that with their material reproduction and credibility hanging in the balance, many scholars take for granted that "the state [is] the foundational unit of analysis" (Abraham & van Schendel, 2005, p. 5). To this end, scholastic heretics are taken in by the revolutionary possibilities of their discursive resistance by failing to recognize that their "heresy" depends on the ideological and linguistic codes of the hegemonic orthodoxy (Wallerstein, 1992). In addition, the narratives of would-be state crafters are given primacy over the chaotic, illegible, and undifferentiated masses, since it is the former who, as "vanguards," give the latter their inertia, direction, and historic meaning (see Gough, 1976; Gouldner 1975-76; Hountondji, 1983, pp. 100–01; Wallerstein, 1992, p. 49). James C. Scott (1985) notes that researchers tend to avoid analyzing and recording the "weak" who mobilize against all organized regimes of domination: "foot dragging, dissimulation, desertion, false compliance, pilfering,

feigned ignorance, slander, arson, sabotage, and so on" (p. xvi). They instead prefer to focus on would-be state-formers given that "[f]ormal, organized political activity, even if clandestine and revolutionary, is typically the preserve of the middle class and intelligentsia" (p. xv).

26. We note below that in the 20 years of his life in South Africa, though he would make periodic trips to Gujurat to drum support for the Hindu cause, for Gandhi, South Africans were props to affirm his passion for the British empire, foils for the development of his ascetism, or were simply invisible. The question of the invisibility of Africans is particularly noteworthy, as the Gujurati-born-and-raised Gandhi never mentions the prominent role that the Siddi played in shaping the history Gujurat (see Segal, 2001, pp. 71–75).

27. It is not by serendipity that Gandhi (1869–1948) would be the causeway to link all these dynamics into a coherent ideology. He was a direct player in their dynamics during his dreary and insular three-year stay in London at law school between 1888 and 1891, where he kept his promise to his mother to abstain from drink, meat, and women. This issue of sex would remain a constant theme in his life; in his 40s, before going back to India and as a married man, he took a vow of celibacy. Naipaul (1977) notes that Gandhi's ascetism and quest for purity were transferred to his commitment to nationalism. Set against Africans and Blackness as hallmarks of unbridled sexuality that stood as a contrast from his days in South Africa, that value was not unfamiliar to the likes of Nehru, the first prime minister of India. Significantly, with sex as a site for the articulation of Hindu supremacist conceptions of nationalism, White women during the Raj were also imagined as over-sexed, presumably more so than "prostitutes," and thus a moral threat to the nation-in-the-making (Chandra, 2011).

28. The myth of the "Mahatma" as an implacable opponent of British imperialism and champion of nonviolent resistance overwhelms the real history of the man's commitment to Hinduism, Indo-Aryan supremacy, British superiority, and militarism. Gandhi, it seems, objected to all colonials lifting a finger against the British, and was stoic in the face of British violence. V.S. Naipaul (1977) documents well his complicity with and encouragement of nationalism, however much he claimed the *harijans*, the "walking carrion," were children of God—so long as they continued to clean toilets, Gandhi could participate in the theatre of doing so alongside them (p. 47). Here, too, Gandhi was not original. Even if he was sincere, his "Hindu nationalism," says Leo Tolstoy, "spoils everything" (cited in Naipaul, 1977, p. 100). For as it turns out, by "[a] remarkable linguistic coincidence: they remained God's chillum" (Naipaul, 1977, p. 47). The contemporary beatification of Gandhi has removed him from the mortal plane, but as we demonstrate in this chapter, this changes little his contribution to anti-Blackness in India.

29. That Fanon is alleged to have made this criticism of Gandhi raises two questions, one empirical and the other political and sociohistorical. First, Gail Presbey (1996) takes up a thoughtful comparative analysis between Fanon's, Gandhi's, and Mandela's approaches to the role of counter-violence in the liberation struggle. There is, curiously, nothing in Presbey's essay to indicate Fanon ever opined on the merits of Gandhi's *Satyagraha*. Hira Singh (2007) also takes up a comparative analysis between Fanon's and Ghandi's approach to racism in the colonial context. Though Singh usefully offers an account of Indian peasants as historically active and

agentic, which is consistent with Fanon's commitment to the peasantry in the "Third World" as a revolutionary force, we find his analysis and historiography wanting in other respects. Despite drawing on David Caute's (1970) biography of Fanon, the same text from which we derive the notation that Fanon strongly disagreed with Gandhi's bourgeois nonviolent approach to decolonization, this difference is not at all recognized in Singh's paper. Singh's account of Gandhi is largely exculpatory and hagiographic—and, dare we say, not very Fanonist. If, nevertheless, it is true that Fanon repudiated *Satyagraha*, what did he make of the nonviolent civil rights movement in the United States and the leadership of Martin Luther King Jr. as a practical matter? We are aware of no record that Fanon commented on the African American civil rights struggle. This is perplexing given that he was intensely attuned to African American life and culture. It is strange, then, that in *Black Skin, White Masks* so much of his autoethnography turns on the history and politics of sexual tropes of African American men.

As a result of that intimacy, especially with Chester Himes and Richard Wright, formulated a good deal of his psychoanalytic thesis on the neurotic manifestations of race and sex on the colonialist-racist context of the United States. In *Black Skin, White Masks*, where he explores when and how Black people in the Americas come to an awareness of their inferiority, Fanon (1952/2008) notes, "I have talked about the black problem with friends, or, more rarely, with American Negroes" (p. 110).

30. We are grateful to Biko Agozino for suggesting the autobiography of M.K. Ghandi (1927/1996) and the travelogue of V.S. Naipaul (1990).
31. Gandhi's anti-Black racism was the reason for the removal of his statue from the University of Ghana in 2018 ("'Racist' Gandhi statue," 2018). We are grateful for one of the confidential reviewers who shared this information in their review. Gandhi's opinions are part of the general reaction of Indians as they came to constitute themselves as much as the process of colonial settlement led to the construction of an "Indian" and diasporic identity in South Africa (see Pillay, 2017). There is no question that the result of the imperatives of colonial settlement and capitalism (which imported, at first forcibly and then "willingly," economic migrants, subcontinent Hindu and Muslim immigrant labour, and indigenous South Africans both as labourers and indigenous peoples) clashed (Hughes, 2007). Though the groups and leaders on both sides were by no means homogeneous, both John Dube (first president of the African National Congress) and Mohandas Gandhi (of a loose consortium of Indian groups) agreed to the necessity of keeping their groups' struggles distinct (Hughes, 2007; cf. Corder & Plaut, 2014).
32. In an 1896 Bombay lecture, ripe with moral outrage about being classed with "raw Kaffirs," Ghandi opined to upper-caste Indians:

> Ours is one continual struggle against degradation sought to be inflicted upon us by the Europeans, who desire to degrade us to the level of the raw Kaffir whose occupation is hunting, and whose sole ambition is to collect a certain number of cattle to buy a wife and, then, pass his life in indolence and nakedness. (cited in Singh & Watson, 2009, p. 15)

Even in 1925, Gandhi (1961) cautioned a German against his wish to be a philosopher in India, thinking it a purer endeavor there. He opined that while philosophy knows no borders, "Europe has reason to hope much from India" (p. 334). To indicate that India was surely on the road to progress (on par with Europe), he asserts: "Though India has her share of wild and soulless two-footed beasts, probably the tendency of the average Indian mind is to discard the wild beast in it" (p. 334).

33. On the issue of nonviolent political action, Singh & Watson (2009) provide a biting critique of Gandhi's selective application of this principle: "Why was it that the blacks 'would not work'? After the British Empire had seized their land and virtually enslaved them, why should they work? Could not the refusal of the black natives to work be viewed as a nonviolent work stoppage? Why did Gandhi so inexplicably oppose this act of civil disobedience as practiced by blacks?" (p. 16).

34. During the Cold War period and well after it, millions of African students studied in one opposing or neutral camp or other. Something of an embarrassment to socialist bloc countries such as China, Jugoslavia, and the USSR, significant tensions arose when African male students dated or married local women. Charles Quiste-Adade (2001) notes a lingering racial animosity toward the children and mothers of relationships "left behind." Indeed, as late as 1993, the Chinese government was embarrassed when Chinese male students at Beijing University rioted and beat African male students for ostensibly "taking their women" (Sautman, 1994). More recently, Wisdom Tettey (2020) has demonstrated how anti-Blackness is mobilized in the new imperial intervention of China in Africa.

35. See also Russell (Chapter 2 in this volume) and Rehal (Chapter 9 in this volume). Rehal, in particular, offers a discussion on intra-Global South homoerotic desire and fear of Black men.

36. Following Dalit critical narratives, a common feature among these high-profile cases were the victims and survivors who were primarily White/Western and savarna women. It is important to note that sexual violence cases involving Dalit women (and men) are routinely erased and have received little to no attention in local and global media as a result of the normalization of violence against lower-caste Dalit, Bahujan, and Adivasi communities (see Munusmy, 2020; Raghavan & Pavithra, 2019). Instances where media coverage has been solicited to violence experienced by African-descended peoples in India highlight how the "libidinal economy of anti-blackness is pervasive regardless of variance, or permutation in its political economy" (Frank Wilderson, cited in Sexton, 2009, p. 37) such that the application of anti-black tropes hypervisiblizes and sexualizes indigenous and diasporic African communities irrespective of historical or geographical specificity.

37. Currently, in the Global North, South Asian intellectuals, social justice activists, and entertainers are taking stock of the salience, melding, and implications of quotidian anti-blackness, anti-Blackness, anti-Siddi, and anti-Dalit narratives and practices for upper-caste and upper-class South Asian identities. These critics are openly criticizing and exposing the convergence of endogenous and exogamous South Asian anti-blackness and anti-Blackness in the shaping of South Asian identity and experience under neoliberal capitalism. It is notable that while

much of these accessible commentaries are from (young) women, key voices of resistance to eroticized spectacles of anti-blackness, anti-Black racism, and casteism include men as well as queer, nonbinary, and trans South Asian activists (see Bhago, 2020; Dalit Queer Project, 2020; Ekhaldi, 2020; Majeed, 2017; Qamar, 2016; Tiku, 2020). These critiques of South Asian anti-blackness and anti-Blackness register at the alchemical articulations of age, class, the "model minority," constructions of Brown men's hegemonic masculinity, colour-based notions of ideal beauty, religion, and the oppression and complicity of upper-caste South Asian women as South Asians struggle to live, resist, and define themselves under neoliberal colonial capitalism. They point out that complicity with the "model minority" thesis is not only empty neoliberal recognition that undermines the collective interests of South Asians in solidarity resistance against multiple oppressions, but that it is also complicit with anti-Black necropolitics, which V.J. Prashad (2000b) calls "weak bad faith anti-Blackness" (see also Fang, 2020). Interestingly, Hassan Minhaj's 2018 Netflix show *Patriot Act* got cancelled immediately following the episode addressing anti-Blackness among South Asians and its implications in the United States, including the complicity of Asian police officers in Derek Chauvin's murder of George Floyd (Images Staff, 2020).

Bibliography

Abraham, I., & van Schendel, W. (2005). Introduction: The making of illicitness. In W. van Schendel & I. Abraham (Eds.), *Illicit flows and criminal things: States, borders, and the other side of globalization* (pp. 1–37). Indiana University Press.

Adi, H., & Sherwood, M. (2003). *Pan-African history: Political figures from Africa and the diaspora since 1787*. Routledge.

Afro-descendants: A global picture. (2015). *Minority Rights International*. http://stories.minorityrights.org/afro-descendants/

Allegra, C. (2019). Unspeakable crime: Rape as a weapon of war in Libya. *Al Jazeera*. https://www.aljazeera.com/programmes/specialseries/2019/09/unspeakable-crime-rape-weapon-war-libya-190903102146596.html

Alpers, E. (2003). The African diaspora in the Indian Ocean: A comparative perspective. In S. Jayasuriya & R. Pankhurst (Eds.), *The African Diaspora in the Indian Ocean* (pp. 19–52). Africa World Press.

Andre, A. (2016, June 26). Being African in India: "We are seen as demons." *Al Jazeera*. https://www.aljazeera.com/features/2016/6/26/being-african-in-india-we-are-seen-as-demons

Anger over "blackface" makeup segment on Pakistan TV. (2018, March 16). *BBC*. https://www.bbc.com/news/world-asia-43429517

Anwar, T. (2014). Delhi's everyday racism: African students recount lynch mob attack in metro. *First Post*. https://www.firstpost.com/living/delhis-everyday-racism-african-students-recount-lynch-mob-attack-metro-1739881.html

Arendt, H. (1970). *On violence*. A Harvest Book.

Armah, A. (1979). *Two thousand seasons*. Heinemann.

Bald, V. (2013). *Bengali Harlem and the lost histories of South Asian America*. Harvard University Press.

Baldwin, J. (1961). The Black boy looks at the White boy Norman Mailer. *Esquire*. https://classic.esquire.com/article/1961/5/1/the-black-boy-looks-at-the-white-boy-norman-mailer

Baldwin, J. (1985). *The fire next time*. Laurel Books. (Original work published 1963)

Basu, H. (2003). Slave, soldier, trader, faqir: Fragments of African histories in Western India (Gujarat). In S. Jayasuriya & R. Pankhurst (Eds.), *The African diaspora in the Indian Ocean* (pp. 223–50). Africa World Press.

Benjamin, P. (2011). On racism and the Arabs! *Commentaries on the Times*. http://commentariesonthetimes.wordpress.com/2011/02/15/on-racism-and-the-arabs/

Bhago, M. (2014, December 3). Especially in the wake of Ferguson, it's time to destroy anti-Blackness in the Sikh community. *Black Girl Dangerous*. http://www.bgdblog.org/2014/12/especially-wake-ferguson-time-destroy-anti-blackness-sikh-community/

Bhaiwala. Z., Hamidi. N., & Bizenjo, S. (2020, August 14). Black Lives Matter—For Pakistan's Sheedi community too. *World Economic Forum*. https://www.weforum.org/agenda/2020/08/black-lives-matter-for-pakistans-sheedi-community-too/

Bhardwaj, V. (Director). (2006). *Omkara* [Film]. Shemaroo Entertainment.

Brown, C.L. (1967). Color in northern Africa. *Daedalus*, 96(2), 464–82.

Brown, J.M. (2003). *Nehru: A political life*. Yale University Press.

Burton, A. (2011). The pain of racism in the making of a "coolie Doctor." *Interventions*, *13*(2), 212–35. https://doi.org/10.1080/1369801X.2011.573219

Burton, A., & Hofmeyer , I. (2016). *Africa in the Indian imagination: Race and the politics of postcolonial citation*. Duke University Press.

Campbell, G. (2006). The African-Asian diaspora: Myth or reality? *African and Asian Studies*, *5*(3–4), 305–24.

Cardoso, H. C. (2010). The African slave population of Portuguese India demographics and impact on Indo-Portuguese. *Journal of Pidgin and Creole Languages*, *25*(1), 95–119. https://doi.org/10.1075/jpcl.25.1.04car

Caute, D. (1970). *Fanon*. Fontana/Collins.

Chandra, S. (2011). Whiteness on the margins of native patriarchy: Race, caste, sexuality, and the agenda of transnational studies. *Feminist Studies*, *37*(1), 127–53. https://www.jstor.org/stable/23069887

Chaudhry, L. (2016). Structural violence and the lives of Pakistani Christians: A collaborative analysis. *Community Psychology in Global Perspective*, *2*(2), 97–113.

Chauhan, P.R. (2010). The Indian subcontinent and "Out of Africa I." In J.G. Fleagle, J.J. Shea, F.E. Grine, A.L. Baden, & R.E. Leakey (Eds.), *Out of Africa I: The first hominin colonization of Eurasia* (pp. 145–64). Springer.

Corder, C., & Plaut, M. (2014). Gandhi's decisive South African 1913 campaign: A personal perspective from the letters of Betty Molteno. *South African Historical Journal*, 66(1), 22–54. http://dx.doi.org/10.1080/02582473.2013.862565

Dalit Queer Project. (2020). https://www.instagram.com/dalitqueerproject/?hl=en/

Davis, A.Y. (1981). *Women, race, and class*. Random House.

De Lauri, A. (2015). "Debtor forever": Debt and bondage in Afghan and Pakistani brick kilns. *SWAB-WPS*. https://shadowsofslavery.org/publications/SWAB-WPS_1-2015_debtor_forever.pdf

Deliovsky, K., & Kitossa, T. (2013). Beyond Black and White: When going beyond may take us out of bounds. *Journal of Black Studies, 44*(2), 158–81. https://doi.org/10.3138/ijcs.56.2017-0005

Deliovsky, K., & Kitossa, T. (2018). Beyond celebration: A critical sociological inquiry of interracial couples research in Canada. *International Journal of Canadian Studies, 56*, 115–40.

Dennell, R. (2010). "Out of Africa I": Current problems and future prospects. In J.G. Fleagle, J.J. Shea, F.E. Grine, A.L. Baden, & R.E. Leakey (Eds.), *Out of Africa I: The first Hominin colonization of Eurasia* (pp. 247–73). Springer.

Desai, J. (2004). *Beyond Bollywood: The cultural politics of south Asian diasporic film*. Taylor and Francis.

Diop, C. (1974). *The African origin of civilization: Myth or reality*. Lawrence Hill and Company.

Ditz, J. (2013). Disappeared: Thousands of Libyan Blacks turn up missing in rebel offensives. *Anti-War.com*. http://news.antiwar.com/2011/09/13/disappeared-thousands-of-libyan-blacks-turn-up-missing-in-rebel-offensives/

Douglas, M. (1970). *Natural symbols: Explorations in cosmology*. Pantheon Books.

Du Bois, W.E.B. (1928/2014). *Dark princess*. Oxford University Press.

Duggleby, L. (2020). *The Sidi project*. http://www.lukeduggleby.com/the-sidi-project

Elias, N. (2000). *The Civilizing process*. Blackwell Publishing. (Original work published 1939)

Elkhaldi. E. (2020). "Arab American psycho" [Podcast]. *Bi-racial identity with Shereen Muhammad*. https://podcasts.apple.com/gb/podcast/80-biracial-identity-with-shereen-mohammed/id1452118650?i=1000495132820

Fang, Marina. (2020, June 30). How Asian Americans are reckoning with anti-Blackness in their families. *HuffPost US*. https://www.huffingtonpost.ca/entry/anti-blackness-asian-americans_n_5ed87ca8c5b6ea15610b5774?ri18n=true

Fanon, F. (1963). *The wretched of the earth* (C. Farrington, Trans.). Grove Press.

Fanon, F. (1965). *A dying colonialism*. Grove Press. (Original work published 1959)

Fanon, F. (1967). *Toward the African Revolution: Political essays*. (H. Chevalier, Trans.). Grove Press. (Original work published 1964)

Fanon, F. (2008). *Black skin, White masks* (R. Philcox, Trans.). Grove Press. (Original work published 1952)

Fatima, N. (2015). Baltimore riots reveal blatant anti-Blackness in the South Asian community. *Brown Girl Magazine*. http://www.browngirlmagazine.com/2015/05/baltimore-riots-reveal-blatant-anti-blackness-in-the-south-asian-community/

Ford, G. (2011, March 9). Race and Arab nationalism in Libya. *Black Agenda Report*. http://blackagendareport.com/content/race-and-arab-nationalism-libya

Gandhi, M.K. (1961). *In search of the supreme* (Vol. 1; V.B. Kher, Ed.). Navajivan Publishing House.

Gandhi, M.K. (1996). *An autobiography, or, The story of my experiments with truth*. Navajivan Publishing House. (Original work published 1927)

Gendzier, I.L. (1973). *Frantz Fanon: A critical study*. Vintage Books.

Getzels, P. (2013). *First out of Africa: The totally isolated tribe of the Andaman* [Film]. Sky Vision.

Ghose, S. (2003). The Dalit in India. *Social Research: An International Quarterly, 70*(1), 83–109. https://muse.jhu.edu/article/558561

Gordon, L.R. (1995). *Bad faith and Antiblack racism*. Humanities Press.

Gordon, M. (1992). *Slavery in the Arab world*. New Amsterdam Books.

Gough, K. (1976). Indian peasant uprisings. *Bulletin of Concerned Asian Scholars, 8*(3), 2–18. https://doi.org/10.1080/14672715.1976.10404413

Gupta, D. (1991). Indian perceptions of Africa. *South Asia Research, 11*(2), 158–74. https://doi.org/10.1177%2F026272809101100203

Harris, J. (1971). *The African presence in Asia: Consequences of the East African slave trade*. Northwestern University Press.

Hegel, G.W.F. (1956). *The philosophy of history* (J. Sibree, Trans.). Dover.

Honan, W.H. (1995, November 5). Book on philosopher's life stirs scholarly debate over her legacy. *New York Times*. https://www.writing.upenn.edu/~afilreis/Holocaust/arendt.html

Hountondji, P.J. (1983). *African philosophy: Myth and reality*. Hutchinson University Library for Africa.

Hughes, H. (2007). "The coolies will elbow us out of the country": African reactions to Indian immigration in the colony of Natal, South Africa. *Labour History Review, 72*(2): 155–68. https://doi.org/10.1179/174581807X224588

Husain. H. (2020, June 5). Pakistan's first Sheedi woman MPA talks about George Floyd and racism. *Cutacut*. https://cutacut.com/2020/06/05/pakistans-first-sheedi-woman-mpa-talks-about-george-floyd-and-racism/

Images Staff. (2020, June 5). Hasan Minhaj calls out anti-Blackness in South Asian communities. *Images*. https://images.dawn.com/news/1185367

India court upholds 2012 Delhi gang rapists' death penalty. (2017, May 5). *BBC*. https://www.bbc.com/news/world-asia-india-39814910

India girl, 16, "brutally gang raped" and thrown from moving train. (2017, June 19). BBC. https://www.bbc.com/news/world-asia-india-40323307

India mob strips Tanzanian student in Bangalore. (2016, February 3). *BBC*. https://www.bbc.com/news/world-asia-india-35483893

Indian army men "gang rape" Kolkata girl aboard Howrah-Amritsar Express. (2015, December 29). *The Daily Star*. https://www.thedailystar.net/world/kolkata-girl-%E2%80%98gang-raped%E2%80%99-army-men-train-194026

Jamal, M., & Band Baja Radio. (2009). *The Black Pakistanis* [Video]. YouTube. https://www.youtube.com/watch?v=Lxaz6hBxf3I

Jayasuriya, S., & Pankhurst, R. (2003). On the African diaspora in the Indian Ocean. In S. Jayasuriya & R. Pankhurst (Eds.), *The African Diaspora in the Indian Ocean* (pp. 7–16). Africa World Press.

Jayawardene, S. (2016). Racialized casteism: Exposing the relationship between race, caste, and colorism through the experiences of Africana people in India and Sri Lanka. *Journal of African American Studies 20*, 323–45. http://doi.org/10.1007/s12111-016-9333-5

Johnson, T. (2000). Ethnic violence and mass deportations of immigrants in Libya. *World Socialist Web Site*. https://www.wsws.org/articles/2000/oct2000/liby-o28.shtml

Johnson, T. (2000). Ethnic violence and mass deportations of immigrants in Libya. *World Socialist Web Site*. https://www.wsws.org/articles/2000/oct2000/liby-o28.shtml

Kareem, M. (2019, May 5). Arabic literature and the African other. *Africa is a Country*. https://www.africaisacountry.com/2019/05/how-do-arabs-talk-and-write-about-black-people

Karmwar, R. (2010). African diaspora in India. *Diaspora Studies*, *3*(1), 69–91.

Khalid, S. (2011, February 3). Egypt's race problem. *The Root*. http://www.theroot.com/views/egypt-s-race-problem

Kitossa, T. (2020, December 4). *Anti-Black sexual racism: Linking White police violence, COVID-19, and popular culture* [Symposium paper]. Intervention Symposium—Black Humanity: Bearing Witness to COVID-19, online. https://antipodeonline.org/2020/12/04/black-humanity-bearing-witness-to-covid-19/

Laffin, J. (1982). The Arabs as master slavers. SBS Publishing.

Le Goff, J. (1974). Mentalities: A new field for historians. *Social Science Information*, *13*(1), 81–97. https://doi.org/10.1177/053901847401300105

Lewis, B. (1971). *Race and color in Islam*. Harper & Row.

Lewis, B. (1986). The crows of the Arabs. In H.L. Gates, Jr. (Ed.), *"Race," writing and difference* (pp. 107–16). University of Chicago Press.

Libyan government says investigating migrant "slave market" report. (2017, November 23). *Reuters*. https://www.reuters.com/article/us-europe-migrants-libya/libyan-government-says-investigating-migrant-slave-market-reports-idUSKBN1DN1ZD

Luedi, J. (2018, September 28). Meet the first African-Pakistani lawmaker. *The Diplomat*. https://thediplomat.com/2018/09/meet-the-first-african-pakistani-lawmaker/

Mackey, R. (2014, September 30). Beating of African students by mob in India prompts soul-searching on race. *The New York Times*. https://www.nytimes.com/2014/10/01/world/asia/beating-of-african-students-by-mob-in-india-prompts-soul-searching-on-race.html

Majeed, J. (2017, January 23). It's time we stopped using "kala" as an insult and respect the African-American community. *Dawn News*. https://www.dawn.com/news/1317116

Man, E.H. (1883). On the Aboriginal inhabitants of the Andaman Islands (Part I). *The Journal of the Anthropological Institute of Great Britain and Ireland*, *12*, 69–116. https://doi.org/10.2307/2841843

Marx, K., & Engels, F. (1978). Manifesto of the Communist Party. In R.C. Tucker (Ed.), *The Marx-Engels Reader* (pp. 473–500). W.W. Norton. (Original work published 1847)

Mason, P. (1971). *Patterns of dominance*. Oxford University Press.

Mazrui, A. (2005). The re-invention of Africa: Edward Said, V.Y. Mudimbe, and beyond. *Africa, and Cultural Criticism*, *36*(3), 68–82.

Menin, L. (2018, February 12). Being "Black" in North Africa and the Middle East: Beyond trafficking and slavery. *Open Democracy*. https://www.opendemocracy.net/en/beyond-trafficking-and-slavery/being-black-in-north-africa-and-middle-east/

Mudimbe, V.Y. (1988). *The invention of Africa*. Indiana University Press.

Naipaul, V.S. (1977). *India: A wounded civilization*. Penguin Books.

Naipaul, V.S. (1990). *India: A million mutinies now*. Viking.

Nair, M. (Director). (1991) *Mississipi Masala* [Film]. StudioCanal Souss.

Nolen, S. (2001, August 9). Cross-caste teen lovers brutally slain. *Globe and Mail*. https://www.theglobeandmail.com/news/world/cross-caste-teen-lovers-brutally-slain/article4151286/

O'Hanlon, R., & Washbrook, D. (1992). After Orientalism: Culture, criticism, and politics in the Third World. *Comparative Studies in Society and History*, *34*(1), 141–67. https://www.jstor.org/stable/178988

Obeng, P. (2011). Siddi street theatre and dance in north Karnataka, South India. *African Diaspora, 4*(1), 1–26. https://doi.org/10.1163/187254611X566080

Pankhurst, R. (2003). The Ethiopian diaspora to India: The role of Habshis and Sidis from medieval times to the end of the eighteenth century. In S. Jayasuriya & R. Pankhurst (Eds.), *The African diaspora in the Indian Ocean* (pp. 189–222). Africa World Press.

Patterson, O. (1982). *Slavery and social death: A comparative study*. Harvard University Press.

Pillay, K. (2017). "The coolies here": Exploring the construction of an Indian "race" in South Africa. *Jounral of Global South Studies*, *34*(1), 22–49. https://doi.org/10.1353/gss.2017.0003

Prabhu, M. (2017, May 3). African victions of racism in India share their stories. *Al Jazeera*. http://www.aljazeera.com/indepth/features/2017/04/african-victims-racism-india-share-stories-170423093250637.html

Prashad, V.J. (2000a). Afro-Dalits of the earth, unite! *African Studies Review*, *43*(1), 189–201. https://www.jstor.org/stable/524727

Prashad, V.J. (2000b). *The karma of Brown folk*. University of Minnesota Press.

Prashad, V.J. (2001). *Everybody was kung fu fighting: Afro-Asian connections and the myth of cultural purity.* Beacon Press.

Presbey, G.M. (1996). Fanon on the role of violence in liberation: A comparison with Gandhi and Mandela. In L. Gordon, T.D. Sharpley-Whiting, & R.T. White (Eds.), *Fanon: A critical reader* (pp. 283–96). Blackwell Publishers.

Qamar, A. (2016, January 27). Confronting anti-Black racism. *SAALT: South Asian Americans Lead Together*. http://saalt.org/confronting-anti-black-racism/

Quist-Adade, C (Director). (2001). *The ones they left behind: The life and plight of African Russians* [Film]. University of Windsor.

"Racist" Gandhi statue removed from University of Ghana. (2018, December 13). *BBC*. https://www.bbc.com/news/world-africa-46552614

Raghavan A., & Pavithra. P. (2019). Dark looks: Sensory contours of racism in India. In Eguchi, S., Calafell, B., & Abdi, S. (Eds.), *De-Whitening intersectionality: Race, intercultural communication and politics* (pp. 223–42). Lexington Books.

Raghavan, S. (2016, September 19). When Indian troops entered Congo 55 years ago. *Livemint*. https://www.livemint.com/Opinion/9D5XT497AEYYluFn3moa2H/When-Indian-troopsentered-Congo-55-years-ago.html

Rajeshkar, V. (1988). The Black untouchables of India: Reclaiming our cultural heritage. In I. Van Sertima & R. Rashidi (Eds.), *African presence in early Asia* (pp. 235–42). Transaction Publishers.

Ramdass, R. (2017). The South African Indian experience as the other. *Journal of Ecumenical Studies, 52*(1), 120–29. http://doi.org/10.1353/ecu.2017.0003

Rao, V.D. (1973). The Habshis: India's unknown Africans. *Africa Report, 18*(5), 35–38.

Rediker, M. (2007). *The slave ship: A human history*. Penguin Books.

Rogers, J.A. (1967). *Sex and race, Volume 1: Negro-Caucasian mixing in all ages and all lands—The Old World*. Helga M. Rogers. (Original work published 1940)

Said, E. (1979). *Orientalism*. Random House.

Sautman, B. (1994). Anti-Black racism in post-Mao China. *The China Quarterly, 138*(June), 413–37. http://www.jstor.org/stable/654951

Scaglioni, M. (2016, July 18). Emancipation and music: Post-slavery among Black Tunisians. *Open Democracy*. https://www.opendemocracy.net/en/beyond-trafficking-and-slavery/emancipation-and-music-post-slavery-among-black-tunisians/

Scott, J.C. (1985). *Weapons of the weak: Everyday forms of peasant resistance*. Yale University Press.

Segal, R. (1995). *The Black diaspora*. Faber and Faber.

Segal, R. (2001). *Islam's Black slaves: The other Black diaspora*. Farrar, Straus and Giroux.

Sexton. J. (2010). People-of-color-blindness: Notes on the afterlife of slavery. *Social Text, 28*(2), 31–56. https://doi.org/10.1215/01642472-2009-066.

Sharda, S. (2017). Black skin, Black castes: Overcoming a fidelity discourse in Bhardwaj's *Omkara*. *Shakespeare Bulletin, 35*(4), 599–626. http://doi.org/10.1353/shb.2017.0046

Sheth, K. (2013). *A certain grace: The Sidi, Indians of African descent*. Photoink.

Shroff, B. (2007). Sidis in Mumbai: Negotiating identities between Mumbai and Gujarat. *African and Asian Studies* 6(3), 305–19. https://doi.org/10.1163/156920907X212259

Siddi, M. (2014a, August 23). *Keynote: African Diaspora in India* [Conference session]. Annual Reparation Conference, Bernie Grant Arts Centre, London, UK.

Siddi, M. (2014b, January 14–16). *Social and economical status of African Diaspora in India* [Conference session]. 8th PAN African Congress, University of Witwatersrand, Johannesburg.

Singh, G.B., & Watson, T. (2009). *Gandhi under cross-examination*. Sovereign Star Publishing.

Singh, H. (2007). Confronting colonialism and racism: Fanon and Gandhi. *Human Architecture: Journal of the Sociology of Self-Knowledge, 5*(3), 341–52. http://scholarworks.umb.edu/humanarchitecture/vol5/iss3/31

Singh, S. (2001). Cultures of exile: Diasporic identities and the "imaginations" of Africa and India in the Caribbean. *Identity: An International Journal of Theory and Research, 1*(3), 289–305. https://doi.org/10.1207/S1532706XID0103_06

Sivathasan, N. (2020, July 13). South Asian anti-Black racism: "We don't marry Black people." BBC. https://www.bbc.com/news/av/newsbeat-53395935

Slate, N. (2012a). *Colored cosmopolitanism: The shared struggle for freedom in the United States and India*. Harvard University Press.

Slate, N. (2012b). The Dalit Panthers: Race, caste, and Black Power in India. In N. Slate (Ed.), *Black Power beyond borders: The global dimensions of the Black Power Movement* (pp. 127–43). Palgrave Macmillan.

Slisli, F. (2012). "The idea that one could come to terms with the Arabs": How Frantz Fanon found common ground with Islam in Algeria. *The Black Scholar, 42*(3–4), 21–26. https://doi.org/10.5816/blackscholar.42.3-4.0021

Soumya, E. (2013, December 2). Africans decry "discrimination" in India. *Al Jazeera*. https://www.aljazeera.com/features/2013/12/2/africans-decry-discrimination-in-india

Teenage German tourist raped on Indian train. (2014, January 15). *The Local*. https://www.thelocal.de/20140115/german-tourist-18-raped-on-indian-train

Tettey, W.J. (2020, December 4). *COVID-19, anti-Black racism in China, and political economy of asymmetrical power* [Symposium paper]. Intervention Symposium—Black Humanity: Bearing Witness to COVID-19, online. https://antipodeonline.org/wp-content/uploads/2020/12/7.-Tettey.pdf

Thangaraj, S. (2012). Playing through differences: Black–White racial logic and interrogating South Asian American identity. *Ethnic and Racial Studies, 35*(6), 988–1006. https://doi.org/10.1080/01419870.2012.661868

Tiku. N. (2020, October 27). India's engineers have thrived in the Silicon Valley. So has its caste system. *Washington Post.* https://www.washingtonpost.com/technology/2020/10/27/indian-caste-bias-silicon-valley/

Trexler, R.C. (1995). *Sex and conquest: Gendered violence, political order, and the European conquest of the Americas*. Cornell University Press.

Tufts SARC. (2020). *Hathras: Caste-based sexual violence and the Dalit feminist movement with Kiruba Munusamy* [Video]. YouTube. https://www.youtube.com/watch?v=er3171LAFks

Van Sertima, I. & Rashidi, R. (Eds.) (1988). *African presence in early Asia*. Transaction Publishers.

Wallerstein, I. (1991). *Unthinking social sciences: The limits of nineteenth-century paradigms*. Polity Press.

Washington, J., Jr. (1984). *Anti-Blackness in English religion, 1500–1800*. The Edwin Mellen Press.

Wells, I.B. (2010). *Ida B. Wells versus Judge Lynch: The anti-lynching trilogy* (J.H. Mitchell, Ed.). CreateSpace Independent Publishing Platform.

Williams, C. (1972). *Destruction of Black civilization: Great issues of a race from 4500 B.C. to 2000 A.D.* Kendall/Hunt Publishing.

World Sindh Congress. (2018). *Forced conversions of minority girls and women in Pakistan* [Submission to the UN Office of the High Commissioner for Human Rights]. https://webcache.googleusercontent.com/search?q=cache:ub74WND6JWkJ:https://uprdoc.ohchr.org/uprweb/downloadfile.aspx%3Ffilename%3D4376%26file%3DEnglishTranslation+&cd=1&hl=en&ct=clnk&gl=ca

Yimene, A.M. (2007). Dynamics of ethnic identity among the Siddis of Hyderabad. *African and Asian Studies*, 6(3): 321–45. https://doi.org/10.1163/156920907X212268

Yimene, A.M. (2012). African cavalry guards: A place for the construction of memory, identity and ethnicity. In E.R. Toledano (Ed.), *African communities in Asia and the Mediterranean: Identities between integration and conflict* (pp. 83–104). Africa World Press.

Contributors

TOMMY J. CURRY is a professor of Philosophy at the University of Edinburgh. He holds a personal chair in Africana philosophy and Black Male studies. He is the author of *Another White Man's Burden: Josiah Royce's Quest for a Philosophy of Racial Empire* (SUNY Press, 2018), which recently won the 2020 Josiah Royce Prize in American Idealist Thought, and *The Man-Not: Race, Class, Genre, and the Dilemmas of Black Manhood* (Temple University Press, 2017), which won the 2018 American Book Award. His research interests are nineteenth-century ethnology, Africana philosophy, critical race theory, and Black male studies.

KATERINA DELIOVSKY teaches in the areas of introductory sociology, qualitative methods, gender and society, and race and racialization. She publishes in the area of critical race feminism with an emphasis on whiteness studies. She is author of *White Femininity: Race, Gender and Power* (Fernwood, 2010) and coeditor of *Back to the Drawing Board: African Canadian Feminisms* (Sumach, 2002).

DELROY HALL is an ordained minister with over 30 years' experience within the pastorate and has similar years of practice as a trained psychodynamic psychotherapist and trainer.

DENNIS O. HOWARD is one of Jamaica's most noted ethnomusicologists, possessing over 30 years of experience in the creative industries. A Grammy-nominated music producer, he holds a PHD in cultural studies and ethnomusicology from the University of the West Indies. He is the managing director at the Institute of Cultural Policy and Innovation. He's also a lecturer at the University of the West Indies and adjunct lecturer at the Media Technology Institute. He's the author of *Rantin Inside the Dancehall* (Jahmento Publishers, 2012) and *The Creative Echo Chamber: Contemporary Music Production in Kingston Jamaica* (Randle Publishers, 2016).

TAMARI KITOSSA is Associate Professor of sociology at Brock University. His research interests include convergences of race, racism, and criminalization, including antiblackness, anticriminology, prison abolition, racial profiling, sociology of knowledge, and interracial unions. Dr. Kitossa is the coeditor, with Erica Lawson and Philip S.S. Howard, of *African Canadian Leadership: Continuity, Transition, and Transformation* (University of Toronto Press, 2019).

KEMAR MCINTOSH earned an MA in African and African diaspora studies at Florida International University. He is currently completing a PHD in global & sociocultural studies, centred in anthropology, at the same institution. Kemar's academic interests are couched in themes such as Caribbean queer politics, critical race, gender, and sexuality theories, feminist political ecology, critical medical anthropology, and critical spatial practice.

LEROY F. MOORE JR. is the founder of Krip-Hop Nation. Leroy is also one of the founding members of the National Black Disability Coalition and has helped start a number of other organizations, including the Disability Advocates of Minorities Organization and Sins Invalid. He is an activist in the area of police brutality against people with disabilities. Since the 1990s, he has written the column "Illin-N-Chillin" for *POOR Magazine*.

ELISHMA NOEL KHOKHAR holds an MA in international political economy from the University of Warwick and an MA in social justice and equity studies from Brock University. She is a contributing editor for *The Missing Slate*.

WATUFANI M. POE earned a BA in Africana studies from Swarthmore College and an MA in Africana studies and history from Brown University. He is currently a PHD candidate in Africana studies at Brown. His dissertation project, tentatively titled *Resisting Fragmentation: Black LGBTQ Movement Building in Brazil and the United States*, looks at Black queer and trans social and political activism in both countries and attempts to understand the ways Black LGBTQ people push for freedom across various movement spaces.

SATWINDER SINGH REHAL is taking his PHD in communication at the University of the Philippines Open University (UPOU). He has a background in health sociology and social development planning. He was previously a lecturer in the HZB School of International Relations and Diplomacy at the Philippine Women's University and the Enderun Colleges, Taguig. His research interests are in the sociology of sports, international health, and Afro-Asian relations in the context of the Philippines.

JOHN G. RUSSELL is Professor of cultural anthropology in the Faculty of Regional Studies at Gifu University, Japan. His research focuses on representations of race and gender in Japanese and American popular culture, the genealogy of blackness in Japan, and the social perception and treatment of otherness. He is the author of *Nihonjin no kokujin-kan* [*Japanese Perceptions of Blacks*] (Shinhyōron, 1991) and *Henken to sabetsu ga dono yō ni tsukurareru ka* [*How Are Prejudice and Discrimination Produced?*] (Akashi Shoten, 1995).

MOHAN SIDDI has been a social worker in the Siddi community of Karntaka and Gujrath, India for over eight years. He is a principal investigator for the Ethnography Study of Siddi Tribes of Karnataka project at Indira Gandhi

National Centre for Arts (Bangalore). He earned his BA in sociology from Spicer Memorial College at the University of Pune, and completed a master's degree in social work at the University of Bangalore.

Index

Figures indicated by page numbers in italics

www.ingramcontent.com/pod-product-compliance
Lightning Source LLC
LaVergne TN
LVHW040755070826
844660LV00025B/1148

* 9 7 8 1 7 7 2 1 2 5 4 3 6 *